MYTHOLOGY

AN ILLUSTRATED ENCYCLOPEDIA

MYTHOLOGY

AN ILLUSTRATED ENCYCLOPEDIA

EDITED BY

Richard Cavendish

CONSULTANT EDITOR

Trevor O. Ling

Professor of Comparative Religion,
University of Manchester

This edition produced exclusively for

WHSMITH

This edition produced exclusively for W H Smith

First published in Great Britain
by Orbis Publishing Limited, London 1980
Reprinted 1984

Printed in Italy by
IGDA, Novara

ISBN: 0-85613-730-8

CONTENTS

INTRODUCTION
Richard Cavendish
PAGE 8

ASIA

HINDUISM
Wendy O'Flaherty *Professor of the History of Religions and Indian Studies, University of Chicago*
PAGE 14

THERAVADA BUDDHISM
M.M.J. Marasinghe *Senior Lecturer in Buddhist Studies, University of Sri Lanka*
PAGE 34

ZOROASTRIANISM
J.R. Hinnells *Lecturer in Comparative Religion, University of Manchester*
PAGE 40

TIBET
Tadeusz Skorupski *Department of the Far East, School of Oriental & African Studies, London*
PAGE 48

CHINA
Anthony Christie *Senior Lecturer in the Art and Archaeology of Southeast Asia, School of Oriental & African Studies, London*
PAGE 58

JAPAN
Susumu Takiguchi *Lecturer in Japanese Language, University of Aston, Birmingham*
PAGE 74

THE MIDDLE EAST

MESOPOTAMIA
M.E.J. Richardson *Lecturer in Semitic Languages and Literatures, University of Manchester*
PAGE 86

SYRIA AND PALESTINE
M.E.J. Richardson
PAGE 92

EGYPT
Rosalie David *Assistant Keeper of Archaeology, Manchester Museum*
PAGE 96

ISLAM
H.T. Norris *Senior Lecturer in Arabic, School of Oriental & African Studies, London*
PAGE 110

THE WEST

GREECE
J.P. Kane *Lecturer in Hellenistic Greek, University of Manchester*
PAGE 120

ROME
John Ferguson *President, Selly Oak Colleges, Birmingham*
PAGE 136

THE MYSTERY RELIGIONS
John Ferguson
PAGE 144

CHRISTIANITY
Richard Cavendish
PAGE 156

THE CELTS
Emrys Evans *Reader in Celtic Studies, University of Manchester*
PAGE 170

SCANDINAVIA
Eric J. Sharpe *Professor of Religious Studies, University of Sydney*
PAGE 178

GERMANY
Francis King *Author of* Ritual Magic in England *and* Satan and Swastika
PAGE 188

THE SLAVS
David M. Lang *Professor of Caucasian Studies, School of Oriental & African Studies, London*
PAGE 192

ARMENIA, GEORGIA AND THE CAUCASUS
David M. Lang
PAGE 198

AFRICA

CENTRAL AND SOUTHERN AFRICA
Jan Knappert *Lecturer in Bantu Languages, School of Oriental & African Studies, London*
PAGE 206

EAST AFRICA
John Kesby *Lecturer in Social Anthropology, University of Kent*
PAGE 214

WEST AFRICA
James Littlejohn *Professor of Social Anthropology, University of Edinburgh*
PAGE 222

THE AMERICAS

THE NORTH AMERICAN INDIANS
James H. Howard *Professor of Anthropology, Oklahoma State University*
PAGE 230

MIDDLE AMERICA
Gordon Brotherston *Professor of Literature, University of Essex*
PAGE 242

THE INCAS
M.J. Sallnow *Lecturer in Anthropology, London School of Economics*
PAGE 254

TROPICAL SOUTH AMERICA
J.O. and M.R. Kaplan
Joanna Kaplan is Lecturer in the Social Anthropology of Latin America, London School of Economics
PAGE 260

VOODOO
Francis King
PAGE 266

THE PACIFIC

POLYNESIA AND MICRONESIA
Christian Clerk *Department of Anthropology, University College, London*
PAGE 272

MELANESIA
Andrew Strathern *Professor of Anthropology, University College, London*
PAGE 278

AUSTRALIA
Catherine H. Berndt *Lecturer in Anthropology, University of Western Australia*
PAGE 284

GLOSSARY
PAGE 292

BIBLIOGRAPHY
PAGE 293

ACKNOWLEDGMENTS
PAGE 296

INDEX
PAGE 298

INTRODUCTION

Interest in mythology has grown steadily throughout the last hundred years, powered by the realization that myths are not childish stories or mere pre-scientific explanations of the world, but serious insights into reality. They exist in all societies, of the present as well as the past. They are part of the fabric of human life, expressing beliefs, moulding behaviour and justifying institutions, customs and values. It is consequently impossible to understand human beings without an understanding of their myths. This is reflected in the wide range of disciplines from which the contributors to this volume are drawn, including anthropology, archeology, religious studies, comparative religion and the history of religions, language and literature. It is also reflected in the arrangement and approach of the book itself, which is divided into six sections and thirty chapters, between them spanning the world. Each chapter deals with the principal myths of a religious or cultural area in relation to the social and historical background from which the myths have sprung.

Myths are imaginative traditions about the nature, history and destiny of the world, the gods, man and society. They are treated here as concepts which deserve serious attention, for what they mean to those who believe in them and as statements about fundamental issues of life. One of the disadvantages of the old-fashioned derogatory use of the word myth, to mean a foolish story or a false idea, is the implication that myths are trivial. The reality is the reverse. It is the things which people regard as important that find a place in their mythology.

At the same time it is impossible to ignore the fictitious clothing which mythology wears. A common rough definition of myth is 'a story about the gods'. Another, broader one is 'a sacred story'. Neither of these definitions is adequate, but certainly many myths are narratives about the exploits of gods and supernatural beings. These myths are stories, not histories. The events related in them did not really happen, yet they may contain truth of a different and deeper kind.

Few people still believe, for example, that the human race is descended from Adam and Eve, the first man and woman, who lived in the beautiful garden of Eden and were tempted by a devious serpent. The story is generally agreed to be fiction, but fiction which is full of meaning. No longer accepted as literally true, as it once was, the story is felt to be poetically true. It says something profound about the human condition, something which cannot be stated as effectively in any other way. It is this which distinguishes the story from the mass of trivial fictions and entitles it to be called a myth.

A religious myth is a way of conveying a sacred truth, but not all myths are religious. Some are primarily social and historical, and the gods may play far less important roles in them, or no role whatever. These myths explain the history and rationale of a community, institution, custom or social development. By telling the story of a people, for instance, a myth supports their sense of solidarity and purpose, of confidence and pride in themselves. The Romans borrowed most of their religious myths from the Greeks. Their own myths were largely concerned with the history of Rome: how the city was founded, how it survived critical dangers and grew strong, and what qualities Romans of the past had displayed which Romans of the present ought to emulate. Though it may be based on actual events, a myth of this kind is again a story with a moral, rather than a history. No attempt is made to distinguish between real and unreal events. The telling of myths is an older art than the construction of histories and the value of myth does not depend on historical accuracy.

Definitions of myth as 'story' fail because a good many myths are not stories at all. The mythology of some societies includes the assignment of different functions or departments of interest to the various gods and goddesses. One deity presides over agriculture, another over war, another over the sea, and so on. Beyond this, the term myth is also applied to religious and secular traditions which exert a powerful influence on attitudes to life, but whose literal accuracy there is reason to doubt. An example is the idea of hell. The traditional Christian picture of hell as a real place, a concentration camp of fire and torment deep in the bowels of the earth, is now regarded by many Christians as a myth. The truth it contains is of a different sort: for instance, that a human being who finally rejects God must inevitably suffer the pain of that rejection. It is in this sense that the idea of hell in Christianity and other religions is treated here as a myth.

A myth is a story or tradition which claims to enshrine a fundamental truth about the world and human life, which is regarded in its own milieu as authoritative, but whose truth is not literal, historical or scientific. The account in the Bible of God creating the world in seven days is scientifically untenable, as are the Indian, Tibetan, Chinese and Greek traditions of the world coming into being from an egg, but the real point of the myth is not affected, nor is its credibility necessarily destroyed. In practice, however, because myths are woven into the fabric of a society in which they are generally accepted as literally true, the impact of new discoveries, new attitudes and new ways of life on myths is usually to undermine them.

When old myths are lost, new ones are needed. Myths flourish and fade and die, but new myths are born, old ones are resurrected, and hybrid forms combining new and old emerge when times change or cultures mingle. Myths are not characteristic only of non-literate or 'primitive' peoples, or of societies of the distant past. Complex modern societies have also thrown up myths. The myth of progress, for instance, has had a profound effect on attitudes and political developments in the modern West. Both left-wing and right-wing political movements have drawn strength from the conviction of being carried forward on an irresistible tide of progress, and both have transformed the old myth of a golden age in the past into a new myth of a utopian future. No society seems ever to have functioned without a set of myths containing its vision of its past, its present and its purposes.

There are innumerable ways of interpreting myths, but the principal varieties of approach can be roughly classified as the functional, the symbolic and the structural. Each provides brilliant and fascinating analyses of particular myths or groups of myths, but whether any one of these systems by itself gives a satisfactory explanation of mythology in general is debatable. In practice, the categories are not clear-cut, and functional, symbolic and structural methods of interpretation often blend into each other.

The functional approach regards myths as justifying social facts. A particular people, for example, traditionally live by fishing. They have a myth which tells how, long ago, a supernatural being taught their ancestors how to catch fish. This story explains how it comes about that they are fishermen, justifies their way of life, and validates their traditional fishing techniques and the beliefs and customs connected with them. It also gives them a sense of sharing in the existence of their ancestors through their way of life.

Many myths provide a similar charter of authorization for groups, institutions, rituals, social distinctions, laws and customs, moral standards, values and ideas. Myths from all over the world account for and sanction kinship rules and marriage customs, techniques of hunting, husbandry, art and war, methods of offering sacrifice, the authority of kings and chiefs, the subordination of women and numerous other facets of a society's structure. They have an important moral function in defining acceptable and unacceptable behaviour. Some of them are unwritten title-deeds, justifying a people's claim to its territory. Some serve the political purposes of a regime, an aristocracy or a priesthood, as in Egypt, Rome and Japan, among the Aztecs in Mexico or the Incas in Peru.

These myths authorize the present state of affairs. There seems to be a deep need in human nature for authority of this kind – an authority that transcends rational argument – and examples are not confined to tribal societies. In England and France in the 17th century the supreme power of kings was justified by the belief that they were appointed to rule by God, a political theory rooted in mythological traditions. The opposite tendency, the rise of democracy, was justified by the myth of the social contract. In Nazi Germany programmes of aggressive expansion and savage race-hatred were 'justified' in part by a revival of ancient Germanic mythology. Japanese imperialism before 1945 had similar sanction, through the revival of myths which promoted nationalism, militarism and belief in the divine authority of the state.

Myths are often closely linked with rituals, though the theory that *all* myths spring from ritual does not command widespread support. The story of Prometheus cheating Zeus out of the meat at the first sacrifice provided a warrant for the customary Greek ritual in which the meat of a sacrificed animal was not burned, and so given to the gods, but eaten by the worshippers. Generally, the ritual repeats and re-enacts the myth, to recreate it with all its beneficent consequences for human beings. In Syria stories of the triumphs of the fertility-god Baal over his enemies were recited, and apparently acted out, in rituals intended to ensure the corresponding triumph of fertility over barrenness on earth. Myths are used in alliance with rituals in this way to tap sources of power and attain experiences otherwise unavailable, for the actors in the ritual participate in the recreated myth. They are taken out of this world and time to become one with the figures in the myth, the gods and the ancestors. Dramatic examples occur in the ceremonies of Voodoo and in the rituals of Australian Aborigines.

Some myths range beyond ritual and custom to confront questions and problems of human life everywhere. They explain how the world came into existence, the origin of mankind and the animals and plants, the origin of the two sexes, how human beings acquired fire, how society began, how work, old age, disease and the last enemy, death, came into the world. Here again, by explaining, the myths also justify the present state of things, the world as it is now. Their practical function may not be so much to satisfy curiosity as to alleviate unhappiness, pain and hardship through an imaginatively satisfying explanation of the world and the condition of man. Set in a comprehensible framework, the evils of life may become, if not welcome, at least less hard to bear.

Whether functional explanations adequately account for the hold which myths have on the mind and for some of their characteristics, is open to question. Symbolic approaches regard mythology as a way of thinking and a poetic method of communication, and look for meanings beneath the surface. In stories of the world born from an egg, for instance, the egg is not meant to be a real egg. The cosmic egg is an effective symbol of life stored within a whole, as a real egg shelters and nourishes the life within it. Similarly, when an Egyptian myth says that the first human beings were made of clay, fashioned on a potter's wheel by a god, the clay shaped on the wheel is a symbol of man's relationship to the divine and of his link with the earth, on which he lives and to which his body returns at the last.

Many myths have a dream-like quality. Strange distorted figures move through them, monsters and hybrid beings. Animals walk and talk like men, men and animals intermarry, change shape and possess magical powers. Women are impregnated and children born in physically impossible ways. There are sinister and disturbing motifs of parricide, fratricide, cannibalism, castration, incest, rape and murder, which often are not condemned. The laws of time, nature and society to which we are accustomed do not apply, which is logical enough when the myths are dealing with a universe before the present order of things was established.

Myths of this kind provided ammunition for the theories of Freud and Jung, and for the belief that myths are creations of the unconscious mind and the dark, primitive well-springs of human nature. Freud thought that myths, and dreams, were projections of thwarted desires which the conscious mind suppressed, so that they came to the surface in distorted imagery. Jung regarded them as products of the 'collective unconscious', shared by all human beings, formed by the experiences of prehistoric man, and containing the 'archetypes' or fundamental patterns of ideas which emerge in myths, dreams, symbolism, art and all other forms of expression.

Freudian and Jungian interpretations have often been criticized for being unduly simplistic, for forcing complicated phenomena into simple, preconceived patterns. They suffer from the more fundamental disadvantage that there is no conceivable way of showing them to be wrong. Since we have access only to the conscious mind, statements about the unconscious are assertions which can neither be verified nor disproved. The prevailing tendency, consequently, is not to explain myths along these lines. They are more often seen as expressions of a philosophy, an outlook on the world, or as creations which, like art and literature in general, are likely to combine conscious and unconscious elements, social and symbolic significance. Especially when they are reactions to pressures and burdens which weigh on all men everywhere, they may have a meaning which transcends their immediate functional relevance in their own milieu.

Freudian theory, however, has influenced structural mythology, which is a comparatively recent development. The structural approach splits a myth into its component parts, its incidents and motifs, and considers the ways in which they are related to each other, to lay bare the underlying structure like a cross-section of the geological strata beneath a landscape. The significance of the myth is not looked for in the narrative as a whole but in the arrangement of the strata beneath.

Structural interpretations are extremely complex and impossible to summarize in brief, but one structural pattern found in myths is an interplay of opposites. For example, the present state of things is the opposite of the state of things 'in the beginning'. Men are dominant today, but women ruled long ago. Or, present-day kinship and marriage rules have developed from a time when incest between parents and children or brothers and sisters was the rule. Or, once upon a time, it was the animals who ate their meat cooked and men who ate it raw, instead of the other way round.

The leading exponent of structural mythology, the French anthropologist Claude Lévi-Strauss, regards myths as structures of opposites, such as nature and culture (the raw and the cooked), male and female, order and disorder. On this view myths state, in a veiled form, contradictions inherent in life which the conscious mind is unwilling to confront. Mythical thought moves from an awareness of contradictions towards their resolution, and stories of the topsy-turvy state of things in the world of myth attempt to mediate between opposites and resolve them. The true function of myth is to provide 'a logical model capable of overcoming a contradiction': which, Lévi-Strauss adds, is an impossible achievement when the contradiction is real.

Myths not only reflect man's experience of life, but have also moulded it, for people naturally interpret what happens to them in the light of their prevailing attitude to reality, which includes their mythology. One reason for taking mythology seriously is that a society cannot be understood in isolation from its myths. Another is the light which myths cast not only on other people's minds but on our own. If mythology is a way of thinking common to human beings in general, then a study of it is a study of ourselves.

Similarities and parallels between myths from different societies, not all of which are readily or completely explainable by the influence of one culture on another, suggest that they embody common patterns of thought. Along with the parallels there are numerous important differences, but the same patterns occur often enough to indicate that human minds tend to supply similar answers to the same basic questions. One factor common to the myths of widely separated peoples is the feeling of living in a world dominated by mysterious, non-human agencies, gods and spirits and supernatural entities. Another common ingredient is the tendency to concentrate on the evils of the human condition, on the unfairness of life and its dangers.

Similar motifs and patterns occur in myths of origin: the dark and watery chaos that first existed, with no light, no sun, moon and stars; the cosmic egg; creation from the dismembered body of a god or a monster; the separation of earth and sky, which were originally joined together; the bringing of order from chaos; the making of man from the ground, clay or mud, or his emergence from the ground.

Again, myths supply broadly similar answers to the question of why we must die. Death came into the world as the consequence of a mistake, sometimes made by a human being or sometimes by a god or a messenger of the gods. Often connected with mortality and immortality is the moon, which appears to die and be reborn again in the sky, and the snake, which renews itself by sloughing its skin.

Other recurring themes include an immense catastrophe in the past, often a great flood, after which the world had to be restored to order or made anew. Another cataclysm may threaten the future, when the present world will be destroyed, as in Hindu, Zoroastrian, Christian, Scandinavian and Mexican myths, for example. The concept of Mother Earth is extremely widespread, and so are the themes of the mutual dependence and mutual hostility between man and woman, between mankind and the animals, and between the members of a family. Or, again, the sense of an order, a balance of cosmic powers on which the world and man depend for life and security, is conveyed in the myths of many different societies.

Myths are of interest not only from a detached point of view, for what they reveal about human psychology and culture, but for their own sake, for the poetic truth which distinguishes great myths, like great works of literature, from trivial fiction. The resurgence of enthusiasm for mythology in our time has drawn strength from the feeling that scientific and technological man has lost his way and that a path to truth lies through the territory of myth. One thing which the reader of this volume will discover is that even when myths come from cultures very unlike ours, they may be strikingly relevant to our own lives and our own situation in the world.

ASIA

CHAPTER ONE

HINDUISM

If myths are stories about the gods, it is difficult to find a Hindu story that is not mythical. 'Here there are more gods than men,' a puzzled European remarked of India centuries ago, and the line between gods and men in Hinduism is as vague and ephemeral as the cloudy trail of a sky-writer. Men obtain divine powers easily in India, as kings, priests or ascetics. The gods, for their part, are so anthropomorphic and so intimately involved in affairs on earth – the establishment of shrines and the rescue of devotees in trouble, as well as the capricious sports which the Hindu gods prefer to indulge in on earth rather than in heaven – that the path from heaven down to earth is as well trodden as that from earth up to heaven.

Gods in India are no better than men, merely more powerful. Indeed, their extraordinary powers allow them to indulge in vices on an extraordinary scale: divine power corrupts divinely. The demons, the third party in the mythological drama, are often similarly hard to distinguish from gods and men. In appearance demons are sometimes deformed or theriomorphic (in animal form), but more often they are just as anthropomorphic as the gods. In behaviour they are sometimes evil (especially the lower orders and cadet branches, blood-drinking goblins and graveyard ghosts), but often far more virtuous than the gods. What makes them demons is the fact that they are the enemies of the gods. Sometimes this makes them the enemies of men as well, but when the gods themselves oppose men, as they frequently do, the allegiance of the demons becomes complex and ambivalent.

The Hindus, however, know very well how to distinguish gods from men, even from 'god-men'. For instance, it is generally known that, unlike mortals, gods do not blink or sweat, their feet do not quite touch the ground, their garlands never wither, and they do not get dirty. Divinity in India, like aristocracy in Europe, is largely a matter of history, birth and inheritance. The gods are those who have always been gods, whose names are enshrined in the ancient texts or, in the case of assimilations from local traditions, whose names were

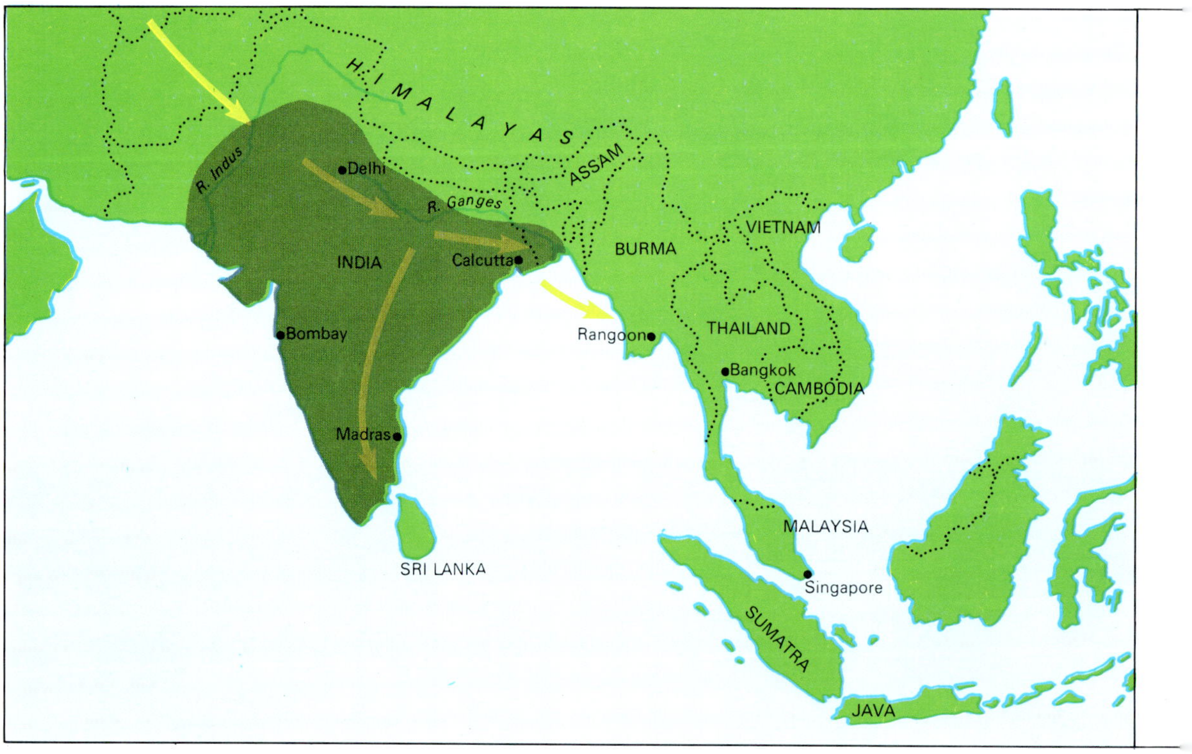

The goddess Chamunda, the Fierce, and Kali, the Black, fighting an army of demons. Chamunda is a title of the goddess Durga, given to her after she had won a battle against two demons. The demons had compelled the god Shiva to give them power and strength greater than that of the gods, but failed to realize that the gift did not make them invincible against goddesses. Conflict between the gods and their rivals and enemies, the demons, is a major theme of Hindu mythology. Miniature painting, Pahari School, 1800.

TIME CHART

Approximate Dates

1500 BC	Indo-Aryans invade northwest India and conquer the Indus Valley civilization: composition of the *Rig Veda*
1500–500 BC	Aryans expand to the southeast across the plains of northern India and along the Ganges valley, establishing Sanskrit (Brahman) culture: composition of the *Brahmanas*
500 BC	Sanskrit culture established in its heartland in the central Ganges plain: rise of Buddhism
500 BC–AD 1	Further expansion southwards in the Indian peninsula and to Sri Lanka (Ceylon), and eastwards into Bengal and Assam
AD 1–500	Sanskrit culture carried by sea to Burma, Thailand and Cambodia, Sumatra and Java: composition of the early *Puranas*

'known to our grandfathers'. The pantheon changes from time to time and place to place, and new gods force their way into it sometimes, but they must be legitimized by stories establishing their birth from, or marriage to, one of the older gods.

Vedic Creation Myths

The *Rig Veda* is a collection of more than a thousand hymns composed in northwest India about 1500 BC, in an archaic form of Sanskrit, an ancient Indo-European language. In addition to this canon, numerous myths appear in commentaries, composed a few centuries later and known as the *Brahmanas*. These texts were not committed to writing for many centuries after their composition, but oral tradition preserved them and later Hindu religious literature draws heavily upon their characters and events.

The central myth of the *Rig Veda* is the myth of creation. This is described in several different ways. Often, the universe is said to have come into being out of chaos when a god – Indra, king of the gods and god of rain, or Vishnu, a solar deity – separated heaven from earth. Then the sun rose and from that spot, the navel of the earth, a great pillar was erected

Indra was the war-god of the Indo-Aryans who invaded India from the north, *c.*1500 BC. Lord of storm and fertility, he is the king of the gods in the *Rig Veda*. He is shown here in his heaven, attended by the Asparases, beautiful nymphs skilled in the arts of love. Razmanama MS, Akbar School, 1598.

to prop apart heaven and earth. This pillar is the axis of the world.

There were now three worlds: heaven, earth and the intervening air or ether. Vishnu is said to have measured out (and thus, in the Vedic view, to have created) these three worlds with three great strides. Although there are some obscure hints of an underworld, little is said about this part of the universe in the *Rig Veda*. The sun travels below the earth at night to return to the east by morning, and this mirror-image world (a world of brightness) is ruled by Varuna, god of cosmic order and lord of the waters. In later literature, the underworld is a dark place and the dwelling of demons.

A late Rig Vedic hymn describes another kind of creation. A cosmic man, Purusha, was dismembered in a primeval sacrifice and from the parts of his body were made the cosmos and the four classes of the social order (priests, warriors, populace and servants). Still later, and more abstract, is a hymn which describes the creation of being from non-being. At first there was neither day nor night, neither death nor immortality. Then, out of darkness and the primeval flood, desire was born, but not even the gods know the source of this creation, for they only appeared after the creation of the world.

Gradually, one god came to be regarded as the author of creation: Prajapati, 'Lord of Creatures', later known as Brahma. In the *Rig Veda*, the god of the sky commits incest with his daughter, the dawn, spilling his seed upon the ground. By the time of the *Brahmanas*, this act was attributed to Prajapati, who was already known as the god of the 'golden seed' in the early texts. The golden seed of the god, placed in the cosmic waters, developed into the universe, a golden egg which split in two: heaven was the upper shell and earth the lower shell, while the sun was the golden yolk. Even in later Hindu cosmology, the universe is called the Egg of Brahma and is regarded as a closed sphere.

The social implications of the incestuous creation were further developed in the *Brahmanas*. Prajapati created four sons (fire, wind, the sun and the moon) and a daughter (the dawn), whom he desired and pursued. She fled from him in the form of a doe, and so he became a stag; she became a cow, he a bull; she a mare, he a stallion; and in this way all the species were created, even the ants. Prajapati's sons also desired the dawn, and spilled their seed on the ground, where it took the form of the fierce god Rudra. Another variant of this myth says that the gods, shocked by the impropriety of Prajapati's act, created Rudra to punish Prajapati. Rudra himself in later Hindu mythology is a god whose golden seed, spilled upon earth, creates the god Skanda.

Later elaborations of the creation myth combined several of these basic concepts. In the beginning the primeval waters desired to multiply, and they heated themselves to produce a golden egg, from which Prajapati was born. He created the words for earth, atmosphere and sky, and from the words the things themselves appeared. He desired offspring and fathered the gods, who became divine by reaching the sky, and the demons, who produced darkness and evil, causing Prajapati to subdue them.

Gods against Demons

Second to the Vedic creation myths in importance and frequency are the myths of the eternal battle between gods and demons. Indeed, the two basic motifs are often combined, for the demons threaten the act of creation and themselves become part of the material out of which the universe is constructed: they provide the necessary power of evil to give meaning to the power of the gods.

In the *Rig Veda*, the demons are often confused

with the human enemies of the invading Indo-Aryans, and Indra as king of the gods simultaneously defeats the human foes, destroys the threatening demons and sets free the creative power of the universe. The arch-enemy of Indra is Vritra, a great serpent who lies coiled about the world-mountain at the navel of the earth, holding back the waters. Indra pierces Vritra, lets loose the rains and shatters the mountains. This act set free the cows who were kept prisoner in the world-mountain (cows being symbolic of wealth and fertility), and released the sun, which was held fast within the rock of the underworld night. The slaughter of the dragon is an act of creation as well as destruction, yet another way of firmly establishing and steadying heaven and earth in their proper places. Indra is also said to have cut off the wings of the mountains, who had previously flown about at will, causing great havoc.

The myth of Vritra is supplemented by an episode in which Indra murders Vritra's older brother, the three-headed Vishvarupa. Vishvarupa is the son of Tvashtar, the artisan of the gods. As Tvashtar is often said to be Indra's father, too, and is killed by Indra (from whom he had hidden the elixir of immortality), the myth is one of a fratricide compounded by a patricide.

Later texts make it clear that all the gods and demons are brothers, the demons being the older brothers cheated out of their patrimony, so that the entire war is a fraternal struggle. The gods and demons share a divine father (Tvashtar, Prajapati or the divine sage Kashyapa) but have different mothers: the gods are sons of Aditi, 'the infinite', a sky-goddess, while the demons are the sons of the demonic Diti. Vishvarupa served as priest of the gods, but secretly he heeded his mother's treacherous advice and acted on behalf of the demons, for which Indra beheaded him. In punishment for the sin of slaying a priest (for even demons could be priests), Indra was weakened and forced to transfer his sin, like some contagious moral virus, to the earth, the waters and women. In return, he granted these receptacles their powers of fertility.

The battle between gods and demons begins immediately after they are created. By performing sacrifices to gain powers, gods and demons vie for superiority, which is inevitably won by the gods. The gods become truthful, the demons false; the gods become the dwellers in heaven, while the demons are banished to the underworld. The gods deprive the demons of the power of ritual and thus defeat them. This ritual power is personified in the form of several deities, of whom the most important are Agni (fire), Soma (the elixir of immortality) and Vach (the goddess of speech), who leave the demons and come to the gods.

Agni's birth is variously described. He is the child of sky and earth, or of Tvashtar and the waters. Sometimes Indra is said to generate Agni by rubbing two stones together. On earth his parents are the two fire-sticks (the upper being his father and the lower his mother) or the ten maidens (the ten fingers). In heaven he is born as lightning, and his third birth is from the waters. Agni burns the demons who

LEFT Vishnu, with Shiva, is one of the two great gods of medieval and modern Hinduism. According to the *Rig Veda*, the demons controlled the earth and the gods asked them for a share in it, as much as the dwarf Vishnu could step over in three strides. The demons agreed and Vishnu strode across the three worlds of heaven, the earth and the intervening atmosphere, so gaining them for the gods. 10th-century carving.

BELOW The principal gods of the Vedic pantheon later became minor figures in mythology, no longer worshipped. Varuna was an ancient god of the sky and cosmic order, possibly related to the Iranian god Ahura Mazda and the Greek Uranus. He was later god of the waters. Figure of Varuna from the Brahmesvara Temple, Bubenesvar, *c.*11th century.

South Indian wood carvings of Soma RIGHT and Sarasvati BELOW. Soma was a hallucinogenic drug, obtained from a plant, possibly the fly agaric. It was by drinking Soma that the gods gained 'immortality', for them a life span of a thousand years. In one myth the gods buy Soma from the Gandharvas, the celestial musicians and magicians, in exchange for Vach, the goddess of speech. Vach was later identified as Sarasvati, the consort of Brahma: goddess of speech and wisdom, she invented writing and the alphabet.

threaten the sacrifice; he carries the sacrifice to the gods and is the mouth of the gods who eat the sacrificial offerings. In this capacity he is said to ride upon a goat, the sacrificial animal, or to be goat-headed. Among mankind he is not the mouth but the stomach, the digestive fire which makes eating possible.

As Agni is the great eater, the eaten is Soma, the second element of the personified sacrifice, the elixir of immortality. Soma was a hallucinogenic drug obtained from a plant that grew high in the mountains. The bringing of this plant from the mountains is a variant of the Indo-European myth of the bringing of fire from heaven. Soma was born in heaven and a swift eagle brought Soma to Indra. An archer shot at the eagle, whose feather fell to earth and became a sacred plant. Once on earth, Soma is still in danger for the demons steal it but are tricked into selling it or giving it back. The Gandharvas, celestial musicians and magicians, are also persuaded to sell Soma to the gods in exchange for the goddess Vach, whom they desire.

The greatest enemy of the gods is not any demon, but death. The one quality which distinguishes gods from other creatures is their so-called immortality, but this quality has neither the permanence nor the inevitability ordinarily associated with the word. When the gods are said to have obtained immortality by drinking Soma, it often means merely that they obtained a full life span, a thousand years for a god. Mortals, too, can win 'immortality', which for them lasts only for a century.

Prajapati was not born immortal. When he had created gods and men, he formed death. Half of him (hair, skin, flesh, bone and marrow) was mortal; the other half (mind, voice, breath, eye and ear) immortal. He fled in terror of death and was made immortal by a sacrificial ritual. Henceforth death ceased to be the enemy of the gods; the danger of death, now 'solved' by the ritual that conquered the god of death long ago and continues to conquer him each time it is performed, is gone, and one is left instead with the problem of avoiding ritual error, a problem to which the priesthood dedicated itself for centuries to come. The gods in turn attained immortality from Prajapati, but the god of death objected that he now had no allotted share, and so the gods ordained that the body of man would be the share of death. Thus the gods obtained their own immortality by sacrificing man to death.

Gods as Benefactors of Men

In addition to the god who is death himself, Vedic texts speak of a king of the dead, who is the first man who died. This is Yama, the son of Vivasvat (the sun). Yama's brindled dogs wander among men as his envoys. When a man dies and his corpse is burned, his soul passes below the earth to the realm of light where Yama rules, a place of rejoicing. Another son of the sun, and thus a brother (and mirror-image) of Yama, is Manu, the ancestor of the human race living on earth. Manu performed the first sacrifice and became the progenitor of mankind through his daughter Ida ('the oblation'), who was

Horses were linked with the sun. Surya, the god of the sun, was one of the principal Vedic deities, and though later identified with Vishnu, was also worshipped in his own right. He crossed the sky in a chariot drawn by seven horses or, in later tradition, by a horse with seven heads. As Vivasvat, the sun stallion, he fathered the Ashvins, the twin horsemen who helped mortals and cured disease. Figure of a horse from the Temple of the Sun at Konarak, Orissa, 13th century.

produced from his offerings of butter and milk. Manu, like his divine counterpart Prajapati, is therefore an incestuous creator. Manu is also said to have been saved in a ship from a deluge which swept away all other creatures. As the waters rose, he was towed to safety on a mountain by a horned fish whom he had earlier protected. (The fish was later identified with Vishnu.)

Manu is not the only mortal to have been saved by the gods. Indeed, almost all the Vedic gods, especially Indra and Vishnu, are on occasion helpful to mankind, but the most important acts of rescue are performed by Manu's twin brothers, the Ashvins ('horsemen'). The relationship between Manu, Yama and the Ashvins is revealed by an ancient myth. Vivasvat, the sun-stallion, married the daughter of Tvashtar, who bore him Yama and his sister Yami. Tvashtar's daughter then fled from Vivasvat's excessive heat, taking the form of a mare and leaving in her place a woman identical to herself. Upon this substitute Vivasvat begot Manu; then, becoming aware of the deception, he took the form of a horse and begot the Ashvins upon the mare. These twins are thus closely related to mortals, though, unlike Yama and Manu, they are regarded as gods.

Their claim to this divine distinction did not go unchallenged at first, precisely because of their unseemly affection for mortals. The secret of the Soma, the elixir which makes the gods gods, was jealously guarded by Indra (who had himself stolen it from Tvashtar) and was kept from the Ashvins, but a human sage named Dadhyanch knew the secret. The Ashvins gave Dadhyanch a horse's head, with which he told them where Tvashtar had hidden the Soma. Indra cut off Dadhyanch's horse-head, but the Ashvins then replaced Dadhyanch's own head and made him whole again.

The mutually beneficial nature of the sacrifice (in which an animal is beheaded) clearly underlies the symbiotic, mutually supportive relationship between gods (Ashvins) and men (Dadhyanch) in this myth. Elsewhere, mere praise or sacrificial offerings (perhaps offerings of the very Soma which Dadhyanch gave) prompt the Ashvins' assistance. When the sage Atri was about to be burnt by demons in a deep pit, the Ashvins restored him with a refreshing drink, possibly Soma. The aged sage Chyavana was made young again by the Ashvins, who prolonged his life and made him the husband of maidens. They saved another sage from a log to which he was clinging in mid-ocean, restored sight to a sage whose father had blinded him, gave an iron leg to a mare whose leg had been cut off in battle, and befriended a woman who was growing old and childless in her father's house. Their general function is that of physicians who heal diseases and ward off death, specializing in obstetrics and gynaecology, for they make the young wife fertile, cause the barren cow to yield milk, and grant children to the wife of a eunuch. Their benevolence toward men, though somewhat exaggerated, is not entirely out of character for a Vedic god but this attitude and the symbiotic sacrificial relationship which underlies it do not endure long in the post-Vedic period.

Epic and Puranic Mythology

The gods of the Vedic pantheon remain as minor players in the Hindu drama in later centuries, though they are no longer actively worshipped. They become literary and metaphorical figures rather than numinous deities. Indra is mocked for his Gargantuan sexual and alcoholic appetites, depicted as a womanizer, a coward and a liar. Yama remains king of the dead, though he now functions, like Indra, as a mere pawn of the true gods, Shiva and Vishnu.

The myths about these two great gods and other minor divinities of the post-Vedic period are found in Sanskrit texts composed from about 500 BC until well into the medieval period, and frequently retold, often still in Sanskrit, to the present day. The two great sources of Hindu mythology are the Sanskrit epics, the *Mahabharata* and the *Ramayana*. These came to be supplemented by 18 lengthy texts called the *Great Puranas*, as well as countless lesser, local *Puranas*, some of which may be of great antiquity. In addition, the myths were recounted in vernacular classics, such as the *Holy Lake of the Acts of Rama* (a Hindi version of the *Ramayana*) or the *Ocean of Love* (a Hindi poem about Krishna). There are also widely loved versions of the Sanskrit classics in Tamil, a South Indian language. Many Hindus know the myths only from these vernacular re-tellings, but others have heard the myths recited in Sanskrit, often with accompanying vernacular glosses, in the local temples.

In his avatars as the fish and the boar, Vishnu saved life on earth from destruction by flood.

ABOVE The sage Manu caught a tiny fish. He was kind to it, and it grew and grew until only the ocean was big enough to contain it, for it was Vishnu in his incarnation as Matsya, the fish. In this form the god saved Manu from a great flood, instructing him to build a boat and take with him on board the seeds of all created things. Later the god killed a monstrous demon who had stolen the Vedas. Vishnu as the fish slaying the demon. Tempera painting, *c.* 1870.

RIGHT As the huge boar Varaha, Vishnu rescued the earth, which had been dragged down to the bottom of the ocean by a powerful demon. Killing the demon, Vishnu lifted the earth up with his tusks. From eastern India, Pala dynasty, 10th century.

Vishnu and his Avatars

Although Vishnu is not one of the most important gods of the *Rig Veda*, he is particularly benevolent to men and noted for his ability to penetrate and pervade all matter 'as a razor fills its sheath'. In the *Brahmanas*, his ability to expand appears in the myth of the dwarf. The demons had won the earth and the gods begged them for a share in it, just large enough for Vishnu, who was a dwarf, to lie upon, or as much as he could cover in three strides. The demons foolishly agreed and Vishnu strode across the three worlds and won them for the gods. This is the oldest of Vishnu's ten avatars, or incarnations.

Other avatars in the *Brahmanas* are not originally associated with Vishnu, but all have to do with fertility and rescue. The fish who saves Manu from the flood is at first unnamed and only later identified with Vishnu. Similarly, the boar who rescues the earth when, overburdened, she sinks below the cosmic waters is at first an ally of the demons, whom Vishnu persuades Indra to kill. Then Prajapati, in the form of a boar, creates the earth, marries her and begets children in her. When Prajapati becomes identified with Vishnu, this act is attributed to Vishnu and further elaborated.

The tortoise avatar, too, was at first a form not of Vishnu but of the abstract universe, its shells being sky and earth. The tortoise was also regarded as a form of the sun (like Vishnu), as the husband of the earth (like the boar), and as the father of all creatures (like Prajapati). Vishnu takes the form of the tortoise to perform the same task he accomplishes in his other aquatic theriomorphic forms: to support the earth in the midst of the cosmic floods. The occasion for the tortoise avatar is the greatest of battles between gods and demons, fought as usual for the sake of the Soma elixir.

The Ocean of Milk

The gods decided to churn the ocean of milk, to obtain Soma, the elixir of immortality. They called in the demons to help, promising them a share. The churning-pole, a mountain, rested on the bottom of the ocean and the great snake Vasuki was used as a rope to turn it, but the violent churning threatened to break the earth to pieces, so Vishnu transformed himself into a tortoise and took the pole on his back. As the ocean was stirred to and fro, a number of wonderful treasures came forth, including the beautiful goddess Lakshmi, who became Vishnu's wife. A virulent poison also came forth from the ocean and threatened to burn up the gods, but Shiva swallowed the poison and kept it in his throat. When the Soma emerged from the churning, as cheese emerges from the churning of milk, the gods and demons struggled for it. The demons carried it off, but Vishnu took the form of a beautiful woman, Mohini the Enchantress. Bewitched by her charms, the demons gave her the precious fluid, and she gave it to the gods.

In addition to these animal forms, Vishnu is renowned as the man-lion, an ambivalent form (half fierce, half tame; half man, half animal) who becomes manifest in order to resolve an ambivalent situation. Prahlada, a good demon and a worshipper of Vishnu, was tormented by his demonic father. When Prahlada declared that Vishnu was omnipresent, his father sarcastically demanded if he was present in the central pillar of the throne room (another form of the world axis). Vishnu emerged from the pillar in the form of the man-lion and disembowelled the wicked demon, to demonstrate both his omnipresence and his wrath.

THE AVATARS OF VISHNU

The great god Vishnu appears on earth in various forms known as avatars, 'descents'. In the most widely accepted tradition there are ten of these incarnations:

1. Matsya, the fish, who saved Manu from the flood
2. Kurma, the tortoise, on whom the churning-pole rested during the churning of the ocean
3. Varaha, the boar, who rescued the earth from the flood
4. Narasimha, the man-lion, slayer of the demon Hiranyakashipu
5. Vamana, the dwarf, who measured out the worlds in three strides
6. Parashurama, destroyer of the warrior class
7. Rama, a prince
8. Krishna, cow-herd and lover of the Gopis
9. The Buddha, a form taken by Vishnu to corrupt the demons
10. Kalki, the rider on the white horse at the end of the Kali age

ABOVE The gods and the demons churned the ocean of milk to obtain Soma. The great snake Vasuki was used to turn the churning-pole and Vishnu, in his avatar as the tortoise, took the pole on his back, to protect the earth from the violence of the churning.

LEFT Vishnu as the man-lion, disembowelling a wicked demon who had challenged his son – a worshipper of Vishnu – to prove the existence of his god. 6th-century carving.

ABOVE Vishnu as the dwarf Vamana. It was in this incarnation that Vishnu measured out the worlds in three strides. According to a later version of the myth, he wrested the worlds from the great demon Bali and sent him down to the underworld. Miniature painting, Jainpur School, 1750.

RIGHT Vishnu's last five avatars, in human form, were undertaken to aid mankind and repress evil, and are based on stories told originally about various popular heroes. One of these heroes was Rama, the model of the good man, virtuous, chivalrous and brave. Rama's beautiful wife, Sita, was the model of the ideal wife and mother. Rama with the dead Sita, from Hola, Pondicherry, 17th century.

Rama and Sita

Vishnu's last five avatars (like the dwarf) are anthropomorphic; they are said to have been undertaken by the god to help mankind, to establish good and to repress evil. In fact, they are based on a motley group of obscure and widely divergent legends originally told about several popular heroes, and their activities are not always reconcilable with the averred moral intention of the god. One of the most popular of these avatars is Rama (sometimes called Ramachandra to distinguish him from another avatar, Parashurama).

Rama was the great human hero of the epic *Ramayana*, a king's son, long before he came to be regarded as an avatar of Vishnu. He is the model of the good man, brave and chivalrous, the virtuous son, the noble king, the righteous and loving husband. His beautiful wife, Sita, is also a model character, the ideal of Hindu womanhood as a loyal and devoted wife and mother.

Rama won Sita as his wife by bending and stringing a great bow which was so huge that an eight-wheeled wagon, pulled by 150 men, was required to carry it. When Rama's father was tricked into passing him over as heir to the throne, Rama cheerfully accepted banishment in the forest with Sita. In the forest Sita was carried off by a powerful demon, Ravana, but with the help of the monkey people and their chief, Hanuman, Rama found Sita on the island of Lanka. In a great battle, Rama killed Ravana and rescued Sita, but he then renounced her, for she had involuntarily become defiled by living in the home of another man. However, he took her back when she proved her purity by entering a fire and emerging unharmed.

The other Rama, Parashurama ('Rama with an Axe'), is a less attractive and less popular figure. Parashurama's father, Jamadagni, discovered that his wife Renuka had been guilty of unchaste thoughts, and at Jamadagni's bidding Parashurama beheaded his mother. Later he obtained the boon of restoring his mother to life again. Parashurama is a member of the class of priests, but he is noted for his acts of violence. As well as beheading his mother (and in marked contrast to the motives of that act), Parashurama commits mass murder to avenge the death of his father. When Parashurama had killed a member of the warrior class who had offended him, another warrior retaliated by killing Jamadagni. Parashurama then exterminated the entire class of warriors and gave the earth to the priests to rule.

The Life of Krishna

The violent nature of the two Ramas is still present, though played down, in Vishnu's third human avatar, Krishna. Originally Krishna was the martial hero of an epic (the *Mahabharata*), destructive, cunning and amoral. When he became identified with Vishnu, the motives for his cruelties were expounded in metaphysical and theological terms. The human kings whom he murdered were actually demons in disguise, who so overburdened the earth that she begged Krishna to exterminate them, and so he became incarnate as a human king. When Krishna neglects to prevent the extermination of his own family, an act of genocide reminiscent of Parashurama, various previous curses and, as a last resort, the force of fate are invoked to excuse him. These classical martial exploits remain part of the Hindu legend of Krishna, but they are overshadowed in the later devotional cults by the emphasis on his childhood pranks and erotic dalliances.

The most popular avatars of Vishnu were Rama and Krishna.

ABOVE Figure of Krishna as a child, from Bengal, 18th century. Krishna came to earth to destroy demons who were disguised as human kings. He was born in a royal palace, but to protect his life he was exchanged with the son of a cow-herd and brought up in a village. The story of the god reared among simple people had a powerful appeal and the cults of Krishna emphasized his mischievous childhood pranks and his youthful erotic adventures, before he left the village to carry out his mission.

FAR LEFT When Rama's wife, Sita, was carried off by a demon, Rama and his brother Lakshmana, who was devoted to him, set off to rescue her. They were helped by Hanuman, the chief of the monkey people. Hanuman carrying Rama and Lakshmana, Jaipur School, 1825.

LEFT Vishnu's incarnation as Parashurama, or Rama with an Axe, a violent figure who, for revenge, wiped out the entire class of warriors. Detail from a miniature painting, Mewar School, 1649.

There are many tales of Krishna's youthful miracles, which caused great wonder among human beings, who thought he was human like themselves.

RIGHT The demons sent an ogress, Putana, to nurse the baby Krishna with poisoned milk, but he drained her life's breath from her through her breasts.

BELOW The village boys swam in a pool in the river and were devoured by the many-headed snake Kaliya. Krishna danced on Kaliya's heads until the snake begged for mercy and promised to leave the pool for ever.

Krishna came to earth to kill demons who had become incarnate as wicked kings. As a child, he was a 'secret' god, for his miracles were unseen or misunderstood or forgotten by human beings, who thought he was a mortal like themselves. From the moment of his birth, Krishna's life was threatened, for the wicked King Kamsa knew that he was fated to be killed by Krishna. Kamsa tried to murder the new-born child, but the baby was smuggled out of the palace and exchanged with the son of a simple cow-herd, who brought the boy up as his own son in a small village. Kamsa sent an ogress to nurse the child with poisoned milk, but Krishna sucked her life's breath from her through her breasts. The serpent Kaliya devoured the village boys who swam in a pool in the river, but Krishna dived in and danced on Kaliya's many heads until the snake begged for mercy. Krishna spared him on condition that he leave the pool for ever.

The mischievous Krishna was dearly loved by the cow-herd women, the Gopis, and the cows (symbols of maternal love) whose milk and butter he stole. The girls of the village loved the adolescent Krishna, who stole their clothes when they bathed in the river. As a young man, he danced with them in the moonlight, but when each of them believed that Krishna loved her alone, he slipped away from her. Their search for the lover who teases them is developed into a metaphor of the worshipper's longing for his god. Later, the group of Gopis was replaced by one Gopi, Radha, mistress of Krishna.

Eventually Krishna left the village and killed Kamsa and many other demons. After numerous battles, his sons and relatives, under a sage's curse, drunkenly killed one another. Krishna himself was mistaken for a deer by a hunter who shot him in the foot, the only vulnerable point in his body, and so Krishna left the earth.

LEFT As a young man, Krishna was loved by the village girls. He teased them, stealing their clothes when they bathed in the river and hanging them on a tree out of reach. He danced with them in the moonlight, slipping away when each girl thought he loved her alone. Their longing for him was developed into a metaphor of the worshipper's longing for his god. Illustration to the *Bhagavata Purana*, Kangra School.

The Kali Age

When Krishna died, the present Kali Age is said to have begun, the last and worst of the four ages of the world. The first age was the Golden Age, when virtue prevailed and man lived on the fruits of the garden of earth. After a steady decrease in both virtue and lifespan during the second and third ages, we find ourselves in the present era of sin, disease and heresy. Among the heresies of the Kali Age, Buddhism was regarded by Hindus of the ancient period as the prime threat, and it was as the Buddha that Vishnu became incarnate after the death of Krishna. Later Hindus have seen in this avatar an attempt at rapprochement with Buddhism, but the avatar was originally designed to damn the Buddhists in Hindu eyes; for Vishnu was said to have assumed the form of the Buddha to mislead, corrupt and ultimately destroy dangerous demons, who were indestructible as long as they remained steadfast in their practice of orthodox Hinduism. The demons became Buddhists and were conquered, but Buddhists remained rife on earth among mortals and will thrive until the end of the Kali Age.

At that moment the earth will be destroyed by fire and flood, and out of the cosmic waters the universe will be created again, with a new Golden Age. The cycles of gradual decay followed by sudden renewal will go on until the end of time. To symbolize the destruction of the evil Kali Age, Vishnu will come in his final avatar as Kalki, the warrior riding on a white horse, who will drive the barbarian kings from India, destroy the heretics and save a remnant of good men, from whom the people of the next Golden Age will be descended. There are ancient resonances in the Kalki avatar. The creature who rescues a 'seed' of good men from the cosmic flood is a development of the fish avatar, a form which is further connected with Kalki by the motif of the horse. An early form of Vishnu (not usually included in the classic list of ten avatars) was that of a horse-headed god and in popular mythology Kalki is often represented as a white horse, rather than as a rider on a horse. The influence of Christianity on the Kalki myth is generally acknowledged, though similar claims of Christian influence on the Krishna avatar are no longer considered valid.

Vishnu also appears in theriomorphic manifestations as the serpent and the bird, which are his 'vehicles'. All the Hindu gods have vehicles: Indra rides on the white elephant of the clouds, the sun rides a bay stallion, Agni a sacrificial goat and Brahma the wild goose. These animals not only convey the gods in a literal sense but are regarded as 'conveying' the essence of the gods wherever the animals appear. Vishnu's two vehicles are two diametrically opposed sacred symbols, both associated with divinity and

BELOW The final incarnation of Vishnu is as Kalki, the rider on a white horse, or sometimes the white horse itself. He appears at the end of the age, when the world is destroyed, subsequently to be renewed. This avatar has been influenced by the image of Christ as the rider on the white horse in the Book of Revelation. Vishnu as Kalki, Basholi School, 1760.

RIGHT At the end of each cycle of time, between the destruction of the world and its renewal, Vishnu sleeps on the coils of Ananta, the serpent of infinity. Above, Vishnu rides the Garuda bird, which carries him through the air. Miniature from Rajasthan, 17th century.

ABOVE The other great Hindu god, Shiva, was at first an outsider. To demonstrate his pre-eminence, he took the form of a column so high that Brahma as a bird could not reach its summit, and Vishnu in the form of a boar could not reach its base. The column is the phallus. Basalt carving, 13th century.

immortality. The Garuda bird which carries him through the air is a descendent of the Indo-European fire-bird who brings the elixir of immortality from heaven; he is a symbol of the sun, of the immortal soul and of divinity, as well as of the golden egg from which the universe develops. But Vishnu is also closely associated with the serpent of infinity, Ananta, on whose coils Vishnu sleeps during the twilight period between the end of each Kali Age and the beginning of the next Golden Age. Though serpents and birds are traditional opponents in Indian folklore, the serpent, like the bird, is a symbol of divinity, rebirth (for he sloughs his skin and is reborn), mystery and eternity. By mediating between these two highly numinous animals, Vishnu demonstrates the wide scope of his own powers.

Shiva and Rudra

In striking contrast with Vishnu, who emerges from the earliest texts as a member of the orthodox pantheon and a god favourably disposed to men, Shiva begins as a dark outsider, demonically opposed to the rest of the gods and to mankind as a whole. His Vedic antecedent is the god Rudra, who punishes Prajapati for his act of incest. Rudra is a god of the wilderness, of wild beasts and jungles, of mountain peaks and dangerous crossroads; he is denied a proper share of the Vedic sacrifice and is worshipped separately, in lonely places. When the gods first offered a sacrifice, they deprived Rudra of a share. In fury he attacked them and forced them to allot him a portion by making him Lord of Beasts.

This myth of unwilling and uneasy assimilation recurs in post-Vedic Hinduism. Shiva married Sati, the daughter of Daksha; Daksha gave a sacrifice and failed to invite Shiva, whereupon Sati committed suicide because of the shame her father had brought upon her; she entered the sacrificial fire and became the first 'suttee' (the rite in which widows burned themselves to death). Shiva then destroyed the sacrifice, beheaded Daksha and cast his head into the fire. When the gods prostrated themselves before him and begged for mercy, Shiva restored the sacrifice, revived Daksha and gave him the head of a sacrificial goat. Thus Shiva was excluded from the sacrifice, performed his own sacrifice (upon Daksha) and was at last admitted to the company of the Hindu gods.

One of the reasons for Rudra's original exclusion from the sacrifice was his close association with death, regarded as a demon to be conquered by the gods, like other demons. In later Hinduism, by contrast, death was accepted as an essential part of the divine plan. As Vishnu appears as Kalki to put an end to the Kali Age, so Shiva performs the same function for his worshippers, assuming the role of Doomsday at the appropriate time. The great myth of Rudra's annihilation of the cosmos is the myth of the triple cities. The three sons of the demon Taraka obtained great supernatural powers and built three cities, one of iron, one of silver and one of gold. Their wish for immortality was denied, but when they asked that after a thousand years their three cities should unite to be destroyed by a single arrow shot from Rudra's bow, this wish was granted them by Brahma. At the end of the fated period the cities joined and were destroyed, just as the triple worlds are destroyed at Doomsday. Yet Shiva plays another, complementary role, as the death of Death. When a worshipper of Shiva was about to be carried off by Yama's messengers, Shiva appeared and killed Death.

He later revived him, but made him promise to spare the devotees of the great god.

The slaughter and revival of Death is modelled on another, earlier myth about Shiva: the slaughter and revival of the god of desire, Kama. Shiva, the god of ascetics, refused to remarry after Sati's death, but the gods wished him to beget a son to become their general in the battle against the demon Taraka. When they sent Kama to shoot his flowery arrows at Shiva to break his trance, Shiva opened his third eye (in the middle of his forehead) and burned Kama to ashes. He revived him later at the entreaty of Kama's wife, and ultimately Shiva did marry a second wife, Parvati, the daughter of the mountain Himalaya. Though Shiva made love to Parvati for many years, he failed to father a child. At length the gods sent Agni in the form of a parrot to interrupt the interminable love-play. Agni took the golden seed of Shiva in his mouth and placed it in the river Ganges. The six Pleiades, wives of the Seven Sages who form the constellation of the Great Bear, found the seed and brought forth a six-headed boy, whom they nursed. This was the god Skanda.

Shiva, the Linga and the Dance

Although he is the great yogi and god of ascetics, Shiva is also a god of fertility; his vehicle is the bull Nandi and he is the god of the phallus, called the *linga*. There are several different stories told by Hindus to justify what they admit to be a non-Vedic cult, the most famous of which is the myth of the Epiphany of the *Linga*. Once when the universe was nothing but water, Brahma and Vishnu argued, each saying that he was the greatest of all the gods. Suddenly there appeared between them a great pillar of flame (yet another form of the world-axis). Wishing to determine the height and depth of the pillar, Brahma took the form of the goose and flew as high as he could, while Vishnu took the form of the boar and plunged into the waters, but neither could find an end to the pillar. Then Shiva appeared from within the pillar, which was the cosmic form of his *linga*, and they bowed before him.

Another, rather less majestic and more anecdotal tale of the origin of the *linga* is the myth of the Pine Forest. Several sages (sometimes identified as the Seven Sages) were practising asceticism in the Pine Forest without truly understanding the greatness of Shiva, who went there to teach them a lesson. He disguised himself as a naked beggar carrying a skull for a begging bowl, and he seduced the sages' wives. The furious sages cursed the 'beggar' to be castrated but as the *linga* fell to the ground, darkness fell over the universe and the sages realized who it was they had insulted. They begged Shiva to restore things as they had been and Shiva agreed, on condition that the sages worship his *linga* ever after. Elements of the Daksha myth (the orthodox priests who disregard Shiva to their peril and are forced to accept him) and the myth of the birth of Skanda (the sexual encounter with the sages' wives) combine to legitimize the cult of the *linga*.

Later variants of the Pine Forest myth are used to explain Shiva's manifestation as Lord of the Dance, Nataraja. When the sages became angry, they performed a sacrifice and hurled a series of destructive objects at Shiva, who turned them all to his own use: they created a tiger, whose skin he took as his loincloth; a ball of fire, which he held in his hand; and

FAR LEFT Shiva and Parvati. Among his other roles, Shiva is god of the phallus and in mythology he had various wives. One was Sati, who burned herself to death on the sacrificial fire and so established the custom of suttee. Another was Ganga, the personification of the river Ganges, which runs through Shiva's hair. The beautiful Parvati, a reincarnation of Sati, was the daughter of the mountain Himalaya. 10th century.

LEFT Shiva and Parvati on Mount Kailasa with their children, the six-headed Skanda and the elephant-headed Ganesha. Kangra School. Nandi, the bull, is Shiva's vehicle and a symbol of his nature.

Shiva in his manifestation as Nataraja, Lord of the Dance. Shiva danced on the head of a demon and as he danced the world was whirled and shaken into chaos. He was begged to stop and he consented to delay the dance until the end of the age, when he comes to destroy the worlds. Bronze from southern India, Chola period.

finally a small demon, whose head Shiva trampled upon. When the demon continued to struggle, Shiva danced upon him as Krishna danced upon Kaliya, and as he danced the universe was shaken and whirled into chaos. Terrified, the sages begged Shiva to stop dancing, and he agreed to postpone the dance until Doomsday, when it would become the dance of universal death.

This story, in which the dance replaces the castration, appears only in the South Indian sources. The northern texts depict Shiva as an enemy of the dance. One day the sage Mankanaka cut his finger on a blade of grass and saw that vegetable sap, instead of blood, poured from the wound. In ecstasy at this miracle, he danced until the worlds shook and the gods sent Shiva to determine the cause of the disturbance. Shiva appeared before Mankanaka, learned from him the reason for his excessive joy, and struck his own thumb with his fingernail. Ashes poured forth from the wound and Mankanaka, realizing his vain folly, stopped dancing and begged Shiva to forgive him.

Shiva's Symbols

The ashes which flow from Shiva's veins are the ashes of corpses. Shiva lives in the cremation ground, surrounded by unclean jackals, and even takes the form of a corpse in later Tantric iconography (Tantrism is an Indian and Tibetan sexual cult). These are attributes derived from his role as god of death. Another symbol of this role is the skull which Shiva carries in his hand and sometimes wears as an ornament in his matted locks. It is the skull of Brahma, whom Shiva beheaded in the midst of one of their frequent arguments. The skull stuck fast to Shiva's hand and he wandered about, begging for alms, until he reached the city of Benares, where the skull fell away. There he established the shrine of the Loosing of the Skull, a shrine which expiates even the great sin of killing a priest. The skull is an ambivalent image – it is murder and also the power that frees one from the stigma of murder – and this image is juxtaposed with another symbol of death and revival: the moon, which Shiva also carries in his hair and which dies and is reborn every month.

The final element of Shiva's coiffure is the river Ganges, which represents fertility, rebirth and purification, as well as Shiva's grace: for the Ganges at first existed only in heaven, as the Milky Way, until a king whose sons had been burned to ashes begged her to come to earth to revive them. She did so, but first she asked Shiva to break her great fall by allowing her to touch earth first on his head, on the peak of Himalaya, and then to wind to earth through his matted locks. The Ganges flows through the skull in Shiva's hair and then through the ashes of the dead princes, reviving them as Shiva revived Kama, and Death, from ashes. In her anthropomorphic form, the Ganges is regarded as yet another wife of Shiva, and her vehicle is the crocodile or sea-monster.

Shiva and Andhaka

Under the influence of medieval devotional cults, the destructive acts of Shiva came to be viewed as acts of grace. Shiva, with Vishnu, is one of the supreme gods of Hinduism. He is both creator and destroyer, erotic and ascetic, mild and mad. The myth of Andhaka, the Blind One, shows how these opposite aspects of Shiva are reconciled.

Shiva had three eyes, the third in the middle of his forehead. Shiva's wife, Parvati, once jokingly covered her husband's eyes with her hands and the universe was plunged in darkness, for the three eyes were the sun, the moon and fire. When a drop of sweat fell into Shiva's third eye, it became a child, who was blind because he had been conceived in darkness. Called Andhaka, he was adopted by a demon and grew up with demonic ways; he lusted for Parvati, not knowing that she was his mother. Shiva impaled him on his trident and held him there for centuries, burning him with the same eye that had engendered him. The fire burned away Andhaka's demonic nature and purified him, and he became one of Shiva's servants.

Interwoven with a thinly veiled theme of incest, the ostensible point of the story is that the god

shows his mercy to those who display emotion toward him, even when that emotion is hatred. And for his part, it is Shiva's intention that those acts of his which seem malevolent or destructive toward us should in fact bring us to him, in the death that frees one from the wheel of rebirth, the cycle of death and reincarnation in which man is held prisoner.

The Goddess

Goddesses of various sorts appear throughout Hindu mythology. The dawn is an important Vedic goddess; Vach, speech incarnate, is one of the chief deities of the *Brahmanas*; the goddess Earth is a consort of Vishnu; and the Ganges, Sati and Parvati are the wives of Shiva. But the Goddess, regarded as a single, supreme divine power, not merely an attribute or chattel of a male god, only comes into her own in the medieval period. By this time, she is a conflation of numerous local goddesses and is the subject of many, often conflicting, village traditions.

The classic myth of the birth of the Goddess is the inverse of the original myth of creation by cosmic dismemberment. The gods, harrassed by a buffalo demon who could not be killed by any god, became furious, and from their angry bodies a wave of energy came forth. These energies merged to form the Goddess, her head formed from the energy of Shiva, her arms from Vishnu, her feet from Brahma, her waist from Indra, her eyes from Agni, and so on; she rode upon a lion. The Goddess killed the buffalo demon, first enticing him to fall in love with her and then beheading him, so releasing his immortal soul from the demonic buffalo body in which it had been imprisoned (a body destroyed by her lion). Thus both his apparent aggression toward her and hers toward him are motivated by love.

Worshippers of the Goddess regard her as the animating force which makes it possible for the gods to accomplish their own deeds. In their versions of the classic myths, for example, Vishnu as the man-lion begs the Goddess and her lion to help him kill Prahlada's father, and Shiva enlists her aid in destroying the triple city. The cycle of myths particularly susceptible to this type of transformation is the one dealing with Shiva and his wives Sati and Parvati. Devotees of the Goddess, particularly Tantric worshippers, add an epilogue to the story of Daksha's sacrifice. After Sati had killed herself, Shiva

ABOVE LEFT In medieval Hinduism Shiva's destructive acts were interpreted as acts of mercy. One of Shiva's children, Andhaka, was born of the god's third eye, in his forehead. Andhaka lusted for Parvati and Shiva impaled him on his trident and burned Andhaka with the same eye that had engendered him. The burning purified Andhaka and he became a servant of Shiva. Mughal MS, *c.*1590.

ABOVE The Goddess killing the buffalo demon. The gods were harrassed by this demon, who could only be killed by a female, and from their angry bodies waves of energy emanated and formed the Goddess. She beheaded the demon, so releasing his soul from the demonic body in which it had been imprisoned. 12th century.

wandered about carrying the corpse, dancing and weeping, disturbing the earth until Vishnu dismembered the corpse. In every place that a piece of Sati's body fell, a shrine to the Goddess arose, the holiest of which is the shrine in Assam where the Goddess's sexual parts (*yoni*) fell. This dance of death appears in an inverted form in Bengal, where it is said that the Goddess in her hideous form as the bloodthirsty Kali dances upon the corpse of her husband, Shiva. By this act, she animates him, changing the corpse (called Shava in Sanskrit) into Shiva, the living god.

This hideous aspect of the Goddess is counterbalanced by her benign, maternal aspect as Gauri, the Golden One, mother of Skanda. A myth explains this apparent schizophrenia. Shiva, whose body is covered with white ashes, once taunted his wife for her dark skin. In fury and shame, she performed asceticism until she was granted the boon of having a golden skin. She sloughed her black skin like that of a snake, and that outer sheath became the cruel goddess Kali. This myth of a 'split' mother recurs in later popular mythology, which extends the tale of Parashurama and Renuka with a significant episode. When Parashurama had beheaded his mother and subsequently obtained the boon of reviving her, he accidentally joined her head to the headless corpse of a low-caste woman, joining that woman's head to his mother's body; and so the two women arose in this mixed form. Clearly this myth, like so many tales of the Goddess, betrays some awareness of historical syncretism and sheds light upon certain caste relationships, but it may also be interpreted in purely symbolic terms as an image of the ambivalent mother, both loving and hateful.

In Bengal, where the cult of the Goddess has always

ABOVE The hideous and bloodthirsty aspect of the Goddess is said to be the black skin which she once shed, like a snake, to reveal the golden skin which is hers in her beneficent and motherly aspect. In her terrifying form as Kali, the Black, she dances on the dead body of Shiva, her husband. By this act she brings him to life, transforming the corpse (Shava in Sanskrit) into Shiva, the living god.

RIGHT Skanda or Kartti-keya, the many-headed god of war, whose vehicle is the peacock. Hindu mythology is still a living force in India and the figures of Mahatma Gandhi and Pandit Nehru can be seen in this relief from the Muragan Temple Tiruchendur, South India.

Ganesha is the god of scribes and merchants. His original head was cut off and replaced by the head of Airavata, the white elephant, mount of Indra. Airavata was killed by Shiva's vehicle, the bull Nandi. Ganesha's title of Lord of Obstacles can be interpreted to mean that he removes obstacles from the path of human beings who worship him correctly, but places them in the way of those who do not pay due homage to the gods.

been particularly prominent, she is glorified at the expense of Shiva. Here it is said that Shiva first married the Ganges and then took the goddess Durga as an additional wife. Durga suffers numerous indignities because of her husband. Shiva smokes marijuana until he is too stupefied even to beg and he sells Durga's jewellery to support his habit. Once a year, at the autumnal festival of Durgapuja, Durga returns to her parents' home in Calcutta and complains about her husband, but at the end of the festival she must return to him in the Himalayas, floating back to him along the very river Ganges which, in anthropomorphic form, is the source of Durga's greatest sorrow.

In South India, the cult of the Goddess is supplemented by the cult of the Seven Sisters and the Little Mothers. Sometimes identified with the gentle, chaste Pleiades who nurse Skanda, sometimes with a larger group of hideous, terrifying ogresses who are placated and kept away rather than invoked, these mysterious figures are widely worshipped in tandem with the more conventional goddesses of the orthodox pantheon. Other goddesses worshipped throughout India and often identified with the Goddess or with one of the Mothers are held responsible for disease and misfortune. Jyeshtha, 'the eldest', is a goddess of evil and bad luck, said to dwell in the homes of those who quarrel. Shitala, 'the cool one', is a euphemism for the feverish goddess of smallpox, who rides on an ass and wears red clothes. Another form of the Goddess in Bengal is Manasha, goddess of snakes. Shashti, 'the sixth', is the goddess of married women and patron of childbirth, worshipped on the sixth day after the birth of a child, when the greatest danger of infant mortality is felt to have passed. Shasti rides on a cat, a domestic animal which, unlike the dog, is regarded with respect by all Indian women.

Skanda and Ganesha

The Little Mothers and the Goddess herself are intimately involved in the mythology of Skanda and Ganesha, two gods regarded as sons of Shiva but worshipped in their own right. Skanda is the great warrior of the gods; he carries a spear and rides on a peacock. As soon as he was born, he pierced the mountains with his arrows and shattered them, causing destruction and worrying Indra (who is the great shatterer of mountains in the early texts). The gods begged Indra to kill Skanda before he overpowered them all. Indra sent the Mothers to kill Skanda, but when they saw his splendour and power they were terrified and nursed him with the milk from their breasts. Indra then attacked Skanda himself, hurling his thunderbolt at Skanda. The weapon

HINDU DEITIES AND MYTHOLOGICAL BEINGS

Hinduism is polytheistic at one level and monotheistic at another, for the numerous deities are often regarded as manifestations of a single principle. There are also many different sects and schools of thought within Hinduism. Some late texts, Indian as well as European, speak of a 'trinity' of gods, the Trimurti, consisting of Brahma the Creator, Vishnu the Preserver and Shiva the Destroyer, but this is not a popular or valid concept, since Brahma is not worshipped. For many Hindus either Vishnu or Shiva is the Supreme Being – creator, preserver and destroyer in one – but other deities have their own worshippers or survive in myths and folklore.

Aditi, the Infinite, a sky-goddess, mother of the gods

Adityas, celestial deities, children of Aditi: they include Indra, Mitra, Rudra, Tvashtar, Varuna and Vishnu

Agni, god of fire: his name is equivalent to Latin *ignis*, 'fire'

Ananta or **Shesha,** the coiled serpent of infinite time

The Ashvins, benevolent gods, twin horsemen, sons of the sun: they are related to the divine twins of Greek and Roman mythology

Asuras, titanic demons, enemies of the gods, possessed of magical powers

Brahma, the post-Vedic form of Prajapati, the creator

Buddha, Gautama, the founder of Buddhism: regarded in Hinduism as an avatar of Vishnu

Durga, a goddess worshipped throughout India but especially in Bengal: wife of Shiva, often identified with Kali and Parvati

Dyaus, early Indo-European god of the sky, related to Greek Zeus and Roman Jupiter, but not an important figure in Hindu mythology

Gandharvas, celestial musicians, demi-gods

Ganesha, Lord of Obstacles, the elephant-headed god of scribes and merchants, son of Shiva and Parvati

Ganges, the sacred river, is personified as the goddess Ganga, one of Shiva's wives, daughter of the mountain Himalaya: before the river reaches earth it is the Milky Way in the sky

Garuda, the king of birds and the mount of Vishnu

Gauri, the Golden One, a benign aspect of the great goddess

Gopis, milkmaids, lovers of the youthful Krishna

Hanuman, chief minister and general of the monkey people

Hari-Hara, a composite god, intended to combine Shiva and Vishnu

Himalaya, Abode of Snow, a great mountain or mountain range, father of Parvati

Indra, in the Vedic period the king of the gods, lord of storm, fertility and war: he later faded into the background

Jyeshtha, the Eldest, goddess of bad luck

Kali, the Black, wife of Shiva, the goddess in her terrifying, cruel and bloodthirsty aspect

Kama, god of desire

Karttikeya, another name for Skanda

Krishna, the Dark One, a cow-herd and a prince, worshipped as an incarnation of Vishnu

Lakshmi, a goddess of beauty and good fortune, born of the churning of the ocean, consort of Vishnu

Manasha, goddess of snakes, worshipped in Bengal

Manu, ancestor of the human race, saved from the flood by a great fish

Mitra, a Vedic god of light, Mithra in Iran, Mithras in the Roman world

Nagas, in legend a race of snakes, ancestors of many Indian princely dynasties: often depicted as cobras, or in human or semi-human form

Nandi, the bull, vehicle of Shiva

Nataraja, Lord of the Dance, a manifestation of Shiva

Parashurama, Rama with an Axe, a human incarnation of Vishnu: his magic battleaxe was given him by Shiva

Parvati, daughter of Himalaya, consort of Shiva

Prajapati, Lord of Creatures, in the Vedic period creator of the universe, father of gods, demons and all creatures: later known as Brahma

Prithivi, goddess of the earth, consort of Dyaus

Purusha, the cosmic man: he was sacrificed and all the parts of the cosmos, including the four classes of society, were made from his dismembered body

Radha, the principal mistress of Krishna

Rama, or **Ramachandra,** a prince, hero of the *Ramayana*, worshipped as an incarnation of Vishnu

Rudra, Lord of Beasts, Vedic god of the jungle and wild nature, god of disease, associated with death: he later evolved into Shiva

Sati, first wife of Shiva: she established the custom of *sati* (suttee)

Shakti, term for the power or the wife of a god and specifically for Shiva's consort as his feminine aspect

Shashti, the Sixth, a goddess who protects children and women in childbirth

Shitala, the Cool One, goddess of smallpox

Shiva, with Vishnu one of the two great gods of post-Vedic Hinduism: among his symbols are the erect phallus and the trident

Skanda, son of the Pleiades, a warrior-god, the six-headed son of Shiva

Soma, the elixir of life, both a god and a drug, made from a plant tentatively identified as a hallucinogen, possibly fly agaric: called Haoma in Iran

Surya, god of the sun, later identified with Vishnu but also worshipped in his own right

Tvashtar, craftsman of the gods

Uma, another name for Shiva's consort

Ushas, goddess of the dawn, in one myth the daughter of Prajapati and by him the mother of all living things

Vach, goddess of speech

Varuna, an ancient god of the sky and cosmic order, possibly related to Ahura Mazda in Iran and Uranus in Greece: later, god of the waters

Vishnu, a Vedic sun-deity, later one of the two great gods of post-Vedic Hinduism

Vivasvat, the sun, an aspect of Surya

Yama, son of the sun, king of the dead

split Skanda's side, from which another warrior came forth, and then Indra worshipped Skanda. This initial rivalry resolved, Skanda went on to accomplish the task for which he had been created, to kill the demon Taraka. Since Skanda is the general of the gods (as Indra was in Vedic times, which may account for their conflict), his wife is the Army of the Gods, though he is also said to be married to various South Indian goddesses as well as to the dancing-girls attached to South Indian temples.

Ganesha, like Skanda, is threatened by Indra as soon as he is born, though the circumstances of his birth reveal a greater threat from his own father, Shiva. Parvati wished to have a child, but Shiva did not want to become involved in family life. At last he scornfully told her to make a child from a piece of red cloth. She did so and the cloth became a handsome young son, but when Shiva touched the child's head, it fell off. To console the desolate Parvati, Shiva sent Nandi, his bull vehicle and his bull-headed doorkeeper, to get another head for the child. Nandi decided to take the head of Airavata, the white elephant who is the mount of Indra. Indra fought Nandi, who broke off one of the elephant's tusks and ultimately forced Indra to admit defeat. Shiva then told Indra to throw the headless body of Airavata into the ocean, whence he would re-emerge whole at the time of the churning. Another version of Ganesha's birth is that Parvati created him from the dirt washed from her body, and stationed him at her bathroom door to keep Shiva from disturbing her. The sexual conflict between father and son is made explicit here, where Ganesha guards Parvati's door (as Nandi guards Shiva's).

The gods gave Ganesha a rat or bandicoot as his vehicle, for Ganesha is the remover of obstacles, and a rat can find or gnaw his way out of any trap. Ganesha's epithet of Lord of Obstacles is sometimes interpreted in a curious way. He is said to be sent by the gods to put obstacles in the path of those who find their way to heaven too easily, by worshipping at shrines without paying due homage to the gods, while he is still supposed to remove obstacles from the path of those who worship him correctly. Ganesha is the god of scribes, invoked at the beginning of any literary work. He is said to be married to the two goddesses Success and Wit. Some texts say that Skanda had fallen in love with them too, and it was agreed that whoever first travelled around the world would have them. As Skanda, the great athlete, raced round the globe, the crafty Ganesha merely waddled round his two parents, who are the whole world, and won the bet. The rivalry of the two gods is often expressed in myths describing the antagonism between their two vehicles, the peacock and the rat.

Mythology in Modern Hinduism

Each of the myths discussed here is told in several different versions. The myths are being retold, reinterpreted and rediscovered everywhere in India to this day and Hindus recognize the modernity and contemporary relevance of the stories even in their original, archaic forms. They are brought up to date from time to time, with revisions stemming from social developments, but the enduring elements of the myths – the human conflicts, the metaphysical enigmas, the symbolic meanings, the ritual enactments – persist even in the most watered-down versions.

Figure of the goddess Durga mounted on the lion, her vehicle. She is being drawn by bicycle to be installed in a shrine during her festival. Durga is a ferocious goddess and a famous slayer of demons, but she is loving and gentle to those who worship her.

The importance of separating abstract classes into their proper order is emphasized in myths which lend support to the Hindu caste system. Similarly, myths depicting the dangers of incest, the inevitability of fraternal rivalry or the contrast between the good mother and the wicked seductress continue to thrive even in urban Indian society. The myths of ritual beheading have lost much of their liturgical power, though they may retain a certain Freudian or horrific appeal, but the contrast between clean and unclean animals, or between the tame and the wild – cows and mares, cats and dogs, birds and snakes, elephants and lions – remains significant in a country still largely rural and agricultural.

In Calcutta one may buy comic books about the marriage of Shiva and Parvati, occasionally bowdlerized or distorted, but often remarkably accurate in preserving the spirit of the myth. Demons appear on the cinema screen in New Delhi, accompanied by blasts of sadly bastardized Indian music, but still demonic from head to toe. Political reformers like Gandhi and Aurobindo drew upon the classical mythology, often twisting it for their own purposes, and were sure of an immediate response from even the most illiterate of their followers. The modern western usage of the word 'myth' to denote a story which is untrue, a fabrication, certainly has no validity in India today. Even the most 'liberated' and westernized of Hindus of modern India still regard their mythology as containing much that is very true indeed.

CHAPTER TWO

THERAVADA BUDDHISM

The founder of Buddhism, Siddhartha Gautama, was born in northern India in about 563 BC. The son of a chieftain of the Sakya clan, he left his home and family at the age of 29 and set out in search of spiritual illumination. After six years of striving, he attained his Enlightenment at the age of 35, at Bodh Gaya in the Indian province of Bihar, and was afterwards known as the Buddha (the Enlightened One) and Sakyamuni (the Sage of the Sakyas). He lived a simple life, travelling about, teaching and winning many followers, and passed away at the age of 80.

Asoka, ruler of the Mauryan Empire in northern India in the 3rd century BC, was a Buddhist and despatched missionaries to several countries, including Egypt and Greece. Asoka's son Mahinda carried Buddhism to Sri Lanka in about 250 BC. Subsequently it spread to Burma, Thailand, Cambodia and other countries of south-east Asia. Buddhism also spread to Central Asia, from there to China, where the first Buddhist temple was built in the 1st century AD, and later to Korea (4th century) and Japan (6th century). Buddhism took firm root in Tibet between the 7th and 13th centuries.

In India, Buddhism was on the decline by about AD 500 and was virtually extinct with the advent of Islam in the 11th and 12th centuries. There are small numbers of Buddhists in India and Pakistan today, and also in Indonesia, the Philippines, North and South America, and western Europe.

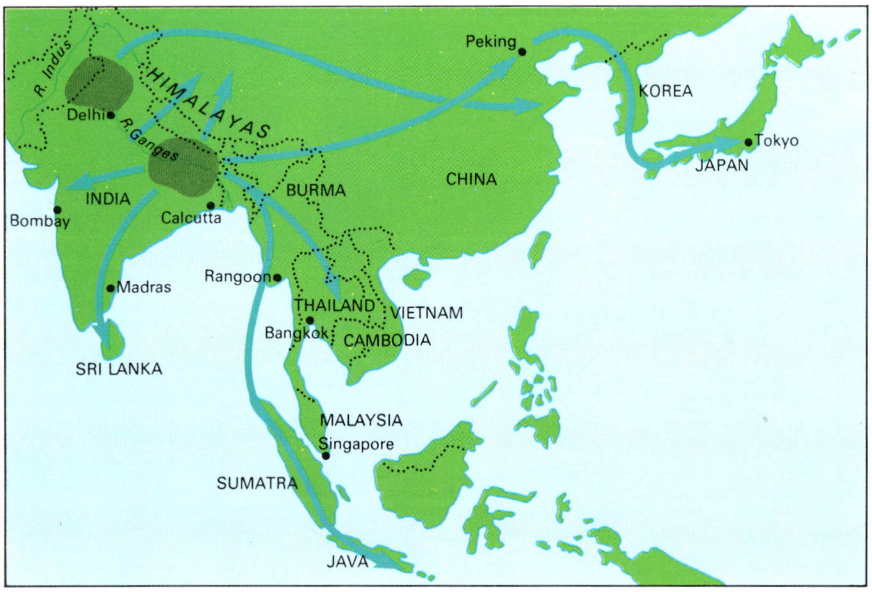

The Buddha's teachings were handed down orally until they were written down in Sri Lanka in the 2nd or 1st century BC. The oldest Buddhist writings are in the Pali language and constitute a collection of texts called the Tipitaka (Three Baskets), which the Theravada Buddhist tradition of Sri Lanka, Burma and south-east Asia regards as authentic. The divergent tradition in Tibet, China, Korea and Japan is known as Mahayana Buddhism.

Buddhism and Hinduism

The religious background in which Buddhism grew up in India was that of Brahmanism, an early stage of Hinduism. Buddhism shared the belief, common in India at the time, that human beings endure many lives, living and dying and being reborn in various forms and conditions of existence, according to the law of *karma* and on the principle that as a man sows, so shall he reap. The supreme purpose of Buddhism was to achieve liberation from this cycle of life, death and rebirth by attaining enlightenment and entering a timeless state, free of both craving and suffering, called Nibbana in Pali, Nirvana in Sanskrit. Indian thought conceived of numerous gods, goddesses and spirits, and of many heavens and hells in which human beings were rewarded or punished according to their deserts. These ideas too were shared by Buddhism, though with a difference.

In time Buddhism developed a mythology of its own. Popular tales grew up about the Buddha himself. It was said that his conception and birth were immaculate. He entered his mother's womb in the form of a snow-white elephant (or according to another story, as a star with six rays). His mother, Maya, saw this in a dream. She gave birth to him after ten months. He emerged from her side, undefiled and without causing her pain, and the udumbara tree, which blossoms only when a Buddha is born, put forth its blooms. On the seventh day afterwards Maya died of joy and was reborn among the gods. Later, while living as an ascetic, the future Buddha subjected himself to privations and austerities which reduced him almost to a skeleton. There were many tales of the miracles he performed after he attained his Enlightenment. He passed away peacefully, surrounded by disciples, among flowering trees beside the river at Kusinagara (in the district of Gorakhpur, Uttar Pradesh province), while the celestial musicians, the Gandharvas, played and sang. The pyre on which his body was burned lighted by itself.

There were also stories of the Buddha's previous births, and it was accepted that others could and did follow his path. The consequence in later Buddhism, in India and outside, was the belief in many Buddhas, manifestations of the spiritual principle of Buddahood, and Bodhisattvas: ideal beings who became Buddhist deities and were worshipped. A Bodhisattva is one who will become a Buddha, but who compassionately delays his liberation from the universe of repeated births and remains in it to help other beings.

The Defeat of the Asuras

The mythological world of the Early Buddhist texts, however, is inhabited primarily by the Devas, the traditional Indian gods. (Early Buddhism here designates the Theravada tradition, which represents the most ancient form of Indian Buddhism.) There is scarcely any difference between the status of the Devas and that of the Asuras, who are supernatural beings of titanic power (often called 'demons'). Both were taken over from traditional Indian mythology, together with the myth of eternal enmity between them (see HINDUISM). References to this enmity occur in the earliest Buddhist texts, but only in the later commentaries are they elaborated into lively stories.

The Asuras, powerful supernatural beings, once lived in the realm of Tavatimsa together with the gods. The king of Tavatimsa, the god Sakka, did not relish the idea of sharing the kingdom with others. He made the Asuras drunk and then had them hurled by their feet on to the steep sides of Mount Sineru. They tumbled into what came to be known as the realm of the Asuras, on the lowest level of Mount Sineru, equal in extent to Tavatimsa. Here grew the

Buddhism originated in India against the background of traditional Indian mythology, but in time it developed a lively mythology of its own. Popular stories grew up about its founder, Gautama Buddha himself.

ABOVE Seated Buddha in the ruins of the temple at Polonnaruwa, Sri Lanka, 12th century.

FAR LEFT Gautama's mother, Queen Maya, was said to have seen, in a dream, the future Buddha enter her womb in the form of a snow-white elephant. Indian carving, c.2nd century AD.

LEFT As a young man, the future Buddha practised austerities which reduced him almost to a living skeleton.

Cittapatali tree, and when it blossomed the Asuras knew that they were no longer in the world of the gods. Determined to regain their kingdom, they climbed Mount Sineru 'like ants going up a pillar'. When the alarm was given, Sakka went out to give battle to them in the ocean, but he was worsted in the fight and fled to his chariot. Fleeing through the Simbali groves, which were the home of the Garudas (mythical creatures, part-bird and part-man), he feared that his chariot would hurt the young Garudas and he turned back. The Asuras, thinking that Sakka had obtained reinforcements, fled back into the Asura realm. Sakka returned to his city and at that moment of victory his palace sprang up from the ground. To prevent the Asuras from coming back again, Sakka set guards in five places, and everywhere were images of the god Indra with the thunderbolt in his hand.

Realms of Gods and Men

In the early texts there are 14 principal types or classes of gods, whose form of existence is considered superior to the human in certain respects. They correspond to the heavenly realms, which are classified in two main divisions, a lower division of six realms and a higher of eight. The gods of the six lower realms live in continuous enjoyment of the senses, but the gods of the eight higher realms live in an unbroken bliss of meditative experience.

The highest of the gods are the Brahmas, whose realm is Brahmakayika. Only a few of them, including Sahampati, regarded as the most senior of them, are described as having any dealings with human beings. The other Brahmas take no interest in human affairs. The gods of the six lower realms are more concerned with the human world and they appear in various myths. Sakka, who is the king of the gods in the realm called Tavatimsa, appears in many of these tales, with or without his divine

ABOVE Gautama attained enlightenment at Bodh-Gaya beneath the Tree of Wisdom, where animals and birds worshipped him. Late 18th-century carving.

RIGHT At the end of his life on earth, at the age of 80, the Buddha passed to Nirvana, lying on a couch in a grove of flowering trees and attended by his disciples. The Parinirvana of the Buddha, relief from the Swat valley, India, 2nd century.

charioteer, Matali. There are several stories of these gods showing an interest in the propagation of the Buddha's teachings.

There is also a class of gods who are inferior to those of the heavenly realms and who live closer to the surroundings of human beings, in forest groves, trees and elsewhere. Of these minor gods, the forest deities (*Vana devatas*) and tree deities (*Rukkha devatas*) keep vigil over the activities of human beings engaged in meditation to attain Nibbana. These gods come from the background of tree-worship which existed in the Buddha's time. Stories of them in the Early Buddhist texts emphasize the watchful ward and care of these kind and sympathetic deities, ever alert to help the meditators.

In addition, there are three realms or classes of existence which are classified as inferior to the human form of existence. The first of them is the Pettivisaya, the realm of the Petas (the ghosts). The second is the animal kingdom, Tiracchanayoni. The third is the Niraya (Purgatory), in which human beings are punished for, and purged of, their misdeeds. It has ten sub-divisions, which are to be understood as different states of suffering, not as spatial divisions within it. A fourth inferior realm, the Asura Nikaya, is a later addition to the system, as there is no evidence in the early texts of the Asuras constituting a distinct realm.

These 'realms' are not spatially distinct from the human world, as in other Indian mythological thought. This is in keeping with Early Buddhist cosmology, in which the universe is not divided into separate compartments, constituting the different regions of human and non-human beings. The mythological beings belong, not to different worlds, but to different types or classes of existence from the human, and the names of the various realms denote particular spiritual characteristics, not places.

Although this is true of the earliest Buddhist writings, the position changes in the later literature. The cosmological ideas of other religions found their way into Buddhist texts, first discolouring the distinctive Buddhist cosmology and subsequently overshadowing it almost completely, especially in the hands of commentators interpreting the original texts several centuries later.

In Early Buddhism, however, the physical world is considered of interest only to the extent that it is related to human beings, and this principle was logically extended to the gods and other mythological beings. Their activities are not centred in far-off heavens or hells, but in the environment of man. They are not of interest in and of themselves, but only in terms of their behaviour towards, and relations with, human beings. This constitutes a significant difference between Buddhist mythology and most other mythologies.

The mythological characters who appear in Early Buddhist stories, consequently, are principally those who have dealings with human beings. Most of these stories seem to have been borrowed from the general stock of traditional Indian mythology and adapted to suit the special requirements of Buddhism. This adaptation led to important alterations in the mythology. The heavens and hells changed from separate and distant worlds to states in which human beings exist after death, and life in them could no longer be eternal. The heavens became places of temporary refuge only and the hells were replaced by the new Purgatory, which is best described as a reform school for evil-doers. The aim of religious endeavour changed from attaining eternal happiness in a heaven to passing beyond the heavens and the condition of the gods. The enlightened man is the highest being in the entire cosmos and the gods and spirits are all subordinated to him.

Mara and the Buddha

Buddhism has no mythology of evil spirits, for it does not believe that any spirits are capable of harming a human being. However, such stories as the Early Buddhist accounts of the demon Mara's futile attempts to prevent the Buddha's Enlightenment led to elaborate tales in the later literature. It was said that when the Buddha sat under the Bodhi-tree, immediately before his Enlightenment, Mara summoned all his forces and advanced against him. Mara's forces extended to a distance of 12 leagues to the front of the Buddha, 12 to the back, nine to the right and nine to the left. The thousand-armed Mara himself rode on his huge elephant, Girimekhala, 150 leagues in height. His followers assumed various fearsome shapes and were armed with terrifying weapons. At their approach, all the gods and spirits who were gathered round the Buddha, singing his praises and paying him homage, disappeared in headlong flight. The Buddha was left alone, and he called to his assistance the ten virtues (*parami*) which he had practised to perfection.

In very late versions of the story, each of the ten divisions of Mara's army is described with a great wealth of detail. Each division was faced by the Buddha with one virtue and was put to flight. Mara's last weapon was the Cakkavudha, a circular weapon which could cut a mountain in half, but when he hurled it at the Buddha, it stood over the Buddha like a canopy of flowers. Still undaunted, Mara

ABOVE LEFT The Apsarases were taken over into Buddhist belief from traditional Indian mythology. They are beautiful nymphs of paradise, trained in the erotic arts. One is seen with an attendant in this fresco from Sigiriya, Sri Lanka, 5th century.

ABOVE After the Buddha had attained enlightenment he remained in meditation for many weeks. To shield him from a violent storm, the great cobra Musilinda came and spread his hood above the Buddha's head for a canopy, and his coils beneath the Buddha's body for a seat.

The Buddha attacked by Mara. The evil Mara attempted to prevent the Buddha's enlightenment. He first sent three beautiful girls, who tried in vain to distract and seduce the Buddha. Then Mara attacked with an army of monsters and demons, but the Buddha was proof against them. Here Mara's white elephant kneels to the Buddha. From a temple at Telvatte, Sri Lanka, *c.*16th century.

challenged the Buddha to show that the seat on which he sat was his by right. Mara's followers all shouted that the seat was rightfully Mara's. The Buddha, having no other witness, asked the Earth to bear testimony on his behalf, and the Earth roared in response. Mara and his followers fled in rout, and the gods gathered round the Buddha to celebrate his victory.

Versions of the tale in the Early Buddhist texts show careful and systematic adaptation from current Indian myths, but in the later accounts there are wholesale and indiscriminate borrowings from the same sources. The simple tale of the Buddha's conversion of a tribal leader, Alavaka, for example, reappears in the later literature with all the mythological embellishments of the Mara myth. These later elaborations seem to have been heavily influenced by the traditions of Jainism (an Indian religion which grew up at about the same time as Buddhism). In the account of the enlightenment of Parsva, a Jain sage and saviour, a god named Samvara or Meghamalin employs all the means at his command to prevent Parsva's enlightenment. The concept of an eternal enemy of enlightenment seems to have been deeply embedded in Jain traditions, as there is a similar story of attempts by a god, who is also described as a demon, to prevent the enlightenment of the Jain prophet Mahavira (a contemporary of the Buddha).

Yama and Purgatory

One of the later texts (the *Vimanavatthu*) describes the splendour of the celestial abodes of the various gods, reborn as a result of meritorious actions in the human world. Another (the *Petavatthu*) contains vivid descriptions of people in states of woeful suffering in the Niraya owing to their misdeeds of the past.

The overlord of the Niraya is King Yama (see HINDUISM). Birth, old age, illness, punishment for crime, and death are regarded as his messengers, sent among men as a warning to do good and abstain from evil. When beings are reborn into Purgatory after death, they are led before Yama and questioned by him. This theme, again, was taken over from traditional Indian mythology, but in the Early Buddhist texts Yama plays no significant role in the operation of the law of *karma*, such as deciding the nature or extent of suffering which a particular individual deserves. He is merely a sympathetic onlooker and one text (the *Devaduta Sutta* of the *Majjhima Nikaya*) says that his questioning of evildoers is not intended to decide the punishment they deserve. By an extension of this idea, a commentary states that Yama's questioning is meant to remind the individual of any good deeds he may have done, and so avert his suffering in the Niraya. According to a story recorded in the commentary, a certain minister who could not remember having done any good deed was reminded by Yama that he had made an offering of jasmine flowers to the Great Pagoda (at Anuradhapura in Sri Lanka) and had transferred the merit of this action to Yama. As a result the minister was reborn in heaven. The concepts associated with this story are untenable by the lights of Early Buddhism but they found sanction and were greatly elaborated in the Buddhist tradition as it developed in Sri Lanka.

Changes of Attitude

Although the Early Buddhist tradition drew freely and profusely on the Indian mythological heritage of its time, it restructured its borrowings to serve as doctrinal devices, used to promote Buddhist teaching, but forming no part of the teaching itself. The earlier texts were remarkably consistent in this, and what remains at the end of this process of 'Buddhistification' is merely the outer shell of the non-Buddhist myths, the entire inner character having been transformed.

Thus the war-waging, bloodthirsty, prayer-heeding gods of Brahmanism, appeased only by massive and costly sacrifices involving extremely complicated ritual, have been transformed into beings whose nature is inherently kind and sympathetic, and who are full of veneration and respect not only towards the Buddha and the arahants (those who have attained liberation), but towards all good men. The fierce king of the dead, Yama, appeased only by elaborate sacrifices, has been turned into a modest onlooker at the operation of the law of *karma*. The evil spirits, infesting man's surroundings and conciliated by offerings, have become beings who are miserably suffering in expiation of their past evil actions, which does away with even the slightest notion that they can harm man. The abodes of the gods are no longer situated in the farthest recesses of space; the gods have the same physical surroundings as man.

The final outcome is that what we see in the Early Buddhist texts resembles the rich non-Buddhist mythology which formed an indispensable part of Buddhist religious traditions, but divested of all its inner characteristics. A close examination of the mythology shows that the resemblances are merely external, the inner character having been changed to serve the special requirements of Buddhism. This system of adaptation extended to both the mythological and the non-mythological spheres, for the sacrifices upon which the gods were feasted, and the various magical means of feeding and placating the lesser mythological beings, were replaced by *dana* – offerings of food made preferably to Buddhist monks – so that no god or demon accepted into Buddhism became the centre of any cult or of ritual observances.

In the opposite direction, however, the later inflow of provincial religious and ritualistic elements into the major Indian religious traditions, especially from Iran and the Greek world, seriously affected subsequent Buddhist interpretations of the mythological material in the Early Buddhist texts. It was in this climate that Mahinda's mission arrived in Sri Lanka. The form of ritualistic Buddhism which he sought to popularize in Sri Lanka seems to have been heavily influenced by what was happening in the Indian subcontinent at the time. As a result, religious rituals and practices which would not have been acceptable to the original Buddhism were now conveniently accommodated, though the original texts were left untampered with. The later commentators and writers were too steeped in their own local traditions to discern the distinctive character of the mythology of the Early Buddhist texts: hence the gulf between the mythology of the original texts and the later interpretations and elaborations of it.

Theravada is the form of Buddhism prevailing in Sri Lanka, Burma and south-east Asia. As in the northern Mahayana countries, belief grew up in numerous Buddhas and Bodhisattvas, who were worshipped as deities.

LEFT Seated Buddha at a temple in Bangkok, Thailand, 18th century.

BELOW At this ruined temple at Angkor, Cambodia, the king is shown as an incarnation of Avalokitesvara, one of the principal Buddhist gods, who aids all beings in distress.

CHAPTER THREE

ZOROASTRIANISM

Zoroaster is the Greek form of the name of the Iranian prophet Zarathustra. He lived in the north-east of Iran, probably about 1500 BC, though his traditional date is the 6th century BC. (Iran is the modern name for Persia.) A fragment of Zoroaster's teaching is preserved in hymns known as the *Gathas,* collected in the Zoroastrian holy book, the *Avesta.* The classic exposition of Zoroastrian teaching is in Middle Persian books, dating in their present form from the 8th to the 10th centuries AD. Zoroastrianism was the official religion of Iran under three great empires: the Achaemenid from the 5th to the 3rd centuries BC, the Parthian from the 3rd century BC to the 3rd century AD, and the Sasanian from the 3rd to the 7th centuries AD. In the 7th century Iran was converted to Islam.

Muslim oppression in Iran forced a group of Zoroastrians to seek a new land where they could practise their religion in freedom. They settled in the north-west of India in the 10th century, and are known as Parsis (meaning Persians). They grew in numbers and strength until they became the numerical centre of Zoroastrianism, and the city of Bombay has come to occupy a position in the Zoroastrian world somewhat like that of Rome in the Roman Catholic Church, as the centre of theological authority. There are now approximately 90,000 Parsis in India and 17,000 Zoroastrians in Iran, with smaller Zoroastrian communities of 3,000 to 4,000 in Pakistan, Britain, the United States of America, Canada, Hong Kong and East Africa.

The Myth of Creation

The starting point for an understanding of Zoroastrian mythology is the theme of good and evil, the age-old problem of so many religions. How can belief in an all-loving, all-powerful God be reconciled with the reality of undeserved suffering in the world? If God is good, perhaps he is not all-powerful. If he is all-powerful, then he cannot be wholly good. The essence of Zoroastrian myth and belief is that God is wholly good. All evil, suffering, misery and death come from the devil.

According to the Zoroastrian myth, the creator was Ahura Mazda, the Wise Lord, later known as Ohrmazd (in Middle Persian). He existed from eternity above in light and goodness. Below in darkness and ignorance lurked Angra Mainyu, the Destructive Spirit, later known as Ahriman. Ohrmazd created first the heavenly beings and then the universe as a trap in which to ensnare evil. He created

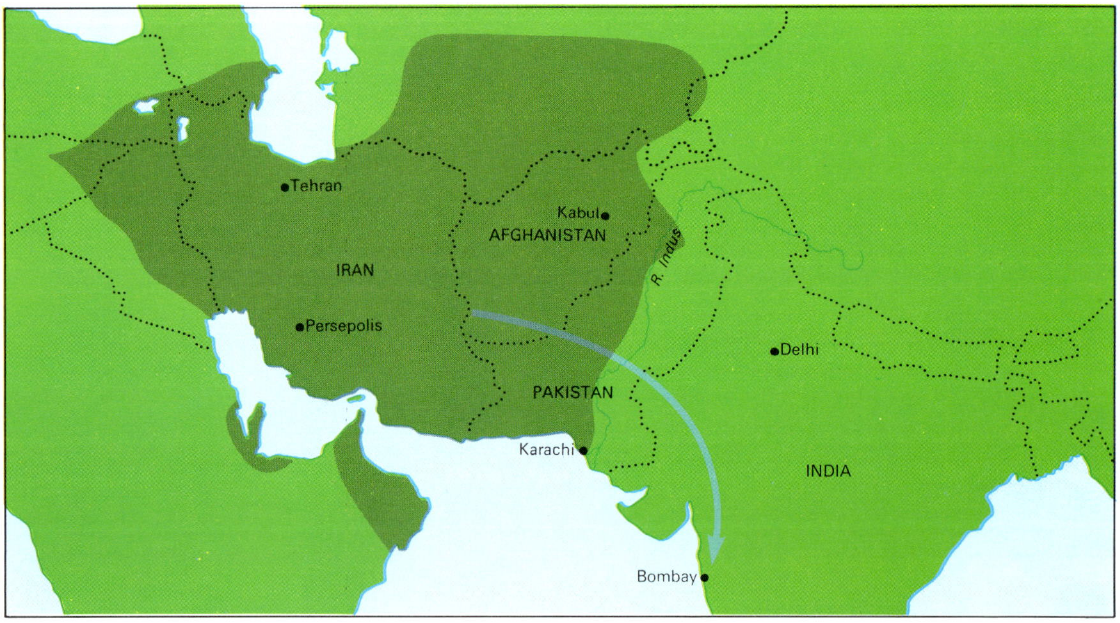

it first in spiritual and then in material form. It was shaped like an egg, with the earth floating flat and round like a dish in the middle. Ohrmazd also created the archetypal, perfect man, Gayomard, and the primeval bull, the source of all animal and plant life. Meanwhile Ahriman was busy miscreating his minions, the demons and the noxious creatures, such as snakes and ants.

Ahriman's instinct is to destroy, and so he attacked the Good Creation of Ohrmazd. He entered the universe through the base of the sky. He released his miscreants on the world and attacked the archetypal man and the primeval bull, inflicting on them suffering and death. But when Ahriman and his forces tried to leave the universe again, they found their exit blocked and were unable to escape. The moribund bull emitted seed, from which grew all beneficial animals and goodly plants. From the man's seed grew a plant whose leaves formed the first human couple.

Evil had now been trapped in a world characterized by life. The battle between the forces of good and evil had begun within the arena of creation and it lasts throughout the course of history, a world 'year' of 12,000 years.

In this myth Ohrmazd and Ahriman exist independently of each other from eternity. Ahriman is not a secondary or subordinate figure; he is not a fallen angel. Good and evil are considered contrary substances, manifesting themselves in such opposites as light and dark, health and sickness, life and death. The originals of these contraries must, in Zoroastrian teaching, be ultimately opposed beings.

Middle Persian writers developed this teaching in conscious opposition to the beliefs of other religions. It was developed in distinction from certain Hindu doctrines, associated particularly with the god Shiva, which sought to reconcile opposites, sought the unity behind the polarity. The Zoroastrians were equally opposed to the belief of some Christians that God grants freedom of action to the devil to perpetrate evil for a period. This, Zoroastrians considered, made God ultimately responsible for evil. They

ABOVE Mount Demavend, to the south of the Caspian Sea. In the ancient myths the monster Azi Dahaka was imprisoned here.

LEFT The throne room of the ancient palace of Zoroastrian Iran at Persepolis. In the centre of the wall can be seen 'The Immortals', the Imperial bodyguard, flanking a royal inscription. Behind them a lion is shown attacking a bull, a mythical motif found at several points in the palace, perhaps symbolizing the sequence of the seasons.

Impression of a royal Achaemenid cylinder seal, showing the great King Darius (522–486 BC) in the favoured Iranian pastime of the hunt. Above the king's chariot hovers the winged symbol of God – expressing the idea that the king is guided by the deity. Notice how an abstract or non-anthropomorphic symbol is used of God. Historically, the symbol was taken over from Egyptian and Mesopotamian religion. The Zoroastrian form has a male human torso, with right hand raised in blessing, surmounting the ring of sovereignty, and with the wings and tail of a bird.

found Muslim teaching on the absolute sovereignty of Allah, and the necessity for human submission to his inscrutable will, equally repugnant.

The Forces of Good and Evil

The good Ohrmazd is supported by his creations, primarily the heavenly beings. Whereas the Christian asserts that 'God is love', the ancient Zoroastrian tended to reverse the statement to 'Love is God'. Many of the Zoroastrian heavenly beings are abstract forces, deified and sometimes personified. Ohrmazd is surrounded by the seven Bounteous Immortals (*Amahraspands*) of Good Mind, Righteousness, Devotion, Kingdom, Obedience, Wholeness and Immortality. They are at once aspects of Ohrmazd's nature, aspects in which man can and should share, and divine beings. The male Vahman (Good Mind), for example, greets the righteous soul at death and conducts it to heaven. The seven *Amahraspands* stand below Ohrmazd in the heavenly hierarchy. Below them are the *yazads*, the worshipful beings. Some of these are ancient Iranian gods associated with nature, such as sun and moon, who have been incorporated into the Zoroastrian faith. Others are abstract gods, like Mithra, around whom the later Mysteries of Mithras centred (see MYSTERY RELIGIONS). Only one mortal is included among the *yazads*, the prophet Zoroaster, through whom the Good Religion was revealed to the Good Creation.

Opposed to the heavenly forces of good are the demonic forces of evil. Corresponding to the *Amahraspands* are the arch-demons of Evil Mind, the spirits of Apostasy, Anarchy, Discontent and two rather obscure figures who poison creation. Corresponding to the *yazads* are the major demons, Fury, Lie, Dearth, the Evil Eye and the female Nasu – the demoness of dead matter, who is depicted as a fly. An evil being who figures prominently in the texts is Azi Dahaka, with three heads, three mouths and six eyes – the most powerful of demons miscreated for the destruction of the Good Creation. In later religious and secular texts he becomes a wicked king of ancient time, a tyrant who brought terrible suffering on mankind in his thousand-year reign.

Corresponding to Ohrmazd's creation of the world is the miscreation of Evil. For everything good there is an evil counterpart. Opposite to the divine fire is the polluting smoke. Opposite to the faithful dog is the rapacious wolf. Opposite to all the beneficent creatures (such as cattle, sheep and horses, animals which aid man), are the biting, poisonous, repulsive and noxious creatures (*khrafstar*), such as snakes, scorpions, spiders, lizards – and cats.

The whole of existence is consequently seen by Zoroastrians as divided between the forces of good and evil. The purpose of creation is to give expression to, and provide an arena for, the conflict which necessarily arises from their mutually destructive natures. 'For where there is good, there cannot possibly be evil. Where light is admitted, darkness is driven away.'

The Myth of the Renovation

The defeat of evil begins with the coming of the Good Religion to the world, when it was revealed to the prophet Zoroaster. The struggle lasts for 3,000 years. The conflict ebbs and flows, but gradually the forces of evil are reduced. The final assault of evil brings about the last great battle. All the natural, God-given order will be overthrown. The sun and moon will not give their light. Religious devotion will wane and respect for elders and family ties will disappear. The world will endure a great and terrible winter and the monster Dahak (Azi Dahaka), the greatest of noxious miscreants, will break free from his mountain prison and terrorize the earth.

Then a virgin bathing in a lake will be impregnated by the seed of Zoroaster, preserved there, and the final saviour, Saoshyans, will be born. He will raise all the dead and assemble the court for the final judgment. The wicked will be returned to hell, whence they came, to be purged of their bodily sin. Then all will pass through a stream of molten metal, to prove the righteousness of all. The heavenly and demonic forces will wrestle in combat until the powers of evil are annihilated and Ahriman himself is rendered eternally impotent. The world will be perfected as the mountains are laid low and the valleys filled up. Ohrmazd and the saviour will offer in sacrifice the last animal to die in the service of man, and from that rite all men will receive the elixir of immortality. Heaven will descend to the moon and earth will ascend to the moon, and all men will dwell in perfection with Ohrmazd for ever.

The Nature of the World

In many traditions, the world is considered evil. It is a prison for the spiritual soul of man, from which the righteous soul must seek to escape. Although Zoroastrianism has a strong dualism of good and evil, it strongly rejects any dualism of spirit and flesh. Ohrmazd first created the world in spiritual (*menog*) form. After 3000 years that world was given material (*getig*) form. *Menog* is the primary existence, but because it is invisible and immoveable it is not totally real. *Getig* is the physical, tangible, sensate expression of the *menog*, from which it derives.

The physical world, therefore, is by nature one with the ideal world. The ills with which it is afflicted are not due to an inherent weakness but to the assault of Ahriman. In the myth of creation it is said that when the world existed in ideal material form, the sun stood still at the noon-day position and the earth was flat and still. The violence of Ahriman's onslaught so shook the earth that the sun was dislodged from its station and began to revolve, causing day and night. The shaking also caused mountains to be thrown up and valleys to appear. That is why, in the myth of the renovation, earthquakes are a 'sign of the end'. They are the tremblings of the earth, comparable to those at the beginning. It is also why the Zoroastrian vision of the renewed earth has the mountains laid low and the valleys filled up, for at the renovation everything will return to its original, ideal form. This is also why it is said that heaven and earth will meet. Neither is done away with, but rather the literal 'best of both worlds' is realized. Zoroastrians do not refer to 'the end of the world', as Christians and Muslims do. In Zoroastrian belief the world is God's and its end would represent the triumph of evil. Zoroastrians look for the renovation of existence, the time when evil will finally be eradicated; when *menog* and *getig* will blend in perfect harmony, and when Ohrmazd, for the first time, will be omnipotent.

The Bridge of Judgment

The true nature of man in Zoroastrian belief is illustrated by the myth of the archetypal man, Gayomard, prior to Ahriman's assault. Gayomard was created immortal, sinless, happy and without need. Ohrmazd was his creator, and to Ohrmazd he will return at the renovation, but throughout life man has complete freedom of will, either to follow his nature or to deny it and align himself with evil.

At death man will face an individual judgment. His thoughts, words and deeds in life are weighed in the scales of justice. If his good thoughts, words and deeds outweigh his evil ones, then his soul will be met at the Bridge of the Separator (the Cinvat Bridge) by a beautiful sweet-smelling maiden, who personifies the soul's conscience. The maiden will lead the soul across the bridge and at the far side it will be met by the *Amahraspand* Good Mind, who will conduct it to heaven. However, if the soul's evil thoughts, words and deeds outweigh its good ones, then it is confronted at the bridge by a personification of its conscience in the form of an ugly foul-smelling old hag. As the wicked soul tries to cross the bridge, it finds that the path becomes as narrow as the edge of a sword and it falls into the abyss of hell.

The punishments in hell are made to fit the crime, for the purpose of hell is corrective. Zoroastrians believe that eternal hell is an immoral concept. The purpose of punishment, in their belief, is to reform. So, at the appointed time, everyone will be raised from the dead, and their souls will be returned from heaven or hell to face the second judgment at the renovation of the universe. Man needs two judgments because there are two aspects of his being, *menog* and *getig*. When man has been judged and corrected in both aspects, then he can dwell with Ohrmazd in the totality of his being. The resurrection of the body is an essential Zoroastrian doctrine, for two reasons: it permits the judgment and correction of the material body, and it reverses Ahriman's apparent victory over the creation of Ohrmazd.

The Nature of Man

As the whole man is judged in body and spirit, so in his life he must hold the two aspects of his being together in harmony. To pursue the life of the spirit at the expense of the body, for example as an ascetic, is to deny the importance of the material creation. This is as sinful as a life of gluttony which neglects the spiritual dimension of existence. The expansion of the Good Creation is the religious duty of the Zoroastrian. As the myth of creation makes clear, Ohrmazd is growth, abundance and life. Ahriman is decay, dearth and death. The holy life for man is that which is dedicated to Ohrmazd in purity, in devotion and in productivity. Agriculture and cattle-raising, marriage and procreation are holy pursuits in which man is a fellow-worker with God.

Whereas Islam teaches that man is the servant of Allah, and Hinduism that human life is a lower plane of existence, in Zoroastrian thought man is 'created better than the stars and moon, better even than the sacred fire, and he is called in revelation greater and better than the spiritual creation'. According to the myth of creation, Ahriman produced a counter-creation to every work of Ohrmazd: counter to the *Amahraspands* he produced his arch-demons, counter to life he produced death, counter to happiness he produced misery. But he could find nothing to counter man. Man's humanity is said to be 'his salvation and his adornment'.

This royal investiture scene is carved in the Iranian 'Valley of the Kings', Naqsh-i Rustam – the place where great monarchs of the ancient dynasty were buried. On the right, Ohrmazd tramples underfoot his defeated enemy Ahriman, whose evil nature is symbolized by the snake head-dress. Ohramzd offers the ring of sovereignty to King Ardashir I (AD 224–241), who mirrors the divine act and tramples on his political enemy. This later representation shows God in human form, unlike the earlier Achaemenid seal. What is also interesting is the changing image of the king – no longer below God but his equal in size and power, his mirror image.

Man's exalted theological position does not make him remote from his physical environment in Zoroastrian belief. The first human couple are said to have grown from the leaves of a plant – a powerful image for the conviction that man is at one with his natural environment. As the archetypal man and bull lived, suffered and died side by side in the original creation, so men and animals are fellow-creatures in the divinely created world we live in. As animals feed men, clothe and guard them and carry their burdens, so men must protect, care for and feed the beneficent animals. Man and the animals which aid him fight together against the noxious creatures and the miscreants of Ahriman.

The Myth of Zurvān

This account of Zoroastrian mythology has been confined to the central orthodox teaching. There were, naturally, a number of ancient interpretations of, or deviations from, this teaching. One of these has been labelled 'Zurvanism', because it focused primarily on Zurvān, or Time. Zurvanism was evidently popular in pre-Islamic Iran, but none of its texts have survived. Zurvanite theology has, therefore, to be reconstructed from such outside sources as orthodox Zoroastrian literature and Christian and Arabic writers. The resulting account must consequently be tentative. The ancient myth apparently related that Zurvān, the great God, existed alone. He offered sacrifice for a thousand years because he wanted a son, but after so long doubted the efficacy of his sacrifice. At the moment of doubt he conceived twins within his hermaphrodite self. Ahriman was the personification of his doubt, Ohrmazd the embodiment of his wisdom. He vowed that he would grant the kingdom to the first-born, whereupon Ahriman leapt forth from his side. Zurvān regretted the vow, but could not avoid implementing it so he granted rulership over the world to Ahriman. To Ohrmazd he granted the high priesthood, sovereignty over the spiritual world, and the final victory.

0 *Creation of Spiritual World*

IDEAL SPIRITUAL WORLD

3000 *Creation of Material World*

IDEAL MATERIAL WORLD

6000 *Assault of Ahriman*

PERIOD OF MIXTURE OF GOOD AND EVIL

9000 *Birth of Zoroaster*

THE OVERTHROW OF EVIL

12000 *Renovation*

Chart of Zoroastrian spiritual history.

The point behind the Zurvanite myth appears to be a dissatisfaction with the Zoroastrian belief in two independent and opposed forces in life. Zurvanism was concerned to find the Undifferentiated One from which the two, the manifold, arose (a spiritual search which was perhaps stimulated by Greek or Indian thought). This interpretation of Zoroastrian mythology wrought profound changes in belief. The ultimate primacy of Time was linked with Babylonian astrology, resulting in the idea of Pitiless Time controlling the world and determining the fate of all men, which denied the fundamental Zoroastrian doctrine of free will.

The belief that Ahriman was the ruler of this world involved a more pessimistic approach to the material world than Zoroaster would have countenanced, but perhaps the greatest change was in the understanding of the godhead. The keynote of Zoroastrian teaching is the overriding conviction that Ohrmazd is wholly, absolutely and exclusively good, whereas Zurvān contains within himself the potential for evil. Zurvanites, therefore, considered that good and evil were not polar opposites, and so questioned the very basis of the Zoroastrian myths of creation and renovation.

Gnosticism is an umbrella term for a number of religious traditions popular in the Roman Empire from the 1st to the 4th centuries AD. Gnostic thought was an amalgam of Greek, Jewish, Christian and Iranian ideas, in varying proportions in different schools of thought. From Iran, Gnostics took the dualistic idea of good opposed to evil in the form of a conflict between light and dark, the myth of the archetypal man and some of the ideas related to salvation. But they interpreted the various mythical details in terms of the Hellenistic Greek belief in the material flesh being a prison for the pure, spiritual soul. Such gnostic interpretations, or perversions, of Zoroastrian teaching were propounded in Iran by Mani in the 3rd century AD. Mani presented himself as the fulfilment not only of Zoroastrian, but also of Christian and Buddhist hopes. His call to the ascetic, celibate life was alien to the spirit of Iran and he was finally executed for heresy. In these extreme interpretations can be seen the spiritual wrestling of different people in ancient Iran with the perennial problem of religion – the problem of evil.

Zoroastrianism in India

Zoroastrians in Iran, over the centuries, have been forced to retreat to remote villages away from Muslim notice, where the ancient traditions have been preserved largely unchanged. The Parsis in British India, however, have been more exposed to the intellectual challenge of the West, and to a range of social upheavals unlike those of their co-religionists in the fatherland.

Under Hindu and Muslim rule the Parsis generally lived in peace and isolation. It was the economic and educational opportunities available under British rule which changed their circumstances. The Parsis came to power in western India as middle-men in trade between the British and the caste-restricted Hindus. The story of their success in the professions and politics from 1750 to 1900 is an amazing one.

Inevitably, the first effect of the change was the materialism it inspired. The ancient myth of creation had taught Zoroastrians that it was their religious duty to expand the Good Creation of Ohrmazd, in order that the negative work of evil might be overcome. This had traditionally been seen in terms of agriculture and the procreation of children in marriage – both religious duties of the devout Zoroastrian. In the mid-19th century Parsis translated this ancient belief into a doctrine which encouraged the development of the material creation of commerce and technology. The latter in particular (the use of steam-powered machinery and electricity for example) they saw as modern man's form of his ancient duty. But most Parsis did not attempt to offer any theological rationale for their pursuit of wealth (which they dispensed with great charity).

Religious knowledge has declined considerably over the last hundred years in the community. It is not so much that Parsis reject the ancient myths, but rather that they are unaware of their existence. Few

Parsis know of the Zoroastrian myth of creation, and even fewer know that the resurrection of the body was ever part of their religion. All the same, many of the fundamental teachings contained in the myths still mould the Parsi character. For example, in the ancient myths the source of evil is known as 'the Lie'. To this day Parsis, religious and non-religious alike, regard lying as a particularly despicable act. Similarly, the ancient Zoroastrian respect for Wisdom (reflected in the divine title Ahura Mazdā, 'the Wise Lord') was an important factor in the Parsi involvement in western education.

The Impact of the West

Because so many Parsis took so enthusiastically to western education, Parsi Zoroastrianism inevitably came under western intellectual influence. This took two main forms: the impact of western religious studies and the intellectual climate created by scientific discoveries. In late-19th century Europe evolution was considered by many to be the master key to numerous problems. In the field of religious studies it was thought that man had evolved spiritually from pagan polytheism to the heights of ethical monotheism. A number of Parsis studied under western scholars who held such views. The best example is M.N. Dhalla, later made high priest (Dastur) of the Karachi community, who studied under A.V.W. Jackson at Columbia University, New York. Dhalla interpreted the Zoroastrian creation myth in this light. The myth of Ohrmazd and Ahriman coexisting together from all eternity seemed to him a dilution of the ideal monotheism. He therefore interpreted Ahriman not as a mythological being, but as an evil tendency within man. This left him with the problem of how to explain death, which in the ancient myth was the ultimate weapon of Ahriman. In some passages Dhalla describes death figuratively as a sinister hunter, and by implication as an evil force, without accounting for its origin. But often in his writings he describes death as Ahura calling men back to himself – an idea totally alien to traditional Zoroastrianism, yet his only recourse once the substantial reality of evil was denied. It also coincided with a view of death often found in popular Christian literature.

Dhalla further attempted to 'demythologize' some of the Zoroastrian teaching. His account of hell is a good example. Hell is vividly described in the traditional myth as a dark abyss, filled with foul smoke and evil food, where men are packed in tight, though they believe they are in total isolation. Such accounts were distasteful to Dhalla's rational spirit. He described hell as the separation of the soul from God and its consequent agony, or as the sufferings of conscience.

Dhalla's interpretation of Zoroastrian mythology was influenced mainly by western religion. Other Parsis were more influenced by western science. When theories of anti-matter were popular in the West, then a number of Parsis used them to explain the traditional myth of the conflict between the good Creator (matter) and the wicked Destructive Spirit (anti-matter). Such Parsis also saw the theory of evolution justified in their own myth of creation – the almost total corruption of the world at Ahriman's first onslaught being progressively eradicated by the efforts of the righteous over the centuries until the time of the renovation, when by human effort (sometimes identified by such Parsis as the work of scientists) evil would be eradicated.

BELOW LEFT A Parsi Fire Temple from Bombay, showing how ancient Iranian artistic motifs are reproduced by the Indian community. The winged symbol over the door and the winged guardian beasts in the doorway both derive from archetypes at Persepolis. Non-Parsis are not permitted to enter Parsi temples, which are kept as clearly defined areas of purity in which the perpetually burning sacred fire, the living, formless symbol of God, is reverenced.

ABOVE Temples were not part of the original Zoroastrian tradition. Zoroastrians are said to have considered a human edifice too small to contain the symbol of God. The ancient nomadic heritage preferred mountain-tops as a place for worship. These fire altars date from the Sasanian era (3rd to 7th centuries AD).

The Backlash

Such westernized interpretations of myth and belief inevitably produced a backlash. Ironically, the backlash against western scholarly influence was first expressed in a movement which began in the West, Theosophy. The Theosophical Society was founded in New York in 1875 by Madame Blavatsky and others, but it soon moved its headquarters to its natural home, in India. Essentially, Theosophists encouraged Hindus and Zoroastrians not to be misled by western scholars who, they said, failed to appreciate the occult significance of ancient rites, prayers and myths. The foremost living exponent of Theosophical Parsi-Zoroastrian teaching is Dastur K.S. Dabu. He explains the doctrine of the resurrection as really meaning the soul 'regaining the former upright status which was lost during the soul's incarnation' in a human body. The myth of the conflict between good and evil he considers an allegory of the soul's struggle against all sorts of handicaps during successive reincarnations. In these interpretations of ancient myth can be seen both Theosophical and Hindu influence.

The common 20th-century attempt to rid religion of mythology leaves many believers unsatisfied, and so new mythologies arise. This has happened among the Parsis, with a movement known as Ilm-i Kshnoom. The founder was Behramshah Shroff (1857–1927). He left home at the age of 17 and, it is said, met members of a secret race of giants who took him to their secret land of Firdos, or heaven, in the mountains of Iran. There everyone lives in a paradisal state in caves with streams of nectar, and ancient Iranian treasures and teachings are stored there. On his return to India, Shroff remained silent for 30 years, and spent the last 20 years of his life teaching.

Kshnoomic teaching bears little resemblance to the ancient mythology. It declares that man's spiritual self is invested with a material body as it enters the process of 'involution' (entry to the material world). It undergoes a series of rebirths on its passage 'through the dark valley of unfoldment in matter', when it is afflicted by the evil 'magnetic' currents of impurity and the blindness inflicted by western scholars of religion. Man evolves through successive rebirths to spiritual unfoldment – release from matter into eternal, universal consciousness. The evolved soul experiences its last rebirth as a Kshnoomic Zoroastrian.

What is particularly interesting about Kshnoomic teaching, viewed in the context of Iranian mythology, is the 'myth' of the founder. In the early 20th century, as Parsi fortunes in Bombay began to wane and as dissatisfaction with the Parsi western orientation began to emerge, there was a strong surge of pro-Iranian sentiment in the community. The Iran League was formed and appeals were launched to persuade the Parsis to return to their fatherland. A number of Parsis contrasted the gross materialism of their community in British India with their rich religious heritage in Iran. These sentiments can be seen in Shroff's account of heaven in the Iranian mountains with stores of ancient treasures and teachings, and streams of nectar.

A Parsi high priest, or Dastur, denoted by the stole, invests a new initiate with the symbols of the religion, the sacred shirt and cord. The ceremony can take place in the home (as here) or temple but, like all Zoroastrian rites, should be conducted in the presence of the sacred fire. The shirt is white as a symbol of the purity of the religion and is to be worn at all times. The cord is untied and retied several times daily to the accompaniment of prayers rejecting evil, worshipping God and vowing to practise good thoughts, good words and good deeds.

Ritual Interpretations

Although these modern interpretations are popular among many Parsis, they are not the beliefs of the majority. The religion of most Parsis is expressed in ritual. It is from the sacred rites that Parsis generally gain what knowledge they have of the ancient myths. There are two rites in particular which affect all Parsis, and which derive from the ancient myths: initiation and funeral ceremonies.

A Zoroastrian child is initiated between the ages of eight and 13. Before that, the child is not held to be morally responsible for his (or her) acts, but after initiation all his cogitations, words and deeds are thought to determine his fate after death. There is nothing remotely resembling infant baptism in Zoroastrianism. The central theme of the mythology, that all creation has complete freedom of choice between the forces of good and evil, requires that initiation should not be permitted until the child is able to choose to undergo the *naujote* (initiation) ceremony for himself.

Initiation is said by Zoroastrians to be joining the army of Ohrmazd; the donning of the armour of the religion and the girding with the swordbelt of faith in order to wage war against evil. Few of the details of the myth of creation are explicit in the ceremony, but it involves, and is understood to involve, many of the fundamentals of the ancient teaching. Above all, there is the emphasis on the conflict between the forces of good and evil. That conflict, which in the myth underlies the whole of history is seen in the rite of initiation as underlying the whole of an initiate's future life on earth. Prayers are offered that he may so conduct that war that his good thoughts, words and deeds may win him a place in heaven. Although the child knows little of the myth of creation and the origin of evil, he has no doubt of the reality of evil, and no doubt that he must fight evil until his dying day.

Towers of Silence

In almost any religion the rites which change least are those associated with death. This is true of Zoroastrianism. The funeral rites are based on the belief that a corpse represents the victory of evil. It is therefore an object in which demons lurk, a source of physical and spiritual pollution. Because the death of a righteous person is a greater triumph for Ahriman than that of a sinner, the corpse of a holy man is particularly impure.

As soon as death occurs the priest should be summoned, bringing with him a dog. In the ancient myths a dog guards the Bridge of Judgment from demons, and the dog's stare is thought to drive away the demons from the corpse. The dead body should be removed on a metal carrier, not on a wooden one which might absorb the pollution. The body is taken straight to the burial ground where it is washed and laid out in white on a marble slab (again non-porous). A sacred fire is kept burning in the room, to keep the forces of corruption at bay by its holy light. There the priest and female relatives and friends offer prayers for the soul on its journey to its judgment.

Wherever possible, the funeral should take place on the day of death, to reduce the period when pollution is present to the minimum. The corpse is carried in procession on a metal bier, led by a priest and a dog. The body is set down for the last time before commital, and the face is exposed so that the bereaved may take their earthly leave of the deceased. Then professional corpse-bearers, and they alone, take the corpse into a Tower of Silence, a *dokhma*, where the corruption of death and the power of evil is strong. Men in such close contact with decay cannot take a normal part in society without the most stringent purificatory rites, including one which lasts for nine nights.

In the tower the corpse-bearers strip the body and leave the vultures to consume the flesh and the sun to bleach the bones. After a few months these are cast into a central pit. During the 30 minutes it is said to take the vultures to devour the flesh, the mourners recite prayers in a nearby hall. During the following three days, while the soul is thought to make its way to the judgment by the divine scales of justice, the family recite prayers to comfort and aid it. The living are expected to mourn for a period, but only for a period. Otherwise, the myth relates, their tears will form a river barrier over which the deceased must struggle. Excessive grief does not help the dead, but harms the health of the living.

Exposing the dead to vultures, or predatory animals, probably dates back to the period between 3000 and 1000 BC, when the ancient Iranians were nomads wandering on foot across the Asian steppes in search of fresh pasture, before they settled in what came to be known as Iran. This ancient practice was given religious authority by the Zoroastrian conviction that death is the work of Ahriman, and therefore the polluting corpse would defile the sacred creations of earth, fire and water if it were buried, cremated or disposed of at sea. It is an increasingly difficult practice to continue in Bombay, where the scarcity of land and a plenitude of poisonous petrol fumes are rapidly decreasing the vulture population of the city. Despite rumours that the scarcity of vultures means that bodies rot for months, and despite the mushrooming of high-rise flats which offer views offensive to bereaved and flat-dwellers alike, the Parsis cling tenaciously to this ancient rite of disposal of the dead which has been sanctified by ancient myth.

Inevitably, the rites have been rationalized. Towers of Silence are said by Parsis to be more hygienic and less morbid than a graveyard where bodies are left to rot over many years. They are more discreet than the cremation rites of the Hindus, where mourners and strangers watch the flames devour the dead publicly. (As one of the few outsiders privileged to visit the *dokhmas* in Bombay, I can confirm the air of natural calm and peace such places have, with none of the horrors the western mind invariably associates with *dokhmas*.) These rationalizations are recent. The basis of the funeral ceremonies is the belief that the pollution of death should not be allowed to corrupt the sanctity of the material creation of Ohrmazd, and this is a central theme of the ancient Zoroastrian myths.

A dokhma, or Tower of Silence, from Yazd in Iran. Such structures should preferably be in remote, barren places and on a hill-top in order that the living community may be kept away from the pollution of death. Nearby there is a building where the mourners pray at the funeral and where a sacred fire burns, its light shining on the tower to keep evil forces at bay.

CHAPTER FOUR

TIBET

Two parallel sets of myths and legends have developed in Tibetan culture: those of the pre-Buddhist religion sometimes referred to as *Bon*, and those of the special form of Buddhism which evolved in Tibet from the 7th century AD on. The term Bon was originally applied to a class of priest-magicians, not to the religion itself, which was known as *lha-chos*, 'sacred matters', as distinct from *mi-chos*, 'human matters'. From the point of view of mythology its principal features appear to have been a cult of gods of the sky, the earth and the lower regions, and a cult of mountains and divine kings. The later *Bon-po* monks (followers of Bon), as known through their literature and living tradition, preserved very little of these earlier beliefs. In the course of their history they absorbed and reproduced all kinds of beliefs with which they met, indigenous and foreign, and between the 7th and 13th centuries – the period of the propagation of Buddhism in Tibet – Bon evolved into a somewhat incongruous form of Tibetan Buddhism. The term Bon now acquired a new meaning, equivalent to that of the Buddhist term *chos* (Sanskrit *dharma*), translatable as 'religion' or 'doctrine'.

The Bon-pos claim that their teachings came from the west, through their founder gShen-rab and ultimately from sTag-gzigs (possibly Iran). This suggests that they first came into contact with a form of Buddhism practised in such countries as Gilgit and Uddiyana to the west of Tibet, and that they were at first unaware of its affinity with the Buddhism introduced directly from India by the Tibetan kings. The Bon-pos and the Buddhists wrote in the same language and both used the same Buddhist literature brought from India, except that the Bon-pos claimed it was their own and would not admit its Indian origins. They accepted the Buddhist pantheon but gave its members different names. The pre-Buddhist gods were absorbed into the new Bon pantheon and as the Buddhists introduced a number of pre-Buddhist gods into their pantheon too, a process of mutual amalgamation took place. An example of this, and of Bon-po ingenuity, is the legend of gShen-rab, their founder, a largely invented personality. It is a fabrication inspired by the life-stories of Sakyamuni (Gautama Buddha, the founder of Buddhism: see THERAVADA BUDDHISM). gShen-rab's life follows the same pattern, although native Tibetan elements were included.

The Founder of Bon

The life-story of gShen-rab is told in *Legs-bshad rin-po-che'i mdzod dpyod-ldan dga'-ba'i char* ('The

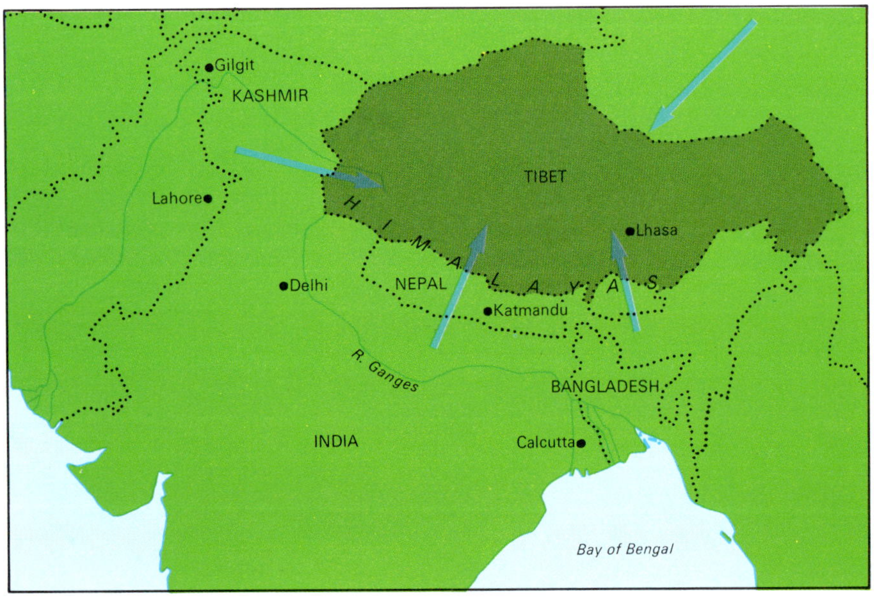

Precious Treasury of Excellent Sayings, Auspicious Rain for the Wise'). After a series of reincarnations gShen-rab is born, in his last life but one, as gSal-ba, the younger brother of Dag-pa, who is his immediate predecessor in a line of seven Teachers. He acquires the teachings of Bon in heaven, while Dag-pa teaches the same doctrine to men on earth. Before being born on earth, he chooses the country and clan in which he will be born. At an auspicious time, transformed into a white syllable A, he enters the head of his father, while at the same time a red syllable MA enters the body of his mother. After nine months and ten days he is born and receives the name of 'Teacher gShen-rab, the Lord of Men, the Victorious One'. At the age of ten he preaches the doctrine in the realm of the earth-gods, the serpents and the air-deities. At the age of 12 he assumes the form of many teachers and proclaims the doctrine in different lands. Next he marries ten women and has eight sons and two daughters.

Thereafter he is disturbed by a demon called Khyab-pa, who abducts one of his daughters, and she in due time gives birth to two sons. gShen-rab regains his daughter and her children, but now Khyab-pa steals gShen-rab's seven horses. gShen-rab sets out in search of his horses at once, but Khyab-pa blocks his way, first with snow, then with fire, and then with sand. gShen-rab overcomes these obstructions one by one, and thus reaches the land of Tibet. Here he gives instruction to the Bon-pos, teaching them ways of exorcizing demons and various rites and supplications to the gods. Khyab-pa now resumes his wicked activities. Disguising his true identity, he becomes gShen-rab's disciple, burns gShen-rab's books and escapes. This time gShen-rab ignores him altogether and, at the age of 31, abandons his family and worldly possessions, becoming a religious mendicant and practising austerities and meditation. Khyab-pa returns once more, but on seeing the hardships endured by gShen-rab he confesses his evil activities and becomes a faithful disciple. gShen-rab spends the rest of his life in solitude and departs from this world aged 82.

Buddhism in Tibet

The introduction of Buddhism into Tibet from India was sponsored by the early Tibetan kings. In the reign of King Srong-btsan sgam-po (died about 650) a temple was founded in Lhasa, known as the *Jo-khang*, 'temple of the Lord', and containing an image of Sakyamuni which was considered the most sacred in Tibet. The king's two consorts, Chinese and Nepalese, were regarded as the first patrons of Buddhism and were later treated as reincarnations of the goddess Tara in her two white and green manifestations. In the 8th century the first monastery was built, Tibetans were ordained as monks and there are accounts of a great debate held to decide whether to follow the Indian or Chinese form of Buddhism, which the supporters of the former are said to have won. By the 13th century the Tibetans had translated all the Buddhist literature of India, Kashmir and Nepal that was available to them.

It is often suggested that the Tibetans accepted

ABOVE Thang-ka, or painted scroll, showing the Great Assembly of Buddhist deities, saints and sages. The central figure is Tsong-ka-pa (d. 1419), founder of one of the principal Tibetan monastic orders.

OPPOSITE AND LEFT Scenes from the life of the Buddha. As an infant he takes his first seven steps and proclaims his universal sovereignty, and is bathed by the gods. As a young man he cuts his hair and becomes a religious mendicant.

only the more debased form of Indian Buddhism, but in fact they accepted it in all its complexities just as they encountered it, including the belief in numerous Buddhas and Bodhisattvas (Buddhas-to-be) who are, in effect, Buddhist deities. Pre-Buddhist gods and cults were taken into Tibetan Buddhism but always, apparently, in a subsidiary manner. For example, local Tibetan gods may be placated at the beginning of Buddhist ceremonies, so that they will remain quiet and attempt no disruption.

One of the main peculiarities of Tibetan Buddhism is the system of reincarnating lamas. Lama (Tibetan *bla-ma*, 'superior') is a polite title given to senior monks and the heads of large monasteries. A reincarnating lama is regarded as the 'manifested body' (*sPrul-sku*) of a particular Buddhist deity or a renowned religious teacher. There are hundreds of them, the most important politically being the Dalai Lama, believed to be a reincarnation of the Bodhisattva Avalokitesvara, and the Panchen Lama, believed to be a reincarnation of the Buddha Amitabha. Since the Chinese invasion of Tibet in 1959, the Dalai Lama and many other Tibetan religious leaders live in exile in India and elsewhere.

RIGHT Costume used in monastic dances, including the mask of the god, a drum and an apron of human bones. Pre-Buddhist deities were taken into Tibetan Buddhism and may be placated at the beginning of Buddhist ceremonies.

BELOW The introduction of Buddhism into Tibet was sponsored by Tibetan kings, one of whom built a temple at Lhasa in the 7th century, containing an image of the Buddha. View of Lhasa from a thang-ka, 19th century, showing the Potala Palace, the residence of the Dalai Lamas.

Origins of the World

The Tibetans took over the Indian Buddhist notion of an endless series of world-ages. Every world-age goes through the process of creation, temporary duration, and decay. In every world-age a Buddha appears at a suitable time to teach the Doctrine (*Dharma*), Sakyamuni being the teacher of the present world-age. The Bon-pos, although their writings are pervaded with Buddhist ideas, preserved several indigenous myths referring to the creation of the world. One was that in the beginning there was an uncreated being. From it a white light shone and from it an egg came into existence. It had no parts, but it had the power to move and fly. After five months it broke open and a man emerged. He sat down on a throne placed in the middle of the ocean and arranged the order of the universe. Another version of this myth describes the beginning of the universe as a void. From the void a being came into existence. From that being a light of many colours permeated space. Then wind, fire, water, foam and a tortoise came into existence, one after the other. The tortoise had six eggs of six different colours and from them six kinds of serpents (*klu*) came into existence as the origin of the six classes of living beings. In two other variations of the myth the universe comes into existence from an egg formed from a blue light shining forth from the void, or the universe is created from a serpent hatched from a primordial egg. In another variant a female serpent was born from the void. From the crown of her head the sky came into existence, from the light of her right eye the moon and from the light of her left eye the sun, from her teeth the planets and the lunar mansions, from her voice thunder, from her tongue lightning, from her breath clouds, from her tears rain, from her nose wind, from her blood the five oceans, from her veins rivers, from her flesh soil and from her bones mountains. In ballads of western Tibet the world is described as a tree with three summits and six branches. On each branch there is a bird laying an egg. These various myths were probably brought into Tibet by different tribes. Tracing the origin of the universe to the void would suggest Indian influence, and to the light an Iranian or Manichean influence.

There are myths which say that Tibet, like Nepal and Kashmir, was a great lake in prehistoric times. According to the Buddhist version, the lake dried out a hundred years after Buddha's death. It was overgrown by a juniper forest and gradually assumed its present form. As for the origin of the Tibetan people, a curious story about a monkey and a rock-ogress received official Buddhist recognition.

The Monkey and the Ogress

The Buddha Amitabha told the Bodhisattva Avalokitesvara that as Sakyamuni had not converted the Land of Snows (Tibet), it was Avalokitesvara's duty to carry out this missionary work. Avalokitesvara sat on top of Mount Potala and looked at the land he was to convert. Its creatures were ignorant and pursued evil ways. He emitted from the palm of his hand a ray of light and from it appeared a monkey (in other versions he himself becomes incarnate as the monkey). He instructed the monkey in the Doctrine and sent him to meditate in the Land of Snows. The country was divided into nine regions: three upper regions inhabited by elephants and deer, three middle ones by rock-ogres and monkeys, and three lower ones by ogres. There were no men at that time. The monkey, engrossed in meditation, was approached by a rock-ogress disguised as a female monkey, but he paid no attention. She changed herself into a beautiful woman, approached him again and asked to be his consort. The monkey refused, but she threatened that if he did not consent she would summon the ogres to devour the creatures of the land, and the ogresses would bear young and, being many, they would take possession of the whole land and devour the whole world.

Perplexed, the monkey went to see Avalokitesvara to ask what to do. The Bodhisattva told him it was proper to mate with the ogress, for their descendants would become human beings, among whom the Doctrine would spread. The monkey obeyed and after nine months the ogress gave birth to six sons. They had bodies covered with hair, like their father, and tails like their mother. Their faces were red and they had a taste for flesh and blood. When they were in want of food their father took them to a forest called the Peacock Woods, where there were other monkeys, and left them there. When he came back after a year he found that they had increased by 500. Their offspring were neither monkeys nor yet men. They suffered from heat and rain in the summer and from snow and cold in the winter, and they had nothing to eat. The father monkey gave them some food, but when they devoured it they were in pain, their hair fell off and their tails disappeared. In distress he went to see Avalokitesvara once more. He was consoled and told that his descendants had now become men and that Avalokitesvara could carry out the mission of converting them. He was given seven kinds of grain, precious dust and other minerals for his children and he went back to them and instructed them how to cultivate land and procure food. The dust and minerals were scattered over the whole land. (From the *Mani bka' 'bum.*)

The Wheel of Life is clasped by Mara, the Lord of Death, for all that lives must die, and live and die again and again. Six sectors of the wheel represent the realms of gods, titanic demons, departed spirits, hells, animals and men. Thang-ka, 19th century.

The King and the Sky-Cord

There are several traditions about the origin of kingship in Tibet. Some of them are aboriginal, others of Indian inspiration. A well known aboriginal version says that after the first ancestor there were six successors, bearing the title of 'Mighty One Enthroned', and also referred to as the 'Enthroned of Heaven'. Each of them descended to earth by means of a sky-cord and went back to heaven by means of the same sky-cord at the end of his reign, disappearing

ABOVE The cult of the Five Buddhas is based on the concept of the four cardinal points plus the centre. The central Buddha, Vairocana, is flanked by the other four Buddhas and two goddesses. Clockwise from the top left, they are Ratnasambhava, Amitabha, Amoghasiddhi, the White Tara, the goddess Vijaya, and Akshobhya. Thang-ka, 18th–19th century.

RIGHT An eleven-headed form of the Bodhisattva Avalokitesvara, the Lord of Compassion and the 'patron saint' of Tibet. Bronze, 17th century.

from earth like a rainbow. Their tombs were believed to be in heaven.

The seventh king lost this power. Being proud of his strength and abilities he proposed a fight with one of his ministers. According to one account, while the preparations for the fight were in progress, the king sent his faithful dog to the minister's house as a spy. The minister, in order to deceive his master, told his friends that if the king was to win the fight he must wear a black turban on his head and a mirror on his forehead, hang the corpses of a fox and a mouse on his shoulders, place a bag of ashes on a bull and wave his sword. Thinking all this was true, the king acted accordingly, but the bag of ashes broke open and blinded him. The two protective deities, who stand by one's shoulders, disappeared on account of the corpses. Swinging his sword in the confusion, the king cut the sky-cord. The minister aimed his arrow at the mirror on the king's head and killed him.

The Buddhists, while aware of myths of this kind, attempted to attach their native traditions of the origins of kingship to India. The following story is recounted by an 18th-century Tibetan scholar, gSum-pamKhan-po. Udayana, the ruler of Vatsala in India, had a son whose eyes were covered by the lower lids, whose brows were blue like turquoises, whose teeth were very white and whose fingers were webbed. On the palms of his hands were the marks of wheels. Fearing that all this might be an inauspicious omen, the king put the child in a copper basket and threw it into the Ganges. The boy was found by a peasant, who took care of him (or in some accounts he was brought up by a hermit). When he grew up and learned about his past, he was greatly distressed and left for the Himalayas. He arrived in Yarlung in Tibet. Twelve men saw him and asked where he came from. 'I am a Mighty One,' he answered and pointed to the sky. Thinking he might have descended from heaven the men made him their king. But according to the secret magicians he came from the land of Mu, and according to the Bon-pos he descended from heaven by means of a sky-cord.

Buddhas and Bodhisattvas appear in numerous different forms, which are related to different activities or manifestations. Among the groups of Buddhas or individual Buddha manifestations well known in Tibet, some are represented in fierce and wrathful forms. One of these is Heruka, who is shown here in a special form as Cakra-Samvara in yab-yum (father-mother) embrace. Thang-ka, 18th century.

Buddhas, Bodhisattvas and Gods

Although Tibetan Buddhism adheres to the later Mahayana teachings, it also preserves the earlier traditions of Sakyamuni Buddha as a historical person. Tibetan versions of his last life, and his previous lives, are based exclusively on earlier Indian versions. In art Sakyamuni appears in different symbolic postures related to various events of his life. He is also worshipped through the medium of the *stupa*, originally a mound containing relics of the Buddha and later a symbol of cosmic Buddhahood.

The cult of the Five Cosmic or Celestial Buddhas is also well attested in Tibet. The set of five derives from an earlier group of three: Vairocana, represented as a preaching Buddha, Amitabha, a meditating Buddha, and Akshobhya, who represents Sakyamuni at the moment when he quelled the forces of Mara, the Evil One, at the time of his Enlightenment (see THERAVADA BUDDHISM). The later concept of five Buddhas, based on the idea of the four cardinal points plus the centre, is expressed in several Indian texts. In the most important of them (the 'Symposium of

The Protectors of Religion are important deities who defend the integrity of the Buddhist religion against its enemies. Many of them appear in fierce or wrathful aspects, with numerous heads and arms, brandishing weapons.

ABOVE Yamantaka, the Destroyer of the Lord of Death. Bronze, 17th century.

RIGHT Mahakala, the Great Black One. Gilt copper, 18th century.

the Truth of all the Tathagatas') Sakyamuni appears as Vairocana ('Resplendent One'), the central Buddha, with the four other Buddhas: Akshobhya ('Imperturbable'), Amitabha ('Boundless Light'), Ratnasambhava ('Jewel-Born') and Amoghasiddhi ('Perfect Accomplishment').

Other groups of Buddhas or individual Buddha manifestations well known in Tibet include: a series of Buddhas in time, seven or 24 in number; the 35 Buddhas of Confession, supplicated in the so-called Confession of Sins; the eight Buddhas of Medicine, with Bhaishajyaguru as their chief; and Amitayus ('Infinite Life'), the Buddha of longevity. There are also wrathful Buddha manifestations, such as Kalacakra, Hevajra, Guhyasamaja, Samvara and Heruka.

The cult of Sakyamuni in his previous lives as a Bodhisattva, 'a being intent on enlightenment' and acting for the benefit of others, developed into the cult of many celestial Bodhisattvas. The most popular of them in Tibet is Avalokitesvara ('Lord of Compassion'). As the 'patron saint' of Tibet, he is worshipped in many forms, of which the best known are the four-armed one with one head and the eleven-headed one with a thousand arms. Maitreya

('The Benevolent One'), the Buddha of the future, is also well known. In art he is represented seated in the European manner.

Many gods, Buddhas and Bodhisattvas appear in different forms related to different activities or manifestations. Avalokitesvara, for example, is known in 108 different forms in iconography. They may also appear under different aspects, such as tranquil, wrathful, or fierce.

An important group of deities known as 'The Protectors of Religion' (*Chos-skyong*) is given the special function of defending the integrity of Buddhist teaching against its enemies. Every religious order, monastery and temple, however small, has its own protective deity. Most of them appear in wrathful or fierce aspects, and even the few who have a tranquil appearance are easily offended. They are depicted with many arms and heads, very often with animal heads, brandishing their characteristic weapons and adorned with ornaments, jewels, tiger-skins, snakes, garlands of flowers or garlands of bones and skulls. One method of classifying them distinguishes between the gods of this world and the gods of the world beyond. Another groups them as 'Protectors of the White Party' and 'Demons of the Black Party', the latter name referring to deities of non-Buddhist origin who were incorporated into Buddhism. This group is also referred to as 'Bound by an Oath', since some of the powerful local deities were subdued and bound by an oath to defend the Buddhist religion.

Mahakala, 'Great Black One' (Nag-po chen-po in Tibetan), a deity of Indian origin, is one of the most prominent protective gods. He has as many as 75 different forms in iconography, the best known being 'Six-Armed One' and 'Four-Armed One'. Two other mighty defenders are Hayagriva, 'Horse-Necked One' (Tibetan rTa-mgrin), and Yamantaka, 'Destroyer of the Lord of Death' (Tibetan sShin-rje-gshed). The most important of the female defenders of Buddhism is Sridevi, 'Glorious Goddess' (Tibetan dPal-ldan lha-mo).

Besides minor feminine powers who are defenders of religion or attendant goddesses, the universal goddess of Indian Buddhism appears under two aspects, as the personification of 'Supreme Wisdom' (Prajnaparamita) and as the 'Mother of All the Buddhas' or 'Universal Mother', known as Tara, 'Saviouress' (Tibetan sGrol-ma). Tara is a very popular goddess among the Tibetans. She has 21 forms, the best known being the Green Tara and the White Tara.

With the development of Tantric Buddhism, in which enlightenment is achieved by the union of Wisdom and Means, symbolically conceived as female and male, a great number of goddesses entered the Mahayana pantheon. The concept of Buddhahood as symbolized by the Five Cosmic Buddhas or other Buddha manifestations was here represented by male and female pairs.

Many of the innumerable indigenous gods and demons were included in the Buddhist pantheon. Their identity and character were often extremely vague, but they were thought capable of interfering with the forces of nature and the lives of men, and most of them were regarded as potentially harmful. Various attempts were made to classify them. One list divides them into nine groups:

1. *gNod-sbyin* – believed to cause epidemics; some of them became temple-guardians
2. *bDud* – evil-tempered demons of the higher spheres, shaped like birds, fish, herbs, stones; their leader, 'The Merciless Blood-Head', inhabits a black castle, nine storeys high
3. *Srin-po* – man-eating giants (corresponding to the Indian Rakshasas)
4. *Klu* – serpent-deities of the underworld
5. *bTsan* (and *The*) – a large group of gods inhabiting the sky, forests, mountains and glaciers; some became protectors of Buddhist doctrine.
6. *Lha* – pre-Buddhist celestial beings, white in colour and generally benevolent; however, many other deities were popularly called *lha*, including those supposed to rest on one's shoulders and gods of food, the hearth, and roads
7. *dMu* – evil demons
8. *'Dre* – malign beings, messengers of death who often cause mortal diseases; almost anything harmful is popularly called *'Dre*
9. *'Gan-'dre* – yet another class of harmful beings

Another list, free of Buddhist inspiration, classifies local deities into three groups:

1. *gNyan* – generally inhabiting the space above the earth, but also mountains, forests and rocks
2. *Sa-bdag* – deities bound to particular places, which they control, including individual mountains, villages and fields; indifferently good and bad in character, they are easily provoked and cause harm
3. *Klu* – serpent-gods of waters and the underworld, very harmful if angered

Arhats and Ge-sar

A set of 16 or 18 Arhats, 'Worthy Ones', has an established tradition in Tibet. Arhat was a title given to Sakyamuni's disciples who attained a state of spiritual perfection. In Tibetan they are called 'Enemy-Conquerors', meaning overcoming the

LEFT Tara, the Saviouress, is a very popular deity in Tibet. She has numerous forms, of which the best known are the Green Tara and the White. Standing figure of the Green Tara, who is regarded as the female partner of Avalokitesvara. Gilt copper, 16th century.

ABOVE A magic dagger used in the ritual slaying of an effigy representing an enemy, or in philosophical terms 'the foe of the self'.

Famous teachers and yogins are worshipped in Tibet.

RIGHT Padmasambhava, 'Lotus-Born', an Indian yogin of the 8th century who propagated Buddhism in Tibet, is credited with using his magical powers to subdue the local gods. Thang-ka, 18th century.

BELOW Milarepa, a renowned Tibetan mystic of the 12th century, whose biography and Hundred Thousand Songs are among the most popular of Tibetan religious books. Bronze, 17th century.

imperfections which prevent one's spiritual progress. Other groups of Arhats developed in later tradition, 108, 500 or a thousand in number.

The 84 Mahasiddhas, 'Great Magicians', are a set of Indian yogins believed to have possessed great magical powers. Padmasambhava, 'Lotus-Born', an Indian yogin of the 8th century, is widely worshipped in Tibet, where he is known as Guru Rin-po-che. He is credited with extraordinary magical powers which he applied to the subjugation of the local gods opposed to Buddhism. The Tibetans also developed special cults of other renowned teachers, Indian and Tibetan, including Milarepa, a Tibetan yogin of the 12th century.

A substantial amount of legendary material has been preserved in the Tibetan epic of the life and adventures of Ge-sar, King of Ling. This hero was popular with the Manchus in China and the peoples of Central Asia as well as in Tibet. His name may be an echo from Caesar and some episodes are borrowed from the legends of Alexander the Great. The version given here comes from the province of Kham.

The assembly of gods in heaven was informed by Padmasambhava, the great magician, that mighty demons would soon be born on earth with the intention of wiping out the true religion and its followers. It was decided that one of the gods who possessed all the necessary magical powers should be born on earth and destroy the demons. Consequently in the land of Ling – close to Hor, the seat of the demons – a boy was born, the son of one of the gods and a serpent-goddess. He was later called Ge-sar. As a child he was persecuted by a local chief, who knew it was prophesied that Ge-sar would become king of Ling. His attempts to kill the boy by beating his head against rocks, by burying him alive, and finally by magic all failed, and Ge-sar was exiled with his mother to a remote country.

Reminded by the gods of his special mission, Ge-sar returned to Ling and, through winning a horse-race by a ruse, became king. He set out to gain possession of hidden treasures and to kill a mighty demon in the north, whom he destroyed with the help of the demon's wife. Returning to Ling after six years away, he found his country devastated by the wicked rulers of Hor and many of his people killed. First flying to India on his horse, transformed into a vulture, to procure all kinds of medicine, Ge-sar then went to Hor to carry out his principal mission.

He was found in Hor by a blacksmith's daughter in a heap of tea-dregs, disguised as a little boy. He became an apprentice to her father and the people of Hor soon learned of his extraordinary abilities. While the demon-king of Hor and the people were watching a set of magic dolls which the young apprentice had made, Ge-sar destroyed their patron-deities. Suspecting the identity of the apprentice, the king of Hor asked a magician to identify him. Ge-sar killed the magician and, appearing before the king as a phantom magician, he gave him misleading information. Appearing again, as an Indian juggler, he foretold the king's early death. Appearing yet again, as the king's patron-god, he said that if the king was to live he must remain in the palace by himself while his warriors and people went to watch dances performed by seven spiders transformed into men. While the people watched the dances, which were illusions created by Ge-sar, the hero went to the palace, revealed his identity and killed the king. A second demon, the king's brother, was destroyed with all his officers by the gods, who reduced them to ashes with thunderbolts. Ge-sar spared the life of the third, the youngest brother, who left the country.

For a time Ge-sar continued with his work of extirpating the wicked. When he had completed his mission, he went to the mountains. There he meditated and finally passed to paradise.

Three kinds of myth can be distinguished in Tibet: cosmological myths describing the origin of the world; religious myths employed to express fundamental religious truths; and myths fabricated to explain traditional beliefs, such as the origins of the Tibetan people. This last category may be regarded as totally fictitious and without real impact on the fundamental issues of life. The cosmological and religious myths, however, convey fundamental truths in a symbolic manner. Tibetan Buddhism (or the Bon-po religion for that matter) cannot be treated as 'mere' mythology, for it presents positive religious values expressed in a living tradition. Scientific knowledge does not necessarily destroy myths of this kind, in so far as they remain the expression of higher religious truths. The richness of myths which we find in Tibet constitutes an essential part of Tibetan culture.

In Tantric Buddhism enlightenment is attained by the union of Wisdom and Means, symbolically represented as male and female. The Bodhisattva Samantabhadra in the embrace of his female partner, surrounded by the Five Buddhas: Ratnasambhava, Vairocana and Amitabha in the top row, Akshobhya and Amoghasiddhi below.

CHAPTER FIVE

CHINA

Not only is China continental in size, covering about the same area as the whole of Europe, but its historical and literary traditions have been written in what is essentially the same language for more than 3,000 years. This tradition knows nothing of the archeologist's prehistory, but attributes the basic human inventions – including agriculture, animal-rearing, pottery, building and writing – to the Three Sovereigns and the Five Emperors. These culture heroes were followed by three dynasties, Hsia, Shang and Chou, of which the first remains shadowy and uncertain. In terms of Chinese culture, the story is one of expansion by the northern peoples into the south, of a succession of struggles for hegemony, of overlapping territories and periods until the 3rd century BC, when China was first united under Shih Huang Ti of the Ch'in dynasty. The western term China comes from the name of this dynasty: the Chinese name is Ch'ung-kuo, or Middle Kingdom.

This first union was re-established under the Han dynasty, when China covered most of its present territorial extent. For most of the period since, the system of government has been one of a centralized state ruled, until 1912, by an emperor and administered by a bureaucracy, led by civil servants who passed a system of public examinations based on a knowledge of the philosophical classics. When the centre was weak, the provinces were more or less autonomous: under a powerful emperor or a strong court the unity of the vast territory was a reality.

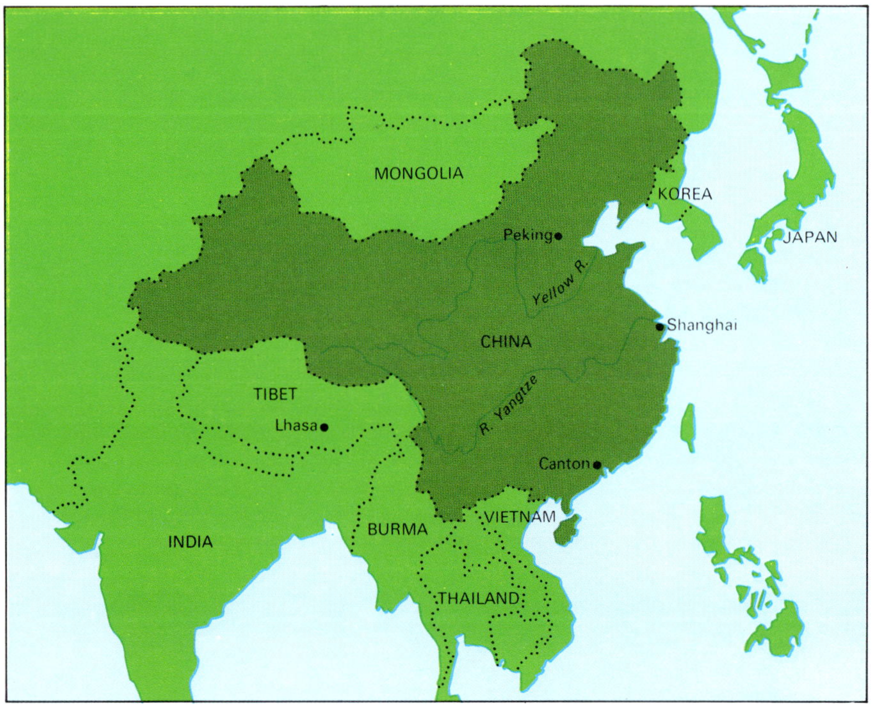

The traditional Chinese cults of the ancestors and of a great variety of deities were influenced over the centuries by the philosophical systems of Confucianism, founded by Confucius (551–479 BC), and Taoism, traditionally founded by Lao Tzu, an older contemporary of Confucius; and subsequently by Buddhism, introduced from India. Later still, Islam and Christianity both gained footholds in China.

Paradoxically, despite the unparalleled duration of the living Chinese tradition, the sources for Chinese mythology are scarce, contradictory and difficult to interpret. For this there are two reasons, both connected with the scholar-administrators. Much of the relevant literature purports to be Shang or Chou in date, but most of it is Han or later, the work of scholars who backdated it to give authority to their own points of view. There is reason to think that one man, Li Szu, a minister under Shih Huang Ti, was largely responsible for this. In 213 BC he persuaded the emperor to burn all books, except for technical manuals on medicine, divination, agriculture and arboriculture. Four hundred and sixty scholars died on charges of evading the order. Li Szu's argument was that scholars were only interested in precedent, studying the past, as he said, to deprecate the present, and opposing all innovations.

That so much survived is a tribute to those who maintained the tradition. That so much of it is Confucian shows how strong that essentially conformist and conservative school was. The decree was revoked in 191 BC and literature was reconstructed, in such a way as to reinforce the position of the scholar class, with their concept of a hierarchical system in which all were subservient to the state in the person of the ruler. The texts were systematized to show what should be, not what actually had been. Old sources were edited to bring them into line with Confucian theory. Much was deliberately omitted: other material was not recovered. It is against this background that the surviving Chinese mythology

has to be considered. This is why there are so many gaps or unresolved problems and queries. Finally, it must be noted that Li Szu himself was a scholar, arguing from precedent: 'The Five Emperors did not copy each other, the Three Dynasties (Hsia, Shang and Chou) did not imitate their predecessors.' And it was to those periods, and to the Three Sovereigns who reigned before the Five Emperors, that all creation and innovation were attributed.

Order from Chaos

Chuang-tzu, a philosopher of the 3rd century BC, relates how the Emperor of the Northern Sea, Hu, and his southern counterpart, Shu, used to meet in the realm of Hun-tun, Emperor of the Centre. Hun-tun, whose name means Chaos, was most hospitable, but lacked the seven bodily orifices which other men have. To repay his hospitality Shu and Hu (whose names together, *shu-hu*, mean lightning) decided to bore the necessary holes in Hun-tun, at the rate of one hole a day. On the seventh day, when they drilled the last hole, Hun-tun died: simultaneously the world as it is now known came into existence.

Six hundred years later we learn that Chaos was like a hen's egg. Neither Heaven nor Earth existed. From the egg P'an-ku was born, while of its heavy elements Earth was made and Sky from the light elements. P'an-ku is represented as a dwarf, clad in a bearskin or a cloak of leaves. For 18,000 years the distance between Earth and Sky grew daily by ten feet, and P'an-ku grew at the same rate so that his body filled the gap. When he died, different parts of his body became various natural elements. The details vary from source to source. In the most elaborate, the cardinal points and the five great mountains derive from his body, rivers and seas from his blood and other fluids, the soil from his flesh. Wind and clouds are his breath, thunder and lightning his voice, his left eye the sun, his right the moon, his hair the stars, his eyebrows the planets. His teeth and bones became metals and stones, his semen pearls and his marrow jade, his sweat the rain. His body fleas became the human race.

This story has Indian parallels, both in the egg of origin and in the use made of the parts of P'an-ku's

ABOVE LEFT Embroidered imperial robe, 18th century, shows a dragon below a medallion of the white hare of the moon, pounding the drug of immortality under the Cassia tree. The drink will make the moon-goddess Heng-o into an immortal toad.

ABOVE Lao Tzu, a probable contemporary of Confucius and founder of Taoism. With Confucianism and Buddhism, introduced from India, this was the basis of China's culture. 16th-century woodcut.

body (see HINDUISM). A tradition from the Yangtze delta says that P'an-ku and his wife represent *yang* and *yin*, as do the two halves of the egg from which P'an-ku was born. In Chinese philosophy yin and yang are two opposing parts which together make a harmonious whole. Examples are female-male, earth-sky, moon-sun, water-fire, square-round, dark-light, compasses, *kuei*-set square, *chu* (*Kuei-chu* = order, proper conduct). One reference makes Yin and Yang deities responsible for the management of Earth and Heaven.

The Physical World

From texts which date mostly from the later Han period (AD 25–220) it is possible to gain some idea of pre-Ch'in notions of the cosmos. There were three schools of thought: *suan ye*, *hun t'ien* and *t'ien kai* or *chou pei*. Of the first, all that is known is that the sun and the other heavenly bodies were believed to move freely in a sky which was not solid. The *hun t'ien* school, whose ideas have obvious connections with the P'an-ku story, believed that the world was like an upright hen's egg. The sky, across which the stars moved, was on the inside of the upper part of the shell. The earth floated upon the primeval ocean, lying on the bottom of the shell.

For the third school, probably the oldest tradition, the inverted bowl of the sky revolved on an axis, the Pole Star, with the other stars fixed to the bowl. Earth was either a flat square or a truncated four-sided pyramid with a sea on each side. (This concept is implicit in the oldest forms of the Chinese character for earth.) Earth is still, square and yin, Sky is revolving, round and yang. The solid bowl of the sky has a support or supports, fixed by guy-ropes which have the same name as the lashings which fasten the body of a chariot to the chassis. An ancient Chinese chariot had a square body with a circular upper part supported by a shaft. *T'ien kai* is the name of this upper umbrella, and metaphors relating the cosmic structure to a chariot are quite common. Sometimes the sky is conceived as a chariot wheel with the Pole Star at its hub, but it is more often like an umbrella, though it frequently has four or eight

MYTHICAL AND HISTORICAL DYNASTIES

Mythical	The Three Sovereigns (Fu-hsi; Shen-nung; Yen Ti)
Mythical	The Five Emperors (Huang Ti, the Yellow Emperor; Chuan Hsiun; K'u; Yao; Shun)
2000–1520 BC	Hsia Dynasty
1520–1030 BC	Shang (Yin) Dynasty
1030–221 BC	Chou Dynasty
221–207 BC	Ch'in Dynasty
202 BC–AD 220	Han Dynasty
AD 221–265	The Three Kingdoms
AD 265–420	Chin Dynasty
AD 420–479	Sung Dynasty
AD 479–581	Six dynasties
AD 581–618	Sui Dynasty
AD 618–906	T'ang Dynasty
AD 907–960	Five dynasties
AD 960–1126	Northern Sung Dynasty
AD 1127–1279	Southern Sung Dynasty
AD 1260–1368	Yuan (Mongol) Dynasty
AD 1368–1644	Ming Dynasty
AD 1644–1912	Ch'ing (Manchu) Dynasty
AD 1912	Republic

ABOVE The dwarf P'an-ku, whose body in mythology became the world. He holds the yin-yang symbol which subsumes cosmic duality. The story has Indian parallels. 19th-century lithograph.

RIGHT Painting on silk of the mythical Emperor Yao, who is said to have regulated the winds. Late 18th century.

supports rather than one at the centre, no attempt being then made to explain how it revolves.

There is an explanation, however, for the observable discrepancy that the Pole Star, the theoretical centre of the system and of the Middle Kingdom, is actually considerably off-centre. According to the *Shan Hai Ching* (the Hill and River Classic), a monster named Kung Kung tried to seize power from Yao, the Fourth Emperor. He failed, and in his fury impaled the north-west support, Mount Pu Chou (the name means Not Round), with his horn. The mountain broke, causing Sky to tip to the north-west and tearing a hole in Sky itself. Earth tilted the other way and that is why waters flow south-eastwards. Floods arose from the attack, giving rise to a series of myths on flood-control, a perennial Chinese problem. The same catastrophe 'explains' the cycle of the seasons, climatic change and day and night. Sun cannot shine when there is no sky: a flaming dragon with a human face takes its place. When its eyes are open it is day, when closed night. Its inhalation is summer, its exhalation winter. Its

PRINCIPAL MYTHOLOGICAL INVENTORS

Fu-hsi, First Sovereign: fishing; domestication of animals; rearing of silk-worms; the divinatory trigrams; measuring instrument; calendar; marriage was invented by his younger sister and wife, Nu-kua

Shen-nung, Second Sovereign; agriculture; herbal medicine

Huang Ti, First Emperor: chariot wheel; potter's wheel; compass; ships; armour.

Yao, Fourth Emperor: regulated the winds, through Yi the Archer

Shun, Fifth Emperor: controlled the floods, through Yu, who succeeded him as ruler

Yu, Hsia Dynasty: succeeded Shun and, on intervention of feudal lords, was succeeded by his son Ch'i; this established primogeniture and the dynastic system, which lasted until 1912

ABOVE LEFT Shen-nung, the second Sovereign, inventor of agriculture and medicine. Glazed pottery.

ABOVE Chu-jung, Heavenly Executioner and Spirit of Fire, who was responsible for keeping order on earth. He received high imperial honours in the 10th and 11th centuries.

RIGHT The Taoist goddess Hsi Wang Mu, Royal Mother of the Western Paradise. Once in 6000 years the magic peaches ripen in the gardens of her palace. Then it is her birthday and all the immortals gather to eat the fruit which renews their immortality. Porcelain plate, early 18th century.

BELOW Ritual staff-head in the form of a dragon. Dragons rise into the skies in the spring and plunge into the waters in the autumn. Gilt bronze, 18th century.

breathing is also the wind, and absence of breathing means there is neither wind nor rain.

According to the *Shu Ching* (Book of History), the central column, which like P'an-ku's body both separated and linked together Heaven and Earth, was a mixed blessing, for because there was traffic between them there was confusion between gods and men. As a result there was no proper order in the sacrifices. So the mythical ruler Chuan Hu ordered Ch'ung, the governor of the South, and Li, the governor of Fire, to break communications between the two realms. The former presided over Heaven and organized the gods, while the latter did the same for men. This story emphasizes the extreme importance of proper order and ritual, and also hints at the complex bureaucracy which was the pantheon in the evolved religious system. It was organized exactly like the imperial administration on earth, with divine departments to control every aspect of the world's activities, whether good or evil, moral or immoral, approved or not.

Of solar, lunar or stellar origins there is nothing. Of lightning we are merely told that it flashes through a hole in the top of the sky. The Lord of Lightning is the executioner in the celestial bureaucracy. There is an old tradition that Sun and Moon have a common ancestor, the Emperor Shun. In fact there are ten suns and 12 moons, the 12 lunar months. Each of these bodies has a mother, who is in charge of its functions. Before dawn the suns are bathed in a lake bordering on the Valley of Light at the extreme eastern edge of the world, where there is an enormous tree called *po*, or sometimes Hollow Mulberry. Newly bathed, nine of the suns lodge in the tree's lower branches, while the tenth climbs to the top and takes its place in a chariot drawn by dragons and driven by its mother. It proceeds across the sky by stages, the daylight hours, until it reaches a tree called *jo*, by Mount Yen-tzu in the farthest west, where the dragons are unyoked. There is no account of its return journey, but the jo-tree has glowing red flowers and may represent the night sky. Elements of this story are reflected in certain characters which can be traced to the earliest Chinese writing: East is a sun in a tree, light is a sun above and darkness a sun under a tree. Dawn is written with nine and a sun – the nine attendant suns lodged in the po-tree.

Traditionally, in ill-omened times more than one sun was seen in the sky, and a myth explains the present single sun. When Yao, the Fourth Emperor, was about to lose his throne to Shun, ten suns appeared in the sky, their heat threatening all living beings. Yao gave a magic bow to Yi the Archer, who shot nine of the suns with it. Yi is the husband of the Lady Heng-o, who lives in the moon in the form of an immortal toad. She stole the elixir of immortality from Yi, who had obtained it from Hsi Wang Mu, the female ruler of the Western Paradise. And it is from the west, after bathing in a western lake, that the moons make their journey across the sky. The moon is made of water and is yin. It is also inhabited by a hare, an earlier tradition than that of the toad. The sun is fire and yang, and is inhabited by a three-footed raven. When Yi shot the nine suns, their ravens fell to earth.

Yi the Archer also restored order to the winds, which are in a great sack controlled by Fei Lien, the Count of the Wind. Fei Lien is said to have been a minister on earth before being made a celestial civil servant. In the latter capacity he is also associated with drought, understandably in Chinese terms since the winds can parch all vegetation as well as bring rain-clouds. Fei Lien rebelled against Huang Ti, the Yellow Emperor, and created great storms. Riding on the wind, Yi reached a mountain top where he subdued the rebel with an arrow and ensured that the winds would be operated in a proper manner in the future.

The rains were controlled by a Lord of the Rain, dressed in yellow scale-armour and a red and yellow headdress, who lived on the slopes of Mount K'un-lun in the far west. According to some traditions he sprinkles rain from a watering-can, while others say that he uses a sword to scatter water from a pot in his left hand. He is said to have been an administrator at the time of one of the Three Sovereigns and, being a successful magic rain-maker, was made Lord of Rain.

Another deity said to have been originally a human being was Ho Po, Count of the River. He gained his power by throwing himself into the Yellow River with a load of stones on his back, a magical act of suicide. Girls were launched onto the waters on a marriage bed as brides for the Count.

FAR LEFT The archer Yi, who helped Emperor Yao to control the unruly winds. When Yao was about to lose his throne, all ten suns appeared at once and their heat threatened the earth. Yao's successor, Shun, gave a magic bow to Yi who shot nine of them out of the sky. That is why there is now only one sun. Yi is the husband of Heng-o. Book illustration, 1645.

LEFT Modern terracotta figure of Heng-o, the goddess of the moon and wife of Yi, from whom she is said to have stolen the herb of immortality. In another story she is said to be immortal because she drank a magic potion made by the hare who lives in the moon. This drink turned her into a toad. She was the daughter of Ho Po, Count of the (Yellow) River. Yi was also concerned with the control of floods and it was through this activity that he met and married Heng-o.

The Creation of Man

According to one tradition, as we have seen, men were originally P'an-ku's fleas. Another story, of uncertain date, says that once Heaven, Earth, plants and animals were in existence, P'an-ku was dissatisfied at the absence of a reasoning being to exploit the potential of creation. He therefore modelled figures from clay which he impregnated with yang and yin. As these embryonic men and women were drying in the sun, clouds gathered in the north-west (where Kung Kung had damaged the sky). P'an-ku gathered up the figures with an iron fork to carry them indoors, but the rain fell before he got them all to safety. Those damaged by the storm became the halt and the crippled.

In another myth Nu-kua, who is sometimes the wife of Fu-hsi, first of the Three Sovereigns, started to model men and women in yellow clay. Becoming bored, she took a rope, dipped it in the clay and trailed it about so that blobs fell off. The modelled figures became the noble and rich, the blobs the humble and poor. In other myths men are created by sexual intercourse, often incestuous. In one case Nu-kua becomes a brother-sister pair. It is relevant that Nu-kua is sometimes described as Fu-hsi's younger sister, but becomes his wife after she has invented marriage. A late story traces the origin of mankind to a pair of attendants of the god of literature, Wen-ch'ang. Their names were T'ien-lung and Ti-mu (Earth Mother) and their union first produced men and subsequently all other beings.

Figure of K'uei-hsing, god of examinations, companion of Wen-ch'ang, god of literature. He is usually shown standing on the head of a turtle. With his brush he marks the list of successful candidates. K'ang Hsi period (1665–1722).

The Control of Nature

Han Fei Tzu, a philosopher of the 3rd century BC, says that when men were few and beasts many, a sage appeared to teach men to make wooden nests for protection. The people made the sage ruler of the world as the Nest Builder. At that time men ate only raw food and many fell ill as a result. Another sage appeared and taught them to make fire with the fire-drill, thus providing them with the means to cook. The people made him the ruler of the world as Drill Man. K'un and Yu of the Hsia dynasty opened channels to control the waters, and Yu led his people in ploughing and digging.

Other sources give different accounts of the way in which men learnt to exploit natural resources, but the discoveries are generally attributed to mythical rulers in the role of culture heroes. The accounts are often contradictory and confused, but there are certain salient features. The most important of these is the maintenance of order, of equilibrium, always a primary concern of Chinese religion and ritual. When Kung Kung upset the universe, the four cardinal points were out of place, earth and sky no longer coincided, fire burned ceaselessly and the waters flowed unchecked. Nu-kua repaired the sky, fixed the cardinal points, using the feet of a tortoise, and piled up the ashes of reeds to check the flow of the waters (reed associated with water and ash with fire may be a symbol of yin-yang). The restoration of order is implicit in many of the invention stories.

The grandson of Shen-nung, Ch'ih-yu, rebelled against Huang Ti. The former invented war and weapons: the latter countered with armour. Ch'ih-yu called down thick fog: Huang Ti invented the compass to guide his troops. Pa, the goddess of drought, aided Huang Ti against the Count of the Wind and the Lord of Rain, who were allied of Ch'ih-yu, but Huang Ti finally exiled her to preserve men from excessive drought. The function of the ruler was to maintain everything in balance.

According to another myth of the control of flooding, at the time of Yao, the Fourth Emperor, K'un tried to control the waters. The dams which he built collapsed, so he stole the Swelling Earth (which grew ceaselessly to block any number of holes). Huang Ti, angered, had K'un executed. After three year's K'un's belly was slashed open with a magic sword and his son Yu emerged. Yu went to Heaven and asked Huang Ti for a gift of Swelling Earth. Equipped with it, he first dammed 233,559 springs. Then he built mountains at the corners of the earth to ensure that it would not be swept away by water and that there would always be dry land somewhere.

Next he cut ditches and bored tunnels to drain the water from the land into the sea.

While tunnelling, Yu penetrated a cavern where he found Fu-hsi, who gave him a jade scale so that he could measure Heaven and Earth. This Yu proceeded to do and, since the task involved travelling, he is credited with the invention of the various means of transport. A section of the *Shu Ching* (Book of History) gives an account of Yu's activities as a geographer. The text, probably of the 5th century BC but based on an older tradition, is a mixture of fact and myth treated on an equal footing. It was further recorded that Yu cast nine bronze cauldrons, one for each of the provinces, where the results of his researches were depicted in low relief. Perhaps Yu's practice of tunnelling was considered parallel to the excavations of those who sought for ores. This related him to the smiths, both as digger and as metalworker. All these elements, smiths, cauldrons, ore from the nine provinces or from the five cardinal mountains (the source of the metal with which Nu-kua repaired the sky), form part of the complex symbolism of imperial rule which is the source of order and harmony. By his own right relationship with the ruler of Heaven the emperor ensures order in the imperial realm. Lesser dignitaries maintain proper relationships with the subordinates of the heavenly power. The rites are observed: harmony prevails. The eight trigrams, whose interpretation is explained in the *I Ching* (Book of Changes), and the circular symbol of yin-yang, all associated with Fu-hsi and Nu-kua, symbolizes this order which is Tao, 'the Way'.

Kan Chiang and Mo Yeh

The somewhat enigmatic story of Kan Chiang and his wife seems to have originated around the delta of the Yangtze river, possibly among Indonesian-speaking peoples, and to reflect ideas about kingship different from those of the Shang dynasty. Ho Liu, king of Wu, ordered the smith Kan Chiang and his wife Mo Yeh to make him a pair of swords. After collecting ore from the Five Mountains they began the work at an auspicious time, but after three months the iron had not yet flowed from the ore. Mo Yeh asked her husband why. He replied that he did not know, but that in similar circumstances his master and the latter's wife threw themselves into the furnace so that the work might be successful. Mo Yeh then threw her hair-clippings and nail-parings into the furnace, the bellows were re-activated, more fuel was added, and the swords were completed in due course. The male sword was called Kan Chiang, the female Mo Yeh.

Then the smith hid the male sword and gave the female one to the king. The latter, after testing it, realized that he had been cheated and, in his anger, killed the smith. Dying, Kan Chiang disclosed the hiding place of the male sword to his pregnant wife and foretold that his unborn son would avenge him. When the boy was old enough, his mother told him what had happened and he sought the sword. When he had found it, he decapitated himself with it. A passing stranger took the boy's head and the sword to the king, who threw the head into a cauldron to

ABOVE Taoist sages with the *yin-yang* symbol, on a K'ang Hsi dish.

LEFT Shou-lao, god of longevity, Old Man of the Southern Star. A Taoist deity, his symbol is the peach, in which he is shown seated on a deer, a symbol of sexuality. The split peach represents the vulva, his coral sceptre the erect phallus. Porcelain, 18th century.

melt. When it failed to do so, the stranger persuaded the king to allow his own head to be cut off: added to the cauldron, it would cause the first head to melt. It did not do so. Finally the stranger decapitated himself into the cauldron and at once the three heads fused into a single lump. This lump is buried at the Tumulus of the Three Kings.

The Pumpkin Girl

Human sacrifice, a common theme in Chinese myths and legends, appears again in the story of the Pumpkin Girl. At the time of the emperor Shih Huang Ti of the Ch'in dynasty, two families Meng and Chiang, who were neighbours, each planted a pumpkin seed by their boundary wall. The two plants grew until they met and united to produce a pumpkin of most unusual size. The two families discussed the ownership of the fruit and finally agreed to divide it. On halving the fruit, they found a beautiful little girl whom they decided to rear jointly, giving her the name Meng Chiang after their two families. Meanwhile the emperor had resolved to build a wall 10,000 miles long to protect his northern frontier from the Huns, but as each section was completed, it collapsed. Finally a sage advised that a human being should be buried alive at each mile of the structure.

The hunt for victims began and terror spread through the land. Then another sage proposed to the emperor that to sacrifice a man called Wan (meaning Ten Thousand) would provide a spirit for each mile without spreading further terror. A certain Wan, fleeing from the threat to those of his name, was hiding in a tree in the garden of Meng Chiang when the latter came out into the moonlight to bathe in the pool there. Happily she said: 'If a man were to see me now naked, then I would gladly belong to him for ever.' And Wan called out: 'I see you.' So they were married, but during the marriage feast, soldiers came and seized Wan, who was duly sacrificed. Meng Chiang, though the marriage had not been consummated, felt bound to her husband and set out for the Great Wall to seek for his bones. Appalled by its length, and not knowing where to begin her search, she sat weeping, when the wall, pitying her, fell down where her husband's remains lay.

Shih Huang Ti, hearing of the widow's devotion, sent for her and seeing that she was beautiful decided to make her his empress. Meng Chiang agreed to the imperial will, provided that there was a 49 day funeral feast in honour of her husband, to be attended by the emperor and the court officials, and that an altar, 49 feet high, should be erected on the river-bank so that she might make offerings for the dead man. The emperor agreed and all was done as Meng Chiang had required. Then Meng Chiang mounted on the altar and denounced the emperor for his cruelty before all the court. Shih Huang Ti sat unmoved, but when she threw herself to her death in the river, the emperor ordered his soldiers to drag her from the water and, having cut her body into pieces, to grind her bones to dust. And as they did so, the fragments turned into tiny silver-coloured fish in which the soul of Lady Meng Chiang lives on.

RIGHT, ABOVE AND BELOW Two representations of the Buddhist goddess Kuan Yin, who is also known as Sung-tzu niang-niang, the lady who brings children. She is the embodiment of compassion and corresponds to the Indian Bodhisattva Avalokitesvara, who is male. It is supposed that she was a Chinese goddess whom the Buddhists adopted. Her cult was not confined to Buddhist households.

BELOW Silver-gilt hairpin with pearl eyes, kingfisher feather inlay, *c.*1820. Meng Chiang's body turned into a shoal of silver fish. Fish, especially carp, are associated with longevity and immortality.

During rice sowing, the grain is scattered in the wet fields and the seedlings are transplanted into the fields where they are to grow under constant irrigation. In popular belief it was the milk from Kuan Yin's breasts which filled the rice ears, and the blood as she pressed out the last drops made red rice. 19th-century print.

The Pantheon

There is no single Chinese pantheon and it is doubtful whether there has ever been a comprehensive catalogue of the gods. Elements from the predynastic period and from regions into which the Chinese expanded, from the centuries before the burning of the books, from the constructs of Confucian scholars, based on theories of hierarchy and order, from Lao Tzu's teachings about the Taoist Way, and from Buddhism, mixed with beliefs in alchemy, drugs of immortality and transmutation, were conflated into a mass of contradictory and unsystematized material.

The compassionate goddess Kuan Yin, for example, seems to have been a local deity whom Buddhists identified with the Indian male Bodhisattva Avalokitesvara. According to one myth, the rice plant has always existed, but at first its ears were empty. Seeing that men lived in hardship and hunger, Kuan Yin went down secretly into the ricefields. There she squeezed her breasts so that the milk flowed into the empty ears. Most of the plants were filled, but towards the end she had to press so hard that a mixture of milk and blood flowed and that is why there are two kinds of rice, white and red.

In another agricultural myth a Bodhisattva is subordinated to a more-or-less Taoist supreme deity who is part of a hierarchical Heaven based on a Confucian model. Ti-tsang Bodhisattva, moved by men's struggle for food, suggested to the ruler of Heaven, Yu-ti, the August Jade One, that the Heavenly Ox should be sent to earth to help in the preparation of the fields. Yu-ti did not agree, for he knew that men would only care for the ox as long as it could pull the plough. Once it grew old, they would eat its flesh and tan its hide. Ti-tsang vowed that he would accept banishment to hell if such a thing were to happen. In fact, Yu-ti proved right. Once the ox became too feeble to pull the plough, he was killed, his flesh was eaten and his hide was tanned, despite his pleas to those whom he had aided. The angry Yu-ti banished Ti-tsang to hell, where he has to keep his eyes closed except on the thirtieth day of the seventh month. Then men light candles and burn incense in his honour.

Another story about a Bodhisattva explains the origin of the red-cored radish, *lo-p'u*. The Bodhisattva Mu-lien (whose personal name was Lo Pu)

Monkey and his companion shown in combat with a female demon. 17th-century woodcut.

had a mother who was both lazy and greedy. She killed animals and ate them. When he reproached her, she cursed him, causing him much grief. When she finally lay dying, she told her son that as a punishment for the destruction of life her soul was to remain in hell for ever. So her son spent all his means on priests to pray for her soul. When his money was exhausted, he became a monk to pray for her himself. By his meritious acts he became a Bodhisattva and was able to go to hell to rescue his mother. Seizing her in his arms, he ran off until he sank exhausted in a field of radishes. His mother, whose torments had included starvation, pulled up a radish and ate it. Mu-lien knew that if the ruler of Heaven were to detect the theft, his mother would stay in hell for eternity. He cut off his finger and pushed it into the hole from which the radish had been stolen. It grew as a red-cored radish.

The Story of Monkey

The way in which Buddhist and Taoist elements combine is again illustrated in the story of Monkey. It reflects the historical journey to India of the great scholar Hsuan Tsang (d. AD 664) to study Buddhism.

On a mountain in Ao-lai, on the eastern side of the Ocean, an egg was fertilized by the wind. From this egg Monkey was born. He became skilled in magic arts and was taught by a Taoist adept to change his shape and to fly through the air. He organized all the monkeys of the world into a kingdom and, having

obtained a magic weapon from the Dragon King of the Eastern Sea, set out to make himself master of the four quarters of the world. Then at a feast given in his honour Monkey drank too much and the servants of hell were able to capture him and he was chained in the infernal regions. Escaping, he stole the judgment register and deleted his own name and those of all the other monkeys. He was summoned to Heaven to explain his conduct and was created Grand Overseer of the Heavenly Stables, to keep him quiet. Discovering this, he started to destroy Heaven itself and then withdrew to Mount Hua-kuo. The gods organized a siege but were repulsed. Monkey proclaimed himself Governor of Heaven and Great Saint. Finally, he was given the post of Superintendent-in-Chief of the Heavenly Peach Garden, the source of immortality, and agreed to accept the divine laws. Failing to receive an invitation to the Peach Festival, he first ate all the food and drink that had been prepared and then stole and swallowed the pills of immortality from the house of Lao Chun.

Rendered thus doubly immortal, Monkey retired again to Mount Hua-kuo. This time, despite all his magic, he was captured after a prolonged siege. The Jade Emperor condemned him to death as a rebel against the throne of Heaven. As he had made himself immortal, he was handed over to Lao Chun, who was ordered to distil him in his alchemical furnace. For 49 days and nights the furnace was heated to white heat. Then Monkey lifted the lid and threatened to destroy Heaven. Despairing, the Jade Emperor sent for the Buddha, who asked Monkey why he thought he should possess Heaven. Monkey replied that he was sufficiently powerful and the Buddha asked him for proof. Monkey asserted that he was invulnerable, immortal, able to assume 72 different shapes, to fly and leap 108,000 *li*. The Buddha doubted whether Monkey could even jump across his palm, but agreed that if he could, then he was surely entitled to rule Heaven. Monkey sprang into the air across Heaven to the ends of the world where, to mark his territory, he pissed at the base of a

LEFT Two of a set of eight New Year Festival lamps in the form of the Eight Immortals. These represent Ho Hsien-ku and Lu Tung-pin. Painted parchment, Shansi Province, 19th century.

BELOW Coloured woodcut of the Eight Taoist Immortals. Their cult seems to have become popular in the 13th century. They form an incongruous group with very little in common. T'ieh-kuai Li, Li with the iron crutch, is said to have been a disciple of Lao Tzu. Han Chung-li, a carefree man of ripe years, is said to have lived in the Han dynasty. The old man Chang-kuo Lao was famous for his donkey, which could travel thousands of miles in a day, but could be folded up like a piece of paper. Lan Ts'ai-ho, a ragged street-singer with one bare foot, was carried to Heaven by a stork. Ts'ao Kuo-chiu, a wealthy young man, was a disciple of Han Chung-li. Ho Hsien-ku is a young girl with a lotus, who went to Heaven. Han Hsiang-tzu was taught the doctrine by Lu Tung-pin, whose story is probably the best known. He is said to have dreamed of his own life and seem himself killed by a brigand. As a result he decided to renounce the world in order to study Taoism. He is shown with a fly-whisk and a sword, dressed as a literary scholar.

ABOVE Porcelain figure of Mi-lo Fo, Maitreya, the Buddha who is yet to come in the present cycle. He is often called the Laughing Buddha and is associated with wealth.

RIGHT Kuan Yu, a general of the San Kuo period (221–65), was canonized as Kuan Ti, god of war. His great popularity was due to his role as preventer, not promoter of war. He underwent a series of posthumous promotions: Duke (1120), Prince (1128), then Warrior-Prince and Bringer of Civilization, and finally Faithful and Loyal Great Deity, Supporter of Heaven, Protector of the Realm (1594). He was also a patron of literature and upholder of justice, in whose temple the executioner's sword was kept. He was much invoked for predictions about the future. Painted screen, 19th century.

great mountain. Then, in a single bound, he returned to the Buddha, who laughed at his claim to have traversed the universe at a leap and showed him that the mountain where he had pissed was no more than the base of one of the Buddha's fingers. He had not even escaped from the palm of the Buddha's hand. Then the Buddha shut Monkey within a magic mountain which he created.

But the time came when T'ang Seng was to leave on his great pilgrimage to the Western Paradise to bring back to China authentic versions of the Buddha's teachings. So the compassionate Bodhisattva Kuan Yin begged for Monkey's release so that, together with Chu Pa-chieh, a Pig-spirit who was to act as the pilgrim's servant, he might accompany T'ang Seng on his journey. Monkey swore obedience to his new master who, as a precaution, fitted an iron helmet on Monkey's head which tightened whenever he contemplated any wayward or wanton act. Despite many temptations and 80 mighty perils, Monkey guarded T'ang Seng safely to the Western Paradise and back, when, after swimming a last river, they landed home in China to be greeted by emperor and people to whom the scriptures were entrusted.

A heavenly committee of welcome, presided over by Mi-lo, the Buddha yet to be born, recognized T'ang Seng as a former chief disciple of the Buddha and awarded him a high rank in Heaven. The horse

which carried the pilgrim and the scriptures was made a four-clawed dragon, chief of celestial dragons. The Pig was created Chief Cleanser of the Divine Altar and Monkey was made God of Victorious Strife. On receiving this title, Monkey asked that, since he was now an enlightened one, the iron helmet should now be removed. T'ang Seng replied that if Monkey were truly enlightened, then the helmet would have disappeared. Monkey touched his head and found that the helmet had indeed gone.

The Heavenly Civil Service

To make matters more complicated, emperors could and did issue decrees which altered the rank and status of the various deities. An example is Kuan Ti, god of war and of literature. He is another god who was believed to have been originally a human being and he figures as a semi-historical character in the *Romance of the Three Kingdoms* (early Ming period), where he is said to have killed a tyrannical official at the end of the Han dynasty. His merit was slowly recognized. Under the Northern Sung dynasty he was granted the title of Duke, and was later promoted to Prince. A Yuan emperor gave him the title Warrior Prince and Bringer of Civilization. In 1594 a Ming emperor created him Faithful and Loyal Great Deity, Supporter of Heaven, Protector of the Realm. Thanks to imperial support in Manchu times, his cult was served by 1600 official temples and countless lesser shrines.

There seems to have been from early times a supreme deity, Shang Ti. Under Confucian rationalization he became T'ien, Sky, but in popular belief he

ABOVE Painting of Yen-lo, the Buddhist Yama, King of Hell, dressed as an emperor. He watches, surrounded by his officials and bureaucrats in the Seventh Hell, while demons and dogs drive those condemned for desecrating graves or selling or eating human flesh into a river. Suppliants offer presents to Yen-lo as petitioners would in an earthly magistrates' court.

LEFT Hanging scroll showing the Four Kings of Hell, who correspond to the Buddhist rulers of the four quarters. Chinese systems of hell are manifold but all are organized like earthly bureaucracies.

Portrait of the Kitchen God and his wife. He reports to Heaven on each household at the New Year. Block print.

remained a deity and was assimiliated to the Taoist Yu-ti, Jade Deity. Yu-ti's principal assistant was Tung-yo ta-ti, Great Emperor of the Eastern Peak, the source of yang. He headed a ministry of some 75 departments, in which the souls of the virtuous were employed as bureaucrats, concerned with every aspect of human and animal life. Similarly the god of the soil had a whole series of deputies, each called Ch'eng Huang. They were responsible for the prosperity of each district, the god himself being concerned with the empire as a whole. They were also empowered to check that the emissaries of Yen-lo, ruler of the dead, carried off only those souls who had completed their life-span, allocated to them by Tung-yo ta-ti's civil servants. (Human magistrates used to consult the local Ch'eng Huang in his temple about difficult cases, because of his intimate knowledge of his district.)

The minute details of life were controlled by hosts of minor deities, co-ordinated by the deputies of Sky and Soil. All activities and livelihoods, from bureaucrats to thieves, prostitutes to soldiers, had their presiding deities. One of the most important for the individual and the family was the Kitchen God, chief of the gods connected with the house and household. Twice a month he received offerings of honey and sweet cakes, which were also presented to him on New Year's Eve, for at that season he went to give the Supreme Deity a report on each member of the household and such offerings would sweeten or impede his delivery, as required. The household was also able to communicate with Heaven through the ancestors, whose tablets in the household shrine received regular attention and reports on family happenings. The immediate ancestors could intervene with the heavenly bureaucracy on the family's behalf. Similarly in the capital, the emperor reported to the imperial ancestors on the affairs of the empire and made offerings to Heaven and Earth, Sky and Soil, for the whole realm. Hierarchy and order, through the mediation of ritual, were thus maintained harmoniously for state and individual alike. In this process the rulers and bureaucrats of heaven and earth were all believed to have their official and appropriate roles.

PRINCIPAL MYTHICAL FIGURES

Ch'eng Huang, name for the god of each district, responsible for the land and people

Ch'ih Sung-tzu, Lord of Rain, who lives on K'un Lun, a mythical mountain in the far west

Chu-jung, god of fire and celestial executioner

Chung-kuei, god of examinations and the protector of travellers against evil spirits

The Eight Immortals, a group of Taoist holy men said to have attained immortality by following the Way

Fei Lien or **Feng Po,** Count of the Wind, associated with winds and drought

The Five Buddhas, associated with the four directions and the centre, comparable with the Taoist concept of the Great Emperors of the Five Peaks

The Four Diamond Kings of Heaven, Buddhist rulers of celestial paradises

The Four Dragon Kings, rulers of the four seas, bringers of rain

The Four Kings of Hell, rulers of departments of hell, deputies of Yen-lo: they may also number ten or 14

Fu-hsing, god of happiness

Heng-o, goddess of the moon, where she lives in the Palace of the Great Cold: consort of Yi the Archer, who lives in the Palace of the Sun

Ho Po or **Ping-I,** Count of the River, god of the Yellow River and the most important of the river-deities

Hsi Wang Mu, Royal Mother of the Western Paradise, a beautiful goddess who lives on K'un Lun

Kuan Ti, god of war and upholder of justice: his cult grew in importance under imperial patronage and reached its peak under the Manchu dynasty

Kuan Yin, a compassionate goddess, the female form of the Indian Bodhisattva Avalokitesvara.

Lei Kung, god of thunder

Lohans, Chinese name for the original disciples of Buddha (called *arhats* in India), who became minor deities in the Taoist system

Lu-hsing, god of salaries or of officials

Lu-pan, god of carpenters and masons

Men Shen, two deities who guard the door of a house against evil spirits and hostile influences

Mi-lo Fo, Chinese name of the Buddha who is to come, 'the laughing Buddha' (the Indian Maitreya)

Nu-kua, goddess sometimes said to have created mankind: also the inventor of marriage

Sakyamuni, the historical Buddha

Shang Ti, originally the supreme god, later known as T'ien (Sky): assimilated to Yu-huang, the Taoist supreme deity

Shou-lao, god of longevity, who determines the length of each man's life

Ti-tsang, Chinese name of the Bodhisattava Ksitigarbha, a merciful being who rescues souls from punishment in hell in Buddhist belief

Tsai Shen, god of wealth

Tsao Chun, the Kitchen God, the most important deity of the family and home

Tung-yo, Great Emperor of the Eastern Peak, the head of the celestial bureaucracy and principal deputy of Yu-huang

Wang Mu Niang-niang, a goddess, consort of Yu-ti: another form of Hsi Wang Mu

Wen-ch'ang, god of literature

Yao-Shih, Chinese name of Bhaishajyaguru Buddha, 'the Master of Healing', who rules a paradise in the east

Yen-lo, ruler of the dead and the underworld (equivalent of the Indian Yama)

Yu Ch'iang, god of the ocean wind

Yu-huang, Yu-ti or **Yu Huang-ti,** the August of Jade or Jade Emperor, ruler of heaven and patron of the Chinese emperors: in one tradition the creator of mankind

A *ch'i-lin*, an auspicious mythical creature, whose appearance indicated divine approval of a dynasty. Detail from a chair cover, 19th century.

CHAPTER SIX

JAPAN

From early times in Japan mythology was used to serve the political aims of the ruling class, which compiled, altered and added to the traditional myths to support its position. The emperors were long believed to be divine in their capacity of Arahitogami, the god personified. The Meiji government (1868–1912) demonstrated how effectively mythology could be used as a political instrument by giving Shinto – the native religion of Japan, from which the bulk of Japanese mythology sprang – a central place in programmes which enhanced the authority of the emperor. Religion and politics became one and the same, and in the 1930s mythology provided spiritual sanction for nationalist and militarist policies.

After the Second World War, things changed. On 1 January 1946 the emperor formally denied that he was a god and pointed out that his ties with his people did not depend on myths. Shinto ceased to be the state religion and it became possible to present Japanese mythology in a less political way, and perhaps in a way closer to its original spirit.

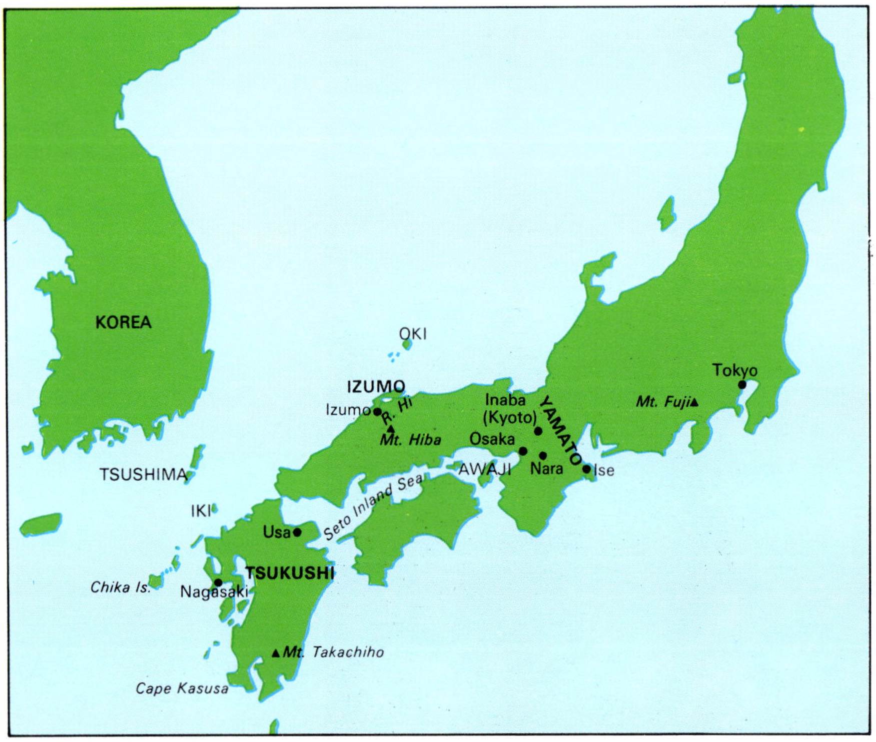

The main body of the mythology is contained in two of the oldest Japanese books still in existence: the Kojiki (Record of Ancient Matters) and the Nihonshoki or Nihongi (Chronicles of Japan), completed in AD712 and 720 respectively. Together they are often called the Kigi. Both these compilations were started some 50 years earlier, on the instructions of the Emperor Tenmu, who deplored the mistakes and falsehoods which had crept into the genealogical and historical records of the imperial family and other leading families of the time. The imperial house needed official records to justify its political power and its claimed descent from Amaterasu, the sun-goddess. In addition, Japan was well on its way to absorbing the traditions and institutions of China, and an official history was needed which would demonstrate that Japan was as great and ancient a nation as China.

Earlier attempts had been made to compile histories, which contained many myths and legends, handed down by oral tradition by priests and influential families, and recited by professional storytellers, the Kataribe. Village elders similarly handed down stories about local deities, ancestors and heroes, and accounts of the origin of religious festivals and other human and natural phenomena. Many of these myths were later recorded in the Fudoki (topographical works), the Norito (liturgical prayers) and the Kogoshui (an ancestral history of the Inbe, a great priestly clan officially in charge of the Shinto religion).

The principal cycles of myths come from three different geographical regions: the Takamagahara or Yamato myths, the Izumo myths and the Himuka or Tsukushi myths. The three cycles were merged into one in the Kigi and an effort was made to present them coherently in 'historical' order. Inevitably the attempt was not always successful and there are some confusions, discrepancies and gaps.

The Japanese translation of 'god' is Kami, but Kami cannot always be translated into other languages as 'god' or 'deity'. Kami meant anything that was awe-inspiring and was believed to possess supernatural power or beauty. Mountains, rivers, trees, rocks, caves, animals and human beings could all be venerated as Kami, and the result is the multitude of gods, spirits and objects of reverence in the spiritual history of Japan.

Fujiyama, a volcano which is the highest mountain in Japan and is associated with the national symbol of the rising sun. The shrine of the goddess Sengen-Sama at the top is visited by many pilgrims, who venerate the rising sun. The Shinto religion holds many natural features sacred, including mountains. In mythology five mountain-gods came into being when Izanagi cut the god of fire into pieces, including O-Yama-Tsu-Mi, the principal god of mountains.

Izanagi and Izanami

At first, according to the Kigi, heaven and earth were not separated and the world was a chaotic mass, shaped like an egg but with no defined limits. The purer and clearer part became heaven and the heavier and grosser part, which took longer to settle down, became the earth. At this stage the land floated about like a fish sporting on the surface of the primeval ocean.

The first three deities came into being, starting with the Centre of Heaven Deity, who reflects the old Chinese concept of Heaven (*T'ien*) which influenced Japanese cosmology and is thought to have been the origin of the Japanese word for emperor (*tenno*). The next two deities represent the creative energy or generative potency or even the creative evolution which 'gave birth' to all things. This triad of highly abstract concepts was followed by a fourth deity in the form of a reed-shoot, symbolizing the birth of all things from a reed-like substance in the primeval ocean of mud. Reed here is a symbol of life shooting up into existence. Then came a fifth deity, who stands for the establishment of Takamagahara, or Heaven. These five high beings are the Separate Heavenly Deities, who for some now unknown reason are separated from the other gods and put in a special category. They are all celestial gods, as distinct from the next group, who are regarded as earthly gods.

In the next period 12 more deities appeared, the last two of whom were a brother-sister pair, Izanagi and Izanami. The heavenly deities commanded Izanagi and Izanami to complete and consolidate the creation of land, and gave them the Heavenly

THE EARLIEST DEITIES

Koto-amatsu-kami (the Separate Heavenly Deities)

The first five celestial deities who came into being after the creation of the world:

Ame-no-minaka-nushi-no-kami (the Centre of Heaven Deity)

Taka-mi-musubi-no-kami

Kami-musubi-no-kami

Umashi-ashikabi-hikoji-no-kami

Ame-no-tokotachi-no-kami

Kamiyo-nanayo (Age of the Seven Generations of Gods)

Twelve gods were now created, the last two being a brother and sister:

Izanagi-no-kami (He who invites)

Izanami-no-kami (She who is invited)

This pair gave birth to the 14 islands of Japan and to 40 deities, related to houses, winds, rivers, the sea, mountains, fields, crops, fire, production and procreation. Subsequently, from Izanagi's body were born many more deities, including:

Amaterasu-o-mi-kami, the Sun-Goddess: the most important single deity in Japan and the central figure of the Takamagahara myths

Tsukuyomi-no-kami, the Moon-God

Takehaya-susano-o-no-mikoto, the Storm-God: a personification of impetuous masculinity and the central deity of the Izumo myths

Jewelled Spear. The two stood on the Heavenly Floating Bridge (explained as the rainbow, the Milky Way, or a boat or raft), thrust the spear down and stirred the ocean with a churning sound. When they lifted the spear again, the brine dripped down from its tip and coagulated into an island. Izanagi and Izanami descended from the heavens to this island and erected a heavenly pillar and a spacious palace. Then they discovered that they were of different sexes and they circled round the heavenly pillar, the male going to the left and the female to the right, in order to consummate their marriage when they met. Unfortunately, in her delight and excitement, Izanami spoke first when they met and said: 'Oh, what a beautiful and amiable youth!' This angered Izanagi and the consequence was the procreation of two children who were in some way defective and whom their parents repudiated.

The young couple went back to heaven to seek advice from the heavenly deities, who decided that the fault lay in the female's having spoken first. Izanagi and Izanami returned to the island and once again circled round the pillar. This time Izanagi spoke first when they met and praised his young wife, receiving praise from her in return. The restored right order in courtship made it possible for them to produce numerous offspring and from this marriage were born Oh-yashima-guni (the great-eight-island-land, an ancient name for Japan) and the smaller islands of the Japanese archipelago.

After bearing the land, the two bore numerous deities, but when Izanami gave birth to the god of fire, Kagutsuchi-no-kami, her genitals were burned so badly that she soon passed away to Yomi-no-kuni, the underworld and land of the dead. Izanagi, weeping and lamenting, buried his beloved wife on Mount Hiba on the border of Izumo Province. He then drew a long sword and cut off the head of the child who had caused her death. Out of the blood and body of the fire-god many more deities came into being.

RIGHT Izanagi and Izanami. This brother and sister pair of deities created land by stirring the primeval ocean with the Heavenly Jewelled Spear. Brine dropped from its tip and formed the island of Onokoro ('self-coagulating'), to which Izanagi and Izanami descended for their marriage. Silk painting, Ukiyo-e School, 19th century.

BELOW The Wife and Husband Rocks at Futami, topped by a Shinto *torii* and linked by twisted ropes which symbolize the union of male and female. These rocks are said to have sheltered Izanagi and Izanami, whose union engendered the islands of Japan and numerous deities.

Izanagi in the Underworld

After this, Izanagi made an unsuccessful attempt to recover Izanami from the land of Yomi. The grief-stricken Izanagi followed her to Yomi and asked her to return to the land of the living. The goddess replied: 'Oh, my beloved husband, why do you come so late? I have already eaten of the cooking-furnace of Yomi and have become the person of Yomi. Nevertheless, I shall discuss the matter with the gods of Yomi. Meanwhile pray do not look upon me.' Breaking this taboo, Izanagi took his many-toothed comb, broke off its end tooth, made a torch of it and looked at her. Maggots were squirming and roaring in the corpse of his wife and eight thunder-deities (or snakes) had taken possession of different parts of her body. Shocked and afraid, Izanagi said: 'I have come unawares to a hideous and polluted land.' He turned and fled. His enraged and humiliated wife said: 'He has shamed me.' She sent the ugly hags of Yomi to pursue and stop him, but Izanagi managed to escape and had reached the entrance to Yomi when Izanami herself came in pursuit of him. Seeing this, he blocked the entrance with a huge rock and the two deities stood face to face and pronounced the formula of divorce. Then Izanami said: 'I will each day strangle a thousand people of your country.' Undaunted by the curse, Izanagi answered: 'In that case I will each day cause fifteen hundred to be born.' This was the cause of the population increase in Japan.

Returning to this world, Izanagi went to Awagihara at the river-mouth of Tsukushi (Kyushu), where he purified himself from the pollution of the underworld. As he stripped off his clothes 12 deities were born, and when he was purifying himself in the water ten more were born. Amaterasu, the sun-goddess and ancestress of the imperial family, was born from the water when Izanagi washed his left eye, Tsukuyomi, the moon-god, from his right eye, and Susano, the storm-god, from his nose. Izanagi was overjoyed with these three noble children and gave his necklace to Amaterasu, ordering her to govern heaven. He ordered Tsukuyomi to govern the realms of the night and Susano to govern the sea. Amaterasu and Tsukuyomi obeyed, but Susano wept and howled, fuming with rage to such an extent that he caused the mountains to wither and the rivers and seas to dry up. The noises of malevolent deities were heard everywhere like summer flies and catastrophes of all kinds occurred. When Izanagi asked his son for an explanation, Susano replied: 'I wish to follow my mother to the land of Yomi.' This infuriated Izanagi and he expelled Susano to the underworld.

Amaterasu and Susano

Susano asked to be allowed to ascend to heaven to visit his sister Amaterasu before going down to the underworld for ever. Permission was given and Susano went up to heaven, but because of his fierce nature there was a commotion in the sea and the hills and mountains groaned aloud. Amaterasu was greatly alarmed and deeply suspicious of her violent brother. She armed herself and challenged him to battle. Susano tried to explain that he had no evil intentions, but Amaterasu demanded proof. Susano suggested that they should swear oaths to prove which of them was in the right. The method of doing this was for each of them to produce children, and if males were born to Susano he would have proved his good intentions and purity of heart. They stood opposite each other, with the heavenly river between them, and swore their oaths. Then they exchanged regalia, Amaterasu taking Susano's long sword, Susano taking his sister's beads. The sun-goddess took the first turn. She broke the sword into three parts, chewed them and spat them out. In the misty spray there came into being three female deities. Susano did the same with the beads and from the misty spray were born five male deities. In this way Susano won the contest, proved his innocence and was permitted to remain in heaven.

Susano now grew conceited over his triumph and his conduct was exceedingly violent. He broke down the ridges between the rice paddies of Amaterasu's heavenly fields and covered up the ditches. When

The two major religions of Japan are Shinto ('the Way of the Gods'), which is of Japanese origin, and Buddhism, which was imported from Korea and China, and which mingled with Shinto. Native Japanese mythology springs from the Shinto tradition. The *torii*, or gateway, is a distinguishing feature of Shinto shrines. This one is in the sacred woods of Ise, where the shrines are dedicated to the sun-goddess and the goddess of cereals, and are rebuilt every 20 years.

Amaterasu was about to celebrate the feast of first-fruits, Susano voided excrement in the New Palace. Amaterasu was surprisingly tolerant of her brother's misbehaviour, until he committed his worst offence. Seeing Amaterasu in the sacred weaving hall, where a heavenly maiden worked at the divine garments, Susano flayed a piebald colt of heaven and, breaking a hole in the roof of the hall, flung it in. Frightened at this extraordinary sight, the maiden struck her genitals against the shuttle and was instantly killed. Amaterasu was so angry that she shut herself up in the heavenly cave. Heaven and earth were plunged in darkness. Constant night reigned, the cries of the myriad deities were heard everywhere and calamities of all kinds ensued.

The eight hundred myriads of gods who lived on the Plain of High Heaven met on the bank of the heavenly river to discuss the best way of appeasing the sun-goddess. Omoigane-no-kami, the god of wisdom, was called upon to think of a way out. Trees were uprooted and placed in front of the cave, decorated with a mirror made by a renowned smith, strings of beads and offerings of cloth. The goddess Ame-no-uzume started to dance on an upturned bucket, exposing her breasts and genitals in ecstasy. The whole heaven shook as the eight hundred myriads of gods laughed and applauded. Overcome by curiosity, Amaterasu opened a crack in the cave door and asked why they were so happy. Ame-no-uzume replied that it was because they had obtained a new deity superior to Amaterasu herself. Other gods brought out the mirror and showed it to the sun-goddess, who saw herself in it without knowing. Gradually she came out of the cave and approached the mirror, at which Tajikara-no-mikoto, the strong-armed god (a deification of physical strength), took her hand and pulled her out. Another god put a rope barricade between her and the cave, and the heaven and the earth became light again. The eight hundred myriad deities deliberated together and put the whole blame on Susano. They imposed a heavy fine on him, cut off his beard and the nails of his hands and feet. As a final forfeit they expelled him from heaven.

The Eight-Tailed Dragon

After he was banished from heaven, Susano descended to Izumo Province, where he met an old couple with a maiden at the headwaters of the River Hi. The couple were crying because the maiden, Kushinada-hime by name, was about to be sacrificed to an eight-tailed dragon, who came every year and had already devoured Kushinada's seven elder sisters. The dragon's eyes were red, like the winter cherry, he had eight heads and eight tails, moss and cypress and cryptomeria trees grew on his body, he was so huge that he spanned eight valleys and mountain peaks, and blood oozed out over his belly.

ABOVE AND FAR RIGHT In earlier times Shinto deities were not depicted, but when Buddhism became the principal religion of Japan images of Buddhist and mixed Buddhist-Shinto deities were placed in some Shinto temples. Wooden figures of Shinto deities.

ABOVE CENTRE *Torii* standing in the sea, the gateway to the Miyajima shrine, near Hiroshima, which is sacred to three goddesses. They were daughters of Susano, the storm-god, a personification of impetuous and full-blooded masculinity.

Susano promised to save the girl from the monster, but asked that she be given to him. The old man and his wife agreed when they knew who it was they were talking to. Susano transformed Kushinada into a comb, which he stuck in the knot of his hair. Then he made the old couple brew sake (rice-wine) and fill eight barrels with it. When the dragon appeared and saw the barrels, each of his heads drank up one barrel and he became completely drunk and fell asleep. Then Susano drew his sword and chopped the dragon into small pieces. When he cut the middle tail the blade of his sword was slightly notched. Thinking this odd, he thrust deeper with the sword and found another sword inside. He thought it was a divine sword and presented it to his sister, the goddess Amaterasu. After this he married Kushinada.

Susano became the ancestor of the ruling family of the province. He did many good deeds in Izumo, where he is associated with fertility, and among his progeny were deities of rivers, cereals, trees and thunder. The most important god among his descendants is another heroic figure of Izumo myths, Okuni-nushi-no-mikoto.

The Adventures of Okuni-nushi

Okuni-nushi had 80 brothers, who wished to marry the beautiful princess Yagami-hime. They set off for her home, in a place called Inaba, making Okuni-nushi carry their bags for them and treating him like a servant. Because of the burden he carried, he lagged behind. His brothers met a sick rabbit with no fur and callously recommended a cure which made the rabbit's condition ten times worse. Presently Okuni-nushi met the unfortunate rabbit, who told him how crocodiles had peeled off all his skin and of the trick the brothers had played. Okuni-nushi sympathized with the rabbit and gave him the right cure, which healed him completely. The rabbit told Okuni-nushi that the princess would marry him, not his brothers. At about the same time Yagami-hime was telling her suitors: 'I will not accept your offers. I will choose Okuni-nushi as my wedded husband.'

Okuni-nushi's brothers were angry and plotted to kill him. When they came to a mountain in the province of Hohki, they told him to catch a red boar which they would drive down to him, but then they rolled down a red-hot rock which resembled a boar. Okuni-nushi caught it and was burned to death. His mother, lamenting, went up to heaven and pleaded with Kami-musubi-no-kami, one of the Separate Heavenly Deities, who sent messengers to restore Okuni-nushi to life.

Seeing Okuni-nushi resurrected, his brothers took him out into the mountains and crushed him to death under a large tree. Once more his body was found by his loving mother and he was restored to life. His

LEFT Amaterasu, the goddess of the sun and the single most important deity in Japan, emerges from the cave to which she had retreated and brings light back to heaven and earth. Print by Kunisada, 19th century.

ABOVE Inari, god of rice and prosperity, who comes to the rice fields every year in spring from his home in the mountains. The foxes are his messengers.

mother then suggested that he visit Susano in the land of Yomi.

Okuni-nushi went to Susano's palace, where the great deity's daughter, Princess Suseri-bime, came out to greet him. They looked at each other adoringly and made love. Susano decided to test Okuni-nushi's courage and wisdom. First he put the visitor in a chamber infested with snakes, and the next night he put him in a chamber infested with centipedes and bees. With the princess's help Okuni-nushi came out unharmed. He was then ordered to bring back an arrow which Susano shot humming into a plain, but when he went to retrieve it, Susano set fire to the grass. Okuni-nushi was saved by a mouse, which showed him how to escape and also brought him the arrow. When he returned with it, Susano was satisfied and went to sleep. Okuni-nushi tied strands of Susano's hair to the ceiling, blocked the door of the chamber with a huge rock and fled with the princess on his back. Susano woke up, but was delayed by having to unfasten his hair. He chased the fleeing pair to the border between Yomi and this world, where he called after Okuni-nushi, telling him to pursue and subdue his brothers: 'Become Okuni-nushi-no-mikoto (the great earth-chief) and make my beloved daughter your chief wife.' Okuni-nushi duly subdued his brothers and made Suseri-bime his chief wife. Yagami-hime was one of his other wives, of whom he had many, and he had many descendants.

FAMILY TREE OF THE FIRST EMPEROR

Izanagi

Amaterasu *sun-goddess* | **Tsukuyomi** *moon-god* | **Susano** = **Kushinada** *storm-god*

Amaterasu → **Oshiho-mimi**

Susano = **Kushinada** → **Okuni-nushi**

Oshiho-mimi → **Ninigi** = **Konohana-sakuya**

Ninigi = **Konohana-sakuya** → **Umisachi**, **Yamasachi**

the sea-god → **Toyotama**, **Tamayori**

Yamasachi = **Toyotama** → **Amatsu**

Amatsu → **Jimmu-Tenno** *legendary first emperor of Japan*

The Tenson-korin

According to the Izumo myths, Okuni-nushi ruled the earth before the sun-goddess Amaterasu dispossessed him and sent her grandson to replace him. The Tenson-korin, the story of how the grandson of Heaven came to govern the earth, is one of the most important episodes in Japanese mythology because it justified the supremacy of the imperial house, descended from Amaterasu.

Amaterasu commanded: 'Ashihara-no-mizuho-no-kuni (Japan) is the land to be ruled by my child Oshiho-mimi.' But it was reported that unruly earth-deities were rampant in the land, which was in

ABOVE LEFT There are seven deities of good fortune and happiness in Japanese popular tradition, shown in a treasure-ship in this print by Kunisada. Among them is one goddess, Benten, who is associated with love, the arts and the sea.

ABOVE Ivory figure of Hotei, one of the gods of good fortune. An amiable, serene and contented deity, he is often represented as a Buddhist priest.

LEFT Porcelain figure of Daikoku, a Buddhist god of wealth and another of the gods of good fortune. In Shinto he is identified as Okuni-nushi, who ruled the earth before the sun-goddess displaced him.

ABOVE In Buddhist belief there are many paradises and hells, in which human beings are rewarded or punished. Scene from one of the hells, late 12th century.

RIGHT Figure of Ninigi, grandson of the goddess Amaterasu. He descended to the earth and governed it for the sun-goddess. This myth justified the supremacy of the Japanese imperial house, which claimed descent from Amaterasu.

an uproar. Several expeditions were sent to subdue the land to no avail, but when the two sons of Okuni-nushi were quelled, the great earth-chief himself surrendered his land on condition that he was to be worshipped in his shrine in Izumo and that his children were to be looked after properly.

Amaterasu again commanded Oshiho-mimi to rule the land, but he suggested that his newborn son Ninigi should take his place. Amaterasu agreed and sent her grandson to earth, giving him some ears of rice from a sacred rice-field, so that he would grow rice on earth and worship the heavenly deities. She also gave him the mirror and the beads which had been used to lure her out of the heavenly cave and the sword named Kusanagi-no-tsurugi, which Susano had taken from the eight-tailed dragon. She told him to regard the mirror as her spirit and worship it. (The mirror, the beads and the sword became the three great emblems of imperial power in Japan.)

Ninigi came down to earth, accompanied by a number of heavenly deities, on the peak of Mount Takachiho (in Kyushu). The god of the mountain offered him a choice between his two daughters, Iwanaga-hime (Princess Enduring Rock), who was ugly, and Konohana-sakuya-hime (Princess Blossoms) who was surpassingly beautiful. Ninigi chose the beautiful younger daughter, but he should have accepted the elder as well, to give him a long and enduring life like a rock as well as a life flourishing like blossoms. This was the cause of the relatively short lives of successive emperors.

Konohana-sakuya promptly told Ninigi that she was with child and would soon be delivered. Ninigi could not believe that he had made her pregnant in one night and suspected that it must be

JAPANESE BUDDHIST DEITIES

Buddhism spread to Japan from China by way of Korea. Missionaries from Korea came to the imperial court in the 6th century AD and the imperial family was converted to Buddhism. Copies of the Buddhist scriptures were obtained from China and Korea, Chinese Buddhist sects established themselves in Japan and native Japanese sects were founded subsequently. Buddhism became the principal religion of Japan and mingled with Shinto. In many Shinto shrines a special sanctuary was reserved for Buddhist worship and Shinto gods were merged with Buddhist deities. For example, the sun-goddess Amaterasu was identified as a manifestation of Vairocana Buddha as the Great Sun. In the 17th century, however, there was a Shinto revival and in 1868 Shinto was declared the state religion and Buddhist deities and priests were banished from Shinto temples. At the present time Buddhism has a rather larger following in Japan than Shinto.

Japanese Buddhas, Bodhisattvas (Buddhas-to-be) and deities include:

Amida: Japanese form of the Buddha Amitabha ('Boundless Light'), the ruler of the Pure Land, a paradise in the west, venerated by certain sects as the saviour of all mankind

Benten or **Benzaiten:** goddess associated with femininity, love, the sea, music and literature

Daikoku: god of wealth, identified with the Indian Mahakala; in Shinto identified as Okuni-nushi

Dainichi Nyorai (Great Sun): the Buddha Vairocana ('the Illuminator'), the supreme Buddha of the Shingon sect

Emma-O: ruler of the underworld and chief judge of hell (equivalent of the Indian Yama)

Fugen Bosatsu: Samantabhadra, the Bodhisattva-form of Vairocana

Hosho Nyorai: the Buddha Ratnasambhava ('Jewel-Born'), guardian of treasures

Ida-ten: protector of Buddhist doctrine, guardian of the law

Jizo Bosatsu: the Bodhisattva Ksitigarbha, protector of mankind and rescuer of souls from hell

Kannon Bosatsu: the Bodhisattva Avalokitesvara ('Lord of Compassion'), one of the most popular deities in Japan, sometimes in male and sometimes in female form; Kannon is from Chinese Kuan Yin

Kishi-Mojin: a goddess who protects mothers and children

Miroku Bosatsu: the future Buddha, Maitreya

Rakan: the original disciples of Buddha (the Indian *arhats*)

Yakushi Nyorai: Bhaishajyaguru, the Buddha of healing

FAR LEFT Wooden figure of Jizo Bosatsu, an extremely popular deity who protects mankind, including children and women in childbirth, and is able to rescue souls from hell and transport them to paradise. The equivalent of Ti-tsang in China, he is the Japanese form of the Indian Bodhisattva Ksitigarbha and is usually portrayed as a Buddhist monk.

LEFT Wooden figure of Kusho-jin, one of the judges of hell. 13th century.

The Suwa-taisha shrine, Nagano Prefecture. For hundreds of years Shinto and Buddhism coexisted in Japan and Buddhist worshippers used Shinto shrines. In 1868, however, the government declared Shinto the national religion and Buddhism and Shinto were separated. Official promotion of Shinto was linked with Japanese nationalism and militarism up to the end of the Second World War.

the child of some earthly deity. Konohana-sakuya entered a palace with no doors, to which she set fire at the moment of her delivery, but she gave birth safely to three perfect children, which proved her faithfulness and their legitimacy.

Two of these children were Umisachi-hiko, who was a fisherman, and Yamasachi-hiko, the younger brother, who was a hunter. They decided to exchange occupations, but Yamasachi was unable to catch any fish and lost the fish-hook in the sea into the bargain. Umisachi said that the tools of one's trade should remain in one's own hands and that the magic powers which bring success are not transferable. Yamasachi smashed his sword and made a thousand fish-hooks out of it, but Umisachi would not accept them and continued to demand the return of his own original fish-hook.

Yamasachi went to consult the god of the sea and Toyotama-hime, the sea-god's daughter, saw him and made love to him. The god liked Yamasachi and gave him Toyotama. After three years with them, Yamasachi remembered the purpose of his visit and asked the sea-god's help. The god summoned all the fish in the sea and the missing hook was found in one of the fish, which had swallowed it. Yamasachi returned to his brother with the hook, but Umisachi still would not forgive him. At this Yamasachi used a magic jewel which the sea-god had given him and caused his brother such anguish and suffering that the latter promised to serve him as his guard day and night.

Toyotama now came from the sea and told Yamasachi that she was about to bear his child, and that it would be improper to give birth to it in the ocean because it was the child of a heavenly deity. She also said that she would revert to her original form to give birth and that Yamasachi was not to look at her. Thinking this strange, Yamasachi secretly watched and saw her turn into a giant crocodile, crawling and slithering about as she gave birth to a boy. When she learned what her husband had done, she was ashamed and fled into the sea, leaving the boy behind. The child later married his aunt, Tamayori-hime, by whom he had four children. One of them was the legendary first emperor of Japan, Emperor Jimmu. This marked the end of the age of the gods and the beginning of historical times.

Characteristics of Japanese Mythology

Japanese mythology is highly political and nationalistic because it is based on the mythology of the imperial court, into which local myths were incorporated. It is often said to lack tragic strength, for peaceful compromise is generally its solution to violent conflicts and confrontations.

The Takamagahara myths concentrate on Amaterasu, the sun-goddess, and include the story of her conflict with Susano, her hiding in the cave, and the Tenson-korin. Broadly, they reflect a hunting culture, with elements of sun-worship. The Izumo myths, dealing with Susano's exploits on earth and the adventures of Okuni-nushi, reflect a farming culture, concentrating on rain rather than the sun, with the worship of gods of the earth and under it.

Besides elements which are purely Japanese, elements stemming from China, Mongolia, Korea and the southern Pacific have entered the mythology. The myth of the Separate Heavenly Deities, for example, is based on Chinese ideas. The story of Izanagi and Izanami giving birth to the land and the gods is the true Japanese creation myth, for Japanese mythology is primarily concerned with the ancestors and the origin of the Japanese nation, rather than with such abstract matters as the origin of the world.

THE MIDDLE EAST

CHAPTER SEVEN

MESOPOTAMIA

For 2000 years the ancient myths of Mesopotamia were almost completely forgotten. Some garbled accounts of them survived, written by classical authors in Greek or Latin, and there are some oblique references to them in the Bible, but the stories had become hopelessly confused in the course of transmission. They had first been recorded by native Mesopotamian scribes, writing on clay tablets in either the Sumerian or Akkadian language, both of which used a complicated script called cuneiform ('wedge-shaped'). This script fell out of use in the last few centuries BC, and Sumerian and Akkadian literature was not rediscovered until cuneiform was deciphered by European scholars in the 19th century.

Despite the decipherment, Sumerian and Akkadian were not easy to understand. Even today there is no reliable complete dictionary of these languages, and any translation which was published before 1939 is almost sure to be unreliable. There have been rapid advances in linguistic research in recent years and archeologists have discovered great numbers of inscribed tablets in the ruins of Mesopotamian cities. It is important to remember this changing state of affairs, because our present knowledge will be considerably expanded during the next decades.

The first literate inhabitants of Mesopotamia referred to the land as Sumer and are called Sumerians. They seem to have been immigrants, though where they came from is not yet certainly known. Perhaps about 3500 BC, they settled in the most easterly part of the world where Semitic languages were spoken. Sumerian was not a Semitic language, but the script used for it was quickly employed for the previously unwritten Semitic language of the area, which is called Akkadian. From the thousands of tablets which have survived, it is possible to reconstruct something of what people believed about the gods, though it is impossible to be certain of the implications of some of these beliefs or of how universal they were in Mesopotamia. Another difficulty is to separate the Sumerian elements from the Semitic ones, for the mixing of the two cultures seems to have affected the content of the myths.

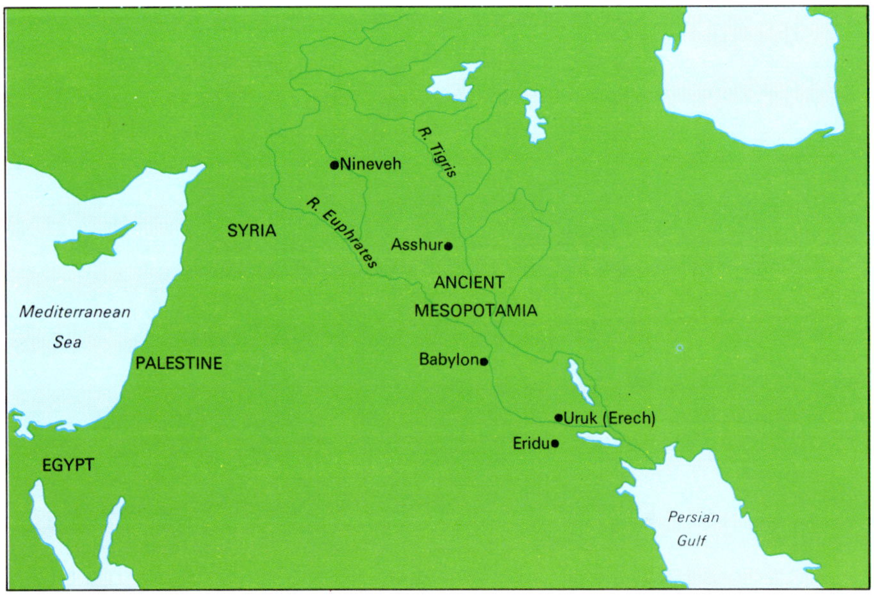

The Creation and the Flood

The most widely known myth from Mesopotamia concerns the flood which was sent by the gods to destroy all life on earth. The Mesopotamian version is very similar to the story in the Bible, but is recorded in poetry not prose. Four gods were involved in the planning of the flood, all of whom have Sumerian names: Anu is described as 'the father', Enlil as 'the counsellor', Ninurta, the son of Enlil, as 'the throne carrier', and Ennugi as 'the canal inspector'. A fifth god, usually known as Ea, revealed the secret plan to a man named Ut-napishtim and told him to build a boat in order to be saved.

Ut-napishtim built the boat according to the precise measurements which the god had given him. He stored in it provisions of all kinds, including silver and gold, and installed his family and some wild animals in it. Then there came a terrifying storm, which frightened even the gods in heaven. 'The gods cowered like dogs, crouching against the outer wall.'

The flood lasted for seven days and nights. When it was over and the boat came to rest on a mountain, Ut-napishtim sent out first a dove, then a swallow and then a raven. The first two returned to him, but the raven did not, which showed that the water had subsided. Ut-napishtim made a sacrifice, to which he invited all the gods except Enlil, who was principally responsible for sending the flood. Enlil was angry that anyone should have survived, but he agreed to bless Ut-napishtim and his wife, and said that they should become like gods. Finally, Ut-napishtim was taken to live in a distant place 'at the mouth of the rivers'.

More information about the gods mentioned in this myth comes from other sources, especially from the myth of creation. There Anu is described as the progeny of two other gods, Anshar and Kishar, and as the father of Nudimmud, who is also called Ea. These are all described as 'great gods', for they were the first group of descendants of primeval Apsu and Tiamat. Of these deities, Apsu represents the mass of fresh water that was thought to exist beneath the earth and from which springs and rivers flowed, and Tiamat the mass of sea-water around the earth.

Most of the narrative in this myth has little to do with the creation of the world, but emphasizes the hostility that existed between different groups of gods. Two battles are described. In the first Ea defeats Anshar, and in the second, on which the whole story depends, the primeval monster Tiamat is destroyed by Marduk, who fashions the universe from her body. Marduk was the national god of Babylonia and after his victory a shrine was erected 'as an abode for Marduk, Enlil and Ea'. Clearly the glorification of Marduk in the myth reflects praise for the achievements of Babylon as a state. The heroic god is given fifty glorious names, and it is Enlil who confers on him the last one, 'lord of the lands'. When this is done, Ea lends his voice in support of the victor.

He whose name his fathers have glorified
Has certainly become like me; his name shall be Ea.
He shall administer all my different rites
And he shall perform all my instructions.

The recitation of this myth was an act of patriotism, as is confirmed by another tablet which describes the ritual with which the Babylonians celebrated the New Year. The celebration lasted for 11 days and on the fourth day the priest is directed to recite this long myth of creation, which consists of more than a thousand lines of text. This was not the only text which had to be recited, but it seems to have been one of the most important. The king was expected to take part in the ritual and the reading of the myth of Marduk's success seems to express the hope for a successful year ahead. Indeed, if for some reason the king did not attend the festival and the myth was not recited this was considered to be of ominous significance for the future.

The Tablets of Destinies

One of the symbols of Marduk's power and authority was his possession of the 'tablets of destinies'. Although it is not clear what exactly these were (probably they were royal symbols of authority), there is a myth above them being stolen by a mysterious bird-god called Zu. The tablets on which this story is recorded are very badly damaged, but from what remains it can be seen that an air of utter hopelessness prevailed among the gods after they had lost the tablets of destinies.

Father Enlil their counsellor was speechless,
A dazzling brightness appeared, silence prevailed,
The whole group of lesser gods was disturbed,
The brilliance of the sanctuary was removed.

Anu took charge of the proceedings and said that if any god could slay Zu his name would become the greatest of all. First they summoned Adad, the storm-god, but he would not fight the terrifying bird. They called Gibil, the god of fire, and Shara, 'the firstborn of Ishtar', who also declined the

ABOVE The story of Gilgamesh is frequently illustrated on cylinder seals. These seals were impressed on legal documents and many thousands of them have been found. Some are simply pictorial while others carry inscriptions. This modern impression of a seal from the 3rd millennium BC shows Ut-napishtim in his boat on the left, and Gilgamesh is fighting a bull-like creature on the right.

LEFT This impression of a very detailed cylinder seal shows the god Ea, surrounded by water with fish swimming around him. He is holding a bird (possibly Zu), who faces Shamash, the sun, rising from behind a mountain before a winged deity. An archer guards a lion on the left while a two-faced figure attends on the right.

conflict. At this point the text is too broken to permit an accurate translation and it is impossible to say who is finally chosen to challenge Zu. Ninurta is mentioned in some tablets. According to some traditions, Marduk was associated with the triumph over Zu.

The final challenger, whoever it was, was encouraged by a speech from a goddess, sometimes called Makh, or Nanshe (which may be another name for Ishtar) or Mammi:

'Let your terrifying cry overcome him,
Let him experience darkness, let his sight change for the worse,
Let him not escape when you meet, let his strength become weakness,
Let the sun not shine above, let his day turn into gloom,
Destroy his life, restrain Zu,
Let the wind carry him to places unknown.'

The story thus far has been taken from the oldest manuscripts available, those written in the Old Babylonian period, about 2000 BC. But much of our knowledge of the old mythology comes from later manuscripts which were copied by scribes of the Assyrian king Asshurbanipal (7th century BC) and deposited in his royal library at Nineveh. These manuscripts give more information about the beginning of the story. It appears that Zu was a servant of Enlil and his tasks caused him to see much of the tablets of destinies. He grew covetous of them and said:

'I will take the divine tablets of destinies.
Then I will control the decrees of all the gods.'

Zu bided his time until one day, when Enlil was washing himself at dawn, he flew off with them to a remote mountain. Enlil, astounded, took counsel with the other gods about who should kill Zu and recover the tablets.

Recently, many fragmentary tablets containing references to the myth have been found. The longest one describes the battle with Zu, and this version has Ninurta as the champion, helped by Adad, the storm-god, who sent storms and floods. 'Clouds of death sent rain, flashes of lightning flew like arrows.' But none of the arrows could reach Zu while he possessed the tablets of destinies, and so Ea, presiding over the battle from a distance, gave orders to use the south wind to overpower the bird. It would then be possible to 'cut off his wings and scatter them to the right and to the left'.

This story shows how our knowledge of Mesopotamian myths has to be built up from a number of different manuscripts, all of which contain important variations in detail. It shows how some gods assumed the role of others in mythological stories, according to the time and place of the recording of a myth. It is also an example of how a myth was used in Mesopotamia not just as a folk-story but in religious practices. There was a special ritual for the construction and consecration of a new drum for the temple. The skin for the drum had to be taken from a black bull and as the bull was slain the priest had to repeat an incantation into the ears of the bull. Into the left ear he said, *alpu illitu Zi attama*, 'You, O Bull, are the offspring of Zu.' After more incantations and ceremonies the bull was slaughtered and its heart was buried in front of the drum, but the reason for the connection between the rebellious Zu and the sacred bull is not clear.

An impression from a seal of the 3rd millennium BC, showing Ea surrounded by water as he is seated on his throne. A figure that appears to be Zu, half bird and half man, is being brought into his presence. The attendant is threatening him with a spear. According to the myth, Zu stole the tablets of destinies from the gods.

Death and the Underworld

The myths of Mesopotamia were known over a vast area in ancient times. Two important ones were discovered during the excavation of the Egyptian city of Tell el Amarna. One of them is about the hero Adapa, who has the chance of gaining immortality, but loses it just when it seems to be in his grasp.

Adapa lived in the city of Eridu in southern Mesopotamia. The god Ea, 'the sage of Eridu', created him as an example of what a man ought to be like. Every day Adapa went to the god's sanctuary by boat, but on one occasion the wind blew him out to sea. His boat capsized and Adapa 'went down to the home of the fish'. Angry, he threatened to break the south wind's wing and, as soon as he uttered the threat, the wind's wing was broken.

After seven days, Anu, the king of the gods, heard what had happened and ordered Adapa to be brought before him. Ea, who had created Adapa, gave him a warning:

'When they offer you the bread of death,
you shall not eat.
When they offer you the water of death,
you shall not drink.
When they offer you a garment, put it on.
When they offer you oil, anoint yourself.'

However, when Adapa came before Anu, the god did not condemn him as expected, but blamed Ea.

'Why did Ea disclose the plan of heaven and earth
To a worthless human being? . . .
As for us, what shall we do about Adapa?
Fetch the bread of life for him to eat!'
When they brought him the bread of life he did not eat.
When they brought him the water of life he did not drink.
When they brought him a garment he did put it on.
When they brought him oil he did anoint himself.

Adapa's refusal to eat the bread and drink the water of life surprised Anu. He ordered him to be taken away and returned to earth. Adapa had forfeited his chance of immortality.

How the myth ends is not yet known, for the tablets are broken, but it seems that the city of Eridu was to enjoy a special position of privilege in the sight of the gods because Adapa 'went up to heaven'.

If this is so, the myth explains the special position granted to the city in civil administration.

The other mythological text found at Tell el Amarna deals with the difficulty of communicating between heaven, which was the dwelling of the chief gods, and the underworld, which was controlled by the lady Ereshkigal.

When the gods were preparing a banquet
They sent a messenger to their sister Ereshkigal:
'We cannot go down to you,
  and you cannot come up to us,
So send someone to collect your portion of food.'

Ereshkigal sent her messenger Namtar to do this but one of the gods, Nergal, showed him disrespect. When he reported this to his mistress she sent him back, saying:

'The god who did not arise before my messenger –
Bring him to me that I may kill him!'

Namtar had some difficulty in finding Nergal again, for he had fled to plead his case before Ea, 'his father'. Ea promised to send demons to protect Nergal in his encounter with the enraged Ereshkigal. Nergal went down to the gate of the underworld and Ereshkigal violently threatened to kill him. Here the tablet is badly broken, but some lines at the end show that Nergal was able to overcome Ereshkigal.

Inside the house he took hold of Ereshkigal,
He dragged her down from the throne by her hair
To the ground to cut off her head.

As she begged for her life, she wept and said:

'Be my husband and I will be your wife.
I will grant you authority in this vast underworld.
I will place in your hand the tablet of wisdom.
You shall be the lord and I the lady.'

Nergal kissed her and comforted her with the brief but moving sentence: 'What you have been seeking from me in these past months shall now be yours.'

The Descent of Ishtar

The underworld is mentioned in many other myths but probably the best description of all is in the story known as the Descent of Ishtar. In this text the underworld is called 'the land of no return'.

Those who enter here have no more light.
Dust and clay is what they have to eat.
They are dressed like birds, clothed with wings.
Dust is spread over the doors and over the bolts.

Ishtar, the beautiful goddess of love, went down to the underworld. The queen of the underworld, Ereshkigal, ordered the gate-keeper to treat Ishtar 'in accordance with the age-old lore'. This meant that as the goddess passed through the seven gates of the underworld she was stripped of her clothes and ornaments, of her crown at the first gate, of her ear-pendants at the second, then of her necklaces, pectoral, girdle, bracelets and anklets, and finally of her body garment. Then she was brought naked before Ereshkigal, who had her tortured by 'the sixty miseries', consisting of afflictions on every part of her body.

Ishtar was the goddess of love and the goddes of war. Here she is seen in one of her more violent attitudes, standing on the back of a lion. This stela was found at Tell Asmar and dates from the 8th century BC. The story of Ishtar's descent to the underworld is one of the best known Mesopotamian myths.

The consequences of Ishtar's captivity were felt in the land of the living, for the earth lost its fertility and, as the gods explained to Ea, 'the king':

'Since Ishtar has descended to the land of no return,
The bull no longer springs upon the cow,

PRINCIPAL DEITIES

Large numbers of deities, of greater and lesser stature, are mentioned in Mesopotamian texts. Some of them represent universal phenomena, such as storm or water, some are local gods of the various cities and states. The following are among the most important gods in the myths so far discovered:

Anu: king of the gods, god of the sky

Enlil: counsellor of the gods, god of winds, storm and rain

Ninurta: 'the throne carrier', son of Enlil

Adad: a Semitic god of storm and rain, equivalent to the Sumerian Enlil

Ea (Enki in Sumerian): god of water and wisdom

Ninhursag: goddess of the earth, consort of Ea

Shamash (Utu in Sumerian): god of the sun

Sin (Nannar in Sumerian): god of the moon

Ishtar (Inanna in Sumerian): goddess of fertility and love, also a warrior-goddess

Tammuz (Dumuzi in Sumerian): god of vegetation, lover of Ishtar

Ereshkigal: queen of the underworld

Nergal: god of war and plague, consort of Ereshkigal

Marduk: the national god of Babylonia

Nabu: Babylonian god of speech and writing, son of Marduk

Asshur: the national god of Assyria

The ass no longer covers his mate,
The man in the street no longer joins the maid.'

Ea created a eunuch, who went to meet Ereshkigal. When he asked for a drink from the skin containing 'the water of life', she cursed him.

'Your food shall be the food in the city gutter,
Your drink shall be the drink in the city sewer,
You shall stand in the shadow under the wall,
You shall dwell on the doorstep
And the drunken and the thirsty shall smite your cheek.'

The eunuch, it seems, was a substitute in exchange for Ishtar, which ironically suggests that in the underworld infertility can be exchanged for fertility. Ereshkigal ordered Ishtar to be sprinkled with the water of life, and she was then escorted out of the underworld. As she passed again through the seven gates, she was given back her garments and her jewellery, and presumably (though the last few lines are extremely difficult to understand) everything returned to normal on earth.

This Semitic version of the myth is very similar to the Sumerian version, in which the goddess Inanna descends to the underworld to liberate her lover, Dumuzi. What is more, the story is clearly parallel to the tale of Orpheus in classical mythology and the Egyptian cycle of stories about Osiris (see MYSTERY RELIGIONS: EGYPT). Because of these parallels, it is natural to wonder whether this myth was recited in some Mesopotamian fertility ritual, but so far there is no direct primary evidence for this. Temples of Ishtar have been found, but what rituals were performed in them is not known.

The Epic of Gilgamesh

All these myths about the gods were written in verse and were doubtless recited regularly on ceremonial occasions. Another myth, which should more accurately be described as an epic, concentrates on the activities of a human hero called Gilgamesh. His adventures are recorded on 11 tablets with a supplementary narrative on a twelfth tablet. Copies were found in the ruins of Asshurbanipal's library at Nineveh and at many other sites where libraries existed in ancient times. Gilgamesh was a king in the city of Uruk, but just when he ruled is difficult to say. A number of building inscriptions mention him, so he must have been a real person, but in the official records of rulers he is described as 'the divine Gilgamesh', who ruled for 126 years. Clearly he had become a legendary figure, superhuman but not quite divine.

'Two thirds of him is god, one third is human' is the way Gilgamesh is described at the beginning of the epic, where he is brought into conflict with Enkidu, a monster created for the gods to check Gilgamesh's power in Uruk. Enkidu's body was covered with shaggy hair, the hair on his head was like a woman's, 'his locks were like a field of corn'. The appearance of this creature caused such confusion in the land that Gilgamesh went out to fight him.

The second and third tablets describe Gilgamesh challenging Enkidu, whom he found enjoying himself with a harlot.

They grappled with each other, gripping like bulls,
They shattered the door-posts, the walls shook.

But evidently neither won the contest, for the third tablet says: 'They kissed each other and made a friendship.' Next, the two friends went to the fearful cedar forest, inhabited by the giant Humbaba, 'who roars like the storm, who has fire in his mouth and breathes out death'. They overcame Humbaba and the victory seems to have attracted the goddess Ishtar, for in the sixth tablet she invites Gilgamesh to be her lover and promises him all kinds of blessings. The hero, rather surprisingly, refuses her advances and castigates her for her inconstancy.

'Which lover did you love for ever,
Which of your shepherds pleased you all the time?
Even for Tammuz, the lover of your youth,
You have decreed a lamentation to be made every year.'

Ishtar, enraged, complains to Anu, 'her father', and Antum, 'her mother', who allow her to send the

The excavation of Babylon was undertaken by a large German team of archeologists before the Second World War and many of the objects from the site are preserved in East Berlin. One of the most spectacular exhibits there is a reconstruction of one of the city gates, the Ishtar Gate, with its beautiful, glazed-brick decoration. This detail from the gate shows one of the famous Babylonian lions as well as the decorative frieze.

'bull of heaven' against Gilgamesh. Helped by Enkidu, he kills the creature.

The seventh tablet opens with a picture of Enkidu in distress, since he has learned in a dream that Enlil has decreed that he must die. In his misery he meets a harlot and curses her.

'You shall sleep in the desert,
You shall stand in the shadow of the wall,
The thorn and the bramble shall wound your feet,
The drunken and the thirsty shall smite your cheek.'

It is interesting that a similar curse is employed by Ereshkigal against the eunuch in the Descent of Ishtar. Enkidu is pacified by Shamash, the sun-god, but then he dreams of descending into the underworld, which is described in detail, just as it was in the Descent of Ishtar, and many more identical phrases are used. As each day passes, Enkidu's pain grows worse and his fear of death intensifies. The eighth tablet records his death and Gilgamesh's grief.

The last part of the story describes how Gilgamesh seeks to escape death himself. First he goes to the 'Mountains of Mashu', where he meets a girl, 'the divine barmaid', who asks why the hero who has conquered Humbaba and slain the bull of heaven should look so weak and old. He explains that, like his friend Enkidu, he too must die unless he can find the secret of immortality from Ut-napishtim, who was granted this blessing by the gods. He decides to cross 'the sea of death' to reach Ut-napishtim's dwelling. Having felled 'twice sixty tree-trunks of sixty cubits each' to serve as punt poles, he successfully crosses the dangerous waters and meets Ut-napishtim. Gilgamesh asks him how he 'joined the assembly of gods'. Ut-napishtim's reply is the tale of the flood. It is a long narrative and when Ut-napishtim finishes it, Gilgamesh has fallen asleep, demonstrating how weak the hero really was. When he wakes, he is determined to find the secret plant which Ut-napishtim told him would give him eternal life. It is at the bottom of the sea.

He tied heavy stones to his feet and they pulled him
down into the sea.
He saw the plant and, though it pricked him,
he took it in his hand.
He cut away the stones from his feet and the sea
threw him back upon the shore.

Gilgamesh then began his journey back to Uruk, where he intended to eat the plant and 'return to my youthful state'. But on the way he stopped by a cool well to bathe. A serpent stole the plant, shedding its skin as it slipped away. Then Gilgamesh wept.

'For whom have I spent the blood of my heart?
There is no gift that I have gained for myself,
The gift I gained was for a serpent
And the waters will carry it twenty leagues away.'

This survey of Mesopotamian mythological literature shows how the sources are interlinked. It is not just a question of different myths sharing the same narrative motifs. They often share identical lines of poetry, but this is a natural consequence of the rich oral tradition which must have existed among the Semites before the Sumerians settled in the area and, as a result of Sumerian influence, the myths were written down. Secondly it indicates how widely these ancient stories were disseminated. Often a reasonably complete myth cannot be recovered from the fragments found at one site alone; those from other sites, in Iraq, Syria, Turkey or even Egypt, are needed to make the text intelligible. The rediscovery of Mesopotamian literature, with its parallels in classical and biblical literature, demonstrates how firmly the literary tradition of the East was established during the classical period of ancient history. When classical Greece first rose as an international power and a civilizing influence on the world, Mesopotamian libraries, their scribes and culture had been flourishing for at least 2000 years.

Ur was one of the most important Sumerian cities, where Nannar, the Sumerian moon god, was worshipped. This stela, now badly damaged, was erected by Ur-Nammu (2112–2095 BC), King of Ur, who is depicted beneath the crescent moon.

CHAPTER EIGHT

SYRIA AND PALESTINE

In the Bible the non-Israelite inhabitants of Syria and Palestine in early times are called Canaanites. Little was known of Canaanite mythology until 1929, when inscribed tablets in a previously unknown language were discovered at the Syrian village of Ras es-Shamrah (ancient Ugarit). The language is now called Ugaritic and the site proved to have been the religious and political centre of a Canaanite kingdom which flourished in northern Syria in the period from about 1500 to 1000 BC. The tablets, which are badly broken, include passages of poetry about the god Baal, known as the Rider on the Clouds, the god of rain and fertility. The texts often also give him the name of Hadad, the storm-god.

Unfortunately, because vowels are rarely indicated in the texts, it is difficult to translate them with confidence and each new version usually differs significantly from previous translations. The order in which the tablets and their episodes should be read is uncertain and since all the tablets are incomplete, a substantial amount of conjectural restoration has to be undertaken. There were three main stories of Baal, which are loosely connected with each other, and it seems clear that these myths were recited and, to some extent at least, acted out, at festivals intended to promote fertility and success on earth by repeating and perpetuating the triumphs of Baal.

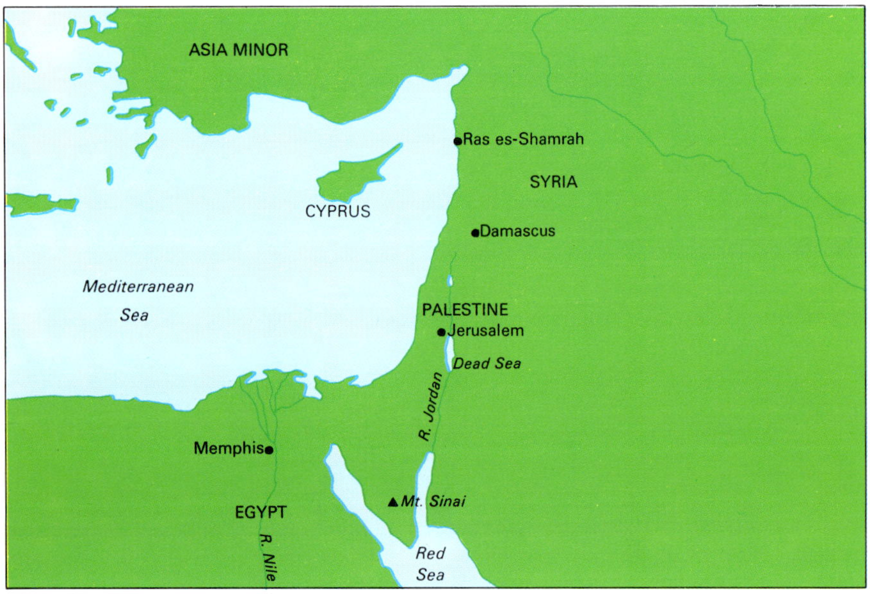

Baal and the Sea

The first story concerns Baal's conflict with Yam, the god of the sea. What appears to be the first tablet records the building of a temple for Yam by the divine craftsmen, Kothar and Khasis. The building seems to have been authorized by El, the chief god, but he is told that there is a danger of Yam, the sea, 'rushing quickly over the earth' and bringing destruction on the land. El supports the work, however, but Yam is told that he will have to challenge the authority of Baal and 'drive him from his throne'.

The second tablet opens with the announcement that Baal is planning an attack on Yam with the help of another god, Horon, and the goddess Athtart. Yam sends messengers to the assembly of the gods on the 'Mountain of Night', saying: 'Surrender Baal and his servants, I will possess the gold of the son of Dagon.' (In the Bible Dagon is associated with the Philistines.) El agrees to make Baal the slave of Yam. Baal resists violently, but is restrained by two goddesses, Athirat and Anat. There is a large break in the tablet at this point, but Baal is apparently surrendered to Yam by the other gods.

When the text becomes legible again, the god Athtar, who seems to be claiming the right to Baal's kingship, interrupts the work on Yam's palace by complaining that he has no house like the other gods, 'no court like the sons of the holy one'. Shapash, the sun-goddess, explains to him that he cannot really be a king, because he has no wife like the other gods.

At the end of this tablet, Baal is in bitter conflict with Yam. He is on the point of being defeated when Kothar and Khasis, the craftsmen gods, give him two magic clubs. Baal names the clubs 'Chaser' and 'Driver', and they chase and drive Yam from his throne. The first 'struck Prince Yam on the shoulders' but 'he did not fall down'. The second, however, struck Yam on the skull.

Yam collapsed, he fell to the earth,
His face trembled, his body crumpled.
Baal dragged away Yam and *laid him down*.

The last words are important, for they could equally well be translated as 'he drank him'. If so, this may indicate that when the myth was recited, sea-water was drunk at this point, to symbolize the victory of

Baal, the rain-god, over Yam, the sea-god. The few fragmentary lines at the end of this tablet contain the proclamation: 'Yam is certainly dead, Baal shall be king!'

Baal's Palace

Having conquered Yam, Baal's second problem is that he has no palace, or temple. To gain El's permission to build one, he uses the charms of two beautiful goddesses. First Anat is described beautifying herself with 'Henna, enough for seven girls, coriander scent and purple make-up'. This preparation is not for love but for battle, and a scene of violence follows when Anat attacks the people of a town in the plain.

Heads roll like balls beneath her,
Hands fly like locusts above her,
Warriors' hands like angry grasshoppers . . .
She plunged her knees in the blood of the guards,
Her dress in the gore of the warriors.

When she has had enough slaughter, Anat ceremonially washes 'with the dew of heaven and the oil of the earth and the rain from the Rider on the Clouds'.

It is to this ferocious goddess that Baal turns for help and she agrees to ask El's permission for a palace. She threatens that if 'El, the bull', her father, does not consent:

'I shall drag him right down to the ground,
like a lamb,
I shall make his grey hair stream with blood,
The grey hair of his beard with gore.'

Anat's mission is not successful, but we do not know whether she attacks El, because the end of the tablet is missing. Disappointed, Baal turns to the divine craftsmen, Kothar and Khasis, who live at Memphis in Egypt. Kothar and Khasis send Baal beautiful furniture, overlaid with silver and gold (probably typical of Canaanite temple furniture). Baal and Anat then approach the goddess Athirat, El's lovely consort, as she sits spinning beside the sea, day-dreaming of El, her lover.

Athirat is frightened when she sees Baal and the fierce Anat, but she is delighted by the gift of the furniture and agrees to approach El on Baal's behalf. Meanwhile, Baal himself goes to 'the heights of Mount Zephon'. This mountain is almost certainly the highest one in the area, the classical Mount Casius, modern Jabal al-Aqra.

Athirat rides to El on a donkey with a silver harness and trappings of gold, and El is so infatuated with her that he cannot refuse her request.

'So, I am a slave, who waits on Athirat.
If Athirat is a slave-girl who moulds the bricks,
Then I am a slave who holds the trowel.
Let the house for Baal be built, like the other gods,
A court like the sons of Athirat.'

Work on the palace starts immediately. At first Baal cannot decide whether the palace should have windows, which he fears might allow his daughters Pidray ('mist') and Talay ('dew') to escape, or his old enemy Yam to enter. Eventually he becomes so confident of his new authority that he has the windows constructed, and he bellows through them with the sound of his thunder.

Several statuettes of Canaanite deities have been found at Ras Shamrah and other sites in the area. The two shown here are in bronze and represent the supreme god El LEFT and the famous warrior god Baal RIGHT. These statuettes were probably used not only as decoration but also as objects of worship. The myths of Baal were recited to promote fertility by repeating his triumphs.

Some aspects of Canaanite mythology are depicted in ivory panels with which furniture in the royal palace was inlaid. The Phoenicians in this area were renowned for their skilled workmanship in ivory and were employed in the royal palaces of Egypt, Israel and Assyria. The detail here is from the royal couch at Ras Shamrah and shows the goddess Anat suckling the royal heir. It is surrounded by other scenes from the royal marriage.

The Contest with Death

Only one problem now remained for Baal, to conquer Mot, the god of death. The myth seems to tell how, during a severe drought, Baal died and was buried, though again the correct translation is doubtful. The agricultural imagery in the scene when El mourns for Baal suggests that the myth was recited at seasonal festivals to make sure of a successful agricultural year, to ensure that the 'death' of winter would be followed by new birth in spring.

In the myth, Mot is described taunting Baal and reminding him that 'when the heavens burn' (when there is a drought, apparently), Baal 'will descend into the throat of Mot, the son of the gods'. Baal appeals to El, but he seems to have been surrendered by the gods to his fate. However, on his way to the underworld, Mot's realm:

He loved a heifer in the pasture,
He lay with her seventy-seven times,
She made him mount eighty-eight times.
She conceived and gave birth to his likeness.

Because the tablet is broken here, it is not clear what happens next. Perhaps Baal escapes and 'his likeness' (the meaning of this word is not obvious) is killed by Mot instead. When the tablet becomes legible again, those who have been looking for Baal report that they have found him fallen to the ground: 'Mighty Baal is dead, the Prince, the Lord of the Earth, has perished.'

At this news El performs a mourning ritual, sitting on the ground in sackcloth, spreading dust on his head and shaving with a flint razor.

He harrowed his arms and ploughed his chest like a garden,
He harrowed his back like a valley,
He lifted up his voice and cried, 'Baal is dead.'

Baal is buried on Mount Zephon and El decides to make the god Athtar king in Baal's place (the same Athtar who claimed the kingship in the story of Baal and Yam). When Athtar is installed on Baal's great throne, he looks ridiculous for his feet do not touch the ground. His reign is so ineffective (meaning presumably that the rainfall is so scanty) that the people have to draw on water stored in casks.

As the drought continued, the goddess Anat searched for Baal and pleaded with Mot to release him. When he refused:

She seized Mot and split him with a sword,
She burned him with fire and ground him with millstones,
She scattered him in a field and the birds ate his flesh.

In other words, she treated him like the seed-corn.

Baal was brought back to life after El had seen a vision of 'the heavens raining oil and the valleys streaming with honey'. Shapash promised to bring Baal back if proper preparation was made.

'Pour sparkling wine from a vat,
Bring wreaths for your family
And I will seek mighty Baal.'

If this is really a seasonally repeated myth, these lines suggest the type of ritual actions that accompanied the recitation.

Because of a break of 40 lines, it is not clear how Baal was revived, or perhaps he was never really dead. Presently Mot also reappears (possibly he too has been miraculously revived) and there is a violent conflict between Baal and Mot. Eventually Shapash tells Mot that further resistance is futile and the myth ends with Baal being recognized as the rightful king. With Baal's victory, presumably, the drought ended and the rains began.

Aqhat and the Bow

Besides several other tablets containing fragments of similar mythological material, there are poems about the activities of human heroes. One of these, Aqhat, was the son of a king called Danel, which is the same name as biblical Daniel, but obviously not the same person. The story centres on a special bow, presented to the young Aqhat by Kothar and Khasis, the divine craftsmen. The goddess Anat offers Aqhat immortality in exchange for the bow. In his reply he seems to ridicule her.

'What will a mortal have as his final end?
What will a mortal have as his last fate?

Glaze(?) will be poured on my head,
  lime on to the top of my head.
I shall die the death of every man,
  even I shall die that death.
One further statement I would make:
  a bow . . . is for warriors,
Can women hunt with something like that?'

With El's consent, Anat resolves to take the bow by force. She eventually succeeds by turning one of her attendants, Yatpan, into an eagle. She then hovers above Aqhat with the other eagles and Yatpan swoops on Aqhat and kills him.

The third tablet tells of a seven-year drought which followed this murder.

For seven years Baal failed,
  for eight the Rider on the Clouds,
There was no dew, there were no showers,
There was no irrigation from the reservoirs of the
  deep,
There was no sweet voice of Baal.

As Danel inspects his poor crops, he hears of his son's death. He sees the eagles flying overhead and prays that Baal will break their wings. When they fall, he finds the remains of Aqhat in the entrails of Sumul, 'the mother of eagles'. This tablet, which may not be the end of the story, finishes with Danel's daughter going to find Yatpan to avenge her brother.

The Hebrew Bible

The Canaanite myths seem closely interrelated. They all involve references to rainfall and drought in association with the life and death, health and sickness of a god or a hero. They are too poorly preserved to make proper comparisons possible, however, especially as the translation of crucial words is so often in doubt.

Geographically, if not historically, the traditions of the Bible are close to those of Canaan, and Syria and Palestine fell within the orbit of Mesopotamian cultural influence. Where the Mesopotamians and Canaanites worshipped many gods, however, the religion of Yahweh, the god of Israel, hailed him as the only true God. Some stories in the Bible use themes which also appear in Mesopotamian and Canaanite mythology and no doubt go back ultimately to early Semitic oral tradition. But in the Bible the themes are stripped of their polytheistic dress, clothed in the garments of Israelite monotheism and employed to stress the unique power of Yahweh, the belief that Israel was Yahweh's chosen people and a sharper sense of God as a moral being.

An example is the story of Noah and the Flood. In the Mesopotamian version five gods are involved, but in Genesis it is Yahweh alone, justly angry at the wickedness of mankind, who sends the flood and who saves Noah. And at the end of the story Yahweh sets his rainbow in the clouds as a sign that he will temper justice with mercy and never again send a flood to destroy life on the earth. Again, in the story of the creation in Genesis, as compared with the Mesopotamian myth, there is no conflict between different generations of gods, no struggle against a primeval monster. Yahweh alone makes the world.

There are many resonances from Canaanite myths in the Bible. The name of the chief Canaanite god, El, is a title of Yahweh. Like Baal, Yahweh rides on the clouds, speaks in the thunder and sends the rain upon the earth, but Yahweh is far more than a god of fertility and there is no story of his death or disappearance and return. Baal is fiercely castigated in the Bible, precisely because his cult, with its emphasis on fertility, provided an alternative to the worship of Yahweh which some Israelites found attractive.

When the Canaanite myths are compared with the stories in the Bible, it seems that parallels exist not so much with the traditional mythological parts of the Bible in the early chapters of Genesis, but rather with the legends of the patriarchs and with the much later stories of Elijah, who spent his life preaching against the cult of Baal. It has been something of a surprise to discover that some verses in the Book of Psalms are almost direct translations from Ugaritic poems, and the poetic style of biblical Hebrew is very similar to that of Ugaritic. It has become clear that many portions of the Bible not only proclaim the greatness of the god of Israel, but are subtle parodies of the literature of Canaan.

(For Mesopotamian myths, see MESOPOTAMIA, for myths in the Bible, see CHRISTIANITY and, for the Flood story, see ARMENIA.)

Many clay plaques have been found throughout Palestine showing a nude goddess. It is probable that they were used in the fertility rituals which were performed in order to secure a good harvest. These two plaques show Astarte (or Athirat), who is referred to in the Ugaritic texts, but her hair style is like that of Hathor, her Egyptian counterpart, whose cult had an influence outside Egypt.

CHAPTER NINE

EGYPT

The mythology of Egypt, with its many references to natural phenomena and nature deities, reflects the unique geographical and environmental context of Egypt, and the country's total dependence on the dual life-giving forces of the River Nile and the heat of the sun. The Nile Valley, isolated from invasion and outside influences during the formative period of Egypt's history, gave birth to a unique civilization. The myths grew out of an environment of sharp contrasts, which constantly reminded the Egyptian of the juxtaposition of life and death.

Winding its way through a narrow valley in Upper Egypt, the Nile fans out into the Delta before finally entering the Mediterranean Sea. The scarce rainfall in Egypt underlines the land's dependence upon the annual Nile flood which, originating in central Africa, causes the volume of water in the river to rise and wash over its banks, covering them with a rich deposit of black mud. Diligent attention to irrigation enabled the Egyptians early on to cultivate a narrow strip of bright green fertile land on either side of the river, supporting people, animals and crops. Beyond this, Egypt was desert. The juxtaposition of fertile land and desert impressed upon the early inhabitants the co-existence of life and death, and also the regular pattern of the land's death and re-birth each year.

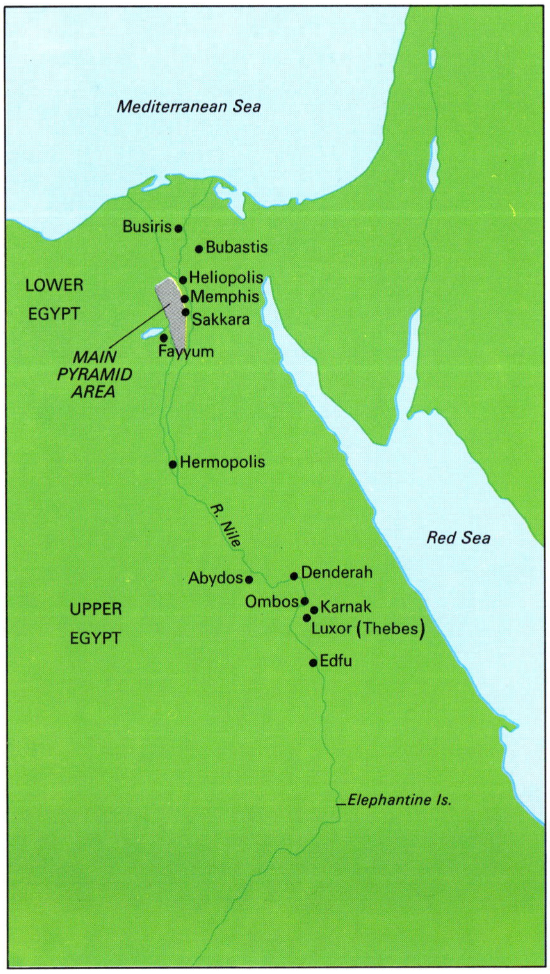

For over 3,000 years, the civilization of the Egyptians – their basic concepts, political institutions, religion and art forms – remained virtually unchanged, although some degree of variation can be determined in the different historical periods. The greatest periods of Egypt's history were the Old, Middle and New Kingdoms. Between these are the two periods known as the First and Second Intermediate Periods – times of internal dissolution and foreign invasion. After the New Kingdom, Egypt entered a period of gradual decline, marked by invasion and occupation by the new great empire-builders, Assyria, Persia, Greece and Rome. Egypt's history is divided into 'dynasties', a term employed by an ancient historian and retained as a useful division today. A dynasty usually consisted of a family of several rulers.

The religion was rooted in the country's historical development. Egypt originally consisted of a number of separate tribes, each with its own local deity. As

THE GODS OF HELIOPOLIS

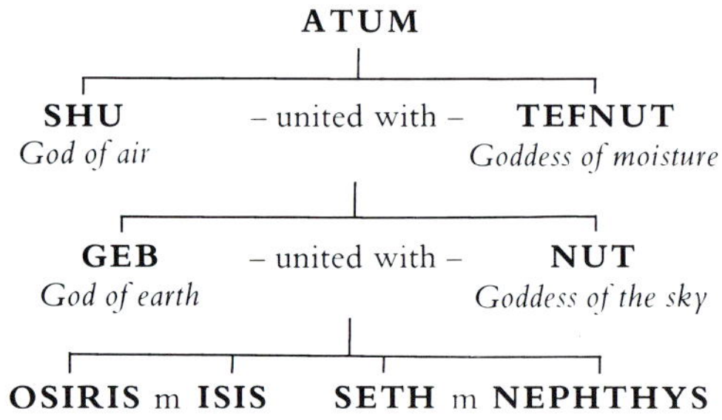

the tribes were politically amalgamated, their deities also became fused with each other. When the final unification of the country took place, in about 3100 BC, the one-time local deities of the north and south were gradually amalgamated into a state pantheon. This also included the cosmic deities, who may have been introduced into Egypt from elsewhere. They were distinguished from the local gods by their lack of animal or fetish forms and their remoteness from the lives of men. Outwardly at least, the Egyptians appeared to worship many gods, whose names and characteristics were often confusing, but an individual worshipper probably habitually approached only the local god and his associates.

Myths of Creation

By the Old Kingdom, three important religious centres had evolved, at Heliopolis, Memphis and Hermopolis. Each was devoted to the cult of a different god. The priesthoods of these cities rivalled each other in attempting to show, in terms of mythology, how their own god and his associated group of deities had originated the creation of the universe. The myths all indicate a belief that the process of creation was gradual and evolutionary, but that on one occasion – 'The First Time' – the god had played a definite and creative role. A golden age then followed, when all the laws, ethics and institutions were handed down to mankind.

The Heliopolitan cosmogony was the most important and most widely accepted. The creator of this Ennead (group of nine gods) was Atum, the original god of Heliopolis. He had emerged from the waters on the primeval island, where he spat forth Shu, god of the air, and vomited out Tefnut, goddess of moisture. They in turn united and brought forth the earth-god, Geb, and the sky-goddess, Nut. From their union were born the non-cosmic deities Osiris, Isis, Seth and Nephthys.

At Memphis, however, it was claimed that Ptah, the city's supreme god, begot Naunet and fathered her son, Atum, from whom sprang the Heliopolitan Ennead. In this way the Memphites attempted to show that it was their deity who had begun the process of creation. At Hermopolis, an Ogdoad (group of eight deities) – consisting of Nun (the primordial ocean), Huh (eternity), Kuk (darkness) and Amun (air) together with their consorts Naunet, Hauhet, Kauket and Amaunet – were believed to have created the world. Alternative versions included the belief that the world had come forth from a cosmic egg or from a lotus flower.

In the later period of the New Kingdom, to establish the omnipotence of their god, Amun, the priests of Thebes declared that Amun had created himself in secret, and that all other gods and cosmogonies had stemmed from him. Another version – associated with Khnum, the ram-headed god of Elephantine, who became a form of Amun – declared that Khnum, the potter, fashioned men on his wheel, making use of the clay in the locality as his basic material.

The Nile countryside shows a vivid contrast between the lush vegetation of the cultivated area and the barren desert beyond. This fertile landscape, near Denderah in Upper Egypt, is typical of scenery which the Egyptians believed existed on the mythical Island of Creation. The palm-trees were translated into the soaring stone columns with their palmiform capitals which can still be seen today in the Egyptian temples.

ABOVE In the Heliopolitan cosmogony, Geb, the earth-god, and Nut, the sky-goddess were children of Shu and Tefnut. Osiris, Isis, Seth and Nephthys were children of the union of Geb and Nut which is shown here, in a painted scene from the Papyrus of Tameniu. 21st Dynasty.

RIGHT A seated figure of Re, with a falcon head. He is crowned with the solar disc and holds a feather, the symbol of Ma'at or Truth. 26th Dynasty.

The Sun-Cult

The worship of the sun may have been brought into Egypt from elsewhere at an early and uncertain date, but during the Old Kingdom an official solar cult developed under the king's patronage at On (later known as Heliopolis). Here the sun-god Re assimilated the features of the earlier local creator-god Atum, and a temple was built to the sun-god. The cult of Re increased in influence until it reached its zenith in the 5th Dynasty, when the kings began to include 'son of Re' in the royal titles. They also built great sun-temples, increased the power of Re's priesthood and made the solar theology the official royal cult. From the 4th Dynasty onwards, the king was buried in a true pyramid – a form which was probably closely associated with the belief in the king's solar afterlife in the heavens.

With the decline in royal power at the end of the Old Kingdom, and the gradual decentralization of political and economic power, the state sun-cult suffered, though the increased power and influence of Re's priesthood as against the king was probably a contributory factor to the eventual disintegration of the society. Replaced in the succeeding periods by the increasingly popular and democratic god Osiris, the cult of Re declined, although the god continued to be closely associated with funerary rituals and resurrection. However, in the New Kingdom, when the kings of the 18th Dynasty advanced their one-time local god, Amun, to the position of 'king of gods',

CHRONOLOGICAL TABLE

Before 3100 BC	Predynastic Period
3100–2686 BC	Archaic Period *Dynasty I–II*
2686–2181 BC	Old Kingdom *Dynasty III–VI*
2181–1991 BC	First Intermediate Period *Dynasty VII–XI*
1991–1786 BC	Middle Kingdom *Dynasty XII*
1786–1552 BC	Second Intermediate Period *Dynasty XIII–XVII*
1552–1069 BC	New Kingdom *Dynasty XVIII–XX*
1069–525 BC	Third Intermediate Period *Dynasty XXI–XXVI*
525–332 BC	Late Period *Dynasty XXVII–XXXI*
332 BC	Conquest of Egypt by Alexander the Great
332–30 BC	Ptolemaic Period
30 BC–AD 641	Roman Period
AD 641	Islamic Conquest

they took care to associate him with the older cult of Re, thus creating the great state god Amen-Re.

At the end of the 18th Dynasty, King Akhenaten tried unsuccessfully to introduce an exclusive form of solar monotheism into Egypt, centred on the worship of the Aten, the disc of the sun. Although this worship differed in many respects from the earlier sun-cult, it may be regarded as an attempt to restore an earlier unique relationship between the ruler of Egypt and the royal sun-god. At all periods, the cult of the sun, perhaps because of its remoteness from the ordinary people and their inability to relate to it, remained essentially a royal and state cult.

Kings and Priests

From very early times, the Egyptians developed a belief in the continuation of life after death, and also realized a need to come to terms with their environment, which they envisaged in terms of nature, vegetation and animal deities. Many of the myths relate to these two aspects of religious belief. At first each locality worshipped its deity in the form of a cult symbol, which was protected by a reed shrine. The tribal chieftain performed the necessary rites on behalf of the community. As the country became united, and the most powerful local chieftain eventually rose to become king, the shrines gradually developed into temples, where the king now performed rituals for the state gods, on behalf of his country and his people. The temple was not regarded as a place of community worship, but as the House

LEFT In this relief from the city of Tell el-Amarna, Pharaoh Akhenaten (Amenophis IV) is shown with his wife Nefertiti and their eldest daughter, making offerings to the Aten, symbolized by the sun's disc. The rays of the sun end in hands, holding ankh-signs, which bestow life on the king and his family. 18th Dynasty.

BELOW An important feature of Re was his sacred eye, which destroyed his enemies. This scene is from the Book of the Dead and occurs in the Papyrus of Hen-taui, a musician-priestess of Amen-Re. It shows Hen-taui and a baboon, representing the god Thoth, making obeisance to the sun-disc which contains the sacred eye, as it rises from the mountain. 21st Dynasty.

RIGHT Pyramid-building reached its zenith in the 4th Dynasty, and the pyramid may have been regarded as a ramp which gave the dead king access to the sky. Part of the original limestone casing of the pyramid of Chephren can still be seen. The closely associated Great Sphinx, carved out of a natural outcrop of rock, is said to bear a likeness of the face of Chephren.

BELOW The king played a vital role in temple ritual, as the son and heir of the gods. This bas-relief from the temple dedicated to Sebek and Haroeris at Kom-Ombo shows Sebek, with a crocodile head and wearing the Atef-crown, embracing the king. Graeco-Roman period.

of the God, where the cult statue was worshipped and attended by priests. The priesthood had no pastoral duties. Its main function was to perform certain rituals for the gods and, in some instances, for the dead and deified kings.

The gods were regarded as beings with human needs: food, drink, clothing, rest and recreation. These were provided in the temples through the daily rituals, when food and clothing were presented to the god's cult statue, and also by the festivals, held at specific intervals throughout the year, when specific events in the lives of the deities were celebrated. Although the festivals varied from place to place, the same daily ritual was performed in all the temples for all the gods. Scenes of the rituals can still be seen decorating the walls of the temples, showing the king performing various rites for the gods. In theory, the king alone could approach the gods, by virtue of his unique position as divine son. It was believed that each king was the offspring of his mother, the Great Royal Wife, by the supreme state god. The Great Royal Wife was herself usually the daughter of the previous king and his great queen. Marriage to such a Great Royal Daughter consolidated the male heir's claim to the throne, and this resulted, not infrequently, in marriage between royal brother and sister.

Despite the king's unique role as divine son, it was the high priest of each temple who attended to the daily performance of the rituals, except perhaps in the main temple of the greatest state god in the king's Residence City, where the king may have fulfilled his filial duties in person. Based on a concept of barter, the performance of the daily ritual for the gods was believed to ensure the king's victory over his enemies and the prosperity of Egypt.

The Island of Creation

However, in addition to the role of the temple as a place of protection for the god's statue, and as a centre of worship and an avenue of approach to the god, in architectural and mythological terms each temple was regarded as a recreation in stone of the Island of Creation, where the first god alighted and was provided with a reed shelter. According to myth, chaos existed before the creation of the universe. Waters covered the earth, darkness prevailed, and there were no gods. Then, a mud island emerged from the waters, and here the first sacred shrine came into being. Demi-gods, emerging from the darkness, picked up a piece of reed that had been washed up on the shore of the new island. They set it up near the water's edge. The island was soon sanctified by the arrival of a divine falcon, which settled on the reed. To protect this deity, a wall was built around the reed, thus forming the first shrine. Gradually the waters receded, exposing a greater expanse of the low-lying Island of Creation.

Eventually, additional rooms were built on either side of the god's original shrine, and other halls and chambers were added in front of it. The original sanctuary, built to protect the divine bird who had first alighted on the reed, remained at a slightly higher level than the surrounding rooms and halls. Each temple represented the island where life had originated, the very centre of creation. The layout of the temple, with its succession of courts and halls, sloping upwards towards the sanctuary and then down again at the rear of the building, and the architectural devices – the papyriform and lotiform columns, the star-painted ceilings, the plant forms carved in stone and rising up, along the bases of the walls, from the ground-level – these were intended to represent the natural forms and setting of the original mud-island with its first shrine. The same basic features were retained for some 3000 years, from the earliest reed shrines to the later monumental temples in stone.

The earliest form of shrine was a hut, probably made of reed matting, positioned at the rear of a small enclosure where the god's symbol was set up. The hut provided a simple shelter for the cult statue. In the 3rd Dynasty monumental building in stone began, and the designs and patterns found in the earlier structures of reeds and brick were now translated into stone. Gradually two main types of temple developed (apart from the solar temples, which were based on a different concept). In the cult temple, worship and rituals were performed on behalf of the deity's statue. The mortuary temple, besides providing for the worship of a god, also accommodated the cult of a dead king. By the New Kingdom, these extensive stone temples had reached their final form, but they still retained the main architectural layout and some of the features which can be traced back to the early shrines. The most complete examples, still virtually intact, date from the Graeco-Roman period.

TOP The temple of Amen-Re at Karnak was dedicated to the great state god. Despite its vastness, it still retains the basic features of the early reed shrines.

ABOVE Statue of Horus, the falcon-god to whom the temple of Edfu was dedicated.

LEFT These columns in the Hypostyle Hall of the Temple of Edfu represent the landscape of the mythical primeval island.

TOP Hathor was the goddess of joy and love, of the sky, and of the west – the abode of the dead. In this detail of a painting on papyrus, she is shown as a cow, wearing a head-dress of two plumes and a solar disc, and decorated with stars symbolizing her role as a sky-goddess. 19th Dynasty.

ABOVE Part of the painted ceiling in the tomb of King Sethos I at Thebes, showing the constellations. The hippopotamus is the goddess Tauert. 19th Dynasty.

Myths and Festivals

Apart from the mythology relating to the origin of the temple, various tales grew up around the festivals of the gods. At Abydos, a yearly pilgrimage brought many people to the cult centre of Osiris, where Mystery Plays were enacted by the priests for the pilgrims, depicting events in the life, death and resurrection of Osiris. In addition, in the most secret area of the temple, rituals were performed which were believed to result in the god's resurrection and the renewal of the vegetation. On a less serious theme, at Thebes, the Feast of Opet took place annually and lasted for almost a month. The great god Amun left his temple at Karnak and visited his wife in the 'Harem in the South', known today as the Temple of Luxor. During the Ptolemaic Period, such festivals were still in existence, and Hathor, the goddess of joy and love, left her temple at Denderah and made the long journey by river to visit her consort Horus in his temple at Edfu, where she remained with him for a fortnight. Such occasions were undoubtedly times of great rejoicing and festivity, and the inhabitants of the villages near the river would have flocked to the banks to view with delight the spectacle of the ornately decorated barque, carrying its precious cargo of the cult statue accompanied by the white-robed, shaven-headed priests.

Birth and Fate

Myths concerning personal deities are less colourful. Certain deities were concerned with the order of the universe and the lesser realm of the fate of the individual. Ma'at, the goddess of truth and justice, was responsible for maintaining the correct balance and order of the universe and its inhabitants. Re, the sun-god, was her father and he had brought her forth to establish unity and order in the world. She was depicted as a woman wearing a single feather as a headdress. Even the king was subject to the dictates of Ma'at and he was expected to uphold her principles. Ma'at also played an important role in the life of an individual after death. At the Day of Judgment, the heart of the deceased was weighed in the balance against the feather of Ma'at to assess his worthiness to pass into a blessed eternity.

Other deities closely connected with the fate of an individual included Shai, Meshkent and Renenet. Shai and Meshkent, regarded as husband and wife, were present at the time of birth and at the Day of Judgment. Shai symbolized destiny, and ordained a man's lifespan and the occasion and circumstances of his death. However, destiny could be changed by an individual's own actions or by divine intercession on his behalf. Meshkent represented the birth bricks, on to which a mother delivered her baby. Her closeness to the child enabled her to predict its future, and she also attended his Day of Judgment, when she was called upon to act as a character witness for the deceased.

Associated with these deities of fortune was Renenet, who had special care for children. She protected them at birth and for the period after birth. Also present at a birth were the Seven Hathors, a group of young women who announced the destiny of the newborn child. However, the goddess to whom most women turned with prayers for a safe delivery in childbirth was Tauert, who is always shown as a pregnant hippopotamus. This grotesque figure was held in great respect and, in common with most of the goddesses present at birth, she was also associated with rebirth after death. Her husband was Bes, the ugly dwarf-god whose areas of influence were love, marriage, music and dancing.

The Conquest of Death

Although birth and its associated perils were areas of great magical and religious activity, it was death which most preoccupied the Egyptian consciousness. The human personality was thought to consist of various distinct elements, some of which were immortal. Death seems to have been regarded as an interruption of life, an obstacle through which man had to pass in order to attain eternity. At death, the

immortal element left the body. The existence which it was believed to experience varied according to the status of the deceased in this world, and also with the period of Egypt's history in which he lived. Whatever form of existence it followed, however, the immortal element still preserved a link with this world through the body in the tomb, and it remained dependent on the food and other offerings left at the tomb for its continued sustenance in the next world. Indeed, the earliest and most enduring concept of the afterlife was centred around a continued form of existence spent in the tomb, or Mansion of the Spirit as it was called.

Evidence from the earliest periods indicates that the Egyptians already had a belief in an existence after death, and pottery vessels and other daily requisites were placed with bodies in the earliest pit-graves. At this date, the bodies of the dead were simply placed in the sand and a natural desiccation of the bodily tissues resulted, so that the bodies retained something of a lifelike appearance.

With the development of an increasingly sophisticated and complex society, the leading members of the early communities were buried in more elaborate brick-lined tombs, lavishly equipped. The body inside the tomb was now no longer in direct contact with the hot, dry sand. Consequently, the body tissues now reached an advanced state of decomposition before this process could be arrested by natural desiccation. However, a belief had by now developed that it was necessary to preserve the body of an individual after his death so that, if he wished, he could return at any time to a location on earth,

ABOVE The Ba, or soul, was depicted as a human-headed bird. It left the body at death but was later reunited with it. This detail from the Papyrus of the scribe Ani shows the Ba hovering over the mummy of the deceased which rests on a bier, flanked by incense stands.

LEFT Painted limestone bas-relief showing Ma'at, the goddess of truth and justice, who wears the feather on her head – the symbol of truth. In the accompanying hieroglyphic inscription, she is called '. . . daughter of Re'. 19th Dynasty.

RIGHT Mummified head of a man. The preservation of the body was regarded an essential preparation for eternity. The soul of the deceased was believed to visit the mummy in the tomb and, through it, to partake of the food offerings left there. Graeco-Roman period.

BELOW A scene painted on papyrus showing Khepri, one aspect of the sun-god, sailing in the solar barque in the company of other deities. He has the head and wings of the sacred scarab-beetle. The god and the scarab were both regarded as symbols of constant self-generation. Thebes, New Kingdom.

provided for him by his preserved body within his tomb. It therefore became necessary to develop a method of preserving the body indefinitely, and by gradual stages, through trial and error, a method was devised. The body was dehydrated by means of natron (a form of salt) and was eviscerated, all the internal organs except the heart, and perhaps the kidneys, being removed from the body and treated separately. This process is now known as mummification.

Two distinct concepts of the other world to which an individual's immortal element could pass gradually developed. During the Old Kingdom, the king's association with the sun-cult reached its zenith, and there came into existence a solar concept of the royal afterlife. Upon death, the king (who was considered partly divine) was reunited with his father Re, the sun-god, in the heavens. The pyramid – his place of burial – may have been regarded as a ramp or other means of access for the king to the sky. His eternity was spent in the heavens in the east, where he joined the other gods, continued with his royal duties and sat in judgment; or he passed his time accompanying the sun-god on his daily journey across the heavens in his solar barque. This solar doctrine offered eternity only to the king, although

A painted scene from a papyrus which shows the Weighing of the Heart. The heart of the deceased is weighed in the balance against the feather of Truth and the scales are supervised by Anubis, the jackal-headed god of embalming, while the Ba of the deceased awaits the outcome of the trial. Thoth the ibis-headed god of writing, records the verdict for Osiris, who is enthroned as judge of the dead and accompanied by his wife, Isis. The fearsome creature who devoured the bodies of those who were unworthy to pass into eternity stands next to Thoth. 21st Dynasty.

his family and favoured courtiers could expect to enjoy a measure of eternity vicariously, through their close association with the king and through the proximity of their burial places to his pyramid. However, even the king had to pass from this world into the other. The gates of the next world were reached by crossing a lake and the king had to use various methods, including his magical powers, to persuade the ferryman to take him across the lake. To ensure a safe journey to the next world, the king was provided with a collection of magic spells (now known as the Pyramid Texts), which were intended to counteract all evils.

Although the king was at first most closely associated with the sun-god, he also became identified with Osiris, the vegetation-god, who was the judge and ruler of the underworld. However, from the Middle Kingdom onwards, it was amongst non-royal believers that the cult of Osiris found widespread acceptance, with its promise of salvation and resurrection from death for everyone, rich or poor. Eternal blessedness was promised to those who worshipped the god and successfully faced the Day of Judgment before a tribunal of gods. The deceased then passed into the underworld where he spent his days, accompanied by his wife, tending a small piece of land.

Attempts by the priests to co-ordinate and rationalize the various concepts of the afterlife were never entirely successful or widely accepted.

The Day of Judgment

Once the funerary rites had been satisfactorily completed, the dead man faced judgment before 42 divine assessors, various other gods and Osiris, the great judge of the underworld. He affirmed the purity of his soul, by reciting the 'negative confession', in which the deceased declared that he had committed no serious offences or sins during his lifetime. If necessary, he would attempt to deceive the gods, in order to pass through this ordeal.

The second part of the trial followed. This was performed in the presence of various deities. Thoth, the ibis-headed god of wisdom and learning, presided over a large balance, while Ma'at, goddess of justice, and Anubis, god of embalming, were present to ensure that the proceedings were fairly carried out. The goddesses of fate and destiny gave testimony with regard to the dead man's character, which was recorded by Thoth on his scribal palette. The dead man's soul, appearing as a human-headed bird, was also present, awaiting the outcome.

The heart of the deceased, regarded as the seat of his intellect and emotions, was then placed by Anubis in one of the pans of the scales. The feather, symbol of the goddess of truth and justice, was put into the other pan. If the heart was balanced equally by the feather, the deceased was declared free from sin, and this verdict was recorded by Thoth. His innocence proven and accepted by the tribunal of gods, the dead man could pass into the blessed afterlife, and spend his eternity in the Osirian underworld. He had escaped the dreadful fate which awaited the guilty. His body would not be thrown to the beast, part-lion, part-crocodile and part-hippopotamus, who lurked near the scales to devour the hearts of those who failed to establish their innocence.

A Democratic Afterlife

By the time of Old Kingdom, to ensure continued provision of the royal and noble burial places, it was expected that a man's heir would provide daily supplies of food and drink at the tomb, and a similar ritual was performed in the mortuary temple

ABOVE Isis suckling the infant Horus. Isis, the symbol of divine motherhood, played an important role in the myth of Osiris. She helped to resuscitate the god and posthumously conceived his son, Horus. 18th Dynasty.

BELOW The god Osiris, as a mummiform figure, wears a feathered crown. His skin is painted green, symbolizing life and rebirth. Wall scene from a tomb at Deir el-Medina. 19th Dynasty.

attached to the pyramid, on behalf of the king. However, this method was open to abuse and neglect and the nobles were forced to find other methods of ensuring a continuing food supply after their demise. The introduction of ka-priests occurred at this time. Paid out of a man's estate, the ka-priest and his descendants were under an obligation to provision the dead man's tomb and to attend to the needs of his Ka, or spirit. Once again, the system was fallible, and eventually the tomb-owner was forced to rely on the wall-scenes in his tomb, including a lavish and detailed menu, and on the small models of workers employed in food production. These, it was hoped, could be activated at will by the tomb-owner after death and commanded to produce the required provisions.

At this period many of the myths regarding the king's solar afterlife and the creation of the universe were formalized, probably by the priests of the most influential gods, and particularly by the priesthood of Re at Heliopolis. Political, economic and religious factors nevertheless contributed to the final decline and disintegration of the Old Kingdom, the great age of pyramid-building. The succeeding periods saw a return to decentralization, with local princes seizing power and ruling as petty kings in their own provinces. The disintegration of the kingdom and the defeat of absolute royal power led to a profound change in the concept of the afterlife. Now, the local princes, and eventually ordinary people who could afford the labour costs, built and equipped local tombs with funerary goods, in the expectation of an individual afterlife not dependent upon that of the king. Even the return of a strong and centralized kingship in the Middle Kingdom did not undermine this belief in a democratic afterlife, available to all. Against this background, the cult of Osiris prospered and spread throughout Egypt. The best known of Egyptian myths sprang from this cult.

The Murder of Osiris

According to Heliopolitan theology, Osiris, Isis, Seth and Nephthys were the children of Geb, the earth-god, by Nut, the sky-goddess. Osiris was married to Isis, and Seth was the husband of Nephthys. Osiris was a human king, who was a good and wise ruler, bringing knowledge of agriculture and advanced arts and crafts to the Egyptians. Seth, however, became jealous of the popularity of Osiris, and plotted his death. He invited Osiris to a banquet, at which he produced a wooden chest which he promised to give to any guest who fitted exactly inside it. Several guests lay down inside the chest in an attempt to win the prize, but when Osiris took his turn, he fitted the chest exactly, for Seth had designed the chest especially for this purpose. Seizing their opportunity, Seth's accomplices closed the chest, trapping Osiris inside. They carried the chest and its burden to the river, where they ferried it downstream to the Delta and then cast it adrift on the sea. Travelling many miles, it was finally washed up at Byblos on the Phoenician coast.

Isis now set out in search of her husband's body. Eventually discovering it at Byblos, she brought it back to Egypt. She had posthumously conceived a son by her husband, and in the secrecy of the Delta marshes Isis awaited the birth of her child. However, she was still in danger from Seth. When out hunting, he discovered the coffin of Osiris, which she was hiding. Seth thereupon cut the body of Osiris into pieces and scattered them throughout Egypt. Isis now set out to rediscover the various pieces. She then reconstituted her husband's body, using her magic arts and anointing the body with unguents. Her sister Nephthys assisted her in this task. Osiris was thus resurrected.

In due course, and after many dangers, Horus was born. Isis brought him up in the Delta marshes, protecting him against the evil machinations of Seth by means of her magical spells. When he was grown, Horus determined to avenge his father's death by killing Seth. A bloody struggle ensued, and Horus castrated Seth while Seth plucked out one of his nephew's eyes. Horus was finally the victor, and the tribunal of divine judges met in the Great Hall of Judgment to decide how the kingdom should henceforth be divided. Thoth, the ibis-headed god of Hermopolis, defended Osiris. The judges made their decision in favour of Osiris. He was acquitted of all evil and was restored to life, not as a living king but in his new role as king and judge of the dead in the underworld. With the gods' endorsement, Horus succeeded his father on the throne as a living king, and his plucked eye was restored to him by Thoth. Seth, however, was disgraced for eternity. Good had triumphed over evil.

The Defeat of Evil

The story of the death and resurrection of Osiris was recorded by the Greek writer Plutarch. The complete form of the myth does not occur in earlier Egyptian sources, although reference is made to Osiris in the Pyramid Texts, which decorated the interior walls of some of the Old Kingdom pyramids,

and other evidence indicates that festivals of Osiris were held regularly at various temples in Egypt. Osiris was a god of vegetation, and consequently of the flooding Nile, the corn and the moon. In this role he represented the annual death of the land and its rebirth, brought about through the flooding of the river. Possibly as a secondary function, he became god of the dead and judge of the underworld, with responsibility for the dead and the ability to grant them eternity. Each king upon death became an Osiris, while his successor ascended to the throne as Horus – the living king, the son and heir of Osiris in the myth.

However, in the myth, Osiris is described as a human king, who brought civilization and agricultural advances to Egypt. He is always depicted as a dead ruler, wearing a crown and carrying royal insignia. His supposed human origin doubtless inspired his worshippers to believe that, through him, they might aspire to eternal life in his realm. Whether Osiris really was a long dead human ruler is not known. Some scholars have suggested that Osiris and Horus in the myth represent two groups of newcomers, who may have entered Egypt in the predynastic period. They would have come into conflict with the indigenous population, who may well have worshipped as their supreme god an early form of Seth (often regarded as an animal deity, with strange unidentifiable features, perhaps representing him as a jackal or boar). Horus and Osiris (the newcomers) defeated Seth (the natives), and the myth may reflect later propaganda against Seth.

The original home of Osiris remains obscure, although it has been suggested that he had links with other Near Eastern nature deities. However, his cult appears to have been established first at two main centres in Egypt – Abydos and Busiris. By the Middle Kingdom, Osiris had replaced Re as the chief god of Egypt but, unlike the royal sun-god, he was capable of appealing to the masses with his promise of resurrection. Also, as a god of the dead, he did not rival the various local deities, for a man could continue to worship both his local god and Osiris. Abydos, his greatest cult-centre and reputed burial place, now became the most sacred centre of pilgrimage for Egyptians. They would attempt to visit Abydos at least once before death, in the hope of increasing their chances of a blessed eternity. Once a year, a great festival was held there, to coincide with the god's resurrection. Similar festivals were

Painted scene decorating the end wall in the tomb of Sennedjem at Deir el-Medina. This depicts one aspect of the Egyptian afterlife – fertile fields are being tilled by the deceased and his wife. In this verdant land, trees and shrubs are heavily laden with fruit and the harvest is abundant. 19th Dynasty.

held elsewhere, but Abydos retained its special importance.

The myth clearly expresses a belief in the eventual defeat of evil (personified by Seth) by good (Horus and Osiris). It also emphasizes the role of Isis as the devoted wife and mother, whose efforts were rewarded by her husband's eventual triumph. Her popularity in Egypt, and later in other parts of the world, was based on her ideal qualities as a mother-figure (see MYSTERY RELIGIONS).

The Osirian concept of the afterlife had a profound effect upon the Egyptians. Not only did it offer a chance of eternity to all believers, regardless of their position and wealth, but it also introduced the idea that a man's continued existence after death was dependent upon his actions, good or evil, in this world. After death, he would be accountable for his deeds, at his Day of Judgment before a divine tribunal. Failure to convince the gods of his worthiness resulted in eternal negation, when his soul would seek in vain for his body. If he passed the test, a blessed eternity awaited him in the fields of the underworld. The prospect of the manual labour involved in cultivating a plot of land throughout eternity did not, however, appeal to those who had never endured such physical hardships. If they were able, these people now provided their tombs with sets of small mummiform figures, usually made of wood or faience and frequently bearing several lines of hieroglyphic inscription. They are now called ushabti-figures. These servant-figures, shown holding agricultural implements, were intended to provide readily available labour for the tomb-owner. They were believed to 'answer' when summoned to undertake agricultural tasks in the Osirian realm. Like the rest of the tomb-equipment, including the mummy, statues and wall-scenes, these figurines were believed to 'come to life' to assist and support the deceased tomb-owner in his continuing existence.

Even when, during the New Kingdom, Amen-Re became the supreme state god with vast wealth and possessions and, in the long years of Egypt's decline, other deities came to prominence, nevertheless it was the belief in Osiris and his ultimate triumph over evil which remained in the Egyptian imagination to inspire and comfort his worshippers.

Detail of a painting on papyrus showing the god Seth killing Apophis, the serpent who was the eternal enemy of the sun-god. Re-Harakhte, another aspect of the sun-god, sits behind Seth in the solar barque. He is shown with a falcon head and the solar disc. From the Book of the Dead belonging to the Lady Cheritwebeshet. 21st Dynasty.

MAJOR EGYPTIAN DEITIES

Amen-Re: Supreme state god of the 18th Dynasty: a fusion of Amun and Re

Amun or **Amon:** Creator-god of Thebes: a god of fertility: associated with the ram and the goose

Anubis: God of embalming: associated with the dog or jackal

Apis: Sacred bull kept at Memphis, where he was tended by priests: each Apis bull was mummified at death

Aten: The sun's disc, decreed to be the only god by Pharaoh Akhenaten (14th century BC): represented as a disc with rays ending in hands

Atum: Creator-god of Heliopolis, where he was merged with Re: his sacred animal was the Mnevis bull

Bast or **Bastet:** Goddess of Bubastis: her sacred animal was the cat

Bes: God of luck, love and marriage, music: represented as a dwarf

Buto: Chief goddess of the Delta: associated with the snake

Geb: God of the earth (Heliopolis)

Hapi: Personification of the Nile, shown with a crown of water plants, lotus or papyrus

Harpokrates: Horus the child, the infant son of Isis: portrayals of him on his mother's lap influenced the Christian iconography of the Virgin and Child

Hathor: Goddess of joy and love, consort of Horus: her sacred animal was the cow: later fused with Isis

Horus: Son of Osiris and Isis: identified with the ruling pharaoh: often represented as a falcon

Imhotep: A god of healing: originally a real man, adviser and architect to Pharaoh Zoser (28th century BC) and builder of the Step Pyramid at Sakkara

Isis: Consort of Osiris, the ideal woman, wife and mother: later worshipped all over the Roman world

Khepera or **Khepri:** The rising sun: associated with the scarab-beetle

Khnum: The potter, creator-god of Elephantine, who fashioned mankind on his wheel: associated with the ram

Khons: A moon god (Thebes), later a god of healing

Ma'at: Goddess of truth, justice and the order of the universe: her symbol was the feather

Meshkent: A goddess of birth, present at the Day of Judgment

Min: A god of fertility, shown with phallus erect: later god of roads and protector of travellers: often identified with Horus

Mnevis: Sacred bull kept at Heliopolis as an incarnation of Atum-Re

Nut: Goddess of the sky (Heliopolis)

Osiris: God of the Nile flood, vegetation, corn, the moon, the dead and renewal of life: often represented as a mummy sprouting corn

Ptah: Creator-god of Memphis, incarnate in the Apis bull

Re or **Ra:** The sun-god, identified with Atum at Heliopolis: the god of the early royal sun-cult: mankind and the animals were said to have come into being from his tears

Renenet: A goddess of children

Sebek: A crocodile-god, worshipped at Shedet in the Fayyum and at Ombos in Upper Egypt

Sekhmet: Goddess of war, a form of Hathor: consort of Ptah: associated with the lioness and the heat of the desert

Serapis: Chief state god in the Ptolemaic period: a fusion of Osiris and Apis: a god of healing and the afterlife

Seth: Brother and enemy of Osiris: sometimes a personification of the desert, barrenness, darkness: came to be regarded as the god of evil

Shai: A god of destiny, present at birth and at the Day of Judgment

Shu: God of the air (Heliopolis)

Tauert: A goddess of childbirth: represented as a hippopotamus

Tefnut: Goddess of moisture, rain, dew (Heliopolis)

Thoth: God of wisdom, arts and sciences, magic (Hermopolis): scribe of the gods: associated with the ibis and the ape

ABOVE Faience ushabti figure from a tomb of the 26th Dynasty. Large numbers of these were put in the tombs of the wealthy to act as agricultural labourers in the afterlife, on behalf of the deceased.

LEFT Brewing and baking were essential activities to ensure a food supply for the dead person, and many models are engaged in such work. This statuette represents a woman grinding corn and comes from an Old Kingdom tomb.

CHAPTER TEN

ISLAM

Islam is sometimes portrayed as a faith cocooned in textual authority. God is made 'word'. Holy writ and not a person is the ultimate authority. God's Prophet, Muhammad, has declared the revelation of God in the Arabic Quran. The Quran is the Almighty's blue-print for his wayward creation.

Few today, however, accept that the social ethic and format of Muslim society are to be found as an entity in the *Suras* (chapters) of the Quran. Years of study have changed the emphasis and altered perspectives. The original view suited the religious prejudice of the western world. The Arabs, like the Jews, are Semites, and Islam, the religion of the Arabs, is historically related to both Judaism and Christianity. Muhammad regarded Moses and Jesus of Nazareth as his forerunners as messengers of God. Consequently, it was once fashionable to dub the Quran a Bedouin version of Semitic revelation, adding little to the structure of a progressive disclosure of God, a disclosure which was first revealed, to quote a well-known Christian hymn, by a Lord of Might to the Hebrews:

Who to thy tribes on Sinai's height
In ancient times didst give the law
In cloud and majesty and awe . . .

Later, the urban sophistication of the civilization to which the Quran related was revalued. It is now known that it was highly developed. In southern Arabia in particular there were skyscraper cities, mighty fortresses and elaborate irrigation schemes. Myths and legends were familiar to men of sophisticated taste who had acquired ideas from Persia, Iraq, Syria, Egypt and Ethiopia.

The French anthropologist Claude Lévi-Strauss has virtually dismissed Semitic 'myth' as of any relevance to the body of primitive or structured myth in primitive societies or surviving in India and eastern Asia as part of complex religious traditions. His reason was that Semitic myths had been subjected to or 'deformed' by intellectual restatements, but he qualified his opinion. If one could discover 'archaic material' and 'mythological residue', it might be possible to attempt a re-examination, and perhaps a rediscovery of some of the most ancient mythology of Semitic peoples. Among major Semitic sources certain stories and characters in the Quran offer clues to the form and content of 'archaic Semitic residue'. In the Quran the most ancient beliefs of Arabia are manifested, reinterpreted or rejected. These beliefs can be compared with survivals in the Bible and with extremely old

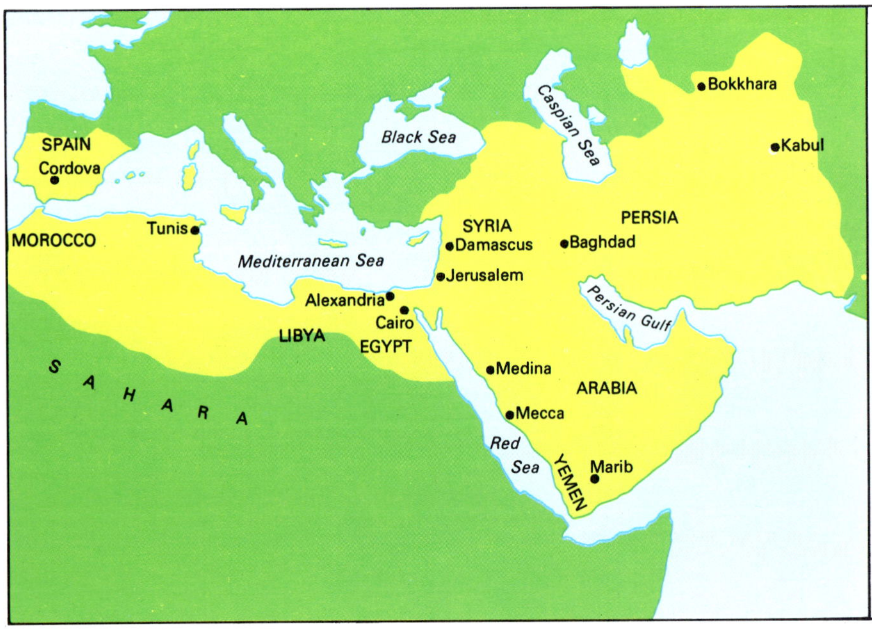

CHRONOLOGICAL TABLE

Dates (AD)	
*c.*570	Muhammad born at Mecca
622	The flight (Hijra) of Muhammad from Mecca to Medina: beginning of the Islamic era
632	Death of Muhammad
633–7	Arab conquest of Syria, Iraq and Persia
639–44	Conquest of Egypt and Libya
661–750	The Umayyad Caliphate, in Damascus: conquest of Tunisia, Algeria, Morocco, Spain, Afghanistan, northwestern India
750–1258	The Abbasid Caliphate, in Baghdad: the 'golden age' of Islam

The story of the ascent of the Prophet Muhammad to the Seven Heavens is briefly referred to in the Quran. According to tradition, the Prophet was mounted on a steed called Buraq, which was smaller than a mule and larger than an ass. It had a woman's head and a peacock's tail. The story of the Prophet's ascent was the model for the description of the journey of the soul after death to the throne of the divine judge. The scene has often been depicted in Islamic painting and this Persian example is from an MS of Nizami, 1504.

Semitic texts outside the Bible, with early Arabian poems and works of myth and legend which pre-dated the Quran or were written down a little later. All this material was the source of greatly elaborated Islamic tales.

One way of exploring Quranic myth and legend is to follow the path of Mircea Eliade and A. Wensinck, or those of kindred spirit. Such writers search for symbols – cosmic pillars, primeval oceans, serpents, cosmological crabs, images of life and death – which they list in their books. That images and symbols are observable in stories told in the Quran, or inspired by it, is to be expected. They are universal and are to be found in all Semitic sources.

The dynamic potential of Islamic symbols as ritual objects is impressive. The annual pilgrimage to Mecca, with the kissing of the black stone, which is embedded in the wall of the Kaaba (the House of God), is possibly unparalleled in this respect, but how many stories has this pilgrimage ritual inspired? How many stories have been inspired by the account of the ascent of the Prophet to heaven, his mystical

The city of Iram of the Columns is a lost relic of man's egoism and folly. Much of the imagery surrounding it in later Islamic stories is derived from the descriptions of the monuments of the Yemen before the coming of Islam. Here, Shaddad Ibn Ad is depicted on his horse, surveying the earthly paradise which he has created.

flight on the back of his fabulous steed, Buraq?

In the Quran symbols are subordinated to people, and the myths of the Quran involve people whose legendary exploits are disclosed to us by commentators on the text. No non-Muslim can pass judgment on the value of Quranic 'myth'. His view will inevitably be subjective and conditioned by the 'mythology' of his own cultural background. The personalities who appear in the Quran have inspired story-tellers, artists and men of literary genius. Characters such as Luqman, King Solomon, Bilqis (the Queen of Sheba), Dhul-Qarnayn and al-Khidr have a peculiarly dynamic appeal. It is they, as people, who are subject to interchange and metamorphosis, who are confused with the *jinn* (beings created from fire), or who manipulate cosmic symbols like players on an instrumental keyboard.

Luqman and Shaddad

One of the most ancient of Quranic figures is Luqman al-Hakim, a legendary sage from the time of Arab paganism before the coming of Islam. According to early legend, he was a wise man who was given the life-span of seven vultures. He fed and cared for seven of these carrion-eaters in succession and died at the same time as the seventh of them. Later, some believed that he had been an Ethiopian slave who told instructive fables, like the slave Aesop, to whom popular Greek fables were attributed.

The vultures appear so attached to Luqman that in some folkloric guise they cannot be excluded as the source for basic features of his character. In pre-Islamic Arabia there was a belief in sacred animals as guests or clients of the god and animals were probably kept at certain Arabian shrines. Gods were related to the *jinn* and the *jinn* to wild animals, and the list of Arabian deities includes a lion-god (Yaghuth) and a vulture-god (Nasr). It is possible that Luqman in one of his varied disguises has been invested with certain marks of divinity or attributes of semi-divine kingship.

Luqman is mentioned briefly in the Quran (*Sura* 31) as one to whom God gave wisdom, and who admonished his son to serve no other god but God. From this one could be forgiven for thinking that Muhammad conceived of Luqman exclusively in the role of Aesop, as a paragon of wisdom and a preacher of God's plan. While it is indisputable that such is the message of this *Sura*, it is twice qualified by its context. The first was the common knowledge of Luqman among the people of Mecca, to whom this *Sura* is addressed. The second is the chapter's attack on him 'who buys sportive legends', meaning Nadr Ibn al-Harith, a rival of the Prophet and a connoisseur of Persian myths. Only an exemplary reference to Luqman, as a model for imitation, was appropriate amidst the personal rivalry manifest in this *Sura*.

The Prophet was no doubt well aware of the complex and often contradictory tales of Luqman al-Hakim. The social climb of Luqman from Ethiopian slave to freebooter, seer, king and 'Prophet' could be significant, but at this point it is pertinent to enquire what he represented to a Meccan living in AD 600, besides being a wise man.

The pre-Islamic Luqman was brother to a pagan hero, Shaddad Ibn Ad (of whom more later), but Luqman was pious and did not reject the warnings of the 'Prophet' named Hud, whom God sent to his people, the Adites, a powerful nation supposed to have lived immediately after the time of Noah. Luqman survived an appalling catastrophe which God visited upon his people and was rewarded with the life-span of seven vultures. He reigned as king and law-giver over the second Adites, who were troglodytes (cave-dwellers), yet he also began to build the Marib dam in the Yemen. His role as 'palace-king' became fused with Luqman as 'troglodyte-seer' and with Luqman as heroic freebooter, intent upon slaying his nephew or his son, yet invariably outwitted by them. He was a giant, jealous of his wife. He combined incompatible patterns of behaviour, aspects of both raw nature and peasant and urban culture. Similar figures in Greek mythology are the Centaurs and the Cyclopes.

Iram of the Columns

Shaddad Ibn Ad, Luqman's brother, was at times confused with the builders of the Egyptian pyramids.

He is best known as the 'titan' whose attempts to construct a columned paradise garden on earth, Iram of the Columns, were ruined by an Almighty 'shout'. Shaddad and his Adites were doomed to destruction, but the henge-city survived as an elusive unseen goal, hidden in the Yemen, Palmyra, Damascus, Alexandria or some remote locality. It was allegedly rediscovered by a cameleer after the Prophet's death, during the reign of the Caliph Muawiya (661–80).

This tale, which finds a modest place in the *Thousand and One Nights*, is originally of pre-Islamic date. It is possible, by comparing references from Abbasid accounts (for example, the *Iklil* of Hamdani, about 945) in which Umayyad verse of the 8th century is quoted, to see evolving the concept of Iram as the abode of a beloved on the one hand, and as the goal of endeavour on the other.

The account of Iram by Wahb Ibn Munabbih, a converted South Arabian Jew who died in 732, in his much edited book the *Kitab al-Tijan fi muluk Himyar* is among the earliest:

When Shaddad Ibn Ad began his reign he gathered his troops together, he being a man of will and determination. He travelled, trampling the earth beneath his feet. He reached Greater Armenia. There he slew every rebel and upriser. Next he crossed the Euphrates towards the east-lands. He reached their remotest limit. Anyone who stood in his way perished. Then he passed over the low plain of Samarqand until he arrived in the land of Tibet. Then he turned aside to Armenia and advanced in depth and with care. Next he crossed to Damascus and reached the Maghrib [North Africa]. He left many traces there, until he arrived at the Atlantic Ocean. He built cities and occupied citadels with their cisterns and store-houses. He stayed two hundred years in the Maghrib. After, he returned to the east.

He was too proud to enter Ghumdan, so he went to Marib. In it he built the noble palace which is named by some story-tellers Iram of the Columns. In the Yemen he left not pearl, nor jewel, nor carnelian, nor onyx, nor likewise in the land of Babylon. In every direction he sent the order for the gathering of that treasure, and he hoarded the riches of the world, gold, silver, iron and tin, copper and lead. There he built his palace. He adorned and embellished it with all that precious stone and wealth. He made its floor of white and red marble, other colours besides. Beneath it he placed cisterns and conduits down which poured the water of the [Marib] dam. It was a palace unlike any other built in the world. Then Shaddad Ibn Ad died after having lived five hundred years. A cave was dug for him in Jabal Shibam. He was buried there, and all his wealth was placed there.

In this passage there is no mention of the divine judgment on the city. In the Quran (*Sura* 89 'of the Dawn'), however, it is emphasized to the exclusion of all else. 'Hast thou not seen how thy Lord did with Ad? with Iram of the Columns? the like of which has not been created in the land?'

Solomon and Bilqis

King Solomon, who ruled Israel in the 10th century BC, became a legendary figure in Jewish, Christian and Muslim tradition, famed for his wisdom, his riches, his many wives and his power over spirits. The story that the Queen of Sheba came to visit him appears in the Old Testament (1 Kings, chapter 10). She came with a great retinue, with camels bearing spices, gold and precious stones, to test Solomon with hard questions. Solomon answered all the questions and the queen was so impressed with his wisdom that 'there was no more spirit in her' and she praised God who had made him king. The queen and Solomon exchanged costly presents and she returned to her own land.

According to Muslim tradition, the queen's name was Bilqis and she ruled in the Yemen, with her

King Solomon is the best example of an idealized Muslim Emperor. He is shown here in his court, surrounded by his courtiers, beasts and birds. The Islamic legends of Solomon show Persian influence.

The Queen of Sheba was brought to Solomon by the *jinn* and she was tested by him to see whether she was a true believer or whether she worshipped the sun. According to some Arabic accounts she returned to her homeland in the Yemen from Jerusalem and was visited by Solomon. He flew to her on his magic carpet which was carried by the winds. This painting of Solomon and the queen is Persian and is found among the poems of Farid al-Din Attar, 1472.

capital at Marib. A bird told Solomon, who understood the language of birds, that the queen possessed a splendid throne and reigned over a people who worshipped the sun instead of God. Solomon sent her a message: 'Do not rise up against me, but come to me resigned.' One of his attendant spirits offered to fetch him the queen's throne, but it was brought by one of his courtiers, who was deeply versed in the scriptures.

Solomon had the throne altered and when the Queen of Sheba came to him, she was asked if she recognized it. She did not, though she said it resembled her throne. Ushered in to Solomon's palace, she thought she was entering a pool of water and bared her legs. The supposed pool was a glass floor, a device employed by the king to see if the queen had hairy legs, as his spirits had told him. She had, and Solomon commanded the spirits to make a special preparation to remove the hair. According to some story-tellers, he then married her.

The legend, considerably modified, also appears in the Ethiopian chronicle Kebra Nagast (Glory of the Kings), which says that the son of Solomon and Makeda (the Ethiopian name for Bilqis) was Menelik I, the first ruler of Ethiopia. The Ethiopian dynasty claimed descent from Menelik.

In Arabian mythology Solomon and Bilqis are treated as a paired king and queen, both exceptional, who command the *jinn* between them. Solomon is their lord, but his control of them depends on his moral behaviour. Bilqis is a more problematic character. Her true faith is in doubt. She is a queen in a normally patrilineal royal succession. Of greater importance is her pedigree. On her father's side she is of the Himyarite Yemenite royal house. Her mother is a *jinniya*, whom her father rescued when she once took the form of a gazelle. Bilqis's hair-covered legs reveal her hybrid birth.

The Quran briefly introduces Solomon and the queen in the chapter 'of the Ant' (*Sura* 27). When the queen is asked if she recognizes her throne, this is a test to try her faith. Disbelief beguiles her: 'But that which she served beside God turned her away; verily she was of the unbelieving people. And it was said to her, "Enter the court", and when she saw it she reckoned it to be an abyss of water, and she uncovered her legs. Said he, "Verily it is a court paved with glass!" Said she, "My lord, I have wronged myself but I am resigned with Solomon to God, the Lord of the worlds!"'

The whole story, paraphrased in the Quran, has been powerful in stimulating the literary and artistic talent of the Muslim East. Muslims have been aware that Bilqis does not properly belong to Islam, and polemics against her supernatural origin are common among Muslim writers.

The legends of Alexander the Great seem to have inspired the exploits of a number of Arabian and non-Arabian warrior kings called Dhul-Qarnayn, one of whom is mentioned in the Quran. In this 14th-century Il-Khanid 'Mongol' painting, Iskandar (Alexander) is shown extending his realm into northern regions perpetually shrouded by fog beyond the Caucasus on the route to Gog and Magog.

The Quran does not name Bilqis, nor does it say that the queen married Solomon, a view common among the Jews at quite an early date. Compared with many eastern sources the Quranic reference is brief. It brings moral lessons to the fore and minimizes those aspects which are irrelevant to religion. Several themes emerge despite the brevity of the account. They include the test of faith, and the merit as well as the illusion of the senses (the glass court like water) for the discovery of the true faith. There are other themes more clearly alluded to in Quranic passages where Solomon alone is the central figure in the narrative.

The Two-Horned

Among the chapters of the Quran, *Sura* 18 'of the Cave' is the richest in the introduction of legendary elements. It is here that Dhul-Qarnayn ('the two-horned'), otherwise Alexander the Great, marches across the pages. The sources of the legend of Alexander are skilfully introduced to present a warrior-king, made mighty by God, his expeditions, his encounter with unbelievers while 'measuring' the earth, and his arrival in the far west where the sun sets in a hot and muddy spring. Then he turns eastward to a land of primitive troglodytes and marches north to the Eurasian steppes, where he erects a barrier of iron and brass between two mountains to protect the inhabitants against the incursions of Gog and Magog. The invaders fail to scale the barrier or break it, but Dhul-Qarnayn warns that on the Day of Judgment God will level it to the ground. His Herculean efforts provide only a temporary respite. Water sources, dykes, dams, solar symbols and the like are conspicuous in this story.

The closest parallel to the summary in the Quran is in the 6th-century Syriac version of Pseudo-Callisthenes (a book which was the core of the Romance of Alexander). As this *Sura* refers so clearly to legendary cycles in the Fertile Crescent and Persia, it is reasonable to assume that it was addressed to Meccan Jews, or if not Jews, then to pagans familiar with these non-Arabian sources. This having been said, there remains a cloud of ambiguities. The commentators disagree as to whom the 'two-horned' reference relates and since Pseudo-Callisthenes itself is a farrago of heterogeneous elements it is not always easy to be precise about where its substance ends, or at what point it becomes fused with ancient eastern, pagan Arabian or Persian material. Professor Philip Hitti once wrote: 'The pagan Arabian developed no mythology, no involved theology and no cosmology comparable to that of the Babylonians.'

The Water of Life

With its theory of a progressively disclosed revelation, Islam sometimes demanded a person fulfilling a mediatory function: mediatory, that is, in a situation where Deity, Prophet and humanity were locked in a complex situation of misunderstood message or an incomprehension of revelation.

If Aaron had not been the brother of Moses, a similar figure would have been discovered to assume his role. If al-Khidr ('the green') had not already existed in the Babylonian epic of Gilgamesh, in Jewish legends of Elijah, in Pseudo-Callisthenes or among South Arabian archetypes, then he would surely have appeared from some other quarter. As Merlin is related to King Arthur in the stories of the Round Table, so al-Khidr advises and leads Dhul-Qarnayn and his company of Yemenite knights. Al-Khidr is an adviser to Muslim mystics and he appears especially in myths in which dilemmas are resolved.

In the *Kitab al-Tijan* al-Khidr seems a different person. Absorbed into the Yemenite elaboration of Pseudo-Callisthenes, with its own heroes, kings and magicians, including Luqman, al-Khidr is now a counsellor, a warrior and in some respects 'a knight of the Quest', a searcher for the ultimate secrets of life. The story of al-Khidr finding the water of life illustrates the swelling body of romance, based on myth enhanced by contact between Arabs and non-Arab nations which formed the growing Muslim community.

ABOVE In this Nizami MS (1529–1530) Alexander has arrived at the source of the water of life. Al-Khidr is standing at the fountain.

OPPOSITE, BELOW Al-Khidr drinking the water of life. The scene is taken from the Persian *Shah-Nameh*, 1438.

Dhul-Qarnayn then followed a way and journeyed along the course of the Valley of Sand until he reached the darkness, where both night-time and day-time were alike. The spring of the sun lay behind him, and he traversed a valley where his horses and camels slipped and all those who were with him. They said, 'Oh, Dhul-Qarnayn, what is this?' He said to them, 'You are in a place where he who takes of it will repent, and he who holds back will also repent.' They travelled in it for many days, the valley turned them aside in an easterly direction. Above them was a white light which almost blinded them. They said to him, 'Oh, Dhul-Qarnayn, what is this valley we have crossed?' He said to them, 'The valley you have crossed is the Valley of the Ruby. He who takes of it will say – would that I had taken more, and he who taketh not will say – would that I had taken a little of it.''

Then he came to the white rock, and it almost took away their sight due to its light and radiation. The obscurity which they found was the effect of the illumination of the rock. Dhul-Qarnayn looked at one of the spurs of the rock, and he saw vultures [or eagles] upon it. He was amazed at the sight of them and the way they clung to that place . . .

Then Dhul-Qarnayn drew nigh to that rock in order to mount upon it. It shook, trembled and rumbled. He drew back from it, and it was motionless. He did this a second and a third time. Then al-Khidr approached it, and it was motionless. He climbed it, and he advanced, watched by Dhul-Qarnayn. Al-Khidr went up skywards until he vanished from sight. A voice from heaven called to him, 'Proceed onwards and drink, for verily it is the fount of life. Be made clean and pure, and then you will live until the day of the last trump, when all in heaven and earth will die, and you taste of final death.' So he advanced until he reached the summit of the rock and found a spring wherein descended heavenly water. He drank of it and was made pure and clean.

The City of Brass

In the 9th century there were in circulation Arabic tales of a city or tower of brass and copper, somewhere in Africa or Spain. It was located near the Pillars of Hercules (the Strait of Gibraltar) or near Cadiz or Algeciras, 'the island of al-Khidr'. This legend, fed by both Muslim and Christian stories, emerged as a key 'travel tale' in the *Thousand and One Nights*. In it appear not only ideas from earlier Arabic folk sources, but also all the Quranic characters we have discussed – Solomon, Bilqis (as Tadmura lying preserved in the city of enchantments), Dhul-Qarnayn (who has now turned into Musa Ibn Nusayr, the Arab conqueror of Spain), Shaddad Ibn Ad, the builder of Iram, and al-Khidr, who plays an elusive, mediatory and sometimes ambiguous role. The late account of al-Mustawfi of Qazwin (about 1340) demonstrates a fusion of Quranic-inspired myth and romance with heterogenous source material. Mingling the Quran with traditions of Solomon and Alexander the Great, it is a classic example of how Muslim tales evolved.

The City of Brass, which is one of the most wonderful constructions in the world, is of these parts. The circuit of its walls is four leagues, and their height to the battlements is more than fifty ells, and there are no gates. Some say that Alexander the Great built it, but the more reliable account is that it was constructed by the demons at the command of King Solomon – upon whom be peace – and this is the view given by the commentators in explanation of the verse of the Quran (*Sura* 34) where God most high says – And we made a fountain of molten brass to flow for Solomon, and of the *jinn* were some who worked in his presence, by the will of his Lord. The walls of this city were made from that fountain of molten brass. But few of the children of men have ever been there; but in the time of the Umayyad

Caliphs one man arrived there, and on his return he gave the Caliph an account of the place.

The military conquests of the Arabs led to an exchange of literary ideas and folklore. The process started with writers who witnessed the advent of Islam and who were known at the Umayyad court, commencing with the Caliph Muawiya. Beginning in the 8th century with Wahb Ibn Munabbih and Ibn Ishaq, followed by al-Kalbi in the 9th century and al-Hamdani in the 10th, the Arabian, and particularly the Yemeni, school of literary 'archeologists' reintroduced the myths of commentators on the Quran as a tool of the biography of the Prophet and in a growing body of fable which integrated the increasing cosmopolitanism of Islamic culture.

As Islam approached the Mamluk era (the beginning of the 13th century), a plethora of romances subordinated the Quranic content to socially determined intrusions fabricated and imported from every corner of oriental legend. Tales from Persia and India were employed. Quranic stories were resited, in the west and the east, and were fused with material from Africa, south-east Asia and the Far East. The repertoire includes Yemenite myths in West Africa, stories of Alexander the Great's adventures told in Malaya, and the reappearance of Solomon and Bilqis in the Kebra Nagast of Ethiopia.

Ali and the Ogre's Head

A feature of late medieval Muslim legends was the cycles in which the central characters were the Prophet and his Companions, his faithful supporters. Ali, the Prophet's son-in-law, was particularly popular, especially in Persia. Among these legends is the tale of Ali and the Ogre's Head (Ras al-Ghul), which also appears in Swahili literature in Africa.

The composition of the legend is attributed to a certain Abul Hasan al-Bakri, who lived in Iraq at the end of the 13th century. The Ogre's Head was an evil king of the Yemen. His real name was Mukhariq, but he was also nicknamed Abul-Lain, 'father of the accursed'. The name attributed to the god of the Saracens in medieval Europe, Appolin (later Apollyon), is possibly explained by this nickname.

Mukhariq slays his father, seizes the throne and rules despotically, armed with the magic sword Al-Samsama, the invincible weapon of the Yemenite

ABOVE The Copper City is captured by the army of Alexander. Its citizens are automata. The episode is from the Oriental Alexander Romance. In later Arabian tales the city was beseiged by an Arab commander, Musa Ibn Nusayr.

RIGHT Many are the stories about the exploits of the caliph Ali Ibn Abi Talib, the Prophet's son-in-law. Here he is shown on the shoulders of Muhammad, destroying the idols in the Meccan Kaaba.

BELOW Amr Ibn Madi Karib, paragon of Yemenite knights, is fighting Malik. Amr is one of the greatest warriors in the legendary literature of the early Islamic conquests.

warrior Amr Ibn Madi Karib. He adores the god Faresh, who speaks to him in fire and thunder and whose image is housed in a temple of emerald, marble and sandalwood. Mukhariq has seven fortresses and his golden palace is in the seventh.

A Yemenite woman complains to the Prophet. She and her family have embraced Islam, and because they have renounced paganism her kinsfolk have been tortured, raped and crucified. The Prophet heeds the woman's demand for just retribution. He summons his followers and his Companions are entrusted with the task of conquering the Yemen. The commander is Ali, armed with his sword, Dhul-Faqar.

The story which follows introduces a series of tales within a tale, escapades and ruses employed to defeat the devilish Ogre's Head. Humorous incidents and buffoonery relieve the narrative of the mighty struggle in which many an iron-clad knight meets his end. As the conflict grows fiercer, the Prophet Muhammad summons the hero Amr Ibn Madi Karib himself to his assistance. The hero is armed with a spear 30 cubits in length and a huge sword.

The first valley is reached and captured. As the Muslims advance the obstacles grow greater. Mukhariq is aided by a blind archer called al-Sakafi, who has a huge bow of hazel-wood cut from a tree watered with milk. It takes four men to carry the bow, which always shoots straight. Yet al-Sakafi fails to hit Ali, and he breaks his bow in seven pieces, much to the grief of Mukhariq.

In the end idolatry is uprooted. Aided by the Prophet's prayers, swarms of bees, gunpowder or Greek fire, Ali eventually achieves the reduction of the seventh citadel. Mukhariq, the Ogre's Head, is split asunder, and his offspring are slain or converted to the True Faith.

THE WEST

CHAPTER ELEVEN

GREECE

The whole of Greek literature and art provides a field for the study of Greek myths. With such an extensive, varied and relatively sophisticated body of evidence, it is hardly surprising that no one theory produced by anthropologists who have studied tribal communities serves as a satisfactory explanation for Greek mythology. These myths have no one form and no single function.

The poems of Homer and Hesiod, the earliest Greek literature, present different categories of myth, contrasting sharply with each other in purpose, spirit and substance, but sharing a systematic complexity. The avowed aim of Hesiod's *Theogony* is to tell how Earth, Sky and Sea came to be; how the gods were born of them, 'givers of good things'; how the gods divided up their plenty and occupied Olympos. The myth starts with primal nature-personification, inherited from Mesopotamian or other pre-Greek traditions. Sky (Ouranos) begot out of Earth (Ge) the older generation of the gods, named Titans, but he would not withdraw himself from Earth to allow her to give birth. The primeval separation of Sky and Earth was achieved by the Titan Kronos with his mother's aid, when he castrated Ouranos with a great sickle. So began the strife and successions of the gods.

For a time the Titans held sway, ruled by Kronos and his consort Rhea. But Kronos too feared a usurper, and swallowed his children. Rhea tricked him, concealing Zeus and giving Kronos a stone to swallow instead, and Zeus forced Kronos to disgorge the other gods, who emerged full-grown. They overwhelmed the Titans, aided by Earth's monstrous offspring, the Hundred-Armed Giants with Fifty Heads. Zeus's own attempt to prevent the birth of offspring failed. Although he swallowed his consort Metis, she still brought forth the terrible warrior-goddess Athena. After this, Zeus coupled with many goddesses and mortal women, siring some children who were gods and some who were mortal heroes.

From the first origin of Earth and the gods, Hesiod explains how the present world-government came to be established. The kernel of the story is the tale of the Titans and the younger gods, how Zeus overthrew Kronos and came to rule the world from Olympos. This story was borrowed, not invented by Greeks. The tale of the younger generation overthrowing the older gods, including details like castration with a sickle and swallowing a stone, is found in myths from western Asia and Mesopotamia, before 1000 BC. What is new, and characteristic of Greek myths in the earliest sources, is the systematic complexity with which disparate material of various types is united to give an understanding of a comprehensible world-order.

The varying offspring of Earth, the great generative Mother, are examples of this process. She brings forth the starry Sky, 'to be a secure dwelling-place for the blessed gods', the Ocean and the Hills, 'graceful haunts of the Nymphs', but also the one-eyed Kyklopes (Cyclopes), the Hundred-Armed Giants and the late-born monster Typhoeos (Typhon). Birth came even from the severed genitals of Ouranos cast into the sea, producing a spume in which grew Aphrodite, 'the foam-born goddess', attended by Eros (Passion). Active powers like Night and Day were involved in this period of generative activity. Night brought forth Day, Sleep and Dreams, but also Death, Pain and Strife. Items like this tend to be presented in bald lists, whose main function is to make the systematic connections already referred to. The two active motifs are those of constant strife and generation.

The *Theogony* is not the origin but the end-product of a process of systematic rationalization

In myth, as in cult, Athena was a warrior. 'Dread is she,' says the Homeric Hymn to the goddess, 'and with Ares she loves deeds of war, the sack of cities and the shouting and strife. She it is who protects the host in their going and in their return.'

LEFT The *tholos*, or rotunda, at Delphi, built *c.*390 BC and standing in a precinct dedicated to Athena. Like most Greek sanctuaries, it is imposingly situated.

BELOW Small statuette of Athena, from the Akropolis at Athens. The goddess, who was the guardian of Athens, is shown in a threatening pose as a warrior. She originally held a spear in her raised right hand and a shield in her left. The figure is less than 30 cm high. Bronze, *c.*490 BC.

SIMPLIFIED FAMILY TREE OF THE GODS

Ouranos = Ge
Sky | *Earth*

Aphrodite

Ouranos *Sky* | **the Hills** | **Pontos** *Sea*

Okeanos | **Iapetos** | **Other Titans** | **Rhea = Kronos** | **Kyklopes** *Cyclopes* | **Hundred-Armed Giants**

Prometheus

Metis = Zeus | **Zeus = Hera** | **Hades = Persephone** | **Poseidon** | **Hestia** | **Demeter = Zeus**

Deukalion | **Persephone**

Athena | **Apollon** | **Artemis** | **Hermes** | **Dionysos** | **Hebe** | **Ares** | **Hephaistos = Aphrodite**

which brings together different types of stories, anthropomorphic gods, fearsome monsters, powers of nature and powers which today we think of as 'abstracts'. These powers and stories were part of an oral poetic tradition inherited by Hesiod. He was not a mythopoeic (myth-making) thinker, but an organizer and selector of traditional material.

Myths as Explanations

In the person of Prometheus in the *Works and Days*, if anywhere in Greek mythology, appears a figure beloved by anthropologists and others, the 'culture hero', who at the dawn of time won for man certain essential advantages of his civilized existence (see also ARMENIA). The Titan Prometheus angered Zeus with men by cheating him of his portion of animal-meat when sacrifice was instituted. This provides the validating charter for the Greek sacrificial ritual, in which the bones and fat were offered to the gods and the meat was kept for human consumption. In retaliation Zeus took fire from men, but Prometheus stole it back. Zeus took his revenge by instructing Hephaistos, craftsman of the Olympians, to fashion woman from clay. Athena decked her with fine clothes and flowers, but she was given a deceitful nature. Woman was a specious gift from the gods to men, in fact a plague and a curse, and the subtlety of the curse was that man can be satisfied neither with her nor without her. This first woman was Pandora. She opened a jar which released ten thousand woes upon men, leaving only Hope behind. 'Before this men lived free from ills, hard toil and oppressive sickness.'

These stories account for fire, sacrifice, human toil and sickness by providing an imaginatively and emotionally satisfying explanation for them, based on the known world-order. Explanation alleviates the hardship by making it comprehensible. The story of woman as both a delight and a curse even hints at the kind of 'mediation of opposites' which, it has been argued, is the universal function of mythopoeic activity. Again, the stories are old, much older than Hesiod.

The Five Races of Man

The story of the Five Races of Man in the *Works and Days* similarly makes the toil of man comprehensible, and this was an obvious theme for Hesiod, who was a farmer, to concentrate on. The story of man is presented as one of continuous decline.

CHILDREN OF ZEUS

Zeus had numerous offspring by goddesses, Titanesses, nymphs and mortal women. The most important of them were:

Athena: by Metis (Thought), daughter of the Titan Okeanos

the Horai (Hours), Eunomia (Order), Dike (Justice), Eirene (Peace) and **the Moirai (Fates):** by Themis (Righteousness), a Titaness

the Graces: by Eurynome, daughter of Okeanos

Kore or **Persephone, queen of the underworld:** by Demeter, Zeus's sister

the Muses: by Mnemosyne (Memory), a Titaness

Apollon and Artemis: by Leto, daughter of the Titan Koios

Hebe, Ares and **Eileithyia, goddess of childbirth:** by Hera, Zeus's consort

Hermes: by Maia, niece of Prometheus

Argos, founder of the city of Argos: by Niobe, a mortal woman

Lakedaimon, founder of Sparta: by Taygete, niece of Prometheus

Dionysos: by Semele, a Theban princess

Herakles: by Alkmene, a princess of Argos, to whom Zeus appeared in the form of her husband, Amphitryon

Perseus: by Danae, a princess of Argos, to whom Zeus appeared as a shower of gold

Minos, King of Crete: by Europa, a Phoenician princess, to whom Zeus appeared as a bull

Polydeukes (Pollux) and **Helen of Troy:** by Leda, a queen of Sparta, to whom Zeus appeared as a swan: Kastor, brother of Polydeukes, and Klytaimnestra, wife of Agamemnon, were children of Leda by her human husband, Tyndarus of Sparta

ABOVE Zeus about to hurl the thunderbolt. Zeus was the most powerful of the immortals. According to Hesiod's *Theogony*, the heavens and the earth reeled when he battled with the fiery serpent Typhoeus, employing 'thunder, lightning and the fiery thunderbolt'. So great was his prowess that the gods pressed him to rule over them. Attic oil-pot, *c.*450 BC.

RIGHT Marble statuette, only 45 cm high, of Aphrodite bathing. Aphrodite was the giver of fertility in sexual generation. In myth she inspired 'sweet passion' in gods and men, beguiling even Zeus to mate with mortal women. Among her notable victims in the myths were Helen, for whose sake the Greeks fought at Troy, and Medeia, the enchantress who aided Jason and the Argonauts.

Five races of man have lived on the earth. The first was the golden race, created by the Titans when Kronos ruled. They lived in ease and peace, free of toil, disease and old age, and when death came to them, as peacefully as sleep, they became benevolent *daimones* (spirits) living on the earth, 'well-disposed, warding off evils, guardians of men, givers of plenty'. The men of the second or silver race, made by the Olympian gods, were removed by Zeus because they were foolish and would not honour the gods. They became underworld spirits, 'the blessed ones beneath earth'.

The last three races were fashioned in turn by Zeus. The third or bronze race was fierce and warlike, and destroyed itself in internecine violence, passing unsung to 'the house of decay', the underworld ruled by 'chill Hades'. The fourth race, to which no metal is assigned, was that of the great heroes or demi-gods who fought at Troy and Thebes. Many of them did not die but were translated to the Isles of the Blessed at the ends of the earth, where they live free from care and sorrow, ruled by Kronos. The present race of men is the fifth race, also destined to pass away. It is the iron race, never resting from labour, born to trouble, sorrow and death, but with some good mingled with its evils.

'Would that I were not among the men of the fifth race,' says Hesiod, 'but had either died earlier or been born later.' In fact the reference to the Greek heroes of Troy and Thebes interrupts the tale of decline and betrays the composite nature of the story, which is used by Hesiod to urge his brother to a life of honest toil.

The *Catalogue of Women* attempts to trace systematically the relationships between Greek heroes, including those referred to above as belonging to the fourth race of men. Their descent is traced back to the founders (eponymous ancestors) of the Greek tribes – Aeolos, Ion and Doros – and to Hellen himself, who founded the race of the Hellenes (Greeks). Hellen was the son of Deukalion, son of Prometheus. Deukalion and his wife Pyrrha were survivors of the Flood, which was sent by Zeus to destroy mankind (the oldest known form of the Flood story is Mesopotamian).

Gods and Men in Homer

With Hesiod we are probably as near as possible to the mythopoeic form, but he hardly preserves that dreamlike dislocation in narrative which belongs to the tales of many tribal communities or even to

Achilles is about to kill Penthesileia, the Amazon queen at Troy. A painting of the 5th century BC at Olympia showed Achilles holding up Penthesileia as she expired. Later sources explain that he was struck with passion for her. The *Iliad* relates the tradition that the Amazons were a tribe of female warriors. Large Athenian amphora, *c.* 540 BC, found at Vulci in Etruria.

some Mesopotamian myths, and which gives a symbolic depth and fantasy to the story concerned. This is even more true of the heroic saga or folk-tale of the Greek epic tradition, notably the *Iliad* and *Odyssey* of Homer. This too is the end-product of several hundred years of oral poetry. It has a historical kernel, which goes back partly to the Greek Bronze Age or Mycenaean period (about 1400–1200 BC) and partly to the Dark Age (about 1000–850 BC). Any historical events have been magnified and distorted beyond recognition by a poetic tradition which aimed at the glorification of the great heroes of the past. The *Iliad* is saga. There are no child-swallowings, castrations or hideous monsters. The poems are about warrior-aristocrats who delight in war, and who are supported or opposed at every turn by the Olympian gods. The setting is an incident during the tenth year of the Greek siege of Troy. At the human level the theme is the wounded honour of Achilles, whose war-prize, the slave-girl Briseis, is taken by Agamemnon, overall commander of the Greek contingents. His wrath, initially justified, is nursed so bitterly that he later spurns generous recompense and causes the death of his closest friend Patroklos at the hands of the Trojans. His revenge on the Trojans is to kill their champion, the prince Hektor, and to leave his corpse to rot unburied. The pleas of Hektor's father, King Priam of Troy, eventually make him relent. But the structure of the story is much looser than this, and many other heroes perform notable deeds of honour and prowess – Menelaos and Paris, Diomedes, Aias (Ajax), Odysseus, Idomeneus.

The society of the gods in their palaces on Mount Olympos reflects that of the heroes, for the gods are men in form and passion, who quarrel, fight, make love and feast. They also take sides in no uncertain manner, as they have their own favourites among the heroes. It is a hard task for Zeus, who rules on Olympos, to control the other gods, whose characters are sharply delineated – Hera, scheming consort of Zeus; Athena, his strong-minded and martial daughter; Poseidon, Lord of the Seas, Earth-Shaker; Aphrodite, who possesses the magic girdle of infatuation and inspires in Helen her passion for the Trojan prince Paris; Hephaistos, lame master-craftsman of the gods, a figure of ridicule on Olympos.

The stature of these gods can be illustrated by a description of Poseidon as he joins the battle. 'He rose and came striding down the rocky slope. The high hills and forests trembled beneath the deathless feet of the descending god. He took three strides and with the fourth reached Aigai, his goal, where his famous palace built of gleaming gold stands deep in the lagoon and will stand for ever. There he harnessed to his chariot his two swift horses, who had brazen hooves and flowing golden manes. He clothed himself in gold, picked up his well-made golden whip, mounted his chariot and drove out across the waves.'

The systematic and detailed presentation of the ebullient Immortals, as the gods are called, is a wholesome achievement of imaginative rationalism. Gods and heroes together form a rich world of

Odysseus and his companions blinding the Kyklops Polyphemos. In the *Odyssey* Polyphemos is a one-eyed giant, a solitary and unsocial monster who thinks himself greater than Zeus and the gods. He traps the Greeks in the enormous cavern where he lives alone, and kills and eats two of them each day. Odysseus befuddles him with wine and drives a heated wooden stake through his single eye. The Homeric Kyklopes enjoy the fruits of their land without toil, and their savagery contrasts with the 'innocence' of nature. Hesiod told of other Kyklopes, who gave Zeus the weapons of thunder and lightning with which he defeated the Titans. Large amphora, *c.*520 BC.

THE TWELVE OLYMPIAN GODS

By at least the 5th century BC the twelve great deities of Olympos were regarded as a group and there was an altar to 'the Twelve', collectively, in Athens. The names vary from place to place and time to time, but the generally accepted list is:

Zeus: chief of the gods, god of the sky, storm, lightning and thunder, but with many other spheres of influence

Hera: sister and consort of Zeus, goddess of marriage and all phases of the life of women

Poseidon: 'earth-shaker', god of the sea and of earthquakes

Demeter: goddess of agriculture, crops and the produce of the earth

Apollon: god of light, reason, inspiration, the arts, prophecy and oracles, healing: connected with the sun

Artemis: goddess of wild beasts and hunting

Ares: 'the shield-piercer', 'sacker of towns', god of war

Aphrodite: 'laughter-loving', 'born of the sea-foam', goddess of love and beauty

Hermes: herald and messenger of the gods, god of commerce

Athena: warlike goddess of wisdom, protector of cities, patron of craftsmen

Hephaistos: the lame smith and craftsman of Olympos

Hestia: goddess of the hearth and home

Dionysos, god of ecstasy, fertility and wine, had taken Hestia's place as one of the Twelve in Athens in the 5th century BC.

Hades, god of the underworld and the dead, was a brother of Zeus, but did not live on Olympos.

Hebe, daughter of Zeus and Hera, was the cup-bearer of Olympos, but was not considered one of the Twelve.

LEFT Parody on a vase with Kirke and Odysseus shown as two grotesques. Kirke was an enchantress, who delayed Odysseus's voyage first by magically transforming his companions into pigs and then through her personal charms. From Thebes, *c.*430 BC.

BELOW Kirke warned Odysseus against the Sirens and this vase shows his encounter with them, as described in the *Odyssey*. Odysseus made his crew stuff their ears with wax and had himself bound to the mast, so that he could hear the Sirens' song. 'Sweetly they sang; my heart longed to go on listening, and I bade my comrades untie me . . . But they leaned forward and rowed.' The bones of men spell-bound by their song lay rotting in the meadow where the Sirens sat. From Thebes, *c.*430 BC.

characters whose honour is sensitive and whose passions are quickly roused. The heroes differ from the gods in their mortality and their dread of old age with its loss of vigour. The Immortals not only live for ever, they never grow old.

There are many hints in the *Iliad* of stories about other heroes, like Herakles (Hercules) or Theseus. Complex as it is, the *Iliad* selects from a much richer tradition. One sub-plot referred to from time to time is the Judgment of Paris. Aphrodite's partiality for the Trojan prince Paris dates back to the time when he judged between Hera, Athena and Aphrodite, and found Aphrodite the fairest. Aphrodite partly won him to this decision by promising him the love of the beautiful Helen, wife of Menelaos. It is to win back Helen that the Greek forces have besieged Troy.

The *Odyssey*, like the *Iliad*, may be regarded simply as an entertaining story. It has traces of serious problem-solving myth in it, but they are heavily overlaid by the purpose of the poetic tradition, to glorify Odysseus. They appear as elements in folk-tale motifs, stories of giant-killings and magical enchantments. Saga is still here in the tale of how Odysseus returns home to Ithaca from the siege of Troy and overcomes his enemies, but even this is a folk-tale motif, as are the hero's son Telemachos, who searches for his lost father, and his loyal wife Penelope, who remains faithful though plagued by suitors. The element of heroic saga lies not in the plot but in the diction and values of the poem. Captured by Polyphemos, the man-eating Kyklops (Cyclops), Odysseus outwits the monster and blinds him by thrusting a stake into his single eye. The sorceress Kirke (Circe), who transforms men into animals, falls in love with Odysseus and helps him. Odysseus escapes the Sirens, whose sweet song lures ships and sailors to destruction on the rocks, by stopping the ears of his crew and binding himself to the mast. These tales are not told so much to make some point about monsters or witches, not even to show a culture hero creating civilization from disorder, but simply as notable exploits of the wily hero.

Prowess and Honour

Bards recited the exploits of heroes like Achilles and Odysseus at the great religious festivals to Zeus, Poseidon, Apollon and the other gods. The Greeks were by no means a race of detached philosophers. They were deeply affected by the examples of heroic

A seated minstrel pours the libation due to Apollon, master of the lyre. The raven associated with the god perches nearby. In myth Apollon was the archer-god who rained arrows on the Greeks before Troy, decimating them with plague until his wrath was appeased by sacrifice and cleansing rituals. He was also the giver of the lyre and minstrelsy to men, and his 'golden lyre' entertained the gods on Olympos. Cup, *c.*470 BC.

excellence or suffering which these traditional myths offered. Songs praising the exploits of the gods were used side by side with those praising heroes for their prowess. In fact 'prowess' is the key to a whole range of Greek values and institutions. Epic poetry honours both heroes and gods for their prowess, and in cult also the Greeks 'honoured' the Olympians. This is the literal meaning of the word normally translated 'to worship'. Thus hymns sung at festivals in praise of the exploits of the gods were meaningful in fundamental ethical and spiritual terms to the Greek community.

Thirty-three such hymns attributed to Homer survive. The longer ones are sung in praise of Apollon, Demeter, Hermes and Aphrodite. The Pythian hymn to Apollon sings of the Muses of Olympos, who 'hymn the unending gifts the gods enjoy, and the sufferings of men, all that they endure from the deathless gods, and how they live witless and helpless and cannot find healing for death or defence against old age'. Such thoughts are constant themes of Greek poetry. Apollon is praised for his skill with the lyre and bow. He 'delights the hearts' of the Olympians with his songs, while the Graces dance, linked hand in hand. The status and powers of the gods – their prowess – are thus contrasted with those of men.

The feats of Hermes include a raid on Apollon's cattle and the fact that he succeeds in cheating Apollon earns him the status of Lord of Flocks and Cattle. The hymn concludes, in a cheerful manner, that the god profits men a little, but mostly cheats and deceives them. This tale reflects the cattle-raiding exploits of Greek princes in the Dark Age. It won the approval of the heroic age, but caused moral problems later, as did the amorous conquests of the gods among mortal women.

Some features of the hymns clearly originated in Greek chthonic rituals, in which earth-spirits and the dreaded powers of the underworld were placated. This darker side of Greek religion was a cult of appeasement and its rituals were quite unlike the 'honours' given to the Olympians. The Pythian hymn relates how Apollon had to overcome a great serpent at Pytho (Delphi) in order to establish his shrine there. It is typical for an earth-spirit to be manifested in the form of a serpent. Perhaps the story helps to explain why Apollon shared this shrine with Dionysos, the daimon (spirit or god) of frenzy, and why Apollon's priestess there, the Pythia, prophesied in trance.

The Exploits of Herakles

It is not possible to present the whole body of heroic Greek myths from a common source as early as Homer or Hesiod. Indeed different poets, and even the same poet in different passages, preserve varying traditions. The ones about Herakles are peculiarly complex. The serious mythical elements absorbed into the tales of his exploits include conflicts with primal monsters, an ambivalence in his own nature – he is prone to fits of bestial frenzy – and his relation to death and the kingdom of the dead. Hesiod refers to several of his adventures. In the *Iliad* he is said to have descended into the underworld and brought back Kerberos (Cerberus), the hound of Hades. Even so, 'Not even the mighty Herakles escaped death, though he was dear to Zeus.' But other brief comments in Hesiod and Homer say that Herakles was translated to Olympos when he had 'performed his great task', and there he feasts with the gods, like them not subject to old age or death, and wed to 'trim-ankled' Hebe.

From the many adventures of Herakles, twelve came to be selected as the tasks imposed on him by Eurystheus, King of Mykenai (Mycenae). They were depicted at the temple of Zeus at Olympia, about 560 BC. Eurystheus and Herakles were cousins and the story was that, before they were born, Hera persuaded Zeus to swear that the younger of the two should be subject to the other. Zeus thought Herakles, who was his own son, would be born first, but the jealous Hera hastened the birth of Eurystheus and he was born before Herakles. Eurystheus feared and envied Herakles and hoped to destroy him by imposing on him twelve impossibly difficult and dangerous tasks. Herakles, however, completed all of them successfully.

1. He killed the lion of Nemea, which was invulnerable to wounds, by knocking it unconscious with his club and then throttling it. He skinned it and afterwards always wore the skin round his shoulders. Eurystheus was so frightened when he saw him that he hid himself in a large pot from then on whenever Herakles appeared.
2. He destroyed the Hydra, the many-headed serpent of the marshes of Lerna.
3. He brought Eurystheus the Keryneian Hind, famous for its swiftness and its golden horns.
4. He netted and brought to Eurystheus the huge wild boar of Mount Erymanthos.
5. He killed the flesh-eating birds of Lake Stymphalos in Arkadia.
6. He cleaned the stables of Augeias in one day, by running a river through them.
7. He caught the wild bull which was laying waste to Crete.
8. He brought Eurystheus the horses of Diomedes, which ate human flesh.
9. He obtained the girdle of Hippolyte, Queen of the Amazons, the warrior-women.
10. He killed the three-headed monster Geryon, who lived near the sunset.
11. He went down to the underworld, seized the many-headed dog Kerberos and dragged him up to earth.
12. He killed the dragon which guarded the golden apples in the garden of the Hesperides and carried off the apples.

King Eurystheus of Mykenai hoped to destroy Herakles by imposing on him twelve impossibly difficult and dangerous tasks.

ABOVE Herakles, who wears the skin of the Nemean lion, attacking the flesh-eating Stymphalian birds with a sling. In other exploits he uses an equally primitive weapon, a club. Amphora from Vulci, *c.* 550 BC.

LEFT Herakles has captured the huge Erymanthian boar and plunges it into an enormous Bronze Age *pithos*, or storage-jar, in which the terrified Eurystheus has taken refuge. Amphora from Vulci, *c.* 510 BC.

ABOVE Formerly thought to represent Herakles, this coin is now known to show Iamos, son of Apollon, who was nourished at birth by snakes. The type is almost identical with coins on which the infant Herakles strangles the serpents which Hera sent to kill him. Gold stater, coin of Zakynthos, *c*.510 BC.

Hera was the implacable foe of Herakles in his exploits, Athena his constant ally. It was in fact a trick of Hera's which subjected Herakles to Eurystheus until his great labours were done. She had even sent two serpents to kill him as a child, but he strangled them. Clearly he well deserved such tributes as 'mighty Herakles, terrible and strong' or 'lion-hearted Herakles', which the Greek poets gave him.

Besides the famous Twelve Labours, another exploit of Herakles was against Troy and is mentioned in the *Iliad*. He rescued the daughter of the Trojan king, Laomedon, from a sea-beast, but later sacked Troy when the promised reward, the renowned horses of Laomedon, was not forthcoming. He had curious and recurrent dealings with the Kentauroi (Centaurs), beasts with the body of a horse but the chest and face of a man. In his relations with these bestial creatures, whose savage passions are quickly roused by the smell of wine or the sight of a woman, Herakles is once more the triumphant hero typical of early Greek poetry, who wins acclaim for his prowess and is an inspiring example of great strength and success.

It is abundantly clear that our earliest sources for the traditional stories of the Greeks (about 700 BC) inherited tales which go back in some form to the Mycenaeans of 600 years or so earlier. It has been suggested that the 'political activities' of Herakles – his relations with various princes of the Mycenaean Peloponnese – demonstrate that some of these stories were originally about a prince of Tiryns, who may perhaps have been a real man. Six of the tasks performed for Eurystheus, King of Mykenai (Mycenae), are located in the Peloponnese. The exploits against Geryon, Kerberos and Hades indicate something quite different: the constant interest of the Greeks in the meaning of death. There are indications in the relations of Herakles with the Centaurs of far earlier preoccupations, which belong to a pre-literate culture concerned with such things as the cooking of food and the use of fire. All this will suffice to indicate the problems of 'origins' and 'strata' in myths. This is not to lose sight of the fact that for the Greeks of the 6th and 5th centuries BC Herakles was the greatest heroic example of strength and prowess, of god-like powers which overcame tremendous obstacles and won for him immortality on Olympos. He alone bridged the seemingly impassable gulf between the short and fateful life of man and the unending splendour of the gods.

BELOW Perseus has cut off the Gorgon's head and has hidden it in a bag. Athena stands by. Medusa is not usually depicted so mildly but is often represented as a fearsome monster. Water-jar, *c*.460 BC, found at Capua.

Perseus and the Gorgon

Herakles, it was said, was descended from Perseus and sailed with the Argo. Thus the Greek poets forged their systematic links between different traditional stories. Perseus was the son of Zeus, who impregnated Danae in a glittering shower of gold, though she was imprisoned in a bronze chamber underground. Mother and child were set adrift on the sea in a chest, but came safely to Seriphos, a rocky isle where Perseus grew to manhood. Then King Polydektes conceived a passion for Danae, and sent Perseus on a quest which was thought impossible to achieve, to fetch back the head of the Gorgon Medusa, whose gaze transfixed the beholder, turning him to stone. But Perseus forced the Old Grey Sisters (Graiai) to tell him how to secure magical equipment – winged sandals which enabled him to fly, a hat that rendered him invisible and a bag in which to put the Gorgon's head. Athena advised him to overcome Medusa by looking not at her but at her reflection in his shield. In this way he cut off her head.

Returning from this adventure, Perseus came to the land of King Kepheus, where he rescued the princess Andromeda from a sea-beast, so winning her hand. A recalcitrant suitor was transfixed by a glimpse of Medusa's head, as indeed was Polydektes when Perseus came back to Seriphos. He and Andromeda became rulers of Tiryns. This story is little more than a magical adventure, a folk-tale in which enchantments overcome the monster and fine deeds win the fair lady.

Jason and the Argonauts

The quest which is intended to get rid of a rival or stumbling-block, but which rebounds on the plotter, is a common theme of this 'adventure story' genre of Greek myths. It occurs again in the story of Jason,

FAMILY TREE OF PERSEUS AND HERAKLES

Abas
King of Argos

Akrisios **Proitos**

Kepheus **Zeus = Danae**

Andromeda = Perseus

Alkaios **Elektryon** **Sthenelos**

Amphitryon = Alkmene = Zeus **Eurystheus**

Herakles

the Voyage of the Argo and the Golden Fleece (see ARMENIA). The first detailed account is that of Pindar and its spirit is the traditional Homeric one, which hymns the famous deeds of heroes past. The strength and god-like form of Jason are praised and his appearance is compared with that of Apollon. The Immortals aid him and he in turn relies on them. Sent in quest of the Golden Fleece by his crafty uncle, who hopes he will never return, he overcomes monsters, fire-breathing bulls and an enormous serpent, and successfully completes his mission.

Jason, son of Aison, was a prince of the true royal line of Iolkos in Thessaly, but the kingdom had been usurped by his uncle, Pelias. Jason was trained to manhood, strength and wisdom by Cheiron, the good Centaur. He claimed his birthright from the usurper, King Pelias, but the king, hoping to be rid of him for good, craftily induced him to bring from far Kolchis the famous Golden Fleece, the magical fleece of a golden ram. Jason gathered about him the flower of Greece, a band of heroes including Herakles, the brothers Kastor and Polydeukes, and Orpheus (who were no doubt added to the original exploit as the tale attracted to itself the names of famous heroes). In their ship, the Argo, favoured by Hera and Poseidon, the heroes mastered the Clashing Rocks, which threatened to crush them, and eventually reached Kolchis. Here King Aietes had possession of the Fleece, but Aphrodite inflamed passion for Jason in Medeia, the daughter of Aietes. Medeia helped Jason in his preliminary task, which was to yoke the fearsome oxen of Aietes and plough a deep, straight furrow with them. She gave him an ointment which was proof against the fiery breath and bronze hooves of these bulls, and he accomplished the task. The Fleece was guarded by a dragon or serpent, as large as a fifty-oared ship, but with Medeia's aid Jason overcame it and seized the Fleece. Jason and Medeia returned to Iolkos, where Medeia murdered Pelias and Jason became king.

The enchantress Medeia was able to rejuvenate the old by boiling and the use of herbs. Here she demonstrates her art on an old ram, but the other figure can hardly be Jason, as the inscription on the vase says. Perhaps it is Aison, his father, or even Pelias, his enemy, for the poets told varied and confusing stories. Some say she made Aison young once more, others that she tricked the daughters of Pelias into cutting him to pieces. In the tragedy *Medea* by Euripides, she is discarded by Jason, becomes almost unhinged and, to punish Jason, murders her children by him. Water-jar from Vulci, *c.*475 BC.

Bellerophon attacking the Chimaira. The *Iliad* describes the Chimaira as 'in front a lion, behind a serpent, in the middle a goat'. Hesiod's *Theogony* has a different description. 'Chimaira was a great and fearsome creature, swift of foot and strong. She had three heads: one that of a grim-eyed lion, one that of a goat, one that of a snake, a fierce serpent.' Terracotta relief from Melos, *c.*450 BC, much restored.

This is the story told by Pindar. Vase-paintings of the 6th century BC add further details. For instance, the heroes are attacked by Harpies or 'Snatchers', monstrous birds with the heads of women, and Medeia is shown renewing the youth of a ram by boiling it in a cauldron, while Pelias, who hopes to be rejuvenated by the same process, stands by.

Many of the myths about heroes are connected with the city of Argos in Mykenai. It was Akrisios, King of Argos, who tried to keep his daughter Danae a virgin, but failed to prevent the birth of Perseus. The *Iliad* mentions Bellerophon, whom Proitos, brother of Akrisios, sent on another 'suicide mission'. Bellerophon overcame the Chimaira, a fire-breathing beast compounded of lion, goat and snake, but the most striking tale told of him was his attempt to soar up to Olympos and join the gods on the winged horse Pegasos, which he tamed with a magic bridle supplied by Athena. He was thrown by his mount, the 'bitter end', Pindar says, that awaits one who seeks 'more than is right'. He was hated by the gods for his overweening ambition and spent the rest of his days as an outcast on the Plain of Wandering (*Iliad*). This expresses the normal gulf between gods and men in the Homeric tradition, which Herakles alone bridged.

Other stories connected with Argos are about the ancestors of Agamemnon, the leader of the Greeks in the Trojan War. There was a tale that Agamemnon's great-grandfather, Tantalos, invited the gods to a banquet and fed them on the flesh of his son, Pelops. Pindar denies that the gods would have eaten human flesh and says the story is a gross slander. According to him, the true story was that Tantalos invited the gods to a feast, from which Pelops disappeared. He was carried off to Olympos by Poseidon, who had conceived a passion for him (the tale is told with the approval of homosexual love which was characteristic of the Greek aristocratic tradition). Later Tantalos tried to steal the food of the gods, ambrosia and nectar, for men to eat, which was foolish:

> If any man hopes, in anything he does, to escape
> the notice of the gods, he is mistaken.

Here the word Pindar uses for 'he is mistaken' conveys also the sense 'he sins'. For his arrogance in attempting to usurp what belonged to the Immortals, Tantalos endured unending punishment – the 'tantalising' threat of a great stone which forever teetered on the brink, about to fall on him. Pindar was 'cleaning up' the old stories, altering folk-motifs in order to give 'honour' and to praise 'prowess', in the same aristocratic tradition earlier expressed by Homer.

Theseus and the Minotaur

Theseus was the national hero of Athens. By the 5th century BC various stories of different types were told about him, including the one that while still a youth he made the dangerous journey from his home at

Trozen to Athens, overcoming on the way the savage Sow of Krommyon and also Skeiron, Kerkyon and Prokrustes, each of whom murdered travellers. Prokrustes stretched them or lopped them to fit his bed; Kerkyon wrestled with them. The poem by Bacchylides which refers to these exploits was sung at a festival of Apollon on the island of Delos. The sow recalls Herakles and the Erymanthian boar, and a number of the adventures of Theseus were modelled on those of Herakles.

Very old was the story of the Minotaur, perhaps the only one originally told of Theseus, which put him alongside Perseus and Bellerophon as a victor against a monstrous foe. The Minotaur is shown as a bull-headed man in paintings and reliefs from the 7th century on. Later Euripides described him as 'half-man, half-bull'. The story was that King Minos of Crete, whose rich palace at Knossos was known to the Homeric tradition, took young men and girls from Athens to be thrown to the Minotaur in the Labyrinth, the maze beneath his palace. Theseus was one of them, but the priestess Ariadne fell in love with him and helped him to kill the Minotaur and escape, giving him a ball of twine which he unravelled as he penetrated to the heart of the maze. This presentation of Ariadne, the Minotaur and the Labyrinth – 'Very Holy Lady', 'Bull of Minos' and 'Place of the Double Axe' – is surely not the original one, which may have involved a goddess, a sacred bull and a shrine. Be that as it may, by the Archaic period (7th and 6th centuries BC) the story had become one of many which demonstrated the prowess of Theseus, and like many of the Greek tales

ABOVE Theseus attacks the Minotaur, represented as usual on Greek vases as human but with the head, neck and tail of a bull: Athenian jar, *c.*550 BC, from Italy.

LEFT A much earlier and very different representation of the Minotaur, in the main a bull, and possessed of horns (or perhaps one horn), but with a human head (badly damaged). Note the twine which stretches between the Athenian tribute-victims, the means by which Theseus will escape from the Labyrinth. Storage-jar from Tenos, *c.*670 BC.

Oedipus and the Sphinx, on a Hellenistic sarcophagus. The Sphinx, a daughter of the Chimaira, was sent to plague Thebes by one of the gods. The Greek Sphinx differs in form from the Egyptian, having the head and breasts of a woman, with wings attached to the leonine body. The story was that the Sphinx killed passers-by who failed to answer the riddle: 'What being with but one voice has now two feet, now three, now four, and when it has the most is the weakest?'. Oedipus found the answer. 'Man, for men crawl on all fours as infants, stand firm on two legs in their prime, and lean upon a stick in their old age.' The defeated monster killed herself.

had strong narrative appeal as an exciting adventure. The name of Theseus was also used to give mythical sanction to the unification of the Attic communities into the single city-state of Athens. He was the greatest of the early kings of Athens and the founder of the state.

FAMILY TREE OF THESEUS AND ARIADNE

Helios *the sun* — children: **Aietes** *King of Kolchis*; **Kirke** *Circe*; **Pasiphae**

Zeus = Europa — son: **Minos**

Pittheus *King of Trozen* — daughter: **Aithra**

Poseidon = Aithra = Aigeus *King of Athens* **= Medeia = Jason**

Medeia — daughter of Aietes

Pasiphae = Minos *King of Crete*

the Minotaur — son of Pasiphae

Ariadne = Dionysos — Ariadne, daughter of Minos

Theseus *King of Athens (son of Aigeus or Poseidon)*

Greek Tragedy

The origins of tragedy are obscure, but most of its themes are selected from the traditional stories of gods and heroes. The myths of the remote past, the ancient sufferings of gods and heroes, provided the terrible events which wrung the emotions of Athenian audiences year after year.

The tragedy *King Oedipus* by Sophokles is based on a myth about the royal house of Thebes. In the *Odyssey* Oedipus (Oidipous in Greek) is said to have married Epikaste, his own mother, in ignorance of their relationship, and to have killed his father, again not knowing who he was. Epikaste, learning the truth, hanged herself. Oedipus continued to rule over Thebes. The main difference in Sophokles is the fate of Oedipus.

Oedipus is presented in the *King Oedipus* at the height of his fortunes. Long ago he rescued the city of Thebes from the tyranny of a monster, the Sphinx, and married the queen, Iokaste, whose former husband, King Laios, of Thebes, had been killed away from home. He has two grown sons and two small daughters by Iokaste. He is accustomed to the easy exercise of power, to wealth, to respect. But then he gradually learns that what the oracle of

Apollon had long before told him – that he would be responsible for the death of his father and would take his own mother to wife – has already occurred. The parents he thought were his, Polybos of Corinth and his queen, had taken in a foundling, for Oedipus had been brought to them by a shepherd and reared as their son. His attempt to confound the oracle by leaving Corinth and his 'parents' had been in vain, for Laios and Iokaste were his true father and mother. As a baby they had exposed him to die in the mountains, because Laios had been warned by an oracle that his son would kill him.

The development of the play lies in the gradual discovery and the horror of these facts. Oedipus is relentless in his efforts to find out the truth and finally discovers that he himself is blood-guilty, a curse upon the city, unwitting killer of his own father, whom he now remembers as a stranger he slew in a chance quarrel long before. Oedipus puts out his own eyes and departs from Thebes. Count no man happy, says the chorus of old men of Thebes, unless good fortune attends him until his death. Oedipus, envied by all, has been laid low. It is a traditional theme of many types of Greek literature. In our own time Freud has suggested that the drive to replace one's father and appropriate one's mother is a universal constituent of human psychology.

The *Bakchai* (Women Possessed) of Euripides, produced in 406 BC, is also about Thebes, but is set in remote antiquity when the rituals of the god Dionysos (or Bakchos) had just been introduced. Dionysos is a new-born god, offspring of Zeus and the Theban princess, Semele. The reigning king of Thebes, Pentheus, is arrogant enough to deny this and suffers the destruction meted out to mortals who oppose the gods. In the tragedy Dionysos, in the human form of a priest, has come to Thebes from Lydia in Asia Minor, where his cult is established. He is attended by the bacchants, the women who are his devotees and who sing of the holy joy which attends the ritual dance, when the god possesses them. The women of Thebes, who reject the new cult, are forcibly possessed and driven out raving into the mountains. Dionysos wearies of the futile resistance of Pentheus. He persuades the king to dress up as a woman, so that he can watch the secret rituals in the mountains without being detected. Then the god leads him – Pentheus sees him now in the form of a bull – to be torn to pieces by his own mother, Agave.

There is no doubt of the power of the god in this play. He possesses both the willing and those who resist, he punishes Pentheus, he weaves illusions and performs miracles. Clearly this myth is closely connected with religious experience, in fact with ritual. It provides a charter and sanction for an ecstatic cult. That the ecstatic religious experience described in the play is genuine and was a reality in Greece there can be no doubt. It was interpreted as possession by Dionysos or as 'madness' (*mania*) in the sense of 'frenzy'. Plato attributed such 'madness' also to poets possessed and inspired by the Muses, and to the priestess possessed by Apollon when she prophesied in trance. The same type of story as the Theban one was also told of King Lykourgos (Lycurgus) of Thrace and of Proitos of Argos. The theme may have had a historic event behind it, a time when 'dancing-madness', such as infected medieval Christendom, swept through Greece from Thrace.

Death and the Philosophers

Greek myths of the dead and ideas about the afterlife involve distinct traditions which are difficult to reconcile. Pindar, for example, refers to the Isles of the Blessed and shares with Hesiod the tradition that some of the ancient heroes now live there, but he introduces a totally different idea of the blessed. They are the souls which in three successive reincar-

Offerings made before the image of Dionysos. In this ritual scene the god is represented by the bearded mask and the garments hung from a pole or tree-stump. Two priestesses make an offering and two more participants hold up the *thyrsos*, a rod tipped with leaves, emblem of Dionysos, while they dance in ecstasy, possessed by the god. The poets say that Dionysos gave man the vine and its fruit, the grape, so that he was also the spirit of drunkenness. Even the ritual ecstasy was an ambivalent gift. In the *Bakchai* of Euripides, the story of how the god first brought the ritual frenzy of the dance to Greece, the ecstasy is perverted to an uncontrolled and destructive fury. Attic vase from Campania, 5th century BC.

nations on earth have chosen a just life. These too win through to the Isles of the Blessed, where Kronos rules. Herakles provides another example of conflicting traditions. His exploit of carrying off Kerberos shows that he was able to descend into the world of the dead and return from it, a most unusual achievement. He was believed to have won translation to Olympos with the Immortals, yet in the *Odyssey* his pallid shade is found in the underworld, an irreconcilable belief which is nevertheless set alongside his translation to Olympos. The normal Greek expectation of death must have been the common Homeric one of descent as a wraith to the underworld, the grim realm of Hades. There was no question that one survived death, but it was a gloomy prospect. In the *Odyssey* Penelope's suitors, killed by Odysseus, are conducted by Hermes to the underworld meadows of asphodel: 'As when bats flit squeaking in the recesses of some wondrous cave . . . so they went together, gibbering.' Elsewhere in Homer the dead are said to be like smoke or a shadow or a dream, without flesh or sinews. The Mysteries of Eleusis, however, and other cults connected with certain gods and rituals, offered better hopes than this (see MYSTERY RELIGIONS).

The emergence of philosophy involved a direct attack on traditional myths. For example, Herakleitos (about 500 BC) denied that the world-order was produced by generative activity, as in Hesiod: 'It

EARLY SOURCES FOR GREEK MYTHOLOGY

Homer (*about 750–700 BC*)

ILIAD: exploits of the gods, Achilles and other heroes at the siege of Troy

ODYSSEY: adventures of Odysseus after the fall of Troy, and his eventual return home to Ithaca

Attributed to Homer

the Homeric Hymns, in praise of the gods (7th and 6th centuries BC)

Hesiod (*about* 700 BC)

THEOGONY: the origins and early history of the gods

WORKS AND DAYS: treatise on farming, containing several myths

Attributed to Hesiod

CATALOGUE OF WOMEN: genealogies of heroes (6th century)

Bacchylides (*5th century* BC)

one of his poems mentions the youthful exploits of Theseus

Pindar (*518–438* BC)

author of odes on victories at the Olympic Games and other festivals in honour of the gods

Aischylos (*525–426* BC), **Sophokles** (*497–405* BC) and **Euripides** (*485–406* BC)

These poets wrote more than 300 tragedies between them, of which only 31 have survived: many of the plays deal with myths of the gods and heroes

In addition, early Greek vase-paintings frequently depict episodes from mythology and sometimes show a different version of a myth from the literary sources.

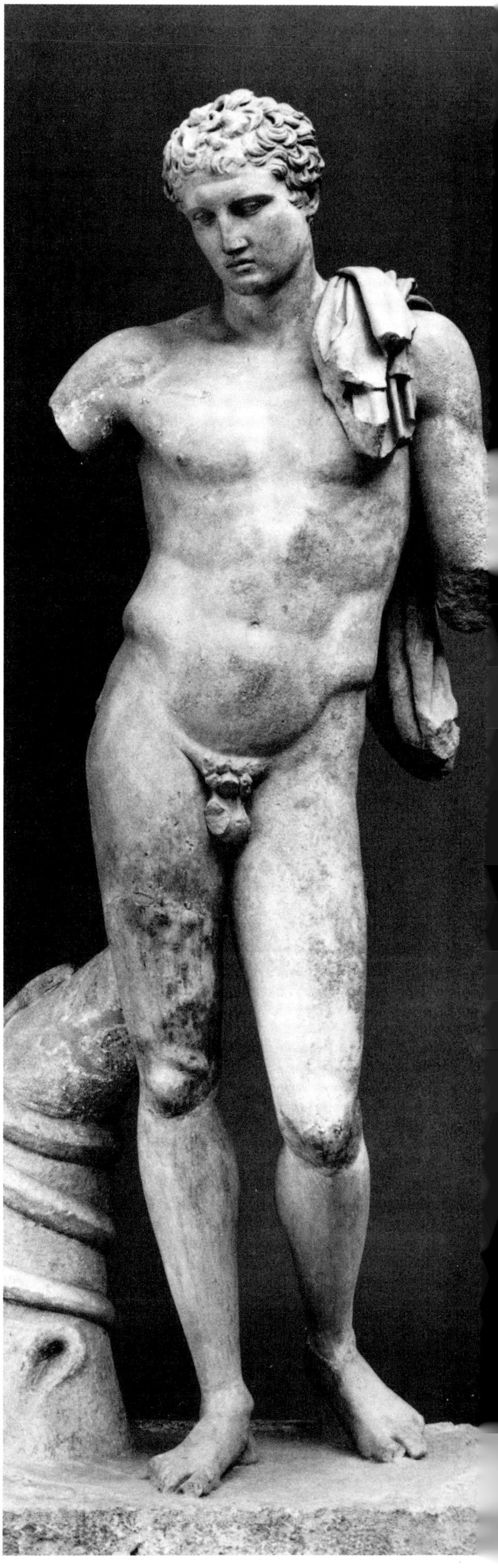

Marble statue, possibly of Hermes, who was certainly represented in this type of pose by Greek sculptors. The Homeric Hymn to Hermes is a rich source of stories about him. It was Hermes, while still a baby, who first made the lyre, for his own delight. Later he gave it to Apollon in return for lordship over herds and flocks; he had previously attempted to steal the cattle of the gods. He also invented the shepherd's pipes. He loved darkness and stealth, and Zeus appointed him messenger of the gods to the dark kingdom of Hades.

always was and is and will be.' It was not only philosophers who expressed dissatisfaction with the myths. Stories in Homer and Hesiod, embodying the heroic ethic, seemed immoral to later generations and the poets were denounced for ascribing stealing, adultery and deceit to the gods. On the other hand, the philosophers did not totally reject myths as a source of knowledge. Plato (about 429–347 BC) employed them when argument could take him no further. For instance, in asserting that the immortal soul undergoes a succession of judgments and reincarnations, he told the myth of Er, which he may well have taken from a body of mystical writings attributed to Orpheus.

The story is told in Plato's *Republic* (book 10). Er, the son of Armenios, a Pamphylian, fell in battle, but afterwards returned to life and told what he had seen after his death. His soul (*psyche*) had travelled with many others to a mysterious place of gaping chasms, where they were all judged by their conduct in life. The souls of those who were benefactors of others and who were just and pious were allowed to enter a chasm which led up through the heavens. There they benefitted from various experiences and sights, and returned cleansed to the place of judgment. The souls of the unjust entered the chasm into the underworld, where they were punished tenfold for their misdeeds, and they too returned cleansed. Some souls proved irredeemable (especially mentioned are those who dishonoured the gods or their parents, and also murderers) and the mouth of the underworld bellowed in protest when they tried to leave it. Fierce attendants seized them, scourged them and threw them down into the depths.

The other souls now travelled on towards a pillar of light, like a rainbow, which was connected to an enormous spindle that rested on the knees of Ananke (Necessity) and caused the eight spheres of the heavens to revolve. Upon each sphere stood a Siren, singing a single continuous note, and the eight notes together made a complete scale, a harmony. There too the souls saw the three Fates – Lachesis, Klotho and Atropos – the daughters of Necessity, singing of things past, things present and things to come. In the gift of Lachesis lay their choice of future lives on earth. Choose well, they were told, for you alone are responsible, not God (*Theos*). The various lives, human and animal, of every condition, were laid out before them, and they chose in turn. One soul, in folly and greed, chose to be a great tyrant, only to discover that his destiny was to eat his own children. At this he blamed fortune and the gods, anyone but himself. Souls which had formerly been just from habit, rather than knowledge, also made unwise choices. Er saw many great heroes, schooled by hardships, choose lives quite different from their former ones. Agamemnon took the life of an eagle, Orpheus the life of a swan, Odysseus the life of an insignificant man.

Then each soul came again before Lachesis to be assigned a spirit (*daimon*) which was to be its guardian in its new life and would give effect to its choice. All drank the waters of the River of Forgetfulness and slept. At midnight, in thunder and earthquake, they were swept away to their new lives. Er himself had watched all this but had taken no part in it, for he was to carry back to men the message of what happened to their souls after death.

Herakles about to chain Kerberos, the three-headed hound of Hades. One tradition was that Kerberos guarded the chasm which led down into his master's kingdom. Alternatively, he patrolled the far bank of the underworld river, the Styx, to which the boatman Charon brought the shades of the dead. Euripides assigned Kerberos three heads, but in Hesiod he has 50. Attic amphora, late 6th or early 5th century BC.

Not many philosophers could employ myths so powerfully. They tended to reinterpret the old tales to rescue what they took to be their meanings. Xenophon in the 4th century BC recalled how a philosopher declaimed a narrative about Herakles which he had written, in which Herakles, as an unformed youth, was confronted by two women, Virtue and Vice: the latter offering him ease and pleasure, while Virtue spoke of great deeds and the goodwill of gods and men. Herakles then listened to a number of lengthy propositions on the nature and consequences of virtue and vice. The great hero had here been transformed into a thinker, rather than a doer of deeds. This and other types of reinterpretation were much developed by later philosophers. Plutarch (about AD 100), for instance, accepted the existence of the Hesiodic daimons (beings between gods and men in nature) and welcomed the thought that these relatively imperfect beings did the deeds attributed by the poets to the gods.

(See ROME and MYSTERY RELIGIONS)

CHAPTER TWELVE

ROME

There is no mythology in the earliest strand of Roman religion, which consisted, as far as is known, in the worship of spiritual powers with limited or special functions. Some of the evidence is late, for the worship was revived by later antiquarians, but the practices were early. Many of these divine functionaries, generally called *numina* (singular *numen*) had to do with work on the farm. An early historian, Fabius Pictor (3rd century BC), says that the priest, when sacrificing to Earth and Ceres, invoked Vervactor for the first ploughing, Redarator for the second, Insitor for the sowing, Oberator for the top-dressing, and for later operations Occator, Sarritor, Subrincator, Messor, Convector, Conditor and Promitor. Some of these names are obscure, but Redarator simply means Replougher, and the last four names are Harvester, Gatherer, Storer and Producer. Other such godlings were Spiniensis (Thorny) for uprooting briars, Puta (Pruner) for pruning, and the odoriferous Sterculius (Dunger) for manuring. Others were connected with rites of passage, the dangerous moments of transition from one condition of life to another. In marriage, there was Cinxia (Girdler) for the girdling of the bride, and Unxia (Anointer) for the ceremony of smearing the bridegroom's door with fat. At birth and later, there were Cunina (Cradler), Vagitanus (Wailer), Rumina (Breastfeeder) and others.

Some of the familiar Roman gods and goddesses seem to have had a similar origin. Ceres (*creare*, creation) is the power of growth in the grain, Flora is the flower-numen, Saturn is connected with sowing, Neptune perhaps with watering, Janus most obviously with the *ianua*, or door. These beings are in origin sexless. A shepherds' numen, Pales or Pares, is found indifferently masculine or feminine. Venus was a garden-numen before she became identified with Aphrodite, the Greek goddess of love, and the name Venus is neuter in form. These spiritual powers with their limited functions had no personality, no interaction with one another, and no mythology.

Gods from Greece

The Romans assimilated their gods and goddesses from the Greeks, who had settled not far from Rome around the bay of Naples, and they came to accept

the great Greek deities under Roman names. Jupiter (Dyaus-piter, or father Dyaus) is the great Indo-European sky-god, who came to Italy independently. There is no trace of a mythology attached to Jupiter which is not taken over from his Greek counterpart, Zeus. His consort Juno, the numen of the power of fertility and growth in the female (corresponding to the male Genius), was identified with Hera. Minerva, an Etruscan patron of crafts, took over from Pallas Athene. Mars is most obviously a numen of war, but he had early connections with agriculture and he was perhaps a storm-numen. His identification with Ares set the war-function uppermost. Mercury was a numen of trade, Vulcan of volcanoes, and Diana was a spirit of the wildwood. The Greek Apollo came to Rome from the Etruscans, but he was not prominent until the time of the Emperor Augustus (who died in AD 14). The Cinderella of the Olympians, Vesta (the Greek Hestia), the spirit of the hearth, seems to have been an Indo-European survival, like the sky-god. In Greece Dionysus usurped her place on Olympus. The Romans called him Bacchus and sometimes identified him with their own Liber, a wine-spirit. Saturn was important enough to survive, linked with Kronos, the god of the old days before Zeus. Janus had no Greek counterpart.

With their new identities the Roman gods took on the myths of their Greek equivalents. The vast majority of the myths which the Romans told of their gods and goddesses are simply taken over from the Greeks.

This is not the whole story, however. In the first place, the Romans had among them some excellent story-tellers. Of them all, the supremely readable repository of Greek myth in Latin is Ovid (43 BC–AD 17). His greatest work in this field is *The Metamorphoses*, in which he recounts some 50 long and 200 short stories, strung together on the loose thread of divinely engineered transformations of shape. Ovid's epigrams are brilliant. Witness his comment on Jupiter's love for the beautiful boy Ganymede (10, 156–7):

> Something was found which even Jupiter
> would rather be than what he was

or on Niobe, who intemperately boasted of her children (6, 155–6):

> Happiest of mothers
> would have been Niobe's title, had she not
> thought of it herself.

But his greatest gift is the variety of his narrative, action and description. To Ovid we owe splendid accounts of Jupiter turning his mistress Io into a cow in an attempt to deceive Juno; Jupiter carrying off Europa in the form of a bull; the nymph Daphne transformed into a laurel tree to escape Apollo's desire; and Jupiter's love for Callisto (1, 423–4):

> 'My wife,' he said, 'will never find the scandal.
> Or if she does, the game is worth the candle.'

Other stories tell of divine vengeance. Actaeon saw Diana naked and was changed into a stag and savaged to death by his own hounds. Semele asked to see Jupiter in his glory and, her wish granted, was burned to death. Pentheus tried to oppose the power of Bacchus and was torn to pieces by the god's raving worshippers. Arachne challenged Minerva to a spinning contest and was defeated and turned into a spider. Marsyas challenged Apollo in music and, on losing, was flayed alive.

A magnificent episode deals with Phaethon, who drove the chariot of the sun off course and was struck with a thunderbolt by Jupiter. Many more have to do with human love. Ovid was interested in, and sensitive to, the psychology of abnormal love, of sister for brother or daughter for father. Or there is the tale of Narcissus, who killed himself for unrequited love of his own reflection in the water. Iphis, a girl in love with another woman, was changed into a man by the gods. Pygmalion, the woman-hater, loved the statue he made and Venus took pity on him and brought the statue to life as the beautiful Galatea. The whole is exuberant, baroque, often witty, sometimes grotesque, racy, rhetorical, brilliantly organized.

One of the most exquisite stories tells how a poor

ABOVE Statue of Diana, a spirit of the wildwood, who was identified with Artemis, the Greek goddess of wild beasts, and portrayed as a virgin huntress. A Roman copy, *c.* AD 300.

OPPOSITE Neptune, the Roman equivalent of the Greek sea-god Poseidon. Holding his characteristic weapon, the trident or fish-spear, he rides the waves in a horse-drawn chariot. Mosaic from Tunisia, 3rd century AD.

couple, Philemon and Baucis, entertained the gods unaware, generously offering them their simple fare, and received their reward. Jupiter and Mercury, disguised as human travellers, were once making their way through the hill country of Phrygia, in Asia Minor. The two gods looked for somewhere to rest, but all the houses they came to were bolted and barred. In defiance of the duty of hospitality which is owed to strangers, no one would take them in. At last they came to the humble cottage of Philemon and Baucis, an old couple who had lived there happily together since their youth. Philemon and Baucis were so poor that they had only the plainest food to offer, but they welcomed the travellers

ABOVE Greek myths were retold with great verve and brilliance by the Roman poet Ovid, including the story of how Jupiter desired the beautiful boy Ganymede and, in the form of an eagle, carried him off to be his cup-bearer. Ganymede with Jupiter, as an eagle. Roman relief, 1st century AD.

ABOVE RIGHT Another famous story told by Ovid was that of Echo and Narcissus. The nymph Echo fell in love with the handsome Narcissus, who was too proud to love anyone. The grieving Echo pined away until she was only a voice, heard in the mountains. Narcissus saw his own reflection in a pool and desired it passionately but could not take it in his arms. Dying of unrequited love, he turned into the flower that bears his name. Wall-painting from the house of Loreius Tiburtinus, Pompeii.

courteously, made them as comfortable as they could and gave them the best they had in the house.

When they all sat down to the meal, every time wine was poured from the flagon it refilled itself of its own accord. The old people were awed by this and decided to kill their only goose in honour of the visitors. The gods now revealed who they were and declared that the goose should not be killed. They brought a flood which drowned all the houses in the area except the cottage, which the gods changed into a temple adorned with marble. Then Jupiter asked Philemon and Baucis what they wished of him. The old couple consulted together and asked two things: that they should be the priests of the temple and that when death came for them, they should both die at the same moment. These wishes Jupiter granted. Philemon and Baucis served the temple all the rest of their lives and when the end came, they turned into two trees, which still grow there, side by side.

Roman Attitudes

The Romans also adapted Greek mythology to their own ends and, in so doing, modified the myths. For example, in one poem Catullus (1st century BC) used a myth from the east about the self-castration of Attis in the service of Cybele (see MYSTERY RELIGIONS). Attis makes a speech which is a lament for his lost sex. It brings together the Greek horror at the loss of physical athleticism and the beauty of the young male body with a Roman horror at the loss of masculine potency.

As another example, take the divine backcloth to Vergil's *Aeneid* (which was left uncompleted at the poet's death in 19 BC). It is borrowed directly from Homer. In one sense it is an inherited piece of epic machinery, and some of the episodes (like the making of Aeneas's armour) are little more than translations or straightforward adaptations. But in other aspects the gods are Roman. Jupiter, as T.R. Glover said, has Homeric traits, but is free from the tyrannical and sensual characteristics of the Homeric Zeus. He has come closer to mankind than Hellenistic poetry allowed: from a Ptolemy he has become an Augustus. Venus is free from the cruelty of Aphrodite in *The Iliad* and the sensuality of Aphrodite in the Homeric hymn. She is the tender, gracious divine mother.

A third example comes from Lucretius's poem *On the Nature of Things* (1st century BC). Lucretius was an Epicurean, and may be drawing upon a Greek allegory. However that may be, he makes of Mars the militarism, ambition and dangerous activism which the Epicurean philosophers loathed, and of Venus the very spirit of peace, tranquillity, *ataraxia* ('freedom from disturbance'). And his opening words place the thing solidly in a Roman context: he invokes Venus as *Aeneadum genetrix*, 'Mother of Aeneas's line'.

Thirdly, the Romans had ritual practices of their own particular brand. Sir James Frazer began his famous book *The Golden Bough* with one of these. The priest of Diana at Nemi, in the Alban Hills outside Rome, was known as the King of the Wood. He held office until a successor killed him. Myths were inevitably told to explain this, for one function of myth is linked to ritual in this way, but they date from contact with the Greeks. It was said that the original King of the Wood was a Greek hero,

such as Hippolytus or Orestes, who came to a violent end. The practice itself, however, was indigenous and antedated awareness of Greek mythology. Another example of Roman ritual may be seen in the Vestal Virgins, who were six in number, chosen between the age of six and ten to serve for 30 years. They had to remain virgin throughout this period and any offence was fearfully punished by burial alive; after retirement they might marry. Details of the ritual are unknown, but it was archaic and of long standing. Water had to be drawn from a pure spring, fire was produced by rubbing two sticks together. Stories of these and other rituals were often traced back to the legendarily pious King Numa.

The Quest for a Past

The typically Roman myths, then, did not pertain to gods and goddesses and the remote past so much as to historical people and historical events, in what Michael Grant has called 'the Quest for a Roman Past'. Let us begin from the foundation of the city. The version of the story by the great Roman historian Livy, who died in AD 17, is a patriotic myth, with many strands.

A Vestal Virgin named Rhea Silvia was raped and named the rapist as the god Mars. She gave birth to twin boys, Romulus and Remus. The twins were exposed to die in a basket on the river Tiber, but the basket was washed up on the bank at a place where a fig tree grew, near a cave called the Lupercal, the Place of the Wolf. A she-wolf found the babies and suckled them, and they were eventually rescued by a shepherd named Faustulus, who took them to his wife, Acca Larentia, to care for.

ABOVE Venus floating on the waters in a shell. Venus was originally connected with gardens, but she was assimilated to the Greek love-goddess Aphrodite, and according to the Greek myth, which the Romans adopted, she was born of the sea-foam. From the House of the Marine Venus, Pompeii.

LEFT The identification of Mars with Ares, the Greek god of war, carried with it the Greek story that the war-god and the love-goddess were lovers. It also emphasized the role of Mars as a deity of war, though the Roman god had important connections with agriculture and was closely linked with the foundation of Rome itself.

Romulus and Remus suckled by the wolf. The characteristically Roman myths, as distinct from those taken over from the Greeks, were concerned with historical events, including the origins of the city and the Roman people. The founders of Rome were Romulus and Remus, twin sons of Mars, who were suckled by a she-wolf. Romulus, whose name means 'Roman', murdered his brother and became the first ruler and law-giver of Rome. It was said that he eventually disappeared mysteriously from the earth and became a god, under the name of Quirinus. Relief, 2nd century AD.

When the boys grew up, they founded a new city, which was to become Rome, at the place where they had been saved from death as babies. They quarrelled, however, and Romulus murdered Remus. One version of the story says that Remus sneered at his brother and jumped over the half-built walls. This was an evil omen, for it implied that enemies might do the same. Romulus's counter was to kill Remus and say, 'So perish whoever else shall cross my walls!'

Romulus now fortified the Palatine Hill, sacrificed to the gods and gave the people laws. He increased the population of the city by establishing a sanctuary for refugees on the slopes of the Capitoline Hill, and he gave the new state political stability by appointing a Senate of a hundred 'Fathers'.

Shortage of women imperilled the survival of the new state. Romulus announced a harvest festival. People came to it from miles around, including many of the Sabines, who lived nearby. At the climax of the festivities the virile young Romans seized the nubile women. This was the famous Rape of the Sabine Women (a scene painted with static perfection by Poussin and with sensual vigour by Rubens). The result was war between the Sabines and the Romans. It ended when the abducted women thrust themselves between the combatants, pleading that their fathers and fathers-in-law should not shed one another's blood (an episode splendidly though inaccurately portrayed by Jacques Louis David, the French Revolutionary painter).

The children in the floating cradle and the suckling by a wild animal are folk-tale motifs. There are elements strongly suggesting that Rome's foundation was an amalgamation of two strands – the twins, the human and animal parentage, the linking of Romans and Sabines. The myth, as often, incorporates a number of divine people and places, including Faustulus (associated with the god Faunus), his wife Acca Larentia (a minor goddess), the Lupercal or wolf-cave, and the Ruminal ('suckling') fig tree. In fact, though the archeological details are still a matter for debate, we know that the hills of Rome were occupied by about 2000 BC, but that any unified city is not to be dated before the 6th century: not the 8th, to which legend assigned these events (the familiar 753 BC is only one of several traditional dates for the foundation).

Exiles from Troy

As time went on and the Romans came in closer contact with the Greeks – whose culture made a surprisingly profound impression on them, but to whom they showed considerable ambivalence – they wanted to link their origins with Greek traditions. By about 300 BC the myth was in circulation that Trojans had escaped from the destruction of Troy and landed in Latium, the area to the south of Rome. The notional date for this was four centuries before the foundation of Rome, the event became associated with the establishment of the town of Alba Longa, from which Rome was founded, and the period in between was peopled with the mythical ancestors of the Roman aristocracy.

The Trojan quest for a new home was told in epic verse with epic grandeur by Vergil in *The Aeneid*. Aeneas was a prince of Troy, son of the Trojan hero Anchises and the goddess Venus. When Troy fell to the besieging Greeks, Aeneas escaped from the burning city, carrying his father, who was lame, on his shoulders and leading his young son Ascanius by the hand. Taking ship, he sailed to the Greek islands,

ABOVE Dido and Aeneas. The origins of Rome were linked with the siege of Troy, in the myth that Trojan exiles landed to the south of Rome and founded Alba Longa, from which Rome itself was founded 400 years later. Vergil told the story of Aeneas escaping from Troy and making his way to Italy. On the way he stayed at Carthage, where Dido, the queen, fell in love with him and tried to keep him with her. Dido symbolizes the challenges of foreign powers to the destiny of Rome. Mosaic, 4th century AD.

LEFT The rape of the Sabine women, on a Roman coin. This was another famous episode in the early history of Rome. The new city needed women and Romulus invited the Sabines, who lived nearby, to a festival. The young Romans then seized the Sabine women.

to Sicily and to Carthage, where Dido, the queen of Carthage, received him. Aeneas and Dido fell passionately in love, but the god Jupiter ordered Aeneas to leave Dido and sail for Italy, where his destiny lay. Aeneas obeyed and Dido, in despair, cursed him and killed herself. (Dido symbolizes the two greatest challenges to the destiny of Rome – Hannibal of Carthage and Cleopatra of Egypt.)

Reaching Italy, Aeneas was taken into the underworld by a prophetess, the Sibyl of Cumae. There he saw the spirit of Dido. He spoke to her lovingly but in blazing hatred she turned her back on him. He also met the spirit of his father Anchises, who told him of Rome's future glory.

Then Aeneas sailed to the mouth of the Tiber and came to the Palatine Hill, where Venus, his mother, gave him armour made by Vulcan, the smith of the gods. Aeneas defeated and killed his enemies among the Etruscans and Latins, who were already settled in the area, and Jupiter decreed that the Trojans and Latins should unite and form one nation. Aeneas founded the town of Lavinium (modern Pratica de Mare, to the south of Rome). His son Ascanius founded Alba Longa (Castel Gandolfo, south-east of Rome) and from Alba Longa, many generations later, Romulus and Remus, who were descended from Aeneas, founded Rome itself.

Vergil turned a patriotic myth into a poem about real people, embodying a vision of destiny, and so gave it the form in which it captured the imagination of future readers. St Augustine (AD 354–430) wept for Dido as the player in *Hamlet* wept for Hecuba, and the name of Aeneas is probably more familiar than that of Romulus.

The Kings and the Republic

The early books of Livy are a storehouse of the myths which caught the imagination of the Romans and which became part of the heritage of Europe. Some of them were retold with splendid verve by Macaulay in the 19th century, in his *Lays of Ancient Rome*.

The traditions named seven kings of Rome: Romulus; Numa Pompilius, who gave Rome her religious institutions, advised it was said by the nymph or goddess Egeria; Tullius Hostilius; Ancus Martius; and three Etruscans, Tarquin the Old, Servius Tullius and Tarquin the Proud.

This last king was an autocratic militarist. He had three sons, Titus, Arruns and Sextus, and a nephew, Lucius Junius, who simulated stupidity to avoid his uncle's jealousy and was known as Brutus (Dunce). The two older brothers and Brutus were sent on a mission to the oracle at Delphi. On their own account, they asked which of them would rule Rome and were told, 'Young men, the highest authority in Rome will be his among you who is the first to give his mother a kiss.' The two princes tossed up for the privilege on their return, but Brutus pretended to stumble and pressed his lips to Mother Earth.

The youngest brother, Sextus, raped Lucretia, the lovely and virtuous wife of Collatinus. She told her husband, her father and Brutus, and stabbed herself. (Titian and Tintoretto have notable paintings of the rape – which Britten turned into an opera – Cranach and Veronese of the suicide.) Brutus raised an army and expelled the king and his family. Establishing a republic, with Collatinus and himself as chief officers or consuls, he won the title of Liberator.

The hardly won freedom was hardly maintained. Brutus's own sons were found conspiring for the return of the Tarquins, and their father inexorably condemned them to death. Then the Etruscan power

ABOVE The divine twins Castor and Pollux, sons of Jupiter, were patron deities of the Roman cavalry and were said to have aided the Roman army to victory in the battle of Lake Regillus, in the 5th century BC. Mosaic from Cyprus, 3rd century AD.

BELOW The two-headed Janus, from a coin. The god's name is connected with *ianua*, 'door', and he was the god of gates and doors, and hence of journeys and the beginnings of things. Because of his connection with entrances and exits he faces both ways.

was raised against Rome. In Macaulay's version:

Lars Porsena of Clusium,
  By the Nine Gods he swore
That the great house of Tarquin
  Should suffer wrong no more.
By the Nine Gods he swore it
  And named a trysting day,
And bade his messengers ride forth,
East and west and south and north,
  To summon his array.

Another of the great myths told how Horatius Cocles ('One-eye') with two others held the approach to the dangerously vulnerable Tiber bridge while it was being demolished and then swam the river in full armour to safety. Nor was this the only story of heroic gallantry to be handed down. Mucius Scaevola ('Cack-handed') offered to get through the enemy lines and assassinate Lars Porsenna, but instead of Porsenna he killed a secretary by mistake. Arrested, he plunged his right hand into a fire to show that he valued honour above safety: to Porsenna's credit, he let him go free.

Stories of Heroism

Peace was patched up with Porsenna, but wars continued. A few years later there was a Roman victory at Lake Regillus where, according to a legend hinted at but not told by Livy, the Romans were supported by two mysterious horsemen. They were identified with the divine twins, Castor and Pollux.

So like they were, no mortal
  Might one from other know:
White as snow their armour was:
  Their steeds were white as snow.

The famous stories continue: the arrogant Coriolanus, refusing to kow-tow to the commons, suffering banishment, leading an army against Rome, persuaded by his mother to desist; Cincinnatus leaving his farm to save his country, the model of the simple fighting farmer, whose *virtus* (literally his manliness) lay in his toughness in the field, whether of the farm or the battle; the arrival of the Gauls to sack the city, finding the senators in full dress, each seated silently in his own courtyard; the cackling of the sacred geese which warned the sentinels on the Capitol of a night attack. During a battle Decius Mus 'devoted' himself, that is offered his own death for his country with the words 'Janus, Jupiter, Father Mars, Quirinus, Bellona, Lares, New Gods, Native Gods, Gods whose power stands over us and our enemy, and you, Divine Power of the Dead . . . on behalf of the state of the citizens, the people of Rome, I devote the legions and auxiliaries of the enemies together with myself to the Gods of the Dead and to Earth.' He then plunged into the thick of the foe and was killed, but his action so overawed the enemy that the Romans won the day.

More curious is the story of Regulus, an incompetent Roman commander in the fighting against Carthage. He was captured and sent back to Rome, under oath to return if Carthaginian prisoners were not released. He went, advised the Senate not to release the prisoners, kept his oath and freely returned to torture and death. This story is told by Cicero (1st century BC) as a Roman illustration of Greek ethical principle (*De Officiis* 3,27). He refers to it in at least six other places and in the next generation Horace similarly uses Regulus as the type of *Romana virtus*, Roman character and courage (*Odes* 3, 5, 41–56):

The story says he pushed aside
his chaste wife's kiss, his little sons,
  a citizen no more, directing
    his strong gaze down,
till he could strengthen the Fathers' uncertain
purpose with unprecedented advice
  and to the tears of his friends
    speed gloriously to exile.
He knew well what the torturers of Carthage
had in store for him, yet thrust away
  his family from his path,
    the people's protests,
just as if, some lawsuit over,
he were leaving behind his labours for his clients,
  making for the fields of Venafrum
    or Spartan Tarentum.

The great Roman myths were not an expression of the unconscious will of a people. They contain folkloric elements but are not folklore. They were rooted in history, and deliberately manipulated by the aristocracy for their own purposes. For example, the son of Aeneas, Ascanius, was also given the name Iulus, to link him with the Julian family, of which Julius Caesar was a member. In general, Roman mythology does not readily fit any of the current theories of myth.

Roman Religious Myths

Some religious myths there were. One, of great potency, taken over from the Greeks, had to do with a golden age of happiness in the past when Saturn reigned, and its possible future return. This was brilliantly used by Vergil in his fourth Eclogue to welcome prospectively the birth of a child to Mark Antony and Octavia:

The last generation of the song of Cumae has
  now arrived;
the great cycle of the ages is beginning afresh.
The maiden Justice is now returning, the rule of
  Saturn is returning,
now a new race is being sent from the height of
  heaven.
A boy is being born, with whom the race of iron
  will cease,
and a race of gold be born throughout the earth.

The 'song of Cumae' refers to the prophecies of the Sibyl. A number of Sibyls, or ecstatic prophetesses, were known to the ancient world, one of whom was housed in a magnificent shrine still to be seen at Cumae, near Naples. In one legend she asked Apollo for life, but forgot to ask for youth, and withered away until she hung in a bottle saying, 'I want to die.' A famous story told how one of the Sibyls sold a

The cave of the Sibyl at Cumae, near Naples. The Sibyls of Cumae were prophetesses. The Sibylline Books, which one of them sold to Rome, were a collection of prophecies and rules for averting disaster. They were kept at Rome and consulted in times of crisis. In the 3rd century BC, for example, when Hannibal of Carthage invaded Italy and threatened Rome, the Sibylline Books were consulted and as a result special sacrifices and rituals were performed, to restore the right relationship between Rome and the gods.

collection of prophecies to Tarquin the Old at an exorbitant price. She offered him nine books; when he refused she destroyed three, and offered the remaining six at the same price; he still refused, and she destroyed three more; he panicked and took the last three at the original price. The books were placed in the charge of a special college of priests, and consulted only in national emergencies on the Senate's instructions.

Emperors too, divine figures as they were believed to be, acquired their own myths. Two will suffice. One covers a number of supernatural occurrences associated with Julius Caesar: the apparition which urged him to cross the Rubicon and attack Rome, the two divine beings who appeared at his funeral, and above all the comet which marked his death in 44 BC and was taken to be his spirit ascended to heaven. The other myth, strong in Greece, was that of Nero Redivivus, the belief in the Second Coming of the Emperor Nero, who committed suicide in AD 68.

Finally there was the myth of Rome's eternity:

As long as the Colosseum stands,
  Rome too will stand.
When the Colosseum falls, Rome too will fall.
When Rome falls, the world too will fall.

It was a potent myth. The Roman empire in the West collapsed. The Colosseum stood. The myth of Rome's eternity remained powerful within the Christian Church (see CHRISTIANITY).

ROMAN AND GREEK DEITIES

ROMAN DEITY	FUNCTION	GREEK DEITY
Jupiter	God of the sky, father of gods and men	Zeus
Juno	Consort of Jupiter, goddess of women and motherhood	Hera
Mars	God of war	Ares
Ceres	Goddess of agriculture, fertility	Demeter
Apollo	God of light, intellect, the arts, healing, prophecy	Apollon
Venus	Goddess of love and beauty	Aphrodite
Minerva	Goddess of crafts, wisdom	Athena
Mercury	God of trade and communications, the divine messenger	Hermes
Diana	Goddess of the wildwood, lady of beasts, goddess of the moon	Artemis
Neptune	God of the sea	Poseidon
Vulcan	The divine smith	Hephaistos
Vesta	Goddess of the hearth, fire	Hestia
Liber	God of wild nature, fertility, ecstasy, wine	Dionysos, Bakchos
Saturn	A god of agriculture, ruler of the golden age	Kronos
Dis Pater	God of death and the underworld	Hades, Plouton
Janus	God of doorways, journeys, beginnings	No equivalent
Faunus	A god of woodland	Pan
Castor and Pollux	The divine twins	Kastor and Polydeukes
Cupid	God of love, son of Venus	Eros

CHAPTER THIRTEEN

THE MYSTERY RELIGIONS

'Mystery' comes from the Greek (*mustes* – initiate, *mus* – close eyes, lips). A mystery religion is a closed society, with initiatory rites, secret proceedings and a private revelation to initiates. The term is applied to a number of religions in the Graeco-Roman world, principally during the Hellenistic period (from about 300 BC), when the political situation had changed and the once proudly independent Greek city-states were pawns in a world of power politics, ruled from Macedonia, Egypt, Syria or Asia Minor. In the old city-states religion and society had been tightly interwoven, part of the 'inherited conglomerate' which was handed down from one generation to another, and so provided stability. Now men and women no longer trusted the old gods. In the 3rd century BC the Athenians gave a Macedonian king, Demetrius the Besieger, the Parthenon for his palace, declaring him the one true god, for the others were asleep, away or non-existent.

In this mood people looked for new gods. Further, psychologically they turned in on themselves, and sought a religion of personal salvation. It was to this attitude that the mystery religions appealed, and their appeal continued through the Hellenistic Age and into the period of Roman domination.

The Myth of Eleusis

The most famous mystery cult of antiquity, the Eleusinian Mysteries, was far older, but some movement from a public to a personal and individual cult can be traced. Behind the cult lay a myth, which had to do with the cycle of the year and the burial of seed in the earth.

Demeter, the Earth-Mother or Corn-Mother (the derivation is not quite certain), had a daughter named Kore, the Maiden, sometimes called by the pre-Greek name Persephone, or in Latin Proserpina. Kore was happily picking flowers one day when the god of the underworld, Pluto (whose name stands for both death and wealth), burst from a fissure in the ground and carried her off to the realm of the dead, where he made her his queen.

Demeter was desolate and wandered over the face of the land in vain search of her lost child. Disguised as an old woman, she came to Eleusis, some 14 miles from Athens. There she lived humbly, like a slave, unsmiling and consuming nothing except a mixture of barley-meal, mint and water. She became nurse to the young prince. She intended to make him immortal by plunging him in fire, but she was interrupted by the queen, and revealed herself. They

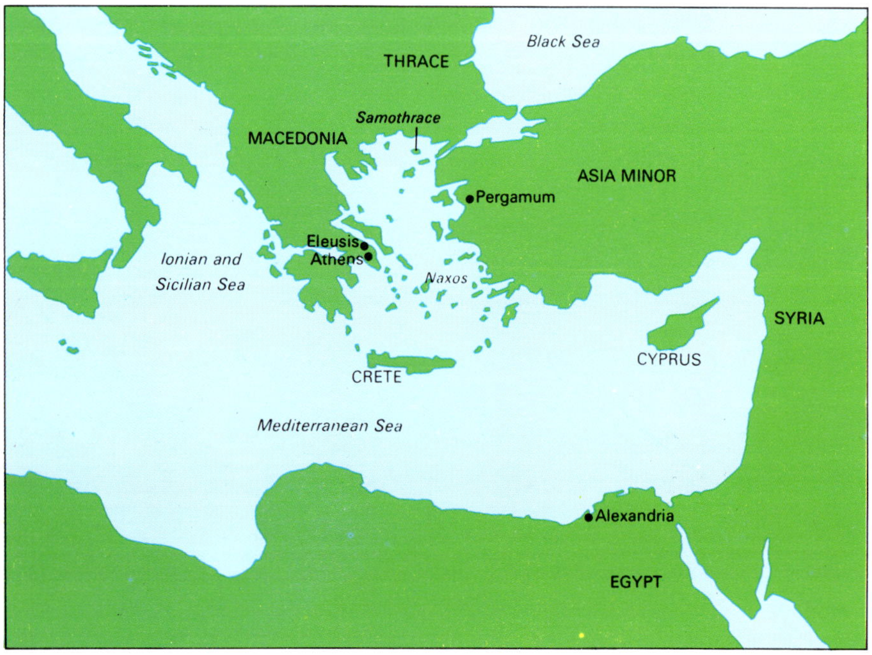

built her a temple-home and there she stayed brooding for a year, while the crops shrivelled and men and animals died.

Zeus intervened and ordered Pluto to release the Maiden. Demeter was joyfully reunited with her daughter, but in the underworld Kore had eaten the sacred pomegranate, and that formed a tie which bound her to return there for a third of each year. Now, like the seed-corn, she spends part of each year under the ground and part on the earth's surface.

This is the myth told in the Homeric Hymn to Demeter. One addition to it must be mentioned. A Christian writer, Clement of Alexandria (2nd century AD), tells how Demeter arrived at Eleusis in grim grief, refusing to eat. A woman named Baubo made the goddess laugh by lifting her skirt and revealing her private parts. It is not clear whether this is a false attribution to the myth, a later accretion, or part of the original.

The myth was taken to hold out a promise of life after death, on the analogy of the seed-corn which is buried in the ground, to grow again in due season.

ABOVE The temple of Isis at Pompeii. The mystery cult of Isis spread across the whole Roman world.

LEFT Pluto and Persephone, enthroned in the underworld, hold plants as symbols of seed buried in the earth and reborn from it. The parallel with life through death for human beings was a theme of the Eleusinian Mysteries.

OPPOSITE The Demeter of Cnidus, mother of Kore or Persephone and a central figure of the Eleusinian Mysteries. *C.*330 BC.

It is not clear whether the period of desolation and death is the winter, when the seed was in the earth after the autumn sowing (as the Homeric Hymn suggests with its reference to spring) or the parched, dry summer, when the seed-corn from the spring harvest was stored in jars underground. It was brought out for the autumn sowing, and autumn was the season of the Mysteries.

BELOW The 'child' with the goddesses of the cult, Demeter and Persephone. At Eleusis a boy or girl known as 'the child from the hearth' was initiated into the Mysteries on behalf of the Athenian state. Relief from Eleusis, 5th century BC.

BELOW RIGHT Demeter and Persephone with Triptolemus. In the myth, Demeter initiated Triptolemus, prince of Eleusis, into the secrets of the Mysteries. Athenian vase-painting by Macron, early 5th century BC.

Initiation at Eleusis

The cult at Eleusis certainly goes back beyond 1000 BC. Once Eleusis came under the control of Athens, it began to expand. The great *telesterion*, or Hall of the Mysteries, with its 42 columns, dates from the 5th century BC.

The cult was entrusted to two families and office was passed on within those families. They provided the Hierophant or chief priest, and his assistant, the Torch-Bearer, the Herald, the Altar-Priest, the Priestess of Demeter and other priestesses.

There was a minor festival in spring. The Greater Mysteries were held in the autumn. As a preliminary, the sacred objects were taken to Athens. On the first day of the festival proper the Herald issued an invitation to those of clean hands, intelligible speech (meaning Greek), and just lives. On the second day the initiates were cleansed in the sea and offered sacrifice of a pig. The third day was devoted to public sacrifice. The fourth was for the purification of late-comers. The fifth saw the great procession from Athens to Eleusis, interrupted halfway by ceremonial insults from watchers on a bridge – a typical ritual for warding off evil influences. The sixth was a day of rest and fasting, leading into the nocturnal celebration, followed by another day of rest. The eighth involved rites for the dead. The ninth was the day of departure.

We can see the combination of public and private ritual in the initiation on behalf of the Athenian state of a boy (or sometimes a girl) known as the *pais aph' hestias*, or child from the hearth, ensuring the goddesses' blessing on the state and its young life.

To reveal the Mysteries was an offence involving the death penalty. The secret was well kept, and we do not really know what happened. We can guess that the myth was enacted as a sacred drama. There was certainly music and dancing, a gong sounding at the name of Kore, a spectacular display of torches, and a theophany (the manifestation of a deity). We know of an antiphonal cry, rhyming in Greek, to the sky 'Rain!', to the earth 'Conceive!' The climax was something seen, probably the display of a golden ear

of corn. The initiates were allowed to handle sacred objects, and took part in some kind of communion-meal of cereal and barley-wine. There is some evidence that the initiate became one with the Maiden: the Roman emperor Gallienus after his initiation put his name on his coins in a feminine form, Galliena Augusta. The promise was that with Kore the initiate descended to the world of the dead and rose to a richer and better life. The condition was moral and ritual purity. So Cicero (1st century BC) after initiation says, 'We have learned to live and die with a better hope'. 'Hope' is a technical term of the mystery religions, almost like 'faith'. So the Homeric Hymn to Demeter puts it:

> Blessed among men on earth is he who has seen
> these things.

But he who is uninitiate and outside the holy rites,
has no like fate, lying in death beneath the
spreading dark.

One initiate put on his tomb: 'Glorious indeed is that mystery vouchsafed by the blessed gods, for death is no ill to mortals, but rather a good.'

Dionysus

Like Demeter, Dionysus was a deity of nature, apparently known early in Greece, but not admitted to Olympus till he stormed in again from Thrace. He is a god of vegetation, and especially of the vine, imprisoned in winter and released in spring. He is a god of animal life who takes on the form of bull, snake and lion, fawn and kid.

His followers were ecstatic women known as Maenads (the mad women) or Bacchants (from his other name, Bacchus). They wore leafy garlands and animal-skins and carried the thyrsus, or sacred staff, wreathed with vine-leaves or ivy. They roamed the mountain in wild whirling dances, at the height of their ecstasy seizing an animal, tearing it apart and eating it raw – undoubtedly a communion in the god's own body and blood. Their frenzy carried them through exposure to the weather and physical weariness.

In the Hellenistic and Roman periods we become increasingly aware of Dionysiac fellowships. Inscriptions name some of the functionaries – Chief of the Mysteries, Chief Herdsman, Bearer of the

TOP Wall-painting of the Bacchanalian dance. Dionysus, or Bacchus, was a god of wild nature and the Maenads, his female followers, attained an ecstatic communion with him through whirling dances and the eating of raw flesh. From the Villa Pamfili, Rome, 1st century AD.

ABOVE Maenads with Dionysus as a bull, one of his principal animal forms.

Four scenes from an initiation into the Mysteries of Dionysus. In the first scene, a boy reads the prelude to the ceremony while the candidate for initiation listens, standing with scarf on head and hand on hip. Next, a Silenus plays the lyre and a Pan the flute, to show that music transforms bestiality. A female Pan offers her breast to a kid, who presumably symbolizes the initiate. In the third scene, a Satyr peers into a bowl and sees, instead of his own reflection, a grotesque mask which represents the grosser side of his nature which has to be put off. On the right, sadly damaged, Dionysus reclines with Ariadne in his arms. In the fourth scene, the initiate bares her back to the whipping which brings her into ritual death, to be followed by spiritual rebirth. Frescoes from the Villa of the Mysteries at Pompeii, 1st century BC.

Phallus, Bearer of the Milk, Bearer of the Torch, and others. One of the god's chief symbols was the *liknon*, a basket filled with fruit, and containing a phallus shrouded in a cloth, speaking of fertility and potency, and ultimately of life gained through death.

This last promise can be seen in a series of superb Roman sarcophagi, dating from the second century AD, and belonging to a wealthy family named Calpurnius Piso. Whether they show the childhood of Dionysus, or Dionysus in triumphant procession with Maenads and Satyrs and panthers, or Dionysus finding Ariadne abandoned and asleep and awakening her to be his bride, they all speak of how our mortality can put on immortality.

Ariadne was the daughter of Minos, King of Crete. She was half-sister to the Minotaur, the monster part-man and part-bull, which was kept penned in the Cretan labyrinth. When the Athenian prince Theseus came to Crete, secretly intending to kill the Minotaur, Ariadne fell in love with him at first sight. She offered to help him if he would take her back to Athens with him as his wife. Theseus agreed and Ariadne gave him a ball of thread, with which he was able to find his way into the heart of the labyrinth, destroy the Minotaur and escape from the maze again. Then Theseus and Ariadne fled from Crete, but when they came to the island of Naxos, he cruelly abandoned her, leaving her asleep on the shore. She was rescued by the god Dionysus, who came with his rout of women and wild animals and drunken Satyrs. Dionysus wakened Ariadne gently with a kiss and made her his consort.

The underlying significance of this myth was believed to be that Ariadne represented the human soul, achieving immortal life and happiness in the loving embrace of the divine.

The Villa of the Mysteries

One of the most remarkable survivals of the Mysteries of Dionysus is to be seen in the Villa of the Mysteries on the outskirts of Pompeii. One room evidently devoted to the Mysteries shows on its walls, brilliantly painted against a bright red ground, the scenes of initiation. The lady of the house sits as a dignified president to the ritual. An initiate stands with scarf on head and hand on hip listening to a boy reading, under guidance, the prelude to the celebration. A maidservant carries ritual offerings from the initiate to a seated priestess, one of whose attendants is pouring a libation.

Now come the Mysteries. A gross Silenus (a drunken old man) is playing the lyre, for music and the divine touch transform even bestiality. A young Pan plays the flute. A charming Panisca (female Pan) offers her breast to a kid, who presumably symbolizes the initiate Then, just before the wall turns at right angles is a terrified woman, for initiation means ordeal as well as grace. Now comes a scene in which a young Satyr is peering into a bowl; behind him another Satyr is holding a grotesque mask. We may presume that he sees the reflection of this mask instead of his own face; he is seeing the grosser side of his nature, which has to be put off.

Now, sadly damaged, are the enthroned figures of Dionysus and his consort Ariadne; these would face the worshipper on entering the room. A kneeling woman beside them is unveiling a gigantic phallus. Beyond, a dark winged figure, perhaps Telete, the very spirit of initiation, is plying a long rod, and far to his left crouches the initiate, her hair dishevelled, her fine robes put off, her head in the lap of one of two comforting women, her back bared to the rod which brings her into ritual death. But now we see her again, the robe of penitence laid by, clashing cymbals and swirling round in the dance of resurrection. Finally we see the preparation for the mystical marriage in which the bride of the god, like Ariadne, is given divine life.

The Orphics

One special Dionysiac group were the Orphics, of whom little is known for sure. There were Orphics, associated with a mystery cult, in the Greek world in the 5th and 4th centuries BC, and later there were

LEFT Vase-painting of Ariadne embraced by Dionysus. The myth of the god rescuing Ariadne, who had been cruelly abandoned on the island of Naxos, was understood to mean that the human soul, like the Cretan princess, could find immortal life and happiness in the loving arms of the divine.

Orphics in a cult-society of the Roman period, perhaps from Pergamum in Asia Minor, which left behind some 80 hymns and some important representations on ritual bowls.

Orpheus is a strange figure, for in some aspects he seems a doublet of Dionysus, in others of Apollo. He was a legendary minstrel, whose music had the power to charm animals and trees, and even persuaded the rulers of the dead to give up his wife Eurydice. He was himself torn to pieces by Maenads, but his head continued to sing after his death. He was a natural centre for a mystery religion which promised life after death.

The Orphics had a myth, according to which man is compounded of two elements, his gross, mortal Titanic body, and his spiritual, divine soul. Zeus made love to his own daughter, Persephone, who bore him a son named Zagreus. Hera, the wife of Zeus, was fiercely jealous and incited the Titans to destroy the child. The Titans were the old powers which had ruled the world before the coming of Zeus. They made friends with the little boy by bringing him a mirror and other toys to play with, and then they tore him to pieces and ate him raw. His heart was saved and brought to Zeus, who swallowed it, and then destroyed the Titans with a thunderbolt. From the ashes of their bodies sprang mankind. Zeus now begot his son again, this time on a mortal woman named Semele, and he was reborn as the god Dionysus.

Relief showing Hermes, Eurydice and Orpheus. One of the roles of Hermes in mythology was to guide the dead to the underworld. Orpheus, the great minstrel, went to the underworld to rescue his dead wife, Eurydice. His music so moved the rulers of the dead, Pluto and Persephone, that they gave him permission to take Eurydice back with him to earth. Unfortunately, he turned to look back at her before she had quite emerged from the underworld, and she was lost to him for ever. The myth could imply, however, that it was not impossible for the human soul to escape the clutches of death and achieve a blessed immortality. A Roman copy, *c.*5th century AD.

Human beings, in consequence, are partly evil and partly divine. Mankind was made from the ashes of the evil Titans, but contains a divine ingredient because the Titans had eaten the child-god. Man's aim in life is to free his Dionysiac part from its Titanic integument. The revealed Mysteries of Orpheus offer him the way, by purity and abstention from animal flesh, ascetic practices and virtuous living. The Orphics believed in reincarnation and the transmigration of souls from one body to another, the weary cycle or wheel of death and rebirth. In becoming divine the initiates became immortal, for the words mean virtually the same thing in Greek.

A number of tablets, some of gold, have been found, mainly though not exclusively in southern Italy, dating from the 4th to the 3rd century BC and inscribed in verse with instructions to the soul as to its behaviour in the world of the dead. These are usually assigned to the Orphics, but it has recently been suggested that they may belong to Mysteries of Persephone.

You will find to the left of the House of Hades a
spring,
and by its side a white cypress standing.
Do not approach near this spring.
You will find another, with cold water flowing
from the Lake of Memory, and sentinels before it.
Say 'I am a child of Earth and starry Heaven,
but my race is of Heaven. You know this already.
But I am parched and perishing of thirst.
Quick, give me the cold water flowing from the
Lake of Memory.'
Then they will freely let you drink from the holy
spring,
and, after, you will have lordship with the other
heroes.

That is from Petelia. The next is from Thurii:

'I come in purity from a pure people,
O Queen of the Dead,
Eucles, Eubuleus, you other immortal gods.
I too claim to be of your blessed race.
Fate and the star-hurled thunderbolt
overwhelmed me.
I have flown out of the sorrow-heavy weary wheel,
I have moved within the crown I desire
with eager steps.
I have sunk into the lap of our Lady,
the Queen of the Dead.'
'Happy and blessed, you shall be a god,
mortal no more.'
'A kid I am fallen into milk.'

This last phrase recurs and, whatever it means, was evidently a ritual formula. We have a geography of the underworld and a system of passwords. We have also a religion of faith and personal salvation.

The Mysteries of Samothrace

The island of Samothrace had its own Mysteries, which attracted worshippers from all over the Graeco-Roman world. The cult dates from about

ABOVE Orpheus and the animals. It was said that the music of Orpheus tamed wild beasts, stopped rivers in mid-flow and caused mountains to move. His power over wild, unregenerate nature and his near-success in rescuing Eurydice from the dead made him the centre of mystery cults which promised a happy life after death to initiates. Mosaic from a villa in Sicily, 2nd or 3rd century AD.

LEFT Ruins of the Hall of Votive Gifts, Samothrace, built 6th century BC. King Philip II of Macedon and his queen, Olympias, the parents of Alexander the Great, were initiated into the Mysteries of Samothrace and so, probably, was the traveller and historian Herodotus. The island was an asylum for political refugees. Many Greek cities sent official observers to the Mysteries, presumably to obtain the blessings of the cult for their own people.

Cybele in her car drawn by lions, the sacred tree, and Attis. The myth was that Attis, Cybele's lover, castrated himself and bled to death. In the Roman festival of Attis, however, served by eunuch priests, the mourning for Attis was succeeded by a time of joy. Attis was sometimes called 'the reaped ear of corn' and the Mysteries had to do with the cycle of the seasons, and so with life after death. From an altar dedicated to Cybele in Asia Minor, late 3rd century AD.

700 BC and lasted a thousand years. The identity of the gods worshipped was part of the Mystery. They are called 'gods', or later 'great gods'. Herodotus (5th century BC) identifies them with divine beings called Cabeiroi from near his own home of Halicarnassus in Asia Minor, but this title is never found on Samothrace. We do however have three cult-titles, Axieros, Axiocersa, Axiocersos; Casmilos or Cadmilos is perhaps another name for one of these.

There were two stages of initiation. The initiate first became a *mystes*, indicating that secrets had been revealed to him verbally; only later did he become an *epoptes*, with the privilege of seeing the sacred spectacle. We do not know the details of initiation, but from the presence of ithyphallic statues and triangular clay objects probably symbolizing the female pudenda, and from some literary references, we may reasonably assume that the revelation had to do with life and its origins, fertility, and rebirth to new life. Initiates were given a purple sash, which was a symbol of protection against storms at sea, and a ring of magnetized iron providing continued contact with the divine power. The initiate had to be pure to be admitted, and was formally questioned to this effect. There was a lustration (ritual purification) also before he was admitted to the higher grade, and there is a general insistence on purity at all points. We do not know what was the spectacle seen by the *epoptes*. It may have been the birth of the divine child.

Initiates were very various. The first we know of for certain are Philip II of Macedon and his future wife Olympias (the parents of Alexander the Great), who are said to have met at the initiation ceremonies, though it is a reasonable deduction that Herodotus was an initiate. Ordinary people, including some slaves, were initiated from many cities of the eastern Greek world. The first recorded Roman initiate dates from 149 BC. From then on, the number of initiates increases.

The Samothracian Mysteries, like the Eleusinian, had their public aspect, and a large number of cities, all Greek, sent official *theoroi*, 'observers', presumably to offer sacrifice and secure blessings for their own people.

Cybele and Attis

In Western Asia a great mother-goddess was worshipped under a number of different names and guises. It was natural that such a power of fertility and life should have her own Mysteries, and it was under the name of Cybele that she came into the Graeco-Roman world as the chief deity of a mystery religion.

The underlying myth deals with the cycle of the year and the seasons, with life and death. While Cybele was asleep, Zeus tried to rape her. She resisted him and he spilled his seed on the ground. But she, who is the earth, became pregnant and gave birth to a bisexual monster named Agdistis. Dionysus overpowered this creature, drugged it and tied its male sex organ to a tree, so that on awakening and springing up the monster castrated itself. From the blood sprang a tree. The daughter of the river-god Sangarius plucked some fruit from the tree and placed it in her lap. She became pregnant. Her father was angry and wanted to kill both her and the child, but Cybele intervened to save them. The child grew to be a handsome young man, Attis. Cybele fell in love with him and took him as her mate, but she found him unfaithful and crazed his mind. In his madness he castrated himself and bled to death.

This was not the end, however. In the Roman festival of Cybele the time of mourning (*tristia*) was followed by a time of joy (*hilaria*). This is a myth of death and resurrection, of the cycle of the seasons, of the death of the old year and the rebirth of the new as a divine child. Attis was sometimes called 'the reaped ear of corn'.

The priests of the cult were eunuchs and self-castration was part of their initiation to the priesthood. The object of the castration is not wholly clear. According to one view, in offering their severed genitals they were offering their fertility permanently to the goddess. Another view is that to ancient thinkers the testes were a channel of emission, not a source of seed, and by removing this the priests were preserving their seed, the life-principle, within their own bodies, dedicated to the Mother's service.

Initiation into the Mysteries of Cybele and Attis in the Roman period was by baptism in bull's blood, the *taurobolium*. Some of those who experienced it described themselves as 'reborn for eternity'. Others renewed the baptism after 20 years. The initiate received milk as a symbol of his rebirth. He participated in a communion meal, in which the familiar cultic instruments of music, the tambourine and cymbal, served as plate and chalice.

Mithras and the Soul

Women were admitted to the Mysteries of Cybele, not to those of Mithras. Mithras came eastwards from Persia in the 1st century AD and his cult spread among soldiers and traders. Persian religion was concerned with the conflict between Order and Chaos, Light and Dark, and in the background to the Mysteries are the great powers of good and evil, Ahura Mazda and Angra Mainyu (see ZOROASTRIANISM). According to the myth Mithras, who is a power of light, was 'born from the rock'. He first

ABOVE Mithras slaying the great bull. The interpretation of this scene is highly controversial. What is certain is that it is a sacrificial act, leading to fertility, blessing and salvation. The god averts his gaze, for he is destroying a brother of the Good Creation. As the creative power of light, Mithras was also the Saviour from darkness and death. A Mithraic hymn says, 'Thou hast saved us also by pouring out the blood eternal.' Roman relief, 2nd or 3rd centuries AD.

LEFT Interior of a Mithraeum at Ostia, near Rome, with a statue of the god slaying the bull. The Mysteries of Mithras were conducted in underground chapels known as 'caves'. The initiation ceremonies involved real or symbolic tests of courage and endurance, and the purpose of the Mysteries was to enable initiates to enter the realms of light.

contested with the Sun and then won him as ally. His great saving act was to catch and kill a wild bull, from whose blood flowed the blessings of fertility for the world. In other stories he saved mankind from flood and drought. Eventually he ascended into heaven. He is the Saviour, the Mediator.

The central Mystery has to do with the journey of the soul. The soul is immortal. It descends at birth through the spheres of the planets accumulating impurities as it passes. Life on earth is a time of trial. The soul has the chance to shed its impurities through moral effort and revealed wisdom. After death the spirits of light and darkness contend for the soul. Mithras intervenes for his initiates. Those who are favoured pass upwards again, persuading the 'Immigration Officials', who block the path, to let them enter the realms of light. The religion is replete with astral symbolism.

There were seven grades of initiate. The lower three, or Servitors, comprised Raven, Bridegroom, Soldier; the upper four, or Participants, were Lion, Persian, Courier of the Sun, Father. Initiation at each stage involved real or symbolic tests of endurance. There is some evidence that initiates wore costumes appropriate to their grade. They met in underground chapels known as 'caves', with a representation of Mithras killing the bull as the focal point of worship. These chapels were mostly small, for Mithraism was never more than a minority cult.

Isis and Osiris

Egypt was 'the gift of the Nile', and it is natural that its myths should reflect this fact (see EGYPT). The goddess Isis represents the land of Egypt waiting for the fertilizing overflow of the Nile, personified as her consort Osiris. Seth, the power of drought, murdered and dismembered Osiris. Isis, sorrowing, reassembled the body, except for the phallus, substituting one of gold. Osiris found new life as lord of the dead, and was resurrected in his son Horus. But Osiris was also the corn. At Philae we see corn springing from the dead body: the inscription runs 'This is the form of him whom one may not name, Osiris of the Mysteries, who springs from the returning waters.' Effigies of corn were buried in tombs: the dead man may even be addressed as Osiris and commanded to raise himself to life. So we have a myth which is linked to the alternation of drought and fertility in the land, and promises that life will follow death as fertility supervenes on drought.

In the Hellenistic and Roman periods the worship of Isis spread far beyond Egypt: she is found from the Euphrates to York. She made universal claims: she was the One who is all things, the goddess of ten thousand names, the single form of all the gods and goddesses.

In the Hellespont she was known as Mystis, the lady of the Mysteries. In one hymn of praise she was made to say, 'I have revealed mystic indications to mankind.' In her own Mysteries the sufferings of Osiris, her own sorrows and their joyful conclusion were re-enacted, so that others too might overcome hardship and put on immortality. We have a valuable

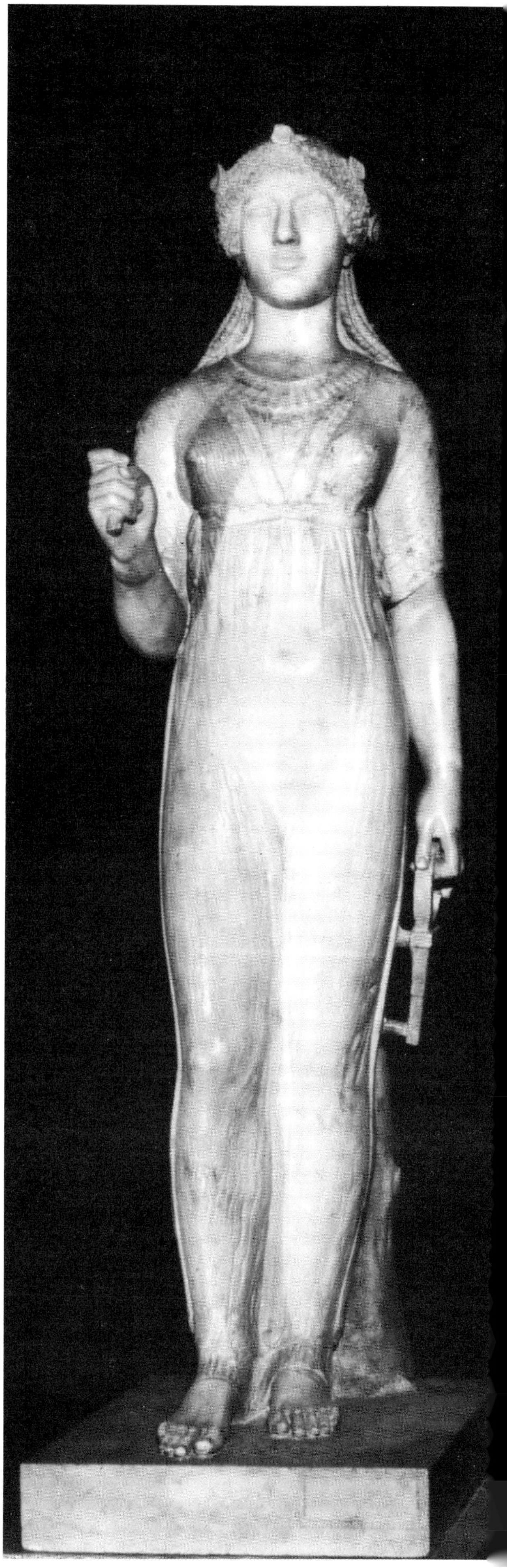

Statue of Isis, or perhaps of one of her votaries, from the temple of Isis at Pompeii. The goddess of ten thousand names was regarded in her Mysteries as the single form of all gods and goddesses. The myth of the killing of her husband, Osiris, of her suffering and sorrow, of her restoration of Osiris to life and the birth of her son, Horus, was re-enacted in the Mysteries so that others too might overcome suffering and tragedy to attain immortal life.

account of initiation at the end of Apuleius's novel *The Golden Ass* (2nd century AD). The hero is shown sacred writing, and is baptized and purified. He does not, of course, reveal the mystic secrets, but he says that he died to his former self, had an ecstatic vision of the cosmos, and experienced the illumination of a brilliant light. Isis's promise to him ran 'You shall live in blessing, you shall live glorious in my protection, and when you have fulfilled your allotted span of life and descend to the underworld, there too you shall see me, as you see me now, shining amid the darkness of Acheron and ruling in the depths of Hades. You shall live in the fields of Elysium and constantly honour me for my favour towards you. And if you show yourself obedient to my divinity by regular observance of religious duties and persistent chastity, you will know that I alone have permitted you to extend your life beyond the time allocated by your destiny.'

From Egypt 18 treatises usually known as the *Corpus Hermeticum* have survived, the scriptures of a small mystic sect, dating from the early centuries AD. Initiation began with a call to repentance, to abandon ignorance, error, the passions, corruption and incontinence, and to put on life and light, self-control and goodness. This involved asceticism, moral probity and silent meditation, and led to a revealed knowledge of God and an ecstatic vision of light. The experience was one of rebirth, of identity with all created things, of unity with God.

Christianity appeared to the Greeks and Romans as another mystery religion from the East, and St Paul was not afraid to use the language of the Mysteries. There was admission on profession of faith, an initiatory rite, a saviour-god, private gatherings of the faithful, a sacramental meal, a revealed wisdom, the promise of life beyond death. But Christianity had its distinctive aspects: a saviour-figure who was clearly historical; a concentration not on *gnosis* (revealed knowledge), but on *agape*, love; a fellowship which paid no regard to sex, wealth, class or status. Initiation was free, which is why A.D. Nock wrote, 'It was left to Christianity to democratize mystery.' (See CHRISTIANITY.)

Wall-painting associated with the cult of Isis. In Egyptian mythology Isis represented the land of Egypt, fertilized by the Nile flood, which was personified as Osiris. She was therefore closely connected with the theme of new life springing up after the 'death' of winter, and so with the hope of new life after death for human beings which was the central promise of the mystery religions. From Herculaneum, 1st century AD.

CHAPTER FOURTEEN

CHRISTIANITY

It is not the purpose of this article to argue that the doctrines of Christianity are untrue, or for that matter to argue the contrary. Christianity contains myths, in the sense of powerful and impressive stories about the world and the human condition which were for centuries generally believed to be literally true, but which few Christians any longer regard in that light. This is not to the discredit of Christianity or of millions of faithful Christians in the past. A great myth, like a great poem, contains truth more profound than the literal.

The first Christians were Jews and the new religion naturally bore the impress of its inheritance from Judaism. The books of the Old Testament were as much sacred scripture for Christians as for Jews, though in time Christians added books of their own to form the New Testament. Of all the books in the Christian Bible, the first and the last, Genesis and Revelation, have been the most important sources of Christian mythology.

The first eleven chapters of Genesis describe the creation of the universe and man; the coming of evil into the world which God had made, when the serpent tempted Adam and Eve in the garden of Eden; the expulsion of the first man and woman from the garden and the origin of work and death; the first murder, when Cain killed his younger brother, Abel; the wickedness of mankind, which caused God to send the great Flood to destroy them; how Noah and his family and the animals were saved from the Flood in the ark and repopulated the earth; the formation of separate nations by the descendants of Noah; and how the different languages came into existence, when God punished the building of the Tower of Babel by confusing the tongues of men and scattering them over the earth. Until comparatively recently this magnificent myth, or collection of myths, about the early history of mankind was common knowledge in the western world and helped to form western concepts of the universe and man.

Creation and Progress

In the opening chapters of Genesis there are two different accounts of how God created the world. According to the first of them, which is thought to date from the 5th century BC, in the beginning the universe was a watery chaos, 'without form and void', shrouded in darkness. God made light and

The creation. In the centre is God, commanding 'Let there be light.' Above him, the dove is the Holy Spirit, moving on the waters of chaos. Next come the creation of light and the separation of the waters. In the lower hemisphere are the creatures of land, sky and sea, with Adam naming the animals, right, and the creation of Eve, left. The circles suggest the wheel of the year, *annus* in Latin, at the top. The sun's chariot, bottom left, stands for the seventh day, the day of the sun or Sunday, on which God rested. Tapestry from Gerona Cathedral, Spain, 12th century.

everything else that exists, and finally he made man and woman. All this had taken six days, and on the seventh day God rested from his labours.

The story of the seven days of creation was accepted by generations of Christians as literally true and in the 17th century an Anglo-Irish scholar, James Ussher, Archbishop of Armagh, calculated the date of creation as 4004 BC. But in the 19th century discoveries in geology and paleontology (the study of fossil animals and plants) made it difficult to think that the universe had existed for less than 6000 years and had been created in a week. On the contrary, the evidence suggested that the world had formed slowly over aeons of time. In 1859 Charles Darwin published *The Origin of Species*, which did more than any other work to replace belief in the literal accuracy of Genesis with belief in the theory of evolution, that living organisms had developed from earlier forms.

The point of the myth in Genesis, however, does not depend on its literal accuracy. It is that the universe owes its existence to God and consequently has meaning, that life is not a tale told by an idiot, full of sound and fury, signifying nothing. The phrase 'And God saw that it was good', which occurs repeatedly in Genesis, implies an optimistic view of life, and man is the highest of God's creations, made in God's own likeness. The scientific theories which replaced it reduced man to a mere animal, the product of blind forces struggling for survival in a fiercely hostile environment, and in his nature as red in tooth and claw as any other predator.

To escape from this pessimistic and uncomfortable conclusion, a new myth took shape, the myth of progress, which was supported by the evolutionary theory of natural selection and the survival of the fittest. Earlier mythologies had often looked back to a golden age in the distant past and regarded the history of mankind as a record of decline. The myth of progress stands this attitude on its head. History is now a record of advance, not decline. As the fittest survive so, slowly but steadily, things improve. The golden age lies in the future and the nearest approximation to it yet reached is the state of affairs now.

The myth of progress reflected and supported the

The making of the sun, in God's left hand, and the moon, in his right, from Salisbury Cathedral. The creation of the universe meant the creation of time. On the fourth day, according to Genesis, God set lights in the sky, to separate the day from the night and 'to be for signs and for seasons and for days and years'. The story of the creation in seven days was accepted as literally true until the 19th century, when scientific discoveries cast serious doubt on it. The point of the myth, however, is that the world owes its existence to God and consequently that life is not empty and meaningless.

vigorous self-confidence and optimism of the 19th century. It produces a social climate of rising expectations, in which people expect the quality of life to keep improving and are alarmed and suspicious if it does not. It lies behind the tendency to regard western industrial civilization as the highest state yet attained by man, and so to look down on societies in the past, and on those in the present which are not industrialized to western standards, as 'backward' and 'primitive'.

Progress and Providence

Left-wing political movements in general, and Communism in particular, have drawn on the myth of progress and the allied notion of the perfectibility of man. The sufferings and miseries of life, in this view, are not the consequence of the innate inadequacy of human nature. They are the result of a wrong structure of society. When this structure is destroyed, as it inevitably will be in the march of progress, human beings will live together in ideal harmony and happiness in the golden age of the future. Right wing movements, like the Nazi party in Germany, have also drawn strength from a conviction of being carried forward on an irresistible tide of progress.

Although the myths of progress and human perfectibility frequently take a non-Christian or anti-Christian form, they have counterparts within Christianity itself. The statement in Genesis that man was made in God's image meant for the Christian that human nature was potentially perfectible, through the grace of God, but human beings would not become perfect in this life. Perfection would be attained in the afterlife, in heaven, not in the heaven on earth of political ideals. The Christian counterpart of the myth of progress is the idea of divine providence, the belief that God is working his purpose out as year succeeds year. God has a plan for the world. Hard as it may sometimes be to understand it, everything which happens is part of the plan, but the power behind the plan is a benevolent, all-seeing and purposeful deity, not the blind mechanisms of natural selection or the impersonal tides of history.

One enduring consequence of the creation myth is Sunday. Keeping the seventh day as the sabbath, a holy day and holiday, may go back ultimately to observation of the phases of the moon. The story in Genesis, however, enshrined the sabbath in Christian law and custom as the ordinance of God, and even in the modern world, for Christian and non-Christian alike, Sunday has a special place in the week. It has survived all the efforts to do away with it of tidy-minded calendar reformers, including those of the French Revolution who introduced a ten-day week. The Jewish sabbath falls on Saturday and it is a legacy of the pagan mythologies among which Christianity grew up that the Christian sabbath is Sunday, 'the day of the sun'. In AD 321 Constantine the Great, the first Christian emperor of Rome, who had previously worshipped 'the unconquered sun', ruled that the day of the sun should be the day of rest.

THE SEVEN DAYS OF CREATION

First Day
Creation of light, separation of light from darkness and the making of day and night.

Second Day
Making of the sky ('the firmament').

Third Day
Creation of the earth and the seas, plants and trees.

Fourth Day
Creation of the sun, moon and stars.

Fifth Day
Making of fish, sea creatures and birds.

Sixth Day
Creation of beasts of the earth, including cattle and insects, wild animals, man and woman. 'And God saw everything that he had made, and behold, it was very good' (Genesis 1.31).

Seventh Day
The day of rest. 'So God blessed the seventh day and hallowed it, because on it God rested from all his work which he had done in creation' (Genesis 2.3).

Adam and Eve

The second creation myth in Genesis is thought to date from the 10th century BC and concentrates on the making of man, which here comes before the creation of plants and animals. It is the familiar story of Adam and Eve, the serpent and the forbidden fruit, a myth of profound beauty and richness which explains how evil, death and suffering came into the good world which God had made.

The Lord God formed the first man, Adam ('man'), from the dust of the ground (*adamah*, so that the name Adam is a pun) and breathed life into his nostrils. Then God planted a garden in Eden, in the east, and put the man there to till it and keep it. The garden contained every tree that is beautiful to look at and good for food, and also the tree of life and the tree of the knowledge of good and evil. God told Adam that he must not eat the fruit of the tree of knowledge.

On the fifth and sixth days God made the animal kingdom in all its richness and variety. The realization that living species had not been created all at once, but had evolved slowly over millions of years, was a principal factor in weakening belief in the literal accuracy of Genesis.

ABOVE *The Creation of Animals*, by Jacopo Tintoretto, 16th century.

FAR LEFT *God Naming the Beasts*, by Francesco Ubertini, called 'Il Bacchiacca', 16th century.

LEFT God resting from his labours on the seventh day. From *Bible Moralisée*, French, *c*. 1250.

God said, 'It is not good that the man should be alone; I will make him a helper fit for him.' So God made all the animals and birds, and brought them to Adam, who gave them all their names, but none of them was a suitable helper for him. God put Adam into a deep sleep and took out one of his ribs. From it God fashioned a woman and Adam called her Eve (another pun, on the Hebrew word for 'living').

The serpent, the subtlest of wild animals, told Eve that if she and Adam ate the forbidden fruit they

The marriage of Adam and Eve. According to the second creation story in Genesis, none of the animals and birds which God made was a suitable mate for the first man, Adam. So God fashioned Eve from one of Adam's ribs and brought her to Adam. Then Adam said, 'This at last is bone of my bones and flesh of my flesh.' The myth provided a warrant for the institution of marriage. Adam and Eve lived happily and innocently, close to God, in the beautiful Garden of Eden. Christian tradition pictured all the animals – here including the fabulous unicorn – living peacefully together there too, for as yet death had not come into the world. From an early 15th-century MS.

would not die, but would become like God, knowing good and evil. Eve ate the fruit and gave some to Adam, who ate it, and their eyes were opened and they knew that they were naked. They were ashamed and made themselves aprons of fig leaves.

Then they heard the Lord God walking in the garden in the cool of the day and they tried to hide themselves. When God taxed them with what they had done, Adam blamed Eve and Eve blamed the serpent. God cursed the serpent and condemned it to go on its belly all the days of its life. Adam and Eve he punished with death, with the toil of wringing a living from the land, with the pain of childbirth and the subjection of woman to man. Then God drove Adam and Eve from the beautiful garden, to prevent them from eating the fruit of the tree of life and becoming immortal, and at the east of the garden God set angels with a flaming sword, to guard the way to the tree of life.

It was after this that Adam knew Eve and she bore him a son, Cain, who was to be the first murderer.

The Fall of Man

Evil entered the world because the first man and woman broke God's law, and they broke it because they wanted to be like God. In the modern age of totalitarianism, nuclear weapons, pollution and over-use of resources, the moral seems clear. The story is about the double nature of man, who stands midway between the animal and the divine, who is half-brute and half-god, made in the divine likeness but made of clay. In his insatiable longing to master all he surveys he tries to raise himself too high, to make himself all-powerful like God. This determination to grasp what he cannot control brings evil on the world and so man knows good and evil, in the sense of experiencing them.

In traditional Christian theology the myth means that man from the beginning has been a rebel against God, that a fissure has opened up between God and man. As Cardinal Newman said in his *Apologia Pro Vita Sua* (1864); '*If* there is a God, *since* there is a God, the human race is implicated in some terrible aboriginal calamity. It is out of joint with the purposes of its Creator.'

To this aboriginal calamity theologians traced the root of 'original sin', a term first used by St Augustine, late in the 4th century. Original sin means that all human beings, quite apart from the individual sins they commit, are infected with an inescapable taint of corruption which cannot be eradicated by human effort alone. Man is a fallen being, evil and guilty from birth. At the same time, in the Christian view, he is redeemable. Through the grace of God and the sacrifice of Christ on the cross, man can be saved from guilt and death, and made perfect in the next world, if not in this. In heaven he becomes what he ought to have been and recovers the state of innocent happiness close to God which, in the myth, Adam and Eve experienced before the Fall.

The story of Eden has had a deep and long-lasting influence in other directions. In Genesis one of the consequences of man's first disobedience was that shame became inextricably linked with sex. The myth provided a warrant for one of the strands in the complicated web of Christian attitudes to sex, the puritanical strand which regards sex and the body with loathing and shame. On the other hand, support has been found in Genesis for the myth of nudism, the notion that nakedness is 'natural', virtuous and healthy, as the state of Adam and Eve in the garden of Eden before they fell.

The fact that God condemned Eve to be subordinate to Adam seemed for centuries to prove the inferiority of women and justify male dominance. The Fall was blamed on Eve, who persuaded Adam to eat the fatal fruit, and her part in the story contributed to the deep-rooted belief in the evilness of woman (which exists far beyond the West), the conviction that women are inherently vicious.

ABOVE The angel shows St John the river of paradise (Revelation 22:1). The lost paradise of the human race's childhood, the Garden of Eden which Adam and Eve forfeited, became the paradise which mankind would regain in the future, beyond death. In the Book of Revelation the heavenly city, New Jerusalem, contains the river of life and the tree of life from Eden. Tapestry from Angers, France, 14th century.

LEFT The expulsion from Eden. The myth of Adam and Eve is a response to the question, how did evil enter the world which the good God made? The myth's answer is the fatal ambition of man. The first human beings tried to gain the powers of God himself. They were tempted to this by the serpent, which traditionally had four legs and could talk. God cursed the serpent to go on its belly. He expelled Adam and Eve from the paradise garden and inflicted on mankind death and the other evils of the human condition. Fresco by Tommaso Masaccio in Sta Maria del Carmine, Florence, 13th century.

Paradise and the Noble Savage

Eden means 'pleasure' in Hebrew. The garden of Eden as a paradise, an ideal place of happiness, free from death, work, conflict, pain, sorrow, guilt and shame, exercised a magnetic attraction as a focus for the longing to escape from the miseries of the human condition to a utopia. In the Middle Ages the garden was often believed to exist in the sky or in a mysterious region 'outside this world', where the souls of the blessed dead lived in idyllic bliss, waiting for the Last Judgment. Alternatively, it was also long believed that the paradise garden was still in existence on earth, just beyond the frontiers of known geography.

The Christian idea of paradise was influenced by the Greek and Roman myth of the Elysian Fields or Isles of the Blessed, a paradise far across the sea, and by Celtic myths of the otherworld. It sometimes coalesced with belief in the millennium (founded on Revelation, chapter 20), the period of a thousand years after the Second Coming of Christ, when Christ would establish a kingdom of ideal happiness on earth.

When Columbus sailed across the Atlantic to reach the East and discovered the Americas, he believed he was close to Eden. Sir Walter Raleigh, travelling up the Orinoco River through beautiful country in 1595, thought for a moment that he had found the earthly paradise. Early reports of the native peoples of the New World inspired comparisons with the mythical golden age and with Eden. The Indians of the Americas were said to enjoy a state of paradisal simplicity and innocence. They lived in freedom, they did little work, they needed few clothes, no money and no weights and measures, and they seemed to have no laws, courts or quarrels.

Christian preachers condemned much of the popular picture of heaven as mythical. Heaven is a spiritual condition, but at popular levels it was imagined as a place in the sky where faithful Christians would live happily in physical bodies. In art, heaven is often represented symbolically. In *The Virgin of the Lilies* by Carlos Schwabe (d. 1926), the Virgin and Child are seen in a sky-garden of lilies among the clouds. White is the colour of purity and the lily is a symbol of the immaculate conception of Christ.

This naive impression was spoiled when the Indians were found to fight wars, but it was the foundation of the myth of the noble savage, the belief that simpler societies are fundamentally superior to civilized societies. This is the converse of the contemptuous modern attitude to primitives, noted earlier, and it has recently come back into fashion.

The concept of the noble savage in turn inspired a new, sympathetic interest in Celtic, Germanic and Scandinavian mythology and influenced the rise of democracy through the myth of the social contract, which explained how governments had come into existence in a world in which man was originally free. The myth was that in the distant past human beings had voluntarily given up some of their freedoms to secure the blessings of orderly government. The corollary was that government should rest not on force but on the consent of the governed.

As the whole earth was opened up by exploration, it became difficult to think that Eden still existed undiscovered. However, the earthly paradise, the millennium and utopia have reappeared in the future heaven on earth of left-wing political movements.

Heaven and Hell

Many Christians now regard hell as a myth and in the past Christian theology condemned much of the popular picture of heaven as mythical. Preachers frequently reproved their congregations for imagining heaven in concrete, physical terms as an improved edition of life on earth. In theology, heaven is not a place but a condition, the state of being with God. In traditional popular belief, however, it was a place in the sky, radiant with light and filled with sublime music. Faithful Christians would live there in physical bodies, forever young and vigorous, feasting, singing and dancing. No one would ever be hungry or thirsty, sad or weary, angry or bored, and no one would ever work.

In Christian art heaven is often pictured as a beautiful landscape, with meadows and trees, the tree of life and the river or fountain of life. Or it may be a sheltered garden of flowers. Both these images are derived from Eden. Another image of heaven is as a city, derived from the Book of Revelation and the Old Testament.

'Now you must note that the city stood upon a mighty hill, but the pilgrims went up that hill with ease . . . The talk they had with the Shining Ones [angels] was about the glory of the place; who told them that the beauty and glory of it was inexpressible. There, said they, is the "Mount Zion, the heavenly Jerusalem, the innumerable company of angels, and the spirits of just men made perfect". You are going now, said they, to the paradise of God, wherein you shall see the tree of life, and eat of the never-fading fruits thereof; and when you come there, you shall have white robes given you, and your walk and talk shall be every day with the King, even all the days of eternity . . .

Now I saw in my dream that these two men went in at the gate: and lo, as they entered, they were transfigured, and they had raiment put on that shone like gold. There were also that met them with harps and crowns, and gave them to them – the harps to praise withal, and the crowns in token of honour. Then I heard in my dream that all the bells in the city rang again for joy . . .

Now, just as the gates were opened to let in the men, I looked in after them, and, behold, the City shone like the sun; the streets also were paved with gold, and in them walked many men, with crowns on their heads, palms in their hands, and golden harps to sing praises withal.' (From *The Pilgrim's Progress*, 1678.)

The celestial city is the New Jerusalem, which in Revelation (chapter 21) is seen coming down from heaven to earth. These are all symbols of a reality which, in theology, is so far from anything known on earth as to be ultimately indescribable. The land-

scape is a symbol of eternal life and beauty, the garden of refuge, the city of security and splendour.

The Church inherited the concept of hell from both Judaism and the classical world, and persisted in it partly from the conviction that hell was needed as a deterrent against crime and anarchy, and partly from a belief in retributive justice, that the wicked deserved to be punished. Hell is the polar opposite of heaven. The damned writhe in fire, boil in cauldrons, freeze in ice, drown in filth. They are torn limb from limb, swallowed and excreted by monsters, stung by snakes and scorpions, mangled, flogged, flayed and hanged. The tortures are endlessly repeated, on and on for ever, and just as the supreme joy of heaven is the presence of God, so the supreme horror of hell is the presence of the Devil.

The traditional picture of the Last Judgment at the end of the world, when Christ comes to judge the living and the dead, is treated by some Christian thinkers as a myth. Some theologians suggest that the doctrine of the Incarnation, that Jesus was God in human form, is also a myth: not meaning that it is untrue, but that its truth is poetic rather than literal. But a great many Christians reject this line of argument.

The Fall of Lucifer

Many Christians now regard the Devil as a myth. The story of Eden found the origin of evil in man's first disobedience. It seems clear, however, that much of the evil and undeserved suffering in the world does not spring from human action. Consequently another story, based on Isaiah and Revelation, traces the taproot of evil to a non-human source. The Devil was originally a great archangel, beautiful and proud.

Coronation of the Virgin in Paradise by Jacobello del Fiore, 15th century. Jesus and Mary are attended by the ranks of the saints and martyrs who, like the Virgin, were believed to have gone straight to heaven when they died. The great majority of ordinary Christians were thought to go first to purgatory, where they were purged of their sins to fit them for heaven, while the irredeemably wicked went straight to hell.

RIGHT Detail from *Hell*, attributed to Hieronymus Bosch in the Palazzo Ducale, Venice. The winged figure with a sword in the right foreground is the Archangel Michael, who defeated the rebel angels in the war in heaven, another myth which accounts for the existence of evil in the world. The rebels and their leader, the Archangel Lucifer, who in his pride had tried to make himself God's equal, were expelled from heaven, as Adam and Eve for the same offence were cast out of Eden. Lucifer, 'light-bearer', is connected with the morning star and the myth of his rebellion may go back ultimately to observation of the morning star apparently trying to defy and rival the rising sun.

OPPOSITE, ABOVE Two details from *The Seven Deadly Sins*, by Hieronymus Bosch, 15th century. In the upper roundel, two angels sound the last trump and Christ comes in majesty to judge the living and the dead, who rise from their graves. The traditional picture of the Last Judgment is regarded by some theologians as poetically rather than literally true. Below, demons torment the damned in a hell of flames and smoke. Many Christians now regard the traditional hell as a myth and its sufferings as symbols of the spiritual and psychological agony of those who have cut themselves off from God.

In his pride he tried to make himself the equal of God. In punishment he was hurled from heaven down to earth, where he has worked evil ever since.

And there was war in heaven: Michael and his angels fought against the dragon; and the dragon fought and his angels, and prevailed not; neither was their place found any more in heaven. And the great dragon was cast out, that old serpent, called the Devil, and Satan, which deceiveth the whole world: he was cast out into the earth, and his angels were cast out with him. And I heard a loud voice saying in heaven, Now is come salvation, and strength, and the kingdom of our God, and the power of his Christ: for the accuser of our brethren is cast down, which accused them before our God day and night . . . Therefore rejoice, ye heavens, and ye that dwell in them. Woe to the inhabiters of the earth, and of the sea! for the devil is come down unto you, having great wrath, because he knoweth that he hath but a short time. (From Revelation, chapter 12.)

Satan's followers, the angels who were expelled from heaven with him, became the demons which tempt men to sin so as to lure them into the Devil's clutches in hell and deny their souls to God. It was said that the great archangel's name was Lucifer, 'light-bearer', in heaven and Satan, 'adversary', after his fall. Satan's crime was the same as Adam's, the attempt to rival God. Both were rebels against God and their two myths coalesced, with the serpent of Eden becoming either an agent of the Devil or the subtle Enemy himself in disguise. There is no suggestion of this in Genesis, but Revelation calls Satan 'that old serpent'.

As Christianity gained pagan converts, the early Church identified the pagan deities as masks worn by Satan and the fallen angels to deceive mankind. Worship of pagan gods was condemned as the worship of demons. On the other hand, Christianity grew up in a pagan world and converts inevitably brought pagan beliefs and myths with them. Christianity had no goddess and to some extent, in popular belief, the Virgin Mary took the place of the pagan mother-goddesses. Similarly, Christ was sometimes assimilated to the dying and rising gods of paganism, though they died and rose from death every year, and Christ but once. Another classical tradition which passed into Christianity, with the establishment of Rome as the headquarters of the Church, was the myth of Rome as the eternal city, which St Augustine transformed into the image of the City of God, the eternal city of the righteous.

LEFT At the Last Judgment the Archangel Michael weighs each human soul in a balance to determine innocence or guilt, a theme which goes back to Egyptian mythology and the weighing of the conscience after death. Stained glass window from Eaton Bishop, early 14th century.

In Giotto's *Crucifixion*, 14th century, in the Lower Church at Assisi, angels catch the blood of the crucified Christ in cups. According to the Grail myth, which developed in the Middle Ages, the Grail was the cup of the Last Supper and was also used by Joseph of Arimathea to collect some of the blood that flowed from the Saviour's wounds. Thus doubly linked with Christ's redeeming blood, the Grail was the supreme talisman of eternal life and union with God. It was guarded in secret in a mysterious castle and only the noblest of knights could succeed in the quest for it.

The Quest of the Grail

In the Middle Ages the fascinating though unorthodox Christian myth of the Grail developed. The earliest surviving story of it is *Le Conte du Graal* by a French author, Chrétien de Troyes, written about 1180 and unfinished. The hero is a young knight named Perceval, who comes to a mysterious castle near a broad river. The lord of the castle is the Fisher King, so called because, crippled and unable to walk or ride, his only pastime is fishing. Entertained by the king in the castle, Perceval sees a procession. First comes a young man carrying a white lance with a white point from which a drop of red blood runs down onto his hand. Then come two more young men holding candelabra and with them a beautiful girl, richly dressed, bearing in her hands a golden grail, studded with precious stones. As she enters with the grail, there is such a brilliant light that the candles lose their radiance, like stars dimmed by the moon or the sun. After her comes another maiden with a silver carving dish. The procession crosses the hall and goes out into another room.

Perceval is consumed with curiosity about what he has seen, but no one makes any comment and he is too polite to ask. Next morning, the castle seems to be completely deserted. As he rides out through the gate, the drawbridge rises under him, apparently by itself. He is later told that he should have asked whom the grail served. If he had, the Fisher King would have been healed and great good would have come of it.

According to later writers, the Grail was the cup of the Last Supper, in which Jesus gave his disciples the wine which was his blood. It came into the possession of a rich follower of Jesus, Joseph of Arimathea, who caught in it some of the blood flowing from the wounds of the crucified Saviour. This great symbol and talisman of eternal life, the container of Christ's redeeming blood, was guarded in secret in a mysterious castle by a succession of Grail Kings, descended from Joseph of Arimathea. In the stories the brave knight of King Arthur's court who fights his way to the Grail through appalling perils and hardships wins immortality and union with God.

The Church cold-shouldered the Grail stories, which imply that salvation can be won otherwise than through the Church. The myth was constructed largely of materials which came originally from pagan Celtic religion. The Grail is usually either the cup or the dish of the Last Supper and is closely linked with the Mass, but its remote ancestors are the magic vessels of immortality in the Celtic otherworld. The Grail King is usually crippled or feeble with age and as a result his land is waste and barren. One of the hero's tasks is to heal the king and so restore life to the waste land, a theme again rooted in pagan Celtic beliefs.

The stories are full of mysterious and enticing motifs. There is the strange title Fisher King or Rich Fisher for the custodian of the Grail. In his castle is the lance that runs with blood, which is the lance that pierced Christ's side on the cross. To heal the Fisher

King the hero must ask a question: in its earliest form it is 'Whom does the Grail serve?' The beautiful Grail Bearer and the Loathly Damsel, a hideous hag who reproaches the hero, are apparently two aspects of a pagan goddess. A theme of revenge is connected with a broken sword which the hero must mend. There does not seem to have been any coherent pagan myth lying behind the Grail stories. Medieval authors built up a Christian myth from loose and shifting pagan traditions.

The Classical Renaissance

During the Middle Ages attempts were made to reconcile classical mythology with Christianity. In the Renaissance, with mounting admiration for Greek and Roman civilization, these efforts were intensified. The myths and legends of the ancient world, so some scholars believed, contained profound wisdom which had been cloaked in fable to conceal it from the common people. Though the myths were pagan, they 'prefigured' or anticipated the truths of Christianity.

This line of approach could have peculiar results. An anonymous French poem of about 1300 reinterpreted Ovid's *Metamorphoses* (see ROME) as a collection of tales prefiguring Christian doctrine. Diana stood for the Trinity and Actaeon for Jesus, Phaethon who stole the sun's chariot was Lucifer, the light-bearer, and Demeter searching for Persephone stood for Mother Church seeking strayed souls. An author in 1531 turned the myth of Zeus raping the handsome boy Ganymede into a symbol of the pure soul finding rapture in the love of God.

ABOVE *The Three Graces* by Raphael, 16th century. During the Renaissance a revival of enthusiasm for Greek and Roman mythology aroused interest in classical groups of three, such as the Three Graces, which were believed to signify the reconciliation of opposites by a third factor that unites and transcends them.

LEFT The Grail, from a French manuscript, 15th century. The three knights are Galahad, Perceval and Bors, the only knights of King Arthur's court who were worthy to achieve the Grail, according to the 13th-century *Queste del Saint Graal.*

The fact that the Christian God is both One and Three excited interest in groups of three in classical mythology, believed to show a pair of opposites with the third factor, the unity that reconciles and transcends them. The classical image of the Three Graces appears frequently in Renaissance art with this connotation. The three goddesses who were rivals for a beauty prize in the Greek story of the Judgment of Paris were treated in the same spirit and the myth of the love affair between Mars and Venus was similarly interpreted, as a union of the opposites of war and love.

The Church was uneasy with the search for truth in pagan mythology. Many churchmen were enthusiasts for classical civilization, but the Church naturally frowned on attempts to revitalize pagan myths and on the unorthodox brand of Christianity which such attempts produced.

Alchemy and the Rosicrucians

The Church was also uneasy about another unorthodox Christian system, alchemy, which shared with the Grail stories the principle that man could find salvation through channels other than those of the Church. On one level, alchemy was an early form of chemistry and an attempt to make gold. On another, it was a mystical quest for God, immortality and a 'golden' state of spiritual perfection.

The central alchemical myth was that of the

ABOVE AND OPPOSITE, ABOVE Two illustrations from an alchemical MS of the 16th century, the *Splendor Solis* of Salomon Trismosin. The beheaded, dismembered corpse represents the destruction of the 'old Adam', the old self. The sun rising above a sleeping town and landscape, bringing light into darkness, is a symbol of life after death, of inward spiritual illumination and rebirth.

Philosopher's Stone. This profoundly mysterious object and spiritual condition, 'a stone and not a stone', was believed to turn everything it touched into gold. It was also the Elixir of Life, a universal panacea which cured all diseases and gave its possessor eternal life and youth. All the chemical processes of alchemy were meant to lead to the production of the Stone, which was also the state of spiritual perfection. In making the Stone, the alchemist became the Stone. Alchemical symbolism mingled Christian, pagan and astrological motifs. There were said to be seven processes in the making of the Stone, corresponding to the seven days of creation in Genesis and to the seven planets, and a parallel was often drawn between the Stone and Christ.

Secrets of Nature, an alchemical text attributed to Arnold of Villanova (1235–1311), draws a parallel between the making of the Philosopher's Stone and the life of Christ. It says that the world was lost through a woman (meaning Eve) and must be recovered through a woman, so the alchemist must 'take the pure mother and put her in bed with the sons according to your intention and there let her do strictest penance until she is well cleansed from all sins'. The pure mother will then give birth to a son. He will preach to all, saying 'Signs have appeared in sun and moon.' The son must be 'taken and beaten well and scourged lest by reason of pride he perish'. Then the alchemist must 'put him in bed to enjoy himself' and subsequently 'take him pure and extinguish in cold water'. Next he must be handed over to the Jews to be crucified. 'And while he is crucified, sun and moon will be seen, and then the veil of the temple will be rent and there will be a great earthquake. So then the fire is to be increased and then he will give up the ghost.'

These instructions refer, on one level, to chemical experiments conducted in the alchemist's laboratory. Their obscurity and their mingling of Christian and erotic symbolism are typical of alchemy.

In the 16th and 17th centuries a gulf opened up between science and religion, as science ate away at the Christian picture of the world and so at Christianity itself. Because alchemy had two sides to it, chemical and spiritual, it appeared to offer a possible bridge across the gap. Hence its importance in three manifestos issued in Germany in 1614 to 1616, which announced the existence of the Rosicrucian Brotherhood, a secret organization of wise men which was almost certainly a fiction. The Brotherhood called for 'a universal and general reformation of the whole wide world', to be achieved through the union of Protestant Christianity with alchemy, magic and advances in science. The supposed founder of the Rosicrucian Brotherhood was Christian Rosenkreutz (Rosy-Cross). Born in Germany in 1378 and brought up in a monastery, he travelled to Syria, Egypt and Morocco, gathering knowledge from great masters of arcane wisdom. On his return to Germany, three brethren from his former monastery joined him to form the Rosicrucian Brotherhood. Five more members were later accepted into the Fraternity, which was pledged to chastity and the healing of the sick. Christian Rosenkreutz died at the age of 106 and was buried in a secret, seven-sided vault. The remaining brethren handed on their knowledge to a few carefully chosen successors, some of whom opened the vault 120 years after the death of Rosenkreutz and found his body perfectly preserved. The story is an interesting example of a myth apparently deliberately created to promote and give authority to a social programme.

The Organized Conspiracy

A witch, in late medieval and early modern Europe, was not merely someone who allegedly caused death, disease and harm by evil magic. He, or more often she, was believed to be a member of a gigantic conspiracy, organized and led by the Devil, whose aim was to destroy Christianity, degrade all decent values, overturn the established order, set the poor against the rich and the young against the old, and bring society down in ruins. Those suspected of this offence were tortured and brainwashed until they confessed to it, and were then executed. Estimates of their numbers range from 250,000 to a million. It is generally agreed that at least the great majority of them were entirely innocent.

At the heart of the witch mania lies the myth of the organized conspiracy. This is based on the belief that the evils which currently afflict the world do not occur in the ordinary course of events, but are caused by a subversive group, responsible for all seriously damaging occurrences. During the witch persecutions these occurrences included bad weather, crop failures and epidemics.

In the late Middle Ages, when witch-hunting on a large scale began, society was changing. Familiar institutions were in decline and the Church was under attack from reformers. A fear grew that the whole fabric of society was in danger. Behind the danger was seen the hand of the Devil. Christians had long tended to blame all the world's ills on the Enemy, who had been built up into a figure of titanic power by theologians. Later, tension between Roman Catholics and Protestants, each convinced of their own brand of truth and consequently of the diabolical malevolence of any opposition to it, contributed to the climate of fear. The fear demanded an outlet. Catholics and Protestants alike found in witches, or supposed witches, Satan's human agents in a huge covert conspiracy against everything they held dear, and reacted with terrifying savagery.

The myth of the organized conspiracy did not die when witch-hunting ended. In the 18th century secret societies, especially the Freemasons, were accused of conspiring against society. In the 19th century the same charge was brought against the Jews. In the 20th century the myth has played its part in anti-semitism, in the Nazi atrocities in Germany, and in the persecution of supposed enemies of society in America and behind the Iron Curtain. Myths are not invariably a force for good.

LEFT Witches and demons. The great witch persecutions in Europe were based on the myth of the organized conspiracy, the belief that the evils which afflict the world are caused by a campaign of deliberate subversion. In this case it was believed that the conspiracy was directed by the Devil and that witches were his human fifth column against Christianity. Mural from Rila Monastery, Bulgaria, 19th century.

CHAPTER FIFTEEN

THE CELTS

The combined evidence of modern archeologists and ancient writers tells us that during the latter half of the first millennium BC a great 'barbarian' people occupied vast areas of western and central Europe. Theirs was an Iron Age culture and they were among the greatest technologists of the ancient world. Craftsmen in metal, builders of roads and makers of chariots, and experts in agriculture and pastoralism, they laid the foundations of western European civilization. The Celts were warriors of unparalleled courage and ferocity, feared even by the Roman legions. They sacked Rome herself around 290 BC and at the zenith of their military power their territory extended from the British Isles in the west to Turkey in the east. It was the imperialistic ambitions of Rome and the free-booting incursions of the German tribes that robbed the Celtic lands – except Ireland – of their political independence, and assimilated or destroyed many of their cultural achievements.

Our knowledge of the religion and mythology of the various Celtic peoples – apparently they were not all of the same ethnic stock, nor did they have a political unity, even though they spoke dialects of the same language – comes from three geographic regions, Gaul (modern France), Britain (particularly Wales), and Ireland.

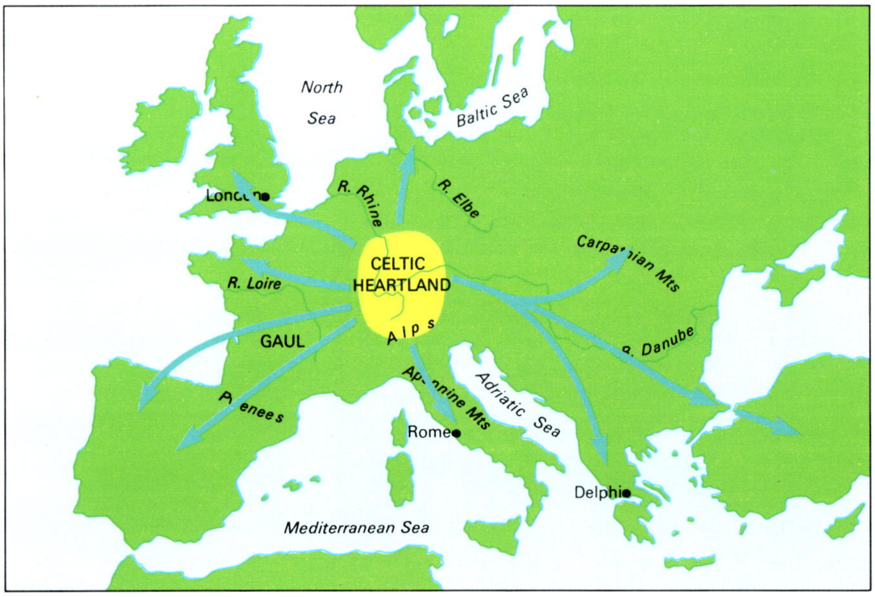

As provinces of the Roman Empire, both Gaul and Britain were influenced by Graeco-Roman culture for some time before the Christian era. Celtic Ireland, in contrast, retained its cultural integrity until the adoption of Christianity during the 5th century AD. It follows that evidence for the mythology of pagan Celtic society has been preserved best in Ireland, but the significance of the Irish material can be understood only by reference to such evidence as survives for the religions of Gaul and Britain.

Celtic Religion

Of the mythology of the Gauls nothing survives. Theirs was an oral and not a written literary tradition. Julius Caesar (1st century BC) reported that the druids, the professional learned men of early Celtic society, actually forbade the writing down of their knowledge, even though they were familiar with the Greek alphabet and used it for other purposes. There can be no doubt that the druids were motivated by no more than the principle of the 'closed shop', by which the skilled and learned sections of all societies in all ages have protected the integrity and status of their professions.

On the other hand, we do have information about the religion of the Celts. It is fragmentary and of limited value, but scholars must refer to it to help them unravel the twisted strands of Irish and Welsh mythology. Such information comes to us from two sources. First, there were the writings of contemporary Greek and Roman commentators. Unfortunately, few of the writers had personal experience of Gaulish society, much less an understanding of it. They relied on hearsay. For the few who actually had direct contact with the Celts – Caesar is a case in point – there were sound socio-political reasons for their commentaries to be biased. We are thus obliged to treat all this evidence with considerable caution.

Second, there are the iconographic representations of the Gaulish deities, and the dedications that sometimes accompany them. Here the difficulty is that the material dates from after the Roman Conquest and was undoubtedly inspired by Graeco-Roman models. This raises the question of how valid in purely Celtic terms the anthropomorphic portrayal of the native deities is, and to what extent this Gallo-Roman art expresses classical rather than Celtic

religious concepts. It is very much an open question, but there is some evidence that the religion of the early Celts was essentially aniconic and that the Celtic deities were originally conceived of as spirits associated with forests, rivers, lakes and other natural features, rather than as anthropomorphic beings. This latter idea seems to have arisen and developed as a result of cultural interference from the Mediterranean world. Here perhaps the story told of Brennus, the Celtic leader defeated at Delphi in 279 BC, laughing in scorn when he heard that the Greeks believed in gods in human form lends support.

Nevertheless, in spite of the obvious shortcomings of our sources, we can establish with fair certainty the following facts:

1. The Celts were a religious people to a high degree.
2. They believed in a life after death (not the Pythagorean transmigration of souls), to the amazement, and indeed envy, of the Roman world.
3. Celtic religion had a large number of female deities of primary importance – mother-goddesses, war-goddesses, tutelary goddesses. This may reflect the prestige of women in early Celtic society.
4. The concept of the triune god, three manifestations of a single deity, was a feature of Celtic religion.

ABOVE The stag-antlered god Cernunnos sits among the animals – bull, stag, wolf and hound. He wears round his neck a torc, a symbol of deity, and holds another in his right hand and a ram-headed serpent in his left. From the Gundestrup cauldron, 2nd century BC, found in Denmark.

LEFT Pre-Roman stone figure of an unidentified, probably local, deity from Euffigneix, Marne, France. The figure has a torc about its neck, and a boar, the most characteristic cult-animal of the Celts, is carved on its torso.

The man-eating monster of Noves, Bouches-du-Rhône, France, has a human arm complete with bracelet protruding from its jaws, while its front paws grasp two human heads. Dating from the 3rd century BC, it is a comparatively small figure, a little over 1 metre high.

THE GODS OF GAUL

Belenus, most widely worshipped Celtic god: equated with Apollo by classical writers, though there is no evidence of Celtic sun-worship: associated with pastoralism, and there may be a link with Irish Beltine (*bel* 'bright', *tine* 'fire'), the fire-festival of purification on 1 May: Welsh ancestor-deity Beli Mawr (Beli the Great) has been identified with him.

Cernunnos, 'Horned One', widely worshipped from an early date: portrayed zoomorphically, wearing stag's antlers: on Gundestrup cauldron (2nd century BC) surrounded by animals: lord of all living creatures: possible prototype of the horned devil of medieval Christianity.

Epona, 'Great Mare' (Welsh *eb-ol* 'colt'), known throughout Celtic world: patron-goddess of horsemen, revered by Roman cavalry: portrayed riding side-saddle on horseback: probably reflects the cultural importance of the horse in early Celtic society.

Lugus, 'Shining One', widely revered as the inventor of all arts and skills, including war and healing: equated with Irish Lug Samildanach, 'skilled in many arts', and Welsh Lleu Llaw Gyffes, 'of the dexterous hand': Caesar identified him with Mercury: abhorred by the early Christians, who destroyed his many temples: the place names Lyon, Loudon, Laon (France), Leyden (Holland) and Leignitz (Poland) derive from Gaulish *Lug(u)-dunon*, 'fort of Lugus', while Carlisle is based on Romano-British *Luguvalium*, 'strong in Lugus'.

Nantosuelta, possibly a river-goddess (Welsh *nant* 'stream'): her iconographic symbol, the raven, suggests a link with Irish war-goddess Morrigan, also associated with rivers: usually appears as consort of Sucellus.

Ogmios, champion of the gods and guide of the dead: carries a club and is identified with Hercules: also shown as an old man with happy followers whose ears are chained to his tongue: explained by the Greek writer Lucian as the god of eloquence: the Celts believed eloquence more powerful than physical strength and the Irish kings dreaded the satire of poets: equated with Irish Ogma.

Sucellus, 'Good Striker': his iconographic symbol is the mallet: also carried a bowl said to signify abundance: Caesar identified him with Dis Pater as the Celtic god of the underworld and ancestor-deity: equated with Irish In Dagda.

Taranis, 'Thunderer' (Irish *torann*, Welsh *taran*, 'thunder'): his iconographic emblems are the wheel and the lightning-flash: greatly revered by the Gauls: sometimes identified with Jupiter.

The Irish Sagas

Unlike the continental Celts, the Celtic-speaking peoples of Ireland and Wales have preserved extensive literatures of considerable antiquity. Of the Irish it has been said that they possess the oldest literary tradition in the vernacular of any northern European people, and that Ireland 'has preserved the richest store of mythological traditions of any country north of the Alps' (Dillon and Chadwick, 134). Most of the early sagas of Ireland contain allusions and incidents of a mythological nature and, in the final analysis, a great many of the personages involved in them are undoubtedly deities or otherworld beings whose original divinity has been substantially compromised in one way or another. They are no longer gods in the accepted sense of the term, to be worshipped and propitiated by sacrifice, but are portrayed as humans with supernatural attributes who take part in pseudo-historical events in actual geographical locations.

This state of affairs may have come about naturally during the process of oral transmission over many centuries, but these obviously pre-Christian sagas received their present form at the hands of monastic scribes, who may not have understood their mythological nature. On the other hand, there is the possibility that the scribes deliberately played down the mythological and pagan aspect in deference to their Christian scruples, or recast the native material on classical models. Modern scholars divide the sagas of early Ireland into four main groups, or cycles.

1. The *Mythological Cycle*, as its name implies, deals with the activities of the pagan Celtic gods and other supernatural beings.
2. The *Ulster Cycle* tells of the exploits of the warrior caste of pre-Christian Ireland and describes a heroic society very similar to that of pre-Roman Gaul.
3. The *Historical Cycles* purport to deal with the activities of 'historical' figures in Ireland during the early centuries of the Christian era.
4. The *Fenian Cycle* tells the adventures of Finn Mac Cumaill and his warrior band, the Fianna.

Much as we might expect, in view of the antiquity of its material, the Mythological Cycle is the least extensive of the four and we can only assume that a large number of stories of this genre had been lost, or had been adapted to other purposes, before the monastic scribes took to recording them. There is also the strong likelihood that quite a number of early manuscripts containing collections of mythological tales have been lost to us as a result of Ireland's centuries of troubled history. Certainly, the famous Book of Leinster (written before 1160 and now kept in Trinity College Library, Dublin) contains an ancient list of saga titles that refer to mythological tales that no longer exist.

In all, some eight tales have survived that may be described as being predominantly mythological in character. Of the eight only four are early in form. They are *Aislinge Oenguso* ('The Dream of Oengus'), *Tochmarc Etaine* ('The Wooing of Etain'), *De Babail int Sida* ('The Taking of the Fairy Mound'), and *Cath Maige Tuired* ('The Battle of Moytura').

The main tale of the Mythological Cycle is 'The Battle of Moytura', which tells how the Tuatha De Danann, or People of the Goddess Danu, overcame their enemies the Fomoiri by means of their superior magical skills. In the elaborate build up to the battle-scene itself, in which the opposing leaders observe the etiquette of the early heroic tradition by facing each other in single combat, we meet the chief figures of the Irish 'pantheon'. As each in his turn makes, or promises, his contribution to the forth-coming battle, we obtain some insight into the original divine function of the character speaking.

The mythological character of the tale is beyond doubt though the question of interpretation remains open. Some authorities see the battle as representing the age-old conflict between the powers of light, the Tuatha De Danann, and the powers of darkness, the Fomoiri. The former are said to have been of great beauty and to have possessed all knowledge, while the latter are portrayed as half-human monsters bent on destroying the established order. Another interpretation resolves the tale to a very simple theme, that of rivalry between an established god represented by Balar, and a younger more gifted deity, Lug Samildanach, and the triumph of the new order over the old. A more recent interpretation views the tale within the context of Indo-European mythology as a whole and involves the concept of the 'three functions'. This is said to mirror the fundamental three-tiered structure of early Indo-European society itself: the priest who represents the magico-religious function, the warrior who signifies physical might, and the farmer who represents fertility and prosperity. The battle of Moytura is then interpreted in terms of a power-struggle between the priest and warrior classes (Tuatha De Danann) on the one hand, and the farmer class (Fomoiri), the providers, on the other. In Indian mythology the struggle is resolved through reconciliation. In the Irish tradition the Fomoiri are vanquished.

ABOVE Statue of the horse-goddess Epona, riding side-saddle. The object in her right hand may be a torc. Epona probably represents the importance of the horse in early Celtic society. From Alise Ste Reine, Côte d'Or, France.

LEFT The origin and significance of this type of hideous and obscene medieval figure, known as Sheela na Gig (Irish *Sile na gCioch*) are obscure. Some believe it to represent the Celtic goddess of creation and destruction, with her voracious appetites. From the Church of St Mary and St David, Kilpeck, Herefordshire, England.

THE GODS OF IRELAND

Brigit, 'High One': three sisters of this name were daughters of In Dagda and patron-goddesses of learning (including poetry and its associated functions of divination and prophecy), healing and smithcraft – three prestigious professions in Celtic society: widely revered in British Isles: St Brigid, a popular saint in Celtic-speaking areas down to modern times, with her patronage of animal husbandry, her curative powers and her sacred fire barred to all males, is probably a Christian reflex of the pagan goddess: one form of the deity was Brigantia, who was the great tutelary goddess of a North British people, the Brigantes.

Goibniu, 'Great Smith': a leader of the Tuatha De Danann and one of a triad of craftsmen, with Luchta the wright and Creidne the brazier, which may reflect the pre-eminence of these crafts in a society that exploited metal-working to a high degree: equated with Roman Vulcan: he provided the feast for the gods, and in the Welsh laws the smith is entitled to the first drink at a feast: appears as Gofannon in Welsh literature and in modern folklore as the Gobban or Gobban Saer.

In Dagda, 'the Good God', a title rather than a name: also known as Eochaidh Oll-athair, 'All-father', suggesting an ancestor-deity, but he is not portrayed as the father of the gods: he carried a club as a protector and owned a magic cauldron as a provider: had an inordinate appetite for food and sex: a leader of the Tuatha De Danann, he controlled druidic magic at the battle of Mag Tuired.

Lug, the Irish form of Gaulish Lugus: known as 'skilled in many arts': commander of the Tuatha De Danann at battle of Mag Tuired: associated with war, magic, commerce and crafts of all kinds.

Morrigan, 'Spectre Queen' or 'Great Queen': a trio of war-goddesses, named the Morrigan, Badb ('scald-crow') and Nemain ('frenzy, fury'), were probably manifestations of the same deity: appeared as ravens, birds of ill omen in Celtic tradition, before and during battles: in her manifestation as 'the Washer at the Ford', the Morrigan foretold the outcome of battle by washing the equipment of those about to fall: the double association with the river and the raven suggests a possible reflex of the Gaulish Nantosuelta.

Ogma, champion of the gods: also described as 'sun-faced', possibly in allusion to the *furor Celticus*, or battle-fury of the Celtic warriors, so dreaded by the Romans: Ogma controlled the element of martial prowess at the battle of Mag Tuired: credited with inventing Ogam, a code of writing (4th century AD onwards) using strokes and notches, whose origin is an open question but may well have had mystical significance, like the Norse runes: the precise linguistic connection between Ogma and Gaulish Ogmios is anything but clear.

Tuatha De Danann, 'the people of the goddess Danu': these are the gods of ancient Ireland, said to have come from overseas: their enemies were the Fomoiri (perhaps 'undersea phantoms'), half-human and half-monster beings who also came from abroad: one theory is that the Tuatha De represent the powers of light and the Fomoiri powers of darkness: in Irish literature the Tuatha De are clearly gods, but their counterparts in Welsh tradition, the children of Don, have been euhemerized, or made human, though their magical skills betray their divine origins: Irish Danu and Welsh Don are probably reflexes of the same Celtic name, which may be preserved in the names of the rivers Don and Danube.

The Tuatha De Danann

The Tuatha De Danann (T.D.D. for short) inhabited the northernmost island of the world, and they possessed all the known skills of that time. They made an alliance with the Fomoiri, and Balar of the Fomoiri gave his daughter Ethne to Cian son of Dian Cecht, chief physician to the T.D.D.

The T.D.D. then invaded Ireland, where they encountered an agricultural people called the Fir Bolg whom they defeated in the first battle of Mag Tuired. However, in the battle Nuada, their king, lost his arm and because of this disfigurement he forfeited the kingship which was offered to Bres, king of the Fomoiri, whose mother was of the T.D.D. The Fomoiri then laid a heavy tribute on Ireland which so impoverished the country that the great champions Ogma and In Dagda were reduced to carrying firewood and to digging ditches. Soon the chieftains of the T.D.D. began to complain against Bres's rule because he did not dispense the hospitality expected of a king.

One day Coirpre, chief poet of the T.D.D., visited Bres's fort where he was inhospitably received. In retaliation he satirized Bres before he departed. This so compromised the kingship and brought such shame upon it that the T.D.D. demanded that Bres abdicate. Bres then appealed to

ABOVE Roman interpretation of the Celtic goddess Brigantia, the tutelary goddess of the Brigantes in North Britain, 3rd century AD. She wears a mural crown and holds a spear, symbol of the Roman deity Minerva. In her left hand is the orb of sovereignty and on her shoulders are the wings of victory. Found at Birrens, Dumfriesshire, Scotland.

RIGHT Two-faced figures with truncated bodies on Boa Island, Lough Erne, Ireland. They are of uncertain date, but may reflect the Celtic belief in the supernatural power of twins.

the Fomoiri to help him keep the kingship by force. The Fomoiri called in their warriors, summoned their allies to their assistance, and invaded Ireland.

The Coming of Lug

Meanwhile, Dian Cecht the physician had made for Nuada an arm of silver that could function like a normal arm – for this reason he was called Nuada Airget-lam, 'Silver Arm' – so that he was now without blemish and could regain the kingship. He then held a great feast at Tara to which a strange warrior came. This was Lug Samildanach, 'of the many skills', son of Cian and Ethne, and grandson to Balar of the Fomoiri. The story of his arrival is a good example of the style and flavour of the saga:

There was a certain warrior on his way to Tara. His name was Lug Samildanach. At that time there were two door-keepers at Tara. One of these saw a strange troop coming towards him, and the leader of that troop was a handsome young warrior dressed like a king. They told the door-keeper to announce their arrival at Tara. 'Who are you?', he asked. 'Lug Samildanach, son of Cian son of Dian Cecht and Ethne, Balar's daughter, is here.'

The door-keeper then asked Samildanach, 'What skill do you practise? No one without a skill may enter Tara.'

'Question me,' said Lug, 'I am a wright.' 'We do not need you,' the door-keeper replied, 'we already have a wright, Luchta mac Luachada.'

'Question me, door-keeper,' said he, 'I am a smith.' The door-keeper answered him, 'We already have a smith, namely Colum Cualleinech of the three processes.'

'Question me,' said Lug, 'I am a champion.' 'We do not need you for we have a champion in Ogma mac Elathan,' replied the door-keeper.

Then he said, 'Question me: I am a harper.' 'We do not need you, we already have a harper, he is Abcan mac Bicelmois.'

Again he said, 'Question me: I am a hero.' The door-keeper replied, 'We do not need you. We have a hero in Bresal Echarlam mac Echach Baethlaim.'

He then said, 'Question me, door-keeper: I am a poet and *senchaid* (a historian, genealogist and folklorist). 'We do not need you. We already have a poet and *senchaid*. He is En mac Ethomain.'

'Question me,' said he, 'I am a sorcerer.' 'We do not need you. We have sorcerers. We have many druids and magicians already.'

'Question me,' said Lug, 'I am a leech.' 'We have a leech in Dian Cecht. We do not need you.' . . .

'Question me,' he said again, 'I am a good brazier.' 'We do not need you, we already have Creidne Cerd as brazier.'

Then Lug said, 'Go and ask the king if he has one man who can practise all these skills. If he has, then I shall not enter Tara.'

The door-keeper went into the fortress and reported it all to Nuada . . . The king then commanded that the chessboards of Tara should be taken out to Lug. The Samildanach won all the games . . . This was told to the king. 'Let him enter,' said Nuada, 'for no man like him has ever come to this fort before.'

The door-keeper then permitted Lug to pass him and Lug went into the court and sat down in the seat reserved for the sage, for he was a sage in all skills.

Example of a trifrons or three-faced deity on a funerary or ritual urn. The number three was important in Celtic mythology and some Celtic goddesses, such as the Morrigan, appeared in groups of three. Found at Bavay, Nord, France.

The Battle

The T.D.D. then took counsel and decided that Lug, because of his superior gifts, should command them in the coming battle with the Fomoiri. Shortly before the battle began, In Dagda met the Morrigan, the hideous war-goddess, at a ford in Connacht where she was washing herself in the river. He had intercourse with her and in return for his favours she gave him a plan of battle for victory. He then went forward under a truce to spy on the enemy's camp. The Fomoiri dug an enormous pit which they filled with porridge (In Dagda's favourite food), whole sheep, goats and swine, and ordered him to eat it all on pain of death. They did not intend that he should have cause to complain of their hospitality. By the time he left the camp In Dagda's stomach was so grossly distended that he could hardly walk and the Fomoiri mocked him for his gluttony.

As the two great armies took up their positions, each of Lug's chief warriors told his commander what he would contribute to the fight. Goibniu the smith would make the spear-heads and the swords, Creidne the brazier would make the rivets, Coirpre the poet would satirize the enemy, Ogma would supply the warrior-power, In Dagda would slay hundreds with his massive club, while Dian Cecht would bring the slain back to life by putting them into a magic well.

Lug himself was to keep out of the battle because of his importance. However, once the main forces were locked together Lug forgot his role and at once came face to face with his grandfather, Balar of the Evil Eye. This eye was opened only in battle because it brought destruction to all who looked on it. As four Fomoiri raised the eye-lid by its handle Lug drove the eye through Balar's head with a sling-stone so that it looked upon the army behind him. The T.D.D. then beat the Fomoiri back into the sea and defeated them.

The victory was proclaimed throughout Ireland by the Morrigan, and Ireland was again under the rule of the T.D.D.

The Welsh Tales

In some respects, the Welsh tales present a rather different picture from their Irish counterparts. Our chief sources of mythological themes and motifs are five of the stories in the *Mabinogion*, a medieval Welsh collection of 11 tales. These are the four stories known as the Four Branches – *Pwyll pendefig Dyfed* ('Pwyll prince of Dyfed'), *Branwen ferch Llyr* ('Branwen daughter of Llyr'), *Manawydan fab Llyr* ('Manawydan son of Llyr'), *Math fab Mathonwy* ('Math son of Mathonwy') – and the tale of 'Culhwch and Olwen'. The Welsh evidence is of no less antiquity than the Irish, but much less of the old material has been preserved and it bears more obviously the stamp of the Christian authors who wrote the old stories down. Compared with the Irish sagas, the amalgam of story themes presents a confused picture and leaves the impression that the compiler of the *Mabinogion* did not understand his material.

Much is common to both traditions, however. Although some parallels are undoubtedly old and derive from a common source, it is uncertain to what extent common themes and personages are due to later Irish influence. Thus, the Children of Don, the family of magicians found in 'Math son of Mathonwy', have their counterparts in the Tuatha De Danann, who are also skilled in the magic arts. Lleu, for example, is easily equated with Lug, and Gofannon with Goibniu. Of the Children of Llyr, who are introduced in 'Branwen daughter of Llyr', only Manawydan has an Irish parallel, the sea-god Manannan mac Lir. In 'Culhwch and Olwen', Lludd Llaw Ereint (probably originally Nudd Llaw Ereint) has been compared to the Irish Nuada Airgetlam and the British god Nodens (or Nodons), to whom dedicatory inscriptions have been found. On the other hand, in a number of native tales and in some early poetry, we have the figure of Arthur – possibly originally a historical figure of post-Roman Britain – who would seem to have provided much of the material for the medieval Arthurian romances and who has in Welsh tradition many of the attributes of the Irish hero Finn mac Cumaill.

Common themes include the cauldron of rebirth in 'Branwen', traditionally a characteristic possession of the ruler of the otherworld, which may be connected with In Dagda's cauldron of plenty. The cauldron of rebirth brings dead warriors back to life. The cauldron of plenty supplies inexhaustible quantities of food which makes those who eat it immortal. Both call to mind a motif on the Gundestrup cauldron (2nd century BC), where a large figure is depicted thrusting warriors into a vat-like vessel.

The otherworld of Celtic mythology is a mysterious realm where there is no death, no work and no winter. It is inhabited by gods or spirits or a fairy people, forever young. In Welsh the otherworld, called Annwn or 'un-world', is presented as no less real and actual than the world of human beings, and passage from one domain to the other is frequent and natural, though sometimes with the aid of magic. Indeed, otherworld beings often call upon humans to help them. Pwyll changes places with Arawn, king of Annwn, so as to kill his adversary, Hafgan. So too in Irish legend, the hero Cu Chulainn aids Labraid of the Swift Sword-hand against his otherworld enemies for a day. In this connection, iron is commonly portrayed as the bane of the otherworld and a metal which the gods cannot wield, and it is conceivable that this represents a folk memory of a culture clash between the Iron Age Celts who invaded Britain and their less advanced predecessors.

As in Irish literature, the figures in the Welsh tales have a half-human, half-divine status. Often possessed of magical powers or specific skills, they act out pseudo-historical events in actual geographical locations. For example, Pwyll is prince of Dyfed (southwest Wales), Math is lord of Gwynedd (northwest Wales) and Manawydan goes into exile in Lloegr (England). In the same way, the story of 'Branwen' tells of intermarriage and war between the royal dynasties of Wales and Ireland.

Bran and Branwen

Bendigeidfran was holding court at Harlech in Wales, his brothers Manawydan, Nisien and Efnisien with him, when 13 ships belonging to Matholwch, king of Ireland, were seen approaching. He had come to ask for the hand of Branwen, Bendigeidfran's sister. Bendigeidfran took counsel and agreed to the match, but Efnisien, the troublemaker, found Matholwch's horses and maimed them, because Bendigeidfran had married his sister off without his consent. Angry at the insult, Matholwch tried to leave, but Bendigeidfran placated him by replacing the horses and giving him gold and silver, and a magic cauldron which brought dead warriors back to life when they were placed in it, though leaving them dumb.

Matholwch took Branwen back to Ireland and a son, Gwern, was born to them. To avenge the insult done to Matholwch in Wales, however, the Irish banished Branwen to work in the kitchens and set a ban on traffic between Ireland and Wales, so that the news could not travel. Branwen overcame this difficulty by sending a letter tied to a bird's leg to her brother. The Welsh mustered their forces and sailed to Ireland. Bendigeidfran, because of his great size, waded across the sea among his ships. The Irish retreated behind the Shannon and demolished the bridge, but the Welsh crossed the river over Bendigeidfran's body and the defenders had to parley.

The Irish then built a house in Bendigeidfran's honour – he had never been contained inside one –

and hid men in bags hung on each of the hundred pillars of the house. But Efnisien, suspecting treachery, went around and crushed the head of each man in them. Then the two armies sat down together and the kingship of Ireland was conferred upon Gwern. At this, Efnisien threw Gwern into the fire and the two sides fell to fighting.

The Irish lit a fire under the cauldron of rebirth and threw their dead men into it to revive them. Seeing this, Efnisien hid among the corpses and, once in the cauldron, stretched himself out so that it burst. The Welsh won the day, but at a terrible cost. Only seven men and Branwen survived.

Bendigeidfran himself was mortally wounded and ordered his head to be cut off and carried to the White Mount in London to be buried with its face towards France. On their return, Branwen looked back to Ireland and died of a broken heart.

The remaining seven spent seven years feasting in Harlech and then stayed in Pembroke for 80 years in blissful forgetfulness. But when Heilyn, son of Gwyn, opened the door towards Cornwall, they remembered their kinsmen and their misery. Unable to rest, they went to London and buried the head.

In Ireland, five pregnant women were left in a cave. They gave birth to five sons, who, when they reached maturity, slept with each other's mother. They then divided and ruled the country between them. This is the origin of Ireland's five provinces.

While the Welsh stories may be compared on the one hand with the Irish tales and on the other with the evidence from the continental Celts and the classical writers, they have come down to us in an exceedingly corrupt form and it is no easy task to draw any firm conclusions about Celtic mythology from them. It is highly unlikely that there will ever be a universally acceptable interpretation of all the disparate strands of myth, folk-tale and pseudo-history which have been woven together.

THE GODS OF WALES

Children of Don, one of the rival dynasties of Celtic mythology (equated with the powers of light), opposed to the Children of Llyr: includes Gwydion, a warrior magician, and Aranrhod, sky-goddess and symbol of fertility: their sons were Dylan, associated with the sea, and Lleu Llaw Gyffes: the family is identified with the Irish Tuatha De Danann.

Children of Llyr, represented by three characters, Bendigeidfran, Branwen and Manawydan, who appear in the story of 'Branwen daughter of Llyr': Benedigeidfran ('Bran the Blessed') is cast as a giant who wades the Irish Sea, since no ship is big enough to carry him: he is slain by a poisoned spear: Branwen's role in the tale is slight and she appears mainly as a victim of ill-treatment: her divinity and antiquity have been called in doubt by some scholars: Manawydan is equated with the Irish Manannan mac Lir, 'son of the sea', the sea-god who travels the waves in a chariot: both names, Manawydan and Manannan, are believed to show some connection with the Isle of Man (Welsh *Ynys Fanaw*, Irish *Inis Manann*).

Pwyll, prince of Dyfed (southwest Wales): visits Annwn, the otherworld, and changes places with Arawn, the king: rules there for a year and a day, and kills Arawn's adversary, Hafgan: earns the epithet *Pen Annwn*, 'Head of Annwn': marries the goddess Rhiannon and has a son, Pryderi: equated with Pelles in the Arthurian legends, where the cauldron of rebirth appears as the Holy Grail.

Rhiannon, 'Great Queen', believed to be the Welsh reflex of the Gaulish horse-goddess Epona, because of her associations with horses in the *Mabinogion*: she first appears riding a mysterious mount that no other horse can overtake, she is later unjustly accused of killing her son and as a punishment is made to carry visitors to the court on her back like a horse, and she is finally forced to wear the collar of an ass about her neck: despite these misfortunes there is sufficient evidence in the Welsh tales to indicate that she was originally a very powerful deity: her son, Pryderi, succeeded his father Pwyll as ruler of Dyfed and of the otherworld.

ABOVE LEFT The Gaulish 'Hercules', carrying his emblem, the club, on his shoulder. He is believed to be identical with the Celtic god Ogmios, champion of the gods and god of eloquence.

ABOVE A large figure, possibly a god, thrusts a smaller figure head-first into a tub. Infantry march towards him, perhaps carrying a tree on their spear-points, while cavalry ride away above. Possible interpretations include sacrifices to the war-god by drowning, resurrection by immersion in the cauldron of rebirth, or a warrior-initiation rite. From the Gundestrup cauldron.

CHAPTER SIXTEEN

SCANDINAVIA

The myths of northern Europe reflect not only an exuberant love of story-telling for its own sake, but a view of man and the universe as being caught in the grip of conflicting powers. Some of these powers were friendly to man, but some were savagely hostile. This attitude was rooted in an acute awareness – common to agricultural peoples in general – of the rhythms of nature: the alternation of day and night, light and darkness, cold and heat, summer and winter, life and death. By boldness and enterprise men might master life to some extent, but it was seldom doubted that human destiny was shaped by powers greater than man.

Scandinavian man evidently felt little security in the world which these powers ruled. Life and happiness were menaced by forces beyond human understanding and control. Between life and death, light and darkness, there was only a fragile barrier. On one side of it, existence was possible and tolerable, if

rarely comfortable. On the other, existence was starkly impossible.

Like other Indo-Europeans, the Germanic peoples tended to see the gods as having complementary functions. A Christian writer named Adam of Bremen said that in the great temple at Old Uppsala in Sweden, as late as the 13th century: 'the people worship statues of three gods; the most mighty of them, Thor, has his throne in the middle; Wodan [Odin in Scandinavia] and Fricco [Frey] have their place on either side. Their significance is of this kind: Thor, they say, rules in the sky, and governs thunder, lightning, the winds, rain, fair weather and produce of the soil. The second is Wodan . . . he makes wars and gives men bravery in the face of enemies. The third is Fricco, distributing peace and pleasure among men, whose idol is fashioned with a gigantic phallus.'

Since the gods had varying and sometimes overlapping functions, there was nothing inconsistent or heretical about worshipping more than one of them. On the contrary, a man might need to maintain good relations with several gods and goddesses. This was a Germanic habit of mind which, at a later date, was not relished by Christians.

The Fury of the Northmen

Scandinavian mythology is one branch, and far the best-known branch, of the pre-Christian mythology of the Germanic peoples in northern and central Europe. Our information about it comes almost entirely, not from Scandinavia itself, but from the outpost of Scandinavian culture in Iceland. Settled mainly from Norway in the 9th and 10th centuries, Iceland was the home of a rich literature in both verse and prose. Clearly there is no guarantee that this is representative of the Germanic peoples as a whole.

The sources date from the Viking Age (from roughly AD 800 to 1100) and later, and the persistent popular impression of the Vikings as bloodthirsty savages makes it hard to appreciate Scandinavian culture on its own terms. The evil repute of the Vikings goes back as far as the 8th century when, after they had sacked the monastery of Lindisfarne, off the Northumberland coast, an English monk named Alcuin wrote: 'Never before has such a terror appeared in Britain as we have now suffered from a pagan race.' To show that old reputations die hard,

in 1911 we find G.K. Chesterton writing about the Norsemen ('Great, beautiful half-witted men') and their gods:

Their souls were drifting as the sea,
 And all good towns and lands
They only saw with heavy eyes,
 And broke with heavy hands.

Their gods were sadder than the sea,
 Gods of a wandering will,
Who cried for blood like beasts at night,
 Sadly, from hill to hill.

This is misleading, however, if it makes us think that because the Vikings showed little respect for the religion and culture they found in Britain, they must have had no religion and culture of their own worth considering.

Before the 9th century Scandinavian contacts with Christian Europe were only sporadic. Their pattern of life was essentially tribal and agricultural. A few people knew how to write, but religion and mythology were transmitted by word of mouth, not through holy scripture. Indeed there are no Germanic holy scriptures, though there are many sacred traditions.

Almost everything we know about the myths comes from two Icelandic texts. Both are called Edda, but the meaning of this word is uncertain. The *Verse Edda* is a collection of thirty poems by unknown authors, dating from about 850 to 1200. There is nothing systematic about its contents and parts of it are obscure.

The *Prose Edda* was compiled in the early 13th century by an Icelandic historian named Snorri Sturluson. Passionately concerned with the past and the traditions of his people, Snorri wrote it as a guide for poets who wished to go on writing and interpreting the old stories in the old manner. It is important to remember that by the time this handbook was written Iceland had been Christian for two centuries. Snorri Sturluson probably never met a pagan in his life. He also entirely fails to place the myths in a context of worship.

Snorri believed the old gods and goddesses to have been no more than great men and women of the past, and he showed not the slightest inclination to worship them himself. There were two families of gods, the Aesir, who included Thor and Odin, and the Vanir, who were closely connected with the dead. Snorri explained the Aesir, quite wrongly, as 'Asiatics', who came from Troy in the wake of the Trojan war. These Trojan exiles were commanded by a chieftain named Odin, who led his conquering army through Germany and Denmark into Sweden, where he was welcomed by a king called Gylfi.

Landscape in Greenland.
In the stony, sea-beaten lands of the north, men confronted snow, ice and extreme cold, and this inevitably influenced their myths. It was said that life first appeared where the heat of the south met the cold of the north. The icy region of Jotunheim was the home of the giants who menaced the world of men, and the goddess Hel ruled a dark land of the dead in the frozen north. Cold was the perpetual enemy of life.

ABOVE Prehistoric rock carvings showing cattle and ploughing. The strong sense of the rhythms of nature in Scandinavian mythology – of the alternation of light and darkness, summer and winter, life and death – reflects the experience of an agricultural people. From Tegneby, Sweden, 5th–3rd centuries BC.

ABOVE RIGHT Gylfi, a legendary Swedish king, comes to the great hall where he learns about the pagan gods. From a 14th-century MS of Snorri Sturluson's *Prose Edda*. Most of what we know about Scandinavian myths is contained in this book, which was written by a Christian historian in Iceland as a guide for poets.

This is where the story of the *Prose Edda* starts. Gylfi inquires about the source of the Aesir's wisdom and prosperity. He finds himself in a great hall, containing three high seats, in each of which there sits a divine figure. He asks them for information, and it is in their answers that we find the bulk of what we know about Scandinavian mythology.

Cosmos and Chaos

In the beginning all that existed was a vast open void, called Ginnungagap. In the south there was a hot region, Muspell, and in the north a cold region, Niflheim. Muspell was filled with fire and heat, Niflheim with ice, frost and snow. Where the heat of the south met the cold of the north life appeared, in the form of a giant, Ymir, and a cow, Authumla, whose milk nourished the giant. The cow fed on salty ice-blocks, and from one block, as she licked it, there emerged a man named Buri, one of whose grandsons was the great god Odin.

Odin had two brothers. Eventually they killed the giant Ymir. They carried his corpse into the middle of Ginnungagap. From it they made the world. Ymir's blood became the sea and the lakes, his flesh became the earth, his bones the mountains, and his teeth and jaws the rocks. From his skull the makers fashioned the sky, supported at each of its four corners by a dwarf. From Muspell sparks and burning embers had emerged, which were placed in the midst of Ginnungagap as the stars and the planets. Ymir's brains, flung into the air, became the clouds. Finally, Ymir's eyebrows were made into the stronghold of Midgard, in which men could live.

One day, Odin and his brothers were walking along the sea shore. They came across two trees, Ash and Elm. From these they created man and woman, giving them spirit and life, understanding and powers of movement, speech, hearing and sight. The gods set them to live in Midgard. Then they made a stronghold for themselves, which they called Asgard. Outside Midgard and Asgard there remains the cold region of Giantland, or Jotunheim, forever threatening the world which the gods made.

Before the world came into being, then, according to Scandinavian mythology (and in most other mythologies as well), matter already existed, but not in a way capable of supporting life. Before the cosmos, there was chaos. Extreme heat in the south confronted extreme cold in the north. Presumably the gods were already present, though there is no definite information on this point. Generally the gods, especially Odin, are said to have organized the world, rather than created it. The world may have emerged from a spontaneous interaction of cold and heat, or it may have been made from the dismembered limbs of a giant. There is no attempt to produce a definitive version.

The gods shaped the world and created a space for themselves, called Asgard, and a space for men, Midgard. At the centre of the world there is a mighty tree, Yggdrasill or Odin's steed (an oblique reference to the gallows). Its branches stretch across the whole world. Its roots extend into the territory of men, into the realm of the dead, and into the world of the frost-giants, who live in the regions of snow and ice, beyond the boundaries of human habitation. At the foot of the tree there is a well, which is the source of the deepest wisdom.

The cosmos is constantly threatened. The main source of the danger comes from Giantland, and it is the particular duty of Thor to hold the giants in check. In the myths Thor is often 'away fighting giants', or there is something close to panic when the giants steal his weapons, especially his formidable hammer. The world of gods and men is unsafe, menaced by hostile powers.

The God of the Ungodly

Thor maintained the order and fabric of the universe by means of his immense strength, the symbols of which were a belt of power, a pair of iron gloves and a hammer named Mjollnir, which represented the lightning or thunderbolt. The name Thor means 'thunder' and he personified the power of the thunderstorm. Because of his connection with storms, he was believed to control the winds and the

rain, and so he was a god of fertility.

Thor was the most popular of the gods in the Viking period. People and places were frequently named after him, presumably to put them under his protection. Violent and unpredictable, he was given to fits of uncontrollable rage, but his anger was usually directed against the giants. To his own people, he was a good and utterly reliable friend, who fought on their side in the struggle of life. He possessed so many of the qualities which the Vikings admired in a leader that the overriding impression of him is as a Viking chieftain larger than life: huge, red-bearded, a titanic eater and drinker, massively strong and courageous, but sometimes over-hasty in his judgment. He was known as the god worshipped by men who believed confidently in their own power and strength, so that paradoxically he might perhaps be called 'the god of the ungodly'.

Thor's symbol, the hammer, is an example of the way in which myths and behaviour interact. It was a short-shafted weapon, intended for throwing. Worn on a thong round the neck it was a protective amulet, and in late Viking times 'the sign of the hammer' was a gesture of blessing, resembling and possibly copied from the Christian sign of the cross. The hammer was also used to bless the bride at a wedding and was placed in graves to protect the dead.

Thor's strength was so great that it was apt to get out of control. One story tells how Thor, disguised as a youth, left Asgard and came to a giant called Hymir, who was preparing to go fishing at sea in his boat. Thor asked to go with him, but Hymir only laughed, because by his standards Thor was so small and would be of little use at rowing. This angered Thor. He persuaded Hymir to change his mind and he took the head of the giant's biggest ox to use as bait. Thor baited his hook with it and succeeded in catching a vast monster of the deep, the Midgard Serpent. The serpent struggled so hard that Thor's foot went right through the bottom of the boat as he fought to haul it on board. Hymir was frightened and cut Thor's line, and the monster sank back into the sea. If he had not done so, the cosmos would have been destroyed.

On another occasion, Thor's hammer was stolen from him by the giant Thrym, who agreed to return it only on condition that he was given the beautiful goddess Freya as his wife. Thor was persuaded by the other gods to dress himself up in women's clothes and pretend to be Freya. He came as a bride to Thrym, who was so besotted by the prospect of the ultimate in married bliss that he did not notice the deception. When Thrym called for the hammer to be brought in and put in the bride's lap, as was the custom, Thor's chance had come. He took Mjollnir and slaughtered the giant and the entire wedding party.

ABOVE LEFT Thor grasps the great hammer, Mjollnir, his principal weapon, which represented the lightning or thunderbolt and was a symbol of his colossal strength as god of storm. The most popular of the gods in Viking times, Thor maintained the order of the universe and warred against the giants who threatened it. Bronze figure from Iceland, 10th century.

LEFT Thor's hammer. With the coming of Christianity to the north, the symbol of the hammer tended to blend into the Christian symbol of the cross. Viking period.

The subtle, wily and dangerous Odin was god of death, magic, wisdom and madness. He was said to appear on earth as an old, one-eyed man in a cloak. He inspired the battle-frenzy of the berserks, and brave fighting men killed in battle went to form his body guard in Valhalla, his great hall in Asgard, where they feasted and drank deep. Bronze figurine from Linby, Sweden, Viking period.

PRINCIPAL SCANDINAVIAN DEITIES

Odin, god of death, wisdom and magic
Frigg, the mother-goddess, wife of Odin
Thor, god of thunder and foe of giants
Njord, god of the sea, fishing and prosperity
Frey, god of fertility, son of Njord
Freya, goddess of love and beauty, sister of Frey
Balder, the good god, son of Odin
Loki, the trouble-maker
Tyr, the one-handed, giver of victory in battle
Bragi, skilled in poetry and the use of words
Idun, keeper of the apples of immortality, wife of Bragi
Heimdall, the watchman of Asgard
Hother, the blind god
Ull, the archer and skier

Odin and the Runes

If Thor was the Viking warrior writ large, Odin belonged to the mysterious region between life and death. He was more subtle and more dangerous. His name may have been connected with words for 'wind', and he was later identified as the leader of the 'wild hunt', the procession of dead souls across the sky, which was connected with the fury of the gale. In Germany he was called Wodan and Adam of Bremen described him as 'fury' or 'madness', while the Old English word *wod* means simply 'mad'. The god's madness was discerned in his followers, the berserks, warriors who wore the skins of bears. Berserk means 'dressed in bear's skin', but came to imply 'possessed by blind fury' because of the raging frenzy in which the berserks went into battle. Odin inspired this mad fury in his followers, and terror in their opponents.

Very few Scandinavians gave their children names derived from or linked with Odin. He was too closely connected with death for comfort, and especially with death in battle. On the battlefield he might show himself as an old man in a cloak. He would be attended by ravens, wolves and the Valkyries, 'the choosers of the slain', the maidens who took the souls of fallen warriors to Valhalla, Odin's hall in Asgard, where they formed his bodyguard. Perhaps because the outcome of hand-to-hand fighting is so chancy and unpredictable, Odin gained a reputation for being treacherous and untrustworthy. There was a story that he taught King Harald Wartooth of Denmark the secret of fighting in wedge formation, but later he turned against Harald, betrayed the secret to his enemies and, when battle was joined, threw the king from his chariot and battered him to death.

Odin was famous for his wisdom and among its many obscure and mysterious sources were his use of a severed head and his mastery of the runes, the letters of the Germanic alphabet. The head was that of Mimir, the wisest of men. According to the myth, Mimir was left as a hostage with the Vanir in the wars between them and the Aesir. They cut off his head and sent it to the Aesir. Odin pickled the head and kept it by him. It talked to him and through it he could consult the spirit-world. There is a further point here, since another source of Odin's wisdom was that he had deposited one of his eyes in Mimir's well, the one at the foot of Yggdrasill, the world-tree. Hence the god is often described as having only one eye.

The runic alphabet, which Odin controlled, was widely used in Scandinavia for magical purposes. There was a story that the god hung on the gallows (also Yggdrasill) for nine days and nights without food or drink. He had been wounded with a spear, which means that he had been sacrificed to himself, in the same way that victims were sacrificed to him in real life, stabbed and hanged on trees. But then he reached down and plucked up the runes. In this way he penetrated to the world beyond death, and so gained mastery of the wisdom of the runes and power over death itself. In the same story there is a hint that Odin could bring a corpse on the gallows back to life by means of the cutting and painting of

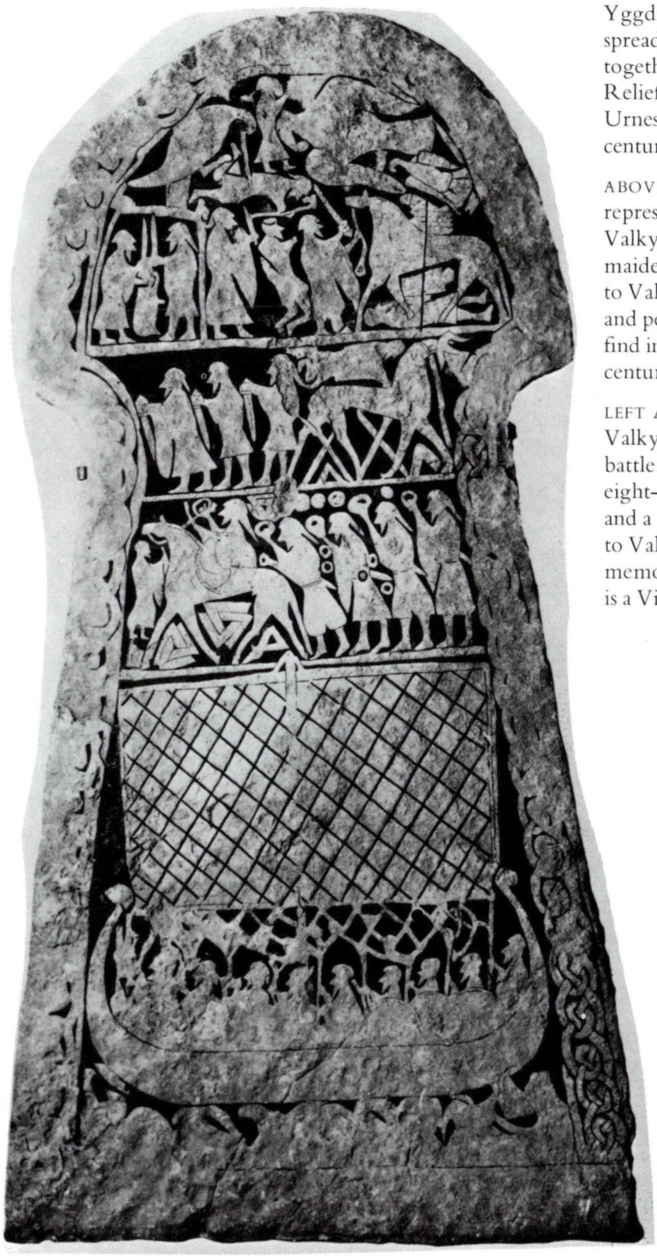

FAR LEFT The great tree, Yggdrasill, whose branches spread through and linked together the whole world. Relief from a church at Urnes, Norway, early 13th century.

ABOVE Figures thought to represent a warrior and a Valkyrie. Valkyries were maidens who took warriors to Valhalla. Silver-gilt amulet and pendant, from a grave-find in Birka, Sweden, 6th century.

LEFT At the top eagles and Valkyries hover above a battle. Below them is Odin's eight-legged horse, Sleipnir, and a procession of the dead to Valhalla. At the foot of this memorial stone from Gotland is a Viking ship.

runes. The 'painting' was probably in blood. There is also a clear connection here with the plant called the mandrake (*alruna* in Old Norse), which was believed to grow beneath the gallows. It screamed when pulled up and it had magical powers.

Frey and Freya

The third of the great gods in the temple at Uppsala was Frey, the god of fertility, appropriately represented with an erect phallus. He was associated especially with Sweden. According to Snorri, he and his sister Freya were powerful and beautiful deities. 'Frey is an exceedingly famous god; he decides when the sun shall shine or the rain come down, and along with that the fruitfulness of the earth, and he is good to invoke for peace and plenty. He also brings about the prosperity of men. But Freya is the most renowned of the goddesses . . . She enjoys love poetry and it is good to call on her for help in love affairs'.

ABOVE Frey was the god of prosperity, plenty, peace and the fruitfulness of the earth. His erect phallus indicates his fertilizing power, and he was also closely associated with horses. Bronze figurine from Sweden, 11th Century.

ABOVE RIGHT Frey's sister, Freya, the beautiful goddess of love, wearing round her shoulders the great necklace, Brisingamen. According to one story, it was made by four dwarves, who gave it to her on condition that she spent a night with each of them in turn. Pendant from Sweden, Viking period.

There is a strange link between the worship of Frey and horses. Sacred horses were kept at his sanctuary at Thrandheim, in Norway. When a Christian king, Olav Tryggvason, went to destroy the sanctuary, he found there a horse which was about to be killed 'for Frey to eat'. Horse fighting and horse racing were practised in Iceland and there are references to horses kept near Frey's temples. Evidently horses were sacrificed to him, and this may be one of the reasons why Christians have always disliked eating horseflesh.

The Killing of Balder

After Thor and Odin, the Scandinavian deity best known in the modern world is probably Balder, called the Beautiful and the Good. He was a son of Odin and he was the most merciful and sweet-tempered of the gods. According to the *Prose Edda*, he was killed through the machinations of the god Loki and this was 'the greatest misfortune that ever befell gods and men'.

Balder, the good god, dreamed of his own death. The gods were alarmed and Balder's mother, the goddess Frigg, protected him by taking an oath from all things not to hurt him: from the earth, from iron and all metals, from stones and trees, from diseases, from animals and birds, from serpents and poison. Once this had been done, the gods amused themselves by throwing things at Balder and, as he was not harmed, everyone was happy. Or everyone was happy except Loki, who was angry. Loki disguised himself as a woman, went to Frigg and asked her if there was any creature which had not sworn. Frigg said there was only one thing, a plant called *mistilteinn,* which seemed too young to take the oath.

Loki found the *mistilteinn* and pulled it out of the ground. He took it back to Asgard and found the blind god Hother. He gave him the plant and directed his aim at Balder. Hother threw the dart, which pierced Balder and he fell dead.

The gods were struck dumb with horror and Balder's wife Nanna died of sorrow. They were burned on a funeral pyre on Balder's ship. The god Hermod rode north to Hel, the country of the dead, where Balder was now an honoured lord. Hermod was told that Balder could leave Hel if everything in the world, alive or dead, wept for him.

The gods sent messengers everywhere and all things wept for Balder, as they do when the frost thaws each spring, when the air grows warm again after winter. But there was one creature which would not weep, a giantess alone in a cave. Balder was no use to her alive or dead, she said, so let Hel keep what it held. Because of her, Balder could not return to the living world. She was probably Loki in disguise.

This myth appears to be a variant of the theme of the dying god of vegetation, though without the element of his annual return to life. The *mistilteinn*, though, can hardly have been the mistletoe, as has long been supposed. Rather it seems to have been a weapon. The story is a drama of life and death, of the inevitable fate which lies in store for beauty and goodness. The villain of the piece is Loki.

Loki the Trickster

There is no stranger figure in world mythology than Loki. Half divine and half demonic, Odin's foster-brother, the begetter of horrors – he is an intricate web of contradictions. He has been compared to the Greek hero Prometheus and in some modern eyes has been given a spurious grandeur as the enemy of constituted authority. Even his sex is in doubt. Perhaps for this reason, he (or she) finds it hard to strike up any normal relationship with gods or with men.

Loki was the son of a giant and by one of his wives, a giantess, he was the father of the Midgard Serpent, the monstrous wolf Fenrir, and Hel, the goddess who ruled the land of the dead in the far north. All these were born and bred in Giantland.

When the gods made Asgard as their home, a giant came and offered to build a great wall round their stronghold, for defence against their enemies. It was agreed that if he finished the work before the end of winter, he should have in payment the beautiful goddess Freya and the sun and the moon. The gods made this bargain thinking that he had no hope of finishing such a massive work in time. They stipulated that he must have no one's assistance, but the giant asked if he could use his horse to help him and, on Loki's advice, the gods agreed. To their dismay, the horse turned out to be a magic stallion, which hauled huge stones at such speed that three days before the end of winter the wall was almost finished.

In panic at the prospect of losing Freya and the sun and moon, the gods rounded furiously on Loki and threatened him with death unless he found a way out. Loki changed himself into a mare and went and lured the stallion away, so that the giant could not complete the work in time. Thor smashed the giant's skull to pieces with his hammer. Loki later gave birth to a foal, which was grey and had eight legs. Named Sleipnir, it was the finest of horses and it became Odin's charger.

To the other gods Loki was a useful but dangerous ally. His relationship to them is graphically portrayed in a poem in the *Verse Edda*, in which he breaks in on them when they are drinking ale and insults each of them in turn. One of the goddesses, Idun, tries to stop an incipient argument, only to have Loki snap at her: 'Shut up, Idun, you are the most promiscuous of women, since you put your arms around the man who murdered your brother.' Frigg he calls a whore, Njord he accuses of incest, Heimdall the watchman he taunts as a layabout. He also boasts of all the harm he has done, which includes seducing Thor's wife, and he ceases only when Thor threatens him with physical violence. This poem gives an insight into Loki's character as a trickster and trouble-maker. Mischievous is too weak a word to apply to him, though at times his malice is merely petty. At other times he is deeply malevolent, as in the story of Balder's death.

In Loki normal values are turned upside down and normal relationships confused. Is it too far-fetched, or too 'modern', to see him playing a role in the cosmic drama similar to that of the skull at the banquet or the jester at the wedding? He personifies the paradoxical, he acts out the inversion of values. A paradox cannot be explained, but it can be acted out. In this case the paradox is that of the god who hates the other gods, and is hated by them in turn. Loki was not a magician, but he knew some of the magician's arts – those of changing shape and flying. Magical powers could hurt or heal, just as the fire can burn but can also give warmth. It is significant that a variant of the god's name is Logi, 'wildfire', which again recalls the myth of Prometheus, who stole fire from the gods and gave it to men.

In the end Loki is seized by the gods, who could not forgive his part in Balder's death, and bound with bonds of iron (like Prometheus). A snake, with venom dripping from its fangs, is fixed above his head. His wife, Sigyn, holds a bowl to catch the drops, but when she has to go to empty it, the venom drips onto his face. At the end of the world he will be released and he will fight against the gods in the last battle. He will struggle with Heimdall, the watchman of Asgard, and each will kill the other.

Sigurd and the Dragon

To move from Loki to Sigurd is to go from the ultimate paradox to a popular heroic legend. According to Snorri, there was a farmer called Hreidmar, who had three sons: Fafnir, Regin and

ABOVE The 'bound devil'. Scandinavian mythology influenced Christianity in the north and the fettered figure may represent Loki, punished by the other gods for his part in the death of Balder. Loki was bound with iron chains and a serpent dripped venom on his head. He would be freed at the end of the world, to fight against the gods in the final battle. Detail from a cross at Kirkby Stephen, Cumbria.

BELOW Sigurd kills the dragon Fafnir, which guarded a fatal treasure-hoard of gold. Scene from the story of Sigurd, from Sweden, 11th century.

Otter. Otter was killed by Loki and his father demanded a ransom for his death. In the home of a dwarf Loki found a treasure-hoard of gold and this was paid to the bereaved father, though Loki warned him that it would destroy its owner. This it quickly did, for Hreidmar was killed for the gold by his two remaining sons, Fafnir and Regin. Then Fafnir drove his brother away and turned himself into a dragon to guard the gold. Regin became a blacksmith and adopted the young hero Sigurd (Siegfried in German), making for him the sword Gram, which was so sharp that it would cut in two a lock of wool carried by the current in a stream.

Regin sent Sigurd to kill Fafnir. He hid himself in a pit by the path which Fafnir took to get water, and when the dragon came crawling down to the water, Sigurd killed him. A drop of the dragon's blood touched Sigurd's tongue and immediately he was able to understand the language of birds. He heard two nuthatches discussing Regin's plans to murder him and seize the gold. Awakened to his danger, he killed Regin and took the gold for himself.

The Sigurd legend, or this part of it, has affinities with many other Indo-European tales. Though not a myth in the fullest sense, it stresses the dangers of excessive amounts of gold and it contains what the Freudians would see as an element of the Oedipus complex – the killing of a father by jealous and greedy sons. Otherwise its features are those of the frontiers between the world of men and the world of vast and mysterious powers.

The whorls in this hunting scene symbolize the sun. There were important Norse midwinter festivals, connected with the sun's recovery of strength and vigour, which have influenced modern Christmas and New Year celebrations. Memorial stone from Gotland, 5th century AD.

The End of the World

The Scandinavians had no more secure a sense of the permanence of things than any other human beings of their time or before. They conceived of the cosmic process, not as a smooth and stable progression, but as a constant struggle between opposing forces, those of creation and order against those of destruction and chaos. The world was habitable by man only in part, and around the borders of the good and fertile land there were threatening powers forever liable to break in and destroy man's work and hopes.

Creation was a process by which the divine powers brought order out of chaos. The end of the world will occur when the forces of order can no longer withstand those of chaos. Natural catastrophes by snow, ice, volcanic eruptions, floods and earthquakes, suggested how the final dissolution would take place and the gods themselves would be swept away in it.

The end of the world will be heralded by three winters of war, and then by three further winters of terrible and unrelenting cold. One wolf will seize the sun and another the moon. The stars will disappear and there will be violent earthquakes. Then the chained wolf Fenrir is loosed and opens his vast jaws to devour the world. The Midgard Serpent spews poison over the sky and the sea, and all the monsters of chaos gather for the attack.

Heimdall, the watchman of Asgard, blows a great blast on his horn and the gods ride out to battle. Thor is soon locked in combat with the Midgard Serpent, Frey with Surt, the fire-giant, Tyr with the huge hound Garm, and Heimdall with Loki. All the gods fight bravely, but in vain, while the world-tree trembles with fear. Odin himself is swallowed by Fenrir and the gods are slain. Surt hurls fire over the world and the earth sinks into the sea.

All that is left is a chaos of fire and smoke, rising into the heavens, and in the end the heat and fire is swallowed up by the ocean. The world has not ceased to exist, but it has returned to the state from which it once emerged.

But perhaps this may not after all be the end. Heaven will still exist, and one day a new earth will arise from the sea, green and fair and rich with fields of corn. The sons of Odin and Thor will have survived and they will be joined by Balder the Beautiful, returned from the dead. They will remember the destruction of Ragnarok only as a bad dream. Two new humans, Lif and Lifthrasir, will be born to repeople the world. The catastrophe may not be final, but the prelude to a new and glorious life.

As with the world, so with the individual man and woman. Each individual was in the grip of incomprehensible powers, from which he could not escape. All the Germanic peoples had a powerful belief in fate, which in Scandinavian mythology was personified as the three Norns, maidens who lived by a sacred spring beneath one of the roots of the world-tree. Their names were Urdi (past), Vedandi (present) and Skuld (future). They later turn up as the three witches in Shakespeare's *Macbeth*. They emerged originally from Giantland, and from that moment the fate even of the gods was sealed, as the world order proceeded inexorably towards its allotted end. No man could combat the influence of fate on his life, for good or for ill, though he could seek omens to give some foreknowledge of what was in store for him.

The vision of the end of the world and the doom of the gods seems to be a grim affirmation that creation has limits which mere mortals cannot comprehend and is subject to forces against which even the gods are helpless.

The End of the Myths

Despite all the work done for two centuries and more on the myth and religion of the North, the area of worship is still very poorly understood. Any impression that the Norsemen listened to passages being read from the Eddas and the heroic sagas, and that this constituted the heart of their faith, is quite wrong. The written material would have played very little part in their worship. We know little about the patterns of worship, but they were clearly bound up with the passage of the seasons and the natural rhythms of an agricultural community, and were directed mainly to those gods and goddesses who were in charge of fertility. There were particularly important festivals at midwinter, some traces of which still survive in modern Christmas and New Year festivities. The underlying attitude would always be that of securing the help of the supernatural powers. Of conventional piety as we understand it, there was probably very little.

The conversion of the Germanic peoples to Christianity was a slow process. In Germany and Britain it was largely, though not entirely complete by the 8th century. Iceland became officially Christian in the year 1000, Norway rather earlier, and Sweden not until two centuries later. In the process the peasant changed his gods, but he did not necessarily change his religion. His attitude to the unseen world might remain the same. Many seasonal rituals continued, the runes kept their power and mystery, sacred places remained sacred. But the great gods were dethroned and the myths passed out of currency. If it had not been for Snorri Sturluson, most of them would have disappeared without trace.

The reasons why the North became Christian are fairly clear. On one level, the conversion made Scandinavia part of Catholic Europe. On another, Christianity offered a security beyond the grave which the old religion did not provide. In the struggle between 'the White Christ' and Thor and Odin, Christ emerged the victor.

In the last resort, the old myths failed because they lacked consistency and seriousness. Odin was treacherous, Christ was not. Thor could be hoodwinked, Christ could not. Frey and Freya were too much of the world, too weak beyond it. The old religion had no centre, either in ritual or organizational terms. It was a conglomeration of separate elements and functions, which remain to challenge and sometimes puzzle us. But there is often a certain nostalgia among us moderns for the memory of men and women who could, for a time at least, shoulder fate aside and worship Thor, because they believed in their own strength.

ABOVE Scene thought to depict Odin attacked and swallowed by the monstrous wolf, Fenrir, at the end of the world. It was believed that after three winters of war and three of unrelenting cold, the forces of chaos would defeat and kill the gods in a great battle and the world would be destroyed. Detail from the Thorwald Cross, Isle of Man, mid-10th century.

LEFT Norse gods in a tapestry. One-eyed Odin holds an axe, Thor wields his hammer, and Frey holds an ear of corn. From Skog Church in Sweden, 12th century.

CHAPTER SEVENTEEN

GERMANY

Germanic mythology is the tree of which Scandinavian mythology is a branch, but little is known about the myths of the pagan Germanic (or Teutonic) peoples in Germany itself. Iconographic material, though always a risky thing on which to base anything more than tentative theories, seems to suggest that the early Germans worshipped an Earth Mother and a Sky Father. There is also evidence of twin gods and of the ritual sacrifice of horned animals.

The Earth Mother, Frija, gave her name to Friday in the Germanic world. The Sky Father was known as Tiwaz. He appears as Tyr in Scandinavia and as Tiw in Anglo-Saxon England. The name is related to Greek Zeus and Roman Jupiter, and the third day of the week (Tuesday) was sacred to him, which led classical authors to identify him with the war-god Mars, to whom the third day was sacred in Rome. It is likely that a German religious ceremony described by the Roman writer Tacitus, late in the 1st century AD, had to do with Tiwaz. Various tribes met once a year to offer human sacrifice in a wood sacred to a god called Ruler of All. Each participant was bound with a cord and, if he fell, was not allowed to get to his feet again but instead had to roll over and over. This binding and falling rule was probably employed either to choose a victim for sacrifice or as an act of divination.

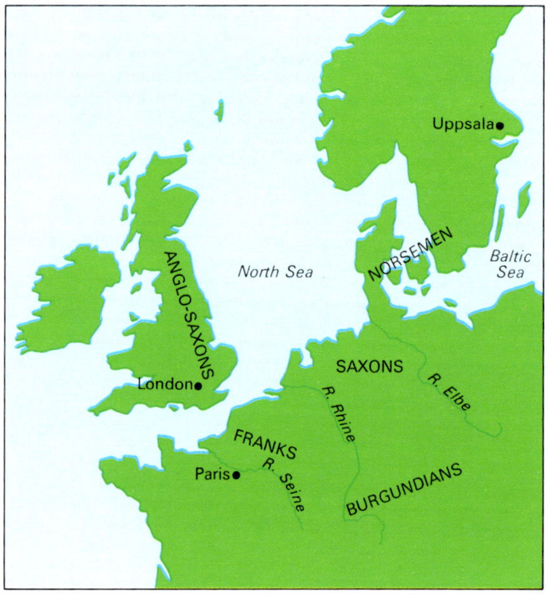

Tacitus says that the Germans sacrificed to Mars and Mercury, meaning the gods Tiwaz and Wotan (or Wodan), the latter being a war-god and the primitive form of the Scandinavian Odin. Such sacrifices were particularly associated with victory in war, captive enemies being slaughtered and captured weapons ritually destroyed. By classical times Wotan had begun to edge Tiwaz from his former pre-eminence. He had come to be considered the ruler of the kingdom of the dead and the god of prophecy and magic. He demanded many sacrifices and his victims were hanged on trees. Sacred to Wotan were the eagle, the raven, the wolf and, of weapons, the spear. His day was the fourth day (Wednesday).

The third of the major German gods was Thunor (or Donar), lord of thunder and lightning, the ancestor of the Scandinavian Thor. His sacred day was Thursday, which caused classical writers to associate him with Jupiter. He was very much a weather-god and his thunderbolts were symbolized by the axe, which later evolved into the hammer. He may also have been linked with fertility, and as late as the present century a North German farmer was found placing stone axes in his first seed-drill to ensure good crops.

The Modern Revival

The modern revival of Germanic paganism was a by-product of the German romantic movement and of German nationalism, following the creation of a united Germany in the 19th century. Pagan mythology was held to justify political and social programmes, frequently programmes of extreme nationalism and anti-semitism concerned to promote the supremacy of the supposed Aryan 'master race'.

The German romantics of the period 1750 to 1850 were not generally greatly interested in the beliefs of their pagan ancestors. Their attention was largely confined to the Gothic culture of the Middle Ages. The first outstanding cultural figure on whom Germanic mythology exerted a major influence was the composer Richard Wagner (1813–83). Pagan myths, he felt, had acted as a thoroughly healthy influence on German history. He wrote: 'In rugged forests in the long winter, in the warmth of the fire upon the hearth of his castle chamber towering far into the air, the German remembers his ancestors, transmuting the myths of the gods into manifold and inexhaustible legend. He does not oppose the influences which press upon him from abroad . . . but he is not content to gaze upon the foreign thing as such, as something purely foreign, rather will he interpret it in German fashion.'

Wagner drew upon Teutonic mythology for his great cycle of operas, *The Ring*. He took the stories on which the cycle is based from a Scandinavian source, the *Verse Edda*, not a German one. The German version of the same myths is contained in the *Nibelungenlied*, a 13th-century compilation based on much older material, and it is odd that Wagner chose to rely on an Icelandic rather than a German source, making little use of the latter except in *The Twilight of the Gods*, the last part of *The Ring*.

The world-order of *The Ring* is that of the Germanic gods, not of Christianity, a doom-laden universe moving inevitably towards a predestined chaos with the death of the gods. Wagner did not take his inclination towards pagan mythology to the point of totally abandoning Christianity in favour of a revival of the worship of Wotan and the Germanic deities. Instead he called for the creation of a reformed Christianity, which would combine the heroic attitudes of the ancient myths with the best (the 'most Germanic') elements of Christianity.

A similar attitude was adopted by Wagner's son-in-law, the British writer Houston Stewart Chamberlain (1855–1926), who became a naturalized German. He held that Jesus had been the son of a German soldier in the service of Rome and that Germany needed a new paganism for its spiritual survival. 'In the want of a true religion,' he wrote, 'that has sprung from, and is compatible with, our own individuality, I see the greatest danger for the Teuton . . . The German stands apart and waits for a god to descend from heaven.'

The Swastika

A far more explicit and thoroughgoing attempt to revive Germanic paganism as a living religion was made by a Viennese journalist, Guido von List (1848–1919). In 1862, when he was only 14 years old, he stood in front of the altar in the crypt of Vienna's Cathedral of St Stephen, solemnly renounced his Catholic faith and swore that one day he would build a temple dedicated to Wotan. He converted a few friends and associates to a belief in the ancient German myths and the group developed their theories into a complete neo-paganism, holding festivals at the equinoxes and solstices. In 1875, for example, von List and his allies celebrated the summer solstice on a hilltop near Vienna, enjoying a 'fraternal feast', adoring the sun as the visible body of 'Baldur incarnate' and burying eight wine bottles carefully laid out in the shape of a swastika. This, interestingly enough, seems to have been the first association of the swastika with revived German mythology.

The word swastika comes from Sanskrit *svastika*, 'well-being, good luck'. The symbol is also known as the fylfot cross, hammer of Thor or hooked cross (German *hakenkreuz*). It has been used from prehistoric times in Asia, Europe and the Americas, often apparently as a symbol of the sun or fire, and so of vigorous life and energy. It was chosen as the official emblem of the Nazi party in 1920, in the belief that it was a purely 'Nordic' symbol, with connotations of heroic German paganism, German manliness and Aryan racial supremacy.

Guido von List discovered, or thought he discovered, the swastika in disguised form in the ancient runic alphabet, as the rune equivalent to the letter G. Perhaps because the swastika was also romantically known as the hammer of Thor, he used it as the emblem of his revived religion of the pagan German gods. By the early 20th century various nationalist groups in Germany had adopted it, including the *Wandervögel* youth movement.

Hitler and Mythology

After the death of his father in 1877 von List, who had previously lived on an allowance made to him by his family, earned his living by journalism. His real interests, however, remained the propagation of Teutonic paganism and the revival of ancient

A float with a swastika, as a symbol of the life-giving sun, at the head of a procession in Munich, celebrating 2000 years of German culture. The swastika was closely associated with the revival of pagan mythology in Germany in the 19th and 20th centuries, and was adopted as the official emblem of the Nazi party in 1920. The Nazi party swastika badge was devised by Friedrich Krohn, a dentist and a former pupil of Guido von List, one of the pioneers of the revival. Krohn's swastika was anti-clockwise, with the top bar projecting to the left as one looks at it, as a symbol of good fortune, but Hitler insisted on having a clockwise swastika, projecting the other way. As has often been pointed out, it did not bring him good fortune in the end.

mythology. To this end he published several books, notably *German Mythological Landscapes* (1891), *The Secret of the Runes* (1908), *The Rites of the Ario-Germans* (1908) and *The Transition from Wotanism to Christianity* (1911). These books attracted admirers, some of them wealthy, and the Guido von List Society was formed to distribute von List's books as widely as possible and to convert the general public to a belief in neo-paganism.

Von List called his version of paganism 'Arminianism', a name derived from the Herminones, a tribe of blue-eyed, fair-haired German heroes described by Tacitus in his *Germania.* According to von List, from the Herminones had been derived a secret society of wise pagan 'priests', which had kept the ancient German mythology alive during the long rule of Christianity and of which he himself claimed to be the last surviving member. Von List asserted that this secret association had left philological traces of its temples and holy places in the names of hills, rivers and valleys. His philology, it is almost needless to say, was as eccentric as his other ideas. For example, he derived the Greek word 'hieroglyph' from a supposed runic 'ir-og-liff'.

The Herminones had supposedly left their traces not only in place names but in much German mystical literature. Such writers as Paracelsus and Boehme had been secret pagans and had written their books in a code only to be correctly unravelled by their fellow members of the Herminones.

Von List died in 1919, but his ideas about German mythology continued to be advocated by his disciple Alfred Schuler, who gave a series of lectures in 1922 at the Munich home of a certain Frau Bruckmann. At the time, the rising politician Adolf Hitler was a frequent guest at the Bruckmann home and it seems possible that he attended the lectures. Certainly he came across such attempts to revive ancient German mythology, for in later life he twice referred to them – paradoxically enough in entirely different ways. On the second occasion, at some time in the 1930s, he informed Rauschning, a Nazi from Danzig, that: 'Our peasants have not forgotten their true religion. It still lives . . . The old beliefs will be brought back to honour again . . . The peasant will be told what the Church has destroyed for him: the whole secret knowledge of nature, of the divine, the shapeless, the daemonic . . . We shall wash off the Christian veneer and bring out a religion peculiar to our race . . . our peasantry still lives in heathen beliefs and values . . . through the peasantry we shall really be able to destroy Christianity because there is in them a true religion rooted in nature and blood.'

Hitler's other reference to neo-paganism, in his *Mein Kampf*, was less favourable: 'Especially in regard to the so-called religious reformers of the ancient Germanic type, I have the feeling that they are sent by dark forces who do not desire the rebirth of our people. For their entire activity leads the folk away from its fight against the common enemy, the Jew, in order that it may expend its energy in internal religious struggles. . . .'

A contemporary and friend of Guido von List, who also attempted to lead a revival of the spirit of German mythology was Lanz von Liebenfels (1874–1954). Born as plain Adolf Lanz, he later claimed, apparently without any justification whatsoever, to be the son of a 'Baron Johannes Lancz von Liebenfels'.

Originally, von Liebenfels was a pious Catholic. Indeed, from 1893 to 1899 he was a member of the Cistercian Order, but he soon abandoned Christianity for a full-blooded paganism and established a society called the Order of New Templars. The membership of this was never large but it did include some wealthy individuals and a number of heathen temples, over which flew the swastika flag, were established; the first in 1907, three others before the outbreak of World War I. In these 'German holy places' the white-robed followers of von Liebenfels carried out pagan rites devised by their leader and studied the writings of both German mystics and von Liebenfels himself. The latter were extremely voluminous, amounting in all to something like 15,000 printed pages, and included *German Psalms*, *The New Templar's Breviary* and the *Bibliomystikon*, a 'secret holy book' in ten volumes.

Many of von Liebenfels's ideas anticipated those of the Nazis, and he assumed that he would be hailed as a German prophet when Hitler came to power. Far from this happening, von Liebenfels was forbidden to publish any of his writings and the New Templars were forced to go underground.

Pagan Germanic religion involved the sacrifice of human beings to the god Tiwaz, god of the sky, and Wotan, god of war, whose victims were hanged on trees. The bodies of those sacrificed were sometimes thrown into swamps and bogs. The early Iron Age mummy of this blindfolded girl was recovered from Windeby Bog in Germany.

The Germanic Belief Fellowship

Besides Wagner, Chamberlain, von List and von Liebenfels, several other German writers called for the rebirth of paganism during the period 1870–1914. Thus in the 1870s the writings of the novelist Felix Dahn led the Catholic Church to accuse him of deliberately fostering a revival of Wotan worship, while in 1880 the sociologist Eugen Dühring published *The Jewish Question*, in which he stated that the Germanic gods were still alive.

In 1907 these and similar influences led Professor Ludwig Fahrenkrog (1867–1952) to found an organization called the Community for Germanic Beliefs, which subsequently united with other small pagan groups, notably the Wotan Society, led by Dr

Ernst Wachler, and the Germanic Religious Fellowship of O.S. Reuter, author of a modern interpretation of ancient German mythology called *The Mystery of the Edda*. After these amalgamations the organization changed its name to the Germanic Belief Fellowship.

As in all small religious groupings there were tendencies to fission – largely based on personality differences – in the Germanic Belief Fellowship, and eventually Reuter broke away to form the *Deutsche Orden*, a pagan group which established a rural commune named after the German god Donar (Thunor). Loosely associated with the *Deutsche Orden* was the Nordungen Fraternity, a pagan youth movement which was founded about 1914.

Fahrenkrog had grandiose plans to build a cathedral to Wotan, Thunor and the other gods of ancient Germany. This, it was intended, should have three aisles meeting at a stone altar behind which, on a sub-altar, would be a copy of the *Edda*, 'Thunor's hammer' and a sacred ring on which oaths were to be sworn. On the altar itself was to be a heap of wood which would be lit with flint and steel at the culmination of each service held in the cathedral. The central point of the services was to be a sermon preached on a text taken from the Edda.

Fahrenkrog's cathedral was never built, but his Germanic Belief Fellowship and the other pagan groups busily celebrated their rites in private houses and in the open air. The principal festivals kept by these heathen revivalists were the *Oster* (Easter) feast, which took its name from the ancient Teutonic goddess Eostre; 'High May', celebrated at a date coinciding with the Christian Whitsun; and Yule, celebrated at Christmas. Pagan ceremonies were also held on Ascension Day and on Good Friday; the latter date was sacred to the pagan Saxons massacred by the Emperor Charlemagne, the former to Thunor's hammer.

Those who entered the Germanic Belief Fellowship were obliged to swear a solemn oath that they were of pure Aryan blood, that they would keep their blood 'pure' in marriage, and that they would bring up their children to follow the same course of action. There was no priesthood as such. Instead every father of a family was a priest towards his own household, conducting ceremonies for weddings, the naming of children and funerals. Sometimes the naming ceremonies were held in public, to make propaganda for paganism. Such a rite, which took place in Munich's Forstenrieder Park, was described in the periodical *Rig*: 'In the centre of five old oak trees we made a table from boulders. On the table is placed a bronze hammer and a bowl of water from the pond close to the beech trees. . . . The mother lays the child at the father's feet. The father bows and takes the child in his arms, saying: "I recognize you as my own, take you into our kindred and give you a name. I sprinkle you with the pure water of the German spring. May all that is un-German be alien to you". . . .'

Another neo-pagan group was the secret society called the German Order, which flourished in the period 1913–22. This had an impressive initiation ritual, conducted by the 'Master of the Lodge' and two assistants. All three were clad in white robes and wore horned helmets upon their heads. The Master bore a ceremonial lance, the 'Spear of Wotan', while the two assistants wore swords. The members of the Lodge, also robed, entered singing the Pilgrims' Song from Wagner's opera *Tannhäuser* and the candidate for initiation was led in, blindfolded and dressed as a pilgrim. He was lectured by the Master, who informed him that they were separated from inferior races by 'our Ario-Germanic concept of the world and life'. Some religious flim-flam followed, culminating in the lighting of a 'sacred torch' and the consecration of the candidate with the 'Spear of Wotan'.

After 1919 most of the groups engaged in the revival of Germanic mythology seem to have suffered a decline in membership. This led various neo-pagan sects to set aside their differences with one another and to unite, in 1931–2, as the Nordic Religious Working Community. The group was tolerated, though not encouraged, by the Nazis.

As in Hitler's own case, there was a conflict of attitudes to neo-paganism at the highest levels of the Nazi party. Some Nazi leaders desired a revival of pagan mythology and others regarded all attempts at such a revival as no more than romantic posturing. For example, Alfred Rosenberg, the leading literary ideologist of Nazism, referred disparagingly to 'Wotan worshippers', while Heinrich Himmler hoped for a rebirth of paganism, devised curious 'Nordic' initiation rituals for his SS men and even made them study the mystic significance of the ancient runes.

After the Second World War, Ludwig Fahrenkrog continued his efforts to win converts to neo-paganism, seemingly with little success, though there are still occasional vague reports of the activities of German neo-pagan groups. Such groups certainly exist in the United States and the *Runestone*, an irregularly published periodical, reflects the beliefs of those for whom Wotan and Tiwaz still live.

The Hitler Youth marching in 1935, under a swastika banner. The *Wandervögel* youth movement had earlier taken the swastika as a badge and shared an ideology which was strongly influenced by the semi-pagan, *völkisch* enthusiasm of the pre-1914 German youth movement. Hitler himself was ambivalent about the revival of ancient Germanic mythology and there was a conflict of attitudes to it at high levels in the Nazi party. The leaders of the revival did not receive the welcome they expected from the Nazi regime.

CHAPTER EIGHTEEN

THE SLAVS

The mythology of the Slavonic peoples is unusually varied, reflecting their far-flung migrations and cultural diversity, their inborn love of story-telling, and their obstinate attachment to ancient beliefs, customs and rituals, persisting to the present day. Although Slavonic writing did not exist before the Christian missionary work of St Cyril and St Methodius in the 9th century AD, the findings of archeology provide evidence from which the origins of the Slavonic pantheon can be partially reconstructed.

The Slavs belong to the vast ethnic family of the Indo-Europeans, who today dominate enormous areas of the world, from San Francisco over the Atlantic Ocean and as far eastwards as Calcutta and Vladivostok. At present there are nearly 250 million Slavonic speakers in the world. Until the 8th century AD or thereabouts, they spoke a common language, though with regional dialects. Today there are 13 separate Slavonic languages, classified into eastern, western and southern blocs. These are the languages of the Russians, Byelorussians, Ukrainians, Poles, Sorbs or Lusatians, Kashubians, Czechs, Slovaks, Slovenes, Croats, Serbs, Bulgarians and Macedonians. The widely differing physical make-up of these peoples and their distinct national languages evolved from their common heritage, largely during the last 12 centuries.

The original Slavs can be traced through the archeological evidence back to the period between 2000 and 1000 BC. They begin to emerge into recorded history in the writings of the Greek author Herodotus (5th century BC), who mentions them under the name of Neuri, dwelling on the upper waters of the Dniester. The location of the original homeland of the Slavs has long been controversial. The best evidence points to a cradle immediately north-east of the Carpathian mountains, in the basins of the Vistula, Pripet and Upper Dniester. To the north, these proto-Slavs maintained contact with ancestors of the modern Baltic peoples. To the east, the Slavs were in relations with the Finns, and to the north-west, with the Germans. Beyond the Carpathians were Thracian tribes.

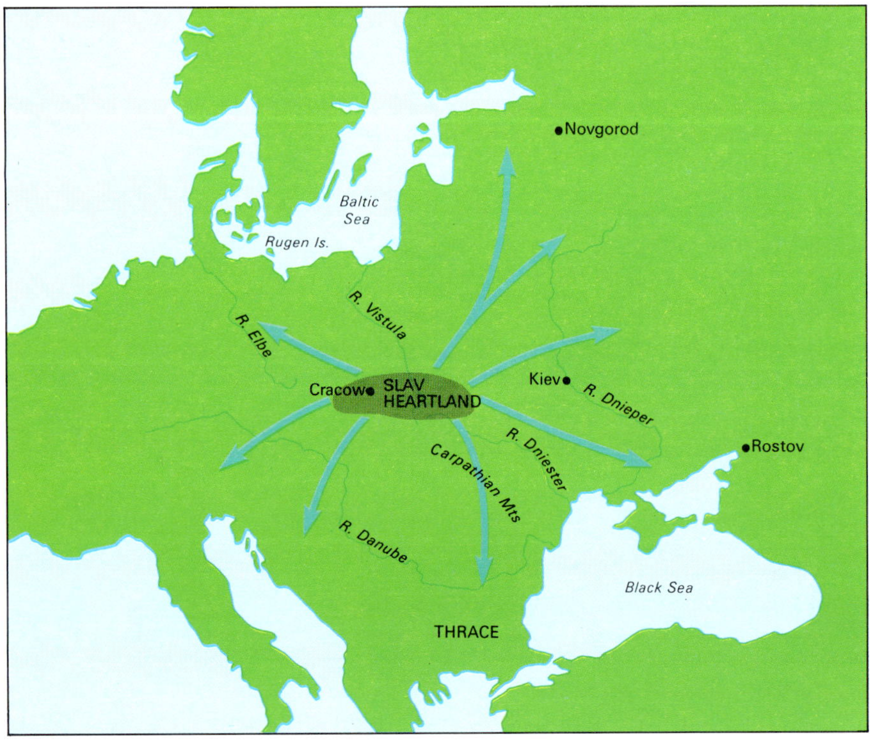

Influences from Iran

Of special significance were early cultural contacts between the Slavs and various Iranian tribes which overran southern Russia (the modern Ukraine), notably Scythians and Sarmatians. During the first century BC the Sarmatians advanced from the east deep into Slavonic territory west of the Dnieper. It was during this period that the Slavs borrowed from the Iranians such words as *bogu* or 'god', *rayi* or 'paradise', and *svyatu* or *sventu*, meaning 'holy'.

Deification of the sun, which was an Iranian characteristic, was also practised by the Slavs. They regarded the sun and fire as children of the god Svarogu, who was believed to generate the heat and light of the sun.

Other Slav deities deriving from the Iranian pantheon include Stribog, the wind god, whose children are the winds of heaven. The Simargl is the Iranian Simurgh, a winged monster, who in Sarmatian mythology guarded the tree producing the seed for every species of plant. Also of vital importance was the female deity Mokosh, who corresponds to Iranian Anahita (the Armenian Anahit). The name Mokosh signifies 'moist' (*mokry*

Small clay chariot from prehistoric Yugoslavia. It bears a goddess with a bird's head, attended by three aquatic birds. From Duplyaya near Vrsac, *c.* 1500–1200 BC.

in modern Russian), showing a connection with the cult of water and rain, and thus of fertility and plenty.

Less clear is the etymology of the name of another key god in the ancient Slavonic pantheon – Veles or Volos, the god of horned animals. Veles is mentioned in 10th-century Russian state treaties and his name is preserved in names of towns as far apart as the Skopje district of southern Yugoslavia and the Novgorod and Rostov regions in Russia. In Christian times, this beneficent god merged with the Byzantine St Blasius, called in Slavonic Vlas or Vlaho: he continues to keep watch over cattle right up to the present time.

During the 6th century AD, the Slavs crossed the Danube and poured southwards through the Balkan peninsula, overrunning Thrace and northern Greece, and reaching the walls of Constantinople. As a result of these incursions, we have accounts of the Slavs from Byzantine chroniclers.

From Procopius (6th century AD), we learn that the Slavs sacrificed animals to their chief deity, the Lord of Lightning, to be identified with the mighty god Perun. The usual offering was a cock, but goats, bears and even bulls were slaughtered and offered up on great feast days. Once sacrificed, the animal had to be eaten by the faithful believers, for it was impregnated with the holy mana, or power, of the god, and in this way the whole group would be ritually strengthened. Belief in this form of transubstantiation may be compared with the thinking behind the Christian service of Holy Communion.

In a key passage, Procopius states that the Slavs 'worship rivers and nymphs and various other demons, offering up sacrifices to all of these; and with the aid of these sacrifices, they carry out fortune-telling and divination'. Many instances are quoted in Slavonic folklore of rivers irritated by some disrespect committed by travellers, and lying in wait preparing to drown them on their homeward path. As late as the 17th century, it is said that the Cossack chieftain Stenka Razin offered a human sacrifice to the River Volga. Casting into the water a beautiful Persian princess whom he had captured, the outlaw cried: 'Oh Mother Volga, thou great river of Russia! Much has thou given me of gold and silver, and of all good things. Thou hast nursed and nourished me, and covered me with glory. But I have done nothing to show you my gratitude. Here is a gift for thee – take it from thy servant, the cossack of the Don.' In spite of this sacrificial act, Stenka Razin soon came to a bad end, being captured and executed by the Tsar's troops.

Animism and Totemism

In ancient Slavonic mythology, life was felt to have an all-pervading unity, embracing all phenomena. This outlook is known as animism. Wherever prehistoric man saw an object in motion, he assumed the presence of a conscious agent, invisible to his eye. In his mind, many inanimate objects also came to be endowed with intelligence. Trees and animals could be revered as man's ancestors, and worshipped as older and wiser than man. Animals were often thought to possess superior powers. There was a category of totemistic animals – mythical beings with supernatural attributes, who assumed animal form for their own mysterious purposes. Every Slavonic clan had its own totemistic ancestor.

The specific animals worshipped could never be killed, nor must their meat be consumed.

The tree of life also occupied a significant place in the Slavonic folk cosmology. Certain trees marked a sacred zone. At one time, the Russians considered it a sin to cut down any tree which was old. According to folk mythology, anyone who cut down a tree would go out of his mind, break his hands or legs, or even die. Trees were thought of as dwelling places for the souls of the departed, who could in case of emergency flit from one tree to another. This gave rise to the notion of wood spirits, called in Russian *lesnye*.

In Slavonic religion, seasonal festivals figured prominently. In winter was celebrated the festival of the winter god, Kolyada, which is still current in the Ukraine and White Russia. Spring witnessed a cycle of sun festivals, testifying to the relief felt at the close of a long winter and the approach of summer warmth. The sun appears in the Slavonic pantheon as Khors. A common solar symbol was a fiery wheel, tarred and then set alight spinning on top of a pole. Summer was sacred to the cult of Perun, god of thunder and lightning, akin to the Greek Zeus and the Scandinavian Thor. Perun was taken over by Orthodox Christianity, in the guise of St Elias or Elijah the Prophet.

Ancient Slavonic mythology is closely bound up with burial customs and rites, and with the cult of the forefathers of the tribe and clan. There were various beliefs as to what happened after death. A few of the Slavs thought that it was the end of everything. The overwhelming majority held that the dead passed into a new country. In this case, the dead were interred ceremonially and the tombs were supplied with articles for their journey. It was the custom in some noble families for a widow to be buried alive in her husband's grave.

The ancestors of a given clan or community were believed to dwell below the earth. In the early and medieval Slav world, cracks and holes in the earth's surface were thought to be gates into the underworld. In relatively modern fairy tales, the open mouth of the monstrous witch Baba-Yaga is conceived as stretching from earth right into the infernal regions.

This wooden idol was discovered in a peat-bog. Most Slavonic idols were demolished when the Slavonic peoples adopted Christianity. From White Russia, *c.* 1750 BC.

From earliest times, a special corner of the family hut was dedicated to the spirits of the ancestors, and at harvest time the little domestic shrine was specially decorated, with freshly embroidered linen cloths. The cult of ancestors merges into that of the domestic deities, called in Russian Domovoi and in Ukrainian Domovik. These guardians of the home and hearth had to be specially propitiated. Belief in the agency of these beings is in turn bound up with the cult of icons, which has persisted in the Slavonic Orthodox world with greater intensity than it attained in the Byzantine homeland.

The Destruction of the Idols

About AD 862, the Viking Rurik and his followers established their dominion over the key cities of Russia. This Scandinavian ruling caste fused many ancient Viking beliefs with those of their Slav subjects. But by the time of Prince Vladimir, the first Christian ruler of Russia, the Slavonic deities had reasserted their supremacy.

At his accession in the year 980, Vladimir is portrayed in the Chronicles as a savage and brutal heathen. He celebrated his accession by erecting figures of the Slavonic gods in front of his palace at Kiev. First of all these stood a wooden figure of Perun, whose head was silver and his mouth gold. Then came Khors and Dazhdbog (gods of the sun) and Stribog, Simargl and Mokosh. An idol of Perun was also erected near Novgorod. A ruined temple, probably that of Perun, was actually discovered in 1951 near a place called appropriately Peryn, four kilometres south of Novgorod. A circular mound for the idol base was enclosed by a ditch containing charcoal, the remains of a ceremonial fire.

At the outset of his reign, Vladimir sacrificed close on a thousand human beings to his idols, but in 989 he adopted Christianity under Byzantine influence, and forced his people to follow suit. This was not achieved without a bitter struggle. The newly converted prince set to work demolishing his idols, burning some and chopping others up. The mighty Perun had a spectacular fate: tied to a horse's tail, he was dragged to the banks of the Dnieper and thrown in. The people wept bitterly, as Vladimir ordered his henchmen to stand by with long poles and make sure that Perun was not washed ashore and salvaged. Eventually Perun floated through the Dnieper rapids, and was blown onto a sandbank by a strong wind. 'From which,' the Russian Primary Chronicle comments, 'that sandbank was known as Perun's Bank, and so it is called even at the present day.'

Such thorough-going destruction, repeated whenever one of the Slavonic peoples adopted Christianity, means that Slavonic idols are rather rare. (The class of female figures carved in stone and called *kamennye baby* are prehistoric fertility goddesses, and are now thought to antedate the Slavonic period.) Perhaps the finest authentic Slavonic idol is that from Zbruch in Galicia, south-eastern Poland. The Zbruch idol is four-sided, each facet carrying relief carvings divided into distinct vertical zones. These zones represent heaven, the world of the gods; earth, home of mankind; and the underworld, whose deity bears

on his back the weight of earth and heaven. The uppermost figures share between them a single flattened conical hat, similar to hats worn by aristocratic saints on medieval icons; the underworld god wears long moustaches.

This cult of idols was also widespread among the western Slavs, right up to the 12th century. The Danish chronicler Saxo Grammaticus (1150–1206) records King Waldemar's destruction of the Slavonic pagan temple of Svantevit or Svyatovit on the island of Rügen in the Baltic Sea. The huge idol stood on a sunken base in an inner sanctuary, hung with purple rugs. The statue held in its right hand a drinking horn, into which wine was poured at the harvest festival, to enable prophecies and divinations to be made regarding next year's crops. Other idols destroyed by King Waldemar were those of Rugievit (patron deity of Rügen island), Porevit and Porenut.

However much zealous converts like Vladimir or King Waldemar might rant against the Slavonic idols and physically destroy them, the people obstinately refused to abandon them. Perun, we mentioned, was reincarnated in Russia as Elijah or St Elias. In the Baltic region, Perun is re-embodied in the popular Lithuanian deity Perkunas, portrayed in folk mythology as a vigorous man holding an axe or hammer. He is a purifier and a fructifier and lives in a castle on a stone hill. If Perkunas strikes a tree, a rock or a man with lightning, the object struck becomes sacred, for the heavenly fire remains inside it. As late as 1652, we read of an old man travelling in Western Lithuania in a thunderstorm and actually eating the ashes of a leather saddle which had been burnt up by lightning: to him, this meant immunity against illness, the gift of oracular powers and the ability to conjure up fire.

Heretical Mythology

After Russia, Bulgaria and other Slavonic lands adopted Christianity, they acquired the art of writing in the Slavonic language. Most of the early literature has a specifically Christian, Orthodox flavour. However, heretical sects also made use of the new-found gift of literacy to undermine the Christian Church, and some of these sects even developed what we may term apocryphal and heretical mythologies.

Perhaps the most important of these religious mythologies was that of the Bogomils. The priest Bogomil appeared in Bulgaria in the 10th century and preached a form of dualism, deriving from the ancient Persian teachings of Mani, to the effect that all tangible objects and human life itself are evil, and that only the invisible world of the spirit is good. Satan, or Satanail, was allegedly the originator of the whole Orthodox community, with its churches, vestments, ceremonies, monks and priests.

The mythological element in Bogomilism includes a fanciful account of the creation, in which Satanail, the evil principle, features as a fallen son of God. Satanail is held responsible for the creation of the earth, and later for the crucifixion of Jesus Christ, his younger brother. This Bogomil mythology was widely preached in Russia as well as in the Balkans. It permeated the ideology of the Cathars and Albigensians in Western Europe. The Bogomils created a whole library of secret books, full of mythological elements.

Prince Igor and Krak

On a much higher plane is the *Lay of Prince Igor's Host*, an anonymous rhapsodic prose poem, thought to have been composed in 1187. It treats of the expedition of Prince Igor Svyatoslavich of Novgorod Seversk against the Polovtsians to the east, and his captivity at their hands. It is doubly important for the study of Slavonic mythology. Besides allusions to ancient Slavonic deities, the exalted style and atmosphere of the work have given rise to a semi-mythological concept of a golden age of chivalry in Russia before the Mongol invasion of the 13th century. In the *Lay* the Russian people are portrayed as the grandchildren of Dazhdbog, and the winds as grandchildren of Stribog. There are allusions to Troyan, a legendary figure regarded as a deification of the Roman emperor Trajan.

A special kind of mythology deals with the foundation of towns and cities by legendary figures of the distant past. In the West the example of Romulus and Remus founding Rome comes to mind. The Slavs did not take naturally to city life, so that towns held for them a special mystique.

In Poland, we have a marvellous story about the legendary hero Krak, founder of Cracow. Krak found the simple folk dwelling near Wawel, the site of the old city of Cracow, under the sway of a malignant dragon. Krak stuffed a sheep, or perhaps

ABOVE LEFT Small bronze idol, found in the Kostroma district, northeast of Moscow.

ABOVE Four-sided idol from Zbruch. The four-faced figure at the top of the stela may represent the deity Svantevit.

Decorative plaque, Scythian work, typical of the art of the nomadic horse-warriors who roamed the steppes of south Russia before the coming of the Slavs. Here the horseman seems to be capturing the enemy with a kind of lasso.

its skin only, with saltpetre, and this the dragon greedily swallowed whole. Perishing with thirst, the dragon drank up half the river Vistula, and promptly burst. Then Krak set to work and founded the ancient citadel and city of Cracow on the Wawel heights. This is supposed to have happened about AD 700, when Poland was still pagan.

Baba-Yaga

During centuries of Mongol oppression, followed by serfdom and priest-ridden autocracy, memories of the old gods grew dim. However, the Russian people felt the continuing need for a body of folk mythology which would supplement the rigid dogma of the Orthodox Church and could assuage the hopes and fears of a simple people, dwelling often in remote places and open to the terrors of dark, cold nights and endless forests. Many of the rich store of Russian fairy tales are built round a recognizable company of fantastic beings, some benevolent, but more of them embodiments of the mysterious forces of evil.

In the flesh-creeping category, no mythological being is more potent than the evil witch called Baba-Yaga. She is a tall gaunt hag with dishevelled hair, who lives in a hut surrounded by a fence made of dead men's bones. On top of the fence are stuck human skulls with eyes in them. Men's legs serve as gate-posts and the bones from human arms are used for bolts. The lock is a human mouth with sharp teeth. At night or at moments of danger, the eyes in the skulls start shining and light up the clearing. After a tasty meal of human flesh, Baba-Yaga will lie down, stretched out from one corner of her hut to the other, her long iron nose projecting through the ceiling like a beak. The hut is supported on revolving legs and can rotate swiftly when the proper spell is recited.

A sinister ally of Baba-Yaga is the Snake, sometimes known as Zmei Gorynich, which means Serpent of the Mountains. Zmei is elusive and gliding, sometimes of mixed reptilian and human nature: he may appear with a serpent's head and a man's body. Sometimes he dwells in mountain caverns or within the bowels of the earth, at others he lives in a luxurious palace or in a revolving hut like that of Baba-Yaga. Zmei loves to abduct some gorgeous princess, who is then rescued by a hero who comes to do battle for her. In one story Zmei is symbolically portrayed as having stolen the light of day. In another the bright moon and many stars come forth from Zmei's body after his death.

Koshchei the Deathless

Another potent incarnation of evil is Koshchei the Deathless, who sometimes appears in reptile guise. When he appears in human form, he is skinny and bony of limb. Koshchei is a great horseman and kidnaps fair princesses and carries them off to his lair. Koshchei is called 'Immortal' or 'Deathless' because he is invulnerable to the normal forces of nature and never grows old.

Another dangerous mythological figure is the Water King, a patriarchal monarch living in subaqueous realms of light and splendour, whence he emerges occasionally to seize a human victim. His daughters are beautiful and intelligent, as in the lively tale of Vasilissa the Wise. When the Water King catches a boy, Vasilissa falls in love with him. She helps the young man to outwit her bad-tempered parent and eventually they escape together to the upper world of dry land.

A malignant figure of a different type is Mother Friday, who embodies the bad luck which is supposed to dog any enterprise undertaken on a Friday (a widespread belief, which goes back to the crucifixion of Jesus on Good Friday). The Orthodox saint associated with Friday – *Pyatnitsa* in Russian – is St Praskovya, so Mother Friday is often known as Mother Pyatnitsa-Praskovya. She is supposed to wander around the houses of the peasants on her holy day, and to be offended if she finds certain kinds of work going on. Spinning and weaving are particularly objectionable to Mother Friday, for the dust injures her eyes. When this happens she punishes the household by afflicting them with sore eyes, styes and whitlows.

Folk Heroes

Faced with hostile Asiatic hordes from without, and terrifying mythological figures within, the medieval Russians evolved in their fertile imagination a breed of supermen, *bogatyrs*, of whom the most famous is Ilya Muromets. These folk heroes were dedicated to the protection of the Russian people from all dangers. Their bravery is contrasted with the feebleness of the pot-bellied nobles, and their master is called Vladimir the Little Red Sun.

Daily life in the Slavonic world is even today impregnated with belief in mythology and the supernatural. In Russia and Poland, people take refuge occasionally against their misery in vodka and other strong drink. Some of them believe that all who drink themselves to death are doomed to serve as carriers of wood and water in the infernal regions.

In Bulgaria the milder climate encourages vine growing. The patron saint of vineyards is called Trifon Zarezan, who is the Christian embodiment of the Greek god Dionysus. On February 14 occurs the ceremonial pruning of the vine-shoots, and wine is poured formally on the earth in honour of the saint.

Even today, a Ukrainian now living in London remembers many details of folk mythology current in her youth about 40 years ago – for instance, belief in the wind god Stribozh, who is the same as the ancient Slavonic deity Stribog. The same lady also recalls being told at her mother's knee about the river god Khopun, who lies in wait for bad men fording or swimming in the stream, and drags them down to their death. Folk-memories of this kind show how such traditions prevail in the 20th century.

In socialist countries today popular interest in folklore sometimes leads to revival of ancient mythological beliefs and customs which had fallen into disuse. Such, for instance, are the processions of the Kukeri mummers in Bulgaria. The participants wear fantastic masks and costumes and perform mimes which conjure up the mythological beings of far off Thracian times, even predating the Slavonic occupation of the Balkans.

ABOVE Ornament in the form of a stag. The Scythians were renowned for their metalwork and stylized representation of the animal world. Early contacts between the Slavs and the Scythians and Sarmatians influenced Slavonic religion and mythology. Bronze, c.500 BC.

LEFT Festival of the pruning of the vine-shoots held, in honour of Trifon Zarezan, in Bulgaria on 14 February, St Valentine's Day. Trifon Zarezan is the Christian embodiment of the Greek god Dionysus and he is credited with magical powers to ensure a good vintage.

CHAPTER NINETEEN

ARMENIA, GEORGIA AND THE CAUCASUS

The immense mountain range of the Caucasus, stretching from the Black Sea to the Caspian, forms a natural barrier separating eastern Europe and the steppes of southern Russia from the Near East. The range can be traversed or bypassed at only about five points, and it was long a bastion shielding the ancient civilizations of Babylonia, Assyria and Iran against barbarian invaders from the north.

Not far to the south of the Caucasus, in Turkish Armenia, is the major peak of Mount Ararat, more than 5000 metres high, with Little Ararat at its side. Mount Ararat is connected with the biblical story of Noah's Ark, which during the Flood was supposed to have travelled several hundred miles from Babylonia in the south to alight at length on the summit of Great Ararat.

According to the book of Genesis (chapters 6 to 9), God saw that man was wicked and violent, and resolved to blot out life on the earth in a great flood. Noah, however, was a righteous man, and God told him to make the Ark to save himself from destruction. Noah obeyed and when it rained unceasingly for 40 days and nights and the flood waters rose to cover the land, Noah and his family escaped death in the Ark. Noah took with him his wife, his three sons, Shem, Ham and Japheth, and their wives. He also took with him in the Ark pairs of every species of animal, male and female.

For 150 days the waters covered the earth until the flood began to abate and the Ark came to rest 'upon the mountains of Ararat'. Noah built an altar to God and offered sacrifice, and God set his bow in the clouds as the rainbow, a sign that he would never again send a deluge to destroy life. Noah tilled the soil and planted a vineyard, and when he drank the wine he became drunk and lay naked in his tent. Ham went into the tent and saw his father naked, for which Noah cursed him, condemning him and his offspring to be slaves to Shem and Japheth.

Even today, mountaineers descending the upper slopes of Ararat bring down pieces of ancient wood and claim to have recovered portions of the Ark. The story in Genesis implies that after the Flood human and animal life began again in the Ararat district and it is interesting that modern archeology has shown that this area was continuously inhabited by the ancestors of modern man for at least half a million years, and that many species of animals and plants found today in Europe originated in the Armenian and Transcaucasian region.

A noteworthy feature of the story in Genesis is Noah's pioneer action in planting a vineyard on the lower slopes of the mountain. The vineyard was shown to visitors until it was destroyed in a disastrous earthquake in 1840. Modern viticultural science has demonstrated that Armenia was indeed one of the countries where the wild vine was first successfully cultivated, so there is more to this wine-making myth of Father Noah than is generally realized.

The tale of Noah cursing Ham and his offspring, and condemning them to be servants of his other two sons, Shem and Japheth, is one of the mainstays of South African clerics and politicians, who have twisted the story into a racial myth, since Ham is pictured as the ancestor of the black peoples. The conclusion drawn is that the black man is divinely condemned to serve the white man for ever, a curious case of a hallowed myth abused in a bigoted and unscrupulous fashion.

Urartu and Armenia

The early phase of Armenian mythology coincides with the rise and fall of the important kingdom of Urartu, centred on the area round Lake Van (now in Turkey). The geographical term Urartu is Assyrian and is another form of Ararat (the Armenian name for Mount Ararat is Masis). First mentioned in the 13th century BC, the Urartian lands were unified by King Aramé (880–844 BC). The kingdom lasted until about 590 BC, when it was annexed by the Persians.

The Urartians adopted from the Assyrians a system of cuneiform writing, and evolved an elaborate pantheon of deities and mythological beings. The chief Urartian god was Haldi, whose consort was the goddess Arubani. Next came Teisheba, god of war, thunder and storms, with his wife Khuba. Third in the hierarchy was Shivini, the sun-god, while the moon was worshipped as the god Shelardi. Like the Armenians and Georgians later on, the Urartians made a special cult of sacred trees and plants. They worshipped fishes and sea-monsters, and took over for ritual purposes a large group of

ABOVE The early kingdom of Urartu centred on Lake Van. Christianity became the official religion of Armenia in AD 301. This Armenian church on the island of Akhtamar on Lake Van was built for King Gagik of Armenia in the 10th century AD. The entire exterior is richly carved with stone reliefs showing biblical scenes, including the story of Jonah and the whale.

LEFT Urartian cast-bronze figurine of a winged bull with human head and torso, *c.*750 BC.

ABOVE Peaks of Great and Little Ararat viewed from the north. Ararat is famous as the place where Noah's Ark landed after the Flood and, to this day, people bring pieces of wood down from the mountain and claim to have recovered portions of the Ark.

RIGHT Noah loading the animals on to the Ark. Glass panel at Wragby Church, Yorkshire, 1682.

Bronze Age megaliths carved with the heads of fishes and sea-dragons, and called Vishaps. These free-standing monuments were originally intended as protective spirits, watching over ancient water and irrigation systems.

The Armenian nation arose on the ruins of the Urartian kingdom, and at first formed part of the Persian Empire of the Achaemenids. After the conquests of Alexander the Great in the 4th century BC, the Armenians gradually built up an independent kingdom under the Artaxiad dynasty. This reached the peak of its power under Tigranes the Great (95–56 BC), who however had to yield to the onslaught of the Roman legions. St Gregory the Illuminator brought about the official adoption of Christianity in AD 301, which was followed a century later by the invention of a distinctive alphabet and the rapid growth of an important national literature, including histories and theological works, and also containing elements of mythology and ancient lore.

A most interesting historian is Moses of Khorene, who is thought to have lived in the 8th century, though his *History of Armenia* contains many elements going back to pagan times. Moses of Khorene helped to codify Armenian mythology and national

ABOVE LEFT Urartian fortress at Van, Turkish Armenia, supposedly founded by the Assyrian queen Semiramis, *c.*800 BC, who built it after the death of the legendary Armenian king she loved.

ABOVE Urartian bronze figure of Teisheba, god of storm and war.

tradition. He recounts the ancient legend of Bel and Hayk, the latter being the legendary ancestor of the Armenians, who call themselves Hayk, and their land Hayastan. Hayk was a descendant of Japheth, son of Noah, and he revolted against Bel (originally a Babylonian term for 'god') after the destruction of the Tower of Babel. Taking with him his clan numbering 300 people, and other followers, Hayk went north to the Ararat district and set up a kingdom there.

Another story concerns a legendary Armenian king, Ara the Fair, who was loved by the Assyrian queen Semiramis – in Armenian, Shamiram. This lady's advances were rejected, whereupon she invaded Armenia to press her suit. When Ara was killed in battle, Shamiram proceeded to Van, where she built the citadel whose ruins can be seen to this day. This tragic story still has a great appeal to the Armenian imagination. A splendid drama holds the stage at the National Theatre in the Soviet Armenian capital of Erevan, in which Ara strides about in a blazing red wig, and Shamiram resembles a sultry and lecherous Cleopatra.

Pagan Armenian Gods

The pantheon of pre-Christian Armenia was largely of Iranian origin, though the Zoroastrian deities developed distinct national features in Armenia. Later on, the Armenian gods also became equated with leading figures in Greek mythology. A case in point is the chief god Aramazd, who derived from the Zoroastrian Ahura Mazda and was later assimilated to the mighty Zeus. The chief goddess was Anahit, goddess of fertility and mother of all wisdom, later portrayed in the guise of the Greek goddess Aphrodite. Vahagn, god of battle, derives from the Iranian war god Verethragna, and is the Armenian equivalent of Mars.

Also much in evidence is the cosmopolitan god Mithra, in Armenian, Mher or Meherr. Memories of the Mithra cult lingered on in Armenia over the centuries. In the Armenian national epic, *David of Sassoun*, Mithra features as the Great Meherr, Lion of Sassoun. Meherr is himself the father of David, the legendary hero of the Sassoun region, a renowned centre of Armenian resistance against alien domination.

Besides the official pantheon of pagan Armenia, there existed a folk sub-culture, rich in mythological

ABOVE Bronze head of Anahit, the Armenian mother-goddess, portrayed in the guise of the Greek goddess Aphrodite. Found near Erzinjan, Turkish Armenia.

elements. Ancient Armenian literature contains frequent mention of Vishaps, acolytes of the dragon and fish-like stone monsters mentioned earlier. These Vishaps could appear either as men or as serpents. They would suck milk from cows and carry away grain from the threshing floor. One early writer says that peasants would run after them vainly shouting, 'Stop, stop!' Water demons lived in the river Aratsani, adopting the form of mermaids, having sexual intercourse with their victims, and then sucking their blood until they died.

A celebrated myth is that of King Artavazd, who fell down a high precipice while hunting near Mount Ararat. The demons seized him and chained him in a cave inside the mountain. Here two dogs gnaw at Artavazd's chains to set him free, that he may bring the world to an end. The chains wear thin about the season of Navassart, the ancient Armenian New Year festival. Therefore the blacksmiths strike a few symbolical blows with their hammers about this time, to strengthen the chains binding Artavazd and save the world from destruction.

Georgia and the Golden Fleece

Bordering on Armenia and lying immediately to the north of it, Georgia is scarcely less rich in myth and legend. Of universal appeal is the tale of Jason and the Argonauts, sailing to Colchis, the western region of Georgia, in search of the Golden Fleece (see GREECE). The myth of the Argonauts must be extremely ancient, since it was known to Homer, who mentions it in the *Odyssey*.

The Golden Fleece itself is a symbol of the fabulous wealth of the Caucasus region, which the Greeks exploited by settling colonies there, from the 7th century BC onwards. A shrewd Greek geographer named Strabo noted nearly 2000 years ago that Medea the sorceress was a historical person, and the wealth of the regions about Colchis, derived from mines of gold, silver, iron and copper, suggested a rational motive for the Argonaut expedition, especially as gold was carried down the mountain torrents and sometimes caught in perforated sieves and fleecy skins.

The main episodes of the Argonaut saga include the sowing of the dragon's teeth, the guilty passion of Medea the enchantress for Jason, the theft of the Fleece, the murder of the Colchian prince Absyrtus, and the terrible retribution of the gods. Among works of art deriving from the Argonaut myth are the *Medea* of Euripides, the splendid treatment by the Austrian dramatist Grillparzer and the magnificent opera *Medea* by Cherubini. Archeological confirmation of the treasure of Colchis has been provided by excavations carried out by the Georgian Academy of Sciences at Vani and other sites in the vicinity of Kutaisi, the district traditionally identified with Aea, capital of ancient Colchis.

In Georgian national mythology, pride of place belongs to the story of Amiran. Son of a Caucasian sorcerer, Amiran is a loud-mouthed braggart, who murders Christians and then engages Jesus Christ in a rock-throwing contest, in which both hurl vast boulders up into the heavens. Christ's rock embeds itself deep in the earth, and he challenges Amiran to

RIGHT Scene from the Argonaut saga, portrayed on an Etruscan drinking vessel. Jason is being spat out by the dragon. The Golden Fleece hangs on the tree behind.

pull it out. When Amiran fails, he is chained to that same rock. Like the Armenian king Artavazd, Amiran has a dog which gnaws away at the chain that binds him. Like the Armenian blacksmiths, the Georgian smiths strike their anvils (this time, on the Thursday before Easter), so as to make the chain solid again.

During the Middle Ages, the Georgians developed a rich and beautiful romantic literature, in which many mythological elements are embedded. The national bard, Shota Hustaveli, is said to have been a courtier of Queen Tamar, who reigned from 1184 to 1213. He wrote a romantic epic, *The Knight in the Panther's Skin*. The main mythological creatures in this poem are the Kajis, or demons, who imprison the heroine in a remote castle. The Kajis belong to the world of the Arabian Nights. They treat the lady in quite a decent and respectable fashion and seem to have commanded a standing army, which is soon put to flight by the valiant heroes of the poem.

Prometheus in the Caucasus

The Caucasus was known in early times as the Mountain of Tongues, and some 50 distinct languages and dialects are spoken in the region to this day, in addition to literary Georgian and Armenian. Many of the smaller nations and tribes have a rich and varied body of mythology, much of which remains in the sphere of oral tradition.

Pride of place goes to the myth of Prometheus which, like the story of the Argonauts, belongs to the mythology of both the Greeks and the Caucasus. In Greek mythology Prometheus was one of the Titans, the old powers which ruled the world before the coming of Zeus. After Zeus had conquered the Titans, Prometheus made human beings out of clay and life was breathed into them by the goddess Athena. Zeus had no love for the race of men. He oppressed them and deprived them of fire. The wily Prometheus stole fire from heaven, carried it down to earth in the hollow stalk of a fennel plant and gave it to men. He also taught mankind the arts and sciences, but Zeus took his revenge. Prometheus he

Funeral monument of King Antiochus I of Commagene, (34 BC). Nimrud-Dagh, Turkey.

ABOVE LEFT East side, heads of Zeus and Apollo. Due to earthquakes the rows of colossal statues have mostly lost their heads.

ABOVE West side, heads of Apollo and the eagle. The Armenian gods were equated with the gods and goddesses of Greek mythology.

Group of Khevsur warriors in tribal costume bearing traditional weapons, from an old photograph taken nearly a century ago. Until recently the Khevsurs wore chain mail and had crosses on their tunics, which led to a belief that they were descended from a lost regiment of Crusaders.

had fettered to a mountain peak. Every day an eagle (or a vulture) came to peck and tear at the chained Titan's liver, and every night the liver grew again, so that there was no end to the torture. Prometheus remained fettered there for thousands of years until at last, in the usual story, he was released by Hercules. According to one classical tradition, the peak to which Prometheus was fastened was Mount Elbruz in the Caucasus.

The question of a relation between the stories of Prometheus and Amiran, mentioned earlier, has long been debated. Some Georgian scholars maintain that the Greeks derived the Prometheus myth from the Georgians after Greek settlements were founded on the Black Sea. As the Amiran story was not written down until the 19th century, it is difficult to come to a definite conclusion on the point. The whole body of tradition, with its theme of the bringing of fire, arts and sciences to men, illustrates the historical significance of the Caucasus region as one of the most ancient centres of metallurgy and ore-smelting.

The Caucasian Albanians (not connected with the Albanians of the Balkans) once occupied much of what is now Soviet Azerbaijan. The Greeks knew them as worshippers of the sun and moon, honouring Helios, Selene and Zeus. They practised human sacrifice, the victim being pierced through the side into the heart with a sacred lance. From the angle of the victim's fall, auguries and divinations were made as to the future of the nation.

A curious medieval myth concerns the Khevsurs, a mountain people living high in the central Caucasus. Until recently they wore medieval chain mail and had crosses emblazoned on their tunics. This led to a tradition that they were a lost regiment of Crusaders who had strayed up into the Caucasus about 800 years ago. There seems to be no factual basis for this myth, however, as the ethnic affinity of the Khevsurs to other Georgian mountain tribes has been established and they speak a well-attested Georgian dialect.

A large and highly original body of mythology has been preserved among the Ossetes, who live on both the north and south flanks of the Daryal Pass in the central Caucasus. These myths concern the mighty deeds of a race of supermen or demi-gods, known as the Narts. The protagonists are both male and female, the main heroes are called Sosruko and Batradz, and there is a mother figure called Satana. These stories have a full-blooded, Wagnerian atmosphere, which is hardly surprising since the Ossetes are descended from the medieval Alans, a people of Indo-European stock. The Nart legends are also current among other Caucasian mountain peoples, including the Kabardians.

AFRICA

CHAPTER TWENTY

CENTRAL AND SOUTHERN AFRICA

It was once customary for Christians to speak of African religions as 'tribal superstitions' and for Muslims to dismiss them as 'ignorance'. Today the beauty and wisdom in these ethnic religions are widely appreciated. Myths belong to a religious community, indeed they are common beliefs which tend to hold the community together. Before the rise of the international conversion religions, such as Buddhism, Christianity and Islam, people were normally born into a religious community. Hence the Roman identification of *natio*, 'birth', with 'nation' in its original sense, a religious community (the Jews in the Roman Empire were called a *natio*). This is still the situation in those regions of Africa where Islam or Christianity has not yet become dominant. A person is born as a member of a tribe and remains a member of it for ever, this membership sometimes being marked on the face or body by scarifications or other mutilations, including circumcision.

Each ethnic (tribal) group has its own religion, which differs from that of its neighbours though there are also similarities, especially if the neighbours speak related languages. In Africa, linguistic relationship is the only yardstick of historical relationship between different peoples, and historically related peoples are likely also to have common elements in their myths. Various groups of peoples in Central and Southern Africa speak related languages. The largest of these, the Bantu linguistic family, includes more than 200 languages. Among them are Zulu, Tswana of Botswana, Swazi of Swaziland, Rwanda, Rundi of Burundi, Swahili, Kikuyu, Ganda of Buganda, Lingala and Kongo in Western Equatorial Africa. Their speakers have all sprung from a single people who spoke the primeval Bantu language, originating possibly in the Cameroun or perhaps further east.

A second coherent family is formed by the Nilotic languages, to which belong Alur in northeast Zaire,

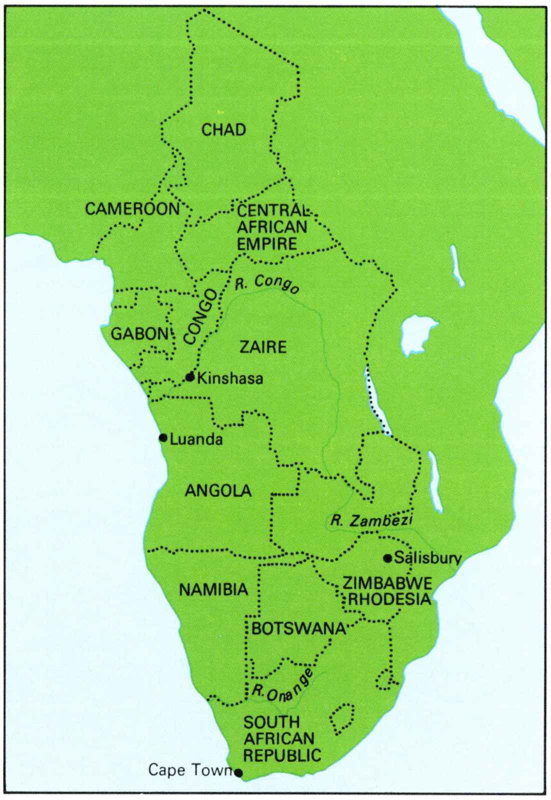

Luo in Kenya, Acholi and Lango in Uganda, and Nuer, Dinka and Shilluk in the Sudan. Along the northern border between Zaire and the Sudan the Zande, Pambia and Barambu languages belong to the Zande family. Further west, the Banda-Gbaya-Ngbandi languages belong together in a family spoken in northern Zaire and the Central African Empire (formerly the Central African Republic). Further north, the Bongo-Bagirmi family includes Sara, a major language of the Central African Empire.

The Hottentots in South-West Africa (Namibia) have a language family to themselves, and so do the Bushmen in the Kalahari Desert. The pygmies in the forests of Zaire and Cameroun speak different languages, each group having its own.

In general, however, African religions have to be discussed in the past tense. Most Africans, willingly or unwillingly, have accepted Islam (for example in North and West Africa, the Sudan and Somalia) or Christianity (in most of Central and Southern Africa). Only a very few nations, like the Yoruba in Nigeria, who have a particularly strong culture-consciousness, have managed to preserve their authentic religion with a complete pantheon. A coherent picture of the 'native' religions of most African peoples has to be put together from old records and surviving oral traditions.

A Plurality of Gods

Most of the tropical African peoples seem to have believed in a plurality of gods. Each religion had its own pantheon and these national gods often belonged together in families, like the Greek gods. There are many interesting resonances in tropical Africa of ancient Egyptian religion. The hippopotamus, once revered as a goddess by the Baronga in southern Mozambique, is strongly reminiscent of the Egyptian goddess Tauert, who was worshipped in the form of a hippopotamus. In ancient Egypt the snake was a symbol of kingship, and it had the same function among the Zulu and several other African peoples. The concept of a river-spirit in many African regions resembles the Egyptian Nile-god Osiris, and the Alur in Zaire used to revere the Nile as a deity.

Many Western missionaries had an axe to grind when writing about the indigenous religions. In the light of their own beliefs, they tended to pay too much attention to the widespread idea of the 'High God', an all-powerful and all-knowing supreme deity, living in or identified with the sky, other deities being regarded as local and unimportant heathen fantasies: as if Greek religion were to be described as 'belief in Zeus and a few local spirits'. Most peoples of tropical and southern Africa did

ABOVE The peaceful waters of the Nile as it flows silently past a village of the Dinka people in the Sudan. The Dinka speak a Nilotic language. Like the other Nilotic peoples, they have successfully resisted all attempts to convert them to Islam or Christianity, but they do accept the existence of a Supreme Being.

OPPOSITE Mask from the Baluba in Southern Zaire which was used during dances at a funeral ceremony for a chief. The lines on the face may represent the scarifications which denoted tribal membership in the old days.

TOP Most villages form a strongly coherent community, which is at the same time a religious 'congregation'. Wood-carving, Zaire.

ABOVE Nails and arrow heads have been stuck in to increase the magical powers of this male image. The horn on its head is also stuffed with magical substances. Wooden statuette from the upper Lomani Region, Zaire.

accept the idea of a 'High God' – or rather, a sky-god, often associated with thunder and lightning – but this did not rule out belief in other deities. More than 20 gods have been listed for the people of Buganda, but most African nations worshipped a more modest range of gods. The sun and the moon were often regarded as divine, and the moon still preserves traces of a female personality, especially in south-western Africa. For the Bantu the most powerful goddess was the Earth herself.

The most prominent divine beings in Central and Southern Africa are the Earth, the Sun, the Moon, the Atlantic Ocean and, in Zaire, the Forest. These are good gods, though the sun sometimes has a double role: it causes life but also drought, and so death. The Earth is always a female deity, who favours those who worship and obey her, but inexorably punishes the disobedient and neglectful. She resembles the Egyptian Isis. The Forest is a mysterious and elusive deity. The forest contains almost everything its inhabitants need: food and drink, wood, bark for clothes, lianas for ropes and snares, roots and juices for medicine. Several Central African nations regard the forest as the abode of the gods, the 'other world' where the spirits live, so that anyone wishing to enter it has to take special precautions and perform certain rituals. The forest is also the abode of evil dwarf-demons, who devour human flesh, preferably alive, and are masters of witchcraft.

The dividing line between gods and spirits is hard to draw but, generally, gods are more human than spirits, have more personality and manifest themselves on a grander scale. Numerous local spirits still live in woods and wells, and are venerated only by the local population. In ancient Greece the local gods and spirits also lived in woods and wells, but as the Greek spirit of national consciousness grew and spread they were merged into the overall pattern of the common Greek religion. This process had not been given time in Africa before it was overtaken by the introduction of Islam and Christianity, and the intrusions of colonial powers which cut state frontiers across tribal boundaries, so that many African nations were split. (The kingdom of the Congo, for instance, was carved into four pieces: two Portugese, one Belgian and one French.) Any natural national-religious development was consequently stifled.

Gods and Animals

A characteristic which the gods of Central and Southern Africa seem to have in common with those of Egypt and India is that they appear originally in animal form but gradually, through the centuries, they become more human. In the oldest versions of the Central African myths, the characters are animals with awesome magic powers. The spider can climb up to heaven, the frog can jump over the forest, the lion can devour an entire village of people, and the python reaches from horizon to horizon.

The next stage in the evolution of the gods seems to be that of half-man and half-animal. In Africa these 'half-castes' are usually evil in character. The leopard-man and the crocodile-man assume their animal shapes to commit crimes. The lion and the snake in semi-human form, however, are often good spirits who help human beings.

Gradually, several of the characters in the myths become almost entirely human and a pantheon of gods and demons evolves, still prone to assume their animal shapes. Like the Greek gods, they marry mortals and have human children. A king of the pigeons has three children with his Zulu wife, a young Ronga man marries a girl who is really a gemsbok-antelope, another young man marries a bushcat, and there is a Zulu saga of the python that gave birth to a prince. The Ngbandi of northern Zaire believe that twins are children of the snake. Many clans claim descent from animal ancestors: for example, the crocodile (the Kwena in Botswana) or the rhinoceros (another Tswana clan). Animal-gods function as protectors of the clan, even when they are not explicitly mentioned as ancestors. Examples include the frog among the Nkundo, the lion among the Tsonga, the hippopotamus among the Ronga, the pigeon among the Sotho and the snake among the Zulu.

Myths of Origins

According to the creation myth of the Bakuba (in Zaire), Mbombo, the white god, ruled when the earth was nothing but water shrouded in darkness. One day he felt a terrible pain in his stomach, and he vomited up the sun, the moon and the stars. The sun shone so fiercely that the water steamed up in clouds and dry hills gradually appeared. Mbombo vomited again and out of his stomach came animals and people and many other things: the first woman, the leopard, the eagle, the falling star, the anvil, the monkey Fumu, the first man, the razor, medicine and lightning.

Nchienge, the woman of the waters, lived in the East. She had a son and a daughter, Woto and Labama. Woto was the first king of the Bakuba. He moved westward with his children and dyed their skins black. He also changed their language by laying a medicine on their tongues. Later his people blamed him for marrying his sister and he withdrew with his followers and founded the nation of the Baluba. He changed their language by means of an incision in their tongues. They settled in the desert. Woto blew his horn and there, out of the barren sand, rose many trees, a whole forest, which still stands today near Salamudimu.

One man found the monkey Fumu licking palm-wine. He killed the monkey Fumu and the leopard killed him. This was the origin of the war between people and animals. Only the goats stayed with people and that is why leopards kill goats.

When Mbongo claimed the kingship a dispute arose, which was settled by Toche, Woto's brother, who gave Mbongo a magic powder. Mbongo strewed the powder along the boundaries of his territory and at once deep crevasses opened in the earth and showed the borders. His next sign of royal descent was to throw an anvil into the lake, where it floated. He coloured the water red, white and yellow, and made the bamboo speak. Finally he called a new animal, and the crocodile crept out of the water. The people cheered and Toche proclaimed: 'This Mbongo is the great-grandson of Woto and his sister.' Still today the Basonge marry their sisters and the king of the Bakuba has the 'right of the first night' with his sister. (Adapted from Knappert, 1977.)

The origin of the world and mankind is a wide-spread theme of myths. The Bakuba creation myth was written down half a century ago. The Bakuba lived in what was then the Belgian Congo, in the wet rain forest traversed by many rivers. This may account for the concept of water as the original, primeval element. The colour white is associated with death and the world of spirits. In this story creation takes place out of the jaws of death, and the association of the stomach with the abode of death is not confined to Bantu groups. The Bakuba and Baluba peoples are rivals. Myths which say that the 'original' human pair were brother and sister are common in the Bantu area, and brother-sister marriages, though extremely rare, have been reported among the Bantu upper classes. The Basonge are regarded as the 'royal' clan. The right of the first night with a sister seems to have the purpose of keeping 'luck' inside the family. The ancestors of the great kings must perforce be culture heroes, inventors of arts and crafts, one of which is magic.

Some details of the myth of Adam and Eve in the Bible have unexpected parallels in African myths. The Shilluk, who live along the Nile in the Sudan, say that Juok (God) created men out of clay. He travelled north and found some white clay, out of which he fashioned Europeans. The Arabs were made of reddish-brown clay and the Africans from black earth. Then Juok said to himself: 'I will give men long legs to run in the shallows while fishing, like the pink flamingoes. I will give them long arms to swing a hoe the way monkeys swing sticks. I will give them mouths to eat millet and tongues to sing with, and I will give them eyes to see their food and ears to hear their songs.' The Pangwe of Cameroun say that God created first a lizard out of clay which he placed in a pool to soak. He left it there for seven days, and then called, 'Man, come out', and a man emerged instead of a lizard.

This is the Eagle-man, with birds' feathers and mask, who will dance the creation-dance in which the sky-god in the shape of an eagle is represented as 'the Spirit of God moving upon the face of the waters'. From the western corner of Zimbabwe Rhodesia.

RIGHT Wooden statue of King Shamba Bolongongo, ruler of the Ba-Kuba-Bushongo people. He lived around AD 1600 and is remembered for his many inventions, such as the cultivation of palm oil, the art of plaiting raffia, the enjoyment of pipe smoking and the game of *Mankala*, which he is here shown playing on a draughts-like board. Before the advent of Christianity, and for a long time after, these statues of the divine kings were worshipped by the Bakuba.

BELOW Human masks from the Sudan, made from clay of different colours. In myths this is the way in which human beings of different skin-colours were created.

During the 19th century several scholars became interested in the mythology of the Zulu people in Natal, so that parts of it were recorded before it was forgotten or overgrown by Christianized myths. The Zulu myth of origin is remarkably similar to the Greek myth of the union of Ouranos and Ge, Sky and Earth, from whom all the gods descend. In the beginning there was a large swamp in the lands to the north, called Uhlanga. In this swamp there grew many types of reeds and rushes, each with its own colour. One morning the sky-god Umvelinqangi descended from heaven and married Uhlanga. Out of this vast valley he 'broke off' many reeds of different colours and made them into people. He made them in pairs, a man and a woman from every type of reed. These original people were all called Unkulunkulu, 'ancestor'. Each pair became the parents of a tribe of human beings, each tribe having its own colour, just as one finds stems and stalks in different shades of brown. So the people of this earth were created from water-plants, which grew from the valley with which Umvelinqangi lived in creative union. Each nation was born from the wet earth and every Unkulunkulu brought his own medicine, that is, his own secret charm of life. (From Knappert, 1977.)

The word *uhlanga* simply means reed. The Zulu call themselves *Abantsundu*, 'the Brown People', and their skin colour is comparable to that of some of the reed growing in the reed-studded pools in the valleys of Zululand.

Man and Immortality

After being created as a human being, the first thing man wants is immortality. Adam and Eve are tricked by the serpent, as a result of which they lose their immortality but are compensated for this loss by their children, who will continue their race on earth. Itonde, the ancestor-god of the Nkundo in Zaire, had to die, for he fell victim to the powerful spirits of the forest. He is the first man whose death is mentioned. He dies in the wilderness, while his wife at home is in labour. Flies are seen for the first time on earth as they creep out of his decaying body. His hunting horn, hanging in his wife's hut, begins to bleed as a sign that he is dead. At that moment his son, Lianja the Radiant, is born out of his mother's calf. The father has risen. The idea of the father coming back as his son, or the grandfather as his grandson, is widespread in Africa and many people call a young boy after his father, if he has died recently, or after his grandfather or an uncle, if the boy resembles them.

The Wafipa in Zaire say that one day God came down to earth and was greeted only by the snake, since all the other creatures were asleep. God rewarded the snake with the secret of immortality. Since that day the snake sloughs its skin every year and so becomes as new, without ever dying. The Baluba in Zaire relate that the first woman was about to slough her skin after a long life of bearing many children. She told her youngest granddaughter that she must not be disturbed, but the girl did not understand and came into her hut to tell her that the rain had started. The old woman had just begun to take off her skin, but she had to stop, and so the secret of immortalizing oneself was lost.

Another myth which attributes the origin of death to a mistake is the Hottentot tale that the moon-goddess sent her messenger, the praying mantis, to earth with the following message: 'Just as I return to life after dying, so you, the people of this world, shall die and rise again.' The mantis was too slow, so she asked the hare to run to the town of People and deliver the message. Unfortunately, the hare was not very intelligent. He garbled the message and told people they had to die just as the moon died, forgetting the promise of reappearance. When called to account, the hare had to confess that he was not worthy of the task, but the promise of immortality could not be given now, for a message from the gods cannot be altered or delivered twice. The moral of the story *as fable* is that everyone must personally discharge the task he has been set. There is no one else he can trust with it. As myth, the story is very old, at least in part. The praying mantis is still known in South Africa as the god of the Hottentots.

Death and the Snake

According to a myth of the Wutu (in Cameroun), one day the Lord God called his special messenger, the chameleon, and told him: 'Go to the people on earth and tell them this good news; they will have to die like all the animals, but later they will rise from their graves again. Now go quickly!' The chameleon travelled down to earth, but chameleons always tread very carefully along the branches and they have a habit of stopping frequently to rest, reflect and look around. So it took the chameleon 14 days to travel from God's city to the Town of People. In the meantime, the snake had heard of God's favours to People and he decided to trick them. He went to the People's town and announced: 'God has sent me to you with the following message. All people who have died will remain in their graves forever after. They will never come back. Death will keep them for good.' Death heard the snake say this and rejoiced, for Death is a greedy character, coveting ever more people as his prey.

When the chameleon finally arrived, he called the townspeople together and solemnly announced what God had told him to say: 'People will rise after death.' The people called him a liar. 'We believe what the snake has told us, for he was here first.' The chameleon replied: 'Impossible, I am God's truthful messenger.' The people then called the snake from his hole in the earth and asked him who had told him that people would die forever. 'God told me that,' lied the snake, without any scruples. The chameleon defied him and said: 'Let us go to God's city together and let him decide who is right.' So they went and appeared before God together. God heard both parties and spoke: 'The snake has lied. I never gave him a message. Yet the message delivered first to mankind will have to stand. It cannot be undone. Death has already begun to kill many people, since he overheard the message. For your punishment, snake, you will be hated by the people forever after, and they will kill you as soon as they see you.' Thus it happens that people die and never rise again.

In the Wutu myth, as in the story of Adam and Eve, it is the snake who tricks people so that they become mortal. The chameleon is regarded in many parts of Central and Southern Africa as the animal that is so cautious that it never makes mistakes. This is seen as a sign of great wisdom, hence God's trust in the chameleon. The snake kept God's gift of immortality to himself, and that is why snakes revive themselves by sloughing their skins.

The Dead

The forces of good and evil are constantly at work to help and harm people. If a person is exceptionally kind, helpful and generous, the Swahili call him or her *malaika*, 'an angel'. Parents and children are supposed always to help each other and when parents and grandparents die, they do not cease to exist. On the contrary, their spirits remain alive and stay near their loved ones, anxious to help them in their needs and worries. Some spirits are stronger than others, but all spirits can work magic. The Zulu say that a man of strong character, an important chief, 'has a large shadow', meaning much power, and after his death they will perform a special ceremony, *ukubuyisa*, to bring his spirit back into the kraal or compound, so that he may continue to help his family. If the descendants do not perform the right ceremonies at the correct time, the ancestral spirits may be disappointed at this lack of reverence. They may withdraw their protection, so that one of the children or grandchildren may fall ill. A diviner will then be called in by the parents, and he may diagnose the disease like this: 'Your paternal grandfather is angry because you have not performed the annual sacrifice of a cock to him.' When the ritual is duly performed, it is believed that the aggrieved spirit will relent and cure the child. This is only one example of the complications caused by the presence

Mask of the Bapuna people in Zaire, representing a white goddess who was worshipped at night. Very little is known about the secret ceremonies which accompanied these religious rituals. White is the colour of the spirits, the beings who belong to the 'other' world where magic comes from. It is the world where the dead people go, which is why the ghosts of the dead are believed to know magic. In Zaire, the forest is believed by many to be the abode of the spirits.

The ceremony of 'witch-smelling' among the Zulu of Natal. The man dressed in full regalia is the *isanukha* or witch-finder. He has been called in to detect the man who is guilty of bewitching his fellows. The culprit has been found and is lying dejectedly in the middle of the circle. Sorcerers are supposed to smell like the flesh of the victims they eat magically. This smell can be detected by the *isanukha*.

of spirits around the house and the compound.

In general, the spirits of the dead are believed to live underground, in a world similar to our own, but ruled by the god of death. It can be entered through a cave or pool, provided certain precautions are observed and certain rituals carried out. Many spirits of the dead, however, wander upon earth as ghosts, either because they have a task to perform or a message to convey to the living, or because they want to avenge themselves upon an evil-doer. Some of them may come back in the form of an animal or other living being.

The Spirit in the Tree

According to another tale, there was once a girl whose mother had died and whose stepmother was very cruel to her. One day, when she was crying on her mother's grave, she saw that the earth of the grave parted and a stalk came out, which grew into a sapling and soon into a tree. The wind rustled its leaves and the tree whispered to the girl, telling her that her mother was near and that she should eat the fruits of the tree. The girl did and the fruits were very tasty and made her feel much better. This happened every day from then on, but as soon as the cruel stepmother discovered what was happening, she went to her husband, the girl's father, and insisted that he had the tree cut down.

The tree lay withering and the girl wept on its maimed trunk for a long time, until she heard a whisper and saw a lump growing up from the grave. It grew and grew until it was a pumpkin. There was a hole in it, from which leaked a trickle of juice. The girl licked up a few drops and found them very nourishing, but again her stepmother soon found out and, one dark night, cut the pumpkin off and threw it on the dungheap. Next day the girl wept and wept until she heard a trickling sound and saw a little stream, which whispered, 'Drink me, drink me!' She did, and felt much refreshed, but now the stepmother made the girl's father throw sand in the stream and bury it. The girl went back to the grave where she cried and cried. She had been sitting there a long time when a man appeared from the bush. He saw the dead tree and decided it was just what he needed to make a bow and arrows, for he was a hunter. He talked to the girl, who told him that the tree had once grown on her mother's grave. He liked her and decided to go to her father and ask for her hand in marriage.

The father consented on condition that the hunter killed a dozen buffalo for the wedding feast. The hunter had never killed more than one buffalo at a time – that was difficult enough. But this time, taking his new bow and arrows, he had not been in the bush long when he saw a herd of a dozen buffalo resting in the shade. Setting one of his new arrows to his bow, he let fly. The first buffalo sank down dead. And the second, and the third. An hour later the hunter came back to tell the father to send men bring the meat to the village. There was a big feast when the hunter married the poor girl without a mother.

This story illustrates the concept of the tenacity of life. The mother's persecuted spirit gradually sinks lower on the ladder of lives, from a human being to a tree, a pumpkin and finally a stream which is blotted out. Even so, there is still some spirit-force left. The wood of the tree can still be used and the arrows which the hunter makes from it never miss. The spirit of the hunter is stronger than the stepmother's evil spirit, so that she is not mentioned any more in the story. The girl's father's spirit is too weak, for he ought not to be so easily managed by his wife. The spirit of the girl's mother is the strongest of all and so manages to look after her child until she is married.

Witchcraft and Sorcery

All human beings have spirits in this way, some strong, some weak. Animals too have 'spirit' and so do plants and the elements of water, wind and fire. The sun and the earth have spirits, for they possess creative forces which affect human lives. Not only are spirits worshipped, however, but magic is used to control them. This is necessary because there are not only good spirits but wicked ones, like the stepmother, who may have been a witch. How else could she have divined each time what her stepdaughter was doing? A witch is a person with an evil spirit. Sometimes a person does not realize how much harm he or she causes to others. The Swahili have a special word for this: *kisirani*, a person who causes ill-luck just by being there.

The original African concept of good and evil is quite different from the one introduced by Christianity. The concepts of good and evil for a person are dependent on his purpose in life. For most Africans the purpose of the individual is to advance the well-being of the family, the clan or the tribe. The purpose of the family, clan or tribe is to multiply. The more children a man has, the more hands to help him with his crops or herds. A numerous family is in Africa a source of pride and prestige. The 'father of many' is evidently favoured by the gods, and less fortunate people will seek him out, hoping to share his good fortune. (This ideal of prolific families is also prominent among the Islamic peoples, who call a family of less than ten children 'unfinished'.)

Everything that enhances the interests of the family is good, everything that causes sickness or death is evil. For instance, a woman whose children die one after another is often suspected of 'eating' them, that is of using their life-strength to work evil magic. Every illness is thought to be the result of spiritual operations. If it cannot be blamed on ancestors or other spiritual beings, it must be the work of a witch or a sorcerer. Both these categories of human beings are workers of evil. 'Human' is a dubious word here, but is used in contrast to bodiless beings such as ghosts or animals with evil capabilities.

A witch is generally a person whose evil spirit has to be fed on the life-strength of other human beings. The term life-strength is used here to express various words in African languages meaning 'that which makes a person live'. Usually, witches will 'take' weak lives, such as those of children. Since infant mortality stands at about 50% in many parts of Africa, it is not surprising that there are numerous accusations of witchcraft. The word witchcraft is misleading: it is not a craft but a congenital characteristic. One is born with it, it is fate. Just as some people are clumsy, accident-prone, kleptomaniac or gifted with telepathy, others are witches, and the emergence of the evil trait is only a matter of time.

These figures are fetishes, wooden images in which the sorcerer has caused a spirit to live. The spirit will serve the sorcerer and kill his enemies for him. In this way the sorcerer can rule whole villages by sheer terror. Nails are driven into the wood in order to make the spirit angrier, and so more effective.

A sorcerer is more powerful than a witch. He is not forced to use magic, he does it for the love of evil. Some believe that a sorcerer is an evil spirit himself, but so powerful that he can control other spirits and make them work for him. He may make a fetish, a wooden statue or other object, and by his incantations compel a spirit to make its home in it. The statue will then fly like a bird to the person selected by its master as his victim and persecute him. In this way sorcerers can control whole communities by sheer terror.

In many parts of Africa this terror is real and frequent. There are numerous reports by missionaries and doctors who have observed it. A teacher in Zambia wrote: 'A young man, a jilted lover, shouted something at night so that the girls in one of the school's dormitories could hear it. Stricken with sudden panic, all the girls jumped out of bed, through the windows, and ran away into the night. Several never came back. The cause of this panic was never ascertained. No one dared speak.' In Malawi a man lost one child after another and came to the conclusion that his mother was a witch. After losing five children he went to a sorcerer and paid him to kill his mother. The sorcerer worked his magic and the old woman died. There are many 'true' stories of this kind. Numerous also are cases of patients who consult a Western doctor requesting a cure against witchcraft. The doctor can find nothing wrong with the patient, but the patient dies in a matter of weeks. More research is needed into these matters, but it is clear that in Africa myths are still alive and continuously influence people's behaviour.

CHAPTER TWENTY-ONE

EAST AFRICA

In East Africa the dividing zone between the two major cultural regions of the African land-mass swings well south of its normal position. The Soomaali and desert Oromo (Galla), for example, in the north-east of Kenya, belong culturally in the North African Near Eastern Major Region, while the majority of East African peoples are part of the Sub-Saharan African Major Region. Each of these major regions can be divided into smaller regions, and these in their turn are made up of a number of ethnic groups. The total number of ethnic groups in the whole of East Africa is about 220, each group having a name for themselves. A large proportion of these groups speak their own distinctive languages, but a number are best described as speaking a dialect of a language which they share with one or more other peoples.

The different ethnic groups vary in size from the Rwanda, the most numerous, with three million people approximately, down to very small groups, such as the Upale, numbered only in hundreds. There are a variety of habitats, spread out along a continuum from very wet to very dry. At the beginning of the century a few groups were hunters and gatherers. Some are still pastoralists, for example the Maasai, but the majority of East African peoples cultivate land as well as keeping some livestock. Until the period 1960–70 the peoples of the west and south were ruled by kings, although some of the states were very small. By contrast, in the north-east and north (apart from a small number of city-states on the coast) there were no kings or states, and all the societies were small, up to only about 300 people.

The passing of the kings is one aspect of striking cultural changes which have affected East African peoples during the 20th century. Among the casualties caused by these changes have been music, dancing and myths. At the present time the myths of a large number of East African peoples which were current in 1900 survive only in books and articles written earlier in the century, by Europeans. Other groups are in the process of losing their older myths. These older forms survive in some places, particularly in the drier areas, where cultural change is slower, while elsewhere new myths are coming into existence, but the conditions of 1900 are gone. Furthermore, large numbers of people in East Africa are now familiar with the Bible and with Islam, and their new knowledge colours their interpretation of events and their recitation of myths. In view of this modern reduction in local colour, the best way to indicate the pattern of myths in East Africa, at their most idiosyncratic, is to examine the situation in the period 1890–1920.

The Pattern of Myths

East African peoples are not culturally isolated, and their myths are strikingly similar to those of other peoples of Sub-Saharan Africa. Indeed so similar are myths in different parts of the world that these African peoples differ from ethnic groups in other major regions not so much in the basic themes of their myths as in their local detail. The animals which figure in certain myths provide an important example. Hyenas and chameleons are very conspicuous in African stories, but not outside Africa (except for chameleons in Madagascar). On the other hand, the *roles* played by hyenas and chameleons in the stories occur in myths all over the world. The role of the chameleons is played by snakes in

Kilimanjaro, the highest mountain on the African land-mass, and the scene of one of the myths told here. The Chaga people live on its well-watered southern and eastern slopes, while the dry plains in the foreground, where the two giraffes are walking, are inhabited by the Maasai.

parts of New Guinea, and that of the hyenas by grizzly bears in parts of North America. Since the mythic themes are so universal, the differences between the regions of Africa which have been so important in terms of, for instance, organization are of little or no importance in the distribution of myths; this is also true of the major cultural regions.

In East Africa, as elsewhere, myths form a pattern which is very complex in detail, but which resolves itself into four major themes. These themes themselves fall into two pairs of opposites:

A. 1. a perfect creation	B. 1. success
2. an imperfect present world	2. failure

Among East African peoples the pattern begins, in an absolute sense, with God creating the world and its inhabitants, including people. But this initial condition, described explicitly or implicitly as paradisal, gives way to the familiar modern conditions, far from paradisal, and marked by famine and illness, a world where people die and where even brothers often hate each other. The relations between brothers indeed are critical in some versions of the second pair of themes (B1. and B2.), as in the Chaga story given here.

A Myth of Two Brothers

There was a man who had two sons, the elder called Mkunare and the younger Kanyanga. They were so poor that they did not own a single cow between them. Eventually Mkunare proposed that he should go up to Kibo (one of the two peaks of Mount Kilimanjaro), because people said that a king ruled up there who was generous to the poor. He took a supply of food and set off up the mountain. After a while he met an old woman who was sitting beside the path. Her eyes were so sore that she could not see. Mkunare greeted her, and she replied, asking why he had come up to this place. He told her that he was looking for the king who lived at the top of the mountain; and the old woman said, 'Lick my eyes clean and I will tell you how to get there.' But Mkunare was too revolted by her sore eyes to lick them, and he went on his way.

Further up, he arrived at the country of the Konyingo (the Little People or Wee Folk) and saw a group of men sitting in their king's cattle-compound. They were the size of boys who herd the goats, and are not yet old enough to go out with the cattle; and Mkunare assumed that they were children. 'Hello, boys,' he said, 'where will I find your fathers and big

Woven mat from the East African coast. The design includes lizards, which figure in some local versions of the origin of death as the chameleon's competitor.

brothers?' The Konyingo replied, 'Just wait here until they arrive.' He waited until evening, but no one came. Before nightfall the Konyingo herded their cattle into the compounds, and slaughtered an animal for their evening meal; but they did not give Mkunare any of the meat. They said that he must wait until their fathers and big brothers arrived. Tired and hungry, he set off again down the mountain, and again passed the old woman sitting beside the path. But she would tell him nothing about what had happened to him, even though he tried to persuade her. On his way back to the settled areas further down the slopes he lost his way in the uninhabited country, and did not get home for a month. He told his kinsmen that there were numerous people on the top of Kibo, with large herds of cattle, but being mean they gave nothing to strangers.

Some time later, however, Kanyanga, the younger brother, decided to go up the mountain in a second attempt to ease their poverty. After a while he too met the old woman sitting beside the path. They greeted each other, and when she asked why he had come up there, he told her he was looking for the king who lived on the top of the mountain. The old woman said to him, 'Lick my eyes clean and I will tell you how to get there.' Kanyanga licked her eyes thoroughly, and she said to him, 'Keep on up, and you will come to the settlement of the king. The men you will see there are no bigger than the boys who look after the goats, but don't jump to the conclusion that they are children. Address them as members of the king's council, and greet them respectfully.'

Further up, he arrived at the cattle-compound of the Konyingo king, and greeted the men there respectfully. They took him to the king, who listened to his plea for help, and ordered that he be given a meal and a place to sleep that night. As a return for their hospitality Kanyanga taught them the incantations and medicines which protect the growing crops against insects and other pests, and also those which invisibly bar the paths against invading enemies. The Little People were so pleased with these new methods that they each gave Kanyanga an animal out of their herds; and he set off down the mountain, driving his cattle in front of him, and singing the Herding-song. (At this point the man who was telling the story might break off and sing the whole of the Herding-song.) And so Kanyanga prospered, and so did his kinsmen; but people composed a song about his elder brother, and this song is still sung at the present time:

O Mkunare, wait till the fathers come.
What right have you to despise the Little Folk?

Thematic Variations

In such stories the younger brother is more successful than his elder brother; or else, in some North American versions, an orphan prospers despite his social disadvantages. In general terms, these myths are about somebody who seems to be destined for failure or obscurity, but who succeeds despite the apparent odds. Closely related to these brother stories are those myths which deal with Trickster, in East Africa a role played by hares, jackals and small antelopes called dikdiks, depending on the area where the story is told.

Within the major themes are grouped together lesser themes. Sometimes God sends people down from the sky, as in one Oromo version; sometimes they come up from the ground, as among the Nyanja. The ending of the original pristine and paradisal condition is described in more than one form. One important theme is that God and people are separated, alienated, physically and morally. Another theme which recurs with great frequency in East Africa is the beginning of death, usually associated in some way with the chameleon. Yet another aspect of the loss of the perfect created order is the deterioration in harmony between men and women, and between brothers.

In practice, this pattern of myths is, or at least was, very complicated. Some ethnic groups lacked parts of the fourfold complex, although other culturally similar peoples nearby had these elements. Not everyone had a specific story of the creation, even though they had a lot to say about the origin of dying, and other features of a corrupted world. Furthermore, since the major themes comprise several specific themes, neighbouring peoples sometimes did not share the same specific theme, but one group had one of them, the next group another.

There is another complication. Some ethnic groups had different, even apparently contradictory, versions of the same specific theme. Such contradictory versions, however, still conformed to the general fourfold pattern. One feature of myths which some people find confusing is that the elements can be combined in several different ways, with the result that specific themes run into each other, and it is impossible to classify whole stories into tidy compartments, because they overlap with stories in other compartments, however these are constructed. It is these opportunities for thematic variation which result in members of one ethnic group reciting different versions of a single story which vary in emphasis or even contradict each other. The account of Kintu which is given here treats him as the first man, but several other Ganda versions assume that he is the first king, people being already in existence when he arrives. In some accounts he comes from the sky, in others from somewhere on the earth's surface.

LEFT Wooden mask, ornamented with fur and with human teeth. Although collected in the country of the Zila people, west of Lake Victoria, such masks were rare in East Africa, and typical of areas further west, for example the Congo Basin, where they represented ancestors and spirits of wild places.

BELOW Wooden head-rest with a stylized antelope design, probably from the Makonde or a neighbouring people. Outside their area there was little wood-carving in East Africa.

Kintu, the First Man

Kintu came into the country with his cow, and found that no one lived there, and that there was nothing to eat. So he kept himself alive by drinking the milk of the cow, and by eating the butter and curd-cheese which he made from the milk. Then one day he saw some people coming down from the sky. They were the sons of the deity Gulu, together with their sister Nambi. She said to her brothers, 'Look, there's a man. Where did he come from?' They asked Kintu, but he told them that he did not know. After they had talked to him for a while, Nambi said to her brothers, 'Kintu is nice; I like him. Let me marry him.' The brothers, however, were cautious, and asked her whether he was really human; but she replied that she knew that he was, since animals do not build houses. And she turned to Kintu and said, 'Kintu, I like you. Let me go home and tell my father that I have met a man out in the forest whom I want to marry.'

The sons of Gulu, however, were still cautious, and they told their father when Nambi was not there that Kintu was very odd and did not eat ordinary food. Gulu's response was to tell his sons to take Kintu's cow away from him, in order to see whether he could live without her. They took the cow, and Kintu was now driven to eating bark from trees in order to survive. But Nambi grew anxious about him, came down from the sky again to look after him, and then took him with her back to the sky. Here he saw large numbers of people, of cattle and banana-plants, of chickens, sheep and goats, and large quantities of other sources of food.

Gulu now decided to impose a series of difficult tasks for Kintu to complete, and he set his servants to work building a house with no door. Inside this house Kintu was confined together with ten thousand packages of mashed plantains (cooking bananas), the carcases of a thousand cattle, and a thousand gourds of banana-beer. Gulu commented to his sons that if Kintu failed to eat all this food and drink all the beer, then he was not really Kintu, but was lying, and so they would kill him. But to Kintu, Gulu said by way of a servant that if the food were not eaten then he was not really Kintu, and so could not have his cow back, nor marry Gulu's daughter.

Kintu sent his thanks to Gulu by the servant, but once alone felt that he was beaten. However, he prayed for help and, as he was praying, he saw the ground on the floor of the house open, revealing a huge pit. He threw in all the food and beer which he could not eat, and the pit closed up again. When he was set a second task he prayed again, and again his difficulties were solved, as they were also for his third task. He was now told that he could have his cow back if he could pick her out from the herds which would be driven in front of him. Since these numbered 20,000 animals, Kintu felt himself again on the brink of failure when he heard a wasp buzzing in his ear. The wasp said, 'Watch me when I fly, and the cow on whose horn I settle is yours.' Since the wasp did not move, Kintu dismissed the first herd to appear, and the second, but when the third was driven up the wasp flew and settled on the horn of one of the cows. Kintu walked up to the animal and hit her with his stick, saying, 'That's my cow.' The wasp flew on to the horn of a heifer. 'And that's a calf of my cow,' said Kintu, 'and that,' he said, as the wasp settled on another animal.

Gulu laughed and said, 'Kintu is amazing! No one can get the better of him, and his claims are true.' So he sent for Nambi, and Kintu married her. Gulu sent them down to live on earth, providing them with a chicken, a banana-plant and the seeds and tubers now most cultivated by the Ganda. He also warned them that once they were on their way they must not turn back, even if they discovered that they had forgotten something.

However, when they had got half way, they discovered that they had left behind the grain for the chicken. Kintu wanted to go back, but Nambi urged him not to, because her brother Walumbe, Death, would be at home by now, and was sure to want to come with them. Nevertheless, Kintu insisted, collected the grain, and returned to Nambi – with Walumbe. The party of three travellers came down to earth here at Magonga. Kintu and Nambi built a house, and began to plant the crops they had brought with them, and in time they had three children.

When Walumbe demanded that one of the girls cook for him, Kintu refused. Walumbe threatened to kill the children, but Kintu still refused Walumbe's

Carved wooden post commemorating a dead ancestor from the country of the Garo people in the south west of the Ethiopian Highlands, on the northern edge of East Africa.

repeated requests. Then the children became ill and began to die, and Kintu turned to Gulu for help. Gulu pointed out that it was Kintu's fault, but sent his son Kaikuzi to capture Walumbe and bring him back to the sky. Kaikuzi's repeated attempts failed, however, and he returned to the sky, while Kintu said that he would go on begetting children, so that Death would never be able to exterminate people. (From an original version collected among the Ganda by J. Roscoe.)

The Coming of Death

Another example of a difference, this time of emphasis, in dealing with a major theme, is that sometimes the hare plays Trickster as an entertaining rogue, a Brer Rabbit, as in a number of Kamba stories, but at others he has far greater intensity as an actor in the process of creation, or at least in its corruption. In a Giryama story, typical of myths found widely in East Africa, hare outruns chameleon, and tells people that they will die. Had chameleon arrived first, people would have heard that they would be deathless.

According to a story collected among the Bararetta Oromo by Alice Werner, in the beginning, when God created people, he sent a message to them by way of the bird now called *holawaka*, the sheep of God. (This is the bird which European naturalists call the white-bellied go-away-bird, *Corythaixoides leucogaster*.) God gave the bird a crest, like a flag, to show that he was a messenger, and said that he must tell people that when they felt themselves growing old and weak they must shed their skins, and then they would be young again. The bird set out on his journey but as he went along he saw a snake eating a newly dead animal. Eager to have some of the snake's

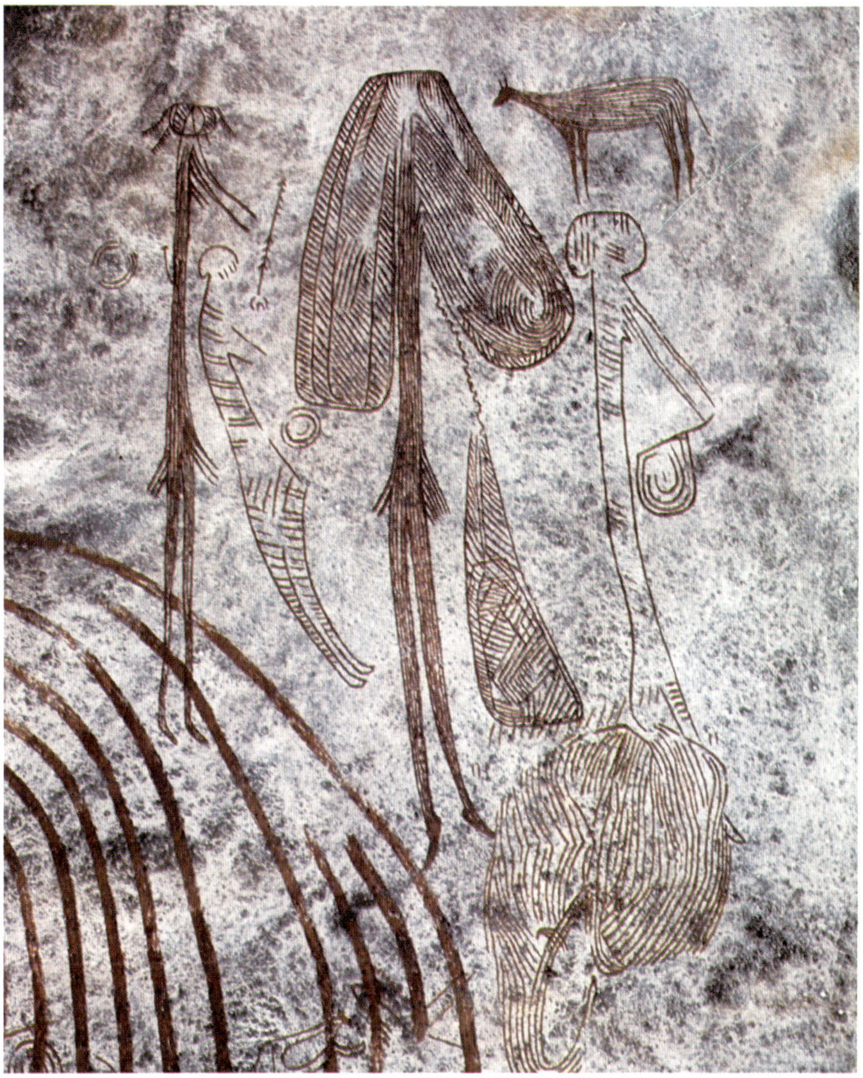

ABOVE Paintings in a rock-shelter in the Kondoa District of Tanzania. The peoples of that area now know nothing of the origins of these pictures, and do not paint themselves, but these figures are not necessarily more than several hundred years old.

LEFT Head of a doll used by a diviner at Entebbe, Uganda. Such figures are not old, and this one probably represents an effort by the diviner to make himself look like the sort of 'witch-doctor' the tourists would expect.

Carved figures of ancestors on a post marking a tomb, from southwestern Madagascar. The island is markedly different in its culture from the main land-mass, and constitutes a distinct major cultural region. The nearest part of Africa is included in the Sub-Saharan African Major Cultural Region, rich in carved masks and figurines in the west and centre, but poor in the east and south. There is, however, one major centre of wood-carving in the east, among the Matambwe, Makonde and Maviha peoples. The North African Near Eastern Major Region is poor in carving, although there is some in the Ethiopian Highlands. These cultural differences, however, hardly affect the themes of myths, which show striking similarities between major regions.

meal for himself, the bird promised that he would tell the snake his message in return for some meat and, more important, some blood. The snake refused the offer, but the bird persisted in his attempts, and eventually the snake agreed. So the bird told him, 'People will grow old and die, but when you grow old you will crawl out of your old skin, and then you will be young again.' As a result people die, but snakes shed their skins and are rejuvenated. God was very angry with the bird, and cursed him with endless pains in the belly. As a result, right up to the present time, *holawaka* flies from tree to tree, bleating out *Wakatia-a-a-a*, 'God help me'.

If the fourfold pattern is constant, and the details so bewilderingly kaleidoscopic, is there any sense that emerges from these myths? There appears to be a coherent body of assumptions which take narrative form in them. People are not self-subsistent, they are created. They are weak, they are morally deplorable, and they are not in charge of their own destinies. Living on earth is full of hazards, and trickery often works, but there is justice in the universe, nonetheless, and life is worth living. The narrative form takes much of the sting out of these sobre truths. Implicit too in myth after myth, and often explicit, is the fact that people live under the power of God, the spirits and the ancestors. The simplest form of myth is the encounter between a man and a spirit in the woods or some other uninhabited place. Numerous such meetings are narrated in East Africa, many of them by the individual who actually saw the spirit.

Myths and Social Order

Within the pattern of the four themes, some stories relate the origin of detailed social conditions. Very important in this context are myths about the origin of kingly rule or of the most recent royal line. All such stories link the royal authority with divine sanctions: the kings rule by the grace of God, and some have even come down from the sky. Others, like Kintu in one of his aspects, came from far away, and the stranger-king, often a wandering hunter, is a familiar figure in African stories. A large number of modern dynasties trace their descent from such a character. One example is Mbega, who is said to have founded the ruling house of the Shambaa, and to have been a hunter. In this instance there is the further complication that there may have been a man from Zigula country called Mbega who did found the recent royal line, perhaps in the 18th century. Stranger-kings, however, cannot be assumed to be the true founders of dynasties in all cases. A stranger is seen as impartial in his administration of justice, and his origin far away places him in the area of superhuman authority, as does a descent from the sky.

In one version of a Rwanda story Kigwa comes down from the sky to Rwanda, with his two sons Katuutsi and Kahutu. The country was then inhabited by members of the Hutu caste, and there were no Tuutsi, and no kings. Katuutsi becomes the first king and founds the Tuutsi caste, while the two brothers together organize the Rwanda as a kingdom and teach the people iron-working. Significantly, Katuutsi's brother is called Kahutu, and it seems more than probable that in an earlier version, which went to make this one, he is explicitly called ancestor of the Hutu caste, who in this version appear as already in Rwanda when the brothers arrive.

Remarkably, there are many peoples in the traditionally kingless northeastern quarter of East Africa who have myths of kings. Examples are the Gikuyu (or Kikuyu) and Kamba. It is not surprising, however, on reflection, that these peoples should know about kings, since people not very far away have had them, and the significance of kings must be clear enough to make them important figures in myths, even to people who have no kings themselves. The peoples of this area, however, also have stories which tell the origins of the ethnic groups of the modern period, and how they came to occupy the place which they now do in each other's estimation. Among the Maasai, Kamba, Gikuyu and their neighbours there is a range of stories which vary around this theme. Such stories, which stress the precedence of the Maasai, however, do not provide an infallible prop to Maasai prestige, any more than stories about the divine sanctioning of the original king put an individual king beyond deposition or the monarchy itself beyond abolition. Myths can be interpreted by revolutionaries as well as traditionalists, and all of these myths of the social order are intimately linked with the fourfold pattern.

Dancers of the Tuutsi caste in Rwanda. As part of their sense of the vast superiority of Rwanda in general and of the Tuutsi caste in particular, these people pride themselves on their skill as dancers.

CHAPTER TWENTY-TWO

WEST AFRICA

When Europeans first became acquainted with the religions of the great civilizations of West Africa, such as those of the Yoruba of Nigeria, the Ashanti of Ghana, or the Dahomeans of what is now Benin, they were amazed to discover pantheons, myths and cults as complex and rich as those of ancient Greece. It has been estimated that the Yoruba can choose from no less than 600 deities to worship. It would be impossible to list all of them here, or those of their neighbours the Dahomeans.

Until the later years of the 19th century the king of Dahomey maintained a resplendent court. Through a class of nobility and a priesthood he ruled a population further stratified into commoners and slaves, and distributed among a variety of occupations. Everyone, to a greater or lesser extent, cultivated a crop or crops – yam, millet, maize, groundnuts, beans, cassava and other vegetables, as well as cotton and palm trees of various kinds. Many also specialized in the basic crafts of a peasant society, in iron-working, pottery, basketry, brass-working, weaving, tailoring, or as wood-carvers, jewellers, grave-diggers and so on. The king and his court are no more, but Dahomean culture still flourishes.

A version of the Dahomean word for a god, *vodu*, is familiar as the name of the Caribbean cult of Voodoo, developed by slaves transported there centuries ago (see VOODOO). In Dahomey most of the *vodu* are organized in three pantheons, of the Sky, of the Earth and Thunder. A creative spirit, Nana-Buluku, to whom no cult is addressed, created a first deity called Mawu-Lisa, sometimes described as an androgynous (double-sexed) being or sometimes as male and female twins. Mawu, the female principle is associated with night, the moon, rest, fertility, gentleness, joy, motherhood. Lisa, the male principle, is associated with day, the sun, heat, strength, labour and, in general, the harder side of existence. This dual deity gave birth to all the other gods and still rules at the head of the most important pantheon, that of the Sky. Most of the gods care for some domain of nature or culture. For example, Age is in charge of uninhabited bush and its animals, and is accordingly a hunter worshipped by hunters. Loko cares for trees, and as most Dahomean medicines are made from roots, bark or leaves, he is the god of medicine. His sister Ayaba is goddess of the hearth. Some have no special domain, however, such as Legba, who is allied with Destiny (Fa). He is the youngest son of Mawu-Lisa and, like all youngest sons in Dahomean thought, is very clever and cunning. The three pantheons have different languages, but Legba knows all languages, both of men and gods. He is accordingly a messenger among all the gods.

The first offspring of Mawu-Lisa were an androgynous being or twins, a male and a female, who

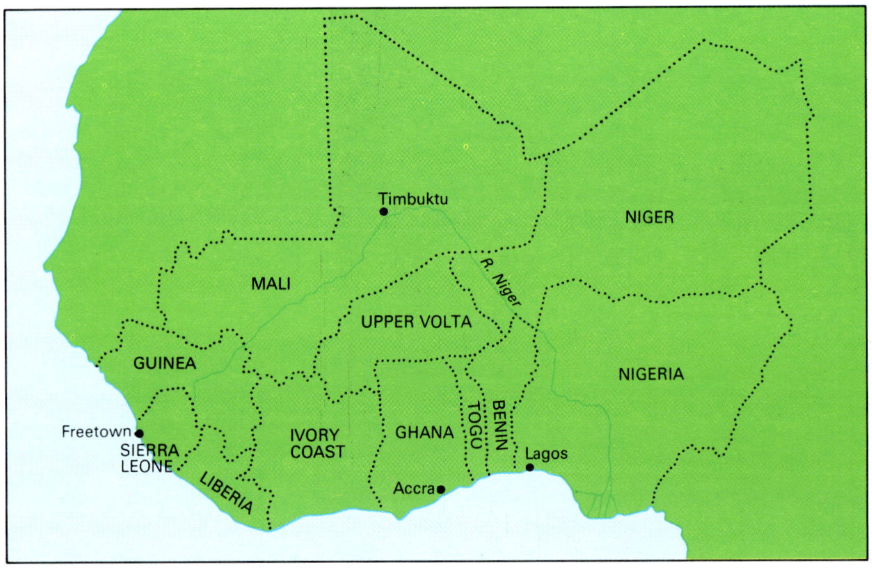

LEFT Myth is not dead in West Africa, despite the influence of European education and technology. Temples and shrines to the gods still flourish and contain masks, figurines and other ceremonial objects. Bronze ornament in the form of a ram's head, with a fringe of mud-fish, worn on the belt of a chief on ceremonial occasions. From Benin, *c.* 17th century.

OPPOSITE Wooden equestrian figure. In many areas of Africa equestrian figures imply wealth and high social status. Among the Senufo of the Ivory Coast figures of this kind represent spirits, which serve as advisers and messengers from the world of spirits to the Senufo specialists in divination.

DAHOMEAN PANTHEONS

Mawu-Lisa
(androgynous being, or twins)
Sky Pantheon

Androgynous being, or twins | **Other deities of the Sky Pantheon** | **Legba**

Under Androgynous being, or twins:

Sagbata
Earth Pantheon

Sogbo
Thunder Pantheon

Similar deities occur among the Yoruba in Nigeria, including Odudua-Orishala (Mawu-Lisa), Soponna (Sagbata) and Shango (Sogbo)

descended to earth and mated. Their children comprise the rest of the Earth pantheon, the generic name of which is Sagbata, a name also applied to the male head of the pantheon. A younger brother of his turned out to be androgynous like his parent or parents, so they kept him in the sky where he founded the Thunder pantheon. He and the pantheon are called Sogbo. In most West African societies elder brothers enjoy precedence over younger especially in matters of succession and inheritance. This situation often gives rise to quarrels between them. Here is a myth telling of the quarrel between Earth and Thunder.

The Quarrel

When Mawu-Lisa were about to choose the child who was to rule the earth, Sogbo was anxious to do so, but Mawu ruled that since earth was far from sky

RIGHT Staff representing Oshe, the god of thunder and lightning of the Yoruba in Nigeria. The staff was carved by a priest to prevent rainstorms.

BELOW Figure of Legba, the messenger and interpreter among the gods of Dahomey. Gifted with the intelligence and cunning credited to youngest sons in Dahomey, Legba understands all languages, human and divine.

it was better that the eldest child went there. Sagbata collected his inheritance from his father and departed. However, he had been unable to put fire and water in his bag, and from jealousy and anger Sogbo caused the rains to stop. He then waited for mankind to plead with his parents to send him to earth instead. Soon the people on earth began complaining, for since Sagbata's coming they could get neither food nor drink.

One day Mawu sent Legba to earth to report on the state of affairs there. He visited Sagbata and was told of the difficulties caused him by Sogbo. Legba replied, 'That's nothing', and promised to send Sagbata a bird who would bring him the word of Mawu about how his trouble might be resolved. Then he climbed back into the sky and sent a bird called Otutu to Sagbata, with the message that a fire so great that the smoke would mount on high should be kindled at once.

Now Legba the trickster had himself suggested to Sogbo that he cause the rains to stop, and to accomplish this had gone to Mawu with a tale that there was no water in the sky, so everyone there was dying of thirst. Mawu had then ordered that no rain should leave the sky.

But now, after visiting Sagbata on earth, Legba had also told the bird Otutu that when Sagbata lighted the great fire and smoke began to rise, Otutu should begin to sing. So when Sagbata got the message from Otutu and kindled a fire, the bird began to sing. Then Legba hurried to Mawu and said that he had not been able to go to earth himself, that he had sent his 'little assistant' Otutu instead, that because no rain had fallen on earth for so long everything had dried up and a great fire was raging there, and Otutu was on the verge of being consumed in it. He added that the sky risked being destroyed in the flames if rain were not made to fall to extinguish them. Mawu at once gave orders that Legba should command Sogbo to cause the rain to fall, so that Otutu should not be burned to death. Rain fell and the earth was saved.

All this time Mawu was kept in ignorance of the feud between the brothers, and to this day knowledge of their quarrel has been withheld from her. But in consequence of what occurred, Mawu decreed that the fall of rain should be regulated from the earth, since the danger of universal conflagration lay there. For this reason Otutu was sent to live on earth, and when this bird finds that the ground is too hot she cries out, and the rain falls. Later Legba effected a reconciliation between the two brothers, so now man lives without fear of another severe drought.

That, at any rate, is the story as related by the Earth priests. Each pantheon has its separate priesthood, however, and some idea of the complexity of the Dahomean myths is indicated by the somewhat different version of the story given by the Thunder priests, who award the victory to Sogbo. They tell of the brothers quarrelling and the conflagration as in the Sagbata version, but there is no intervention by Mawu. Instead, Sagbata is made to give much of his wealth to Sogbo, through Otutu. Sogbo takes it and sends a message back to Sagbata that, as the elder, he had inherited most of the wealth of his father, but that he had been foolish enough to leave behind him the two things which are the power of the universe, fire and water; and with these two things he, the younger, had acquired dominion over Sagbata's realm. Then he sent rain and the brothers were reconciled.

The First Human Children

In these societies myths not only reflect necessary conditions of society's existence, such as fire and water in due proportion, and features of social life such as quarrels between elder and younger brother, they also validate beliefs about a great many subjects, as a myth from Ashanti shows.

The Ashanti are a matrilineal people. Children belong not to their father's lineage but to their mother's, so that a person inherits rights through the line of descent of his mother, his mother's mother and so on. The Ashanti believe that a person is formed from the blood of the mother's line and the spirit (*ntoro*) of the father's, as well as by the gift of a soul from the supreme God. There are twelve *ntoro* lines, each with its own set of surnames and responses to greetings, its own sacred day and its own taboos on killing and eating certain animals. The father's *ntoro* is held to be instrumental in the conception of the embryo in the womb, and *ntoro* are said to have been given to men by gods under the direction of the supreme Sky God. Long ago one man and one woman came down from the sky and one man and one woman came up from the earth. From the Sky God came also a python, which made its home in the river now called Bosomuru (*bosom* meaning a god, a child of the Sky God). At first these men and women did not bear children, they had no desire, and conception and birth were not known at that time. One day the python asked them if they had no offspring, and on being told they had not, he said he would cause the women to conceive. He bade the couples stand face to face, then he plunged into the river and, rising up, sprayed water upon their bellies with the words *kus kus*. He then ordered them to return home and lie together. The women conceived and brought forth the first children in the world, who took Bosomuru as their *ntoro*, each male passing on this spirit to his children.

A Bosomuru *ntoro* man or woman would never kill a python. If they see a dead python, they sprinkle white clay upon it and bury it.

As in this case, the serpent plays a major role, quite different from its role in the Old Testament, in many West African myths. Mawu-Lisa of the Dahomey Sky pantheon, for example, in fashioning the world made use of a creative force called Da, which controls all life and motion. Da simply means 'serpent', and it is always conceived as a snake, the symbol of sinuous flowing movement.

Twins and Pairs

Twins and the theme of unity in duality, of perfect existence as the union of male and female, also figure largely in West African myths. In the myths of the

ABOVE In West African myths powerful deities are frequently described as double-sexed beings or as pairs of male and female twins, representing the idea of unity in duality, of perfect existence as the union of male and female. Wooden figures of the primordial couple, Senufo, Ivory Coast.

LEFT The snake has a major creative role in many West African myths. Plaque from the palace of the Obas, Benin, 17th century.

RIGHT Not only are twin deities common in West Africa, but twins born to human parents are considered uncanny and are the object of cults. Yoruba doorway, showing a pair of twins.

BELOW The Nommo in Dogon mythology are twins, prefigurations of human beings, who took form in the cosmic egg. Dogon figure of a Nommo, from Mali.

Dogon the universe starts before the emergence of personalized beings with a movement of matter within 'the egg of the world'. At a certain point in the process beings become conscious of themselves and the course of creation grows more complicated. The first personalized being was Amma, and his sons, called Nommo, were prefigurations of man. The egg within which the primordial events took place was divided into two twin placenta, each of which should have contained a pair of twin Nommo. Each twin as a spiritual being was composed of both male and female principles, though in bodily form either a male or a female.

In the Dogon account, earth got off to a bad start. In one placenta the male Nommo, called Yurugu, was impatient for birth. He could not wait for the period of gestation decreed by Amma, and forced his way out. He tore off a piece of his placenta and with it came hurtling down through space outside the egg. The fragment of placenta became the earth, but Yurugu's impatience, had seriously disorganized Amma's plans for creation, for the earth was now provided with only a predominantly male soul, and hence was incomplete, imperfect. From this situation arose the idea of impurity; earth and Yurugu were solitary and impure. Yurugu had been impatient to establish a domain over which he would rule, but he eventually realized that he could not do it without his twin soul. He clambered back to heaven to try to find the rest of his placenta with his twin in it, but he was too late. At his revolt Amma had handed over his twin soul to the other half of the placenta, and Yurugu could not find her. From that time he has vainly searched for her. He returned to the earth and began to procreate in his own placenta, that is with his mother, and from this horrible act there came into existence single, incomplete beings.

However, Amma retrieved the situation. He sent to earth the Nommo of the other half of the egg, who created the sky and the stars. They came to earth on a gigantic arch, at the centre of which stood two Nommo of the sky in the form of blacksmiths. Four pairs of Nommo, avatars of the first, took up their stance at the four cardinal points and became the first ancestors of man. The Dogon consider themselves to be formed of four 'tribes'. The arch was the new undefiled earth, and with it came light and rain. The ancestors brought with them the 'seeds' of everything on earth – humans, animals and plants. Yurugu and his misdeeds, however, could never be wholly annulled. As a consequence of his actions death became a feature of life on earth. He is a being of night and darkness, ruling over the dry uncultivated wasteland.

Idle speculations? Not at all, for many features of Dogon life and culture conform to specifications apparent in the myths. The Dogon are organized in patrilineal lineages, as well as in village wards, villages and districts. Every lineage has its 'big house', modelled on the images projected in the myths. It is built in an oval shape, which the Dogon expressly say reproduces the shape of the great placenta from which everything emerged. The building itself, they say, represents a Nommo in his human form. It has four towers, for example, which are his limbs. Similarly, villages are conceived as twins, being always built in pairs, one of which is referred to as Upper and the other as Lower. The district is similarly organized as a unity of two halves. Blacksmiths among the Dogon have a somewhat exalted status, corresponding to their illustrious ancestry, and they do not marry other Dogon but only each other's sisters and daughters. Shrines to the various Nommo are found in every village.

Living Myths

Some millions of West Africans have received an English or French type of education or are employed in modern occupations involving machinery or bureaucratic procedures. It is a mistake on that score to imagine that myth in West Africa is dead. On the contrary, myths are still known to, and recited by, devotees of the gods associated with them. Temples and shrines to these gods still abound and associated cults still flourish. Inside the temples are found statuettes, masks and paraphernalia which, when placed in European museums and art galleries, do indeed become dead, under the name of 'art'.

An example is a myth I heard from several Temne in 1977. The Temne are rice cultivators living in the northern area of Sierra Leone. The population is distributed among some two dozen small chiefdoms. In each chiefdom the right to chiefship is the property of one or two royal lineages. The myth is the charter entitling the Kabia lineage to rule the chiefdom of Marampa. A chief called Bai Rampa was fighting a desperate war against invaders from another tribe, and was losing. One day his wife met a demon who inhabited a deep pool. The demon, called Koblo, offered to help her husband, provided a sheep was sacrificed to him. The queen agreed, the demon helped her husband and he won the war.

When he returned from the fighting, she told him about the demon and asked him to sacrifice a sheep. He refused to believe her, claiming that he had won the war by his own prowess. She told the demon her husband's answer. The demon said, 'If I don't get a sheep, I will have you instead.' She returned and pleaded with her husband to sacrifice a sheep to Koblo, but he still refused. So, wearing her finest clothes and gold ornaments, she entered the pool, where she still lives. Bai Rampa realized his mistake and changed his name to Bai Koblo. Ever since, the chiefs of Marampa have called themselves by that name and have offered an annual sacrifice to Rampa's queen.

West African cultures are noted for their wealth of folk-tales, stories told for amusement and clearly distinguished from myths such as those above. Some recitations one hears, however, combine elements of both story and myth. Here is one such recitation, again from the Temne, which I wish to tell for two reasons, the first being that throughout West Africa river gods, goddesses and demons figure prominently in religion and myth. It is about the Temne river demon, called Anyaroli, an androgynous being like all Temne demons. Though it has no 'official' cult it is often sacrificed to, as in return for sacrifice it bestows wealth.

Long ago, after men were created they asked God to create animals too. So God created animals, and they lived a long time without a proper king, for God had only created a temporary king, the lion. Now after a time all the animals got angry because Lion was eating all the others. At that time there were only specimen animals on earth, one of each kind. So the rest went to Lion and said they wanted a proper permanent king, and Lion held a meeting. But it was difficult – there was Elephant for example, he wanted to be king because he was the biggest. There was Whale, and even many of the lesser animals also wanted to be king. So Lion said they were to fetch a big iron pot and light a fire. They filled the pot with water and put it on the fire. All the animals wondered at this. When the water boiled, Lion said, 'If there is any animal who can take this pot in his hands and drink half the water – he will be king.' At that time all the animals had limbs.

The elephant started to try but the pot and the water were too hot. He said he did not want to be ruler. Others tried but none succeeded. Then Monitor Lizard stood up. He told them he would try, but first he wanted them to sing a song. What he had in mind was that when they were singing he would go from one to another, while the water cooled. None suspected this, so they started singing. Then he went to one and said 'See, I'm going to drink', then to another and so on. When he'd gone round the circle the water was a lot cooler and he drank half of it.

Then Lion called Monitor Lizard into the middle of the circle and they started beating the drum and Lion said, 'Monitor Lizard is going to be king.' So they beat the drums furiously. But Monitor had burned his limbs holding the pot, because it was still hot, and so that the rest wouldn't see, he withdrew his limbs into his gown. There were many smaller animals in the world then and all had limbs. Lion raised his hand and there was quiet. He said, 'I now declare that Monitor Lizard is your ruler.' Then many smaller animals jumped up to see Monitor, and as soon as they did so they were in the same lineage; they became snakes, without limbs, or lizards or crocodiles with small cramped ones. That was how Monitor got his family.

Before all this Monitor had gone to Anlubu (the soldier bird, held to be a kind of diviner) and in fact it was Anlubu who had given him the idea of how to

ABOVE The first Nommo came to earth on a huge arch, at the centre of which stood two Nommo of the sky in the form of blacksmiths. Each Dogon village has a 'big house', which represents a Nommo in his human form, and blacksmiths have a high status among the Dogon corresponding to their exalted ancestry. The wooden object in front of this blacksmiths' shrine at Irelli represents a serpent and the stairway to the sky.

BELOW Dancing figure, an altar iron, from Mali.

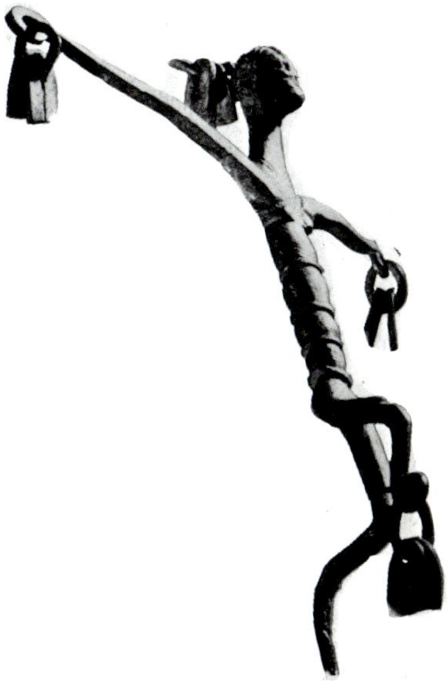

A fetish is a statue or other object which is held in awe, not as the symbol of a god, but because it is believed to contain superhuman power in its own right. Fetish from Gabon.

drink the water. Now Anlubu said 'What can you pay me for all I've done for you?' Monitor said, 'Whatever you want, I'm king'. Anlubu said 'I had a friend you've made into a snake. I want him back in the same form as he was.' Monitor was so happy that instead he said 'Your friend will now be very beautiful', and he shouted, 'I want Anlubu's friend to be beautiful, as beautiful as a human being.' As soon as he said that, God sent a messenger to tell him he was not to create human beings. But the snake already had the face of a human being; so God ordered it to stop there. That is how Anyaroli comes to have a human face and a snake's body. Then Monitor was asked if he wanted to live on land or on water. He said either. So his family can live either on land or in water, as he does.

Myth and Experience

Not only is myth very much alive but, along with beliefs, it moulds experience, to such an extent that sometimes an individual's account of a particularly dramatic experience cannot be distinguished from a recitation of a myth. Throughout West Africa twins figure prominently in pantheons, and twins born to mortals are the object of cults, of various sorts. Temne twins, for example, are carried round the town on a winnowing fan soon after birth, with dancing and singing, while people toss silver coins onto the fan. A shrine is erected to them where parents of twins offer sacrifice. Now, twins are believed to be demons belonging to the family of Monitor Lizard. They are river demons who have managed to enter their mother's womb while she was bathing in the river, and have been born in the form of mortals. The members of this family, as recounted, can live either on land or in water, and include all snakes.

Any Temne baby born badly deformed is regarded as a demon, and is 'returned to the bush', which means abandoned. A deformed twin, however, is so treated with special ritual. A Temne woman told me of such a ritual she participated in only a few years ago. 'I gave birth to twins and one was returned. His head was huge and kept growing to an unusual shape. He never learned to stand, and was never satisfied suckling. It drew my breast so hard I was afraid. A woman came and advised me it was a demon. She was a mother of twins and advised me to return it to the bush. So we invited this man and he came and made the ritual. He was expert in all medicines. He and I and a friend went to a big cotton tree in the bush. We had a piece of white cloth and spread it under the tree, we had a bottle of wine and some rice-flour and some chickens' eggs. Then the doctor put on some special clothes, red in colour. We laid the baby on the cloth, with the wine, flour, eggs and a special ring. Then the doctor started singing some songs and we (the two women) answered. The baby started to change his shape from a person to a demon. His head changed to a snake's and it started to eat the rice-flour, then it changed into a snake, its whole body, and it ate the rice-flour. In front of the tree was a hole, where the snake went. The doctor said we should run away, the spot would soon be too terrible. So we ran back to town. When we returned both the doctor and me were sick. My friend later became sick and died. During this time we asked some people for leaves and washed with them, for the demon usually comes asking for his mother. Also some holy water from the alphas (men learned in Islamic lore). That was this doctor's last job doing this, he died in Mabersanek Hospital soon after. I only survived because leaves were given me.

What actually happened? I do not know, but the woman spoke in all sincerity, and several Temne listening to her with me sometimes nodded or grunted approval of her words. When she left us, they explained that it was the doctor's own fault that he had died and that the other two had become ill. 'He should have taken them away before the baby turned to a snake,' they said, 'mortals are not supposed to witness such things.'

THE AMERICAS

CHAPTER TWENTY-THREE

THE NORTH AMERICAN INDIANS

The myths of Native North America come from an area which is not only vast and variegated in terms of climate and topography, but in which there are at least 236 recognized ethnic groupings, speaking at least 134 different languages or dialects. Usually each ethnic group has, or had, its own characteristic mythology and religion, closely tied to local topographic features and reflecting the local fauna and flora. Though there are often close similarities between different groups, resulting from a common cultural and linguistic heritage, or from borrowings, the general rule is diversity, not uniformity.

No brief treatment, consequently, can do justice to the variety and range of the myths. This article describes the principal deities in the major culture areas of North America, together with some of the myths in which they figure. All the myths presented here are still current among conservative Native Americans, though in most groups only a few individuals can recount them properly.

The Eastern Woodlands

That part of North America first explored and colonized by Europeans was a more or less continuous forest extending from the tree line of Labrador and Hudson's Bay to the Gulf of Mexico and westward to about the longitude of the Mississippi. The common political organization of this region was the tribe, varying in numbers from a few hundred to one or two thousand. Members of a tribe spoke a common language and were united under a common government. In some parts of the East a number of such tribes were loosely bound together in 'confederacies', such as the Iroquois Confederacy in the north and the Creek Confederacy in the south. Beyond these limits, affinity of speech delimited certain major groupings. There is a great similarity in the myths and legends of the Algonquian speakers of the northern Woodlands, and again among the tribes of the Iroquois Confederacy. There is also a considerable sharing of concepts and myths by the Muskhogean speakers of the Southeast, though here the Iroquoian-speaking Cherokee and other non-Muskhogeans shared many of these concepts and myths as well.

All the tribes of the Eastern Woodlands believed in a supreme deity, sometimes referred to in English as the Great Spirit. The Great Spirit created the world and is the author of life. Invisible and immaterial, he is invoked with reverence, but is not a definite personality about whom myths are told. Generally aloof from the world of sense, he is probably best named the Great Mystery. Most tribes in the Eastern Woodlands believe in a multi-tiered heaven, varying from four to 12 layers. In the uppermost of these, it is said, the Great Spirit dwells.

Closer to man are the Sun, the Four Winds, and Mother Earth. These six are commonly addressed during the smoking of the sacred pipe or calumet. The total number of these major deities, plus the standpoint of the petitioner, makes seven. *Four* and *seven* are the most important ritual numerals in aboriginal North America, and recur constantly in Native American myths.

The tribes of the Eastern Woodlands commonly referred to the world as 'this island', and both the Algonquian-speaking groups and the Iroquois tribes conceived of it as flat and resting upon the back of a giant turtle. The sky is regarded as the roof of man's

world, but as the floor of the lowest tier of heaven. This stratum, that just above the earth, is the home of the Thunderbirds. These are usually conceived of as giant birds with human faces. The beating of their wings is what men call thunder, and the flashing of their fierce eyes is lightning. They have enormous destructive power, and sometimes inadvertently kill men and destroy their crops, but they are generally benevolent, since they bring the rain necessary for both horticulture and browse for wild beasts which man hunts. Several ceremonies are dedicated to them, the best known being the War Dance, still performed today by the Iroquois tribes, the Shawnee and other Woodland groups, as a weather-controlling ceremony. All birds, since they fly above the earth near the home of the Thunderbirds, are thought to be their agents and helpers, and also messengers between man and the Powers Above. For this reason bird feathers, particularly those of the powerful and high-flying golden eagle, are featured prominently in ceremonial head-dresses, on the sacred calumet and in other religious paraphernalia.

ABOVE Mecicine-mask dance by Indians at Esquimault, Vancouver Island, British Columbia. In the Northwest, shamans summoned medicine-spirits to cure diseases.

LEFT An Underwater Panther, on a buckskin bag. The zigzag quilted line above the panther represents water. In myths of the Eastern Woodlands the 'underwater' creatures mirror those of the earth. The Underwater Panthers are generally malevolent figures, held responsible for deaths by drowning, but are also a potential source of wisdom and healing power.

The Underwater Panthers

Powerful deities also live under the earth and beneath the waters of lakes and streams. Some of these creatures are 'underwater' mirrors of creatures living on the surface of the earth, such as the underwater wolf and the underwater bear. Just as heaven is multi-tiered, so is the underwater-underground region. In the lowermost of the lower domains is the home of the chiefs of the underwater-underground creatures, the powerful gods known variously as the Underwater Panthers or Giant Horned Snakes. As described in myths throughout the Eastern Woodlands, these creatures appear much like the dragons of medieval Europe or the Far East. A Shawnee myth describes one as having the head of a large buck with horns and the body of a snake. The Ojibwa, Menomini, Potawatomi and Eastern Dakota picture them as panthers of enormous size with horns like bison and bodies covered with either short yellow hair or coppery scales. The snakes, fishes and all other underwater and underground creatures are their subjects and messengers. The Underwater Panthers or Giant Horned Snakes are generally considered to be malevolent, and deaths by drowning are credited to their evil hunger. They are, however, a potential source of great wisdom and healing power, particularly healing with herbs, which grow from beneath the ground and hence derive their power from these Powers Below.

The Thunderbirds are constantly at war with the Underwater Panthers and Giant Horned Snakes. Great storms, earthquakes, floods and other violent natural phenomena are considered the result of battles between these two opposing but complementary cosmic forces. Both are considered necessary or at any rate inevitable parts of the scheme of things, and man himself shares attributes of both.

Lesser deities in the Eastern Woodlands are spiritual prototypes of the various animal and plant species. Often diseases are attributed to the disfavour of the spirit of one or another animal species. Particularly important were the spirits of the Bear, Deer, Bison, Beaver, Underwater Wolf, Snake, Turtle and Fish. In the case of animals, albinos were regarded as the 'chiefs' of their respective species and a potential source of great power to the Indian 'blessed' by them. Of the plants, only Corn (maize) and Tobacco emerge as major deities, though each plant species has its particular spiritual prototype.

Nanabush and the Medicine Dance

The central personage in the major Algonquian myth cycle is Nanabush, the Great Hare (also known by many other names, such as Manabozho, Wisaaka and Glooscap). Nanabush is the incarnation of vital energy and the inventor or discoverer of many things useful to mankind. Sometimes described in heroic terms, he is more often a devious and blundering anti-hero, a not particularly admirable character who is constantly searching for his next meal but usually failing in his attempts to find it. Nanabush is intimately associated with his grandmother Nokomis, the Earth, and with his younger brother Chibiabos, the Wolf, who appear in the principal myth of the cycle.

Nanabush returns from hunting to find that Chibiabos, the Wolf, is missing. Suspecting foul

ABOVE Cherokee dance mask, of painted wood, once worn by the leader of the Snake Dance. The spirit of the Snake was a lesser deity in the Eastern Woodlands, with the spiritual prototypes of other species of animals and plants.

RIGHT A Mandan village. The lodges of the Plains Indians recreated in miniature the plan of the world. The plan of the lodge was flat with a circular base, over which hung the tent of the sky. The door was to the east, the direction of the rising sun. Tipi encampments were also circular, and circles or 'hoops of the world' recur frequently in ceremonies and myths. Oil-painting by George Catlin, 1832.

play, he travels far and wide searching for his lost brother. He questions various animals and birds, but is given evasive answers. Finally he holds the (previously white) raven in the smoke of a fire and the tortured bird reveals that the Underwater Panthers have killed Chibiabos. Changing himself into a tree-stump, Nanabush approaches the rocks where these monsters sun themselves and slays several of them before the alarm is given. In retaliation the Underwater Panthers bring a great flood which engulfs the earth. Only by climbing a tall pine-tree, which he magically extends four times, is Nanabush able to keep his nose above water. Seeing various aquatic mammals swimming nearby, Nanabush begs them to dive for a bit of earth. Otter and Beaver dive first, but drown in the attempt and float lifeless to the surface, bleeding from the nostrils. Nanabush restores them to life by blowing upon them. Muskrat tries next. He too drowns, but between his claws Nanabush finds a tiny bit of mud. He blows upon this the ritual four times, and at each breath the dirt increases at such a rate that finally the dry land is restored for men and animals to live on. Defeated in this contest of power, the Underwater Panthers sue for peace. By way of reparation, they teach Nanabush and his Grandmother, the Earth, the use of herb remedies and how to perform the life-extending Midewiwin, or Medicine Dance. Chibiabos is restored to life, but is assigned the guardianship of the land of souls in the west.

Buffalo hunt, on a painted elkskin robe from Montana. The life of the Plains Indians was revolutionized in the 18th century by the introduction of the horse, which facilitated the hunting of the buffalo. The animal's importance in the Indian economy is reflected in numerous myths.

How Corn Came

Corn or maize was undoubtedly the most important food crop of aboriginal North America, and many of the horticultural tribes have stories concerning its advent. The Creek and their neighbours in the Southeastern Woodlands regard maize as the body of Corn Woman. Corn Woman is described as living, incognito, with a human family which is not aware of her identity. She feeds them corn dishes and they do not know where she is getting the food. They spy upon her and discover that the corn comes from her own body. According to one version, the corn consists of scabs which she scratches from her thighs, an obvious analogy to shelling corn from the cob. In another version it is the washings from her feet. All versions are equally revolting. Corn Woman realizes that she has been spied upon when the individuals she has been feeding suddenly lose their appetite for her food. Her solution to the problem varies widely. In one version she tells them to build a corn crib and lock her inside for four days. They do so, and from inside the crib there is a noise like distant thunder. At the end of the fourth day they open the door as directed and she comes out. The crib is filled with corn and she instructs them in its use (Swanton 1929: 9–13).

The Great Plains

Extending westward from the Eastern Woodlands to the Rocky Mountains, and from the Canadian prairies to the Texas coast, lies the Great Plains region of North America. Previous to White settlement this vast sea of grass supported innumerable herds of bison, as well as many other animals – pronghorn antelope, two species of deer, rabbits and birds. Along its streams it was possible to raise crops of corn, beans and squash, and horticulture was imported into the region as early as AD 500. The introduction of the horse by Europeans in the 18th century caused a revolution in the life of the Plains Indians by facilitating the hunting of the bison on horseback by highly mobile groups. This way of life proved to be so attractive that many tribes from surrounding areas entered the Plains. The colourful life-style which subsequently developed among these Plains nomads, with their graceful warbonnets, gorgeous buckskin clothing and lofty tipis, has provided the model of the typical American Indian in the minds of most Europeans and Americans.

Many of the deities of the Plains tribes and the myths in which they figure are closely akin to those of the Eastern Woodlands, and were in fact imported from that region. Here, too, is the Powers Above/Powers Below dichotomy, with the Thunderbirds and Underwater Panthers waging their eternal cosmic wars. Much, however, is unique and attributable to the flat, relatively treeless topography. The Plains Indian world is one of majestic completeness of almost every view of earth and sky. The circle of the horizon is complete and whole, with no valley wall or forest to impede the view. Above is the incredibly blue dome of heaven, crossed each day by the sun. To the Plains Indian his world, though colossal, was entirely intelligible. Its plan, like that of his lodge,

ABOVE The new Ghost Dance religion, originating in the 1870s among the Paiute in Nevada, spread to the Sioux and other peoples in reaction against the threatened destruction of American Indian culture by the encroaching Whites. The Sioux hoped for a great leader who would restore the state of things before the coming of the white man. This photograph of Ghost Dance worshippers at prayer was taken among the Arapaho, c.1893.

ABOVE RIGHT Part of the Sun Dance ritual among the Sioux. The dance was dedicated to the Thunderbirds and was intended to bring rain to nourish the life of the prairies. The dancers imitated Thunderbird nestlings.

was flat with a circular base, over which was hung the tent of the skies. Its door was to the east, the direction of the rising sun. Tipi encampments were likewise circular, and circles or 'hoops of the world' are a recurrent concept in myth and ceremony.

The most characteristic religious ceremony of the Plains tribes was the Sun Dance, dedicated to the Thunderbirds. It was held in a circular lodge dominated by a sacred cottonwood pole in its centre. In a fork near the top of this pole was a bunch of willow boughs known as the 'thunderbird's nest'. The dancers, garbed to represent baby thunderbirds and constantly piping on eagle-bone whistles to imitate the sound of nestlings, danced for four days and three nights without food or water, all the while gazing at the 'thunderbird's nest' above. On the final day some were attached to the centre pole by means of thongs threaded through slits made in the flesh of their shoulders. They jerked backwards in their dancing until their flesh gave way and they were released. The idea is simple – by their dress, their bobbing dance, their birdlike piping on whistles, and by their fasting, thirsting and other sacrifice, the Sun dancers hope to entice the Thunderbird to stop and bring rain to nourish the grass of the prairies. This will in turn bring the bison and other game upon which the people depend. The rain will also nourish the gardens of corn, beans and squash which the women have planted near the streams.

Bison and Maize

So important were maize and the bison to the Plains Indians that it is not surprising to find the two linked in many of the myths told by Plains tribes. In a Cheyenne myth, two young men enter a hill by diving into a spring which gushes from it. Inside they find an old woman cooking bison-meat and maize in two separate pots. Inside the magical hill are great herds of bison and other game animals and vast fields of growing maize. The Old Woman gives them the two pots, commanding them to feed all the tribe, leaving an orphan boy and an orphan girl to the last. The contents of the vessels remain undiminished until it comes to the turn of the orphans, who empty them. Then buffalo arise from the spring and, from seed given to the young men, maize is grown each year by the Cheyenne.

A Dakota myth says that two men were out hunting when they saw in the distance something wondrous approaching them. As it came closer, they saw it was a beautiful woman dressed in white buckskin and carrying a bundle on her back. She was so attractive that one of the men wanted to rape her, but when he approached her he was enveloped in a mist. When it lifted, he was reduced to a skeleton being eaten by terrible snakes. She told the other man to return to his camp and prepare a great lodge for her reception.

The hunter returned and the chief ordered a great lodge prepared. All assembled there dressed in their finest garb. The woman entered and spoke, saying: 'I came from Heaven to teach the Dakota how to live and what their future shall be . . . I give you this pipe. Keep it always.' She also gave them a package containing four grains of maize, with the words: 'I am a buffalo, the White Buffalo Cow. I will spill my milk (the maize) all over the earth, that the people may live.' She taught the people the use of the pipe, and assigned colour symbolism to the four winds or directions, red for north, yellow for east, white for south and black for west. She taught them seven sacred ceremonies to prolong their lives. She then walked away and as she disappeared, she turned into a reddish-brown bison calf. The White Buffalo Calf pipe is still reverently maintained to this day as the tribal palladium of the Dakota, and is an object of pilgrimage for members of the tribe.

The Son of the Sun

Another common tale in many Plains tribes involves the marriage of a mortal to a celestial god, the Sun. It has obvious affinities to world-wide myths of a similar type, of which Jack and the Beanstalk is the familiar example in English folklore.

An Arapaho version of the story begins with a sky-world family of gods, a man and a woman and their two sons, Sun and Moon. In search of wives, Sun and Moon travel in opposite directions. Moon takes for a wife a water animal, the Toad, but Sun decides to marry a mortal woman. Looking down from on high, he sees two Indian girls gathering firewood. Descending, he transforms himself into a porcupine and climbs a tree. One of the girls, desiring quills for her embroidery, follows the animal up the tree, but it keeps ascending and the tree continues growing. Finally the sky is pierced, and Sun, resuming the form of a young man, takes the girl to wife in the sky-world lodge. There a son is born to her. Her parents-in-law present her with a digging stick, but her husband forbids her to dig a certain plant. Out of curiosity she disobeys and uncovers a hole through which she looks down on the earth and sees the camp circle of her people.

Homesick, she decides to descend by means of a sinew rope, but just before she reaches the earth with her son, her husband throws a stone down at her, killing her. The child survives and is cared for by an old woman, Night. She calls the boy Little Star, and makes a bow and arrows for him. With these he kills an Underwater Panther, the husband of Night. Night transforms the bow into a lance and Little Star continues killing serpents, which infest the world. He is incautious, however, and while he is sleeping on the prairie a snake enters his body and coils itself in his skull. His flesh falls from him, but his skeleton remains articulated and he remains conscious. He prays for two days of rain and two of intense heat, and these force the serpent to thrust its panting head out from his mouth. He seizes the serpent and pulls it forth, and is restored to living form. The reptile's skin he affixes to his lance, and returns to the black lodge of Night, where he becomes the morning star.

The Southwest

Some of the most spectacular archeological sites and the best preserved aboriginal cultures in the United States are found in the arid but magnificently scenic region known to anthropologists as the Southwest. At first the Southwest culture area was defined to include only Arizona and New Mexico, but it has now been extended to include adjacent areas in southern Utah, southwestern Colorado and northern Mexico. Next to the Southeast, it possessed the most highly developed culture north of Mexico. This high cultural development, based upon farming, is even more remarkable in view of the desert character of most of the region.

Perhaps the best known of the cultural subdivisions of the Southwest is that represented by the so-called 'pueblo' tribes. They live in pueblos, or towns, along the Upper Rio Grande in New Mexico, in the Hopi villages of northeastern Arizona, and at Zuni in western New Mexico. They adhere tenaciously to their traditional way of life, which in many respects persists with little change from that reported by the Spanish 400 years ago. Their government is a true theocracy, and each pueblo follows a strict ceremonial calendar rooted in mythology. Despite the increasing encroachment of the White world, the Pueblos continue to find satisfaction in their rich and complex ceremonial life, around which their cultures are integrated as functional wholes. Since an adequate rainfall is crucial to Pueblo life, it is not surprising to find that

Prehistoric cliff dwellings at Mesa Verde, Colorado. The Pueblo Indians lived in permanent settlements and sometimes occupied communal houses constructed in caves by their predecessors, the Basket Makers. Despite the barrenness of the region, the Southwest had a high cultural development, based on farming and linked with a rich and complex religion.

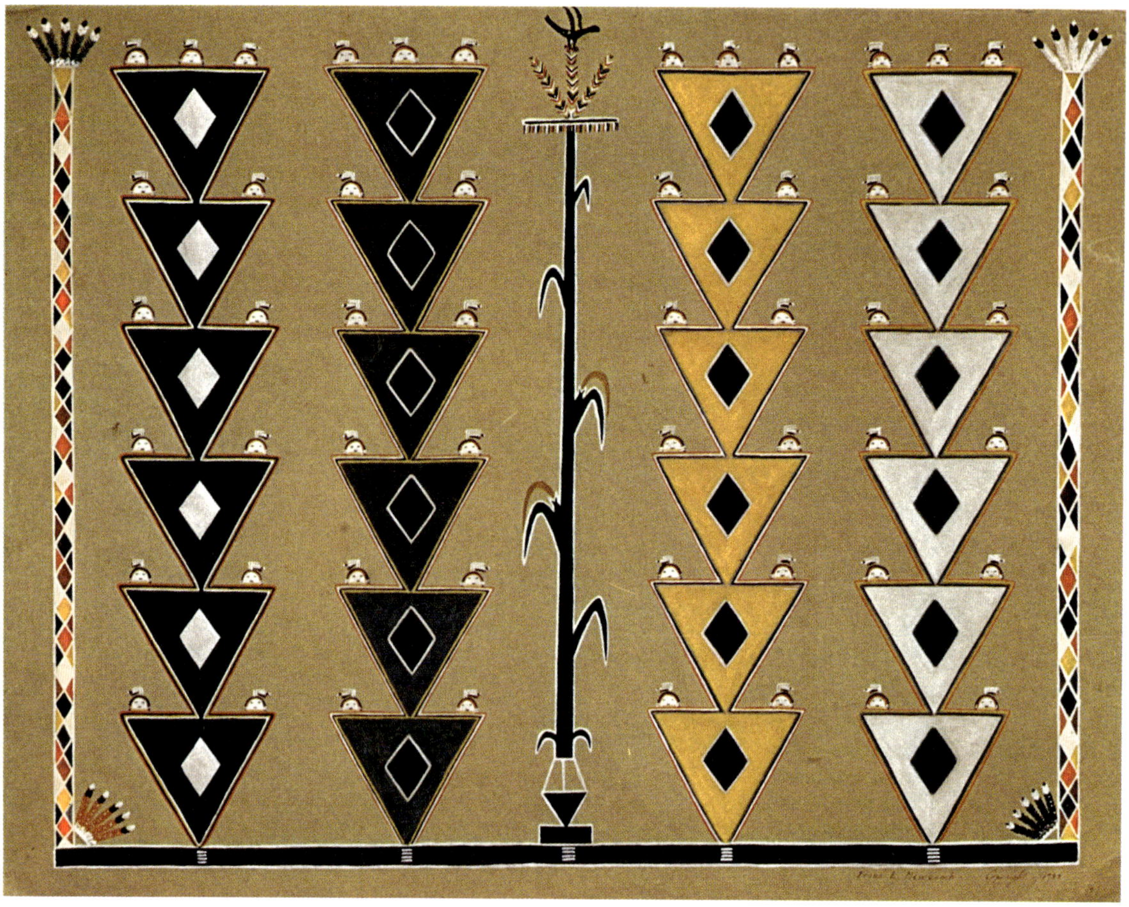

RIGHT Rain and rain-clouds, vital to the growth of corn and other plants, are naturally important in the myths of the arid Southwest. In this Navaho sand-painting from New Mexico, the black corn at the centre has three white roots growing out of a symbol of earth. On either side are two columns of clouds, with symbolic hailstones in the centre of each cloud and the Cloud's People's heads peeping over the edge. At the bottom is a bar of black water with seeds in it, and at each side are sections of rainbow-rope.

BELOW The deities of the Pueblo people are the principal powers of nature. This Navaho sand-painting from Arizona shows two great deities, Mother Earth and Father Sky. The blue Mother Earth has a spring of water and four plants on her body. The black Father Sky has the Milky Way on his body, with the sun, moon and stars below. A line of pollen unites the pair, suggesting their mutual responsibility for fertility.

most ceremonies, and the myths which they re-enact, are concerned with rain and the fertility of their crops.

The Pueblo people divide their deities into two great categories. The gods themselves represent the powers and divisions of nature. The *kachinas* are primarily the spirits of ancestors, but in a secondary usage are the spirit-powers of other beings, even of the gods. Father Sun and Mother Earth are the greater deities of the pantheon, but each is known by many names and assumes a number of personalities. Among the Hopi, for example, the Sun is called Heart of the Sky, and Earth is termed Mother of Germination, Mother of Seeds, Old Woman, Spider Woman, Corn Maiden and Goddess of Growth. Along with the Sun are other celestial gods, and the Knife-Feather monster. These and the meteorological gods, the Cloud-Masked Rain-Bringers, are termed 'Those Above'. The complementary deities which dwell in the bosom of Mother Earth, termed 'Those Below', include the twin gods of War, who once delivered mankind from monsters, the Corn Father and Corn Mother, and the mineral 'Men' and 'Women' representing Salt, Red Shell, White Shell and Turquoise. Also included are animal gods, or Ancients, which are intermediaries between men and the higher gods, and patrons of religious fraternities. Another deity, associated with both subterranean and celestial powers, is the Plumed Serpent, a deity connected with lightning, rain and fertility. This last is clearly related to Kukulcan of the Maya and Quetzalcoatl of the Nahua (see MIDDLE AMERICA), likewise to the Giant Horned Snakes and the Underwater Panthers of eastern North America.

The second group of higher powers is composed of the ancestral and totemic kachinas. Originally limited to the spirits or personified medicine power of the ancients, personifications of a similar power in other objects have come to be known by the same name. In general the kachinas are anthropomorphic. In ritual and in pictorial representation they appear as masked, and a great number of Pueblo Indian dances involve masked dancers impersonating kachinas. They are very numerous, yet each has its distinct attributes of costume and behaviour. Small kachina dolls were made by parents for their children to acquaint them with the characteristic masks and dress of these supernatural beings.

The Corn Maidens

Two characteristic Pueblo myths are quoted here. Both, in different ways, emphasize water and the growth of plants, the dominant concerns of desert farmers.

According to a Hopi myth, man once lived in an underworld paradise. People were prosperous and happy, until they grew licentious. In punishment the waters rose in the underworld. The people escaped by following Spider Woman up a reed, two kinds of pine trees and a giant sunflower that reached above the flood. As the people climbed to safety, the Mocking Bird assigned each to a tribe. But Mocking Bird grew exhausted and stopped singing before all the people had been assigned, and the latecomers tumbled back into the underworld, where all dead things were to go. The others set off in search of the sunrise, the white men going south, the Pueblos staying in the centre, the other Indians going north. It was agreed that when one of the parties arrived at the sunrise, the others would stop where they stood. The whites, who created horses to aid them, were the first to reach their destination. When they did so, a great shower of stars informed the others, so both the Pueblo people and the other Indians settled where they are now.

A Zuni myth says that when the forefathers of the Zuni came up from the underworld they were accompanied by ten lovely Corn Maidens, who were invisible to ordinary eyes. The maidens travelled with the tribe for four years, unseen and unknown, but at Shipololo, the Place of Fog, witches discovered them, gave them seeds of the different kinds of maize and squash, and transformed them into human shape. The Zuni travelled on, but the Corn Maidens lingered in a magical dance-bower, walled with cedar and fringed with spruce, dancing with their bright stalks of corn with white plume-like leaves, and bathing in the dew.

Discovered by deer-hunters, the Corn Maidens were brought before the Zuni to dance, but as they danced, the people all fell asleep. Payatamu, the little flute-playing god who places blooms on flowers, had come to watch. He was charmed by the dancing girls and yearned especially for Yellow Corn Maiden, the loveliest of the ten. The Corn Maidens read his thoughts and in fear kept dancing until he too had fallen asleep, whereupon they fled away to the Mist and Cloud Spring. Plagued by a great famine, the Zuni prayed for their return, and finally they were persuaded to come back and dance again. The famine ended and ever since the beauty and dancing of the Corn Maidens have been celebrated in Zuni ritual.

Kachinas are personifications of supernatural powers. These Hopi dolls are painted to resemble the masked dancers in religious rituals and represent the kachinas of lightning LEFT and corn RIGHT. The dolls are given to children, to teach them to recognize the characteristic masks and costumes of the spirits.

Western North America

West of the Great Plains, and extending almost the full length of the continent, rises the long spine of the Rocky Mountains – the Great Divide of North America. West of it are the three culture areas known as the Plateau, the Basin and California. The Plateau lies between the Rockies and the Cascades of Oregon to the west. The Basin is the dry southern extension of the Plateau, bordered on the west by the Sierra Nevada of California and the Cascades. The California area is that of the present state. The native cultures of these three areas are impressive not so much for what they possess but for what they lack in terms of eastern North America. All three were essentially non-agricultural in nature, depending upon the hunting of local animals and the gathering of wild plant foods. Social organization was likewise poorly developed and an organization into local bands was the characteristic form in most of the region. In spite of their technological and social simplicity, it is sobering to remember that these Indians were able to wrest a living from even the most inhospitable portions of their territory – places where most of us would starve.

The animal-powers bulk large in the myths of these groups. As in aboriginal Australia (see AUSTRALIA), the Indians west of the Rockies generally believed in an Age of Animals, before men existed, when the beasts themselves had human form. Nevertheless they were truly animals in nature and disposition, and among all of them Coyote is chief. Coyote, the anti-hero and trickster, is clearly analogous to the Great Hare or Nanabush of the north-

TOP Apache warrior's cloak, showing a god and spirits.

ABOVE Tsimshian flying frog headpiece, from the Northwest Coast. According to one myth, a woman was seen floating on a lake. Her eyebrows, breasts, hands and knees were covered with frogs and she became the ancestress of a clan which took the frog as its badge.

eastern Algonquians. In many stories he is represented as contemptible – deceitful, greedy, bestial, with an erotic mania that leads him even to incest. He is often outwitted by the animals he endeavours to trick and is totally without gratitude to those that help him, yet he is a mighty magician, reducing the world to order and helping man with innumerable benefactions. Like the Algonquian Nanabush, Coyote frequently has a close associate or helper, sometimes Fox, Wolf, or Eagle. This associate's character is, on the whole, more dignified and respectable than Coyote's.

Coyote and the Dead

According to a Wishram myth, of the Plateau area, in the Age of Animals, Coyote was sad because people died and went away to the land of the spirits. His sister had died and some of his friends. Eagle's wife had died and Eagle was mourning her. Coyote and Eagle started out together to the land of the dead. They came to a big body of water. Waiting until dark, Coyote began to sing, and in a short time four spirit men came and ferried them across to the land of the dead.

They entered a great tule-mat lodge where the spirits of the dead, beautifully dressed and painted, were dancing and singing to the beating of drums. The moon, hanging from above, filled the lodge with light. Near the moon stood Frog, the master of the lodge of the dead. Early in the morning the spirits left the lodge for their day of sleep. Then Coyote killed Frog and put on his skin. At twilight the spirits returned and began another night of singing and dancing. Coyote, in Frog's clothing, stood beside the moon.

When the dancing and singing were at their gayest, Coyote swallowed the moon. In the darkness Eagle caught the spirit people and put them into Coyote's basket and closed the lid tightly. Then the two started back to the land of the living. Coyote carried the basket and Eagle flew overhead. On the way they heard noises from inside the basket. The spirits were complaining, and several called together: 'Open the lid and let us out!' Coyote was tired, for the basket was getting heavier and heavier. 'Let's let them out,' said Coyote. 'No, no,' answered Eagle. A little later Coyote set the basket down. It was too heavy for him. 'Let's let them out,' said Coyote again. 'We are so far from the spirit land now that they won't return.' So he opened the basket. The people took their spirit forms and, moving like the wind, went back to the island of the dead.

Eagle scolded Coyote at first, but then he remarked: 'It is now autumn. The leaves are falling, just as people die. Let us wait until the spring. When the buds open and the flowers bloom, let us return and try again.' 'No,' replied Coyote, 'I am tired. Let the dead stay in the land of the dead forever.'

So Coyote made the law that after people have died, they shall never come to life again. If he had not opened the basket and let the spirits out, the dead would have come to life every spring, just as grass and flowers and trees do.

Another story of Coyote, a Paiute myth, from the Basin area, says that in the Age of Animals, in what is today called Bryce Canyon, Utah, there lived many birds, animals and lizards. At that time animals were much like humans, and like humans they began stealing and fighting among themselves. Coyote, who was in charge of the world, observed their behaviour and became very angry. He decided to punish the creatures of the valley by turning them to stone. Visitors to Bryce Canyon today can see the brightly painted faces and bodies of the stone animals lining the walls of the canyon – the victims of Coyote's wrath.

Kwakiutl mask from the Northwest Coast, depicting the sun, with the head of an eagle at its centre. It was used in dances of the Dluwulaxa dancing society, which was associated with the spirits of the sky.

The Northwest Coast

The Northwest Coast culture area extends up the Pacific Coast from the northern border of California to Yakutat Bay in southern Alaska. A region of spectacular beauty, with snow-capped peaks rising abruptly from the seashore, it is also one of the most unusual in North America in terms of its aboriginal culture. Although no agriculture was practised, and loom-weaving and ceramics were absent, a wealth of fish, sea mammals and wild plant foods enabled the groups of this area to live very well, and in fact to accumulate great surpluses of food and capital goods. These surpluses were later given away to other groups in elaborate and ostentatious 'potlatch' ceremonies. The elaborate art style of the region is now recognized as one of the great native art traditions of the world. Based upon completely different principles from the art of the Western world, it shows relationships to the art of the Ainu of Japan and of Shang dynasty China. No less interesting is the demonstration that the basic form of Northwest Coast culture seems to be derived from the same core of traits and complexes which characterize early Eskimo culture, though the Northwest Coast people are Indian, not Eskimo, in physical type.

The Northwest Coast people recognize an overall sky-god named Power-of-the-Shining-Heavens.

ABOVE Sisiutl, the double-headed snake, with a snake's head at each end and a human head in the middle, was a supernatural helper of warriors. Carved in 1920 by Dick Price of the Vancouver Island Kwakiutl in British Columbia.

BELOW Kwakiutl house front with a painting of a thunderbird lifting a whale. The thunderbird was a gigantic mythological creature which caused thunderstorms when it moved. Photographed at Alert Bay, British Columbia, before 1889.

Below him are uncountable lesser spirits, including almost every type of being known to mythology. There are the one-eyed Cyclops, the headless giant with eyes in his breast, the bodiless but living heads and talking skulls, sea-serpents, mermen, Circes, and cannibal spirits of many types. There are also numerous animal spirits and these, particularly, often appear as totemic or family badges in the fantastic totemic art of the region. The animal spirits themselves are not held to be clan ancestors, but only to have been connected in some significant way with the family or clan progenitor. Thus an Eagle clan chief appeared at a feast with a necklace of live frogs, and his family forthwith adopted the frog as a badge. Many mythical creatures appear as clan badges as well, and the double-headed snake (represented with a head at each end and a human head in the middle) known to the Kwakiutl as Sisiutl, is one of the most important of these beings.

The most characteristic feature of the mythology of the Northwest Coast is the cycle of legends in which the protagonist is Raven. Raven, the anti-hero and trickster, is our old friend Coyote or Nanabush in a littoral and insular form. Like these other tricksters he is engaged in an insatiable food-quest, travelling from place to place and meeting animals of every description. In contests of wit he destroys or eats them or drives them off and secures their stores of food. Yet, despite his greedy and treacherous nature, it is Raven who created the earth and established the

laws that govern life upon it. The following is the Tsimshian version of a widespread and characteristic Raven myth.

Raven Steals Daylight

When Raven was born, his father tried to teach him and train him in every way, and after he grew up, told him he would give him power to make a world. There was no light at that time in this world, but Raven was told that far up the Nass River was a large house where a selfish chief kept the light just for himself.

Raven thought of all kinds of plans for getting the light into the world. Finally he changed himself into a cedar leaf and dropped into the water that the chief's daughter was about to drink. The girl swallowed the leaf and became pregnant. When her time was completed they made a hole for her, in which she was to bring forth her child. They lined it with rich furs, but the child did not wish to be born on these fine things. In the end they put moss in the hole and the baby was born on it. Its eyes were very bright and moved around rapidly.

Round bundles of varying shapes and sizes hung about the walls of the house, and the baby cried and pointed to these bundles. This lasted for many days. Finally the grandfather said, 'Give my grandchild what he is crying for. Give him that one hanging on the end. That is the bag of stars.' So the child played with this, rolling it about on the floor behind the people, until suddenly he threw it up through the smoke-hole. It went straight up into the sky and the stars scattered out of it, arranging themselves as you now see them.

Some time later he began crying again. Then his grandfather said, 'Untie the next one and give it to him.' He played and played with it around behind his mother. After a while he threw it up through the smoke-hole as well, and there for all to see was the big moon.

Now there was just one more thing remaining, the box that held the daylight, and he cried for that. His eyes turned around and showed different colours and the people began thinking that this was no ordinary baby, but it always happens that a grandfather loves his grandchild just as he loves his own daughter, so the grandfather finally said, 'Oh well, untie the last thing and give it to him.' When the child had the box in his hands he uttered his raven cry 'Ka, ka,' and flew out with it through the smoke-hole. Then the chief from whom he had stolen it said, 'That old shit-ass Raven has gotten all of my things.'

Rattle in the form of a raven with the head of a hawk on its breast and a human figure on its back. Raven, the trickster, is the protagonist of a cycle of Northwest Coast myths. Cunning, greedy and treacherous, it was Raven who created the earth and established the order of nature.

CHAPTER TWENTY-FOUR

MIDDLE AMERICA

Middle America is an area defined not so much by physical geography as by cultural history. Joining Mexico (which lies in North America) to Guatemala and the neighbouring Central American republics, it corresponds roughly with the region christened New Spain by Hernando Cortes and his companions when they sailed there from Cuba in the early 16th century. This part of the New World has a complex history of city-states and empires, and shares certain ritual and calendrical conventions agreed upon far back in pre-Columbian times. These have survived the impact of Christianity to some extent and have modified religious teachings imported from Europe. Their force was such as to override differences between the languages and cultures native to the area: between the Nahua, who include the Aztecs and Toltecs of highland Mexico; the Maya in Guatemala and Yucatan; and the intervening Otomanguan groups, Mixtec, Zapotec and Otomi.

Beyond this, Middle America may also be defined as the bibliographical centre of Native America. Long before the Europeans arrived with the alphabet, Middle Americans built up libraries of paper and parchment books, paginated in screenfold or accordion fashion and recording such matters as the timing of rituals and the ancestry of powerful families. The Spaniards burned these books on principle, as pagan threats to Christian doctrine, but some survived through being sent to Europe and are now known by the names of the libraries and families which came to own them (Borgia, Vienna, Dresden, Paris, Bodley). Others survived in Mexico, along with more enduring texts incised on stone and wood.

Most Middle American texts are written in either Toltec or Maya script. Both these types of writing make use of certain sets of Figures, Numbers and Signs peculiar to Middle American ritual, and both are related to complicated calendars. Though books in native script continued to be used in Middle America at least until the 19th century, after the Spanish invasion several authors turned to the alphabet to write down their languages, chiefly Nahua and Maya. Middle American literature in native and in alphabetic script serves as the authoritative guide to ways of living and thinking long untouched by the Old World. In it myth is seen to be not so much the fantasy of the 'unconscious' as agreed belief; not just imaginative narrative, but a social charter and philosophy.

The Ages of the World

Throughout the New World there is a belief in multiple creations, of which the present world is but one. In Middle America there are normally four of these creations or 'world-ages' (a total also acknowledged by the Navaho and the Pueblo in North America and by the Quechua in Peru). Movement through these ages is usually progressive and the present age may acquire a special status as a fifth age which is the sum of the others.

This notion of five-in-four is expressed in the carving known as the Aztec Sun Stone, where the sign which names the present age, Movement (XVII in the Twenty Signs of ritual), is constituted by the signs which name the four previous ages: Water

Temple of the Sun, Palenque, constructed of limestone and characteristic of the gracious architecture at that ancient Maya city. Note the high roof comb with its delicate tracery effect. This is one of a group of three sanctuaries, each of which contains an elaborately carved hieroglyphic panel.

(IX), Jaguar (XIV), Rain (XIX) and Wind (II). These signs are enclosed in the unending ring of the Twenty Signs, running anticlockwise and itself enclosed by two Year-Snakes. In the design as a whole, each of the named 'positions' in time is implied by and implies the others.

The 16th-century Nahua manuscript known as the Legend of the Suns tells us more about these world-ages ('Suns') and their cataclysmic endings. In the first, of Water, men were invented and moulded from ash by the great Toltec and Aztec god Quetzalcoatl. Then everything was overtaken by water and people turned into fish. In the Jaguar-age the sun was eclipsed and in the darkness jaguars ate the people up. Then came the Rain-age, which ended in a rain of volcanic fire and ash, the Wind-age with its hurricane, when people turned into apes, and the present age, Movement, doomed to earthquake and famine.

The same sequence of cataclysmic events – Flood, Eclipse, Eruption and Hurricane – occurs in texts from other parts of Middle America. In the *Popol Vuh* (Book of Counsel) of the Quiche-Maya in highland Guatemala, the men of the first age, made of earth and mud, never fully escaped the watery element; soggy and absorbent, they 'dissolved in the water'. Those of the second age, made of wood, were by contrast too stiff and 'heartless'; after 'the face of

THE TWENTY SIGNS OF RITUAL

Middle American ritual and divination depend originally on sets of symbols, which were conventionally agreed upon in pre-Columbian times between various languages and cultures. The chief of these sets, related respectively to Venus, moon and sun, are the Nine Figures, points of origin in cosmogony; the Thirteen Numbers, harbingers and bird auguries; and the Twenty Signs, shown here, which subsume the other two sets and fall into two decimal halves (for example, IX and XIX are sometimes interchanged).

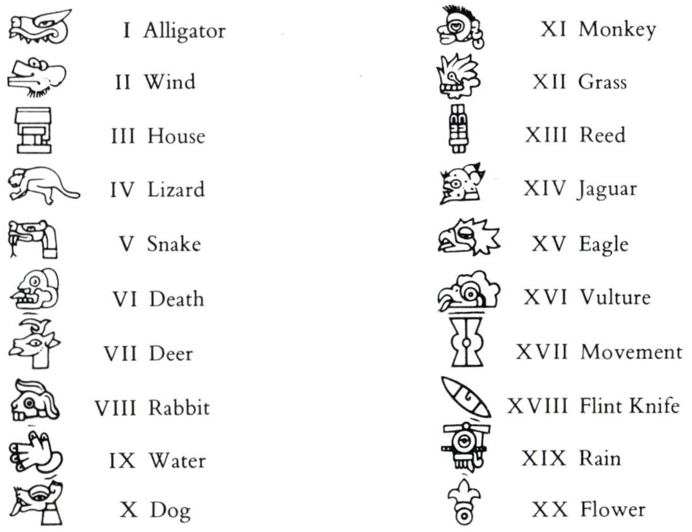

the earth was darkened' by the gods, they were eaten up and destroyed by jaguars and other creatures of the wild.

Among those who attack them in this account are the archetypal domestic animals of Middle America: Dog and Turkey. Complaining of being treated as mere food, they turn on their masters and are joined even by domestic grindstones and cooking pots, whose complaints are especially vivid. The grindstones say: 'We have been shattered by you every day, every day, night and day, all the time; crunch, crunch, scrape, scrape, on our faces you went.' The cooking pots say: 'Pain it was you inflicted on us. Sooty our mouths, sooty our faces. Always we were dumped on the fire. You burned us. We felt no pain, so you try it. We shall burn you.'

Beyond the onomatopoeic excitement in these speeches lies an important moral statement about attitudes to what we use. A character in Alejo Carpentier's novel *The Lost Steps* remarks that this text anticipates the myth of the robot and the threat of the machine. An attack by a similar combination of domestic creatures and objects occurs at the end of the second world-age in a Quechua myth from Peru, though in this case Dog and Turkey are replaced by llamas.

A counterpoint emerges between the endings of the first two ages, Flood and Eclipse, and those of later ones. For while the endings of the later ages involve mainly terrestrial forces like volcanoes and hurricanes, the fates of the first two depend more on the sky, on the proper balance and course of celestial powers.

ABOVE The opening or title-page of the Laud screenfold, one of the principal ritual documents of ancient Mexico. Probably written in the 14th century, it once served as a reference work for priests of the Toltec faith. The ceremony shown here involves eight priests attired as gods and ranged in pairs. They support another of their number, costumed as Mictlantecuhtli, who is curing the sun of eclipse by sucking the darkness from it in shaman fashion.

RIGHT The mighty 'Sun Stone' of the Aztecs, unearthed at the heart of their capital Tenochtitlan (Mexico City) at the site of the Great Pyramid. It commemorates the past and present ages of the world, the sign of the present age Movement (XVII) ingeniously incorporating those of the four ages of the past, shown in boxes on its limbs.

The title-page of the Fejervary screenfold, possibly the most complex symbolic diagram of America. At the centre stands Xiuhtecutli, Fire or Year Lord and 1st of the Nine Figures of cosmogony, the rest of which are ranged in pairs about him: Itztli (2nd) and the Sun as Piltzintecutli (3rd) at east (top); Cinteotl (4th) and Mictlanteucuhtli (5th) in the underworld (right); the two women Chalchihuitlicue (6th) and Tlazolteotl (7th) at west (bottom); and Tepeyollotl ('Hill Heart' 8th) and Tlaloc (9th) at the zenith or heart of heaven (left). The diagonals co-ordinate emblems of the past world ages with the four year-signs of the Toltec calendar (XIII, XVIII, III and VIII).

In the Flood which ends the first age, the waters above merge with those below, obliterating the horizons and making of everything a timeless cosmic ocean. In the larger scheme of things, then, prime importance is attached to the task of separating the waters and keeping them separate. The Vienna screenfold shows Quetzalcoatl performing this task as the planet Venus. The cycle of Venus's movement between the western and eastern horizons, as the evening and the morning star, is taken as a guarantee of the world's continuing existence in time. In parallel texts in Nahua, Venus rising in the east as the herald of the sun is said to 'wound the sources of water' with his arrows of light, to emerge as the triumphant opponent of the rain-gods, who work for the return of the Flood.

More obviously celestial is the catastrophe of Eclipse, when the sun falters on his daily path from east to west and is 'consumed', eaten by the envious and hostile forces of hell. Emerging monstrously in the darkened day-sky, the very stars sit ready to descend and devour, with their jaguar claws and teeth. In Toltec ritual, just as worship of Venus kept Flood at bay, so the cure for Eclipse was the heart and lifeblood of man, offered to the sun, Tonatiuh or Royal Lord, to strengthen him and in gratitude for his regular and untiring illumination of the world.

Counting Reality

Among the Maya, concern with the catastrophes of Flood and Eclipse led to the most advanced astronomy and mathematics known in the New World. This same Maya tradition provides the most overtly philosophical treatment of the belief in successive world-ages. The *Community Book of Chumayel* contains a 'song' about the creation of the present world and finds a way to start counting or enumerating our reality. The sum of this reality is the Twenty Signs, articulated in the body of the *uinal*, the 20-day week of the Maya calendar (compare *uinic*, 'man', with his 20 digits). When the *uinal* appears in the east, these Signs are correlated with the Thirteen Numbers (the number of lunations in a year is 12 or 13).

He started up from his inherent motion alone.
His mother's mother and her mother, his mother's
  sister and his sister-in-law, they all said:
How shall we say, how shall we see,
  that man is on the road?
These are the words they spoke as they moved
  along, where there was no man.
When they arrived in the east they began to say:
Who has been here? These are footprints.
  Get the rhythm of his step.
So said the Lady of the world,

And our Father, Dios, measured his step.
This is why the count by the footstep of the whole world was called 12 *Oc*.
This was the order born through 13 *Oc*,
When the one foot joined its counter-print to make the moment of the eastern horizon,
Then he spoke its name when the day had no name . . .

In this sophisticated passage the motif of the footsteps of the 'man on the road' solves the paradox of a 'beginning' to continuous time. *Oc* means foot or footprint and from 12 *Oc* we move immediately to 13 *Oc* as the other foot comes forward, corresponding to that undefinable moment of static equilibrium when the one foot is exactly even with the other foot moving past it. This is 'the moment of the eastern horizon', the edge of the day-unit, when the day is 'named' or created. It is the start position of right with left, of even with odd (12 and 13), not a beginning out of nothing (0 to 1). This initial parity is characteristic of Middle American cosmogony and of the parent figures, like the Lady and the Father here, who supervise the world's existence through its several beginnings and endings.

The Creation of Man

At Palenque, atop a small pyramid, there is a sanctuary dedicated to maize, the substance from which the people of this world-age are made, according to Maya doctrine. A panel shows ceremonies related to the plant, which stands, anthropomorphic, with arms extended, worshipped by two priests. In the history of American agriculture maize has a special place. It was (and is) admired for its growth by stages, defined by separate words in many American languages and numbered at 13 in Middle America; for the tassels of blond hair adorning the cob; for the evenness of its kernels and for the fact that these may occur in four colours – white, yellow, red-blue or black. While red and black symbolize the east and west horizons and celestial movement, white and yellow are prized as the colours of the kernels which were chosen to make the flesh of man at the start of this age in the history of the world.

In Middle American creation stories, finding the right material for man's flesh is presented as a demanding business, especially after the failures of the past. The *Popol Vuh* records how Gucumatz ('Feather Snake' or Quetzalcoatl) and his companions deliberated at length on the question of who should inhabit the present world, and how the white

ABOVE A maize plant correctly placed in the earth, in the agricultural chapter of the Fejervary screenfold. There are four sections in the chapter, in each of which the anthropomorphic plant is guarded by one of the Nine Figures. Here Tlaloc guards Chalchihuitlicue. The earth is friable and the burnt offerings are a ball of natural rubber and a wooden hand-plough, whose phallic character is confirmed by the loin cloth adorning its upper end.

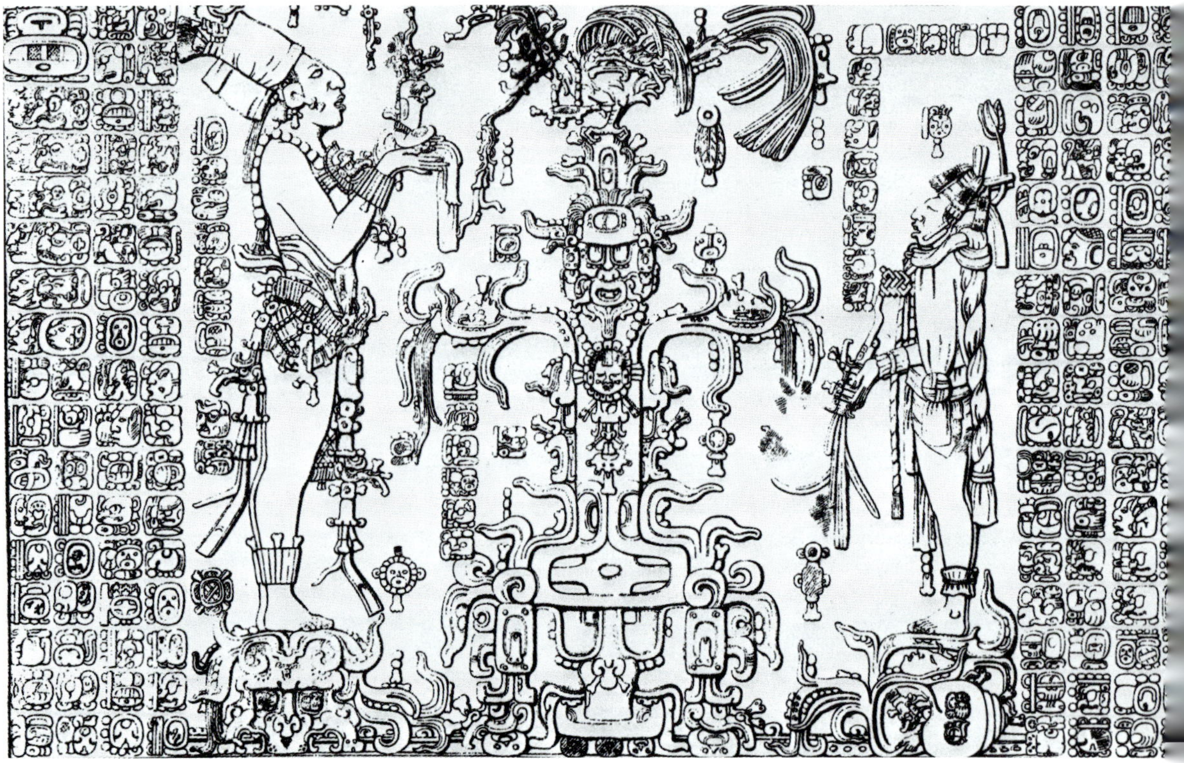

RIGHT Worship of maize depicted on the main panel in the Temple of the Foliated Cross, Palenque. To either side Maya hieroglyphs explain the central ceremonial scene. On the left the text opens with a Maya Era date and discusses events of the 3rd millennium BC; on the right it moves to contemporary times and refers to affairs at Palenque in the 7th century AD. Maize is the substance of which the people of the present world-ages are made, according to Maya doctrine.

and yellow maize ground up to make their flesh was discovered only with cunning in the heart of the 'Food Mountain'. Once formed, these maize-men caused a further problem by turning out too well. They had god-like vision and thoughts, could perceive the secrets of the four world-ages and knew instantaneously what was happening anywhere in space. In order to preserve their own superiority and to ensure that men felt the creative impulse in their bellies as well as their heads, and reproduced their kind, the gods decided to 'chip their eyes'. In the *Community Book of Chumayel* this act is referred to as 'the loss of vision', one of the tasks of the artist and writer being to make it good. The *Popol Vuh*, indeed, records just those secrets of the world-ages of which the gods deprived the first men.

The 'maize doctrine' of the Maya, as it might be called, has shaped their life in many ways, not least in the cultivation of maize itself. The screenfolds treat in detail of the fortune of the maize crops and of the propitiation necessary at each stage of cultivation. One of the chief reasons for the political resistance offered by the Maya to foreigners has been the defence of the traditional economy, in which maize plays a central part. Even now in Yucatan, villagers debate the morality of forsaking maize for sugar, a cash crop, in terms which invoke the ancient myth about the creation of man from maize.

Maize has a special place in American agriculture, and is symbolically connected with the human body, the sky and the calendar. Here is a goddess of young maize, seated in native fashion. Her head-dress of plaited paper is adorned with a maize cob, like Cinteotl's. The cast of her features reveals her home on the Gulf Coast, the area named Cuextlan in Nahua, after the Huaxtec Maya who live there. Late Classic period.

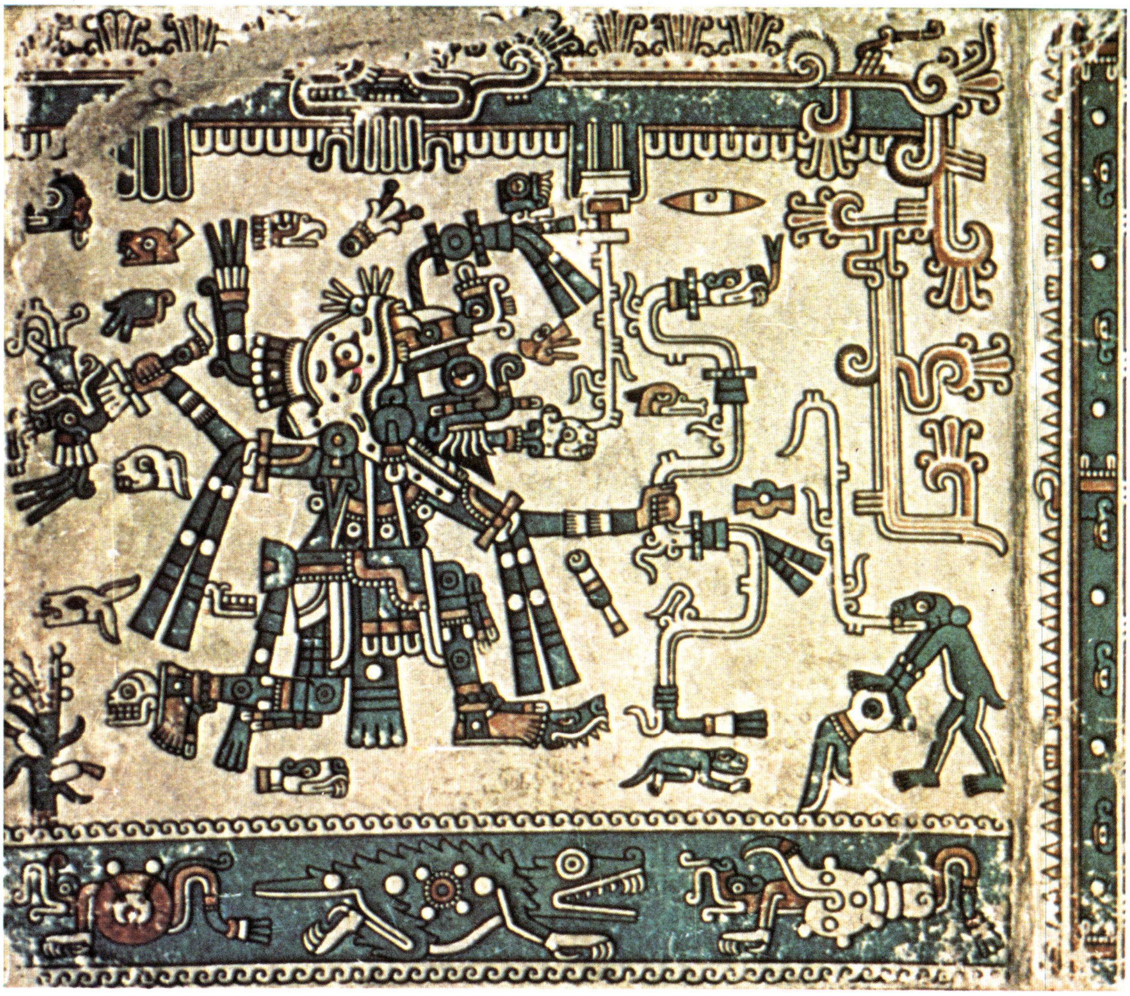

RIGHT An image of the rain-making god, known as Tlaloc in Nahua, who is celebrated for his capacity to bring together the waters above and the waters below. His assistant is the lizard-frog of Sign IV; standing opposite a maize plant, he pours out a jar of water. Shell-fish, reptiles and fish in the water below also act in concert by frothing up the water. From the Laud screenfold.

BELOW A 14th-century image of Tlaloc, from Mixtec territory around Oaxaca. He is readily identifiable by his mask, with its long drooling teeth and its goggling frog eyes.

The Precious Bones

As in the Maya tradition, maize appears as a man-like creature in the Toltec screenfolds and the maize-god Cinteotl is portrayed as both plant and man. However, the chief extant Nahua myth about the creation of man (in another part of the manuscript which contains the Legend of the Suns) ascribes to him another original substance, bone-meal. The god Quetzalcoatl, while passing from west to east as the planet Venus, encountered Mictlantecuhtli, the Lord of the Dead Land, the underworld, and asked him for the 'precious bones' or manioc, from which man was to be made. He was asked: 'What do you want to do with them, Quetzalcoatl?' He answered: 'What worries the gods is who shall live on earth.' The Dead Land Lord gave him a conch to blow and told him to carry the bones four times round a jade circle, but the conch was blocked up. Quetzalcoatl summoned the worms, which hollowed it out, and the bees, which forced their way through it. He blew the conch and the Dead Land Lord told him to take the bones, but instructed his vassals to order Quetzalcoatl to leave them in the underworld. On the advice of his *nahual* (his animal form, or double) Quetzalcoatl pretended to have left the bones.

But then he really went back up, clutching the
precious bones, male bones on the one side,
female on the other.
He took them and wrapped them up,
and took them with him.

And the Dead Land Lord again spoke to his
vassals:
'O gods, is Quetzalcoatl really taking the bones?
Dig him a pit.'

They dug him one; he stumbled and fell in,
And Quails menaced him and he fainted.
He dropped the precious bones and the Quails tore
and pecked at them.

And then Quetzalcoatl came to and weeps and
says to his *nahual*:
'O my *nahual*, what now?'
And the reply came:
'What now? Things went badly; let it be.'

Quetzalcoatl gathered the bits, wrapped them in a bundle and took them with him. The bits were ground up by the goddess Cihuacoatl (Woman Snake). Then she placed the meal in a jade bowl and Quetzalcoatl dropped blood on it by piercing his penis. Mankind was made from the ground bone-meal.

Despite the tricks played on him, Quetzalcoatl succeeds in fetching the 'precious bones' of his buried father from the underworld, a service to men which they repay by worship and penance. The bleeding of the penis, a penance prescribed in Toltec religion, is intimately related to the blood-cults for which the Aztecs became so odious in Spanish eyes. There is another level of meaning in the story, however, at

LEFT A stone statue of the type known as 'chacmool' seen before the columns of the Temple of the Warriors, Chichen Itza, Yucatan. The design of both the chacmool and the nearest two columns is definitive of Toltec architecture, found here deep in Maya territory as a result of invasions around AD 1000. The two columns, 'coatlaquetzalli', also found at Tula in Mexico, consist of snakes with jaw thrust on to the ground and tail arched forward as beam-bearers.

BELOW LEFT A smiling skeleton in fired clay, made by the Totonacs, neighbours of the Huaxtec on the Gulf Coast. Its form is characteristic of the lord of the Middle American underworld, Mictlantecuhtli in Nahua.

which the 'bones' are understood to be manioc, a vegetable, like the maize of Maya myth. Quetzalcoatl's blood is then also the heat needed to rid the vegetable of its volatile poison.

Other Middle American accounts of the creation of man concern themselves less with the substance of which he is made than with the place at which he first appeared and his arrival on earth. With this emphasis, the Vienna screenfold, from the Mixtec town of Tilantongo, lays claim to the territory occupied by that people. The ancestors of the Mixtecs – or better, of their ruling class – are shown emerging from a body which is both vegetable and human and which serves as the place-sign for Apoala, at the heart of Mixtec territory. Naked like Adam and Eve, the Mixtec ancestors stake their claim through this place-sign and through the fact that the whole event is witnessed by Quetzalcoatl.

Rain-Makers

In the Toltec tradition the master of rain and water is Tlaloc. He has goggle-eyes and a toothy mouth (like the rain-god doll of the Hopi further to the north). Finding favour with the rain-gods is an occupation as old as agriculture itself, and throughout Middle America Tlaloc-like figures appear on stone carvings and other texts of great antiquity. Tlaloc's great power is to bring down the waters above, as in the Flood which ended the first world-age. The Laud screenfold portrays him as the one with this power on a page which makes use of all the Twenty Signs of ritual. In his hands he holds the Snake (V) of lightning; his mouth utters a Jaguar (XIV) roar – thunder, which has its House (III) in the sky and which traps the Wind (II) proper to his rival Quetzalcoatl, to produce the static atmosphere in which Rain (XIX)

BELOW An Aztec model of Xipe-Totec dressed in the flayed skin of a sacrificial victim, as he appeared during the agricultural festival of Tlacaxipeualiztli. The two layers of skin represent vegetal renewal.

The 'Feather-Snake' or Quetzalcoatl figure of Middle American religion, represented as a basalt monolith. Aztec.

will fall (the sign Rain is Tlaloc's mask, which indicates his function).

In the religion of the Toltecs, and even more of the Aztecs, Tlaloc's rain was not freely given. It was bargained for, in exchange for the blood of sacrificed victims whose flowing tears would simulate and so stimulate the flow of rain. Before dying, the victim would imagine his journey up to Tlalocan, the 'house of quetzal plumes', Tlaloc's abode at the heart of the sky, passing on the way through the 'place of the unfleshed', the abode of 'the frightening prince' or the Dead Land Lord. This underworld is distant by four days, or four years in spirit-time, from the western horizon. In one of the *Twenty Sacred Hymns of the Aztecs* he says:

My brother, Tozcuecuexi,
I am going forever, it's the time of weeping,
send me to wherever it is.
Under his command I have already said
to the frightening prince I am going forever;
it is time for weeping.
Over four years we shall be carried on the wind,
unknown to others by you it is told,
to the place of the unfleshed.
In the house of quetzal plumes
transformation is effected;
it is the due of the one who vivifies men.

Among the lowland Maya of Yucatan and Peten (northern Guatemala), rain-gods have a less sanguinary aspect. Long-nosed creatures known as Chacs, they carry the axes of thunder and lightning like Tlaloc, but are associated less with clouds and the heart of the sky than with the moist coastal winds of Yucatan. In the Dresden screenfold they are 'walkers in the maize fields', who help the farmer with his digging and sowing. They were believed to be expert in the knowledge of fish-manure and on incised bones found in a 7th-century tomb at Tikal the Chacs actually appear as fishermen, wearing bird head-dresses and wielding tackle.

Quetzalcoatl of Tula

The motif of the snake and the bird is one of the most ancient in Middle America, an expression of the lowly and the high, the sexual and the spiritual conjoined. The name Quetzal-coatl, feather-snake, directly evokes this notion, the quetzal being a bird uniquely valued for its feathers. In Nahua the name also means 'precious twin', an allusion to Quetzalcoatl's role as the planet Venus appearing on both the west and the east horizons. In addition to being a major actor in Middle American cosmogonies, Quetzalcoatl has close links with the city of Tula, the capital of the Toltecs. Born of Itztli (Obsidian), but of uncertain fatherhood, Quetzalcoatl arrives there as a mysterious stranger with a 'craggy face'. Always pious, he becomes famous for his rejection of human sacrifice. He is also the great 'culture-bringer' and inventor, the originator of the city's artistic wealth, woven textiles, feather-work, jade, gold, superior strains of plants like cotton, and the arts of dancing, painting and writing.

Quetzalcoatl's position at Tula did not go undisputed. Rivals within the city, militarist in tendency, harass, shame and drive him out. The story of his disgrace is told at length in the Florentine Codex. Made drunk by his enemy, the warrior-sorcerer Tezcatlipoca, Quetzalcoatl sinks to incest with his sister and self-disgust. Leaving Tula, he travels through the snow-covered mountains to the southeast and finally disappears on a raft of woven snakes. Other Nahua accounts of his departure from

ABOVE Alternating masks of Tlaloc, the rain-maker, and his opponent in highland Mexico, Quetzalcoatl, the drying wind. The masks II and XIX of the Twenty signs, are set into the outer walls of the 'Quetzalcoatl' pyramid. From the southern end of the great causeway at Teotihuacan, 6th century.

BELOW Pottery whistle figurine representing a bound sacrificial victim, offering his own heart. From Teotihuacan.

Tula deal less with the human drama and more with its significance in geography and astronomy. The route he travels is traced eastwards past Cholula to the Nahua outposts of Xicalanco and Acallan, at the Maya frontier. In the *Annals of Cuauhtitlan* he is said to have burned himself to death there, at the 'Land of the Black and Red'. In a passage of extraordinary beauty his heart, burned to incandescence, becomes the planet Venus, among embers which scintillate as bird plumage, and the earthly hero thus regains celestial power.

'When they reached the place they were searching for, now again there he wept and suffered. In this year 1 Reed (so it is told, so it is said), when he had reached the ocean shore, the edge of the sky-water, he stood up, wept, took his attire and put on his plumes, his precious mask. When he was dressed, of his own accord he burned himself, he gave himself to the fire. So that where Quetzalcoatl burned himself is called the Place of Incineration.

And it is said that when he burned, his ashes rose up and every kind of precious bird appeared and could be seen rising up to the sky: roseate spoonbill, cotinga, trogon, blue heron, yellow parrot, scarlet macaw, white-fronted parrot, and all other precious birds. And after he had become ash the quetzal bird's heart rose up; it could be seen and was known to enter the sky. The old men would say he had become Venus; and it is told that when the star appeared Quetzalcoatl died. From now on he was called the Lord of the Dawn.'

An obvious question about these accounts is how far they reflect historical events. There is no doubt that upheavals in Tula towards the end of the 1st millennium AD resulted in an exodus from the city along exactly the route Quetzalcoatl is said to have taken, and in Toltec penetration of Yucatan. Maya texts record this invasion and associate it with a figure called Kukulcan (which is Quetzalcoatl in Yucatec), but they give a very different view of the hero. He is not so much the victim as the propagator of militarism, possibly because near-contemporaries from Tula shared the same name. In any case, as far as the Toltecs themselves are concerned, the Quetzalcoatl who mattered was the god who set an example of self-sacrifice and who endowed Tula with its wealth and civilization.

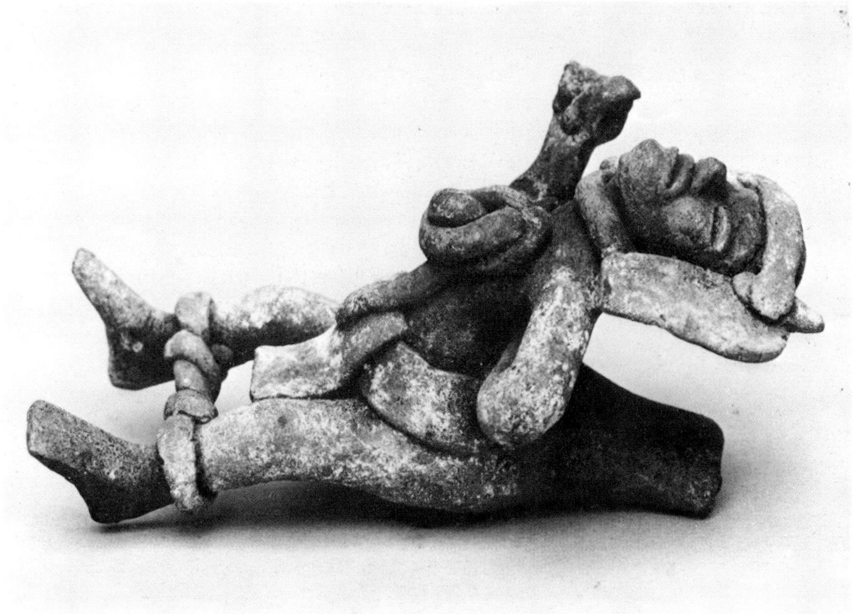

ABOVE A Gulf-Coast brazier, appropriately upheld by the Fire God, who is both the youngest of the gods as Xiuhtecutli and, as here, the oldest, Huehueteotl, the 'Old God'. Note the well-articulated fingers, which serve to perform the act that first distinguished man from other animals: kindling fire by means of a fire-drill.

RIGHT A massive Aztec sculpture of the fearsome and earthy goddess Coatlicue, mother of the immaculately conceived Huitzilopochtli. Like the Sun Stone, it was found at the centre of Tenochtitlan. As well as the woven 'snake-skirt' of her name, Coatlicue wears a necklace of hearts and hands. Her head may be seen as single or double, in a visual pun typical of native American art.

War-Lords

Quetzalcoatl's principal rival at Tula, Tezcatlipoca, is another of the great gods of the Toltec pantheon. His name means 'mirror' or 'glinting' (*tezcatli*) 'smoke' (*poca*), a quality proper to him as the shaman who 'sees all' and can therefore instigate strife. He is club-footed because, as the Great Bear constellation, his 'leg' came to dip below the horizon, in the view of the Nahuas as they moved south into the tropics. Portrayed in the Borgia, his deformity is covered up by the mirror-smoke of his name, and his untied umbilical cord reminds us that he was born as he is here: fully-armed, the paragon of the Toltec warrior. Like Tlaloc, his particular powers are specified by the Twenty Signs in the screenfolds. They indicate the sharpness of his death-dealing spear, his speed and his keenness of eye. The Snake (V) of potency protrudes from his loins. The Eagle (XV) at his head and the Jaguar (XIV) at his foot are the emblems of the two military orders of the Toltecs. On his breast is the sacrificer's Flint Knife (XVIII) and on his banner is Rabbit (VIII), the sign of the captive victim. His shield protects Vulture (XVI), emblem of merchants and trade, and behind him the House (III) or sanctuary of the settled community is safeguarded.

Tezcatlipoca served as a model for other war-gods of ancient Mexico, notably for the Aztec hero Huitzilopochtli. In the Aztecs' account of their migrations from Aztlan (somewhere in northern Mexico or the southern United States), when they were poor and despised, Huitzilopochtli is an unprepossessing character, carried with them along the road. This is how he appears in the Boturini screenfold, bundled up like a mascot and with a modest Hummingbird (*huitzilin*) disguise. When they attained power in Tenochtitlan, however, the Aztecs provided the world with a much grander image of the patron who had urged them on to glory. He was made into a solar god and was given a sanctuary next to Tlaloc's atop the Great Pyramid at Tenochtitlan. He was also said to have been miraculously conceived by Coatlicue (Snake Skirt), the earth-mother, who was impregnated by a ball of fluff or down when she was sweeping. Her family felt dishonoured by her unexplained fat belly and swore to kill her. As they closed in, Huitzilopochtli leaped out of Coatlicue's womb, fully armed like Tezcatlipoca, and slew them to a man. This feat has the solar analogy of sunrise 'killing' the stars and epitomizes the power to strike instantly and definitely.

In his annals of Tenochtitlan and the Valley of Mexico, the Nahua author Chimalpahin, writing about 1600, discussed this transformation of Huitzilopochtli from tribal mascot to sun-king. He showed how the Aztecs (like the imperialists of our own century) deliberately created and reshaped myths for political ends. In this respect, Huitzilopochtli is especially notable as one who was claimed to have been conceived miraculously. The moral and kinship problems caused by this special origin are resolved in his tremendous martial energy alone, this being provoked by doubts about legitimacy which are never explicitly denied.

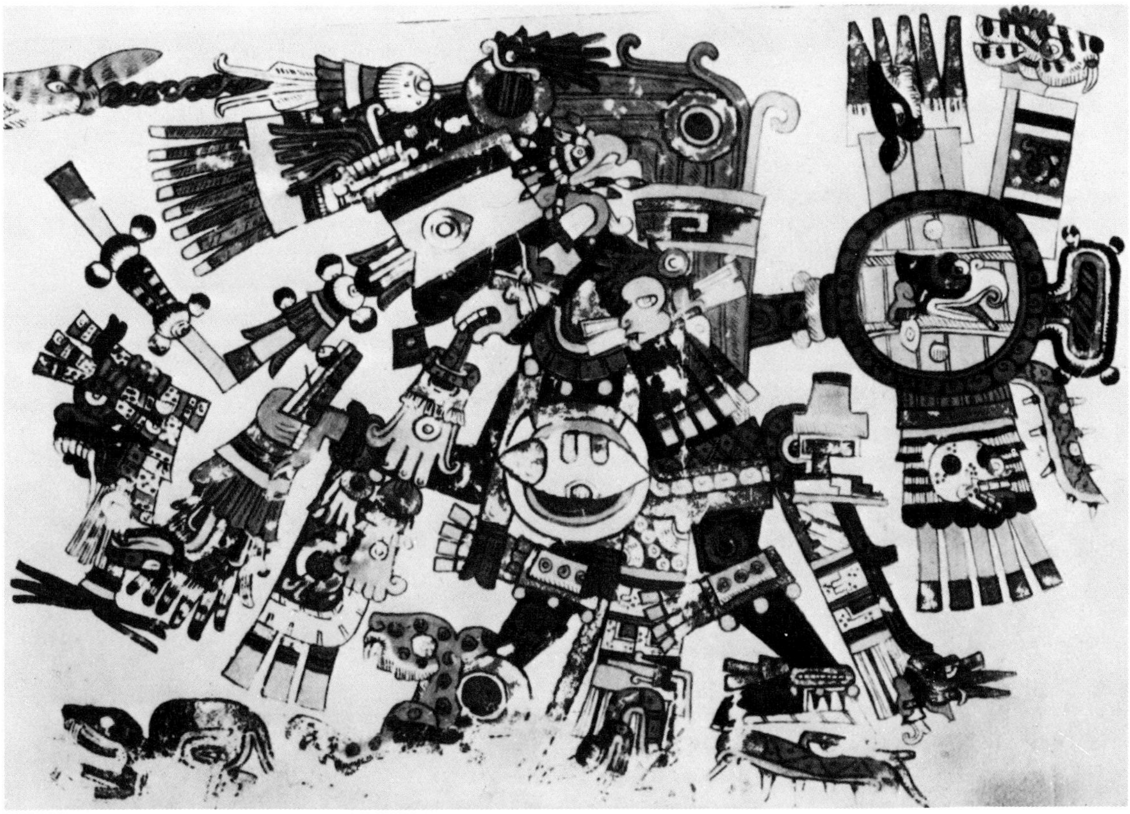

LEFT The Toltec warrior Tezcatlipoca, 'Mirror Smoke'. Like that of Tlaloc, Tezcatlipoca's might is celebrated through the Twenty Signs of ritual, so arranged as to specify the powers particular to him. From the Borgia screenfold.

ABOVE Pottery figurine showing a woman and child. Note the woman's finely woven skirt and her ear plugs, a mark of nobility. Some authorities regard this as a representation of Chalchihuitlicue, a water-goddess and consort of Tlaloc.

PRINCIPAL GODS

The following are some of the principal figures among the numerous deities of the Maya in Yucatan and Guatemala; of the Toltecs, a Nahua people from the north, who settled in central Mexico and founded the city of Tollan (modern Tula); and of the Aztecs, another northern Nahua people, who moved into central Mexico in the 12th century AD, founded their capital city of Tenochtitlan (Mexico City) and eventually built up an empire, adopting many of the gods and myths of the peoples they subdued. Except for Huitzilopochtli, the Nahua deities listed here were common to both the Toltecs and the Aztecs.

Chac (Maya): long-nosed rain-gods of Yucatan; the name also means 'red' or 'large'

Chalchihuitlicue, 'Jade Skirt' (Nahua): goddess of fresh water, rivers and lakes, consort of Tlaloc

Cihuacoatl, 'Woman Snake' (Nahua): goddess of childbirth

Cinteotl, 'Maize God' (Nahua): perfect incarnation of maize

Coatlicue, 'Snake Skirt' (Nahua): one of many earth-goddesses, mother of Huitzilopochtli; as a mother-goddess represented with a child in her arms

Gucumatz, 'Feather Snake' (Quiche-Maya): a major creator-god, counterpart of Quetzalcoatl

Huitzilopochtli, 'Hummingbird on the Left' (Nahua): sinister Aztec war-deity, god of the sun as patron of the Aztec empire

Hunab Ku, 'One God' (Maya): creator-deity of Yucatan

Itzamna, 'Iguana House' (Maya): lord of the heavens and culture hero, son of Hunab Ku

Itztli, 'Obsidian' (Nahua): the sacrificial Flint Knife (XVIII of the Twenty Signs), associated with the birth of the earthly Quetzalcoatl

Kukulcan, 'Feather Snake' (Maya): counterpart of the historical Quetzalcoatl

Mictlantecuhtli, 'Dead Land Lord' (Nahua): ruler of the underworld, through which the soul must pass after death

Quetzalcoatl, 'Feather Snake' or 'Precious Twin' (Nahua): a creator-god, identified with the planet Venus; also a priestly ruler and culture hero of Tula, about AD 900; god of the wind (his mask is Wind, II in the Twenty Signs)

Tezcatlipoca, 'Mirror Smoke' (Nahua): warrior-sorcerer figure; historical opponent of Quetzalcoatl at Tula

Tlaloc, 'the One Who Makes Things Sprout' (Nahua): controller of thunder and rain (his mask is Rain, XIX in the Twenty Signs)

Tlazolteotl, 'Dirt Goddess' (Nahua): an earth-goddess and goddess of love, also known as 'Mother of the Gods'

Tohil (Quiche-Maya): counterpart of Tlaloc

Tonatiuh (Nahua): the sun, also known as Pilzintecutli, 'Royal Lord'

Xipe, 'the Flayed One' (Nahua): god of vegetation; his priests put on the flayed skins of sacrificed captives to simulate new growth on the earth

Xiuhtecutli, 'Year Lord' or 'Fire Lord' (Nahua): god of fire and primal god of ritual and the calendar, also known to the Aztecs as Huehueteotl, 'Old God'

Xochipilli, 'Flower Prince' (Nahua): god of flowers, feasting and pleasure

Xochiquetzal, 'Flower Feather' (Nahua): goddess of flowers and craftsmen

Yum Kaax, 'Forest Lord' (Maya): maize-god, counterpart of Cinteotl

CHAPTER TWENTY-FIVE

THE INCAS

The Andes mountains of South America have witnessed the rise and fall of many civilizations in the last 3000 years. That of the Incas developed relatively recently, for they embarked on their imperial expansion from their base in the Cuzco valley less than 100 years before the execution of their emperor by the Spanish conquistadors in 1533. None of the South American civilizations possessed the art of writing and our knowledge of pre-Incaic culture rests mainly on archeological evidence. Inca culture at the time of the Spanish conquest, however, was documented in detail by the Spanish chroniclers, whose concern with Christian evangelization direced their attention in particular to the 'idolatrous' beliefs and rituals of the people they encountered. Much of the mythology of the Cuzco region which they recorded appears to have been assembled under Inca supervision around the middle of the 15th century as the empire expanded.

The Creation

The place of creation in Inca myth is the area around Lake Titicaca, 150 kilometres southeast of Cuzco. It is quite possible that the original Inca tribe migrated from here to the Cuzco valley in the 12th century. The architectural style of the Incas was similar to that of the famous ceremonial centre of Tihuanaco, close to Lake Titicaca, which dates from around AD 500 and which was already in ruins at the time of the Incas. All versions of the creation story unite into a single scheme the various myths of origin, languages and cultures of the different peoples which were brought under Inca domination.

As one version has it, the god Viracocha created the earth and the sky and peopled the earth with men. There was no sun and the people walked in darkness. But they disobeyed their Creator and he chose to destroy them, turning some into stones and drowning the rest in a flood which rose above the highest

mountains in the world. The only survivors were a man and a woman who remained in a box and who, when the waters subsided, were carried by the wind to Tihuanaco, the chief abode of the Creator. There he raised up all the people and nations, making figures of clay and painting the clothes that each nation was to wear. To each nation he gave a language, songs and the seeds they were to sow. Then he breathed life and soul into the clay and ordered each nation to pass under the earth and to emerge in the place he directed. Some came out of caves, others from hills, others from fountains, others from the trunks of trees. Each nation made a shrine of the place from which it had issued.

As it was dark the Creator made the sun, moon and stars and ordered them to go to the island of Titicaca, in the lake of the same name, and thence to rise to heaven. When the sun, in the form of a man, was ascending into heaven, it called to the Incas and to their chief Manco Capac and said: 'Thou and thy descendants are to be Lords, and are to subjugate many nations. Look upon me as thy father, and thou shalt be my children, and thou shalt worship me as thy father.' With these words he gave to Manco Capac a headdress for his insignia and a battle-axe for his arms. At this point the sun, moon and stars were commanded to ascend to heaven and to fix themselves in their places, and they did so. At the same instant Manco Capac and his brothers and sisters, by command of the Creator, descended under the earth and came out again in the cave of Pacaritampo, at the point where the sun rose on the first day after the Creator had divided night from day. (Adapted from Molina, 1573.)

This myth has obvious parallels with the story of Noah's Ark and the possibility of Christian influence cannot be discounted. The notion of a primeval cataclysm, however, is undoubtedly native to the region. It recurs in various forms in contemporary Andean mythology; in the Q'ero origin myth quoted later it is attributed to the power of the sun, which significantly is here no longer regarded as the originator of the Inca lineage.

The Journeys of Viracocha

After the sun had emerged from the island of Titicaca there came from the south a white man, large of stature, who aroused much respect and veneration. He had great powers, making plains of the hills, and of the plains high mountains, and brought forth springs in the living rock. He instructed people how they should live, exhorting them to be good and not to do one another harm or injury. He passed northwards over the highlands and was never seen again. This was Viracocha.

ABOVE Machu Picchu, the Inca city which the Spaniards never found and which was discovered only in 1911, in a near-perfect state of preservation. It is situated in a saddle with precipitous drops on either side, and is dominated by the peak of Huayna Picchu. The houses and temples of the city are set amidst elaborate agricultural terracing. Machu Picchu is one of a chain of Inca settlements in the temperate Urubamba valley which probably served the emperor as luxurious pleasure resorts.

OPPOSITE This *kero*, or wooden beaker, would probably have been used for ceremonial libations. The decorations suggest associations with a cult of the birds. Late Inca period.

Some time later a similar man was seen, who wherever he went healed the sick and restored sight to the blind with only the words he spoke. But as he approached a village called Cacha the people rose up and prepared to stone him. As they drew near he knelt and raised his eyes to heaven as though imploring divine aid. At that moment a great fire appeared in the sky. Filled with fear and trembling the people crowded towards him and begged him to have mercy and save them. The man ordered the fire to cease and it went out, but the flames had so scorched the stones that even today the largest ones are as light as cork.

The man passed on from Cacha to the seashore where, spreading his cloak, he moved on it over the waves, and never again appeared. (Adapted from Cieza de León, 1553.)

As with the creation story, the myths relating the earthly travels of Viracocha incorporate into their narratives existing features of the landscape such as ruins and unusual rock formations. The stones at Cacha are in fact cinders and lava from the volcano at Tinta. Other myths in the cycle tell how Viracocha was refused food and drink by a wedding party and in retaliation turned the revellers into stone. Certain rock outcrops are still explained by the highlanders with reference to this story.

Andean Indians are dark-skinned and grow no facial hair. Theories concerning the European or Asiatic provenance of the white-skinned, bearded Viracocha go back much further than modern speculations; some Spaniards believed that St Thomas the Apostle had visited the Andes, a suggestion which the chronicler Cieza de León scornfully rejected. What is certain is that the bearded conquistadors who captured Atahualpa were at first hailed as gods, *viracochas*, by the partisans of his rival Huáscar, who were making sacrifices for the deliverance of their leader from the hands of Atahualpa's generals. The greed and brutality of the

CHRONOLOGICAL TABLE

*c.*1200	Inca group of tribes settles in Cuzco valley in Andes mountains: start of Inca dynasty with chieftain Manco Capac
*c.*1200–1400	Reigns of semi-legendary Inca rulers: intermittent raids and wars between Incas and neighbouring tribes, but no permanent conquests
*c.*1400–1438	Reign of Viracocha Inca: Incas ally with Lupaca of Lake Titicaca area: Quechua tribe, neighbours and allies of Incas, defeated by the Chanca: Viracocha Inca's son, Pachacuti, repulses and defeats Chanca: Incas now in position of power
1438–71	Reign of Pachacuti Inca: city of Cuzco rebuilt: concerted military expansion begins: empire extended southeast to Lake Titicaca, northwards to Quito, westwards to the coast: Quechua imposed as common language
1471–1527	Military expansion continues: southern boundary of empire fixed at about 35°S· Ecuadorian highlands north of Quito conquered: the Inca empire consolidated
1528–32	Civil war between Inca half-brothers Huáscar and Atahualpa: capture of Huáscar by Atahualpa's generals
1532	Atahualpa captured at Cajamarca by Pizarro and Spanish conquistadors
1533	Huáscar assassinated on Atahualpa's orders: Atahualpa executed by Pizarro
1533–72	Spanish conquest of Inca empire
1553	Publication of *Parte Primera de la Crónica del Perú* by Pedro de Cieza de León
1573	Publication of *Relación de los Fábulas y Ritos de los Incas* by Cristobal de Molina (of Cuzco)

ABOVE A monolithic statue at Tihuanaco, Bolivia, the mythical place of origin of the Incas.

RIGHT The Gateway of the Sun at Tihuanaco, cut from a solid block of lava. The central carved figure at the top is generally held to represent the creator-god Viracocha.

Spaniards soon led to their being reclassified as 'devils'. The word *viracocha*, however, is today a polite term of address used by Quechua speakers towards men of higher social status.

The Foundation of Cuzco

From the cave at Pacaritampo there emerged three brothers and three sisters. They were dressed in long blankets and shirts of the finest wool, and had many gold vessels. One of the brothers, Ayar Cachi, was so brave and strong that he levelled the hills with his sling and shot stones to the clouds. His brothers were jealous of him and deceived him into returning to the cave to retrieve a goblet of gold. When he was in the cave they blocked the entrance with stones and trapped him inside the mountain. They then founded the settlement of Tampo Kiru.

The two brothers, full of remorse at what they had done to Ayar Cachi, suddenly saw him come flying through the air on great wings of coloured feathers. They tried to run away but he said, 'Don't be afraid; I come only that the empire of the Incas shall begin to be known. Therefore leave this settlement and go farther down until you come to a valley where you will found Cuzco. And as I shall always pray to God so that you may quickly achieve great power, in a nearby hill I shall remain in the form you now see, and it shall always be sanctified and reverenced by you and your descendants, and the name you shall give it is Huanacauri. The sign you will display from now on to be esteemed, honoured and feared is that you pierce your ears in the manner you now see me.' When he said this, they saw that he was wearing gold earrings.

The brothers went to the hill called Huanacauri and at the peak they saw Ayar Cachi once more, who told them that those who were to be invested as knights and considered nobles should assume the fringe or crown of the empire. When Ayar Cachi had said this he and another brother were turned into two figures of stone. The third took his sisters and came to where Cuzco now stands, and called himself thenceforth Manco Capac, meaning king and rich lord. There he founded the new city, the beginning of which was a little stone house covered with thatch which he called Coricancha, 'enclosure of gold'. There were many other tribes living in the

The walls of the temple of Coricancha, 'enclosure of gold', in Cuzco, now supporting the sanctuary of the Dominican church. Coricancha was the richest booty of the Spanish conquest. Its walls were covered in sheets of gold, and in its gardens the plants, animals, people, even the lumps of soil, were all wrought in gold and silver. In its inner sanctuary was kept a huge gold disc representing the Sun, Inti. The walls are a triumph of Inca masonry; in 1950 an earthquake reduced the Dominican church to rubble (it was later rebuilt), but the walls of Coricancha stood firm.

The shrine of Intihuatana, 'hitching place of the Sun', at Machu Picchu. Many Inca cities contained shrines of this kind, which served as solar observatories and as sacrificial altars.

PRINCIPAL INCA DEITIES

Viracocha, the Creator, being without beginning or end, the 'incomprehensible god' who created the universe, all other supernatural beings, animals, plants, men and women: also a culture hero who instructed human beings in the arts of civilization: human manifestation in myth usually as a bearded white-skinned man, dressed in a long tunic: the gold statue of him in Cuzco was the size of a boy of ten, 'in the shape of a man standing up, the right arm raised and the hand almost closed, the fingers and thumb raised as one who was giving an order'.

Inti, the Sun, divine ancestor of the Inca dynasty: usually regarded as male, represented by large gold discs with rays and human face: focus of official Inca ceremonial, though this was directed to other sky-gods as well.

Ilyap'a, the Weather God, male deity usually associated with thunder and identified with a constellation: pictured as a man in the sky with a sling, who made rain fall by shattering with his slingshot a pitcher of water held by his sister: the crack of his sling was the thunder, his slingshot the lightning bolt.

Kilya, the Moon, female deity, wife of the Sun: originally brighter than the Sun, who in mythology threw ashes in her face to outshine her: she was mainly of importance in the calendar.

Huacas (Shrines), generic term for all other supernatural beings or forces associated with material objects and having local spheres of influence: mountains, trees, lakes, streams and unusual rock formations might be regarded as *huacas*, as well as places associated with myths and legends: there were 500 *huacas* in the immediate vicinity of the city of Cuzco alone.

region of Cuzco but Manco Capac did them no harm; for their part they did not interfere with him, but rather were pleased with him.

Manco Capac attracted many people to his service with love and kind words. When he died a statue of him was made and he was worshipped as a child of the sun. (Adapted from Cieza de León, 1553.)

The cycle of myths relating the activities of Manco Capac and his brothers and sisters after their emergence from the cave of Pacaritampo ('camp of origin') establishes the prerogatives of the Inca ruling class, such as the sister-marriage of the emperor himself and the various ornaments and insignia of his warrior nobles. The latter's investiture rites included a pilgrimage to the hill of Huanacauri. In some versions Manco Capac chooses the site of Cuzco with the aid of a golden staff which he uses to test the fertility of the soil. It is interesting that the version quoted above, despite the warlike pretensions of Ayar Cachi, stresses the peaceful nature of the initial colonization; indeed such was the reputation of the Incas in the 15th century that many tribes capitulated to them without a fight.

Viracocha and Inti

Students of Andean history are agreed that a fundamental reworking of Inca mythology took place around the time of the accession of the ruler Pachacuti in 1438, but they disagree as to the nature of this reformation. Pachacuti's victory over the Chanca, which left the Incas poised for imperial expansion, was said to have been preceded by a vision of a figure dressed like the Inca with serpents twined around his arms and pumas between his legs and around his shoulders. The figure told Pachacuti that he would conquer many nations. According to John Rowe, this vision was subsequently said to be that of Viracocha, with the institution of whose cult Pachacuti is usually credited. The introduction of a creator-god into the pantheon over and above the more ancient Inca deities of the Sun and the shrine of Huanacauri was a sophisticated attempt to formulate a pluralistic theology more suited to an expanding empire. Rowe cites evidence that Viracocha was originally a local creator-god, or *huaca*, of the people in the Urcos area, 20 kilometres from Cuzco, whose name the eighth ruler assumed after it had appeared to him in a vision, and which was converted by Inca intellectuals into a universal deity.

Franklin Pease, on the other hand, argues that the idea of this type of creator-god was pre-Incaic and was associated in particular with the great coastal sanctuary of Pachacámac, south of Lima. He maintains that Pachacuti's vision was of the sun-god, which usurped the preeminent position of Viracocha in the spiritual hierarchy as a prelude to the Incas' military conquests. Pease maintains that this usurpation was symbolized in legend by Pachacuti's wresting of power from his ineffectual father, the namesake of the creator-god. The disappearance of the solar cult with the demise of the Inca ruling class in the Spanish conquest is seen as evidence for its relatively recent imposition on the subject peoples by an imperial elite.

Contemporary Andean Mythology

Through all the vicissitudes of political and religious domination of the Andean peoples, first by the Incas and then by the Spaniards, it is the local cults of the *huacas*, rather than those of the Creator or the Sun, which have shown most resilience. The Incas, however, have not been forgotten and the figure of Inkarí (the word is a compound of Inca and *rey*, Spanish for king) is an important element in contemporary Andean mythology.

According to a myth collected in the community of Q'ero, near Cuzco, there was a time when the sun did not exist and the earth was populated by powerful primeval men. Roal, the creator-spirit and chief of the mountain spirits (Apus), offered to invest these primeval men with his power. They responded that they had their own and needed no other. In annoyance, Roal created the sun and ordered it to rise; its light blinded them and its heat dried up their bodies. But they did not die, and today they sometimes come out of their refuges at sunset or at the times of the new moon.

The Apus then created a man and a woman, Inkarı and Collari. They gave to the former a golden crowbar and to the latter a spindle, as symbols of power and industriousness. Inkarí had received orders to found a great city in the place where, when it was thrown, the bar would remain upright. He tried the first time and it fell badly. The second time it fell at an angle but he nevertheless decided to build a town, which was Q'ero. But the conditions were not propitious and in the same region he built a capital, Tampo.

The Apus, annoyed at Inkarí's disobedience, allowed the primeval men to come to life again. Full of envy of Inkarí, they rolled blocks of stone towards him to kill him. Inkarí fled to the region of Titicaca to meditate for a while. Then he returned and threw the bar for a third time. It fell vertically in the centre of a fertile valley, and there he founded Cuzco.

Inkarí's eldest son was sent to populate Q'ero and the rest of his descendants originated the lineage of the Incas. His labour completed, Inkarí together with Collari passed through the land teaching the people his knowledge, finally disappearing into the jungle. (Adapted from Núñez del Prado, 1974.)

The primeval beings in this myth are identified with the desiccated pre-Hispanic mummies which can still be found in shallow graves in the mountainsides. Inkarí in Q'ero corresponds closely to the figure of Manco Capac in the Inca dynastic myths. In other areas he is identified with the last emperor, Atahualpa, and acquires millennial significance. One myth relates how Atahualpa's head was cut off by Pizarro, carried to Cuzco and buried. But under the ground, the head is still alive and a body is growing on to it. When it is fully reconstituted the Inca will rise out of the earth, the Spaniards will be driven from the land, and the ancient empire restored.

Two female figurines, the one LEFT in gold and the other RIGHT in silver. Metal objects, such as these were probably made for Incaic religious cults by artisans from the Chimú civilization, which was incorporated into the Inca empire in the mid-15th century. Many aspects of the Inca culture, both their material arts and their religion and mythology, were absorbed from conquered peoples.

CHAPTER TWENTY-SIX

TROPICAL SOUTH AMERICA

The Indians of the tropical forest of South America are tribal peoples whose subsistence includes hunting, gathering, fishing and gardening. They live in small societies, each of which has its own unique set of myths. No set of gods and culture heroes is common to all the Amerindians of this vast area. We are also dealing with mythic worlds where men are animals and animals are men; with such deliberate confusion of identity between the human and animal realms, it is perhaps more relevant to consider the symbolic values of the anaconda or the jaguar than the adventures of their human counterparts. The anaconda, for instance, is often depicted as Master of Cultivated Plants and the jaguar as Master of Fire. Although the gods, culture heroes and other mythic beings vary from one society to another, one can talk generally about South American mythology. Claude Lévi-Strauss, the noted French anthropologist, has shown that the myths from one society are but a transformation of those from another, being modified in an orderly way by variations in understanding of the world and differences in social organization. As we move from one Amerindian culture to the next, the myths of one are understandable in terms of the other in so far as they both embody a set of common concerns and entail a common logic.

Very generally speaking, myths from South American jungle societies are complex statements about what there is in this world: they tell what items exist in the universe, how they came to be, and what their nature is. Their main concern is to define the ideal or harmonic relations which must hold among such items for society to be. For society to exist, items categorized as dangerous to one another must mingle – men with women, humans with animals, kin with in-laws – and this mingling must follow the proper rule, usually one given by a culture hero of mythic time. As a case in point, the Piaroa myth of the origin of menstruation, quoted later, comments on the danger for men of menstruating women and the consequent necessity for food taboos. A myth of the origin of society, often encountered among South American Indians, tells of the creation, usually from fish, of separate groups of people. In their separateness, the groups existed in an asocial and infertile state. Social life, and thereby fertility, could emerge only through the coming together of these groups; they became one people, though dangerously so, through intermarriage. Among the Shavante of Central Brazil the bond between kin and in-laws is broken again after death; for then one returns to one's own group of origin, which is free from in-laws. Thus dangerous entities are once again separated from one another in the afterworld, and in this separation comes non-life: an eloquent statement in itself on the nature of life.

The myths, then, are concerned with what it means to be human and alive within human society, and it is the inherent dangers of society that are consistently stressed. Social life was made possible through the creation of cultivation, of cooking fire, of cultural artifacts, hunting, the generative powers of man and woman; but in the wake of such creations came not only knowledge and law, but death, disease, cannibalism, misfortune and suffering.

The Origin of Horticulture

This myth comes from the Trio of Surinam and Brazil. The culture hero Paraparawa went fishing at the edge of the river. At first he caught nothing, but at long last he caught a small fish, called *waraku*. As he caught it, it hit the ground behind him and flopped around. He looked for it, but it had gone. Then he

Roof disc placed on the central pole in a dancing house of the Wayana Indians, who live on the border of Surinam and French Guiana. South American Indians often view their houses as microcosms of the universe, and the disc depicts mythologically significant creatures from the universe's three domains – land, sky and water. Represented are the bushy-tailed ant bear, the turtle, the fish, morocoto, a fishing bird, and two double-headed caterpillars which are said to cut off and devour human heads.

heard a voice behind him say, 'It is I', and he was startled because his fish had become a woman. The woman, Waraku, said, 'I want to see your village.' So they went, and at that time Paraparawa's village was among the *waruma* reed.

Waraku was surprised when she saw the village and said, 'Where is your food? Where is your drink? Where is your house?' 'I am without a house,' said Paraparawa, 'and my bread is the soft pith inside the *waruma* reed.' Waraku said she had seen enough and they returned to the water. She said, 'Wait a minute, my father is coming, and he is bringing food, bananas, yams, sweet potatoes and yuca.' (Yuca is the staple root plant of many tropical Amerindian societies, from which bread and drink are made.)

When Waraku's father came, Paraparawa first saw the yuca plant. Her father came up and up through the water, and they saw the leaves of the yuca plant coming up out of the water. Waraku's father came as a giant alligator (or sometimes as a large water-snake, probably an anaconda). As he came closer Paraparawa saw his red eyes and was so frightened he ran away. But the woman stayed and took the food plants from her father. Then she gave them all to Paraparawa.

'How shall I fix them?' asked Paraparawa. 'Cut a place for them. Cut a field for them,' answered Waraku. 'Right,' he said, and then he planted them. He planted yuca, bananas and all the other things in his field. They grew. They all grew until they had finished growing. Waraku then told Paraparawa how to make all the utensils needed to make bread from the yuca root, for he was ignorant and did not know about these things, how to cook food. Waraku made bread for Paraparawa, but when he tried some of it he vomited. He was not accustomed to it, but he tried everything; he had to swallow all the new foods. Finally he grew accustomed to eating these things and stopped eating the inside of the *waruma* reed. That is how it was.

When Men Received Fire

This myth comes from the Kayapo-Gorotire of Central Brazil. Noticing that a pair of macaws had built their nest on top of a steep rock, an Indian took his young brother-in-law, Botoque, with him to capture the nestlings. Botoque climbed up an improvised ladder, but he could find only two eggs in the nest. His brother-in-law insisted he take them,

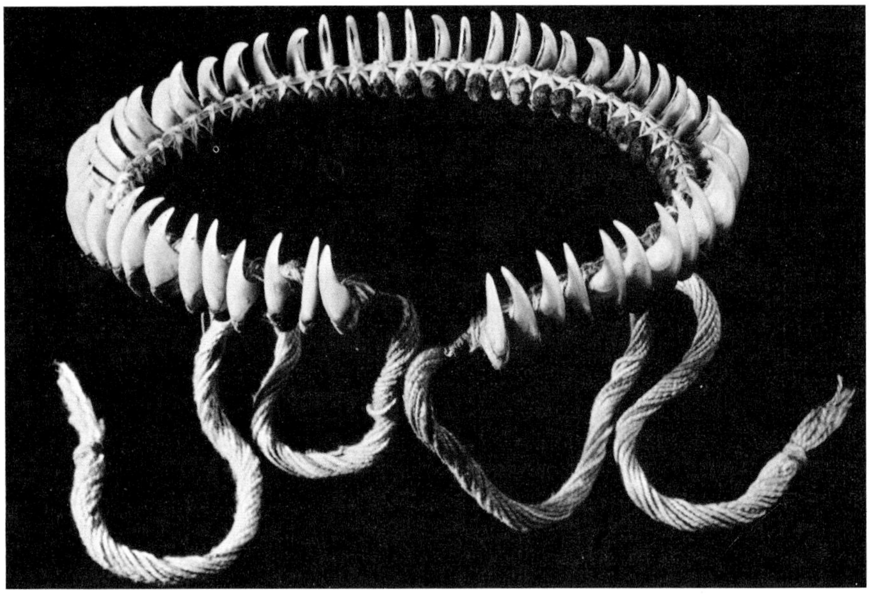

A necklace made of jaguar's teeth, from the Mato Grosso of Brazil. Necklaces such as these are commonly symbols of power for the warrior or shaman. The jaguar is important in the myths of most South American Indians as the giver of hunting and fire and, with them, of society to man. Frequently, the warrior or shaman is said to be able to transform himself into a jaguar.

but as the eggs fell down, they changed into stones which hurt the older man's hand. This made him furious and he dismantled the ladder and went away.

Botoque remained caught on top of the rock for several days. He grew thin; hunger and thirst obliged him to eat his own excrement. Eventually he noticed a spotted jaguar carrying a bow and arrow and all kinds of game. The jaguar saw the hero's shadow and, after trying in vain to catch it, looked up, asked what had happened, repaired the ladder and invited Botoque to come down. Botoque was afraid and hesitated, but in the end he came down and the jaguar, in friendly fashion, suggested that if he would sit astride its back, it would take him to its home to have a meal of grilled meat. In those days the Indians were unacquainted with fire and ate their meat raw. So at the jaguar's house Botoque ate his first meal of cooked meat.

The jaguar's wife, who was an Indian, disliked the young man, but the jaguar, being childless, decided to adopt him. The wife gave him old wizened pieces of meat to eat and scratched him in the face when he complained. The jaguar scolded his wife to no avail. One day it gave Botoque a brand-new bow and some arrows, taught him how to use them and advised him to use them against the woman. Botoque killed her by shooting an arrow into her breast. He fled in terror, taking with him the weapons and a piece of grilled meat.

He reached his village, where he told his tale and shared the meat. The Indians decided to get possession of the fire. When they arrived at the jaguar's home, no one was there and the game caught the day before had not been cooked. They roasted it and took away the fire. For the very first time it was possible for them to eat cooked meat.

But the jaguar, incensed by the ingratitude of his adopted son, who had stolen 'fire and the secret of the bow and arrow', was to remain full of hatred for all living creatures, especially human beings. Now only the reflection of fire could be seen in its eyes. It used its fangs for hunting and ate its meat raw, having solemnly renounced grilled meat. (From Lévi-Strauss, 1969.)

The Jaguar's Son-in-Law

According to the Mundurucu of Northern Brazil, a deer married the daughter of a jaguar, without realizing who she was, because at that time all animals were in human form. One day he decided to pay a call on his parents-in-law. His wife warned him that they were vicious and would want to tickle him. If the deer could not refrain from laughter, he would be devoured.

The deer withstood the ordeal successfully, but he realized that his parents-in-law were jaguars when they brought back a deer they had killed while out hunting, and sat down to eat it.

The next day the deer announced that he would go hunting, and he brought back a dead jaguar. It was now the jaguars' turn to be frightened.

From then on the deer and the jaguars kept a watch on each other. 'How do you sleep?' the jaguar asked his son-in-law. 'With my eyes open,' was the reply, 'and when I am awake I keep my eyes closed. What about you?' 'I do just the opposite.' Consequently the jaguars dared not run away while the deer was asleep, but as soon as he woke up, they thought he was asleep and took flight, while the deer ran off in the opposite direction. (From Lévi-Strauss, 1969.)

The Origin of Menstruation

This myth comes from the Piaroa of the Orinoco Basin in Venezuela. The wives of Wahari, the culture hero, were playing on a swing in the jungle. They were swinging over a ravine, taking turns. Buoka, Wahari's older brother, came and played with them. He had no woman, but enjoyed those of his brother. One after another the women came down to the bottom of the ravine, inviting Buoka to make love with them. Each time Buoka swung across, he made love with a woman. He had a very long penis that he wrapped round his shoulders and he was able to make love from a distance and very often.

Wahari, irritated by his brother's behaviour, transformed himself into a beautiful woman and joined his playing wives. He took his turn on the swing and Buoka, sitting on the bank, sent his penis out to Wahari on the swing and tried to get into him, but there was no opening. The penis hit Wahari on the thigh and on the belly-button, seeking a hole. When it hit Wahari's thighs again, Wahari cut it into five parts until it was down to normal size. Blood flowed from Buoka's penis and he was so sad that he isolated himself in a small house apart from his regular house. He lay in the hammock with his menstruation and brooded, just as a woman does today with her first menstruation.

Wahari went hunting in the mountains, and on the way back he visited his brother, not knowing that Buoka was menstruating. When he saw the small house with smoke coming from it, Wahari cried out, 'Who is there?' 'It is I,' Buoka answered, 'I am menstruating.' Wahari lamented, 'What is going to happen to us? It is not right that men have periods.'

Meanwhile, Wahari's wives went to play again with the swing, but Buoka was not there and they returned home to their hammocks, sad because they could not find him. Wahari returned and told them that Buoka was menstruating. The women jumped from their hammocks and asked, 'Where is he? And where is he menstruating? From the head, the ears, the mouth, from the point of his fingers, from the knees, the feet, the anus, the penis?' They did not know about menstruation.

The women hurried to Buoka's house, where each quickly made love with him. And that is how they received menstruation. Wahari said, 'Now women will have menstruation.'

The women returned to Wahari's house. They began to prepare the game Wahari had brought for eating, but one by one each of them announced that she was menstruating and retired to her hammock. A menstruating woman must not touch the food to be eaten by a man, or he will sicken and die. Wahari said, 'Men should not menstruate; women should.' Therefore all women menstruate and men do not.

Time and Myth

History and myth are one and the same for the Amerindian. Often the myth introduces a pre-mythic state of being, tells of a transformation and in so doing ends in post-mythic time. This transformation from pre-mythic to post-mythic time represents historical time for the Indian, while the post-mythic state of being, described in the myth, is perceived as the proper or inevitable state of present-day life: man eats meat cooked, not raw; jaguar eats meat raw, not cooked.

The following set of myths from the Piaroa of the Orinoco Basin illustrates how myth mediates between pre-mythic and post-mythic time. The first myth, about how the Piaroa lost their hard shiny blue anuses, is the primary one and the rest elucidate its meaning.

A (This is one version of the myth about the culture hero Wahari committing incest with his sister, Cheheru.) Paruna could find no yopo (a common South American hallucinogenic drug) near his house, so he went searching for it. While Paruna was away, Wahari went to visit his sister, Cheheru, who was Paruna's wife, to obtain yopo. He copulated with his sister and afterwards Cheheru removed the yopo plant from her vagina. Paruna had a vision of Wahari grinding the yopo drug, and he saw his wife nearby lying naked in her hammock. He quickly returned home to ask Wahari where he had found this yopo. Wahari answered that it was growing all around the house, which Paruna knew to be a lie. The two brothers-in-law quarrelled over this incestuous affair ever after. When the quarrel began, the Piaroa lost their hard shiny blue anuses.

B (This is part of a lengthy myth about the origin of sleep and also, appropriately enough, about the origin of the sloth.) Wahari created the sloth. He transformed himself into the large sloth and his brother, Buoka, into the small one, so that they could guard the house which contained their sacred musical instruments, the ones which women were not allowed to see. After creating the large sloth Wahari had second thoughts; because of its large head it was too dangerous an animal. To render it harmless he reversed the positions of head and buttocks. When Wahari had first transformed himself into a sloth, the head was where the anus is and the anus where the head is. Thus today the sloth has a small head and it will not eat people.

C Among the Piaroa, blue eyes are associated with the red deer, an incarnation of Buoka, the elder brother of the culture hero, and with the absence of knowledge. Buoka created Wahari and Cheheru by withdrawing his brother from his right eye and his sister from his left eye. In so doing, he withdrew his own thoughts, leaving his eyes blue and empty, and himself in ignorance.

D Finally, throughout Middle and South America mirrors are often a symbol for eyes. The Piaroa have a myth about the large anteater, who creates himself, and to make his eyes he uses mirrors (mica?). Mirrors are shiny and hard, as well as reflecting.

Men of the Kamiura tribe of the Xingu River, Brazil, adorned with ceremonial head-dresses and playing wooden flutes. The yellow head-dresses are symbols of the sun, from which it is often held that men derive their fertility. The sounds of the flutes are the voices of mythical beings.

This unique piece is a cap (or plug) for a ritual flute. The cap is an anthropomorphic representation of the mythological being whose voice is the sound of the flute.

This series of myths sets up the following equivalences:

Blue eyes = ignorance
Mirror (hard, reflecting) = eye
Eye = anus
Buttocks = head
Incest taboo = society/knowledge

With the first myth (A) the significant question is not so much why did the Piaroa lose their hard shiny blue anuses, as why did they ever have them? We are dealing with a set of symbols contrasting a primordial state with a social state of being. In the 'upside-down' world of pre-society, people lived in ignorance, symbolized by man having a blue eye situated on his bottom (B and C). Standing up, man would look down towards the 'lands of the animals' which exist beneath the earth, and not up towards the 'lands of the gods', the source of knowledge.

In the primary myth (A) the transformation from the primordial asocial world to the social one comes with the recognition of sexual exchange. Incest is viewed as a relationship of non-exchange. Society cannot exist if men keep their daughters and sisters to themselves. With this recognition came both the loss of innocence (the loss of shiny blue anuses) and the acquisition of knowledge (taboo against incest).

The Rule of Women

The topsy-turvy world of pre-society is also represented in the Kayapo myth of the origin of cooking fire, where it was jaguar who ate grilled meat and man who ate meat raw, and in the Piaroa myth of the origin of menstruation, where it was man who menstruated, not woman. A myth which is widespread among the tropical forest societies tells of a world once ruled by women, not men.

An example comes from the Tupi of Amazonia, Brazil. In very remote times, when the world was ruled by women, the Sun, indignant at this state of things, decided to remedy it by reforming mankind and subjecting them to his law, and then choosing a perfect woman, whom he could take as his companion. He needed an emissary. He therefore arranged for a virgin named Ceucy to be fertilized by the sap of the cucura or puruman tree, which streamed over her breasts. The child, who was called Jurupari, took power away from women and restored it to men. To emphasize men's independence, he instructed them to celebrate feasts from which women would be excluded, and he taught them secrets to be handed down from generation to generation. They were to put to death any women who learned these secrets. Ceucy herself was the first victim of this pitiless law promulgated by her son, who even today is still in search of a woman sufficiently perfect to become the wife of the Sun. (From Lévi-Strauss, 1973.)

Having stated the inverse, the myth then tells the story of how affairs were set right in the world: how man acquired cooking fire and jaguar lost it, why women menstruate and men do not, how men acquired the ritual and sacred knowledge necessary to maintain law and order in society and how women lost such skills. In myth the nature of man and animal, or men and women, is defined and their differences distinguished. Women are fertile naturally, whereas men achieve fertility by cultural means through the acquisition of religious knowledge.

The symbolic equivalence of the menstruating woman and the knowledgeable man is overtly recognized by the Tukano of the Northwest Amazon, who call boy initiates 'menstruation people'. South American religious leaders, the shamans, are responsible for the fertility and general well-being of their land and people. Knowledge and fertility are linked concepts. The myths state the nature of man's fertility as opposed to the fertility of woman. Each is responsible for distinct domains; both are necessary for the existence of society.

Woman, Nature and Culture

Although women are associated with natural fertility, and men with that which is cultural, the complexity of metaphors in the myths means that women cannot categorically be classed with nature. A myth widespread in the Guianas relates how man, living in a state of nature, acquired cultivated food from woman, her ability to plant being a distinctive feature of her sex. The culture hero is always a fisherman who catches fish/woman, who in turn gives him the art of cultivation, as in the Trio myth where she gives him cooking fire and cultural artifacts as well. The implication is that man, having no knowledge of fire, eats his food raw, whether it be the fish he catches or the wild plants he gathers.

Symbolism in the myths of tropical South America is not fixed in meaning but highly fluid. Depending on the opposition at hand, 'woman' can be placed on the side of nature or, to the contrary, on the side of culture. Both the following groups of oppositions can emerge from a set of myths taken from any one society (see Rivière, 1969).

Nature	*Culture*
WOMEN	MEN
naturally fertile	culturally fertile
sexual promiscuity	sexual control
chaos	order
ignorance	sacred knowledge

Nature	*Culture*
MEN	WOMEN
naked	clothed
hunting	cultivation
forest	village
sun	cooking fire
incest	marriage rule

The myths of the origin of cultivation shed further light upon the widespread South American myth of the time when women ruled society. In the Trio myth fish/woman scolds the culture hero for not living in a village, for not eating bread, for not being properly civilized. The culture hero acquired not only cultivation from woman but the art of civilization itself – cultural artifacts and social relations.

When man acquires cooking fire, cultivation and cultural artifacts, he also achieves society, its achieve-

A ceramic made by the Karaja of the Rio Araguia, Brazil, depicting a scene from their ceremony of Aruana, in which masked male dancers invite women of the tribe to dance with them. Ceremonies such as these commonly serve several ends at once: they assure the fertility of nature and of man; they reconstruct the mythic past, regenerating society; and they initiate the young into society.

ment being contingent upon the acquisition of in-laws. Fish/woman becomes the culture hero's wife, and so he enters into a relationship of exchange with other men. Fish/woman has a father, the anaconda, the alligator or the jaguar, who becomes the hero's father-in-law. An exchange relationship is thereby established, which is always precarious; for a theme common to many myths is that the relationship with wife's brother, with sister's husband, and with father-in-law – in short the in-law relationship – is inherently dangerous. Note the message of the Mundurucu myth of the jaguar's son-in-law where marriage and the threat of being devoured are conjoined: in-laws are strangers who may eat you.

Society and Danger

The myths of the origin of cultivation and society, then, are also about the dangers man encounters by entering into a social state. In the Piaroa cycle the father-in-law transforms himself at will into jaguar or anaconda. Indeed, when the focal relationship of the myth is between the culture hero and his father-in-law, and not between the hero and his wife, the father-in-law is generally depicted as jaguar, not as anaconda. Thus the culture hero, a fisherman, marries the woman who is the daughter of the guardian of fire, the hunter, a meat eater (the jaguar in the Kayapo myth). The culture hero is prey to the latter, yet through his social relationship with the jaguar becomes of a kind with him. As predator of one of his own kind, the jaguar has a relationship with his son-in-law, the culture hero, which is cannibalistic in nature. Cannibalism is thereby identified with the origin of the in-law relationship and hence of society.

Normally we would expect to find cannibalism placed in opposition to social order, but here they are conjoined. However, if we read the myth closely, we see that cannibalism occurs not just with the establishment of an in-law relationship, but because the relationship is a non-reciprocal one. In the Kayapo myth of the origin of fire the culture hero receives from the jaguar, his father-in-law, fire, cultivation and cultural artifacts. He gives very little in exchange. For this reason his father-in-law tries to eat him. The proper social relationship is a reciprocal one: one gives and one receives. If not, disaster is the consequence.

An important aspect of the myths is that any given myth is about a multiplicity of topics, not a single topic. Myths about the acquisition of cultivation are also about the origin and nature of in-law relationships. Themes are intertwined, with each theme being used to explain the next. Kin and in-law relations can be talked about in terms of the opposition between knowledge and ignorance, which in turn can be explained in terms of controlled and chaotic behaviour, which can be reduced to proper as opposed to cannibalistic eating, the cooked and the raw, which is apt symbolism for talking about kin and in-law relations. The teller of myths uses critical mythic events creatively and the construction of a myth is a highly creative process, one of mankind reflecting upon itself.

From the perspective of Western categories, we could say that it is in myths that we can discover Amerindian philosophies of causality, their classification of elements in the universe, their concepts of time and space, and their unique vision of man's destiny. Whether such labels help in understanding the Amerindian world view, however, is questionable. The abstract theories of our culture about the ordering of society and the universe are so alien to those of the tropical forest Indian that we can use them only as the loosest of guides.

CHAPTER TWENTY-SEVEN

VOODOO

Voodoo is the religion of the peasant masses of Haiti, who number something like 97% of the total population. Most of the inhabitants of Haiti are descended from slaves, who were imported from Africa to work the plantations, where they came under Christian influence. Both African and Christian influences are evident in the religion, and the word Voodoo itself comes from a West African word for a god or spirit (see WEST AFRICA).

The outstanding characteristic of Voodoo worship is the central importance attached to the 'possession' of the worshippers by the gods of the cult. At the high point of almost all Voodoo ceremonies one or more of the worshippers attains a dissociation of consciousness and goes into a trance, during which he or she is believed to be 'ridden' or controlled by a god. In the trance the worshipper follows the conventional pattern of behaviour which is traditionally associated with the god. This type of experience, in which a superhuman power is felt to invade the body and mind of a human being, and replace the human personality with its own, has a long history in many other parts of the world besides Haiti.

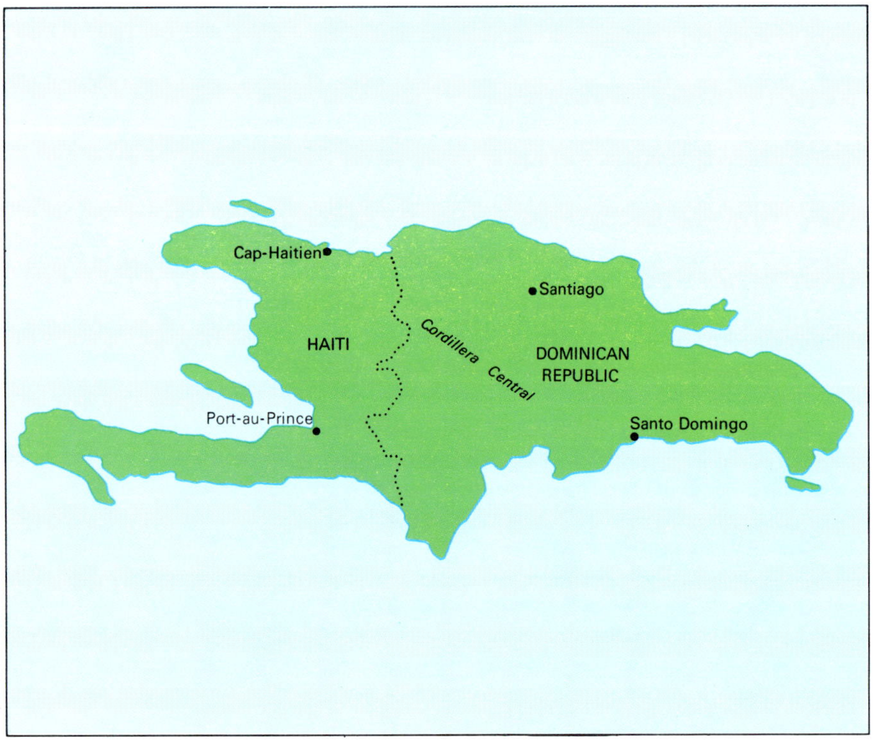

There are thousands of Voodoo *loa* (gods and spirits). They include not only gods of African origin, but personified natural forces and objects – 'Saint' Sun and 'Saint' Wind, for example – and voodoo-ized Christian saints. The god Legba is always the first *loa* to be invoked in any ceremony. He came originally from Dahomey in West Africa and his function was to be the spokesman and interpreter of the gods, without whose aid they could not communicate with either human beings or each other. Traces of this function as a go-between can still be discerned in the Legba of Voodoo. No *loa* can enter into the worshippers unless he has Legba's permission, for Legba is the guardian of the gate that joins the worlds of men and *loa*. He holds the key to this gate, and is therefore often identified with St Peter. The preliminary invocation at all ceremonies hails Legba as the controller of the barrier between the physical world and the world of spirit.

Atibon-Legba, remove the barrier for me . . .
Papa Legba remove the barrier
So I may pass through.
When I come back I will salute the *loa*.
Voodoo Legba, remove the barrier for me
So that I may come back.
When I come back I will thank the *loa*.

By extension from his command of the spirit-gate Legba is regarded as the guardian *loa* of all gates and boundaries. As such, he exercises a benevolent protective function over the home. He is also the god of pathways and 'Master of the Crossroads'. In the latter role he presides over the activities of ritual magicians who, in Haiti as in medieval Europe, regard a crossroads as a particularly suitable place for their operations.

Legba's appearance is that of a weak, poorly dressed old man, puffing a pipe and supporting himself on a crutch. As a symbol of Legba a crutch is kept in many Voodoo sanctuaries. In spite of his physically feeble appearance, Legba is enormously strong and possession of a worshipper by him is extraordinarily violent, the entranced devotee often falling to the ground as though pole-axed.

Spirits of Death and War

The god of vegetation is Loco, who is often worshipped under the form of a tree. It is he who gives knowledge of the secret properties of herbs, and consequently he is also the god of healing. In appearance he is something like a prosperous peasant, smoking a pipe and holding a stick in his right hand.

Loco was responsible for the existence of Nibo, one of the Guede, the gods of death. One day, so the story goes, Loco was out walking when he came upon a parcel. Unwrapping it he found a stone which, when he had taken it home, turned into a child. The amazed Loco asked his neighbour Ogu, god of war and of blacksmiths, what he should do. Ogu had the child baptized and, standing as the boy's godfather, gave him the name Nibo. Subsequently he adopted the boy. Nibo often claims to be the brother of Ogu's son, Ogu-badagri. The latter dislikes him intensely, however, and should the two *loa* ever take possession of two worshippers at the same time a violent quarrel frequently breaks out.

The Guede, the family of death spirits to which Nibo belongs, are about thirty in number. Besides Nibo himself, other prominent members of the family are Baron Saturday, Baron Cemetery, Baron Cross and Maman Brigitte. In appearance the Guede often resemble undertakers' men, in full mourning, wearing black top-hats, frock-coats and dark glasses. Alternatively they dress up as corpses, stuffing their mouths with cotton, tying up their chins with linen bandages and giving voice to death-rattles.

The Guede combine their functions as gods of death with being the gods of obscenity and licentiousness. Those possessed by them – such possessions being very frequent around the time of the Festival of All Souls, the feast of the dead – not only dress as corpses but, on occasion, strap imitation penises to their loins and with these either pretend to rape women worshippers or dance the *banda*, probably the world's most flagrantly sexual dance. The conversation of those possessed by the Guede is almost invariably obscene. They tell dirty jokes, sing equally dirty songs and mispronounce ordinary words to give them a sexual connotation. The Guede – or rather, the worshippers possessed by them – always behave in an outlandish fashion. They pour rum into their ears, drink an excruciatingly hot beverage made from 21 different types of pepper, and steal the worshippers' property.

Ogu, the *loa* who adopted Nibo, was the divine blacksmith in Dahomey. But ironworking has never had any great importance in the Haitian economy and in Voodoo only vestiges of this function are left. An iron bar stuck into a brazier, for example, is called 'Ogun's Forge' and his interest in fire is indicated by the fact that those possessed by him often 'wash' their hands in blazing *clairin* (cane spirit). In the main, however, the Haitian Ogu is a war-god. His most common symbol is a machete or sabre stuck upright in the ground and he is regarded as a veteran of the many civil wars of Haiti's history. Those possessed by him put on old military uniforms or, if these are not available in the sanctuary, they tie red rags round their heads and waists. When Ogu manifests himself he talks like a soldier, using military slang and larding his speech with much swearing. He demands rum in a soldierly way – 'My testicles are cold,' he shouts – and he is extremely fond of women.

Most Haitians are descended from slaves brought over from Africa to work on the plantations, where they were exposed to Christian influence. The Voodoo religion mingles African and Christian elements, and its deities include gods of African origin and Christian saints. The god of vegetation, Loco, is often worshipped in the form of a tree. Such outdoor meetings were common at times when the Haitian government, anxious to prove itself 'progressive', was attempting to suppress the Voodoo faith. *Voodoo Ceremony Around the Holy Tree*, painting by Gerard Valcin, 1963.

The Zombies, painting by another Haitian artist, Hector Hyppolite. It is widely believed in Haiti, and elsewhere in the West Indies, that a corpse can be animated by the evil will of a black magician. It is known as a zombie, a word of African origin. In an apparently trance-like or drugged condition, the zombie can be forced to do simple menial work for its owner.

A song sung in his honour illustrates this quality.

Ogu works, he does not eat.
He puts money on one side
In order to sleep with a pretty girl.
Yesterday evening Feraille went to bed without supper.
Ogu works.
Ogu does not eat.
He has bought a dress to give to his girl.
Yesterday Ogu went to bed without supper.

Zaka the Peasant

In marked contrast to the warlike Ogu is Zaka, the peaceful peasant-god of agriculture. He dresses as a typical Haitian peasant, in denims and a straw hat, smoking a pipe and carrying a machete in his hand. Those possessed by him talk in an exaggeratedly rural accent and are usually very friendly to the other worshippers in the sanctuary, who greet him familiarly as 'cousin Zaka'. Sometimes, like all peasants, especially those living in such a highly stratified society as Haiti, in which the life of the farmer is a continual struggle for a bare existence, Zaka's outward calm breaks down and he reveals the violence lurking underneath. This violence is the subject of a Voodoo hymn.

Cousin Zaka, you are in a rage,
O devil.
You are in a rage,
O devil.
You want to leave a good woman
And go and live with vagabonds.
Cousin Zaka, you are in a rage,
O devil.

The Rage of John the Baptist

Many of the *loa* are personifications of natural forces and there are, for example, no less than six storm-gods. In the south of Haiti the most notable of them is Shango, a god of African origin, but in the north his place has been taken by St John the Baptist. This is probably because storms are especially prevalent in Haiti around St John's day. A Voodoo myth quoted by an anthropologist who lived in Haiti during the 1930s attempts to explain this:

'On a given day in the year God permits each saint to have control over the universe. St John the Baptist, however, is so irresponsible and his rage so violent that God fears the consequences if he were allowed to exert his power on his day. By plying him with drink the day before, he is made so drunk that when he falls asleep he does not waken for five days. When he is told his day is already passed, his rage is so terrible that great storms flay the earth, and it is a commonplace . . . that this day is marked by thunder and lightning storms of almost hurricane proportions . . .'

The relationship between the Christian saints and the Voodoo 'saints', or *loa*, is explained in a myth which the French anthropologist Alfred Métraux heard in Port au Prince, the capital of Haiti:

'When he had created the earth and the animals in it, God sent down twelve apostles. Unfortunately they behaved too stiffly and powerfully. In their pride they ended by rebelling against God. He, as a punishment, sent them to Africa where they multiplied. It is they and their descendants who, as *loa*, help their servants and comfort them when they are unhappy. One of the apostles who refused to leave for Africa gave himself up to sorcery and took the name of Lucifer. Later God sent twelve more

LEFT The Guede are the death-spirits of Voodoo. In appearance they resemble undertaker's men, in black frock-coats and top-hats, with dark glasses. *The Guede*, painting by Andre Pierre.

BELOW Poster outside a Voodoo temple offers 'contact with the invisible world'. This contact is achieved in ceremonies during which worshippers go into a trance and are 'ridden' or possessed by the gods. The experience, in which a superhuman power is felt to invade the worshipper's mind and body, is the central characteristic of Voodoo worship. The African emblems, the French language, and the advertisement for American soft drink illustrate the blend of cultures seen in Voodoo.

apostles, who this time behaved like dutiful sons and preached the gospel. They and their descendants are what we call the saints of the Church.'

The Love-Goddess

One of the oddest associations between Christian figures and the *loa* is the identification of the Virgin Mary with Erzulie, the Voodoo goddess of love. Erzulie is said to be a half-caste from the Antilles. Originally she was in fact a member of a family of sea-spirits (and it is interesting that Aphrodite, the Greek love-goddess, was born of the sea), but her connection with the ocean has been almost completely forgotten and she is now almost exclusively concerned with romantic love. When she appears in a Voodoo sanctuary – when she takes possession of a worshipper, that is – a song is sung in her honour.

Ah! The beautiful woman
Who is Erzulie!
Who is Erzulie!
Oh, I will give you a present
Before you go away. Abobo!

As the song is repeated again and again, Erzulie is led to a corner of the sanctuary dedicated to her and her cult, where glamorous dresses are laid out, with make-up, a toothbrush and a comb. She combs out her hair so that it hangs loosely, she puts on a dress and, if they are available, jewels, makes herself up and walks back into the sanctuary. Here she flirts with her worshippers, demands sweet refreshments – small sugar-cakes and sweet champagne especially delight her – sniffs perfume and speaks in an exaggeratedly high 'feminine' voice.

Erzulie is apt to behave generally in an exaggeratedly feminine way. For example, if she is refused a gift for which she has asked a worshipper, she is inclined to break into floods of tears, a storm of grief which only ends when Erzulie leaves the head of the worshipper she has possessed. She has had many love-affairs with other gods, including the war-god Ogu. Nibo, the Guede *loa* who was adopted by Ogu, is deeply in love with Erzulie but she, being a half-caste and light of skin, always rejects his advances, for he is very black. Sometimes Nibo possesses one worshipper at the same time as Erzulie is possessing another. When this happens, Nibo follows Erzulie about complaining: 'You know well that I love that woman, but she won't have anything to do with me because I am black.'

RIGHT Erzulie, the central figure in this painting by Andre Pierre, is the Voodoo goddess of love. Damballah, the serpent-god, and Jean Dantor, a minor *loa*, accompany her. Someone possessed by Erzulie speaks in an exaggeratedly high voice, flirts with other worshippers and demands sugar-cakes and sweet champagne.

The Hissing Serpent

Another of Erzulie's lovers is Damballah, a serpent-*loa* who lives in trees, especially those near springs. Like many of the *loa*, Damballah originated in Dahomey, but there he was more of a primordial force than a personal god. The Dahomean precursor of Damballah was Da, the force of life, who takes many forms but principally one in which he circles the earth giving motion to the stars and planets. In Voodoo this earth-circling force has been reduced to the status of a mere snake-god and he is greeted as such in the sanctuaries.

Worshippers possessed by Damballah never speak, but only hiss and whistle. They wriggle along the ground like snakes or climb trees. They are offered white things to eat and drink, for white is Damballah's colour. Silver is sacred to him and those who find favour with him discover hidden treasures or become rich in some other way.

Damballah is a friend of Agwe, the sea-god, to whom are sacred not only the oceans but all which is in them or on them – fish, seaweed, boats and ships. The symbols of Agwe, present in most Voodoo sanctuaries, are model boats, shells and oars painted green or blue. In the murals found in sanctuaries he is represented by pictures of cargo boats and heavily armed warships. Agwe is a green-eyed half-caste who dresses as a naval officer. He is the patron *loa* of fishermen and all who earn their living from the sea, and is hailed as such in a hymn:

Master Agwe, where are you?
Don't you see I'm on the reef?
Master Agwe, where are you?
Don't you see I'm on the reef?
Don't you see I'm on the sea?
I've a rudder in my hand,
I can't go back.
I'm already going forwards,
I can't turn back.
Agwe, where are you?
Can't you see I'm on the reef?

It is a truism that men make their gods in their own image and that a mythology reflects the social complexities of the culture which gave it birth. Voodoo is no exception. The *loa*, though most of them have an African origin, have been deeply affected by the Roman Catholicism of the Haitian middle classes and by the influence of what, for all its shortcomings, is basically a western free-enterprise political system.

BELOW Painting from the interior of a Voodoo temple, Port-au-Prince. Damballah lives in trees and his possessed worshippers climb them and imitate the behaviour of a snake. The sacred tree is a common Voodoo symbol.

THE PACIFIC

CHAPTER TWENTY-EIGHT

POLYNESIA AND MICRONESIA

The islands of Polynesia and Micronesia span some 5000 miles of the Pacific Ocean. Though it may be possible to trace ancestral common elements, shared to varying degrees, different islands and island groups have developed their own distinctive cultural styles in relative isolation. Despite its greater size, Polynesia shows the greater homogeneity in its culture. Doubtless the more recent settlement of much of Polynesia and the greater isolation of its central oceanic vastness are major factors in this effect. Yet even in Polynesia, there are not inconsiderable variations on themes, whether in social structure, in culture generally, or in myth. Within a group of islands, or even within a single island, there may be several differing versions of the same myth. So it is clear that none of the myths offered here can be taken to be common to the whole of Micronesia or the whole of Polynesia, let alone both. They have been chosen either because they represent a general theme of very wide distribution or because they bring out important points in the cultural and social background.

The Forming of Earth and Sky

The Nauruan myth of Areop-enap and the formation of heaven and earth from a clam shell provides a good example of the 'sky-raiser' theme which is common in Polynesia and in eastern Micronesia. At first there was only the air and the ocean and one living being, Areop-enap, Ancient Spider, who wandered about in limitless space. One day he found a vast rounded object, a clam shell. He took it in his hands and examined every side, looking to see whether there was an opening by which he might enter it, but he found none. Areop-enap struck the shell. There was a hollow sound and he knew that it was empty. He tried to force it open, but failed. Then he made an incantation and, trying once more, succeeded in opening up the shell enough for him to go inside, but he could see nothing. All was dark for there was neither sun nor moon. There was not enough space to stand upright in the shell and so he had to crawl.

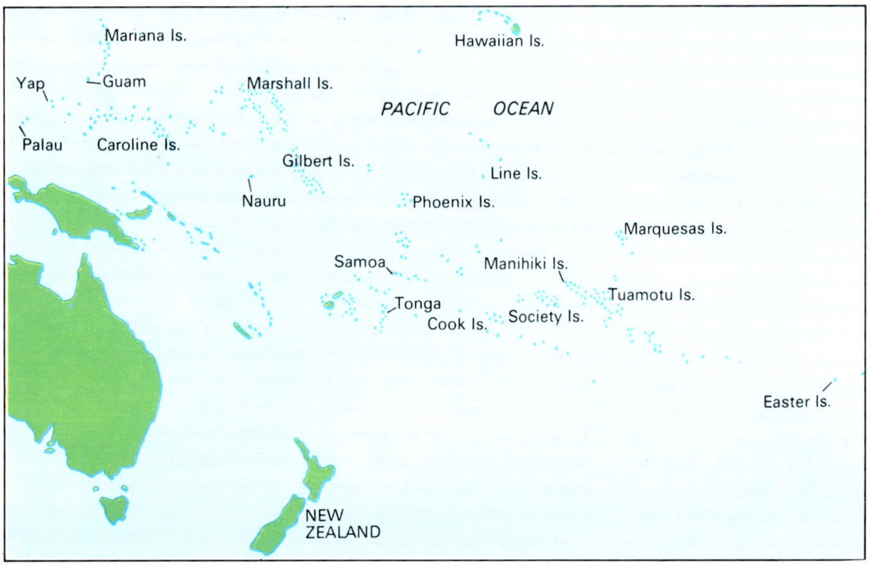

Areop-enap searched about, hoping to find something. At last he found a Triton's horn shellfish. He took it up and, placing it under his arm, slept upon it for three days to instil it with magical powers. Then he set it aside to seek for some other thing. He found a larger Triton's horn, which he dealt with in the same way. Next, taking up the first shellfish, he said to it, 'Can you lift the ceiling a little to make it possible to sit up?' The Triton's horn said 'Yes', and raised the top half of the clam shell a little. Areop then took the creature out of the Triton's horn shell and placed it in the western half of the clam shell to become the moon, which he called *maramen*.

There was now a little light in the shell and Areop-enap saw a large caterpillar, Rigi. He said to him, 'Can you raise the ceiling a little higher?' The caterpillar, stirred to life by being spoken to by Areop, said 'Yes.' He strained to force the shell further open and salty sweat ran down his body to gather in the lower half of the shell, where it became the sea. When he had raised the upper half of the shell, which became the heavens, the caterpillar fell down and died.

Now Areop took the creature from the larger Triton's horn shell and put it in the eastern sky to become the sun, *ekuan*. The lower half of the clam shell became the earth. Thus it was that earth and heaven were formed.

Closest to this particular version is a story from the Gilbert Islands in which the first being, Nareau, sets about the separation of earth and sky. The sky, which lies just over the earth, is raised by Riiki (Eel).

Hale o Keawe, repository of chiefly bones and valuables, part of a reconstructed temple complex, the City of Refuge, at Honaunau, Hawaii. Within the precincts of the 'City', criminals and other fugitives gained priestly protection and were safe from punishment. This is a distinctive Hawaiian development of the ritual centres, *marae*, found throughout Polynesia.

Rangi and Papa

In Polynesia sky and earth are more usually presented as living beings, often called Rangi (Raki, Langi) and Papa. In New Zealand Maori creation myths they are the parents of the principal gods. Originally, Rangi and Papa clung close to each other and their children were unable to see or move about freely in the dark close space between them. Eventually all these children except the god of wind and storm, Tawhiri-matea, agreed to separate their parents. This separation was finally achieved by Tane, who assumed the form of a tree to force the sky upwards. The sorrow of the parted Rangi and Papa takes a material form in the mists rising from the earth and the rain falling from the sky. Tawhiri-matea's anger at the sorrow of his parents leads to a war of the gods, through which natural events such as the ravages of storms or the attacks of the sea against the land are explained.

Rangi and Papa become the starting point for a family tree which includes nearly the whole of creation, from their children (not just the six major gods, but many more), to animals, plants, inanimate natural objects and human beings. Myths reflect the importance of genealogies in Polynesian societies. The position of an individual in a genealogy was important in determining his social relations, particularly in establishing his rank relative to others sharing a common ancestor. Often it was those descended in a line of first-born males from an original ancestor who had highest rank. (The issue of the status of the firstborn is at the crux of the Mangaian myth of Tangaroa and Rongo, to be discussed shortly.) There is a genealogy of a Cook

ANCESTRY AND SETTLEMENT

The exact nature of the link between the peoples of Micronesia and Polynesia is still far from clear. Their languages are descended from a common 'Austronesian' stock, and some features of physical type also suggest a common ancestry. Micronesia shows greater evidence of cultural mixing, with possible influences from Melanesia, the Philippines and Indonesia. Some believe that the Polynesian ancestral stock developed in Micronesia, but many think this is more likely to have taken place in Melanesia. The early migration routes are uncertain.

Suggested dates of settlement:

1. Movement of people of Austronesian language stock from South China area into western Micronesia, 3500–2500 BC.

2. Canoe voyaging from the west into central and eastern Micronesia, 2000 BC onwards.

3. Proto-Polynesian colonies established, in Tonga 1200 BC, in Samoa before 800 BC.

4. Polynesian culture develops in the west, then further voyaging sets up an eastern Polynesian centre in the Marquesas, 150 BC.

5. Expansion of Polynesian culture in the east, for example in Hawaii AD 100, Easter Island AD 450, New Zealand AD 800.

Ferdinand Magellan discovered Guam, in western Micronesia, in AD 1521. Spain was the early colonial power in Micronesia, followed by Germany, Japan, the United States of America, and Britain (in the Gilbert Islands).

In Polynesia major European influence began in the 18th century. In the 19th century the activities of whalers, traders and missionaries expanded across the region. Britain and France had the largest colonial holdings.

Islands chiefly family which covers 65 generations back to Atea, who occupies Rangi's position there, and Papa. This could be reproduced in other parts of Polynesia as real and mythical genealogies merge in establishing rank.

Mana and Tapu

The Maori account of the first woman helps to highlight another aspect of Polynesian society, the notions of *mana* and *tapu*. Following the advice of his mother, Papa, the god Tane formed a female being, Hine-ahu-one, from earth and took her as his wife. Their first child was the egg, Tiki-tohua, from which all birds are descended. Their next child was a woman, Tiki-kapakapa. She was well cared for and, when she grew up, was given the name Hine-a-tauira. Tane took her as his wife and their daughter was Hine-titamauri.

Then, one day, Hine-a-tauira asked Tane who her father was. He laughed. She asked again and Tane pointed to his genitals. She understood, then, that her husband was her father. Overcome with shame and distress at this incestuous relationship, she fled into the darkness below, where she became known as Hine-nui-te-po, Great Woman of the Night. As she departed she called out, 'Stay, Tane, to draw our descendants into the world of light, I will go below to gather them into the darkness.' Their descendants are men, and Hine-nui-te-po is goddess of death.

Mana was a person's effective power and was related to rank in society. The ultimate *mana* was that of the gods. Though practical success was important in establishing a person's *mana*, it was often seen as an abstract quality in need of protection. *Tapu* (taboo) involved a set of rules which restricted the contact between the relatively pure and powerful and the impure and demeaning. Though among the Maori women could become *tapu* in circumstances such as childbirth, *tapu* was primarily associated with the pure, masculine forces of the universe. Women were one of the main sources of the 'common-ness' that could remove *tapu*. This could either be dangerous to male powers or ritually useful. Death is the ultimate

ABOVE *Moai paapaa*, a wooden female figure from Easter Island. Such figures are said to represent ancestral spirits, *akuaku*, the first being carved by the ancestor hero Tu'u-ko-ihu after a meeting with spirit beings.

ABOVE RIGHT Wooden figure of a god, with shell inlay and human hair, from Kealakekua Bay, Hawaii.

SOME PRINCIPAL CHARACTERS

Polynesia

The children of Rangi and Papa, the principal gods of the Maori in New Zealand.

Rangi = **Papa**
Sky | *Earth*

Tangaroa	**Rongo-ma-tane**	**Haumia-tiketike**	**Tane-mahuta**	**Tawhiri-matea**	**Tu-matauenga**
Oceans/fish	*Cultivated foods*	*Foods growing wild*	*Forests, trees, birds, insects*	*Winds, the elements*	*War, man*

Micronesia

Olofat and Luk, two gods who are protagonists of a cycle of myths, principally in the Caroline Islands. They are usually brothers. Luk is handsome, good and creative. Olofat is ugly, jealous and a trickster, who transforms the world by his tricks. In some islands Olofat is god of fire. Olofat is also known as Yalafath, Iolofath or Yelafaz. Luk is also known as Lukunor, Lugeilang or Lukelang.

Nareau the Elder and **Nareau the Younger,** major figures in myths of the Gilbert Islands. The elder Nareau is responsible for the earliest stages of creation, the younger for the later stages. Nareau the Younger later becomes a trickster figure, like Olofat and the Polynesian Maui.

removal of power and, in the myth, we see the Great Woman of the Night assuming her role in pulling men into death. Rank, status and the positive life-powers were essentially for and of the men. Women are represented as relatively impure and a source of negative influences on power. In the male power-orientated world, they may be man's origin but also his death.

In some Polynesian myths man was originally to be reborn, as the moon is, but one of the gods decreed it otherwise. Similarly in Micronesia in the Caroline Islands, it is Olofat who rejects Luk's proposal that men should be reborn. Elsewhere in Micronesia immortality is lost through mischance or forgetfulness. In the Palaus a malicious bird causes the water of life to be spilled. In the western Carolines negligent children forget to exhume in time the body of their mother, so the possibility of continued life is lost.

The Origin of Fire

In the origin of fire story from Yap in Micronesia, Yalafath is its source though the unfortunate thunder-god is the direct donor. The root vegetables, taro and yam, were eaten in Yap but fire to cook them was not known. They had to be baked in the sun. The people were wracked with internal pains and asked Yalafath for help. At once a red-hot thunderbolt fell from the sky into a pandanus tree. Prickles burst out of the sides and middles of the pandanus leaves. The thunder-god, Dessra, found himself caught in the tree and called out for someone to come and release him. A woman named Guaretin, who was sun-baking taro nearby, came and helped him. He asked her what work she was doing. When she told him, he sent her to fetch some moist clay and he formed a cooking pot. Then he told her to get some sticks from the arr tree which he placed under his arm, implanting in them the seeds of fire. This is how clay pots came to Yap and how it became possible to make fire by the friction of wood.

The trickster element in Yalafath (Olofat) is not very evident in this tale, but in Polynesia the trickster demi-god Maui gives full evidence of his character in gaining fire from the underworld. In the Samoan version Ti'iti'i (Maui tikitiki) gains the secret of fire from the god Mafuie by ransoming Mafuie's right arm which he has torn off.

Maui Fishes up Land

According to a myth from Hawaii (Polynesia), Maui used to go fishing with his brothers. He was not a very good fisherman, but he was an excellent trickster. Often, just as one of his brothers was pulling in a fish, Maui would jerk it off the line with his own hook and claim it for himself. At last, annoyed by his tricks, his brothers refused to take him fishing with them any longer. His mother then scolded him for his failure to provide her with fish. Eventually she told him to go to his father to obtain a fish-hook of great power, called Manai-ka-lani, which would provide all the fish they needed. This he did and, jumping on-to the end of their canoe, tried to join his brothers as they went fishing. Calling out that the canoe was too

ABOVE The Polynesian trickster-hero, Maui, fishes up the North Island of New Zealand. Maori meeting house wall-panel, carved and painted wood, eyes inlaid with shell, from Whakarewarewa.

LEFT Maui is destroyed between the thighs of Hine-nui-te-po, goddess of death, as he attempts to enter her body and gain eternal life for all. Carved wooden lintel, New Zealand Maori.

Animal themes, plentiful in myth, sometimes find expression in art.

ABOVE Bird-shaped food bowl, wood inlaid with shell, from the Palau Islands, Micronesia.

RIGHT A *marakihau*, a carved mythical man-fish sea monster, which can suck in men and canoes through its tubular tongue. New Zealand Maori meeting-house panel, Ngati Porou tribe.

BELOW *Moai moko*, a wooden lizard-man figure from Easter Island. Pairs of these figures were hung in house doorways. They seem to have represented lizard guardian spirits giving protection from intruders. Certain lizards were regarded as spirit animals in many parts of Polynesia.

small, they threw him overboard and he had to swim back to land. On that trip the brothers caught only a shark. Maui told them that they would have had far finer fish had he been there.

Finally they allowed him to come out in their canoe, far out to sea off the coast of Maui Island. But still they caught only sharks and the brothers scornfully asked Maui where his fine fish were. He then dropped the hook Manai-ka-lani into the sea with bait from the red-billed mud-hen, *alae*, the bird special to his mother, Hina. He made an incantation, saying that the power of the hook would enable him to catch the great *ulua* (a large kind of jackfish). The sea bottom began to move and the sea became violently disturbed. For two days, with the line taut, the fish pulled the canoe through the great waves. Then the fish tired and, the line slackening, Maui told his brothers to pull hard against it. This they did and land began to rise from the water. Maui told them that, in order to keep the fish, they must not look back. But one brother disobeyed, the line broke and the land lay behind as a string of islands.

The Maui stories are immensely widespread. The basic outline of the land-fishing story is probably as close as one can get to a pan-Oceanic myth. Even in Micronesia, in the western Carolines there is a land-fishing character called Motiktik, a name clearly related to the Polynesian Maui tikitiki. Maui's other feats include, in various islands, sky-raising, snaring the sun to make it move more slowly through the sky, the creation of the first dog (often from his brother-in-law), and an attempt to destroy the goddess of death, which fails and brings about his own destruction. Maui is essentially a popular hero with no emphasis on chiefly powers. The Maui stories are not part of priestly mythology, but were clearly immensely popular with ordinary people all over the Pacific.

The fishing myth helps to emphasize the fact that the cultures of Micronesia and Polynesia are essentially island cultures, New Zealand being the largest land mass. The sea and the things of the sea are of major importance. Themes of canoes and fishing are recurrent in myth and legend. In the Nauru story it was a clam shell that became the basis for the universe. Fish, animals and birds often play mythical roles. In Polynesia particularly, they may become the physical manifestation of a god or spirit. For instance, the Maori feared certain lizards which were said to be the material form of the evil god Whiro.

A Question of Seniority

Conflict between brothers is an element that often appears in the Maui cycle, and again in the division between Olofat and his elder brother, Luk, in Micronesia. Groups of brothers often acted as

Figures thought to represent three sons of the Polynesian primal parents.

ABOVE LEFT Wooden figure from Rurutu, Austral Islands, representing the god Tangaroa as creator of other beings, or possibly the ancestor A'a. A hollow in the back contained other images.

ABOVE CENTRE A wooden staff-god from Rarotonga which represents either Rongo or Tangaroa, the eldest sons of Avatea, the Cook Islands equivalent of Rangi.

ABOVE RIGHT Figure of Tangi'ia, fourth son of Abatea and Papa, from Mangaia, Southern Cook Islands. It is made of braided coconut fibre and bark-cloth, decorated with feathers of the red-tailed Tropic Bird. Younger brother of the prominent Tangaroa and Rongo, Tangi'ia was a lesser tribal god.

property-holding cooperative units, but questions of individual rights and relative status were frequently divisive. The story of Rongo and Tangaroa shows a conflict over seniority and the rights of the firstborn.

The story comes from Mangaia in the Cook Islands (Polynesia). Tangaroa and Rongo were the twin sons of Vatea (The Wide Expanse) and Papa (Earth). Tangaroa should have been the firstborn son, but he gave precedence to his brother and emerged, a few days after Rongo's birth, from a boil on his mother's arm. The ingenious Tangaroa taught his brother all the practices of agriculture. His father, Vatea, wanted to make him the sole inheritor of all his parents' possessions, but Papa said that this should not be, since if the power of the rightful firstborn, Tangaroa, was to rest on all their property, they would not dare to touch it and would be unable to eat the food. Therefore, when they distributed their possessions, the greater part went to Rongo, but all the things which were reddish in colour became Tangaroa's. Red fish were Tangaroa's, all others were Rongo's. A reddish-leafed chestnut and reddish types of yam and coconut became Tangaroa's but far more varieties fell to Rongo. All bananas were Rongo's, but the reddish plantain was his brother's. Rather than hanging down like a banana, the plantain stands upright. This is a mark of the dignity of the senior god.

Tangaroa and Rongo held a feast, to which Vatea and Papa were invited. Each made a pile of his own foods. Rongo's pile was by far the bigger. Examining the heaps of food, the parents decided that Rongo carried the prize for plenty, but Tangaroa, with his piles of red food, won that for beauty.

Tangaroa was greatly displeased at the preference shown to Rongo, and was even more displeased when Rongo usurped his rights by stealing the affections of his wife. Tangaroa decided to leave A'ua'u (Mangaia). He set off in a canoe loaded with his red foods and visited many islands until he finally settled in Rarotonga and Aitutaki.

The possession of superior *mana* was often attributed to a firstborn son. This is so much the case for Tangaroa that his parents could not even touch those goods that passed into his possession. The emphasis is on rank through seniority in a group of brothers and seniority of descent line. In Micronesia, particularly in the western part of the region, the importance of wealth for the creation of status is emphasized. This is brought out in myth as poor and despised families gain wealth from supernatural helpers and become powerful and influential. Thus, as usual, we can see both contrasts and similarities between Polynesian and. Micronesian myths and societies.

CHAPTER TWENTY-NINE

MELANESIA

The area known as Melanesia stretches from the tip of Irian Jaya, belonging to the Indonesian Republic, in the west, as far as the New Hebrides and New Caledonia in the east. It includes Papua New Guinea (P.N.G. for short) and the Solomon Islands. Within its innumerable local societies and language groups there is, naturally enough, much diversity and countless specific myths have proliferated. Yet they reveal a limited and consistent set of themes.

From classical tradition we tend to think of myths as tales of the exploits of pagan deities. In Melanesian myths we have, similarly, stories of culture heroes and heroines, whose doings initiated and still validate contemporary practices. As 'charters' for such practices, the myths tell us the people's ideology and values, in connection with magic, kinship, warfare and ceremonial exchanges of wealth. They explain the origins of life, death, culture and the environment. They sometimes posit actions which are the reverse of current norms, as when they describe incestuous or murderous relations between parents and children, or between siblings, as a primeval state from which proper kinship rules emerged. Customs are thus seen as developing out of an opposite original situation.

Myth may link with ritual but may also range further, as a means of explaining the cosmos. In most societies of Melanesia, myth is important, although there are variations in the degree of importance and in the spread of mythological knowledge. Often important myths are known only to senior men, and are tied to display of, or control over, ritual objects or artistic carvings. Nowadays, mythical ways of thinking show also in 'cargo cults', aimed at acquiring the wealth and status of incoming Europeans. Prophets develop new myths by combining traditional themes with bible stories learned from Christian missions.

Myth is a fundamental source of power which cultists seek to tap. As origin stories of particular groups, myths link the group to such sources of power, explaining not only how the group began but how this power is also still necessary to sustain and perpetuate it. Sacred myth bridges over into epics, ballads and folk-tales, elaborated for their narrative interest beyond the purpose of explaining origins. The Baining people (New Britain, P.N.G.), for instance, possess a body of legends about two families, one good and the other bad. The good man is Sirini, his wife Sichi. The evil woman, Sinapki, kills everyone except for a single man, who becomes a 'tree of life', the cordyline. From the cordyline's fruit Sirini emerges and takes revenge on Sinapki and her husband: several stories trace their adventures. Such narratives, like those of Ambwerk and Tuman (elder and younger brother) among the Tangu people (Madang Province, P.N.G.), are intended to point morals as well as entertain.

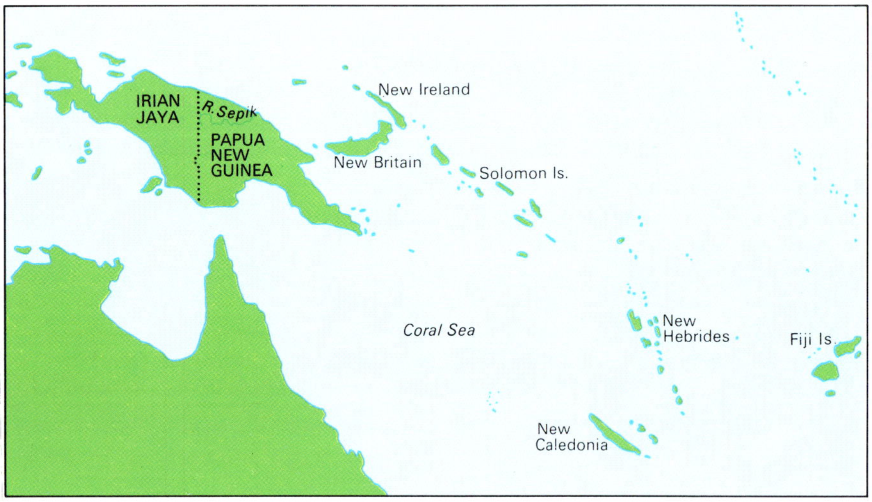

The Ogre-Killing Child

There is no overall pantheon. In Papua New Guinea alone (population about 2,756,000 in 1975) there are over 700 separate languages, and the names of mythical personages are correspondingly legion. Certain motifs, though, are spread very widely, such as the 'myth of the ogre-killing child'. Among the Orokaiva (Northern Province, P.N.G.), Totoima is represented as an original monster, half man half wild pig, who killed and ate his children, until his wife had twins and hid them from him in a taro garden. Totoima became suspicious, searched the garden and killed his son, but the daughter escaped. She brought back a powerful magician, who restored the son to life and enabled him to kill his father, himself marrying the daughter. Totoima's body was butchered and distributed, like that of a pig, to all the different Orokaiva groups. Thus they

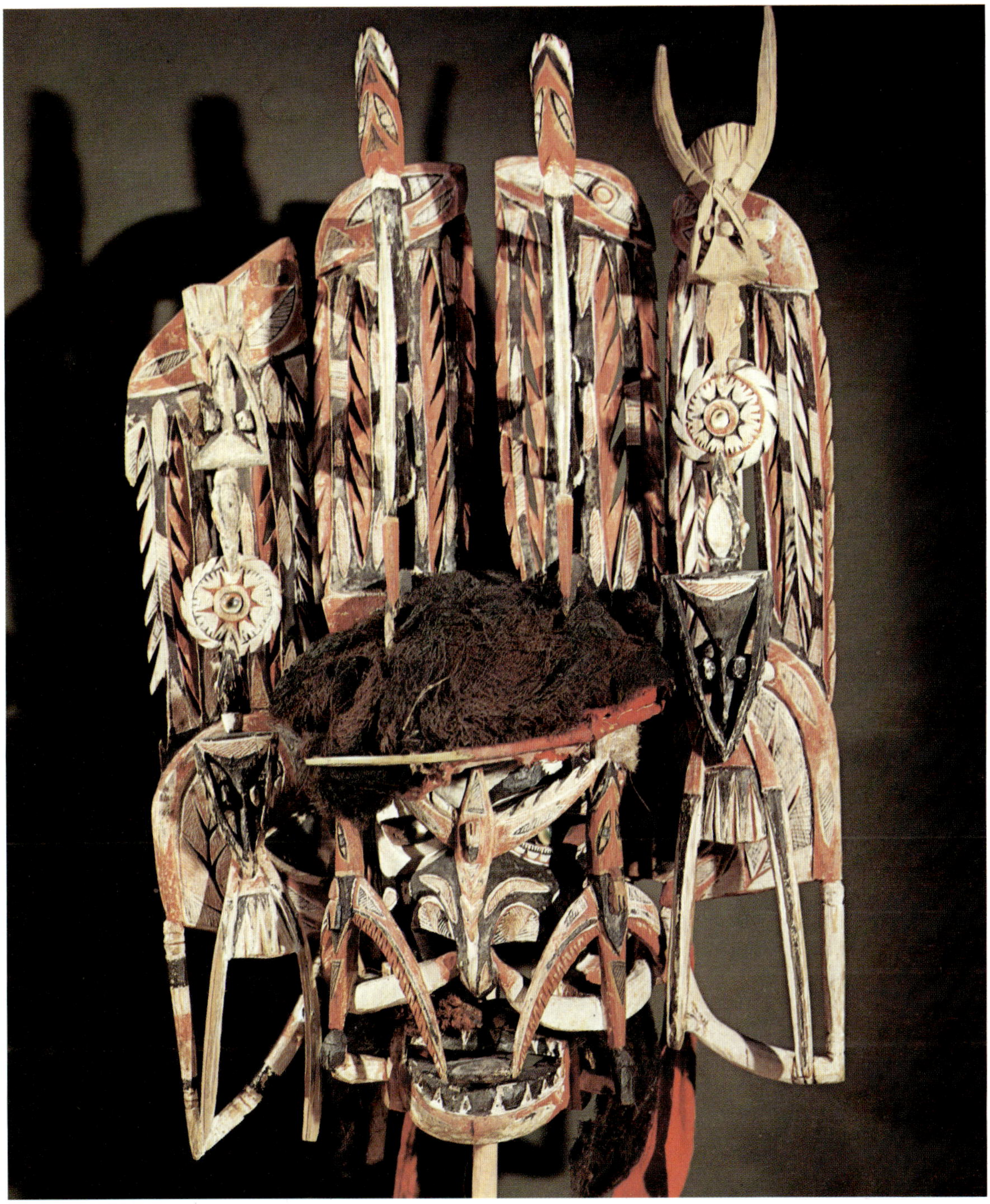

benefited from his strength and were united in communion, though they remained divided by the same spirit of internecine strife as Totoima caused.

Sex and Death

Totoima shows similarities with Sosom, Tiro, Sido, Iko or Hido, whose stories occur widely among the Kiwai, Orokolo, Toaripi and Marind-Anim peoples (southern coast of Papua and Irian Jaya). Sosom is pictured as a giant, who travels over Marind-Anim territory each year, fertilizing the earth and its people. He is patron of an initiatory cult for boys, and his penis is associated with the bullroarer instrument, whirled as a warning to women to keep away from the initiates. He is spoken of as brother of the sun.

The Sido stories explain both fertility and death. In the Kiwai and Toaripi versions he travels widely, dying and achieving rebirth. He has two mothers, joined together as Siamese twins until he severs them. Trying to avoid death, he sloughs off his skin in a trench as snakes do, but some children break his secret by spying on him, and he dies. His mothers sadly dig up his skull, clean it, and wear it around their necks. They follow his spirit on its journeys, but make the mistake of giving him water from the skull to drink, so he can never be reborn as a man. As a spirit he marries a girl, and his semen causes horticultural plants rapidly to grow. He also gives his wife fire, which he makes by rubbing his teeth on wood. He finally becomes a huge pig, and the pig a house, to which all dead people thereafter must go.

A similar hero, Soido, kills his wife and from her blood grow taro and yam tubers, while from her

Ancestor mask of enamelled wood from New Ireland. These masks, called 'Matua', represent the funeral rites of forebears. In some Melanesian myths all the dead go to a house, which is the body of a dead giant.

ABOVE Shrine effigy of John Frum, white-faced and scarlet-coated, with a model of an airplane at his side. On the island of Tanna in the New Hebrides many stories were told about a mysterious messianic figure called John Frum. Since first appearing to a gathering of headmen in 1940, he has been expected to return in an airplane laden with goods. 'Cargo cults' of this kind, aimed at acquiring European wealth and artefacts, are a modern development in Melanesia.

RIGHT Face mask worn in dances to celebrate the wild plum harvest. A parallel between fertility of nature and human sexuality is drawn in many myths. Carved and painted plum-tree wood with fibre hair, from Saibai Island, Torres Straits, late 19th century.

flesh and bones spring sweet potatoes and bananas. He eats these plants, then travels to find his new wife, Pekai. His penis sprays vegetables over the land, diffusing horticulture. The parallel between garden fertility and human sexuality is plain here.

In further versions (for example, Daribi people, Eastern Highlands Province, P.N.G.) the hero's large penis causes a young girl to cry out, so he is ashamed and leaves, thus causing people to lose their immortality. The penis is described as a snake, which links Sido again with the idea of a snake as ancestor, either male or female. In this cycle of stories, a set from the Sepik area (Wogeo and Murik Lakes, P.N.G.), Malaita (Solomon Islands) and New Hebrides all describe the ancestral snake as female. She bears a daughter, who with her beauty attracts a man; he marries her, not knowing who she is, and she has a son. She gives the child to her mother, the snake, while she works, but the husband, coming upon the snake, is horrified and kills his serpent mother-in-law. If he had accepted her, he would have achieved fame and wealth. His wife, in grief, leaves him and returns to the earth.

In the Murik Lakes story the daughter is called Jari and her mother Gogo. The husband kills and cooks Gogo, so in revenge Jari cooks their son for him to eat and leaves him. She travels through all the villages, bestowing birth-magic and creating tidal rivers. She marries a man of the bush, to whom she gives knowledge of the arts of housebuilding, betel-nut chewing and tobacco-growing. She takes fire from her genitals and shows him how to cook food. She fashions his own genitals from betel nuts and bread-fruit, so that they can have intercourse. A carving

which represents her is thought to contain great power and she also is said to possess a prophetess and diviner belonging to the family which owns the carving. We see here a definite connection between myth, art and ritual, which is typical of the Sepik area as a whole.

The idea that man's genitals were made for him by woman appears in reverse form in the Highlands societies of P.N.G., where men claim dominance over women. In Mount Hagen (Western Highlands Province) a myth which is the basis of the contemporary Female Spirit cult tells how a man inserts a sharp stone and fragments of pearl shell into the stem of a banana tree. A number of girls rub themselves on the stem and cut themselves open, and the man and his brothers marry them. Their youngest sister, however, avoids this and remains a spirit. She returns to them in a storm and gives the man a pack of ornaments and magical substances, to be used in setting up her cult. Interestingly, one of the purposes of the cult is to protect men against the menstrual fluids of their wives, descended from the sisters who were first cut open. Only the spirit who remained unformed and a virgin can give this protection.

Incest and Fertility

The Huli (Southern Highlands Province, P.N.G.) link this same motif of cutting open women's genitals with the themes of incest and the origins of sun and moon. In their myth, Ni secretly watches his sister Hana rub herself on a tree trunk; he inserts a stone and she cuts herself. They copulate, and are ashamed to face their mother Honabe, so they ascend to the sky, where he becomes the sun and she the moon. While they themselves had no children from their incestuous intercourse, they are treated in cults as major deities whose rituals centre on fertility.

The theme is comparable to the myth of brother-sister incest among the Trobrianders (Milne Bay Province, P.N.G.). In this, a sister brushes her head accidentally against a vessel of charmed coconut oil and scented leaves, which her brother has prepared as love-magic. Inflamed, she chases him, and they have repeated intercourse on the shore, where they die of

ABOVE Wooden figure of a sea-spirit, with the head in the form of a shark. In the Solomon Islands it was believed that human souls might be reborn as sharks. From San Cristobal, Solomon Islands.

LEFT Malanggan carving of a fish with a flying fish and a snake as companions, ridden by the deities Solang (in male and female form) and preceded by the god Lemesisi. From New Ireland.

ABOVE Interior of *Haus Tambaran* (cult house) containing drums and carved figures at Kalabu, Maprik, Papua New Guinea.

RIGHT Hornbill carving for spirit house, with central moon symbol. The beak may be seen as phallic, while the moon design on its body is female. The figure is thus a composite male/female symbol. From Maprik, Papua New Guinea.

hunger and shame, while through their breasts a mint flower sprouts. A man from elsewhere sees this in a dream, and travels to obtain the boy's powerful magic and a sprig of the mint. Since then boys have used the magic to attract girls whom they can marry.

From the forbidden act, then, or more precisely the magic which caused it, comes what is lawful and fertile. In Trobriand society brother-sister incest is very strongly forbidden, yet in one sense the sister does reproduce for her brother, since group membership is traced matrilineally through women, and her children thus belong to her brother's sub clan, not to her husband's.

A further parallel is found among the Tangu, whose myths reiterate themes of relationships between father and son, elder brother and younger brother, brother and sister, and husband and wife, revealing both interdependence and hostility within these ties. In one myth a brother-sister pair of orphans are saved from a gigantic flood by climbing into a coconut tree. All others die, and these two have to mate in order to renew life. They build a new men's club-house and hold a feast, at which they strike the earth with a digging stick and all the new people, their descendants, emerge. Again, life is renewed perforce from a forbidden act.

Creation and Custom

Relations within the whole cosmos are often conceived of as on the same binary model of relations of kinship and marriage. Cosmological beings, such as the sun, are similarly explained in personified terms, as when the sun's heat is spoken of as coming from the anus of an old man in the sky (Imbongu people, Southern Highlands Province, P.N.G.), or from his forehead, which he rubs with a rough leaf to make it shine (Mount Hagen); or when the moon is said first to have been kept privately in a pot, from which it was stolen or escaped and ascended into the sky (Manus, New Ireland, and Sepik areas, P.N.G.).

Such stories may carry a deeper reference. The sun, as a primal ancestor, may be the ultimate keeper of morality. In Tolai myths (New Britain, P.N.G.), the sun is called To Kabinana, and he is the origin of proper custom, while his brother the moon breaks the correct rules of marriage. In the Eastern Highlands Province (Fore people) the earth is represented as a creative mother, called Jugumishanta, and her husband is Morufonu. Like Jari, she shapes the husband's genitals for him, and they have intercourse in a garden. Then they travel together, creating people, landscape and custom. Jugumishanta owns a sacred flute, hiding in it a piece of her pubic hair. Morufonu steals it to play, and as he touches the hair his own facial and body hair begins to grow. The myth reflects men's current control of such flutes and their use in initiation rituals for boys, from which women are excluded. It also tells us that male growth nevertheless depends on the fertilizing and creative power of women's sexuality.

In other Highlands societies, a creative role is ascribed to Sky Beings, known as *Tei-wamb* in Mount Hagen. They reveal themselves by sudden onset of mists or cracks of lightning. According to the origin myths of particular tribes, they reveal to an ancestor the tribe's *mi*, or totem, by which they swear oaths. In one group the *mi* is the cordyline plant, which appears also as the 'tree of life' in Baining myth.

Cargo cult myths show the same concern with fundamental sources of power. A Biak myth (Irian Jaya) tells of Manarmakeri, who entered the spirit world of Koreri and had a vision of immortality. He wandered, bringing blessings on those who accepted him despite his appearance as an unkempt old man (the symbolism of his journeys also connects him with the moon as a sign of immortality through its regular death and rebirth). Other people's lack of faith in him prevented their attainment of entry into Koreri and contact with the deity, Manseren Manggundi. The myth became the basis for recurrent religious movements through which Manseren was expected to return. The myth appears to be entirely indigenous.

Cargo myths in Madang Province, P.N.G., have been more influenced by Christian teaching from the Catholic and Lutheran missions established there since 1885. In accordance with indigenous ideas, the secret of the white man's wealth is presented as dependent on the hidden names of the Creator God, who is really the indigenous Dodo or Anutu, and of Christ, who is Kilibob or Manup, two sons of Anutu in traditional mythology. Both sons are culture heroes, Kilibob inventing useful arts such as canoe-building and wood-carving, Manup making love-magic, sorcery and warfare. Christ is seen as an equivalent hero for Europeans.

Generalizations over the whole spectrum of Melanesian mythology are obviously difficult. Nevertheless, three themes stand out: (1) initial creation, usually involving the creation of sexuality and sexual intercourse, which brings with it horticulture and customs of conduct towards kin; (2) the subsequent spread of knowledge, powers of fertility, and customs by extensive journeys made by heroes and heroines; and (3) the explanation of death and poverty as resulting from wrongdoing or mistakes placed in mythical time. Such themes, mirroring the individual cycle of birth, maturity and death, link Melanesian myths clearly with mythology and the problems of human life everywhere.

Ceremonial shield from Sepik, Papua New Guinea.

CHAPTER THIRTY

AUSTRALIA

Captain Cook's arrival at Sydney Cove in 1770 has become the nucleus of a new mythology. The official bicentenary celebrations in 1970 promoted him as a discoverer, a culture hero of Australian nationalism. Aborigines boycotting these rites denounced him as a villain, a symbol of conquest and dispossession.

The early European settlers were mostly hostile or indifferent to Aborigines and their culture, and expected both to die out. That actually happened around the southern and eastern coasts, as the remaining Aborigines became partly European, physically and in life-style. Traditional Aboriginal society was non-literate, depending on word-of-mouth transmission, supplemented by graphic representations, emblems, dance, drama and mime. In the southeast a few Europeans recorded what they could. Where European settlement was less heavy, in the centre and north, and especially in Arnhem Land and the Western Desert, Aboriginal culture had a breathing space. But mining and other pressures are bringing drastic changes.

Officially, the 'Aboriginal' label now covers everyone who identifies as such, whether 'full' or 'part' Aboriginal. The 1977 population estimate of about 136,300 included 13,600 Torres Strait Islanders. At first European settlement, the conventionally accepted guess is 300,000, made up of about 300 or 500 tribes, depending on how specific languages or dialects are grouped. The Aborigines were semi-nomadic, each group keeping within a certain range of territory. Goods, not people, moved along the trade routes that spanned the continent.

Many Aboriginal myths describe the travels of mythical characters (some of whom are ancestors) who play a creative role, naming places, altering the landscape, causing animals and human beings to appear, and establishing customs. Their tracks, superimposed on a map of Australia, would make a close-meshed criss-crossing pattern over every part of the land. These myths provided an outward-looking orientation, complementary to the focus on local sites and local identity. Regional variations in myths include different sequences in the travels of their characters, different names, different content,

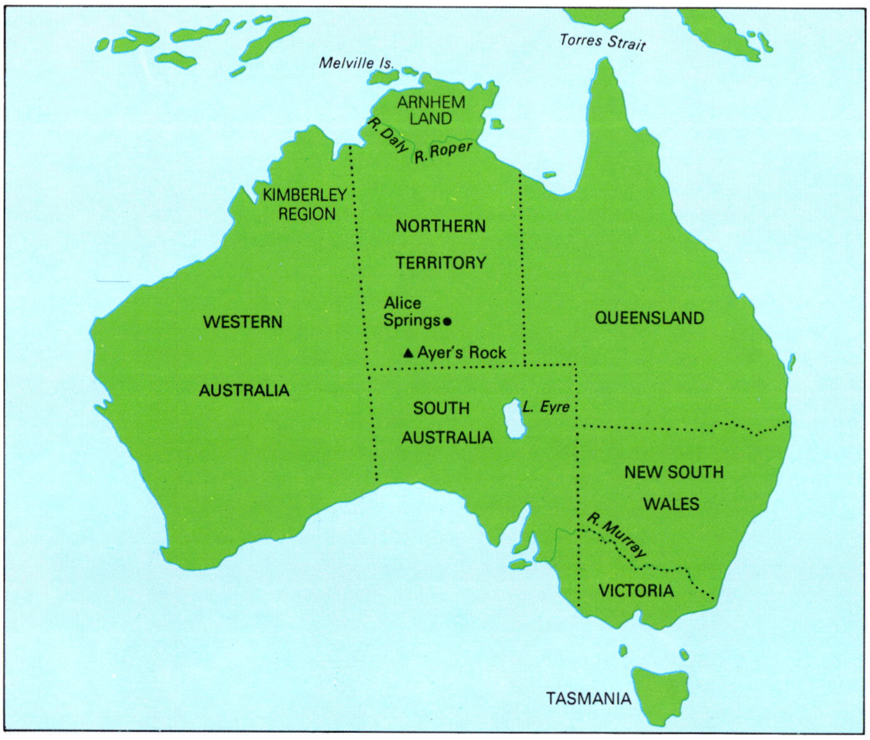

even different meanings. The main myths were tied to specific sites with local custodians and rules and penalties to check deviation. Men were the principal controllers and executives in sacred affairs, though women had important roles and responsibilities.

Straightforward plot-and-climax narratives were less common in Australia than in, say, Papua New Guinea. Most myths, in song or prose versions, or both, are long sequences of territory-linked episodes, concluded when a character takes on a new shape, or goes into the ground or into the sky, or moves out of the region. (Not knowing the end of a 'story-line' means not having close links with the people who are assumed to know it.)

Father, Mother and Snake

Everything people regarded as important had a place in their myths. Overall, there were thousands of characters. In each region, some were more prominent than others. An important figure throughout the south-east was the All-Father or Sky Hero, known by such regional names as Baiami, Daramulun, Koin, or just Papang ('Father'). A near-equivalent on the lower Murray River in South Australia was Ngurunderi. The various Mura-mura beings of the Lake Eyre Basin were typically able to change shape. So were most of the mythical travellers through the Western Desert. Emphasis on dominant male figures is most noticeable among the northern Aranda, in central Australia, though there the earth itself is a nurturing, life-giving mother. Farther north, female characters get more attention. So does the female role in creation and fertility. There are the two Djanggau (Djanggawul) Sisters, who on their travels populated the Arnhem Land coast; Wara-murunggundji, the Mother who came from the north-west via Melville Island to western Arnhem Land; and old blind Mudungkala, who emerged from the earth at Melville Island with three babies, the first human beings. The Old Woman or Fertility Mother, Kunapipi (Gunabibi), Gadjari, Karwadi or other names, often combined with the Lightning Snake, is central to a religious complex that has spread through the north of the Northern Territory into Western Australia.

On the northwest coast the most powerful figures are the Wandjina, made famous through their representations in rock art. Associated with rain and seasonal fertility, and with Ungud the Rainbow

ABOVE Great snakes, living in watercourses, pools or underground, sometimes manifestations of the rainbow, are powerful and feared beings of Aboriginal mythology. There are many myths of them swallowing up people and animals. Myth of the Rainbow Serpent, from Port Keats, Northern Territory.

OPPOSITE Performers during the Irrikara totem ceremony of the Aranda in central Australia. The Aranda are divided into totemic groups, each connected with an animal or plant. Women and children are banned from these ceremonies, which are confined to men. A common mythological theme in Australia, as in South America, is that women once controlled sacred rites which were taken over by men.

ABOVE Wandjina figure, on bark, from Kimberley, Western Australia. The Wandjina are associated with rain and fertility.

RIGHT Aboriginal bark painting from eastern Arnhem Land, Northern Territory. In the bottom section and the second section up the Djanggau Sisters are giving birth to the first human beings. In the third section are sacred poles and trees which provide shade for the children. At the top, the two Sisters stand by the sacred spring, and on the right is the artist, Mawalan, himself.

Snake, they resemble other characters throughout the north. Huge snakes living in billabongs, or watercourses, or underground, sometimes manifestations of the rainbow, such as Kaleru, the great Rainbow Snake of the Kimberley region, are an almost constant feature of myth and fragmented tradition all through the continent (except Tasmania, where no such evidence is available). Wanambi in his deep pools in and around the Western Desert is still powerful and feared. The Snake-Man Jarapiri and his companions, who made a creative journey from Winbaraku, northwest of Alice Springs, are now part of that landscape. The giant northern Aranda Snake of Emianga, after swallowing numbers of people, including some ancestral edible-seed women who had emerged from the same pool, is now deeply and dangerously coiled beneath the waters at his final resting place.

Myths and Territory

Aboriginal myths have several generally accepted characteristics. Many, not all, are connected in some way with sacred ritual. They provide a charter, or complex of charters, for ritual events or sequences, including initiation rites such as circumcision, and mortuary and fertility rites. Ritual events dramatically celebrate episodes of the Dreaming, the mythical time in the past which is also present now, the eternal past-in-the-present, so that the actors in the ritual become, temporarily, the mythical characters themselves.

The myths map out verbally the dimensions of particular territories, noting which mythical characters are where, or where they emerged, or where they went. They emphasize the ties between specific territories and specific groups of people. They represent ownership and custody statements, an equivalent of written title-deeds. And they underline the *idea* of identification with territory as an inevitable 'fact of life'.

The Wapiya Girls

Myths include statements about relations between individuals and between groups; similarities and contrasts, as in language or marriage rules; proper and wrong ways of behaving. The story of the Wapiya Girls brings in several features: the groups of girls, the song-demonstration, language-change, food collection, the girls' circumcision of a youth and the killing of the girls for breaking a religious taboo.

This story is a Wonkamala myth from the Lake Eyre district, South Australia. After the old Mura-mura Madaputa-tupuru died, his daughters mourned for him and buried him. Then they went north to Ukaralya ('Girls') Creek. On the opposite bank they saw the Wapiya ('Boomerang') girls. They exchanged greetings and each group gave a representation of their respective *Mura*, or sacred songs. Then the first group danced across the creek and joined the others, adopting their language, Wonkamala. They went north together, dancing and laughing.

Some time later, after gathering sweet tree-gum

LEFT Many Aboriginal myths tell of mythical characters who wandered about, altering the landscape and causing humans and animals to appear. The journey of the great Snake is recreated in ceremonies and paintings by the Warramunga people. This painting is at the place where the Snake ended his journey.

BELOW In northeastern Arnhem Land the dead are believed to go to an island somewhere in the Torres Straits, where they are greeted by the Kultana, a spirit associated with the north wind and rain. The design on the Kultana's body represents falling rain.

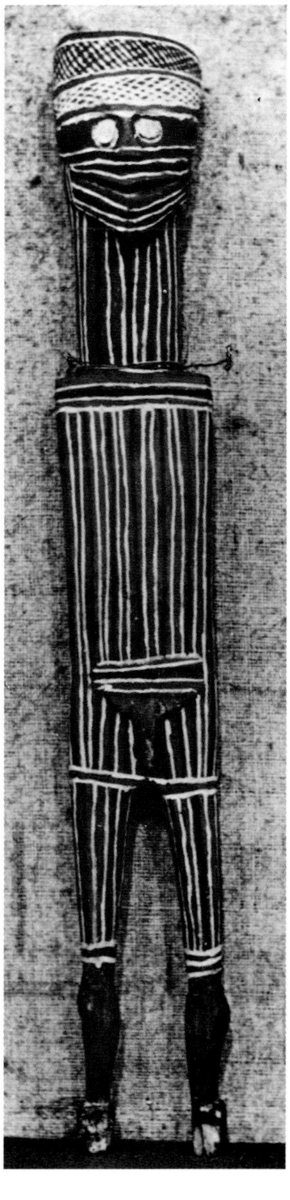

and drinking some mixed with water, they came to a vast sheet of water with high tumbling waves. They hurried forward and joyfully bathed in the waters. Then they followed the shore until they were stopped by a steep hill, which rose from it. Some of them turned homeward and met a youth, whom they circumcised. They sent him to a nearby camp to get wood for their fire but, though his wound was still unhealed, he wished to have access to the women there, who were enraged by his immodest behaviour and killed him. The girls waited for him, but finally decided he must be dead. Continuing on their journey, they came to a place where a number of men had assembled for the sacred Wodampa dance. The men, angry that the girls had seen what it was not lawful for them to see, strangled them.

The girls who had not feared the steep hill danced to it in a line. The oldest of them struck it with her digging-stick so that it split, and they all danced through the opening. Arawotya, who lives in the sky, let down a hair cord and drew them up to himself, folding up the cord as he did so. But one of the girls, climbing up the cord, cut her hand with her digging-stick and let her bowl fall. She climbed down to get it, but now Arawotya had drawn the cord up, out of her reach. So she had to remain below. She met two young men who threw their weapons at her, but because she was covered with shining scales they glanced off her harmlessly and returned to them. Finally one of them burst her covering of scales with the stem of a tree, so that she was without covering. Then she gave herself up and became his wife.

Arawotya at one time wandered over the earth, making the deep springs which are to be seen in otherwise waterless parts of western Queensland. It was after he had done this that he went up to the sky. (Adapted from Howitt, 1904.)

Myths and Reality

Basically myths draw on the ingredients of everyday living: food, water, firewood and other materials, terrain, taboo places. From this point of view, they are actual and potential survival-kits. The information they contain can be spelled out or noted in passing (as in teaching children). Stories of the origin of fire, for example, can tell how to make fire.

Some myths deal directly with transcendental issues. What is life, what is its meaning and purpose? What is death? Where do the dead go? How did it all begin? Who is responsible? Living creatures come in various shapes, but what is behind these appearances, these physical forms? Are they essentially or potentially one, different but interdependent manifestations of the same life-force? Myths supply final answers, either in short statements or in more discursive accounts with symbolic and perhaps ritual ramifications. Stories which connect Moon with death are examples, though not all explanations of death include Moon.

A Wotjo myth from Victoria says that at the time when all animals were men and women, some died, and the moon used to say, 'You up-again', and they all came to life again. There was at that time an old man who said, 'Let them remain dead.' Then none ever came to life again, except the moon, which still continued to do so. (Howitt, 1904.)

According to a Lungga/Gidja myth from East Kimberley, Moon tried to seduce Snake, but she was in the category of women he called mother-in-law. Therefore, she was taboo to him. She and the other women with her attacked Moon in fury and cut off his organs, which turned to stone. Then he declared angrily: 'When I die, I shall come back in five days; when you die you will not come back, you will stop dead.' (Kaberry, 1939.)

In a Gunwinggu story from western Arnhem Land, Yagul, a red-eyed Pigeon man, was sick. He was dying. Moon tried to help him. 'Do what I do!

I die, but I always come alive again. Look at me. Here I am now, new!' Djabo, the Spotted-Cat man, was sceptical about this. He persuaded Yagul not to try. 'No, I shall just die,' Yagul told Moon. So that is now the custom for all human beings. When Djabo himself was sick, Moon tried to help him too. 'Drink my urine,' he urged him, 'and then you will be like me, you will come back to life.' But Djabo wouldn't. If Yakul and Djabo had listened to Moon, nobody would have died.

Because they concern 'ought' as well as 'is', myths bring in contrasts of 'ought not' behaviour. They include 'bad examples' as well as 'good examples'. Incest, breaches of marriage rules, rape, treachery, murder, may not be punished, nor even stated to be wrong. Here problems of interpretation can be difficult, and not only for outsiders.

References to the movements of mythical characters need not be taken as reports of where the actual population of a region originally came from. When Seagull made the Torres Strait Islands by 'stepping over the sea', this illustrates the cultural link between them and the mainland, and with Papua. The characters who came to western Arnhem Land from Manggadjara (Macassar) via Melville Island reflect the contact with Indonesian traders that ended early in this century; but even more such characters came there from the mainland itself, from all directions. The Aranda emphasis on local origins for so many of their heroic figures conforms with their strong belief in local continuity, through the partial reincarnation of those actual beings in ordinary human form.

Whether the distance they covered was small or great, many of the mythical travellers left visible marks in the landscape. The basic substance of earth and sea was there when they came, or when they

ABOVE Aranda initiation ceremony. The totemic ancestors established the rites of initiation for young men, in which they are taught the myths and sacred ceremonies.

RIGHT Bark painting, belonging to an Aboriginal medicine-man, showing the goose-men who were totemic ancestors. From the swamp country near Elcho Island, Arnhem Land.

emerged from it. They shaped, added to, rearranged it, made rivers and billabongs, hills or trees, or simply left footprints or buttock imprints. The jagged western escarpment of Arnhem Land is full of mythical characters who turned themselves into rocks; or the rocks are their bones, vomited by the Rainbow Snake, who had swallowed them, drowned them in a great flood, after being disturbed by some noise they were making – a child crying, for instance, or people shouting or knocking on the ground. Myths of potential disaster have been reinforced by preparations for uranium mining in this region, and myths of land ownership have taken on a new meaning in land-rights claims and anti-mining protests.

Male-Female Relations

Not all the main creators produced human beings in a final and near-perfect state. In some Dieri myths, from South Australia, the first creatures of human type were 'quite unformed'. In some south-eastern myths they had no sex organs or the sexes were not differentiated. In a Wotjbaluk example from Victoria, a man 'altered himself and one other so that he was the man and the other was the woman'. In a Mungkan myth from northern Queensland, Moon turned his younger brother into a woman, to be his wife. (Moon is always male in Australia, while the sun is almost everywhere female.) In north-eastern Arnhem Land the Djanggau Sisters and their Brother had abnormally large genitals. But the children they made were normally sexed from birth, though women's roles in child-minding and in religious rites were at first the converse of what they are now. This illustrates the common theme that women once owned or controlled all or some of the secret-sacred songs and rites, but these were stolen or otherwise taken over by men.

The myth of the Wawalag Sisters, also from Arnhem Land, shows a different facet of male-female relations. In the beginning, two Sisters came north from the Wawalag country near the Roper River. Some people (but not, traditionally, in women's versions) say they left there because they had an incestuous relationship with a man. The elder, Waimariwi, had a small child, and she was pregnant. The younger, Boaliri, had just reached puberty. They travelled through many places, naming them as they reached them. Their long baskets were heavy with stone spearheads. Along the way they collected roots, and their two female dogs helped them to catch small animals. They gave them all names. At last they reached a sacred waterhole where, tired, they put down their things. They didn't know that this was the home of the great python, Yulunggul.

Waimariwi's child was born. Boaliri tried to cook supper, but all the food jumped from the fire and dived into the waterhole – roots, goannas, blanket lizards, glider possums, wallabies, everything! 'Oh, sister, something is wrong. Maybe there's a Snake here?' But it was too dark to leave that place. A great storm broke, with lightning, thunder and heavy rain. They washed the baby quickly, to remove the smell of the afterbirth blood, but some blood must have fallen into the waterhole. (Or, as some people say, menstrual blood from the younger Sister.) Now it was night. Inside the hut, by their fire, they danced and sang sacred songs to calm the storm. The storm became quieter. But they couldn't stay awake. Perhaps they thought the Snake had gone. But he was there, waiting. He was singing, making them drowsy. They slept.

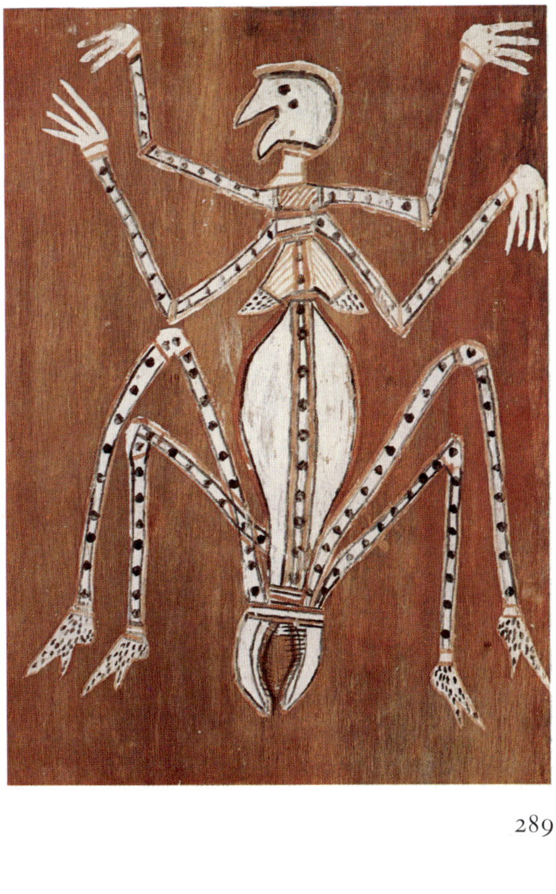

ABOVE Initiation ceremonies often involve circumcision and an ordeal by fire. A boy is raised on a shield to be circumcised in this Aranda initiation rite.

LEFT Bark painting from Croker Island, Northern Territory, showing a pregnant female spirit. Many Aboriginal mythical figures formed or gave birth to human beings, though not always in a final state. Sometimes the first creatures of human type were 'unformed', or had no sex organs.

RIGHT Aboriginal rock paintings recreate and perpetuate the adventures of the mythical figures of the Dreaming, the time in the past which is also present now. Many rituals celebrate episodes of the Dreaming and those who take part in them become, for the moment, the mythical characters themselves.

BELOW The Rainbow Snake swallowing children of one of the Wawalag Sisters, in a bark painting from northeast Arnhem Land. In the myth the two Sisters camped unawares by the waterhole in which the great python Yulunggul lived. The Snake sang them to sleep and then devoured the Sisters and the children, afterwards vomiting the children up.

Yulunggul emerged from his waterhole. He stretched himself, standing erect, then lowered himself again. He put his head into the hut. He wrapped his body around and around it (as a python does with its prey). Water came flooding over the ground. And he swallowed them all: the Sisters, the dogs, the children, and the stone spears. They slept inside his stomach. An ant bit him. He jumped and vomited them up. Then he swallowed the Sisters again. He stood erect again, his head reaching toward the sky. Facing east, he spoke with the other great pythons who lived at sacred places in that region. At first Yulunggul lied to them. Then he confessed: 'I ate those two Wawalag!' He lowered himself to the ground again, and retreated into his waterhole. And there he is today, with the two Wawalag, in that sacred water.

That is how the monsoon came, to bring the wet season. And that is how the rituals for circumcising boys began.

The Sisters lost to the Snake (acknowledged as a phallic symbol even when reported to be female) the creatures they had named and their ritual songs as well. In men's versions, they tried to resist men's ritual authority and the loss of their male children to the world of men, for circumcision.

The Djanggau and Wawalag myths are complex in details and in interpretations, underlining the point that the myths of any region should not be

considered separately but in conjunction. The Wawalag mother-child (father absent) situation differs from the large-scale, more impersonal creation of people by the Djanggau. Myths from other areas, in contrast, may emphasize the family unit or highlight sex antagonisms and men's attitudes to women as sexual objects, with the family as less important.

Detailed analysis of these and other themes has barely begun. Straightforward symbolic and ritual interpretations are only a jumping-off point. For instance, the Old Woman or Mother who swallows novices during initiation rites is a familiar, accepted mythical figure, but in a Daly River myth, from the Northern Territory, the Old Woman, Mutjinga, was killed for swallowing all the novices she was guarding – killed because she did not vomit them up alive?

The problem is one of relating myth-content to local explanations and local 'reality' without being confined to these. It is exemplified in the Aranda myth of a bleached Skull-Ancestor, among 'dark rocks slippery with blood', and an 'ancestral sire' who killed his own sons who had behaved hostilely to him: a myth with 'a strong element of savage fierceness and cruelty and treachery' (Strehlow, 1971: 551–60), and this in a region where ordinary life, despite its conflicts, was not marked by the warlike aggressiveness evident in some societies. But 'catharsis' is not an adequate explanation, and this myth too must be seen within the context of the entire Aranda repertoire.

Currently, some myths are being simplified or reframed for tourist consumption. Uluru, Ayers Rock, in central Australia, is one famous site involved in this process. But conversely, because it is home to an assortment of mythical characters (snakes, lizards, hare-wallabies, dingo, marsupial moles, willy-wagtail), it has potential as well as actual links with Aboriginal traditions from other areas. Aboriginal myth is still a dynamic force, with enough momentum and enough support to reshape its regional relevance to meet today's changing circumstances. The current emphasis on cultural revival and Australia-wide Aboriginal identity draws on still-living local traditions to supply more generalized content and symbols. The rich mosaic of Aboriginal myth and its dramatic and artistic counterparts demonstrate the complexity, depth and poetic genius of Aboriginal traditional life, as a positive foundation for the future.

Carved wooden figures of the elder Wawalag Sister, centre, and the younger Wawalag Sister, left. The other figure, right, is Laindjung, who rose from the sea, his face stained with foam and his body running with water. Figures like these are sometimes used in rituals linked with myths.

GLOSSARY

aetiology, or **etiology** The study of causes. Aetiological myths explain how something came to be (the origin of a custom, for example).

androgynous Uniting male and female, hermaphroditic.

aniconic Represented symbolically rather than pictorially (a god represented as a rock or a stump of wood, for example).

anthropomorphism Attribution of human form and personality to something non-human, as a deity or animal.

avatar A deity's descent to earth in a visible form, a manifestation or incarnation of a deity.

catharsis Purging of the emotions by vicarious experience, as through hearing a myth.

chthonic Connected with the earth. From Greek *chthon*, 'earth'.

cosmogony A theory of the origin of the universe.

cosmology A theory of the origin and construction of the universe.

culture hero or heroine A mythological being who first bestowed civilization on human beings, giving them knowledge of arts and crafts, social institutions, laws and customs.

dichotomy Division of a whole into two parts.

epiphany The manifestation of a deity.

eponym One for whom a people, place or institution is named. A hero invented to explain a name. The eponymous ancestor of a people is the one whose name they bear (Aeolus as ancestor of the Aeolian Greeks, for example).

euhemerism The theory that the gods were originally real men and women. The interpretation of myths as based on real events. From Euhemerus, a Greek philosopher of the 4th century BC.

fetish A statue or object believed to contain a spirit and so to have magical power. From a Portuguese term for the gods of West Africa.

iconography Pictorial representation of a deity or mythological being.

incarnation Embodiment in flesh.

indigenous Originating in a given locality, not introduced from outside.

ithyphallic With erect phallus.

karma (in Sanskrit) or **kamma** (in Pali) 'Actions'. In Hinduism and Buddhism, the sum total of a person's actions, thoughts and feelings, whose consequences are worked out in successive lives.

liturgical Connected with public ritual.

lustration Ceremonial purification, by sacrifice or often by washing.

mana Mysterious spiritual power residing in a person, animal, object or place. The term comes from Polynesia, but is used for similar concepts in other societies.

metamorphosis Change of shape, transformation of one creature into another.

millennium Period of a thousand years. More specifically, the thousand-year reign of Christ on earth predicted in the Book of Revelation (Chapter 20). Millennial myths are those related to the future return of some great figure of the past who will preside over a period of happiness and peace.

monotheism The belief that there is only one deity.

mythopoeic Myth-making, myth-creating.

numinous Pertaining to divine power and inspiring profound awe. From Latin *numen*.

palladium An object on which the safety of a people or institution is believed to depend. From the image of the goddess Pallas kept in the city of Troy.

pantheon Literally 'all the gods', a people's deities considered as a group. Also used for a group of deities closely related by kinship or domain.

polytheism The belief that there are many deities.

rites of passage Rites conducted to ensure a safe passage from one place, state or condition to another, as at birth, puberty, marriage and death.

shaman Priest-magician, who is also a doctor and diviner. Medicine-man.

syncretism The blending together of beliefs or practices from different traditions.

taboo Sacred and consequently prohibited or hedged with restrictions. Banned or set apart. From a Polynesian term, *tapu*.

theocracy Government by priests.

theogony The genealogy of the gods.

theophany The manifestation of a deity.

theriomorphic In animal form.

totem The emblem or badge of a group or individual, an animal, plant or object with which the group or individual is closely connected. Originally a North American Indian word, from the Algonquian group of languages.

trickster A crafty and cunning deity or mythological figure, who persistently plays tricks and engages in wily stratagems. In some myths he plays an important role in the creation of the world or in its subsequent corruption. Often described as greedy, lustful, treacherous and contemptible.

zoomorphic In animal form.

BIBLIOGRAPHY

HINDUISM AND BUDDHISM

Bhattacarji, S. *The Indian Theology: A Comparative Study of Indian Mythology*, Cambridge, 1970
Danièlou, A. *Hindu Polytheism*, London, 1964
Dikshitar, V.R.R. *The Purana Index*, 3 vols, Madras, 1955
Dimmitt, C. and van Buitenen, J.A.B. *Classical Hindu Mythology*, Philadelphia, 1978
Dowson, J. *A Classical Dictionary of Hindu Mythology and Religion*, London, 1961
Hopkins, E.W. *Epic Mythology*, Wiesbaden, 1978 reprint
Keith, A.B. *Indian Mythology* (in *The Mythology of All Races*, vol 6, New York, 1964 reprint)
Kosambi, D.D. *Myth and Reality*, Bombay, 1962
Kosambi, D.D. *The Culture and Civilization of Ancient India*, London, 1965
Law, B.C. *The Buddhist Conception of Spirits*, Calcutta, 1923
Law, B.C. *Heaven and Hell in Buddhist Perspective*, Calcutta, 1923
Ling, T. *Buddhism and the Mythology of Evil*, London, 1962
Macdonell, A.A. *Vedic Mythology*, Delhi, 1963 reprint
Mani, V. *Puranic Encyclopedia*, Delhi, 1975
Marasinghe, M.M.J. *Gods in Early Buddhism*, Sri Lanka, 1974
Moor, E. *The Hindu Pantheon*, Delhi, 1968 reprint
O'Flaherty, W. *Hindu Myths*, London, 1975
Sörensen, S. *Index to the Names in the Mahabharata*, Delhi, 1963 reprint
Wilkins, W.J. *Hindu Mythology, Vedic and Puranic*, London, 1973 reprint
Zimmer, H. *Philosophies of India*, New York, 1957
Zimmer, H. *Myths and Symbols in Indian Art and Civilization*, New York, 1968 reprint

ZOROASTRIANISM

Boyce, M. *A Persian Stronghold of Zoroastrianism*, Oxford, 1978
Boyce, M. *Zoroastrians, Their Religious Beliefs and Practices*, London, 1978
Frye, R.N. *Heritage of Persia*, London, 1976 reprint
Hinnells, J.R. *Persian Mythology*, London, 1973
Jackson, A.V.W. *Zoroaster the Prophet of Ancient Iran*, New York, 1965
Jackson, A.V.W. *Zoroastrian Studies*, New York, 1965 reprint
Zaehner, R.C. *The Dawn and Twilight of Zoroastrianism*, London, 1976
Zaehner, R.C. *The Teachings of the Magi*, London, 1976 reprint

TIBET

Clark, W.E. *Two Lamaistic Pantheons*, New York, 1965 reprint
David-Neil, A. *The Superhuman life of Gesar of Ling*, London, 1958
Evans-Wentz, W.Y. *Tibet's Great Yogi Milarepa*, London, 1951
Evans-Wentz, W.Y. *The Tibetan Book of the Dead*, London, 1957
Getty, A. *The Gods of Northern Buddhism*, Oxford, 1963 reprint
Karmay, S.G. *The Treasury of Good Sayings: A Tibetan History of Bon*, Oxford, 1972
Nebesky-Wojkowitz, R. *Oracles and Demons of Tibet*, The Hague, 1956
Nebesky-Wojkowitz, R. *Where the Gods are Mountains*, London, 1956
Snellgrove, D. *Buddhist Himalaya*, Oxford, 1957
Snellgrove, D. *Nine Ways of Bon*, London, 1967
Snellgrove, D. and Richardson, H. *A Cultural History of Tibet*, London, 1968
Stein, R.A. *Tibetan Civilization*, London, 1972

CHINA AND JAPAN

Anesaki, M. *Japanese Mythology* (in *The Mythology of All Races*, vol 8, New York, 1964 reprint)
Birch, C. *Chinese Myths and Fantasies*, Oxford, 1962
Christie, A. *Chinese Mythology*, London, 1968
Eberhard, W. *Folktales of China*, London, 1965
Fitzgerald, C.P. *China, a Short Cultural History*, London, 1935
Granet, M. *Festivals and Songs of Ancient China*, London, 1932
Kojiki, transl. B.H.Chamberlain, *Transactions of the Asiatic Society of Japan*, vol 10, 1882
Kojiki, transl. D.L. Philippi, London, 1968
Mackenzie, D.A. *Myths of China and Japan*, London, 1923
Nihongi, Chronicles of Japan, transl. W.G. Aston, London, 1956 reprint
Saunders, E.D. 'Japanese Mythology' (in *Mythologies of the Ancient World*, ed S.N. Kramer, New York, 1961)
Waley, A. *Monkey*, London, 1961
Werner, E.T.C. *Myths and Legends of China*, London, 1922

MESOPOTAMIA, SYRIA AND PALESTINE

Albright, W.F. *Yahweh and the Gods of Canaan*, 1968
Brandon, S.G.F. *Creation Legends of the Ancient Near East*, London, 1963
Cross, F.M. *Canaanite Myth and Hebrew Epic*, 1973
Frankfort, H. (ed) *Before Philosophy*, London, 1949 (first published as *The Intellectual Adventure of Ancient Man*, Chicago, 1946)
Frankfort, H. *The Problem of Similarity in Ancient Near Eastern Religions*, 1951
Gaster, T.H. *Thespis: Ritual, Myth and Drama in the Ancient Near East*, New York, 1961
Gibson, J.C.L. *Canaanite Myths and Legends*, 1978
Gray, J. *The Legacy of Canaan*, London, 1965
Heidel, A. *The Babylonian Genesis*, Chicago, 1951
Hooke, S.H. *Babylonian and Assyrian Religion*, London, 1953
Hooke, S.H. (ed) *Myth, Ritual and Kingship*, Oxford, 1958
Kapelrud, A.S. *Baal in the Ras Shamra Texts*, 1952
Kapelrud, A.S. *The Violent Goddess*, 1969
Kramer, S.N. *Sumerian Mythology*, Philadelphia, 1944
Ringgren, H. *Israelite Religion*, 1969
Rogerson, J.W. *Myth in the Old Testament*, 1974
Saggs, H.W.F. *The Greatness that was Babylon*, London, 1962
Sandars, N.K. *The Epic of Gilgamesh*, London, 1960

EGYPT

Brandon, S.G.F. *Creation Legends of the Ancient Near East*, London, 1963
Edwards, I.E.S. *The Pyramids of Egypt*, London, 1965
Erman, A. *The Ancient Egyptians*, New York, 1966
Frankfort, H. *Ancient Egyptian Religion*, New York, 1948
Gardiner, A.H. *Egypt of the Pharaohs*, Oxford, 1961
Green, R.L. *Tales of Ancient Egypt*, London, 1967
Griffiths, J.G. *The Origins of Osiris*, Berlin, 1966
Morenz, S. *Egyptian Religion*, London, 1973
Plutarch *De Iside et Osiride*, ed J.G. Griffiths, Cardiff, 1970

ISLAM
Eliade, M. *Images and Symbols*, London, 1961
Engnell, I. *Studies in Divine Kingship in the Ancient Near East*, Oxford, 1967
Faris, N. *The Antiquities of South Arabia*, Princeton, 1938
Gerhardt, M. *The Art of Story-Telling*, London, 1963
Hamori, A. *On the Art of Medieval Arabic Literature*, Princeton, 1974
Hitti, P.K. *History of the Arabs*, London, 1946
Leach, E. *Genesis and Myth and Other Essays*, London, 1970
Lévi-Strauss, C. *The Savage Mind*, London and Chicago, 1966
Nicholson, R.A. *A Literary History of the Arabs*, Cambridge, 1969
Norris, H.T, *Saharan Myth and Saga*, Oxford, 1972
Serjeant, R.B. *South Arabian Hunt*, London, 1976
Wensinck, A.J. *The Ocean in the Literature of the Western Semites*, Amsterdam, 1918

GREECE
Dodds, E.R. *The Greeks and the Irrational*, Berkeley, 1971 reprint
Fontenrose, J.E. *Python: A Study of Delphic Myth*, Berkeley and London, 1959
Grant, M. *Myths of the Greeks and Romans*, London, 1962
Graves, R. *The Greek Myths*, 2 vols, London, 1955
Guthrie, W.K.C. *The Religion and Mythology of the Greeks* (in *The Cambridge Ancient History*, vol 2, 1961)
Hesiod *Theogony*, ed M.L. West, Oxford, 1966
Homer *The Odyssey*, transl. E.V. Rieu, London, 1946
Homer *The Iliad*, transl. E.V. Rieu, London, 1950
Kirk, G.S. *Myth: Its Meanings and Functions in Ancient and Other Cultures*, Cambridge, 1970
Kirk, G.S. *The Nature of Greek Myths*, London, 1974
Lloyd-Jones, H. *The Justice of Zeus*, Berkeley, 1971
Nilsson, M.P. *The Mycenaean Origin of Greek Religion*, New York, 1963
Otto, W.F. *Dionysus: Myth and Cult*, Bloomington, 1965 reprint
Otto, W.F. *The Homeric Gods*, London, 1955
Pinsent, J. *Greek Mythology*, London, 1969
Rose, H.J. *A Handbook of Greek Mythology*, London, 1964
Schefold, K. *Myth and Legend in Early Greek Art*, London, 1966

ROME
Gjerstad, E. *Legends and Facts of Early Roman History*, Lund, 1962
Grant, M. *Myths of the Greeks and Romans*, London, 1962
Grant, M. *Roman Myths*, London, 1971
Livy *The Early History of Rome*, transl. A. de Selincourt, London, 1960
Ogilvie, R.M. *The Romans and Their Gods*, London, 1969
Oswalt, S.G. *Concise Encyclopaedia of Greek and Roman Myth*, London, 1969
Ovid *Fasti*, transl. J.G. Frazer, London, 1929
Ovid *Metamorphoses*, transl. R. Humphries, London, 1957
Perowne, S. *Roman Mythology*, London, 1969
Vergil *The Aeneid*, transl. C. Day Lewis, London, 1952

THE MYSTERY RELIGIONS
Angus, S. *The Mystery Religions and Christianity*, New York, 1925
Campbell, J. (ed) *The Mysteries*, London, 1955
Cole, S. *The Samothracian Mysteries*, High Wycombe, 1975
Cumont, F. *The Mysteries of Mithra*, Chicago, 1910
Ferguson, J. *The Religions of the Roman Empire*, London, 1970
Festugière, A.J. *Personal Religion Among the Greeks*, Berkeley, 1954
Guthrie, W.K.C. *Orpheus and Greek Religion*, London, 1952
Hinnells, J.R. *Spanning East and West*, Milton Keynes, 1977 (on Mithraism)
Kerenyi, C. *Dionysus: Archetypal Image of Indestructible Life*, Princeton, 1976
Kerenyi, R. *Eleusis*, London, 1967
Linforth, I.M. *The Arts of Orpheus*, Berkeley, 1941
Mylonas, G.E. *Eleusis and the Eleusinian Mysteries*, Princeton, 1961
Willoughby, H.R. *Pagan Regenerations*, Chicago, 1929
Witt, R.E. *Isis in the Graeco-Roman World*, London, 1970

CHRISTIANITY
Brandon, S.G.F. *Creation Legends of the Ancient Near East*, London, 1963
Cavendish, R. *Visions of Heaven and Hell*, London, 1977
Cavendish, R. *King Arthur and the Grail*, London, 1978
Hick, J. *Evil and the God of Love*, London, 1966
Hick, J. (ed) *The Myth of God Incarnate*, London, 1977
Holmyard, E.J. *Alchemy*, London, 1957
Jung, C.G. *Psychology and Alchemy*, London, 1953
Levin, Harry *The Myth of the Golden Age in the Renaissance*, London, 1970
Loomis, R.S. *The Grail: from Celtic Myth to Christian Symbol*, New York and Cardiff, 1963
Patch, H.R. *The Other World According to Descriptions in Medieval Literature*, Harvard, 1950
Russell, J.B. *Witchcraft in the Middle Ages*, Cornell, 1972
Seznec, J. *The Survival of the Pagan Gods*, New York, 1953
Simon, U. *Heaven in the Christian Tradition*, London, 1958
Trevor-Roper, H.R. *The European Witch-Craze in the 16th and 17th Centuries*, London, 1969
Williams, N.P. *The Ideas of the Fall and of Original Sin*, London, 1927
Wind, E. *Pagan Mysteries in the Renaissance*, New York, 1958
Yates, F.A. *The Rosicrucian Enlightenment*, London, 1972

THE CELTS
Chadwick, N.K. *The Celts*, London, 1970
Cross, T.P. and Slover, C.H. *Ancient Irish Tales*, New York, 1936
Dillon, M. *Early Irish Literature*, Chicago, 1948
Dillon, M. (ed) *Irish Sagas*, Cork, 1968
Dillon, M. and Chadwick, N.K. *The Celtic Realms*, London, 1972
Filip, J. *Celtic Civilisation and Its Heritage*, Wellingborough, 1977
The Mabinogion, transl. G. & T. Jones, London, 1972 reprint
MacCana, P. *Celtic Mythology*, London, 1970
Murphy, G. *Saga and Myth in Ancient Ireland*, Cork, 1971
Piggott, S. *The Druids*, London, 1974
Powell, T.G.E. *The Celts*, London, 1958
Rees, A. & B. *Celtic Heritage*, London, 1961
Ross, A. *Pagan Celtic Britain*, London, 1967

SCANDINAVIA AND GERMANY
Davidson, H.R.E. *Gods and Myths of Northern Europe*, London, 1964
King, F. *Satan and Swastika*, London, 1976
The Nibelungenlied, transl. A.T. Hatto, London, 1965
The Prose Edda, transl. J.I. Young, Berkeley, 1966
Tacitus *Germania*, London, 1970
Turville-Petre, E.O.G. *Myth and Religion in the North*, London, 1964

THE SLAVS
Dvornik, F. *The Slavs*, Boston, 1956
Gimbutas, M. *The Slavs*, London and New York, 1971
Hoddinott, R.F. *Early Byzantine Churches in Macedonia and Southern Serbia*, London, 1963
Lang, D.M. *The Bulgarians*, London and Boulder, 1976
Ralston, W.R.S. *Russian Folk-Tales*, London, 1873
Rayfield, D. 'The Heroic Ethos of Russian and Georgian Folk Poetry' (in *The Slavonic and East European Review*, vol 56, London, 1978)
The Song of Igor's Campaign, transl. V. Nabokov, London, 1960
Wosien, M.G. *The Russian Folk-Tale*, Munich, 1969

ARMENIA, GEORGIA AND THE CAUCASUS
Apollonius Rhodius *Argonautica*, transl. E.P. Coleridge, New York, 1960
Baddeley, J.F. *The Rugged Flanks of Caucasus*, 2 vols, Oxford, 1940
Burney, C. and Lang, D.M. *The Peoples of the Hills*, London 1971
Downing, C. *Armenian Folk-Tales and Fables*, Oxford, 1972
Lang, D.M. *The Georgians*, London and New York, 1966
Lang, D.M. *Armenia, Cradle of Civilization*, London, 1978
Maclean, F. *To Caucasus, the End of all the Earth*, London, 1976
Rustaveli, S. *The Man in the Panther's Skin*, transl. M.S. Wardrop, London, 1966
Rustaveli, S. *The Knight in Panther Skin*, transl. K. Vivian, London, 1977
Surmelian, L., *Daredevils of Sassoun*, London, 1966
Surmelian, L., *Apples of Immortality*, London, 1968

AFRICA
Argyle, W.J. *The Fon of Dahomey*, Oxford, 1966
Bleek, W.H. and Lloyd, L.C. *Bushman Folklore*, London, 1911
Bryant, A.T. *Olden Times in Zululand and Natal*, London, 1965 reprint
Doke, C.M. *Lamba Folklore*, New York, 1927 (Zambia)
Evans-Pritchard, E.E. *Witchcraft, Oracles and Magic Among the Azande*, Oxford, 1937

Evans-Pritchard, E.E. *The Zande Trickster*, Oxford, 1967
Forde, D. (ed) *African Worlds*, New York, 1954
Gelfand, M. *Shona Religion*, Cape Town, 1962
Herskovits, M.J. *Dahomey*, New York, 1938
Junod, H.A. *The Life of a South African Tribe*, 2 vols, London, 1927 (Ronga)
Kesby, J.D. *The Cultural Regions of East Africa*, London and New York, 1977
Knappert, J. *Traditional Swahili Poetry*, London, 1967
Knappert, J. *Myths and Legends of the Swahili*, London, 1970
Knappert, J. *Myths and Legends of the Congo*, London, 1971
Knappert, J. *Bantu Myths and Other Tales*, London, 1977
Mbiti, J.S. *Akamba Stories*, Oxford, 1966 (East Africa)
Parrinder, G. *African Mythology*, London, 1967
Reynolds, B. *Magic, Divination and Witchcraft Among the Barotse of Northern Rhodesia*, London, 1963 (Zambia)
Schapera, I. *Praise Poems of Tswana Chiefs*, Oxford, 1965 (Botswana)
Werner, A. *African Mythology* (in *The Mythology of All Races*, vol 7, New York, 1964 reprint)
Werner, A. *Myths and Legends of the Bantu*, London, 1933

THE NORTH AMERICAN INDIANS

Alexander, H.B. *North American Mythology*, Cambridge, Massachusetts, 1916
Barbeau, M. *Tsimsyan Myths*, Ottawa, 1961
Barnouw, V. *Wisconsin Chippewa Myths and Tales*, Madison, 1977
Benedict, R. *Zuni Mythology*, New York, 1935
Brown, J.E. *The Sacred Pipe*, Norman, Oklahoma, 1953
Clark, E.E. *Indian Legends of the Pacific Northwest*, Berkeley, 1933
Coffin, T.P. *Indian Tales of North America*, Journal of American Folklore, 1961
Curtin, J. *Seneca Indian Myths*, New York, 1923
Swanton, J.P. *Tlingit Myths and Texts*, Washington D.C., 1909
Swanton, J.P. *Myths and Tales of the Southeastern Indians*, Washington D.C., 1929

MIDDLE AMERICA

Bierhorst, J. *Four Masterworks of American Indian Literature*, New York, 1974
Brotherston, G. *Image of the New World*, London, 1978
Burland, C. *Magic Books from Mexico*, London, 1953
Burland, C. (ed) *Codex Laud*, Graz, 1966
Burland, C. *The Gods of Mexico*, London, 1967
Caso, A. *The Aztecs: People of the Sun*, Norman, Oklahoma, 1954
Coe, M.D. *The Maya*, London, 1966
Edmonson, M.S. (ed) *The Book of Counsel: the Popol Vuh of the Quiche Maya of Guatemala*, New Orleans, 1971
Krickeberg, W. *Pre-Columbian Mexican Religions*, London, 1968
Leon-Portilla, M. *Aztec Thought and Culture*, Norman, Oklahoma, 1963
Leon-Portilla, M. *Pre-Columbian Literatures of Mexico*, Norman, Oklahoma, 1968
Roys, R.L. (ed) *The Book of Chilam Balam of Chumayel*, Washington, 1933
Sahagun, B. de *Florentine Codex: General History of the Things of New Spain*, transl. C. Dibble and A.J.O. Anderson, 11 vols, Santa Fe and Salt Lake City, 1950–69
Thompson, J.E.S. *The Rise and Fall of Maya Civilization*, Norman, Oklahoma, 1967
Thompson, J.E.S. *A Commentary on the Dresden Codex*, Philadelphia, 1972
Vaillant, G.C. *The Aztecs of Mexico*, London, 1965
Wolf, E. *Sons of the Shaking Earth*, Chicago, 1959

THE INCAS

Cieza de León, P. de *Parte Primera de la Crónica del Perú*, transl. H. de Onis as *The Incas of Pedro de Cieza de León*, Norman, Oklahoma, 1959
Métraux, A. *The History of the Incas*, New York, 1969
Molina, C. de *The Fables and Rites of the Incas*, transl. C.R. Markham, Cambridge, 1873
Nunez del Prado, J.V. 'The supernatural world of the Quechua of southern Peru' (in *Native South Americans*, ed P.J. Lyon, Boston, 1974)
Pease, F. *El Dios Creador Andino*, Lima, 1973
Rowe, J.H. 'The origins of creator worship among the Incas' (in *Culture in History*, ed S. Diamond, New York, 1960)
Wachtel, N. *The Vision of the Vanquished: The Spanish Conquest of Peru through Indian Eyes*, Hassocks, 1977

TROPICAL SOUTH AMERICA

Boas, O.V. and C.V. *Xingu: the Indians, their Myths*, London, 1974
Farabee, W.C. *The Central Arawaks*, Philadelphia, 1918
Fock, N. *Waiwai: Religion and Society of an Amazonian Tribe*, Copenhagen, 1963
Kaplan, J.O. *The Piaroa: a People of the Orinoco Basin*, Oxford, 1975
Lévi-Strauss, C. *The Raw and the Cooked*, London, 1969
Lévi-Strauss, C. *From Honey to Ashes*, London, 1973
Maybury-Lewis, D. *Akwe-Shavante Society*, Oxford, 1967
Nimuendajú, C. *The Apinaye*, Washington, 1939
Rivière, P. *Marriage Among the Trio*, Oxford, 1969
Reichel-Dolmatoff, G. *Amazonian Cosmos*, Chicago, 1971
Reichel-Dolmatoff, G. *The Shaman and the Jaguar*, Philadelphia, 1975
Wilbert, J. *Folk Literature of the Warao Indians*, Los Angeles, 1970

VOODOO

Deren, M. *Divine Horsemen*, London, 1953
Huxley, F. *The Invisibles*, London, 1966
Métraux, A. *Voodoo in Haiti*, London, 1959

POLYNESIA AND MICRONESIA

Alpers, A. *Legends of the South Sea*, London, 1976
Andersen, J.C. *Myths and Legends of the Polynesians*, London, 1928
Dixon, R.B. *Oceanic Mythology* (in *Mythology of All Races*, vol 9, New York, 1964 reprint)
Grey, G. *Polynesian Mythology*, Christchurch, 1956 reprint
Lessa, W. *Tales from Ulithi Atoll*, Berkeley, 1961
Luomala, K. *Voices on the Wind*, Honolulu, 1955
Reed, A.W. *Treasury of Maori Folklore*, Auckland, 1963

MELANESIA

Berndt, R.M. *Excess and Restraint*, Chicago, 1962 (on the Fore people)
Burridge, K. *Tangu Traditions*, Oxford, 1969
Hesse, K. *Baining Legends*, Port Moresby, 1977
Hogbin, I. *The Island of Menstruating Men*, London, 1970 (Wogeo people)
Hogbin, I. (ed) *Anthropology in Papua New Guinea*, Melbourne, 1973
Kamma, F.C. *Koreri*, The Hague, 1972 (Biak people)
Lawrence, P. *Road Belong Cargo*, Melbourne, 1964 (Madang people)
Lawrence, P. and Meggitt, M.J. (ed) *Gods, Ghosts and Men in Melanesia*, Oxford, 1965
Malinowski, B. *The Sexual Life of Savages in North-Western Melanesia*, London, 1929 (Trobriands people)
Sun and Moon in Papua New Guinea Folklore, ed U. Beier and P. Chakravarti, Port Moresby, 1974
Van Baal, J. *Dema: Description and Analysis of Marind-Anim Culture*, The Hague, 1966
Vicedom, G.F. *Myths and Legends from Mount Hagen*, Port Moresby, 1977
Wagner, R. *Habu*, Chicago (Daribi people)
Williams, F.E. *Drama of Orokolo*, Oxford, 1940

AUSTRALIA

Berndt, R.M. (ed) *Australian Aboriginal Anthropology*, Canberra, 1970
Berndt, R.M. and C.H. *Man, Land and Myth in North Australia: the Gunwinggu People*, Sydney, 1970
Berndt, R.M. and C.H. *The World of the First Australians*, Sydney, 1977
Hiatt, L.R. (ed) *Australian Aboriginal Mythology*, Canberra, 1975
Howitt, A.W. *The Native Tribes of South-East Australia*, London, 1904
Kaberry, P.M. *Aboriginal Woman, Sacred and Profane*, London, 1939
Lamilami, L. *Lamilami Speaks*, Sydney, 1974
McConnel, U. *Myths of the Mungkan*, Melbourne, 1957
Mountford, C.P. *The Tiwi – their Art, Myth and Ceremony*, London, 1958
Mountford, C.P. *Ayers Rock*, Sydney, 1965
Mountford, C.P. *Winbaraku and the Myth of Jarapiri*, Adelaide, 1968
Robinson, R. *The Feathered Serpent*, Sydney, 1956
Robinson, R. *Aboriginal Myths and Legends*, Melbourne, 1966
Spencer, B. and Gillen, F.J. *The Native Tribes of Central Australia*, London, 1938 reprint
Stanner, W.E.H. *On Aboriginal Religion*, Sydney, 1959–63
Strehlow, T.G.H. *Songs of Central Australia*, Sydney, 1971
Warner, W.L. *A Black Civilization*, New York, 1958 reprint

ACKNOWLEDGMENTS

The publishers would like to thank the following for providing the illustrations on the pages listed below:

Key: T top; B bottom; R right; L left; C centre; and combinations, e.g. TR, BL

Antikvarisk-Topografiska Arkivet, Stockholm: 181R, 183TR, 183BR, 185B
Antikenmuseum, Basel: 131B
Archeological Survey of India, New Delhi: 17T, 27L
David Attenborough: 280T
Australian Information Service: 287B, 288B, 290–1T
Belzaux-Zodiaque: 171B, 175
Bodleian Library: 159BR (Ms. Bodley 270B), 244T (Ms. Laud misc. 678), 248T (Ms. Laud misc. 678)
British Library: 114, 117T, 117B, 118B
Trustees of the British Museum: 60T, 68T, 71B, 127B, 128B, 130, 168, 169T, 202T, 210T, 216, 226T, 251B, 253B, 276TL
Bulloz: 67, 98B
Cambridge University Museum of Archeology and Anthropology: 277C, 277R
Chandler-Pohrt Collection: 231B
Chester Beatty Library, Dublin: 116, 118T
Christie's, London: 159BL (A.C. Cooper), 274L (A.C. Cooper), 276B (A.C. Cooper)
Colorphoto Hans Hinz, Basel: 281B
Cooper-Bridgeman Library: 162, 208T, 223
Dr Audrey Coulson: 261
Department of Antiquities and Museums, Damascus: 94
Detroit Institute of Arts: 240–1T
Kerry Dundas: 286R
Edinburgh University Library: 112, 115
The Syndics of the Fitzwilliam Museum, Cambridge: 160
Werner Forman Archive: title page, 26T, 26B, 31, 42, 52B, 54T, 56L, 66BL, 77, 102T, 106T, 108, 171T, 177R, 179, 180R, 181L, 182, 183BL, 184L, 184R, 185T, 186, 187B, 206, 211, 213, 219T, 222, 224R, 225T, 225B, 226B, 227T, 227B, 235, 238T, 238B, 239, 241, 244B, 245, 246T, 248B, 249BL, 249BR, 252B, 273
Giraudon: 18T, 18B, 63R, 93R, 111
Gulbenkian Museum of Oriental Art: 51, 53, 56R, 62B, 81B
Haddon Collection, Cambridge University Museum of Archeology and Anthropology: 284, 287T, 288T, 289T
Sonia Halliday Photographs: 136, 142T, 142C, 158, 161T, 165B, 166, 169B, 199, 200B, 201L, 203L, 203R
Claus and Liselotte Hansmann: 21B, 22B, 50T, 52T, 65B, 68–9B, 69T, 193, 267, 270T, 279, 283
Robert Harding Associates: 41T (Richard Ashworth), 45R (Christina Gascoigne), 190 (Christina Gascoigne)
Dr John Hinnells: 41B, 45L, 46
Hirmer Fotoarchiv: 101BL, 106B, 109B, 122B, 128T, 134, 135, 157
Michael Holford Library: 59L, 70B, 71T, 73, 78–9B, 80–1, 88, 89, 98T, 99B, 103T, 123, 124, 127T, 129, 131T, 142B, 146R, 147T, 262
Horniman Museum, London: 55R, 72
Alan Hutchison Library: 207 (Sarah Errington), 209 (Piers Hamick), 220–1 (Bernard Gerard)
I.G.D.A.: 35T (N. Cirani), 48 (G. Dagli Orti), 49B (G. Dagli Orti), 50B (G. Dagli Orti), 76B (G. Ricatto), 82T (G. Dagli Orti), 87B (A.C. Cooper), 99T (Seemuller), 100B (G. Dagli Orti), 101BR (G. Dagli Orti), 102B (Seemuller), 104B, 121B (C. Bevilacqua), 122T (R. Lalance), 125B (A.C. Cooper), 138R (R. Pedicini), 139T (C.Bevilacqua), 141B (A. Buscaglia), 145T (C. Bevilacqua), 146L (C. Bevilacqua), 159T (G. Nimatallah), 163 (G. Dagli Orti), 164–5 (C. Bevilacqua), 165T (G. Dagli Orti), 165C (G. Dagli Orti), 167T (Seemuller), 167B (C. Ciccione), 195L (G. Tomsich), 196 (G. Dagli Orti), 197T (G. Dagli Orti), 200T (E. Turri), 212, 243, 247 (G. Dagli Orti), 250, 264 (M. Carrieri), 289B (G. Dagli Orti)
I.G.D.A./Bulloz: 98B, 113
I.G.D.A./Scala: 161B
Israel Department of Antiquities and Museums: 95T, 95B
Trustees of the Lady Lever Art Gallery, Port Sunlight: 64, 66BR
Professor David Lang: 197B, 198, 201R, 202T
Larousse: 80L, 195R
Linden Museum, Stuttgart: 217T, 218
MacQuitty Collection: 36T, 97, 101T, 107, 210B, 219B
Manchester Museum: 104T, 109T
Mansell Collection: 36B, 137, 139B, 147B, 150, 151T, 202B
Manx Museum, Isle of Man: 187T
John Massey Stewart: 204
Metropolitan Museum of Art, New York: 60B
John Moss: 263, 265
Musée de l'Homme, Paris: 217B, 220L, 228
Musée Romain, Avenches: 140
Musée Royale de l'Afrique Centrale, Tervuren: 208B
Museum für Völkerkunde, Hamburg: 275T
Museum of Fine Arts, Boston. Bigelow Collection: 76T
Museum of the American Indian, Heye Foundation, New York: 233
National Monuments Record, London: 173B
National Museum of Antiquities of Scotland: 174T
Peter Newark's Western Americana: 234R
Novosti Press Agency: 194
W.H. Pederson: 291
Anne and Bury Peerless: 15, 16, 17B, 21T, 22T, 23BL, 23BR, 24T, 24B, 25T, 25B, 27R, 30B, 33, 100T
Percival David Foundation of Chinese Art, London: 70T
Photoresources: 29L, 35BL, 38, 62T, 65T, 87T, 93L, 121T, 125T, 126, 132, 138L, 152, 153T, 237, 274R, 277L, 280B, 281T
Axel Poignant: 180L, 275B, 276TR, 282T, 282B, 285, 286L, 290B
Popperfoto: 191
Michael Ridley: 19, 20B, 23T, 28, 29R, 37L, 59R
Jean Roubier: 172, 173T, 177L
Royal Ontario Museum: 231T
Sakamoto Photo Research Laboratory, Tokyo: 78L, 79R, 82B, 84
Scala: 35BR, 37R, 57, 103B, 145B, 148L, 148R, 149TL, 149TR, 148B, 155
Ronald Sheridan's Photo-Library: 143, 153B, 154
Edwin Smith: 144, 174B
Smithsonian Institution, National Anthropological Archives: 234L, 240B

Smithsonian Institution, National Collection of Fine Arts: 232B
South American Pictures: 255 (Marion Morrison), 256B (Tony Morrison), 257 (Marion Morrison)
Staat Museum, East Berlin: 90
University Museum, Philadelphia: 91
University of Hong Kong: 63L
Mireille Vautier: 39T, 39B, 78–9T (Vautier-Decool), 83R (Helene Decool), 232T (Vautier-de Nanxe), 249T (Vautier-Decool), 251T (Vautier-Decool), 252T (Vautier-Decool), 256T (Vautier-Decool), 258 (Vautier-Decool), 259L (Vautier-Decool), 259R (Vautier-Decool), 268 (Vautier-de Nanxe), 269T (Vautier-de Nanxe), 269B (Vautier-de Nanxe), 270B (Vautier-de Nanxe)
Victoria and Albert Museum, Crown Copyright: 20T, 49T, 54B, 55L, 61R, 66T, 81T, 83L
Roger-Viollet: 105
Warburg Institute: 141T
John Webb: 30T
Wellcome Institute: 61L
Wheelwright Museum of the American Indian, Santa Fe, New Mexico: 236T, 236B
Wiener Library: 189
Frank Willett: 224L
Roger Wood: 43, 47, 151B
Zefa: 75, 215

We would like to acknowledge with thanks the following museums and collections:

Anspach Collection, New York; Archeological Museum, Florence; Archeological Museum, Jerusalem; Art Gallery of New South Wales; David Attenborough Collection, London; Australian Institute of Anatomy, Canberra; Australian Museum, Sydney; Ayudha National Museum; Collection of Kurt Bachmann, New York; Baroda Museum; Bibliothèque Nationale, Paris; British Library, London; Trustees of the British Museum, London; Bodleian Library, Oxford; Cairo Museum; Cambridge University Museum of Archeology and Anthropology; Cathedral Museum, Gerona; Chandigarh Museum; Chandler-Pohrt Collection; Chester Beatty Library, Dublin; Dallas Museum of Fine Arts; Delphi Museum; Detroit Institute of Arts; The Syndics of the Fitzwilliam Museum, Cambridge; Galleria dell' Accademia, Venice; Philip Goldman Collection, London; Gulbenkian Museum of Oriental Art, Durham; Hermitage Museum, Leningrad; Horniman Museum, London; Indian Museum, Calcutta; Khajuraho Museum; Collection of Mr and Mrs David Lloyd Kreeger, Washington D.C.; Kyoto Museum; Lady Lever Art Gallery, Port Sunlight; Lahore Museum; Le Bardo National Museum, Tunis; Linden Museum, Stuttgart; Liverpool City Museum; Louvre, Paris; Madras Museum; Manchester Museum; Fosco Maraini Collection; Metropolitan Museum of Art, New York; Musée Alésia, Alise-Sainte-Reine; Musée Calvet, Avignon; Musée Condé, Chantilly; Musée de l'Homme, Paris; Musée Granet, Aix-en-Provence; Musée Guimet, Paris; Musée Nationale des Arts Africains et Oceaniens, Paris; Musée Romain, Avenches; Musée Royale de l'Afrique Centrale, Tervuren; Museo Capitolino, Rome; Museo Castello, Milan; Museo Gregoriano Etrusco (Vatican Museums), Rome; Museo Nazionale, Naples; Museo Nazionale, Palermo; Museum für Völkerkunde, Basel; Museum für Völkerkunde, Berlin; Museum für Völkerkunde, Hamburg; Museum of Fine Arts, Boston; Museum of Haitian Art, College of St Pierre, Port-au-Prince; Museum of the American Indian, Heye Foundation, New York; Museum of the Cherokee Indian, North Carolina; National Archeological Museum, Reggio Calabria; National Gallery of Prague; National Museum, Athens; National Museum, Belgrade; National Museum, Copenhagen; National Museum, Damascus; National Museum, Reykjavik; National Museum of Anthropology, Mexico; National Museum of Antiquities, Scotland; National Museum of Villa Giulia, Rome; Palazzo Ducale, Venice; Percival David Foundation of Chinese Art, London; Pio Clementino Museum (Vatican Museums), Rome; Prince of Wales Museum, Bombay; Pruniger Collection, Lucerne; Katherine White Reswick Collection, Cleveland; Rhodes Museum; Royal Ontario Museum, Toronto; Schimmel Collection, New York; Staat Museum, East Berlin; State Museum, Lucknow; Statens Historiska Museet, Stockholm; Smithsonian Institution; Museum of History and Ethnography, Tbilisi; Ubersee Museum, Bremen; University Library, Uppsala; University of Hong Kong; University Museum, University of Pennsylvania.

We are particularly grateful to:

Professor Gordon Brotherston; Christie's, London; Dr Audrey Coulson; Dr Rosalie David; the Gulbenkian Museum of Oriental Art, Durham; Sonia Halliday; the Lady Lever Art Gallery, Port Sunlight; Professor David Lang; Tony Morrison; Bury Peerless; Michael Ridley; Tadeusz Skorupski; Sotheby's, London; Mireille Vautier and the Wheelwright Museum of the American Indian, Sante Fe.

INDEX

Page numbers in *italics* refer to illustrations

A

A'a *277*
Aaron 115
Abcan 175
Abel 156
Absyrtus 202
Abul-Lain 117
Abydos 102, 107–8
Acca Larentia 139, 140
Acheron 155
Achilles 124, 125, 134; *123*
Actaeon 137, 167
Adad 87, 88, 89
Adam 9, 156, 158–61, 164, 209, 210, 211, 249; *157, 160, 161*
Adam of Bremen 178, 182
Adapa 88
Adites 112, 113
Aditi 17, 32
Adityas 32
Aea 202
Aeneas 138, 140–1, 142; *141*
Aeolos 123
Aeschylus, Aischylos 138
Aesir 179, 180, 182
Aesop 112
Africa *see* Central and Southern Africa; East Africa; North Africa; West Africa
Agamemnon 122, 124, 130, 135
Agave 133
Agdistis 152
Age 222
age of the animals *see* animals
ages of the world *see* world-ages
Agni 17–18, 25, 27, 29, 32
Agwe 270
Ahriman, Angra Mainyu 40–7, 152; *43*
Ahura Mazda *see* Ohrmazd
Aias *see* Ajax
Aietes 129, 132
Airavata 33; *31*
Aischylos *see* Aeschylus
Aison 129; *129*
Aitutaki 277
Ajax, Aias 124
Akhenaten 99, 109; *99*
Akrisios 130
Akshobhya 53, 54; *52, 57*
Alavaka 38
Alba Longa 140, 141
Albanians (Caucasus) 204
Albigensians 195
alchemy 67, 69, 167–8; *168, 169*
Alcmene, Alkmene 122, 128
Alcuin 178
Alexander the Great 57, 98, 115, 116, 117, 152, 200; *115, 116, 117*
Alexandria 113
Algeciras 116
Al-Hamdani 113, 117
Ali 117–18; *118*
Al-Kalbi 117
Al-Khidr 112, 115–16; *116, 117*
Alkmene *see* Alcmene
alligator 243, 261, 265
Al-Mustawfi 116
Al-Sakafi 118
Alur 207
Amahraspands 42, 43
Amaterasu 74, 75, 77–8, 80–2, 83, 84; *79*
Amaunet 97
Amazons 127; *123*
Ambwerk 278
Ame-no-uzume 78
Amen-Re 99, 108, 109; *101*
Americas *see* Incas; Middle America; North American Indians; South America, tropical; Voodoo
Europeans in, 161, 230, 233, 235, 237, 242, 256–7, 259
Amida 83
Amiran 202–3, 204
Amitabha 50, 51, 53, 54, 83; *52, 57*
Amitayus 54
Amma 226
Amoghasiddhi 54; *52, 57*
Amon 109
Amphitryon 122, 128
Amr Ibn Madi Karib 118; *118*
Amun 97, 98–9, 102, 109
anaconda 260, 261, 265
Anahit, Anahita 192, 201; *202*
Ananke 135
Ananta 26, 32; *26*
Anat 92, 93, 94, 95; *94*
Anchises 140, 141
Andhaka 28; *29*
Andromeda 128
Anglo-Saxons 188
Angra Mainyu *see* Ahriman
animals:
age of 227–8, 237, 238, 260, 287
helpful animal motif 79, 80, 218; *37*
hostile to man 42, 44, 209, 244, 262, *see also* snake
animism 193
Anlubu 227–8
Annwn 176, 177
Anshar 87
Antum 90
Anu 86, 87, 88, 89, 90
Anubis 105, 109; *105*
Anutu 283
Anyaroli 227, 228
Apache *238*
Aphrodite 120, 121, 124, 125, 126, 129, 136, 138, 143, 201, 269; *122, 202 see also* Venus
Apis 109
Apoala 249
Apollin *see* Apollyon
Apollo, Apollon 121, 122, 124, 125, 126–7, 129, 131, 133, 137, 142, 143, 150, 172; *126, 134, 203*
Apollyon, Apollin 117
Apophis *108*
Apsarases *16, 37*
Apsu 87
Apuleius 155
Apus 259
Aqhat 94–5
Ara 201
Arabia 110–18
Arabian Nights *see Thousand and One Nights*
Arachne 137
arahants *see* arhats
Arahito-gami 74
Aranazd 201
Aranda 283, 286, 288, 291; *284, 288, 289*
Aranrhod 177
Arapaho 235; *234*
Ararat, Mount 198, 199, 201, 202; *200*
Aratsani, River 202
Arawn 176, 177
Arawotya 287
Ardashir I *43*
Areop-enap 272
Ares 121, 122, 124, 137, 143
Argo, Argonauts 128, 129–30, 202; *202*
Argos 122, 130
arhats, arahants 39, 55–6, 73, 83
Ariadne 131, 132, 148; *149*
Arianrhod *see* Aranrhod
Ark *see* Noah
Armenia 113, 192, 198, 199–202; *199–202*
Arminianism 190
Arnhem Land 284, 285, 287, 289; *286, 287, 288*
Arnold of Villanova 168
Artavazd 202, 203
Artemis 121, 122, 124, 143
Arthur, King 115, 166, 176, 177
Aruana ceremony *265*
Arubani 199
Ascanius 140, 141, 142
Asgard 180, 181, 182, 184, 185, 186
Ashanti 222, 224–5
Ashvins 19, 32
Asoka 34
Assam 15, 30
Asshur 89
Asshurbanipal 88, 90
Assyria *see* Mesopotamia
Astarte *see* Athirat
Asuras (demons) 14, 16–17, 18, 20–1, 32, 35–6, 37
Atahualpa 256, 259
Atea 274
Aten 99, 109; *99*
Athena, Athene 120, 121, 122, 124, 125, 128, 130, 137, 143, 203; *121, 128 see also* Minerva
Athens 130–2, 144, 146, 148; *121*
Athirat 92, 93; *95*
Athtar 92, 94
Athtart 92
Atlantic Ocean 208
Atri 19
Atropos 135
Attis 138, 152; *152*
Atum 96, 97, 98, 109
Augeian stables 127
Augustine St 141, 160, 165
Augustus 137, 138
Aurobindo, Sri 33
Australian Aborigines 237, 284–91; *285–91*
Austral Islands *277*
Authumla 180
Avalokitesvara 50, 51, 54, 55, 67, 73, 83; *39, 52*
Avesta 40
Awagi-hara 77
Axieros, Axiocersa, Axiocersos 152
axis mundi see world-axis
Ayaba 222
Ayar Cachi 257, 258
Ayers Rock 291
Azi Dahaka 42–3; *41*
Aztecs 10, 242–3, 248, 250, 252, 253; *244, 249, 250, 252*; Aztec Sun Stone 242–3; *244*
Aztlan 253

B

Ba *103, 105*
Baal 10, 92–4, 95; *93*
Baba-Yaga 194, 196
Babylonia *see* Mesopotamia
Bacchants *see* Maenads
Bacchus, Bakchos 133, 137, 143, 147
Bacchylides 131, 138
Badb 174
Baiami 285
Baining 278, 283
Bai Rampa 226–7
Bakchos *see* Bacchus
Bakuba 209; *210*
Balar 173, 174, 175, 176
Balder, Baldur 182, 184, 185, 186, 189
Bali (Indian demon) *22*
Baluba 209, 210; *206*
Bantu 206, 208, 209
Bapuna *211*
Baron Cemetery, Baron Cross, Baron Saturday 267
Baronga 207
Basonge 209
Bast, Bastet 109
Batradz 204
battle *see* war
Battle of Moytura *see* Mag Tuired
Baubo 145
Baucis 138
Bel 201
Belenus 172
Beli Mawr 172
Bellerophon 130, 131; *130*
Bellona 142
Benares 28
Bendigeidfran *see* Bran
Bengal 15, 30–1, 32
Benten, Benzaiten 83; *81*
Bes 102, 109
Bhaishajyaguru 54, 73, 83
Biak 283
Bilqis *see* Queen of Sheba
bison *see* buffalo
Blasius, St 193
Blavatsky, Madame 45
Boaliri 289
Bodh Gaya, Bodhi-tree 34, 37; *36*
Bodhisattvas 35, 50, 54–5, 67–8, 83
Boehme, Jacob 190
bogatyrs 197
Bogomils 195
Bombay 40, 46, 47; *45*
Bon 48–9, 50, 52, 57
Book of Leinster 173
Bosomuru, River 225
Botoque 261–2
Bounteous Immortals 42
Bragi 182
Brahma 16, 25, 26, 27, 28, 29, 32; Brahmas 36
Brahmanas 15, 16, 20, 29
Brahmanism 15, 34, 39
Bran 176–7
Branwen 176–7
Brennus 171
Bres 174
Bresal 175
Bridge of Judgment 43, 47
Brigantia 174; *174*
Brigid, St, Brigit 174
Brigitte *see* Maman Brigitte
Briseis 124
Brisingamen *184*
brothers *see* fraternal rivalry; twins
Brutus 141
Bryce Canyon 238
Bubastis 109
Buddha (Gautama) 21, 25, 34–5, 37–8, 39, 48, 49, 50, 51, 53, 54, 55, 69–70, 73; *35–9, 48–9*
Buddhas 35, 50, 53–5, 72, 83; *52, 57*
Buddhism:
Chinese 34, 49, 58, 67–71, 72–3, 83; *66, 70, 71*
Indian 15, 25, 34–9, 44, 48–50, 68, 206; *35–9*
Japanese 34, 83; *81, 82, 83*
Mahayana 34, 55
Theravada 34–9; *35–9*
Tibetan 34, 48–57; *49–57*
buffalo, bison 233, 234; *233*
bull, archetypal or heavenly 41, 44, 67, 90, 91, 154; *153, 198*
Buoka 262–3
Buraq 112; *111*
Buri 180
Burma 15, 34
Busiris 107

Buto 109
Byblos 106

C

Cabeiroi 152
Cacha 256
Cadiz 116
Cadmilos, Casmilos 152
Caesar, Julius 57, 142, 143, 170, 172
Cain 156, 160
Cakkavudha 37
Calcutta 31
Callisto 137
Cambodia 15, 34
Canaanites 92–5; *93–5*
cannibalism 150, 265, 278, 280
cargo cults 278, 283; *280*
Caroline Islands 274, 275, 276
Carpentier, Alejo 244
Carthage 141, 142
Casius, Mount 93
Castor, Kastor 122, 129, 142, 143; *142*
castration 27, 28, 106, 120, 124, 138, 152
Catalogue of Women 123, 138
catastrophe, primeval 12, 61, 243–4 *see also* flood
Cathars 195
Catullus 138
Caucasus range 198, 202–4
Celts 161, 162, 166–7, 170–7; *171–7*
Centaurs, Kentauroi 112, 128, 129
Centre of Heaven deity 75
Cepheus, Kepheus 128
Cerberus, Kerberos 127, 128, 134; *135*
Cercyon, Kerkyon 131
Ceres 136, 143 *see also* Demeter
Cernunnos 172; *171*
Ceryneian, Keryneian hind 127
Ceucy 264
Chacs 250, 253
Chaga 215
Chalchihuitlicue 253; *245, 246, 253*
Chamberlain, H.S. 189
Chamunda *see* Durga
chaos, primeval 12, 15, 16, 50, 59, 75, 95, 101, 156, 180, 186, 208
Charlemagne 191
Charon *135*
Cheheru 263
Cheiron 129
Ch'eng Huang 72
Cherokee *232*
Chesterton, G.K. 179
Cheyenne 234
Chibiabos 232–3
Chichen Itza *249*
Ch'ih Sung-tzu *see* Lord of Rain
Ch'ih-yu 64
ch'i-lin *73*
Chimaira 130; *130*
Chimalpahin 252
China 34, 49, 50, 57, 58–73, 74, 75, 83, 84, 239; *59–73*
Chrétien de Troyes 166
Christ *see* Jesus
Christianity 9, 12, 40, 41, 42, 43, 44, 45, 109, 133, 143, 156–69, 193; *157–69*
in Africa 206, 207, 208, 210, 213, 214
in the Americas 242, 254, 255, 256, 266, 268–9
in Armenia, Georgia 200, 202–3; *199*
and Celtic myths 170, 172, 173, 176
in China 58
and Germanic myths 178, 179, 181, 184, 187, 189, 190; *185*
in India 25; *25*
in Iran 44
and Islam 110, 113, 116
in Melanesia 278, 283
and mystery religions 155
and Slavonic myths 192, 193, 194, 195, 196, 197; *197*
Chuang-tzu 59
Chuan Hu 62
Chu-jung *see* Lord of Lightning
Ch'ung 62
Chung-kuei 72
Chu Pa-chieh 70, 71
churning the ocean 21, 32, 33, 76; *21, 76*
Chyavana 19
Cian 174, 175
Cicero 142, 146
Cieza de Léon, Pedro de 256
Cihuacoatl 248, 253
Cincinnatus 142
Cinteotl 248, 253; *245*
Cinvat Bridge 43
Cinxia 136
Circe, Kirke 125, 132, 240; *125*
Cittapatali tree 36
City of Brass, Copper 116; *117*
Clashing Rocks 129
Clement of Alexandria 145
Cleopatra 141, 201
Clotho, Klotho 135
Cloud-Masked Rain-Bringers 236
Cloud People *236*
Coatlicue 252, 253; *252*
Coirpre 174, 175
Colchis, Kolchis 129, 202
Collari 259
Colum 175
Columbus, Christopher 161
communism 158, 169
Community Book of Chumayel 245, 247
Community for Germanic Beliefs 190
Condítor 136
Confucius, Confucianism 58, 67, 71
Constantine the Great 158
Convector 136
cooked food *see* raw and cooked food
Cook, Captain 284
Cook Islands 273–4, 277; *277*
Coricancha 257; *257*
Corinth 133
Coriolanus 142
corn, maize 145–6, 152, 154, 232, 233, 234, 246–9, 250, 253; *236, 237, 246, 247, 248*; Corn Father 236; Corn Maidens 236, 237; Corn Mother 236; Corn Woman 233
Corpus Hermeticum 155
Cortes, Hernando 242
cosmic egg 9, 11, 12, 16, 26, 41, 50, 59–60, 75, 97, 226, 274
cosmic pillar *see* world-axis
Coyote 237–8, 240
Cracow 195–6
creation myths:
African 208–10, 215, 222, 226; *209*
American 230, 240–1, 242, 245–6, 254–5, 258, 259
Chinese 9, 59–60
Christian 9, 156–7, 158; *157, 158, 159*
Egyptian 97, 98, 101; *97, 101*
Greek 9, 120, 134–5, 210
Hindu 9, 15–16, 17, 29, 32, 59–60
Japanese 75–6, 84; *76*
Jewish 9, 95, 156–7, 158
Mesopotamian 87
Pacific 272–3, 274, 279–80, 283, 285
Scandinavian 180
Tibetan 9, 50–1, 157
Zoroastrian 40–1, 43, 44–5, 46
out of chaos *see* chaos
by creative journeys 255, 279, 280, 283, 284, 285, 286, 287, 288–9; *287*
by dismemberment 12, 16, 29, 32, 50, 59–60, 87, 180, 279–80
egg motif *see* cosmic egg
fishing up land *see* fishing
of mankind *see* man
separation of earth and sky 12, 15–16, 59, 62, 75, 120, 272–3
Creek 233
Creidne 174, 175
Crete 127, 131, 132, 148; Cretan bull, 127
Crommyonian, Krommyonian sow 131
Cronus, Kronos 120, 121, 123, 134, 137, 143 *see also* Saturn
Cu Chulainn 176
culture hero, heroine:
African 209
American 232, 238, 250, 253, 258, 260, 262, 263, 264, 265
Chinese 58, 64
Greek *see* Prometheus
Pacific 278, 280–1, 283, 284
Cumae 141, 142; *143*
Cunina 136
Cupid 143 *see also* Eros
Cuzco 254, 256, 257, 258, 259; *257*
Cybele 138, 152; *152*
Cyclopes, Kyklopes 112, 120, 125, 240; *124*

D

Da 225, 270
Dabu, K.S. 46
Dadhyanch 19
Dagda *see* In Dagda
Dagon 92
Dag-pa 49
Dahak 42
Dahn, Felix 190
Dahomey 222–4, 225, 266, 267, 270; *224*
Daikoku 83; *81*
Dainichi 83
Dakota 232, 234
Daksha 26, 27, 29
Dalai Lama 50
Damascus 110, 113
Damballah 270; *270*
Danae 122, 128, 130
Danel 94–5
Danu 173, 174
Danube, River 174
Daphne 137
Daramulun 285
Daribi 280
Darius *42*
Darwin, Charles 157
David of Sassoun 201
Dazhdbog 194, 195
death:
god or personification of
African 211, 212, 218–19
American 238, 267; *269, see also* Mictlantecutli
Canaanite 94
Egyptian 105
Germanic 182, 188; *182*
Greek and Roman 120 *see also* Hades; Pluto
Hindu 18, 26–7, 28, 32
Pacific 274, 276; *275*
Tibetan *51*
origin of
African 210–11, 215, 217, 218–20, 226; *216*
American 238, 260
Christian 156, 158–60
Hindu 18
Jewish 156, 158–60
Pacific 275, 279, 280, 283
Zoroastrian 45, 47
Decius Mus 142
Delos 131
Delphi 127, 141, 171; *121*
Demavend, Mount *41*
Demeter 121, 122, 124, 126, 143, 144–6, 147, 167; *144, 146*
Demetrius the Besieger 144
Denderah 102
Dessra 275
Deukalion 121, 123
Deutsche Orden 191
Devas 35
Devil 40, 41, 163–5, 168–9, 172, 195, 268
Dhalla, M.N. 45
Dhul-Qarnayn 112, 115–16; *115*
Diana 137, 138, 143, 167; *137*
Dian Cecht 174, 175
Dido 141; *141*
Dieri 289
Dinka 207; *207*
Diomedes 124, 127
Dionysos, Dionysus 121, 122, 124, 127, 132, 133, 137, 143, 147–50, 152, 197; *133, 147, 149*
Dios 246
dismemberment, creation by *see* creation myths
Dis Pater 143, 172
Diti 17
Djabo 288
Djanggaus, Djanggawuls 285, 289, 290–1; *286*
Dodo 283
Dogon 226; *226, 227*
Domovik, Domovoi 194
Don 174, 176, 177
Don, River 174
Donar 188, 191
Doros 123
dragon 17, 61–2, 68, 71, 72, 78–9, 127, 129, 164, 186, 195–6, 200, 202, 232; *59, 62, 185*
Dreaming, the 286; *290*
Drill Man 64
druids 170
dualism 42–3, 44, 45, 152, 173, 195, 231–2, 233
Dühring, Eugen 190
Dumuzi 89, 90
Durga 31, 32; *15, 33*
Dyaus 32, 137
Dylan 177

E

Ea 86, 87, 88, 89, 90; *87, 88*
Eagle 238
Earth (goddess) 12, 20, 29, 32, 89, 120, 121, 136, 141, 144, 152, 188, 208, 210, 230, 232, 236, 277, 283, 285; *236* (*see also* entries for individual goddesses)
Easter Island 273; *274, 276*
Echo *138*
Eddas 179, 180, 184, 185, 189, 191
Eden 9, 156, 158, 160, 161, 162, 163, 164, 249; *160, 161*
Edfu 102; *101*
Efnisien 176, 177
Egeria 141
egg *see* cosmic egg
Egypt 10, 11, 34, 88, 90, 91, 93, 96–109, 110, 112, 141, 144, 154–5, 168, 207, 208; *42, 97–109, 154, 155*
Eight Immortals 72; *69*
Eileithyia 122
El 92, 93, 94, 95; *93*
Elbruz, Mount 204
Elephantine 97, 109
Eleusis, Eleusinian Mysteries 134, 144–7, 152; *146*
Eliade, Mircea 111
Elias, St 194, 195
Elijah 95, 115, 194, 195
elixir of immortality 42, 63, 67, 115–16, 162, 168, 275 *see also* Soma
Elysian Fields, Elysium 155, 161
Emma-O 83
En 175
end of the world 25, 26, 27, 42–3, 45, 163, 186–7; *187 see also* world-ages
Enki 89
Enkidu 90, 91
Enlil 86–7, 88, 89, 91
Ennugi 86
Eostre 191
Epikaste 132
Epona 172, 177; *173*
Er 135
Ereshkigal 89–90, 91
Eridu 88–9
Eros 120, 143
Erymanthian boar 127, 131; *127*
Erzulie 269–70; *270*
Eskimo 239
Ethiopia 110, 111, 114, 117
Ethne 174, 175
Etruscans 137, 141–2
Euripides 131, 133, 138, 202
Europa 122, 132, 137
Eurydice 150; *150*
Eurystheus 127, 128; *127*
Eve 9, 156, 158–61, 168, 209, 210, 211; *157, 160, 161*
evil, problem of 11, 16, 40–1, 44, 156, 160, 163, 213, 215, 216–17, 226, 247, 283
evolution, theory of 45, 157–8
exposure of infants 133, 139, 228

F

Fa 222
Fabius Pictor 136
Fafnir 185, 186; *185*
Fahrenkrog, Ludwig 190, 191
Faresh 118
Fates 122, 135 *see also* Norns
Father Sky *236*
Father Sun 236
Faunus 140, 143
Faustulus 139, 140
Feather Snake 246, 250, 253
Fei Lien 63, 64, 72
Female Spirit cult 281
Feng Po 72
Fenrir 185, 186; *187*
Finn 173, 176
Fir Bolg 174
Firdos 46
fire, hearth 43, 63, 118, 139, 224; *45, 46*
gods of 17–18, 55, 62, 76, 124, 143, 185, 253, 260, 274; *61, 245, 252*
origin of 17, 26, 64, 76, 122, 185, 192, 203, 275, 279, 280, 287 *see also* raw and cooked food
Fisher king 166–7
fishing up land 275–6; *275*
fish-woman 260–1, 264–5
Five Buddhas *see* Buddhas
Five Emperors 58, 59, 60, 72
flood myths:
Australian 289
American 233, 237, 243, 244–5, 249, 254–5
Chinese 61
Christian 156, 198, 255; *200*
Greek 123
Hindu 19, 25, 32; *20*
Jewish 86, 95, 156, 198, 255
Melanesian 283
Mesopotamian 86–7, 91, 123; *87*
Mithraic 154
Flora 136
Fomoiri 173, 174–6
food *see* raw and cooked food
Food Mountain 247
Fore 283
Four Diamond Kings 72
Four Dragon Kings 68, 72
Four Kings of Hell 72; *71*
fraternal rivalry, fratricide 17, 79, 80, 106, 140, 186, 215–17, 223–4, 257–8, 262–3, 267, 275–6, 276–7
Frazer, Sir James 138
Freemasons 169
Freud, Sigmund 11, 33, 133, 186
Frey 178, 182, 183–4, 186, 187; *184, 187*
Freya 181, 182, 183, 185, 187; *184*
Fricco 178
Frigg, Frija 182, 184, 185, 188
Frog 238

Frum see John Frum
Fudoki 74
Fu-hsi 60, 61, 64, 65
Fu-hsing 72
Fujiyama, Mount 75
Fumu 209
Fungen 83

G

Gadjari 285
Galatea 137
Galla see Oromo
Gallienus 146
Ganda 217
Gandharvas 18, 32, 34
Gandhi, Mahatma 33; *30*
Ganesha 31, 32, 33; *27, 31*
Ganga 32
Ganges, River 15, 27, 28, 29, 31, 32, 52
Ganymede 137, 167; *138*
Garm 186
Garuda, Garudas 26, 32, 36; *26*
Gathas 40
Gauls 170–1, 172, 174, 177; *171, 172, 173, 175, 177*
Gauri 30, 32
Gautama see Buddha
Gayomard 41, 43, 44
Ge 120, 121, 210
Geb 96, 97, 106, 109; *98*
Genius 137
Georgia 199, 202–4
Germanic Belief Fellowship 191
Germanic myths, peoples 10, 12, 162, 170, 174, 178–87, 188–91, 192; *179–87, 189–91*
German Order 191
Germany, modern 188–91; *189–91*
Geryon 127, 128
Ge-sar 57
Ghost Dance *234*
Giantland (Scandinavian) 180, 185, 187
Gibil 87
Gibraltar 116
Gikuyu see Kikuyu
Gilbert Islands 272, 273
Gilgamesh 90–1, 115; *87*
Gilgit 48
Ginnungagap 180
Girimekhala 37
Giryama 219
Glooscap 232
Glover, T.R. 138
gnosticism 44, 155
Gobban Saer, Gobban 174
Gofannon 174, 176
Gog 115
Gogo 280
Goibniu 174, 175, 176
golden age 10, 25, 26, 97, 142, 157, 195
Golden Fleece 129, 202; *202*
golden race 123
Gopis 24, 32; *25*
Gorgon 128; *128*
Graces 122, 126, 167; *167*
Graiai 128
Grail, Holy 166–7, 177; *166, 167*
Grant, Michael 139
Great Bear constellation 27
Great Emperors 72
Great Hare see Nanabush
Great Spirit 230
Great Woman of the Night 274, 275
Greece 9, 10, 90, 91, 112, 120–35, 188, 192, 193, 207, 208, 210, 222; *121–35*
and Armenia, Caucasus region 201, 202, 203–4; *202, 203*
and the Celts 170, 171, 172
and Christianity 161, 167
and gnosticism 44
and India 32, 34, 39
and mystery religions 144–55; *145–6, 149*
and Rome 136–8, 142, 143; *137–9*
Gregory the Illuminator, St 200
gSal-ba 49
gShen-rab 48–9
gSum-pam Khan-po 52
Guaretin 275
Guatemala see Middle America
Gucumatz 246, 253
Guede 267, 270; *269*
Guhyasamaja 54
Gulu 217–19
Gunabibi 285
Gundestrup cauldron 172; *171, 177*
Gunwinggu 287
Guru Rin-po-che 56; *56*
Gwern 176, 177
Gwydion 177
Gylfi 179–80; *180*

H

Hadad 92
Hades 121, 123, 124, 127, 128, 134, 143, 150, 155 see also Plouton; Pluto
Hafgan 176, 177
Haiti see Voodoo
Haldi 199
Ham 198
Hana 281
Han Fei Tzu 64
Hannibal 141
Hanuman 22, 32; *23*
Haoma 32
Hapi 109
Harald Wartooth 182
Hari-Hara 32
Harlech 176, 177
Haroeris *100*
Harpies 130
Harpokrates 109
Hathor 102, 109; *95, 102*
Hauhet 97
Haumia 274
Hawaii 273, 275; *273, 274*
Hayagriva 55
Hayastan 201
Hayk 201
hearth see fire
Heavenly Ox 67
heavens and paradises:
American 237
Celtic 161, 166, 176
Chinese 62, 63, 70, 73; *62*
Christian 158, 160, 161, 162–3; *161, 162, 163*
Egyptian 105; *107*
Greek and Roman 123, 133–4, 135, 155, 161
Indian 34; *16*
Islamic 111–12, 113; *111, 112*
Japanese 83
Jewish 158, 160
Scandinavian 182
Slavonic 192
Tibetan 51–2, 57
Zoroastrian 42, 43, 46
Hebe 121, 122, 124, 127
Hector, Hektor 124
Heilyn 177
Heimdall 182, 185, 186
Hektor see Hector
Hel 184, 185
Helen 124, 125
Heliopolis 96, 97, 98, 106, 109
Helios 132, 204
Hellen 123
hells 9, 34, 37, 38, 42, 43, 45, 67, 68, 73, 135, 162–3, 164; *51, 71, 81, 83, 164*
Heng-o 63, 72; *59, 63*
Hephaestos, Hephaistos 121, 122, 124, 143
Hera 121, 122, 124, 125, 127, 128, 129, 137, 143, 150 see also Juno
Heraclitos, Herakleitos 134–5
Hercules, Herakles 122, 124, 127–8, 129, 130, 131, 134, 135, 172, 204; *127, 128, 135*
Hermes 121, 122, 124, 126, 134, 143; *134, 150* see also Mercury
Herminones 190
Hermod 184
Hermopolis 97, 106, 109
Herodotus 152, 192
Heruka 54; *53*
Hesiod 120–3, 127, 130, 133, 134, 135
Hesperides 127
Hestia 121, 124, 137, 143
Hevajra 54
Hi, River 78
Hiba, Mount 76
Hido 279
'High God' 207–8
Himalaya, Himalayas 27, 28, 31, 32, 52
Himmler, Heinrich 191
Himuka myths 74
Hina 276
Hinduism 12, 14–33, 34, 41, 43, 44, 45, 47, 59–60, 173; *15–33*
Hine-ahu-one 274
Hine-a-tauira 274
Hine-nui-te-po 274; *275*
Hine-titamauri 274
Hippolyta 127
Hippolytus 139
Hiranyakashipu 21; *21*
Hitler, Adolf 190, 191
Hitti, Philip 115
Ho Liu 65
Holy Lake of the Acts of Rama 20
Homer 120, 124–5, 126, 127, 128, 129, 130, 131, 134, 135, 138, 202
Homeric Hymns 126, 134, 138, 145–7
Honabe 281
hoops of the world 234; *232*
Hopi 235, 236, 237, 249; *237*
Ho Po 63, 73
Hor 57
Horace 142
Horai 122
Horatius 142
Horon 92
horticulture, origin of 260–1, 264, 280, 283
Horus 102, 106, 107, 108, 109, 154; *101, 106*
Hosho 83
Hotei *81*
Hother 182, 184
Hottentots 207, 211
Hreidmar 185, 186
Hsi Wang Mu 63, 73; *62*
Hsuan Tsang, T'ang Seng 68, 70–1
Hu 59
huacas 258, 259
Hua-kuo, Mount 69
Huanacauri 257, 258, 259
Huang Ti 60, 61, 63, 64
Huascar 256, 257
Huayna Picchu *255*
Hud 112
Huehueteotl 253; *252*
Huh 97
Huitzilopochtli 252, 253
Huli 281
Humbaba 90, 91
Hunab Ku 253
Hundred-Armed Giants 120, 121
Hun-tun 59
Hydra 127
Hymir 181

I

Iamos *128*
Ibn Ishaq 117
Iceland 178, 184, 187, 189
I Ching 65
Ida 18
Ida-ten 83
Idomeneus 124
Idun 182, 185
Igor, Prince 195
Iko 279
Ilm-i Kshnoom 46
Iya Muromets 197
Ilyap'a 258
Imbongu 283
Imhotep 109
immortality 18, 29, 69, 88, 91, 99, 102–6, 108, 125, 127, 128, 133–5, 166, 167–8, 182, 194, 251 see also death, origin of; elixir; heavens; hells; judgment; moon; mystery religions; snake
Inaba 79
Inanna 89, 90
Inari *80*
Incas 10, 254–9; *255–9*
incest myths:
African 209
American 238, 250, 258, 263–4
Chinese 64
Egyptian 96, 97, 100, 106
Greek and Roman 132–3, 137, 150
Indian 16, 19, 20, 26, 28, 33
Japanese 76
Pacific 274, 278, 281–2, 288, 289
Scandinavian 185
In Dagda 172, 174, 175
India 43, 51, 110, 117, 189 see also Buddhism; Hinduism; Parsis
Indra 15, 17, 18, 19, 20, 25, 29, 31–3, 36; *16*
Inkari 259
Insitor 136
Inti 258; *257, 258*
Io 137
Iokasta see Jocasta
Iolkos 129
Iolofath 274
Ion 123
Iphis 137
Iram of the Columns 113, 116; *112*
Iran, Persia 32, 39, 40–4, 46, 47, 48, 51, 110, 112, 115, 117, 152, 192, 195, 198, 200, 201; *42–5, 47*
Iraq 110, 117
Ireland 170, 172–7; *174*
Irian Jaya see Melanesia
Iroquois 230, 231
Ishtar 87, 88, 89–90, 91; *89*
Ishtar Gate *90*
Isis 96, 97, 106, 108, 109, 154–5, 208; *105, 106, 145, 154, 155*
Islam 34, 40, 42, 43, 44, 58, 98, 110–18, 206, 207, 208, 213, 214, 228; *111–18*
Isles of the Blessed 123, 133–4, 161
Ithaca 125, 134
Itonde 210
Itzamna 253
Itztli 250, 253; *245*
Iulus 142
Iwanaga 82
Izanagi 75–7, 80, 84; *76*
Izanami 75–7, 84; *76*
Izumo myths 74, 75, 79, 84

J

Jack and the Beanstalk 235
Jackson, A.V.W. 45
jaguar 243, 244, 245, 249, 252, 260, 262, 263, 264, 265; *262*
Jainism 38
Jamadagni 23
Janus 136, 137, 142, 143; *142*
Japan 10, 34, 74–84, 239; *75–84*
Japheth 198, 201
Jarapiri 286
Jari 280, 283
Jason 128–30, 132, 202; *129, 202*
Java 15
Jerusalem 162
Jesus Christ, Jesus of Nazareth 110, 161, 163, 164, 165, 166, 167, 168, 187, 189, 195, 197, 202, 283; *162, 163, 164, 166*
Jews see Judaism
Jimmu 80, 84
jinn 112, 114, 116
Jizo 83; *83*
Jocasta, Iokasta 132, 133
John the Baptist, St 268
John Frum *280*
Joseph of Arimathea 166
Jotunheim see Giantland
journeys, creative see creation myths
Judaism, Jews 44, 86, 92, 94, 95, 110, 113, 115, 156–7, 158–61, 163, 168, 169, 190, 198, 206, 255
judgment of the dead 42, 43, 47, 102, 105, 108, 109, 115, 135, 161, 163; *105, 111, 164, 165*
Jugumishanta 283
Julius Caesar see Caesar
Jung, C.G. 11
Juno 137, 143
Juok 209
Jupiter 32, 137, 138, 141, 142, 143, 172, 188; *138*
Jurupari 264
Jyeshtha 31, 32

K

Ka 106
Kaaba 111; *118*
Kabardians 204
kachinas 236–7; *237*
Kagutsuchi 76
Kahutu 221
Kaikuzi 219
Kailasa, Mount *27*
Kajis 203
Kalacakra 54
Kaleru 286
Kali 30, 32; *15, 30*
Kali Age 21, 25, 26
Kaliya 24, 27; *24*
Kalki 21, 25, 26; *25*
Kama 27, 28, 32
Kamba 219, 221
Kami 74
Kami-musubi 75, 79
Kamiura *263*
Kamiyo-nanayo 75
Kamsa 24
Kan Chiang 65
Kannon 83
Kanyanga 215–16
Karaja *265*
Karnak 102; *101*
Karttikeya see Skanda
Karwadi 285
Kashmir 49, 51
Kashyapa 17
Kastor see Castor
Katuutsi 221
Kauket 97
Kayapo 261, 264, 265
Kebra Nagast 114, 117
Kentauroi see Centaurs
Kepheus see Cepheus
Kerberos see Cerberus
Kerkyon see Cercyon
Keryneian hind see Ceryneian hind
Khapun 197
Khasis 92, 93, 94
Khepera, Khepri 109; *104*
Khevsurs 204; *204*
Khnum 97, 109
Khons 109
Khors 194
Khuba 199
Khyab-pa 49
Kiev 194
Kigi 74, 75
Kigwa 221
Kikuyu, Gikuyu 206, 221
Kilibob 283
Kilimanjaro, Mount 215–16; *216*
Kilya 258
King of the Wood 138
kingship, myths of 10, 51–2, 100, 104–5, 106–7, 112, 174, 209, 217, 221, 226–7, 255, 257–8; *39, 42, 43, 100, 210*
Kintu 217–19, 221
Kirke see Circe

Kishar 87
Kishi-Mojin 83
Kitchen God 72, 73; *72*
Kiwai 279
Klotho *see* Clotho
Knife-Feather monster 236
Knossos 131
Koblo 226–7
Kogoshui 74
Koin 285
Kojiki 74
Kolchis *see* Colchis
Kolyada 194
Konohana-sakuya 80, 82–4
Konyingo 215–16
Kore 122, 144–5, 146
Korea 34, 83, 84
Koreri 283
Koshchei 196
Kothar 92, 93, 94
Koto-amatsu-kami 75
Krak 195–6
Krishna 20, 21, 23–4, 25, 27, 32; *23, 24, 25*
Krohn, Friedrich *189*
Krommyonian sow *see* Crommyonian sow
Kronos *see* Cronus
Ksitigarbha 73, 83
Kuan Ti 71, 73; *70*
Kuan Yin 67, 70, 73, 83; *66, 67*
K'uei-hsing *64*
Kuk 97
Kukeri mummers 197
Kukulcan 236, 251, 253
Kultana *287*
Kum-Ombo temple *100*
K'un 64
Kunapipi 285
Kung Kung 61, 64
K'un-lun, Mount 63, 72
Kurma 21; *21*
Kushinada 78–9, 80
Kusho-jin *83*
Kusinagara 35
Kutaisi 202
Kwakiutl 240; *239, 240*
Kwena 208
Kyklopes *see* Cyclopes

L

Labama 209
Labraid 176
Lachesis 135
Lady of the World 246
Laindjung *291*
Laios 132, 133
Lake Regillus, battle of 142
Lakshmana *23*
Lakshmi 21, 32
lamas 50
lance, holy 166
Land of the Black and Red 251
land-fishing *see* fishing
Langi 273
Lanka 22
Lanz von Liebenfels, Adolf 190
Laomedon 128
Lao Tzu 58, 67, 69; *59*
Lares 142
Lavinium 141
Leda 122
Legba 222, 223–4, 266; *224*
Legend of the Suns 243, 248
Lei Kung 73
Lemesisi *281*
Lerna 127
lesnye 194
Leto 122
Lévi-Strauss, Claude 12, 110, 260
Lhasa 49; *50*
Li 62
Lianja 210
Liber 137
Lif 186
Lifthrasir 186
Ling 57
List, Guido von 189–90
Li Szu 58, 59
Little Mothers 31
Little Star 235
Livy 139–40, 141–2
Lleu Llaw Gyffes 172, 176, 177
Llud Llaw Ereint 176
Llyr 176, 177
Loathly Damsel 167
Loco, Loko 222, 267; *267*
Lohans 73
Loki 182, 184–5, 186; *185*
Loko *see* Loco
London 177
Lord of the Dawn 251
Lord of Lightning 62; *61*
Lord of Rain 63, 64, 72
Luchta 174, 175
Lucian 172
Lucifer 164, 167, 268; *164*
Lucretia 141
Lucretius 138
Lug, Lugus 172, 173, 174, 175–6
Lu-hsing 73
Luk 274, 275, 276
Lukelang, Lukunor 274
Lungga 287
Lu-pan 73
Lupercal 139, 140
Luqman 112, 115
Luxor 102
Lycurgus, Lykourgos 133
Lydia 133
Lykourgos *see* Lycurgus

M

Maasai 214, 221
Ma'at 102, 105, 109; *103*; symbol of *98, 105*
Mabinogion 176–7
Macassar 288
Macaulay, Lord 141, 142
Macedonia 144, 152
Machu Picchu *255, 258*
Madagascar 214; *220*
Madaputa-tupuru 286
Maenads, Bacchants 133, 137, 147, 150; *133, 147*
Mafuie 275
Magellan, Ferdinand 273
Magog 115
Magonga 218
Mag Tuired, Moytura 173, 174, 175–6
Mahabharata 20, 23
Mahakala 55, 83; *54*
Mahasiddhas 56
Mahavira 38
Mahinda 34, 39
Maitreya 54–5, 83
maize *see* corn
Majjhima Nikaya 38
Makeda 114
Makh 88
Malaya 117
Maman Briggite 267
Mammi 88
man:
archetypal or cosmic 16, 32, 50, 59, 226; *60*
creation myths:
African 208, 209, 210, 216, 219, 225, 226, 227; *210*
American 243, 246–7, 248–9, 255, 258, 260
Chinese 59, 64, 73
Christian 156, 157, 158–61
Egyptian 97, 109
Greek 122, 150, 203
Hindu 16, 18
Jewish 156, 157, 158–61
Mesopotamian 88
Pacific 273, 283, 285, 289, 291
Scandinavian 180
Tibetan 51, 57
Zoroastrian 41, 43, 44
emerging from below ground 12, 209, 216, 225, 255, 283
made of clay, earth 11, 12, 64, 97, 109, 122, 158, 160, 203, 209, 255
races of 122–3, 188, 189, 190, 191, 198, 237
skin colour 209, 210; *210*
Man, Isle of 177
mana 274, 277
Manabozho 232
Manannan 176, 177
Manarmakeri 283
Manasha 31, 32
Manawydan 176, 177
Manco Capac 255, 256, 257, 258, 259
Mandan *232*
Mangaia 273, 277; *277*
Mani 44, 51, 195
manioc 248–9
Mankanaka 28
Manseren Manggundi 283
Manu 18–19, 20, 32; *20*
Manup 283
Maori 273, 274–5, 276; *275, 276*
Mara 37–8, 53; *38, 51*
Marampa 226–7
Marduk 87, 88, 89
Marib 112, 114
Marind-Anim 279
Mars 137, 138, 139, 142, 143, 167, 188, 201; *139*
Marsyas 137
Mary, Virgin 109, 165, 269; *162, 163*
Masai *see* Maasai
Mashu, Mountains of 91
Masis *see* Ararat
Matali 37
Math 176
Matholwch 176
Matsya 21; *20*
Maui 274, 275–6; *275*
Mawu-Lisa 222–4, 225
Maya (Buddha's mother) 34; *35*
Maya (people) 236, 242, 243, 245–7, 248, 249, 250, 251, 253; *243, 246, 247, 249*
Mbega 221
Mbombo 209
Mecca 110, 111, 112, 115; *118*
Medea, Medeia 129, 130, 132, 202; *129*
Medusa 128; *128*
Meghamalin 38
Meherr, Mherr 201 *see also* Mithra
Melanesia 278–83, 285, 288; *279–83*
Melville Island 285, 288
Memphis 93, 97, 109
Menelaos 124, 125
Menelik I 114
Meng Chiang 66
Menomini 232
Men Shen 73
menstruation, origin of 260, 262–3, 264, 281
Merciless Blood-Head 55
Mercury 137, 138, 143, 188
Merlin 115
Meshkent 102, 109
Mesopotamia 86–91, 95, 113, 115, 120, 123, 124, 198, 201; *42, 87–91*
Messor 136
Metis 120, 121, 122
Métraux, Alfred 268
Mexico *see* Middle America
Mexico City 253
Mherr *see* Meherr
Michael, archangel 164; *164, 165*
Micronesia *see* Polynesia and Micronesia
Mictlantecuhtli 248, 250, 253; *244, 245, 249*
Middle America 10, 12, 236, 242–53; *243–53*
Midewiwin 233
Midgard 180; Midgard Serpent 181, 185, 186
Milarepa 56; *56*
Milky Way 28, 32; *236*
Mi-lo Fo 70, 73; *70*
Mimir 182
Min 109
Minerva 137, 143
Minos 122, 131, 132, 148
Minotaur 131, 132, 148; *131*
Miroku 83
Mist and Cloud Spring 237
Mithra, Mithras, Mitra 32, 42, 152–4, 201; *153*
Mixtecs 249; *248*
Miyajima shrine *78*
Mjollnir 180, 181; *181*
Mkunare 215–16
Mnevis 109
Mocking Bird 237
Mohini 21
Moirai *see* Fates
Mokosh 192–3, 194
Molina, Cristobal de 256
Monitor Lizard 227–8
Monkey (China) 68–71; *68*; Monkey Fumu 209
moon, death and immortality 12, 28, 42, 63, 211, 238, 275, 283, 287–8; *59, 63*
Morrigan 172, 174, 175, 176
Morufonu 283
Moses 110, 115
Moses of Khorene 200–1
Mother Friday 197
Mot 94
Motiktik 276
Mo Yeh 65
Moytura *see* Mag Tuired
Mu 52
Mucius Scaevola 142
Mudungkala 285
Muhammad 110, 111, 112, 113, 117, 118; *111, 118*
Mukhariq 117–18
Mu-lien 67–8
mummification, Egyptian 104, 108, 109; *103, 104, 106*
Mundurucu 262, 265
Mungkan 289
Mura-mura 285, 286
Musa Ibn Nusayr 116
Muses 122, 126, 133
Musilinda *37*
Muspell 180
Mutjinga 291
Mycenae, Mykenai, Argos 122, 124, 127, 128, 130, 133
mystery religions 134, 144–55; *145–55*
Mystis 154

N

Nabu 89
Nadr Ibn al-Harith 112
Nagas 32
Nahua *see* Middle America
Nambi 217–18
Namtar 89
Nana-Buluku 222
Nanabush 232–3, 238, 240
Nandi 32, 33; *27*
Nanna 184
Nannar 89; *91*
Nanshe 88
Nantosuelta 172, 174
Naples 136, 142
Naqsh-i Rustam *43*
Narasimha 21; *21*
Narcissus 137; *138*
Nareau, Elder and Younger 272, 274
Narts 204
Nasr 112
Nasu 42
Nataraja 27–8, 32; *28*
Naunet 97
Nauru 272, 275
Navaho 242; *236*
Naxos 148
Nazi party 10, 158, 169, 189, 190, 191; *189, 191*
Nchienge 209
Nefertiti *99*
Nehru, Pandit *30*
Nemain 174
Nemean lion 127; *127*
Nemi 138
Nepal 49, 51
Nephthys 96, 97, 106
Neptune 136, 143; *136*
Nergal 89
Nero 143
Nest Builder 64
Neuri 192
New Caledonia 278
New Guinea *see* Papua New Guinea
New Hebrides 278, 280; *280*
New Ireland *279, 281*
Newman, Cardinal 160
New Zealand 273, 276 *see also* Maori
Ngabandi 208
Ngurunderi 285
Ni 281
Nibbana *see* Nirvana
Nibelungenlied 189
Nibo 267, 270
Niflheim 180
Night 120, 235; Mountain of 92
Nihongi, Nihonshoki 74
Nile, River 96, 107, 109, 154, 207, 209; *97, 207*
Ninhursag 89
Ninigi 80, 82; *82*
Ninurta 86, 88, 89
Niobe 122, 137
Niraya 37, 38
Nirvana, Nibbana 34, 36, 37
Nisien 176
Njord 182, 185
Nkundo 208, 210
Noah 95, 112, 156, 198, 201, 255; *200*
noble savage, myth of 161–2
Nock, A.D. 155
Nodens, Nodons 176
Nokomis 232–3
Nommo 226; *226, 227*
Nordic Religious Working Community 191
Nordlungen Fraternity 191
Norito 74
Norns 187
North Africa 110, 116, 168, 207 *see also* Egypt; Ethiopia
North American Indians 216, 230–41, 242; *231–40*
Noves, monster of *172*
Novgorod 194
Nuada 174, 175, 176
Nudimmud 87
Nu-kua 61, 64, 65, 73
Numa 139, 141
numen, numina 136
Nun 97
Nut 96, 97, 106, 109; *98*
Nyanja 216

O

Oberator 136
Occator 136
Ocean of Love 20
Odin 178, 179, 180, 182–3, 184, 185, 186, 187, 188; *182, 187*
Odudua-Orishala 223
Odysseus 124, 125, 134, 135; *124, 125*
Oedipus 132–3, 186; *132*
Ogam 174
Ogma, Ogmios 172, 174, 175; *177*
ogre-killing child 278–9
Ogre's Head 117–18
Ogu 267, 268, 270
Ogu-badagri 267
Ohrmazd, Ahura Mazda 32, 40–7, 152, 201; *43*; symbol of *42, 45*
Ojibwa 232
Okeanos 121, 122
Okuni-nushi 79–80, 82, 83, 84; *81*
Olav Tryggvason 184
Old Grey Sisters 128

Old Mother, Old Woman 291
Olofat 274, 275, 276
Olympos, Olympus 120, 124, 126, 127, 128, 130, 134, 137, 147
Ombos 109
Omoigane 78
On 98
opposites, theme of 12, 25–6, 40, 41, 42, 55, 122, 167, 178, 215, 222, 225, 260, 264, 265, 278; *57, 167, 225* *see also* dualism; yang and yin
Order of New Templars 190
Orestes 139
organized conspiracy, myth of 168–9
original sin 160
Orokaiva 278
Orokolo 279
Oromo 214, 216, 219
Orpheus 90, 129, 135, 150; *150, 151*
Orphics 148–50
Oshe *224*
Oshiho-mimi 80, 82
Osiris 90, 96, 97, 98, 102, 105, 106–8, 109, 154, 207; *105, 106*
Ossetes 204
Otter 186
Otutu 224
Ouranos *see* Uranus
Ovid 137–8, 167
O-Yama-Tsu-Mi 75

P

Pa 64
Pacaritampo 255, 257, 258
Pachacamac 259
Pachacuti 256, 258–9
Padmasambhava 56, 57; *56*
Paiute 238
Palau Islands 275; *276*
Palenque 246; *243, 246*
Pales 136
Palestine *see* Syria and Palestine
Palmyra 113
Pan 143, 148; *148*
Panchen Lama 50
Pandora 122
Pangwe 209
P'an-ku 59–60, 62, 64; *60*
Papa 273, 274, 277
Papang 285
Papua New Guinea 285, 288 *see also* Melanesia
Paracelsus 190
paradises *see* heavens and paradises
Paraparawa 260–1
Parashurama 21, 22, 23, 30, 32; *23*
Pares 136
Paris 124, 125, 167
parricide 17, 120, 132–3, 278
Parsis 40, 44–7; *44, 46*
Parsva 38
Paruna 263
Parvati 27, 28, 29, 32, 33; *27*
Patroklos 124
Paul, St 155
Payatamu 237
Pease, Franklin 259
Pegasos 130
Pekai 280
Pelias 129, 130; *129*
Pelles 170
Pelops 130
Penelope 125, 134
Penthesileia *123*
Pentheus 133, 137
Perceval 166; *167*
Pergamum 150
Perkunas 195
Persephone, Proserpina 121, 122, 144, 150, 167; *145, 146* *see also* Kore
Persepolis *41*
Perseus 122, 128, 130, 131; *128*
Persia *see* Iran
Peru *see* Incas; Quechua
Perun 193, 194, 195
Peter, St 266
Pettavatthu 38
Pettivisaya 37
Phaethon 137, 167
Philemon 138
Philip II of Macedon 152
Philistines 92
Philosopher's Stone 168
Phrygia 138
Piaroa 260, 262, 263–4, 265
Pidray 93
Pilgrim's Progress 162
Piltzintecutli 253; *245*
Pindar 129–30, 133–4, 138
Pine Forest 27
Ping-I 73
Pizarro, Francisco 256, 259
Plain of Wandering 130
Plato 133, 135
Pleiades 27, 31
Plouton *see* Pluto
Plumed Serpent *see* Quetzalcoatl
Plutarch 106, 135
Pluto, Plouton 143, 144, 145; *145*
Pole Star 60, 61
political use of myths 10, 71–2, 74, 80, 84, 88–9, 114, 140, 142, 169, 188, 252, 258 *see also* kingship
Pollux, Polydeukes 122, 129, 142, 143; *142*
Polybos 133
Polydektes 128
Polydeukes *see* Pollux
Polynesia and Micronesia 272–7; *273–7*
Polyphemos 125; *124*
Pompeii 148; *138, 139, 145, 154*
Popol Vuh 243, 246
Porenut 195
Porevit 195
Porsena, Porsenna 142
Poseidon 121, 124, 125, 129, 130, 132, 143 *see also* Neptune
possession 10, 133, 266, 267, 269, 270, 281
Potala, Mount 51
Potawotami 232
Power-of-the-Shining-Heavens 239
Prahlada 21, 29
Prajapati 16, 17, 18, 19, 20, 26, 32
Prajnaparamita 55
Praskovya, St 197
'Precious Treasury' 48–9
Priam 124
Prithivi 32
Procopius 193
Procrustes *see* Prokrustes
progress, myth of 9, 157–8
Proitos 128, 130, 133
Prokrustes 131
Prometheus 10, 121, 122, 123, 185, 203–4
Promitor 136
Proserpina *see* Persephone
Protectors of Religion 55; *54*
Pryderi 177
Pseudo-Callisthenes 115
Ptah 97, 109
Pu Chou, Mount 61
Pueblo Indians 235–7; *235–7*
Puranas 15, 20
Purusha 16, 32
Puta 136
Putana *24*
Pwyll 176, 177
Pygmalion 137
pyramids, Egyptian 98, 104, 106, 112; *100*
Pyramid Texts 105, 106
Pyrrha 123
Pythia 127
Pytho 127

Q

Q'ero 255, 259
Quechua 242, 244, 256, 257
Queen of Sheba 112, 113–15, 116, 117; *114*
Quetzalcoatl 236, 243, 245, 246, 248–9, 250–1; *250, 251*
Quiche-Maya *see* Maya (people)
Quirinus 142

R

Ra *see* Re
races of mankind *see* man
Radha 24, 32
Ragnarok 186; *187*
rainbow 52, 76, 95, 198; *236*; Rainbow Serpent *see* snake
Rakan 83
Raki 273
Raleigh, Sir Walter 161
Rama, Ramachandra 21, 22–3, 32; *22, 23*
Ramayana 20, 22, 32
Rangi 273, 274
Rarotonga 277
Ras al-Ghul 117
Ras es-Shamrah 92
Ratnasambhava 54, 83; *52, 57*
Ravana 22
Raven 240–1
raw and cooked food 12, 64, 128, 262, 263, 264, 265, 280
Razin, Stenka 193–4
Re 98–9, 102, 104, 106, 107, 109; *98, 99, 108*
Redarator 136
Regin 185, 186
Regulus 142
Remus *see* Romulus and Remus
Renenet 102, 109
Renuka 23, 30
Reuter, O.S. 191
Rhea 120, 121
Rhea Silvia 139
Rhiannon 177
Rigi 272
Rig Veda 15, 16, 20
Riiki 272
rites of passage 136
ritual, myths and 10, 18, 39, 46, 62, 87, 88, 90, 92, 94, 102, 126, 133, 138–9, 179, 181, 278, 281, 286; *93, 95, 265, 287, 288, 290, 291* *see also* mystery religions; sacrifice
River of Forgetfulness 135
Roal 259
robot 244
Romance of the Three Kingdoms 71
Rome 9, 10, 32, 44, 98, 136–43, 144–55, 161, 167, 170–1, 172, 174, 188, 206; *137–43, 145, 147, 148, 150–5*
  city of 9, 40, 136, 139–41, 143, 165, 170, 195
Romulus and Remus 139–40, 141, 195; *140*
Ronga 208
Rongo 273, 274, 277; *277*
Rosenberg, Alfred 191
Rosenkreutz, Christian 168
Rosicrucian Brotherhood 168
Rowe, John 259
Rudra 16, 26, 32
Rügen Island 195
Rugievit 195
rule of women *see* man
Rumina 136
Ruminal 140
runes 174, 182–3, 190, 191
Rurik 194
Rustaveli, Shota 203
Rwanda 214, 221

S

sabbath 158
Sabines 140; *141*
sacrifice, myths of 10, 16, 17, 18, 19, 20, 26, 32, 33, 42, 44, 65, 66, 122, 182, 245, 251; *153*
Sagbata 223–4
Sahampati 36
Sakka 35–6
Sakyamuni *see* Buddha
Salamudimu 209
Samantabhadra 83; *57*
Samoa 273, 275
Samothrace 150–2; *151*
Samvara 38, 54; *53*
Sangarius 152
Saoshyans 42
Sarasvati *18*
Sarmatians 192
Sarritor 136
Satan, Satanail 164–5, 195 *see also* Devil
Satana 204
Sati 26, 27, 29, 30, 32
Saturn 136, 137, 142, 143
Satyrs 148; *149*
Saxo Grammaticus 195
Scandinavia 12, 162, 174, 178–87, 188; *179–87*
Schuler, Alfred 190
Sciron *see* Skeiron
Scythians 192; *196, 197*
Seagull 288
Sebek 109; *100*
Sekhmet 109
Selene 204
Semele 122, 133, 137, 150
Semiramis 201
Sengen-Sama 75
Senufo *222, 225*
Separate Heavenly Deities 75, 79, 84
separation of earth and sky *see* creation myths
Serapis 109
Seriphos 128
serpent *see* snake
Seth 96, 97, 106, 107, 108, 109, 154; *108*
Seven Hathors 102
Seven Sages 27
Seven Sisters 31
Shaddad 112–13, 116; *112*
Shai 102, 109
Shakespeare, William 187
Shakti 32
Shamash 89, 91; *87*
Shambaa 221
Shamba Bolongongo *210*
Shamiram 201
Shango 223, 268
Shang Ti 71–2, 73
Shan Hai Ching 61
Shapash 92, 94
Shara 87
Shashti 31, 32
Shavante 260
Shawnee 231, 232
Sheba *see* Queen of Sheba
Shedet 109
Sheela na Gig *173*
Shelardi 199
Shem 198
Shen-nung 60, 61, 64; *61*
Shesha 32
Shih Huang Ti 58, 66
Shilluk 206, 209
Shinto 74–84; *75–84*
Shipololo 237
Shitala 31, 32; *32*
Shiva 20, 21, 26–31, 32, 33, 41; *15, 26–30*
Shivini 199
Shou-lao 73; *65*
Shroff, Behramshah 46
Shu (China) 59
Shu (Egypt) 96, 97, 109
Shu Ching 62, 65
Shun 60, 61, 62, 63
Sibyl, Sibylline books 141, 142–3; *143*
Sichi 278
Sicily 141
Sido 279
Sigurd, Siegfried 186; *185*
Sigyn 185
Silenus 148; *148*
Simargl, Simurgh 192, 194
Simbali groves 36
Sin 89
Sinapki 278
Sineru, Mount 35–6
Sirens 125, 135; *125*
Sirini 278
Sisiutl 240; *240*
Sita 22–3; *22*
Skanda, Karttikeya 16, 27, 30, 31–3; *27, 30*
Skeiron 131
Skuld 187
Skull-Ancestor 281
Slavs 192–7; *194–5, 197*
Sleipnir 185; *183*
sloth, creation of 263
snake, serpent:
  in creation 17, 50, 225; *225*
  and death, immortality 12, 26, 91, 159–60, 210, 211, 220, 235, 279, 280, 287
  and evil 9, 41, 42, 156, 158, 159–60, 164, 228; *43*
  Giant Horned 232, 236
  and infinity, time 25–6, 243, 270; *26*
  and kingship 207
  Lightning 285
  Midgard 181, 185, 186
  of the Mountains 196
  Nagas 32
  Plumed *see* Quetzalcoatl
  Rainbow 285–6, 289; *286, 290*
  and sexuality 160, 225, 250, 280, 290
  Sisiutl 240; *240*
Snorri Sturluson 179, 183, 185, 187
social contract, myth of 10, 162
Sogbo 223–4
Soido 279–80
Solang *281*
Solomon 112, 113–15, 116, 117; *113*
Solomon Islands 278, 280; *281*
Soma (elixir of immortality) 17, 18, 19, 20–1, 26, 32; *18, 21*
Sophocles, Sophokles 132, 138
Soponna 223
Sosom 279
Sosruko 204
Sotho 208
South America, tropical 260–5; *261–5*
Sphinx 132; *100, 132*
Spiniensis 136
Sridevi 55
Sri Lanka 15, 34, 38, 39
Srong-btsan 49
Sterculius 136
Strabo 202
Stribog, Stribozh 192, 194, 195, 197
Stymphalian birds 127; *127*
Styx, River *135*
Subrincator 136
Sucellus 172
Sumatra 15
Sumerians 86, 90, 91
Sumul 95
Sun Dance 234; *234*
Sunday 158
Surt 186
Surya 32; *19*
Susano 75, 77–9, 80, 84
Suseri-bime 80
suttee 26, 32
Suwa-taisha shrine *84*
Svrantevit, Svyatovik 195; *195*
Svarogu 192
Swahili 117, 206, 211, 213
swastika 189, 190; *189, 191*
Swelling Earth 64
Syria and Palestine 10, 92–5, 110, 115, 144, 168; *93–5*

T

Tacitus 188, 190
Tadmura 116

Tajikari 78
Takachiho, Mount 82
Takamagahara, 74, 75, 84
Talay 93
Tamayori 80, 84
Tammuz 89, 90
Tampo 259
Tampo Kiru 257
Tane 273, 274
Tangaroa 273, 274, 277; *277*
Tangi'ia *277*
T'ang Seng *see* Hsuan Tsang
Tangu 278, 282
Tantalos 130
Tantrism 28, 29, 55; *57*
Tao, Taoism 58, 65, 67, 68, 72, 73
tapu 274
Tara (Ireland) 175
Tara (goddess) 49, 55; *52, 55*
Taraka 26, 27, 33
Taranis 172
Tarquin the Old 141, 143
Tarquin the Proud 141, 142
Tauert 102, 109, 207; *102*
Tavatimsa 35, 36
Tawhiri-matea 273, 274
Tefnut 96, 97, 109
Teisheba 199; *201*
Tei-wamb 283
Telemachos 125
Telete 148
Temne 226, 227, 228
Tenmu 74
Tenochtitlan 252, 253
Tenson-korin 80, 84
Tepeyollotl *245*
territorial myths 10, 249, 286, 289
Tezcatlipoca 250, 252, 253; *253*
Thailand 15, 34
Thebes (Egypt) 97, 102, 109
Thebes (Greece) 122, 123, 132, 133
Themis 122
Theosophy 45
Theseus 124, 130–2, 138, 148; *131*
Thomas, St 256
Thor 178, 179, 180–1, 182, 184, 185, 186, 187, 188, 189, 194; *181, 187*
Thoth 105, 106, 109; *99, 105*
Thousand and One Nights 113, 116, 203
Thrace, Thracians 133, 147, 192, 193, 197
Thrandheim 184
Three Sovereigns 58, 59, 60, 63, 64
Thrym 181
Thunderbirds 231, 233, 234; *234, 240*
Thunor 188, 191
Tiamat 87
Tiber, River 139, 141, 142
Tibet 28, 34, 48–57, 113; *49–57*
T'ien 71, 73, 75
T'ien-lung 64
Tigranes the Great 200
Tihuanaco 254, 255; *256*
Ti'iti'i 275
Tiki-kapaka 274
Tiki-tohua 274
Ti-mu 64
Tipitaka 34
Tiracchanayoni 37
Tiro 279
Tiryns 128
Titans 120, 121, 122, 123, 150, 203
Titicaca, Lake 254, 255, 256, 259
Ti-tsang 67, 73
Tiw, Tiwaz 188
Tlaloc 249–50, 252, 253; *245, 246, 248, 251*
Tlalocan 250
Tlazolteotl 253; *245*
Toaripi 279
Toche 209
Tohil 253
To Kabinana 283
Tolai 283
Tollan 253
Toltecs *see* Middle America
Tonatiuh 245, 253
Torres Strait 284, 288
totems 193, 236, 240, 283; *238, 284, 288*
Totoima 278–9
Totonacs *249*
Tower of Babel 156, 201
Towers of Silence 47; *47*
Toyotama 80, 84
tragedy, Greek 132
Trajan 195
tree-deities 37
tree of life *see* world tree
Tree of Wisdom *see* Bodhi-tree
trickster 185, 216, 219, 224, 237, 240, 274, 275
Trifon Zarezan 197; *197*
Trimurti 32
Trio 260
Triptolemus *146*
Trobriand Islands 281, 282
Troy 123, 124–5, 128, 130, 134, 140, 179
Troyan 195
Trozen 131, 132
Tsai Shen 73
Tsao Chun *see* Kitchen God
Tsimshian 241; *238*
Tsonga 208
Tsong-ka-pa *49*
Tsukushi myths 74
Tsukuyomi 75, 77, 80
Tuatha De Danann 173, 174–6, 177
Tukano 264
Tula 250, 251, 252, 253
Tuman 278
Tu-matauenga 274
Tung-yo 72, 73
Tupi 264
Tu'u-ko-ihu *274*
Tuutsi caste 221; *221*
Tvashtar 17, 19, 32
Twenty Signs of Ritual 242–3, 245, 249–50, 252, 253; *244, 248, 251, 253*
twins 19, 32, 44, 129, 139–40, 142, 143, 222, 223, 225–6, 228, 250, 253, 278, 279; *140, 142, 174, 226*
Typhoeos, Typhon 120
Tyr 182, 186, 188

U

Udayana 52
Uddiyana 48
Ugarit 92
Uhlanga 210
Ukaralya Creek 286
Ull 182
Uluru 291
Ulysses *see* Odysseus
Uma 32
Umisachi 80, 84
Umvelinqangi 210
underwater deities 232
Underwater Panthers 232, 233, 235, 236; *231*
Ungud 285–6
Unkulunkulu 210
Unxia 136
Uppsala 178, 183
Uranus, Ouranos 32, 120, 121, 210
Urartu 199–200; *199, 201*
Urdi 187
Ur-Nammu *91*
Uruk 90; *91*
ushabti-figures 106, 108; *109*
Ushas 32
Ussher, Archbishop 157
Ut-napishtim 86–7, 91; *87*
Utu 89

V

Vach 17, 18, 29, 32; *18*
Vagitanus 136
Vahagn 201
Vahman 42, 43
Vairocana 53, 54, 83; *52, 57*
Valhalla 182; *183*
Valkyries 182; *183*
Valley of Light 62
Valley of the Ruby 116
Valley of Sand 116
Vamana 21; *17, 22*
Vanir 179, 182
Varaha 21; *20*
Varuna 16, 32; *17*
Vasilissa 196–7
Vasuki 21; *21*
Vatea 277
Vatsala 52
Vedandi 187
Vedic myths *see* Hinduism
Veles, Volos 193
Venus, goddess 136, 137, 138, 140, 141, 143, 167; *139*; planet 245, 248, 250, 251, 253 *see also* Aphrodite
Verethragna 201
Vergil 138, 140–1, 142
Vervactor 136
Vesta 137, 143 *see also* Hestia
Vestal Virgins 139
Vijaya *52*
Villa of the Mysteries 148; *148*
Vimanavatthu 38
Viracocha 254–6, 258, 259; *256*
Virgil *see* Vergil
Virgin Mary *see* Mary
Vishaps 200, 202
Vishnu 15, 16, 19, 20–2, 23, 25–6, 27, 29, 30, 32; *17, 20–3, 25, 26*
Vishvarupa 17
Vivasvat 18, 19, 32
Vladimir, Prince 194, 195
Vladimir The Little Red Sun 197
Vlaho, Vlas 193
Volga, River 193
Volos *see* Veles
Voodoo 222, 266–70; *267–70*
Vritra 17
Vulcan 137, 141, 143, 174

W

Wachler, Ernst 191
Wafipa 210
Wagner, Richard 188–9, 201, 204
Wahari 262–3
Wahb Ibn Munabbih 113, 115, 117
Waimariwi 289
Waldemar 195
Wales 170, 172, 174, 176–7
Walumbe 218–19
Wan 66
Wanambi 286
Wandervögel movement 189; *191*
Wandjina 285–6; *286*
Wang Mu 73
Wapiya Girls 286–7
war or battle of the gods:
American 232, 233
Canaanite 92–3, 94, 95
Celtic 173, 174, 175–6
Christian 164; *164*
Greek 120
Indian 16–17, 20–1, 35–6; *15*
Mesopotamian 87, 88
Polynesian 273
Scandinavian 185, 186–7; *187*
Zoroastrian 41, 42, 45, 46
Waraku 261
Waramurunggundji 285
Warramunga *287*
Washer at the Ford 174
Water King 196–7
water of life 88, 90, 115, 116; *116, 117* *see also* elixir
waters, primeval 16, 17, 20, 50, 61, 75–6, 87, 101, 111, 156, 208, 210
churning of *see* churning
fishing up land *see* fishing
Wawalag Sisters 289–91; *290, 291*
Wayana *261*
weighing of the soul 43, 47, 102, 105; *105, 165*
Wen-ch'ang 64, 73
Wensinck, A. 111
Werner, Alice 219
Whiro 276
White Buffalo Cow 234
Winbaraku 286
Wisaaka 232
Wishram 238
witchcraft, witches 125, 168–9, 196, 213, 237; *169, 212*
Wodan, Wotan 178, 182, 188, 189, 190, 191 *see also* Odin
Woman:
and man, tension between 122, 160, 217, 262–3, 264, 274–5, 281, 287, 289, 290
rule or dominance of 12, 264, 280, 283
Wonkamala 286
world-ages 25, 41, 42–3, 44, 50, 122–3, 242–5, 246, 247, 249; *25, 26, 244, 245*
world-axis 15–16, 27, 76 *see also* world-mountain; world-tree
world-mountain 17
world-tree, tree of life 50–1, 62, 180, 182, 186, 278, 283; *183*
Wotan *see* Wodan
Wotjbaluk 289
Wotjo 287
Woto 209
Wutu 211

X

Xenophon 135
Xipe 253; *249*
Xiuhtecutli 253; *245, 252*
Xochipilli 253
Xochiquetzal 253

Y

Yagami 79, 80
Yaghuth 112
Yagul 287–8
Yakushi 83
Yalafath 274, 275
Yam 92–3, 94
Yama 18, 19, 20, 26, 32, 38, 39, 73, 83
Yamantaka 55; *54*
Yamasachi 84
Yamato myths 74
Yami 19
Yang and yin 60, 63, 64, 65; *60, 65*
Yangtze, River 60, 65
Yao 60, 61, 63, 64; *60*
Yao-Shih 73
Yap 275
Yarlung 52
Yatpan 95
yazads 42
Yelafaz 274
Yellow River 63, 73
Yemen 112, 113, 114, 115, 117–18
Yen-lo 72, 73; *71*
Yen-tzu, Mount 62
Yggdrasill 180, 182, 186; *183*
Yi 63, 72; *63*
Yin *see* yang and yin
Ymir 180
Yomi 76–7, 80
Yoruba 207, 222, 223; *224, 226*
Yu 61, 64–5
Yucatan *see* Maya (people)
Yu Ch'iang 73
Yu-Huang 73
Yulunggul 289–90; *290*
Yum Kaax 253
Yurugu 226
Yu-ti 67, 69, 72, 73

Z

Zagreus 150
Zaka 268
Zarathustra *see* Zoroaster
Zbruch idol 194–5; *195*
Zephon, Mount 94
Zeus 10, 32, 120, 121, 122, 123, 124, 125, 127, 128, 132, 133, 137, 138, 143, 145, 150, 152, 167, 188, 194, 201, 203–4, 207; *122, 203*
Zila *217*
Zion, Mount 162
Zmei Gorynich 196
zombies *268*
Zoroaster, Zarathustra 40, 42
Zoroastrianism 12, 40–7, 152, 201; *41–7*
Zu 87–8; *87, 88*
Zulu 206, 207, 208, 210; *212*
Zuni 235, 237
Zurvan 44